# REMEMBERING THE TIMES
# OF OUR LIVES

*Memory in Infancy and Beyond*

# The Developing Mind Series

### Series Editor
**Philip David Zelazo**
*University of Toronto*

### Co-Editors
**Dare Baldwin,** *University of Oregon*
**David F. Bjorklund,** *Florida Atlantic University*
**Judy DeLoache,** *University of Virginia*
**Lynn Liben,** *Pennsylvania State University*
**Yuko Munakata,** *University of Colorado, Boulder*

---

---

The Developing Mind Series brings you readable, integrative essays on fundamental topics in cognitive development—topics with broad implications for psychology and beyond. Written by leading researchers, these essays are intended to be both indispensable to experts and relevant to a wide range of students and scholars.

# REMEMBERING THE TIMES OF OUR LIVES

## Memory in Infancy and Beyond

Patricia J. Bauer

*Duke University*

**LEA** LAWRENCE ERLBAUM ASSOCIATES, PUBLISHERS
2007 Mahwah, New Jersey                                    London

Copyright © 2007 by Lawrence Erlbaum Associates, Inc.
    All rights reserved. No part of the book may be reproduced in
    any form, by photostat, microform, retrieval system, or any other
    means, without the prior written permission of the publisher.

Lawrence Erlbaum Associates, Inc., Publishers
10 Industrial Avenue
Mahwah, New Jersey 07430
www.erlbaum.com

Cover illustration by Jeanne Cowan
Cover design by Kathryn Houghtaling Lacey

**Library of Congress Cataloging-in-Publication Data**

Bauer, Patricia J.
    Remembering the times of our lives : memory in infancy and beyond / Patricia J. Bauer.
        p.   cm.
    Includes bibliographical references and indexes.
    ISBN 0-8058-4040-0 (cloth : alk. paper)
    ISBN 0-8058-5733-8 (pbk. : alk. paper)
    1. Autobiographical memory.   2. Memory in infants.   3. Memory in children.
I. Title.

BF378.A87B38   2006
155.42'2312—dc22                                                    2005043526
                                                                        CIP

Books published by Lawrence Erlbaum Associates are printed on acid-free paper,
and their bindings are chosen for strength and durability.

Printed in the United States of America
10  9  8  7  6  5  4  3  2  1

*To J. Steven Snow, with whom I share the times of my life.*
*Thank you for being the person you are.*

# Contents

# Acknowledgments

This volume has only one author, but many contributors. I extend my sincere thanks to the postdoctoral students, graduate students, and staff members who took part in a seminar in the spring of 2002, during which we had lively discussions of many of the issues covered in this volume: Melissa Burch, Jean Burr, Mari Strand Cary, Carol Cheatham, Jane Couperus, Tracy DeBoer, Holly Eibs Bunje, Jennifer Haight, Erica Kleinknecht, Marina Larkina, Angela Lukowski, Christina Phill, Kelly Snyder, Rebecca Starr, Leif Stennes, Nicole Talge, Elise Townsend, Heather Whitney Sesma, and Sandra Wiebe. This cast of characters helped to ensure a strong start for this project.

My appreciation to Melissa Burch, Mari Strand Cary, Carol Cheatham, Tracy DeBoer, Holly Eibs Bunje, David Forman, Rachel Friedlieb, Angela Lukowski, Abigail Muehleck, Rebecca Starr, Leif Stennes, and Sandra Wiebe, for reading and commenting on drafts of one or more (and in some cases, several) chapters. The work stands improved for your efforts. My thanks also to Philip D. Zelazo, a terrific editor! Thank you, Phil, for encouraging me to write this volume, and for your support and patience throughout the process.

I have been fortunate for most of my career to have received support for research from the National Institute of Child Health and Human Development (HD-28425). My research enterprise also has been aided by support from the Graduate School of the University of Minnesota; a McKnight-Land Grant Professorship from the University of Minnesota; and the Center for Cognitive Sciences, the Center for Neurobehavioral Development, and the Center for the Study of Neurobehavioral Development in the Context of

Adversity, all at the University of Minnesota. Financial support for the preparation of this volume was provided by the College of Education and Human Development, University of Minnesota, in the form of a single-semester leave in the fall of 2002. During the final stages of preparation of the volume, I also received support from the National Institutes of Health, in the form of an Independent Scientist Award (HD-42483). In actuality, the thanks extend to the taxpayers of the United States of America: Thank you for supporting my research program and those of so many others whose efforts are reported in this volume. May we continue to value basic research, even as other needs press.

I also extend my appreciation to the larger community of scholars in which I have been privileged to work on a day-to-day basis. The spaces of the Institute of Child Development (where this work was conceived and drafted) are occupied by faculty colleagues, students, and staff members whose dedication to inquiry is infectious, whose doors are (almost always) open, and whose examples of high achievement have inspired and sustained me. Thanks to Jean Mandler and Cecilia Shore for providing early rearing environments full of protective factors and for helping me to appreciate the challenge of the infant mind. Thanks to Charles Nelson, and to Leslie Carver, Carol Cheatham, Tracy DeBoer, Michelle de Haan, Angela Lukowski, Kathleen Thomas, and Sandra Wiebe, for aiding in my appreciation of the developing brain. Special thanks to Robyn Fivush and Katherine Nelson, whose thinking on the development of autobiographical memory has substantially influenced my own. Finally, boundless gratitude to my loving husband, Steve Snow, for sustaining me in this and all endeavors.

—*Patricia J. Bauer*

# I

# AUTOBIOGRAPHICAL MEMORY AND ITS SIGNIFICANCE

# 1

# Remembering the Times
# of Our Lives

*"The horror of that moment," the King went on, "I shall never, never for-
get!"*

*"You will, though," the Queen said, "if you don't make a memorandum
of it."*
—Lewis Carroll, from *Through the Looking Glass and What Alice
Found There* (1872/1982, p. 94, emphasis in original)

In his brief dialogue between the King and the Queen—two of the chess
piece sovereigns of the Looking Glass House—Lewis Carroll captured the
complementary sides of the coin we term *memory*. The King, having experienced a "horrifying" event (being set on a table by Alice, a relative giant
whom the King could neither see nor hear), expresses absolute faith in the
durability of memory. The Queen, in contrast, presents a less flattering view
of the capacity: that without some intervention (a memorandum), even a salient event will be forgotten. In a rare instance, the reality experienced by
the King and Queen on their side of the looking glass is reflected on the
drawing room side as well. Memory is at times seemingly indelible and at
other times frustratingly fallible. What is more, in true looking glass fashion,
the same past experience can at one moment impinge on consciousness un-
bidden and at another elude deliberate attempts to recollect it.

The phenomenon of memory—in its mercurial splendor—is the subject of
this book. That said, on this, the first page of this volume, I have misled you
(just as Alice is often misled). To say that this book is about memory is to
imply that there is a single entity called *memory*. In fact, memory is not a unitary construct. There are many different kinds and types of memory, and
what is to be said as "truth" about one type of memory may not be truth

3

about any other. To borrow a favorite metaphor of a colleague at the University of Minnesota, Michael Maratsos, memory is not pudding. Pudding is a homogeneous entity. When you put a spoon into a bowl of pudding, you draw out pudding. Each spoonful looks like the last spoonful. Comments, characterizations, and truths that you declare about one spoonful are equally true of the next, and the next, and the next. Michael Maratsos admonishes that language is not pudding—there are many different aspects of language, including phonology, morphology, semantics, syntax, and pragmatics. Laws that apply in the domain of phonology do not necessarily hold true, or even have relevance, in the domain of syntax, for example. Thus, one cannot sample language and make broad characterizations (see Maratsos, 1998, for discussion of the conceptual pitfalls of considering heterogeneous domains such as language to be essentially homogeneous, or qualitatively the same throughout).

Professor Maratsos' point is valid about language. It is equally valid about memory. There are many different types of memory and many ways that it can be divided. One common division is along a temporal dimension—some memories are short term: They last only seconds. Other memories are of the sort anticipated by the Lewis Carroll's King: memories that are long term and may even last a lifetime. A "rule" that seems to hold true of short-term memory is that it is capacity-limited. Although estimates vary, it is commonly thought to hold seven "units" of information—such as digits in a phone number—plus or minus two. In contrast, long-term memory is virtually limitless in its capacity. For all practical purposes, there is no upper limit on the number of items, pieces of information, or personal experiences that one can maintain in long-term memory stores.

There are several other divisions of the thing we call *memory*, ranging from the type of content of the memory (e.g., whether it is of facts and figures or personally relevant events), to the brain structures that we think are responsible for it. If memory were pudding, then we could select any given memory phenomenon and use it to describe and characterize all of memory. As a consequence, this would be a much shorter book. Memory is not pudding, however, and because time is not infinite, this book is not about all types of memory. Instead, it is about a particular type of memory, one near and dear to all of us—namely, *autobiographical memory* or *personal memory*. Autobiographical or personal memories are the memories of events and experiences that make up one's life story or personal past. They are the events that we share as we get to know new people, as we reconnect with loved ones after long absences, or as we greet coworkers on Monday morning. They are the stories that we tell about ourselves that reveal who we are and how our experiences have shaped our characters. They are the stories that we use to convey to others the person we want them to see. Indeed it is not an overstatement to say that "Recall of events is a phenomenon of crucial importance to humans. It is the basis of individuality: we are our memories" (White, 2002, p. 604).

The purpose of this volume is to trace the development from infancy through adulthood of the capacity to form, retain, and later retrieve autobiographical or personal memories. Over this wide developmental span, the capacity changes dramatically. Whereas very young children produce halting stories that are barely recognizable as autobiographical, older children and adults produce eloquent narratives that bring past experiences to the present, as if they were being relived in brilliant Technicolor. Throughout the developmental period, the major characters of remembering (played by the King) and forgetting (played by the Queen) share the stage, yet take turns as the lead. The changes in the relative significance of their roles are the result of multiple factors and forces that together support autobiographical memory and determine competence in conveying to others its contents. Analyzing the skill from a developmental perspective permits examination of each of its components and the contributions they make to the entire complex. Because the developmental story is about a particular type of memory, as opposed to "memory pudding," it is essential that the territory to be explored be clearly demarcated. To that end, I consider some of the major divisions of memory in more detail.

## MEMORY AS AN ELEPHANT, NOT A PUDDING

Many readers are familiar with John Godfrey Saxe's poem "The Blind Men and the Elephant." It is based on a Hindu fable about six blind men's first encounter and initial exploration of a previously unknown creature—an elephant (this fable in turn was based on a Chinese parable from the Han dynasty [202 BC–220 AD], featuring three as opposed to six blind men). Because the men cannot see with their eyes, they explore the animal with their hands. Unlike the eyes, which can take in the whole of the elephant with one glance, the scope of the hands is more limited: Only the part of the elephant that fits into the tactile field can be appreciated at a time. As each man explores the portion of the creature with his hands, he describes it to the others. Their descriptions are depicted pictorially on the cover of this volume. The first man, feeling the side of the elephant, says that an elephant is like a wall. The second man, feeling the tusk of the elephant, concludes that the creature is like a spear. The third man, feeling the trunk of the elephant, says that an elephant is like a snake. The fourth man, feeling the knee of the elephant, concludes that an elephant is like a tree. The fifth man, feeling the ear, says that an elephant is like a fan. The last man, feeling the tail of the elephant, says that an elephant is like a rope. In Saxe's words, "Though each (man) was partly in the right, (they) all were in the wrong!"

In other words, each man was right about the small portion of the elephant that he was feeling. No man was right about the whole of the elephant. So it is with memory. That is, facts may be true about one type of memory, but may be wrong (or irrelevant) when applied to a different type of memory.

The suggestion that memory is not a unitary construct has been with us for a long time. Indeed Daniel Schacter and his colleagues (Schacter, Wagner, & Buckner, 2000) attributed the first suggestion that there might be multiple forms of memory to a 1804 paper by Maine de Biran, a French philosopher. Formalization of the notion was advanced at the beginning of the 20th century with studies of wounded veterans from World War I. Karl Kleist (1934), a German physician, performed detailed behavioral examinations of veterans who had received head wounds from gun shots or shrapnel. He found that some mental capacities were spared or left intact, whereas others were disrupted. Moreover, he observed that there were systematic relations between the site of the wound (and resulting brain lesion) and the type of impairment experienced by the veteran. Kleist's studies supported speculation that different parts of the brain subserve different cognitive functions, including different types of memory.

For the contemporary literature, the strongest impetus to consideration of different memory skills as representative of different types of memory came from studies of a patient known as H. M. As told by journalist Philip Hilts (1995), Henry M.'s early life was rather ordinary. He was born in or around Hartford, Connecticut, on February 26, 1926. He was raised in a working-class neighborhood, enjoyed hunting and fishing, and as a child thought he would grow up to be an electrician like his father. Researcher Suzanne Corkin and her colleagues (Corkin, Amaral, González, Johnson, & Hyman, 1997) tell of an event in Henry M.'s otherwise unremarkable early life that, in retrospect, is thought to have changed everything.

In 1935, when Henry M. was 9 years old, he was knocked down by a boy riding a bicycle. As a result of the accident, Henry lost consciousness for approximately 5 minutes. Within a year of the accident, Henry experienced a minor (petit mal) seizure. At the age of 16 years, he suffered a major, generalized convulsive episode. By the time Henry was a young adult, his seizures had become more frequent and more severe. He was experiencing as many as 10 minor and 1 major seizure each week (Hilts, 1995). None of the anticonvulsant medications that were available at the time could successfully control the seizures. Henry had to abandon his goal of becoming an electrician: He could not climb or work on a ladder for fear of falling during a seizure.

In a desperate attempt to relieve the seizures, in August 1953, when Henry M. was 27 years old, his neurosurgeon, William Scoville, performed an experimental operation that involved removal of large portions of the temporal lobes on both sides of Henry's brain (Scoville & Milner, 1957). In that era, experimental brain surgeries were almost common. They were heralded as treatments for a range of disorders, including schizophrenia and depression. For psychiatric disorders, the area of the brain that was most frequently targeted was the front part of the brain, the frontal lobes; the surgery was known as a frontal lobotomy. In the case of Henry M., the tissue that Scoville removed was from the side of the brain, just above the ears. Figure 1.1 is a diagram of the lesion. Although the lesion was made bilaterally, in the diagram, the right side is shown intact to illustrate the structures removed. The surgery was successful as a control for Henry's seizures. Since the surgery, Henry has suffered significantly less seizure activity (he is reported to experience no more than two major seizures per year; Corkin, 2002). From the standpoint of memory, however, the surgery was a personal tragedy for H. M. even as it was a boon for researchers.

From the time of his surgery, which took place when he was a young adult, H. M. has had great difficulty learning new facts and forming memories of new public or private events (Milner, Corkin, & Teuber, 1968; Scoville & Milner, 1957). For example, he is unable to remember a list of words he studied only minutes before. His recognition of a word on the list when paired with a word that was not on the list is no better than chance. H. M.'s difficulty in learning new things extends to many different types of materials, including strings of digits; faces of famous people; series of musical tones; public events; and even private events and personal facts, such as how old he is, that his hair has grayed, or how many years have passed since his surgery. Although H. M. does show some ability to remember new information that he encounters over and over again—such as the spatial layout of the house in which he went to live 5 years after his surgery (Corkin, 2002)— he is unable to acquire new information on the basis of a single or small number of exposures to it. It is not that information does not register in H. M.'s conscious mind: He is able to remember over a matter of seconds (i.e., his short-term memory is preserved), but he fails to establish new long-term memories.

Despite the fact that H. M.'s surgery was personally devastating, he generously turned the experience to scientific advantage by collaborating in the study of his particular mnemonic syndrome. In so doing, he permitted the field to advance substantially. Since William Scoville and Brenda Milner's (1957) original assessment of him, researchers have administered to H. M. a multitude of different memory tasks. They have found that, although he performs poorly on many types of tasks, he does well on others. For example, in an early study, H. M. demonstrated that he was able to learn a new motor skill. Specifically, over the course of 3 days, H. M. learned to copy a geometric figure reflected in a mirror, making fewer and fewer errors on each copying attempt (Milner et al., 1968). H. M.'s performance improved each day despite the fact that he had no conscious recollection of ever having at-

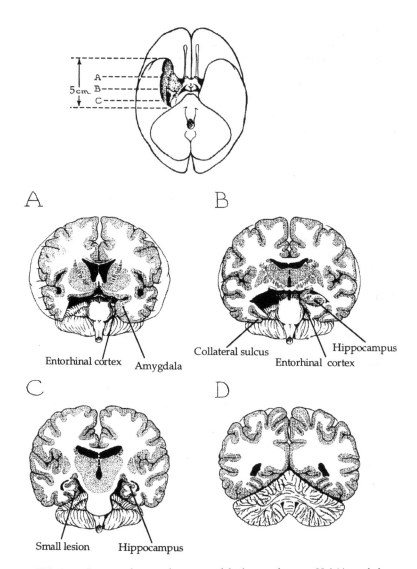

FIG. 1.1.   Diagram showing the extent of the lesion of patient H. M.'s medial temporal lobe based on MRI studies. The inset at the top of the figure is a ventral (bottom–up) view of the human brain showing the rostro-caudal (front-to-back) extent of the lesion. A through D are drawings of slices through the brain, arranged from rostral (A) to caudal (D), showing the extent of the lesion. Note that, although the lesion was made bilaterally, the right side is shown intact to illustrate the structures that were removed. From "H. M.'s Medial Temporal Lobe Lesion: Findings From Magnetic Resonance Imaging," by S. Corkin, D. G. Amaral, R. G. González, K. A. Johnson, and B. T. Hyman, 1997, *The Journal of Neuroscience, 17*, 3964–3979, Fig. 1. Copyright © 1997 by the Society for Neuroscience. Reprinted with permission.

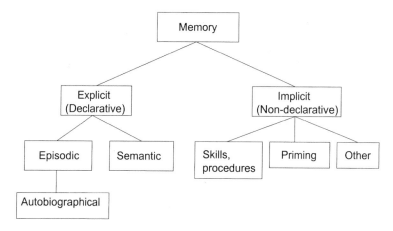

FIG. 1.2.   Taxonomy of different types of memory. Based on Squire (1987).

tempted the task before! As a result of years of study of H. M., researchers have found common elements in the wide range of memory abilities that are preserved versus those that are disrupted in H. M. and other patients like him (e.g., R. B.; Zola-Morgan, Squire, & Amaral, 1986). The major type of memory that is impaired in H. M. has come to be known as *explicit* or *declarative*; the major type of memory that remains intact in H. M. has come to be known as *implicit*, *nondeclarative*, or *procedural*. As depicted in Fig. 1.2, autobiographical memory, the subject of this volume, falls into the category of explicit memory.

## Declarative and Nondeclarative Memory

One of the most significant distinctions between declarative (or explicit) and nondeclarative (or implicit) memory is that we are consciously aware of the former, but not of the latter. Ironically, this distinction is the most contentious in part because there is no agreed-on definition of *consciousness*. As an approximation, Morris Moscovitch (2000) offered that, ". . . consciousness is a mental state that permits one to have a phenomenological awareness of one's experience" (p. 609). We are consciously aware that when we are driving a car and we want to stop the car, we use the brake. We are not, however, consciously aware of how many pounds of pressure we apply to the brake or how we change the amount of pressure if we need to come to a rapid stop versus a more gradual stop. Skilled braking does not come from conscious reflection; it comes only with practice. Nor can we easily describe to someone else how to be a skilled braker. Rather, we tell the novice driver, "You'll get the feel of it." More important, from the standpoint of memory, the concern is not as much with the mental state, but with the contents that can be brought to consciousness. In other words, the concern is with ". . . those aspects of memory that can inform conscious experience, that are the object of phenomenological awareness, and about which the person can reflect and comment" (Moscovitch, 2000, p. 609). How do we know when we are consciously aware? Stefan Köhler and Morris Moscovitch (1997) suggested that, ". . . one is conscious or aware of [a memory] when a verbal or nonverbal description can be provided of [it] or a voluntary response can be made that comments on it" (p. 306).

Köhler and Moscovitch's (1997) rule for how we can tell when we are consciously aware of a memory or past experience entails another distinction between declarative and nondeclarative memory: the contents with which the different types of memories are associated. Declarative memory is devoted to processing of names, dates, places, facts, events, and so forth. These are entities that we think of as being encoded symbolically and that can be described with language. In contrast, much of nondeclarative memory is devoted to perceptual and motor skills and procedures. Smooth braking while driving is not a name, date, place, fact, or event, but a collection of finely tuned motor patterns, behaviors, and perceptual skills that we cannot verbally describe.

Declarative and nondeclarative memory also differ in terms of their *functions*, *rules of operation*, and as becomes apparent in chapter 5, in the brain regions and systems that support them. From the standpoint of its *function*, declarative memory is specialized for fast processing and learning. The instructor need tell us only once (or perhaps a few times) that the brake is what we push to stop and the accelerator is what we push to go. After a brief period of study, this basic distinction is mastered explicitly. The instructor can give a written examination, and we can fill in the blank: "To stop, you depress the _____." In contrast, acquisition of most of the mnemonic abilities subsumed under the nondeclarative umbrella proceeds more slowly: Behavior is modified only with practice, experience, or multiple trials. That is, it is only with extensive practice that we learn how much pressure to apply to the brake pedal to stop or how to skillfully pump the brakes to stop on ice or snow.

Declarative and nondeclarative memory differ in their *rules of operation*. Declarative memory is fallible: We forget names, dates, places, and so forth. In fact as becomes apparent in subsequent chapters, much forgetting from declarative memory occurs literally minutes, hours, and days after an experience. Although there are compelling demonstrations of long-term remembering of lessons learned in high school and college (e.g., foreign language vocabulary; Bahrick, 2000), we are all painfully aware of just how much is lost even within a semester. In contrast, nondeclarative memory seems to be infallible. A typical example is riding a bicycle—we may not have ridden a bicycle in many years, but when we ride one again, we "just know how." Indeed breaking an old nondeclarative pattern can be quite difficult, as exemplified by the tendency to, in a moment of panic, slam the pedals backward (as we did on our old one-speed bikes) instead of squeezing the hand brakes (as we should on our adult, multispeed bikes). This is not to say that declarative memory is invariably fallible and nondeclarative memory is invariably infallible: They are relative terms.

Declarative memory operates in a flexible, context-independent fashion. We can learn a fact in Location 1 and declare the fact later in Location 2. From my office at Duke University in Durham, North Carolina, I can declare that the capital of North Carolina is Raleigh—a fact that I learned in my elementary school in Indianapolis, Indiana. Thus, declarative memory is portable and transferable. In contrast, nondeclarative memory tends to be tied to a particular context. For example, out of the context of my computer keyboard, I could not possibly tell you how to get from the "j" key to the "o" key. Yet as I type, 99 times out of 100 I execute the operation without error. The inflexibility of nondeclarative memory is perhaps nowhere better illustrated than in the domain of priming. *Priming* is said to occur when a behavioral response to a stimulus is stronger following prior exposure than it would have been absent prior exposure. A typical scenario for demonstration of priming effects is to have participants study lists of words, such as that in Table 1.1. For some participants, a target word is included on the list (e.g., *elephant*), whereas for other participants, the target word is not included. After some intervening task, the same participants are given the test of completing a number of word-fragment problems. Among them is the fragment "e l _ p _ _ n t." Participants who have studied the list that included *elephant* are more likely to complete the fragment than are participants who studied the list without the word on it. Critically, the effect is diminished if there are surface-feature changes between study and test. For example, if, as depicted in the bottom half of Table 1.1, at study the font of the word list is blurred but at test the fragment is in focus, the amount of priming is diminished (e.g., Roediger & Blaxton, 1987).

With respect to the distinction between declarative and nondeclarative memory, it is important to keep in mind that, in most cases, one derives both declarative and nondeclarative knowledge from the same experience. Learning to type is a good example. In typing class, students learn the key positions quite explicitly. Demanding typing instructors even give tests in which, outside the context of the keyboard, students are required to indicate the keys on home row in order, whether "t" is to the left or right of "o," and other such specific features. Yet one would never become a good typist based on this kind of experience alone. To become a good typist, one must practice executing the motor movements of typing. Although I am explicitly aware that the "j" key is on the second row of the keyboard (and is, indeed, the resting state position for the index finger on the right hand) and that "o" is on the top row, this ex-

TABLE 1.1
Sample Stimuli for a Priming Study

| | Condition | |
|---|---|---|
| Effect Strength | Study (List of Words) | Test (Word Fragment Problems) |
| Stronger priming (study and test share surface features) | elephnt | m _ _ g i _ a l |
| | emotion | e l _ p _ _ n t |
| | convert | l _ _ s _ d e d |
| | optometry | p _ u _ a _ |
| Weaker priming (study and test have different surface features) | *elephant* | m _ _ g i _ a l |
| | *emotion* | e l _ p _ _ n t |
| | *convert* | l _ _ s _ d e d |
| | *optometry* | p _ u _ a _ |

*Note.* The fragments can be completed with the words *marginal, elephant, lopsided,* and *plural.*

plicit knowledge is not what permits me to skillfully move my fingers from "j" to "o" as I type "j-o-l-l-y." That skill is acquired through practice, practice, and more practice at hitting the keys on the keyboard.

Another important point is that, in most cases, declarative and non-declarative knowledge not only are acquired in parallel, but they continue to coexist even after execution of the behavior no longer seems to require conscious awareness. Many skills, such as typing and driving, start out very demanding of attentional resources, yet eventually can be performed almost automatically—that is, without conscious attention paid to them (e.g., one can walk and chew gum at the same time!). Such changes tempt the conclusion that, once these skills no longer require conscious attention to execute, they have "become implicit." A moment's reflection reveals the flaw in this logic, however: If declarative knowledge were to become nondeclarative, that would mean it was no longer declarative. The fact that I can tell you that the "j" key is on home row, between the "h" key on the left and the "k" key on the right, proves that my knowledge is accessible to consciousness, although I do not have to think about where the "j" key is to type. In other words, I still have the explicit knowledge even though it is not that knowledge on which I depend to execute the behavior. In the intact organism, declarative and nondeclarative knowledge and memory coexist. Many behaviors are executed based on nondeclarative memory alone, but that does not mean that one type of knowledge has "turned into" another. Rather, at the time of learning, both types of knowledge were acquired; skilled performance of the motor behavior may be supported by one (nondeclarative), yet the other (declarative) continues to exist.

## Different Types of Declarative Memory

Although the distinction between conscious, symbolic, fast, fallible, and flexible explicit or declarative memory and unconscious, nonsymbolic, slow, infallible, and inflexible implicit or nondeclarative memory takes us a major portion of the way, it does not yet capture the specific type of memory that is the subject of this volume—namely, *autobiographical memory*. To get to autobiographical memory requires that we consider the two major subtypes of declarative memory: *semantic memory* and *episodic memory* (Schacter & Tulving, 1994).

*Semantic memory* supports general knowledge about the world (Tulving, 1972, 1983). We are consulting semantic memory when we retrieve the fact that the capital of North Carolina is Raleigh, that the largest city in the state is Charlotte, and that in the month of August it is very hot in North Carolina. Like the other type of declarative memory (episodic memory), semantic memory is long term. That is, humans seem capable of storing bits and pieces of information (sometimes embarrassingly trivial information) over long periods of time. For practical purposes, the capacity of semantic memory seems infinite. By way of contrast with episodic memory, semantic memory is not tied to a specific event or time. We know that (a) birds fly; (b) elephants are a type of pachyderm; (c) despite their resemblance to fish, whales are mammals; and (d) the heart and the lungs work together. However, in most cases, we do not know when and where we learned this information. We might be able to reconstruct how old we were or what grade we were in when we gained these valuable gems; but unless there was something unique about the experience surrounding the acquisition of this information, we carry it around without address or reference to a specific episode.

*Episodic memory*, in contrast, supports retention of information about unique events (Tulving, 1972, 1983). Episodic memory is what permits us to remember that, earlier in the day, a Downy Woodpecker flew to the feeder, extracted a peanut, and flew off. It allows us to remember whether the word *elephant* was on a list we studied in the context of a memory experiment. It supports memory for the time we went whale watching off the coast of San Diego, California. It is episodic memory that permits me to remember that I learned that "the heart and lungs work together" from Mr. Lakes, my fifth-grade science teacher at MacArthur Elementary School.

Some episodic memories, such as memory for whether a particular word was on a study list, do not stay with us for very long and are not especially personally relevant or significant. Such memories are episodic because they are linked to a specific place and time. In the case of the word *elephant*, semantic memory supports knowledge that it is a type of pachyderm (a timeless, placeless bit of information), yet episodic memory supports whether the word was on the list studied earlier in the day in the context of that memory experiment. Generally speaking, however, these episodic memories do not have a great deal of personal significance, and thus are not especially good candidates for becoming autobiographical or personally defining. In contrast, others of our episodic memories are highly personally relevant and, indeed, are the episodes we reference when we define ourselves. Why do I remember that I learned about the cooperation of the heart and lungs when I was in fifth grade? I learned many other things in the fifth grade, yet I have a vivid memory of learning this particular fact and not others. This episode has stuck with me because of the reaction of Mr. Lakes to a challenge I put to him when he imparted to the class this fact. My challenge was, "If the heart and lungs work together, why doesn't my heart stop when I hold my breath?" Mr. Lakes' response was to the effect that I had asked a really good question and that I should become a scientist and find out why. This episode frequently comes to mind when I think about the forces that shaped my educational and career choices. In this regard, the episode is highly personal and autobiographical. It is this particular kind of episodic memory—namely, autobiographical memory—that is the primary subject of this volume.

## WHY ISN'T PUDDING ENOUGH?

In the space of a few pages, I have introduced a number of distinctions within the domain of memory. Whereas virtually every student of memory would agree with divisions along the temporal dimension (i.e., short- vs. long-term memory), not all would agree with division of memory into two different systems—declarative and nondeclarative—or with division of declarative memory into semantic and episodic. Indeed in the late 1980s and early 1990s in particular, a debate waged over whether, through different tasks (e.g., recall of word lists vs. priming), researchers were studying fundamentally different systems of memory, as claimed by some scholars (including Graf & Schacter, 1985; Mishkin & Petri, 1984; Squire, 1987), or whether they were studying what was basically a single kind of memory under different cognitive demand conditions, as argued by Henry Roediger and his colleagues, for example (e.g., Roediger & Blaxton, 1987; Roediger, Rajaram, & Srinivas, 1990). Generally, the latter argument did not go so far as to imply that memory was pudding, but it did question division into different memory systems characterized by different rules of operation and supported by different neural structures, for example.

A major reason for the debate was the manner in which research purporting to demonstrate two different memory systems was conducted. Not infrequently, researchers took representatives from a patient population (such as H. M.), tested them on a task thought to tap Memory System A, and then tested them on a different task thought to tap Memory System B. Finding that the patients could perform one of the tasks but not the other, researchers concluded that there was support for the proposal of different memory systems: one that was intact and another that was impaired. Yet as pointed out by Henry Roediger and his colleagues, there is a major problem with this approach in that inherent in it is a confound between the purported system and the task used to measure it: Different tasks were used to measure different memory systems (e.g., Roediger et al., 1990). Moreover, frequently, only one task was used to measure each hypothesized system. In such studies, because task was confounded with memory system, it was impossible to differentiate the operation of different memory systems from the operation of a single system under conditions of different cognitive demands.

In the years since concerns such as these were articulated, researchers positing different memory systems have strengthened their investigative approach substantially. As discussed in detail in chapter 5, the case that there are multiple systems of memory today rests on a stool with not one, but with at least three legs. Researchers now routinely combine data from patient populations with that from animal models of trauma and disease and with that from studies in which the brains of patients and healthy research participants are imaged as they engage in different memory tasks (these different methodological approaches are discussed in chap. 5). Both within and across studies, each memory system is tested with not one, but with multiple different tasks. The data from these different sources converge to suggest patterns of breakdown and sparing, and patterns of activation and co-activation across different neural structures, that sort themselves along lines consistent with the major division between memory systems. As a result, there is growing consensus (although not universal acceptance) that there are multiple systems of memory specialized for different mnemonic tasks (e.g., Schacter et al., 2000).

It is likely that these different memory systems either evolved to deal with competing demands for different kinds of information storage, or that nature took fair advantage of structures that had evolved for other reasons to deal with the demands. Either way, one memory system seems specialized for rapid encoding of information that is subject to equally rapid forgetting, whereas the other seems specialized for acquisition of information at a slower rate, yet seemingly permits more robust retention. Why could not a single system accomplish both tasks? Although this question cannot be answered definitively, as discussed in more detail in chapter 5, computer simulations have revealed that a system which can change rapidly to accept new inputs has difficulty maintaining old inputs. Conversely, a system that is good at maintaining old inputs has difficulty "learning" new things (e.g., McClelland, McNaughton, & O'Reilly, 1995). This analysis suggests that two complementary memory systems work in concert to avoid interference with existing knowledge, yet still maintain flexibility. In full recognition that not all scholars of memory see merit in the argument for multiple memory systems, I use the distinction because, in my opinion, the perspective provides the best fit to data from the wide variety of sources described in this book (as well as data that fall beyond the scope of the volume).

## PLAN FOR THE BOOK

There have been many books and articles written about autobiographical memory. What sets this book apart is its scope. Most existing treatments address autobiographical memory in adults or autobiographical memory in children, but do not unite the literatures. Yet autobiographical memory spans childhood to adulthood, and there are interesting and important similarities and differences in the autobiographies of younger and older individuals. Moreover, treatments of autobiographical memory have not attended to the years of development that go on before verbal children share their first autobiographical experiences. In this volume, these disparate literatures are brought together under a single cover. A major focus is on the developmental events that link the separate life phases. In this domain (as in many others), a developmental perspective is especially valuable because, examined from its mature state, it is not at all clear how or why autobiographical memory takes the forms that it does. By considering autobiographical memory in its infancy through its mature years, we are able to witness the individual developmental trajectories as well as the convergence of the multiple facets of the complex ability that permits preservation of the past into the present.

The scope of this volume is relatively unique in another way as well. Most treatments of autobiographical memory deal with a single level of analysis. That is, they consider the brain regions that seem to be responsible for the experience of reliving past events, they focus on the phenomenological experience of the individuals doing the remembering, or they examine the effects on autobiographical reports of the sociocultural milieu in which reminiscing takes place. Each type and level of analysis makes an important contribution to our understanding of the phenomenon of autobiographical memory. Yet because the ability is multifaceted and multiply determined, no single type or level of analysis is sufficient; all are necessary. In this volume, I consider many of the myriad influences on autobiographical memory—from those at the level of nerve cells to those at the level of culture. That so much ground can be covered in one volume is a strong testament to the health of this field of inquiry.

The book is divided into four major sections. In Part I (chaps. 2 and 3), I provide a description of autobiographical memory and its significance. Ironically, autobiographical memory is so central to who we are as human beings that, the majority of the time, most of us blithely ignore it. Yet as becomes apparent, it is through autobiographical memory that we as individuals maintain a sense of connection with our own past and thus a sense of continuity over time. Case studies such as that of Henry M. make this clear: Without the ability to form autobiographical memories, we have no sense of who we are relative to who we were. The loss of autobiographical memory is part of a larger complex of ailments that falls under the rubric of amnesia—loss of memories of past events (*retrograde amnesia*) and the inability to form new memories (*anterograde amnesia*). These types of amnesia frequently go hand in hand and are the result of trauma or disease.

Although we can be grateful that most of us will not suffer an anterograde or retrograde amnesic syndrome, most of us do suffer from another form of amnesia—namely, infantile or childhood amnesia. *Infantile amnesia* and *childhood amnesia* refer to the relative paucity among adults of verbally accessible memories from the first years of life. In other words, infantile or childhood amnesia represents a period of time for which continuity of self is lost or disrupted: Without memories of what happened early in life, we effectively have no early life. In the first section of the volume, I describe the amnesia more fully and summarize the most influential theories as to the source(s) of infantile or childhood amnesia. I then begin evaluation of the theories by examining the characteristics of the early memories that we do have, as well as some intriguing individual and group differences in early autobiographical memory.

Part II (chaps. 4, 5, and 6) concerns memory function and development in the period of time from which, as adults, we typically have few if any autobiographical memories—the first 3 years of life. As is seen, one of the most tenacious theories as to the source of this almost total amnesia is that children younger than 3 to 3½ years of age simply do not form memories that endure and are accessible over time. In other words, the suggestion is that, throughout infancy, individuals are unable to encode, store, and subsequently retrieve memories of the events that take place in their lives. What is more, it has been widely believed that even after children finally develop the ability to remember events, their memories are poorly organized and unreliable.

To evaluate these suggestions, I review data on long-term memory in infancy and very early childhood and how it changes over the first years of life. I also review one of the major contributors to change in it—namely, developments in the brain structures that support the broader class of memory to which autobiographical memories belong (declarative memory). As becomes apparent, use of nonverbal methods for testing memory in young children has revealed that, although infants are not able to speak, they can remember specific past events. The findings make clear that, in their strongest form, suggestions that adults lack memories from early in life simply because none were formed cannot be true. Nevertheless, there are pronounced changes in memory function throughout early childhood, as well as in the neural structures that support it. Links between the structures and functions, as well as their implications for developments in autobiographical memory, are explored.

Part III (chaps. 7, 8, and 9) focuses on developments in memory in the period of time from which, as adults, we have some, but not a large number, of memories—the preschool years. As becomes apparent, contrary to the impression gathered from examination of adults' recollections of this period of time, preschool-age children have very active mnemonic lives. They remember the activities in which they engage on a daily or routine basis, and they also remember unique experiences of the sort that make up one's autobiography. Their memories are accurate, long lasting, and, in their organization and structure, remarkably similar to those of older children and even adults. Nevertheless, over the course of the preschool years, there are age-related changes in autobiographical memory—changes that help explain why adults remember less from this period of time relative to the later years.

As is the case in the period of infancy, in the preschool years, changes in autobiographical memory are related to developments in the brain structures that support declarative memory. Also during this time are important developments in a number of conceptual domains related to autobiography, such as in the child's self-concept. A child's developing sense of self allows her or him to appreciate that some events have personal relevance or significance, thus lending the *auto* to the *auto*biography. In addition, there are substantial and significant changes in the skills that allow children to tell others about their life experiences. In contrast to children's earliest, rather "minimalist," autobiographical reports, the narratives of older preschoolers are chocked full of details of who did what to whom, when, and why. All of this development takes place within particular familial and cultural milieus that interact with the characteristics of the individual child to produce truly unique tellers of individual life tales. The patterns of individual and group differences in autobiographical memory that emerge in the preschool years are wholly consistent with those that populate the literature on autobiographical memory in adults.

In Part IV (chaps. 10 and 11), I review the literature that concerns the fates of memories as individuals make the critical transitions from infancy to early childhood, and from early to later childhood. These points in developmental time are prominent in the phenomenon of infantile or childhood amnesia and in the achievement of adultlike autobiographical memory. Ironically, they are the periods in development from which we have the least data. As a result, although we now have evidence that preschool-age and younger children remember the times of their lives, we have little data on whether those early memories cross the great divides that seem to separate the period of infancy from that of the preschool years, and the period of the preschool years from that of middle and later childhood (and adulthood). As it accrues (slowly), the evidence is proving to be largely consistent with the expectations derived from an examination of adults' autobiographical records.

In the final chapter, I take stock of the entire body of available evidence and use it as the basis for an account of the development of autobiographical memory that also serves as an explanation for the phenomenon of childhood amnesia. Changes in both remembering and forgetting have prominent roles to play in the conceptualization. On the remembering side of the coin are developmental changes that render memories increasingly autobiographical in appearance, such as greater self or personal relevance and association with a particular place and time. The net effect is that, with increasing age, the number of memories recognized as clearly autobiographical increases substantially and significantly.

The complementary side of remembering—forgetting—also is involved in shaping the course of development of autobiographical memory. In fact, early in development, the role of forgetting could be said to be more prominent than that of remembering. For a variety of reasons, including limitations imposed by the immature brain on the encoding, storage, and subsequent retrieval of memories in the first years of life, the memories of early childhood are more vulnerable to forgetting, relative to those from later childhood and adulthood. As a result, although memories are formed, they are not retained with the reliability or robustness of later-formed memories. An adultlike autobiography is achieved when the rate of formation of "typical" autobiographical memories outstrips the rate at which memories are lost to forgetting. It is the cross-over point of the functions of remembering and forgetting that in the literature is recognized as the "offset" of childhood amnesia and the "onset" of autobiographical memory.

In the conceptualization fashioned over the course of this volume and brought together in the final chapter, the point in developmental time when the functions of remembering and forgetting cross over is the product of continuous changes in a number of different elements. The elements are associated with different levels of analysis. Together they permit maintenance of a personal past that grows and develops with its author.

# 2

# Autobiographical Memory in Adults

> *I would have you imagine, then, there exists in the mind of man a block of wax . . . and that when we wish to remember anything which we have seen, or heard, or thought in our minds, we hold the wax to the perceptions and thoughts, and in that material receive the impression of them as real, the seal of a ring; and that we remember and know what is imprinted as long as the image lasts; but when the image is effaced, or cannot be taken, then we forget and do not know.*
>
> —Plato, from *Collected Works of Plato* (~354 BCE)

Plato's wax provides a perfect medium for preserving beyond the moment the details of the times of our lives. "As long as the image lasts," we can remember and know the weddings, graduations, births, and deaths that constitute our life stories and personal pasts. The details of these events—when they occurred, who participated in them, where they took place, and so forth—are matters of public record. A critical feature of our autobiographical memories for events such as these is that they go beyond the public record, however. Like Plato's wax, in addition to the objective details of who did what to whom, autobiographical memories feature information about the perceptions, thoughts, and emotional reactions of the participants in the events, and indications of the significance the events had for their personal lives. By way of analogy, we may say that autobiographical memories are to event memories as diaries are to public records. Whereas memories of events and public records are potentially faithful impressions of what happened at a particular place and a particular time, autobiographical memories and personal diaries ". . . are infused with the idiosyncratic perspectives, emotions, and thoughts of the person doing the remembering" (Wheeler, 2000, p. 597).

The difference can be illustrated with reference to this excerpt from an adult female's narrative, describing the birth of her son:

> I remember the amazement (I) felt when my son was born. He was red and wrinkly with bright blue eyes staring into my eyes. He was tinier than I expected. The room around me kind of disappeared and I stared at my new baby feeling excited, nervous, and shocked. I didn't feel tired at all. My son was bundled up very tight in a blanket wearing a rainbow cap. I was wearing a hospital gown. I was sweaty and my hair was very messy. It was the most amazing moment of my life. (From the data set reported in Bauer, Stennes, & Haight, 2003; West & Bauer, 1999)

The events that would be entered into the public record of the birth of this baby boy are readily apparent and would be the same for all who participated in it. That is, all present would have been able to observe that the infant was small and that the author of the narrative was wearing a hospital gown. What would not be contained in the public record, however, are the emotions, thoughts, reactions, and reflections of the new mother. These features of the event could not be objectively observed, and thus would not appear in the public record, but they would appear in the mother's diary account of her experience. It is the presence (or absence) of these "diary features" that distinguishes autobiographical memories from "run-of-the-mill" event memories. The purpose of this volume is to describe this specific type of memory and its development in the individual, and to work toward a multilevel explanation of its form and function. As argued in chapter 1, if we are to make progress in understanding autobiographical memory, we must be clear about what "it" is. Thus, I begin with a detailed definition of *autobiographical memory*.

## DEFINING AUTOBIOGRAPHICAL MEMORY

As implied by the contrast between public records and personal diaries, autobiographical memories differ from event memories in that *autobiographical memories are infused with a sense of personal involvement or ownership in the event.* They are memories of events that happened to one's self, in which one participated, and about which one had emotions, thoughts, reactions, and reflections. It is this feature that puts the *auto* in *auto*biographical.

In addition to the defining feature that autobiographical memories are about one's self, there are a number of characteristic features that mark memories as autobiographical. One of the characteristic features of this particular type of episodic memory is that *autobiographical memories tend to be of unique events that happened at a specific place, at a specific time.* In other words, they are memories of particular episodes, as opposed to general se-

mantic memories (i.e., knowledge of the world; see chap. 1). By this definition, recollection of the moment of first meeting your child is an autobiographical memory, whereas the self-relevant fact that you have a child is
not. The latter may be a true fact and it is a fact about one's self. However,
it is not a recollection of a specific episode. By this criterion, memories of
such things as the physical layout of the house in which you grew up, or
that when you were a child you were extraordinarily fond of mint choco-
late-chip ice cream, are not autobiographical memories. These examples
are of memories that are relevant to the self, but they are not memories of
unique events or experiences.

Another feature of autobiographical memories is that they entail a *sense of
conscious awareness that one is reexperiencing an event that happened at some
point in the past* (Rubin, 1998; Tulving, 1985a, 1985b, 1993; Wheeler, 2000).
As discussed in chapter 1, conscious awareness is one of the defining features
of explicit or declarative memory. Thus, it alone does not differentiate autobiographical memory from event memory (or the diary entry from the public
record). Rather, the distinguishing feature is that the individual is aware that
she or he is reexperiencing an event that happened in her or his own past. In
the excerpt provided earlier, this sense is conveyed by the narrator's statements that she "remembered (her) amazement," that "the room around (her)
kind of disappeared," and that "it was the most amazing moment of (her)
life." This specific type of awareness, termed *autonoetic* or *self-knowing*, has
been associated with memory from the time of William James (1890). Indeed
for James, "Memory requires more than the mere dating of a fact in the past.
It must be dated in *my* past . . . I must think that I directly experienced its
occurrence" (p. 612). Many other phenomena that, by the end of the 20th
century, were widely recognized as indicative of memory, including motor
learning, for example, were described by James, but were not considered evidence of memory by him.

The requirement that retrieval of a memory entail a sense of conscious
awareness of it having happened in one's own past also figured prominently
in Endel Tulving's (1985a, 1985b, 1993) seminal definition of *episodic memory*. His major division between episodic and semantic memory hinged on
the type of awareness that accompanied it: Episodic memory was characterized by autonoetic (self-knowing) awareness, whereas semantic memory was
characterized only by noetic (knowing) awareness. Ironically, however, although Tulving defined episodic memory in terms of its personal relevance
and phenomenological reexperience, historically, much of the work conducted in the semantic-episodic framework lacked the sort of personal relevance that was part of the definition of a memory as episodic. That is, rather
than asking participants to recall significant events of their lives, researchers
had them remember lists of words and other personally insignificant stimuli.
For this reason, although autonoetic awareness is associated with episodic

memory more broadly, discussion of it figures most prominently in the domain of autobiographical memory.

In summary, a defining feature of an autobiographical memory is that it is about one's self. Autobiographical memories also tend to be of particular episodes or events that happened at a specific place, at a specific time. In addition, autobiographical memories are characterized by a sense of conscious awareness on retrieval of them: One is consciously aware that one is reexperiencing an event from one's personal past. As is seen in chapter 11, this "family resemblance" definition of autobiographical memory (i.e., a concept specified by characteristic as opposed to defining features; Rosch & Mervis, 1975) has important implications for how we conceptualize its developmental course. In consideration of the defining and characteristic features of autobiographical memory, in the context of this volume, when reference is made to *autobiographical memory*, the focus is on memories for unique experiences in which the individual has a sense of personal involvement. Because specific queries of individuals about the phenomenological features of their retrieval are not common, less emphasis is placed on the feature of autonoetic awareness. The definition of *autobiographical memory* in the present volume corresponds to what William Brewer (1986, 1996) referred to as *recollective* or *personal* memory. The term *autobiographical* is preferred for present purposes because it conforms to current usage (Larsen, 1992), especially in the context of the developmental literature.

Although the focus of this volume is on development, it is wise to begin discussion of autobiographical memory with adults to gain a sense of perspective on the phenomenon, the development of which we are attempting to describe and explain. However, because of the developmental focus, the treatment of adult autobiographical memory provided is relatively brief. The interested reader is referred to reviews of the adult autobiographical memory literature by Ulric Neisser and Lisa Libby (2000) and David Pillemer (1998) for more comprehensive treatments.

In the sections that follow, I briefly describe some of the techniques that have been used to study adults' autobiographical memories. This discussion is important because the answer to any question is determined in part by how the question is posed. In other words, what we "know" about autobiographical memory is through the eyes of particular methods. Critical evaluation of the literature requires that we have some appreciation of the strengths and weaknesses of the methods on which it is based. After a brief review of the methods used to study autobiographical memory in adults, I discuss some of the characteristics of adults' memories that have been discovered through the use of the techniques and describe some of the features that well-remembered events seem to have in common. The chapter ends with consideration of some of the sources of systematic individual and group differences that have been observed in adults' autobiographies. Over the course of the balance of the volume, a major goal is to bring developmental data to bear to aid in explanation of why adults' autobiographical memories take the forms that they do.

## TECHNIQUES FOR STUDYING AUTOBIOGRAPHICAL MEMORY IN ADULTS

A representative (although certainly not exhaustive) list of techniques for studying adults' autobiographical memories is provided in Table 2.1. The first known experimental study of memory for a naturally occurring event was carried out by Sir Francis Galton (1880), the founder of *Differential Psychology* (the study of individual and group differences, rather than common traits) and developer of the statistical methods of correlation and regression. In the service of the study of individual and group differences in visual imagery, Galton distributed questionnaires to colleagues in the scientific world and to members of the general public, asking them to rate the phenomenological properties of a particular image based on past experience. Specifically, Galton asked respondents to recollect the appearance of the breakfast table "as you sat down to it this morning" and then to rate the mental image on the dimensions of illumination (e.g., "Is the image dim or fairly clear?"), definition ("Are all the objects pretty well defined at the same time, or is the place of sharpest definition at any one moment more contracted

**TABLE 2.1**
**A Sample of Techniques for Studying Adults' Autobiographical Memories**

*Retrospective Techniques*

Describe and/or rate the phenomenological properties of mental images
    (e.g., "Rate the clarity of the mental image.")
Free recall
    (e.g., "Tell me [or write down] what you remember about the time you _____.")
Cue word
    (e.g., "Think of a specific memory associated with the word _____.")
*Autobiographical Memory Interview* or *Autobiographical Interview*
    (e.g., "Describe an incident that occurred [in a specific life period].")
"Reception" events
    (e.g., "Describe how you first heard the news of [specific event].")

*Prospective Techniques*

Diary
    (maintain records of events as they occur for later tests of recognition, recall, or both)
"Beeper"
    (record events of the moment in response to external signals, for later recognition, recall, or both)

than it is in a real scene?"), and coloring ("Are the colours of the china, of the toast, breadcrust, mustard, meat, parsley, or whatever may have been on the table, quite distinct and natural?"). He remarked on two notable results of the study: ". . . the proved facility of obtaining statistical insight into the processes of other persons' minds; and . . . that scientific men as a class have feeble powers of visual representation. There is no doubt whatever on the latter point, however it may be accounted for" (p. 304). (Galton went on to contrast the "feeble powers" of the men of science he sampled—19 of whom were noted to have been Fellows of the learned Royal Society—with those of a group of elementary school boys. He used the contrast between the samples to speculate on developmental changes in visual imagery.)

In contemporary studies, participants are frequently asked to rate the qualities of their autobiographical memories. In some cases, the focus of the research is (as it was for Galton) the phenomenological properties of the memories themselves (e.g., Larsen, 1998). In other cases, the ratings are used to predict some other feature of the memory, such as its robustness and resistance to forgetting (e.g., Thompson, 1998).

Other common techniques for studying autobiographical memory include free recall and the use of cue words. As the name implies, in free recall, respondents are given an open-ended prompt and then asked to provide a narrative description of the event: "Tell me what you remember about your first day of college." The cue-word technique was originally proposed by Galton (1879) as a means to study free association. It involved reading a word (e.g., *ice cream*) and then expressing whatever ideas the word elicited. Herbert Crovitz and his colleagues (Crovitz & Quina-Holland, 1976; Crovitz & Schiffman, 1974) adapted the technique to the study of memory by asking participants to "think of a specific memory" associated with a given word (e.g., Rubin, Wetzler, & Nebes, 1986). Especially for their work with patient populations, researchers sometimes desire more standardization than these rather unconstrained techniques permit. In such cases, they may rely on instruments such as the *Autobiographical Memory Interview* (AMI; Kopelman, Wilson, & Baddeley, 1989, 1990), in which participants are asked to provide information from each of three life periods: childhood, early adulthood, and recent life. Autobiographical reports are elicited with such probes as, "Describe an incident that occurred while you were attending elementary school" (see also Levine, Svoboda, Hay, Winocur, & Moscovitch, 2002, for description of a similar instrument, the *Autobiographical Interview*). Greater standardization also can be achieved by asking all participants to report on the same experience, such as their recollections of receipt of the news of historic events such as the assassination of President John F. Kennedy (e.g., R. Brown & Kulik, 1977), the explosion of the Challenger Space Shuttle (e.g., Neisser & Harsch, 1992), or the tragic events of September 11, 2001 (e.g., Pezdek, 2003).

What all of the techniques just described have in common is that they are *retrospective*: They require that participants "think back" to a previous experience. In some cases the target event is from the recent past (i.e., the morning's breakfast table), whereas in others it is from the distant past (i.e., an incident from elementary school). In the case of recollection of events from an individual's personal life, rarely is there an objective record of the event in question. This makes it difficult to evaluate whether what the participant reports is what "really happened" or to verify when the event occurred. This problem is overcome in cases when the target event is a matter of public record or when informants are available to verify the accuracy of the report. Even in these circumstances, however, what can be verified are the details of the events themselves; what cannot be verified are the elements that make the memories autobiographical. Despite these limitations, these techniques are the source of much of the rich data we have on adults' autobiographical memories. As becomes apparent over the course of this chapter, open-ended, free-recall probes yield narratives that can be analyzed for their form and content; responses to cue-word probes can be used to plot the distribution of memories from different phases of life, yielding insight into the function and determinants of autobiographical memory; and asking participants to report on their memories of historic events is a major source of information concerning autobiographical memories for traumatic or highly stressful events.

Whereas much of the literature on adults' autobiographical memories is derived from retrospective accounts, *prospective* studies are also represented in the literature. In prospective studies, respondents keep records of the events of their lives and later query themselves or are queried by others for their memories of the experiences. One distinct advantage that such studies offer over retrospective studies is that the date and circumstances of the events in question, as well as the respondents' impressions of them, can be clearly identified because they were recorded at the time of the experience. One major disadvantage, however, is that they are labor-intensive—requiring as they do that participants record the events of their lives for later tests. As a result, prospective studies tend to be of single participants or small groups of participants. Perhaps the best known prospective study of one's own autobiographical memory is that of Marigold Linton (1975), who kept a diary of personal events each day for several years. At various intervals, she submitted herself to memory tests for subsets of the events that had happened during the recording period. Similar efforts were carried out by Willem Wagenaar (1986) and Richard White (2002), some results of which are discussed in a subsequent section.

One potential problem with self-directed prospective studies is that respondents may wittingly or unwittingly select events that are likely to be highly memorable. Indeed Linton (1975) did exactly this: The items she selected for later tests were precisely those she anticipated would be most memorable. This procedure introduces a source of bias in the results, one that may obscure normative patterns of remembering and forgetting. To circumvent this potential problem, William Brewer (1988) introduced a clever "beeper" technique. For the term of the study, Brewer had participants wear a pager-type beeper that went off at times determined by the researcher. When the beeper sounded, participants were to record on a response card information about their ongoing activities, such as the time, their location, their actions, and their thoughts and emotions (a criterion for selection into the study was that the participant had to have legible handwriting!). The participants were later tested for their recognition, recall, or both, of the entries on the response cards (see also Thompson, 1998). Such studies effectively eliminate the problem of self-selection of events to record. In summary, there are a number of techniques that permit various "windows" on the contents of adults' autobiographical memories. Both retrospective and prospective approaches have their strengths. No approach is without is limitations.

## CHARACTERISTICS OF ADULTS' AUTOBIOGRAPHICAL MEMORIES

Although across studies the techniques that have been used to examine adults' autobiographical memories have differed, the studies tend to converge to suggest regularities in the form in which autobiographical memories are reported and represented, especially as it relates to the function of autobiographical memory. They also highlight areas of apparent strengths and weaknesses in adults' autobiographical records.

### The Form and Function of Autobiographical Memories

*Form.*  Memory can be displayed in a number of ways. For example, nondeclarative memory is exhibited when we drive a car, tie our shoe, or hit the right keys on the keyboard even though we are looking out the window as we type (see chap. 1 for discussion). Individuals such as Henry M. (introduced in chap. 1), who have amnesia due to damage to the medial temporal lobe structures implicated in declarative memory (discussed in chap. 5), exhibit memory for procedures such as copying geometric figures seen only in a mirror, although they have no recollection of ever having performed the task before. Even in the first months of life, infants exhibit memory when they, for example, kick their legs vigorously after having learned the contingent relation between kicking and the movements of a mobile suspended above their cribs (discussed in chap. 4).

Although we are willing to accept a variety of behaviors as evidence of memory, there is almost universal agreement that *autobiographical memory is expressed in only one way—namely, verbally* (although see Howe & Courage, 1993, for an exception). As David Rubin (1998) succinctly argued, ". . . language and especially narrative structure are necessary components of autobiographical memory" (p. 53). The narrative structure to which Rubin referred is the familiar form of a newspaper story, one that includes the components of *who, what, where, when, why*, and *how*. As individuals produce autobiographical narratives, they typically adhere to the temporal order in which the events unfolded. They use the past tense to tell the story, except perhaps when reliving an especially salient aspect of the event or experience, at which point they may switch to the present tense (Pillemer, 1992). How the conventional form for telling and retelling autobiographical narratives is acquired is the subject of chapters 8 and 9.

Although autobiographical memories are *expressed* verbally, that does not mean they are represented in memory only as narratives or exclusively in verbal format. On the contrary, imagery—especially visual imagery—is thought to play an important role in the maintenance and recollection of autobiographical events (see Brewer, 1996; Larsen, 1998; Rubin, 1998, for discussions). Powerful images are clearly evident in the excerpt provided at the beginning of this chapter—as a mother recalls the birth of her son. Reports from participants in controlled studies of adults' autobiographical memories indicate that the process of recollection of an event frequently gives rise to visual images (e.g., Brewer, 1988). In his 1996 review, Brewer indicated that, among undergraduate research participants, ". . . the frequency of occurrence of imagery is frequently close to 100% . . ." (p. 36). Participants' ratings of the strength or vividness of the image are higher for accurate relative to inaccurate recollections. Moreover, memories about which participants are very confident are rated as having a stronger imagery component, relative to memories about which participants are less confident (Brewer, 1988). Similar indications of the role of strong visual images in memories are to be found in Brown and Kulik's (1977) conceptualization of *flashbulb memories* (in which memories of certain events are likened to a photograph of the experience). Thus, it seems that events that are well remembered likely have a strong visual component to them. Indeed a strong visual image is one of the features that makes some memories especially vivid (Rubin, 1998).

**Function.**   The form of autobiographical memories says something about their function, the most obvious of which is social. That is, it is through telling the events of our lives to others that we as individuals share ourselves with others. The *social function* of autobiographical memory more than anything else dictates that the form be verbal: Unless the person with whom we are communicating was there at the time of the event, one of the only ways to paint the picture and share the event is through language (representational art is, of course, another medium, but the temporal unfolding of events is especially challenging to convey even for the artistically talented among us). More accurate copying of geometric forms and more vigorous leg kicking cannot convey what happened, to whom, why, or how the participants felt about the experience. Language is virtually the only means of expression that can do that. For a listener to appreciate the event, the narrator needs to provide a setting for it (the narrative *where* and *when*), tell *who* was there, *what* happened, and the narrator needs to provide the causes and consequences of the event (*why* and *how*). In addition to making it possible to tell others what happened, the narrative form also serves an organizational function, making it easier to remember the times of our lives (i.e., as a coherent story, as opposed to an arbitrary list of characters and actions).

Autobiographical memory also serves an *explanatory function*: We justify and rationalize our present behaviors by appeals to events in our pasts. Some nice illustrations of this function of autobiographical memory are available in personal memory narratives about college experiences collected by David Pillemer and his colleagues (e.g., Pillemer, Picariello, Law, & Reichman, 1996). Respondents in these studies sometimes have been current college students and in other studies graduates of academic institutions. In a typical study, students and former students are asked to provide a description of an influential educational experience. Many of the examples illustrate turning points in students' academic careers, such as this excerpt from a student who explained her change of major:

> In my sophomore year, I took an English literature course. I loved the course material, enjoyed writing papers, and felt pretty good about it until . . . I wrote an essay on my interpretation of a poem. I felt I had great insight into a special meaning within the verse. When the paper was returned, the teacher told me I didn't have any understanding of the material and she hoped I wasn't going to be an English major. I remember her pinched face and small, tight mouth as she said these things to me. I thought no way do I want to be like her. So I changed my major from English to Sociology. (Pillemer et al., 1996, p. 333)

Formative experiences may be positive as well, as illustrated by another excerpt from Pillemer and his colleagues (1996), this one taken not from their own work, but from a 1972 autobiography of noted developmental psychologist Jerome Kagan:

> My commitment to chemistry was also weakened by a psychology professor's idle comment in the introductory psychology course. He had posed a question I cannot remember, but to which I apparently gave a good answer. He asked me to stay and as we walked across the campus he said I had an apperceptive feeling for psychology and added, "You would probably be a good psychologist." The sentence rings as clearly now as it did that afternoon 22 years ago. I began to think about psychology more seriously. (Kagan, 1972, p. 140; cited in Pillemer et al., 1996, p. 319)

The explanatory function of autobiographical memory actually belongs to a larger functional category—that of *personal identity*. As noted earlier in this chapter, autobiographical memory is quintessentially personal. As Ulric Neisser, one of the fathers of modern cognitive psychology and noted scholar of autobiographical memory, once said: "We are our memories" (Neisser, 1982). It is the collection of personal events that defines us as individuals. Autobiographical memory is our personal past, our historical self. What we have experienced is who we are. In this sense, autobiographical memory *is* self:

> First of all, everyone uses the past to define themselves. Who am I? I have a name, a family, a home, a job. I know a great deal about myself: what I have done, how I have felt, where I have been, whom I have known, how I have been treated. My past defines me, together with my present and the future that the past leads me to expect. (Neisser, 1982, p. 13)

Perhaps no place is the critical role of autobiographical memory in one's self-concept more obvious than in cases in which the personal past is lost. In his popular 1985 volume, *The Man Who Mistook His Wife for a Hat*, Oliver Sacks told the tale of Jimmie G. who, like Henry M. introduced in chapter 1, suffered a profound case of amnesia. In the case of Jimmie G., the memory loss was not the result of surgery, but of years of alcohol abuse, which caused damage to some of the neural structures implicated in autobiographical memory (see chap. 5, for discussion; amnesia is one of the features of a larger alcohol-related clinical syndrome known as Korsakov's). Jimmie G. had no difficulties with short-term memory—he could remember lists of words or strings of digits for a few seconds at a time. He also had excellent long-term memory of events from the distant past. Specifically, he remembered his early childhood and himself as a young man. However, because he had essentially lost the capacity to form new declarative memories, he was unable to "update" his life history (although the etiologies of the amnesic syndromes are different, the reader will note similarities in the patterns of loss and sparing in the cases of Jimmie G. and Henry M.). Although Jimmie G. was in his 50s when he met Sacks for the first time, he presented himself as a 20-year-old. Not only did he talk about his life in the navy during World War II as if it were the present, but he had no comprehension of what he was doing in the hospital talking to Dr. Sacks. A quotation from Sacks makes the point very poignantly:

Sacks:      . . . I'm the neurologist here.
Jimmie:   Neurologist? Hey, there's something wrong with my nerves? And "here"—where's "here"? What is this place anyhow?
Sacks:      I was just going to ask you—where do you think you are?

Jimmie:   I see these beds, and these patients everywhere. Looks like a
          sort of hospital to me. But hell, what would I be doing in a hos-
          pital—and with all these old people, years older than me. I feel
          good, I'm strong as a bull. Maybe I work here . . . do I work?
          What's my job? . . . No, you're shaking your head, I see in your
          eyes I don't *work* here. If I don't work here, I've been *put* here.
          Am I a patient, am I sick and don't know it, Doc? It's crazy, it's
          scary. . . . Is it some sort of joke? (Sacks, 1985, p. 26; italics orig-
          inal)

## "Black Holes" and "Bright Spots" in Adults' Autobiographical Memories

Although thankfully few of us suffer from the amnesia that Oliver Sacks' patient Jimmie G. experienced, we nevertheless have "black holes" in our autobiographical memories. That is, we frequently forget events that at the moment seemed incredibly important. Conversely, we have "bright spots" of
remarkable memories for some of the events of our lives. These impressions
that we have of our own memories are born out by studies employing the
various retrospective and prospective techniques described earlier.

*Black Holes.*   There is one major black hole with which all researchers of
autobiographical memory are familiar and into which some of the memories
of virtually all adults have fallen: Most adults recall few experiences from the
first years of life. This phenomenon, known as *infantile amnesia* or *childhood
amnesia*, is the subject of chapter 3. For present purposes, the focus is on
adults' recollections of the more recent past. Given that long-term memory,
of which autobiographical memory is a subset, is considered to have infinite
capacity and duration, it may seem that forgetting should be an anomaly.
However, a moment's reflection makes abundantly clear that we do not remember all the times of our lives! (Although see Luria, 1968, for a description of a man with an extraordinary memory, known as "S", who among
many other feats maintained in memory a virtually complete record of the
events of his life, dating from infancy.)

Lapses of autobiographical memory are most readily apparent in studies
employing prospective methods—in these cases, there is documentation that
an event occurred and, thus, we know there was something to recall. We can
then ask whether the event is recalled at a later time. Because of the dedi-
cated efforts of psychologist Richard White (2002), we are able to track over
a period of 20 years the fate of one individual's memories of the events of his
life in the year 1979. Each day for the entire year, White wrote a 20- to 50-
word description of one event that had happened that day. He attempted to
select a range of events, from unusual to, in his words, "humdrum." In addi-

tion to the description, he rated the event on seven characteristics, including its frequency, his level of participation in the event, how vivid the event was, how personally significant it was, its association with existing knowledge, the intensity of physical sensations associated with the event, and the intensity of emotion associated with the event.

White then tested his memory for the events of 1979 after four different delays: 1 year (test in 1980; reported in White, 1982), 2 years (test in 1981; reported in White, 1982), 6 years (test in 1985; reported in White, 1989), and 20 years (test in 1999; reported in White, 2002). For each test, White read the descriptions he had written of the events, in random order, and for each, he rated the quality of his recall of the event on a 5-point scale, with 5 indicating *total recall*, 4 indicating a *high degree of recall*, 3 indicating *some details recalled, but substantial loss of information*, 2 indicating *awareness of event, but few details*, and 1 indicating *no recollection of the event*.

As reflected in Table 2.2, even at the first test, after a delay of only 1 year, White had *total recall* of few events. In fact there was only one event for which he judged himself to have *total recall*. In contrast, he had no recollection of 40% of the events that he had described in his own words! White had roughly the same level of recall of the events of 1979 when he tested himself again a year later (i.e., after a 2-year delay). By the time 6 years had passed (i.e., the 1985 test), White had no recollection of 60% of the events. Twenty years later, he had forgotten 83% of the experiences he had recorded. White (2002) acknowledged this rather astounding rate of forgetting and also noted its contrast with rates estimated by Linton (1975) and Wagenaar (1986), both of whom employed similar methods, yet had high rates of recognition for events they had recorded. The difference may be accounted for by the fact that White purposefully recorded a variety of events, as opposed to those that were most distinctive. The findings are all the more illustrative for precisely that reason, however: Most of the days of our lives are a mixture of unusual and "humdrum" events.

TABLE 2.2
The Percentage of Events From the Year 1979 Remembered
by Richard White After Delays of 1, 2, 6, and 20 Years

| Rating of the Quality of the Memory | Recall Test (and Retention Interval) | | | |
|---|---|---|---|---|
| | 1980 (1 year) | 1981 (2 years) | 1985 (6 years) | 1999 (20 years) |
| 5 (Total recall) | 1% | 0% | 0% | 0% |
| 4 | 25% | 16% | 4% | 1% |
| 3 | 16% | 15% | 15% | 6% |
| 2 | 19% | 23% | 21% | 9% |
| 1 (No recall) | 40% | 45% | 60% | 83% |

*Note.* Based on White (2002), Table 1.

*Bright Spots.*    Although adults clearly do not remember all (or even the majority) of the events of their lives, they nevertheless have rich memories of many experiences. One of the most common ways to estimate how much of their pasts individuals remember is to use the cue-word technique. When autobiographical memory is sampled in this way, without restrictions on the time period from which individuals are to draw experiences or on the types of experiences they are to retrieve, an interesting retention function is revealed. The function obtained from mature adults is depicted in Fig. 2.1. The solid line reflects the number of memories mature adults are *observed* to retrieve from each year of life. The broken line reflects the number of memories that adults would be *expected* to retrieve based on forgetting alone (i.e., with the passage of time, some forgetting is expected). The first thing to notice about the function is that events from the first few years of life are not well remembered: The observed number of memories from the early years is below the number expected. This infantile amnesia or childhood amnesia is the subject of chapter 3. The second notable aspect of the function is that events from the ages of 10 years to 30 years are well represented, even among respondents in their golden years. This so-called *reminiscence bump* is frequently observed in studies with respondents 40 years of age and older (see Rubin, Rahhal, & Poon, 1998, for a review). As discussed in more detail later in the chapter, it is thought that it might be associated with the period during which a mature sense of personal identity begins to form. It is during this time that individuals decide on academic majors and careers and make

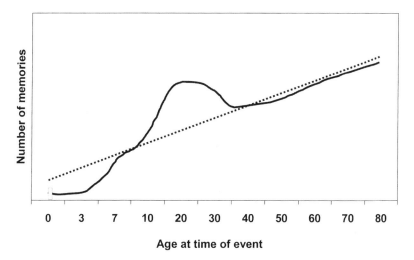

FIG. 2.1.    Schematic representation of observed and expected retention functions from mature adults. The number of memories observed is represented by the solid line. The number of memories that would be expected based on forgetting alone is represented by the broken line.

major relationship decisions, for example (as illustrated by the excerpts from Pillemer et al., 1996). Throughout life there may be frequent reflections on this period, which essentially function to strengthen memories of the events of the time.

The typical retention function is, of course, an abstraction drawn over many memories and many individuals. Within such a function, some events are better remembered than others. In addition, because retention functions are estimated based on retrospective studies, there is always the question of whether the events are remembered accurately or whether there are significant errors in them. Moreover, because the functions are abstracted across individuals, they do not capture the individual variation in adults' autobiographical memory reports. In the next section, I discuss the types of events that adults seem to remember the best. Over subsequent chapters of the volume, it becomes apparent that some of the features which seem to work to make events especially memorable by adults represent developmental challenges for children. Because the challenges are met slowly, over the first decade of life, they represent significant constraints on the ability of individuals to remember events from early in life.

## QUALITIES OF THE EVENTS ADULTS REMEMBER

A moment's reflection, not to mention the results from studies like Richard White's (2002) analysis of the strengths and weaknesses of his own memory, makes clear that, in the domain of autobiographical memory, not all events are created equal: Some events are better remembered than others. Although there are clear (and not infrequent) exceptions, there are nevertheless some commonalities across events that are well remembered. After discussing some of the features that seem to increase the likelihood that an event will be retained over time, I consider the issue of whether the events are remembered accurately.

### What Contributes to Later Autobiographical Recall?

In Table 2.3 are listed a number of factors that have been implicated as predictors of adults' memories of the events of their lives.

*Personal Significance.*    Perhaps the most obvious factor to contribute to formation and long-term maintenance of an autobiographical memory is the personal significance of the event: Events that are important to individuals

TABLE 2.3
Factors Implicated as Predictors of Adults' Recollections of Events

| Factor | Expected Effect |
| --- | --- |
| Personal significance | Events that are important to individuals will be well remembered |
| Distinctiveness | Events that are unique will be well remembered |
| Affective intensity | Events that are "affectively charged" will be well remembered |
| Life phase | Events from the ages of 10 to 30 years will be well remembered |

should be well remembered. Indeed this feature figures prominently in folk theories of autobiographical memory. That is, personal significance, relevance, or importance is one of the features that individuals nominate as a predictor of the strength of their own memories (e.g., Csikszentmihalyi, Larson, & Prescott, 1977), and it is invoked as an explanation for why some events are well remembered and others are forgotten. In actuality, personal significance is not an especially satisfying explanation, however. Empirically, ratings of the personal significance of an event are not very predictive of later recall. For example, for each entry, Richard White recorded in his diary a rating of the *importance to self* of the event of the day. Whether memory was tested 1 year later or 20 years later, the ratings were essentially unrelated to later recall. In two studies from my own laboratory, adults' retrospective ratings of how personally meaningful events were to them bore virtually no relation to what they remembered about the events (Weigle & Bauer, 2000; West & Bauer, 1999). Thus, whether tested prospectively (as in White, 1982, 1989, 2002) or retrospectively (as in Weigle & Bauer, 2000; West & Bauer, 1999), how personally significant an event is judged to be seems to bear little relation to later recall.

The feature of personal significance or personal relevance is also less than satisfying conceptually because of the danger of circularity: If an event is well remembered, it must have been personally significant; if the event is forgotten, it must *not* have been especially personally relevant. Yet as just discussed, judgments of importance to self made at the time of an event are not strongly related to later memory for an episode (e.g., White, 2002). Although the feature of personal significance is not predictive of adults' memories of autobiographical experiences, and it is a less-than-satisfying explanation for why some events are remembered and others are not, the construct may have significance *developmentally*. As is seen in chapter 8, the self for whom events are more or less significant undergoes a protracted course of development. The extent to which individuals reference events to themselves thus changes over time. The larger number of events from later in life, relative to early in life, remembered by adults (see Fig. 2.1) may be explained in part by this aspect of development.

*The Distinctiveness of the Event.*   One of the most consistent predictors of later recall of events is their uniqueness or distinctiveness. Specifically, events that are unique tend to be better remembered, relative to single episodes of events that occur more frequently (e.g., Brewer, 1988; Wagenaar, 1986). For example, in White's (1982, 1989, 2002) examinations of his own memories from the year 1979, the uniqueness of an event at the time it was experienced was strongly related to how well it was remembered: The less unique the event, the worse was White's recall of it. This pattern may be accounted for by interference, schematization, or both. Interference from other, similar experiences makes it more difficult to retrieve the features of any specific experience. Similarly, schematization occurs as the features that are common across experiences are abstracted and the representation condensed to include only the common elements. The result is that, ". . . repeated encounters of similar kinds blend, and the details of any single event may be forgotten . . ." (Barclay & DeCooke, 1988, p. 106). As is seen in chapter 7, the extent to which children *mark* events as distinctive, relative to one another, increases with age. It is likely that the developing ability to preserve the distinctive features of events contributes to the larger number of events from later in life, relative to early in life, remembered by adults (see Fig. 2.1).

*The Affective Intensity of the Event.*   The affective intensity of an event is another predictor of later recall: Events that are "affectively charged," or have high levels of emotionality associated with them, either positive or negative, tend to be well recalled (e.g., Brewer, 1988; Thompson, 1998; Wagenaar, 1986; White, 2002). The vivid picture of the affectively intense event of the birth of her son painted by the narrator at the beginning of this chapter is indicative of this relation. Although the effect is observed for both positive and negative affect, much of the research on the relation between affect and memory has concerned negative emotions. As discussed by researchers Sven-Åke Christianson and Martin Safer (1996), greater attention to negative relative to positive emotions and their relation to memory likely stems from the interests of clinical and forensic psychologists, whose work tends to concern negative life experiences. In addition, it is easier to induce negative emotions in the laboratory because reactions to negative experiences are less variable relative to reactions to positive experiences (i.e., there is greater consensus among individuals as to what makes us sad, angry, or unhappy than there is about what makes us happy).

Studies of recall of events with negative emotion associated with them reveal relations between the intensity of the event and subsequent memory for it. For example, participants who rate events as intensely emotional tend to have greater confidence in their memories of them (e.g., Reisberg, Heuer, McLean, & O'Shaughnessy, 1988). Participants who indicate that they felt more emotion in an event remember more central (but not peripheral) details about it (e.g., Christianson & Loftus, 1990). In addition, a number of studies have found that individuals who indicated that they had strong emotional reactions to events of national significance, such as the assassination of President John F. Kennedy (e.g., R. Brown & Kulik, 1977; Winograd & Killinger, 1983), the explosion of the space shuttle *Challenger* (e.g., Neisser & Harsch, 1992), and the events of September 11, 2001 (e.g., Pezdek, 2003; Smith, Bibi, & Sheard, 2003), tend to have better memory for the events.

Whereas memories for affectively charged events tend to be robust, memory for the emotion itself does not necessarily maintain its intensity over time; *"blunting" of emotion is especially pronounced for negative events.* The pattern is nicely illustrated in a study reported by W. Richard Walker and his colleagues (Walker, Vogl, & Thompson, 1997), conducted with students at Kansas State University. The researchers asked a number of students to record one unique event per day for periods of time ranging from 3 months to 2½ years. They asked the participants to rate the pleasantness of the events both at the time they made the diary entries and at the time their memories of the entries were tested. Ratings were made on a 7-point scale, ranging from −3 (*unpleasant*) to +3 (*very pleasant*).

Some of the participants in the study were tested after a retention interval of 3 months, others were tested after a retention interval of 1 year, and one participant was tested after a retention interval of 4½ years. Consistent with the literature already reviewed, Walker and his colleagues found that events initially rated as extremely pleasant or unpleasant were better remembered, relative to less emotionally intense events. As illustrated in Fig. 2.2 (based on Walker, Skowronski, & Thompson, 2003), over time participants' ratings of the emotional intensity of the events they recorded in their diaries faded (i.e., with increased retention interval, pleasant events were rated as less pleasant and unpleasant events were rated as less unpleasant); and the emotion associated with unpleasant events showed greater change relative to the emotion associated with pleasant events. This effect is observed even for events that originally were rated as highly arousing of negative emotion and highly personally significant (e.g., Fivush, Edwards, & Mennuti-Washburn, 2003). To quote Charles Thompson (1998), ". . . the memory for unpleasant events remains but the emotion is forgotten" (p. 40). In effect then, these data provide empirical support for the adage that "time heals all wounds" (see also Holmes, 1970; see Walker et al., 2003, for a review).

Why are affectively charged events well remembered even in the face of lessening of the intensity of the emotion over time? One category of hypotheses to explain this pattern concerns the effects of arousal on memory: The arousal associated with intense emotion is thought to focus the individual's attention on the central features of the experience, resulting in a net increase in memory for them. Consistent with this suggestion, the central features of affectively charged events tend to be better recalled, relative to more

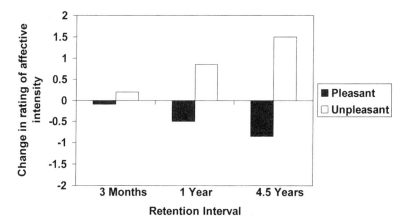

FIG. 2.2.    Changes in ratings of affective intensity after 3 months, 1 year, and 4½ years. Ratings were made on a 7-point scale (−3 to +3), with negative values indicating unpleasant affect and positive values indicating pleasant affect. Negative change indicates that the affect was rated as less pleasant after the delay relative to the time of the event; positive change indicates that the affect was rated as less unpleasant after the delay relative to the time of the event. Based on Walker, Skowronski, and Thompson (2003); values are approximate.

peripheral features (see, e.g., Christianson & Safer, 1996, for a review). Some possible neural mechanisms for this effect are discussed in chapter 5.

Whereas the influences of arousal and attention on memory almost certainly play significant roles in enhancement of memory for affectively intense experiences, it is unlikely that they offer a complete account of the effects. First, highly emotional events tend to be infrequent. In studies in which the independent contributions of frequency and emotionality have been examined, frequency, rather than emotionality, has been found to be the most important determinant of later recall (Brewer, 1988; White, 1982). The suggestion that affective intensity does not determine recall is supported by findings that a large proportion of the early memories reported by adults are rated as having no emotion associated with them (West & Bauer, 1999). Second, highly emotionally arousing events tend to engender memory narratives that are more causally and temporally connected, relative to events that are less emotionally arousing (e.g., Ackil, Van Abbema, & Bauer, 2003). There is a well-documented advantage in memory for stories, texts, and events that are highly causally connected (see van den Broek, 1997, for a review; see also chap. 7, this volume, for discussion). Thus, whereas effects of arousal almost certainly contribute to superior memory for events that are affectively charged, relative to events that are less intense, other factors—such as the distinctiveness of infrequent events and the tendency to create causally coherent narratives about them—likely play a role as well.

*The Phase of Life When the Event Occurred.* It is well documented in the literature that adults over 40 years of age have better recall of events experienced between the ages of 10 and 30 years, relative to events experienced before the age of 10 years or in later adulthood. As already mentioned, I reserve discussion of adults' memories from their childhoods (i.e., before the age of 10 years) for chapter 3. Here I consider the so-called *reminiscence bump* for events occurring between the ages of 10 and 30 years. Actual data reflecting the bump (as opposed to the schematic representation in Fig. 2.1) are provided in Fig. 2.3, from an article by David Rubin, Tamara Rahhal, and Leonard Poon (1998), based on data from Fitzgerald (1988). The figure reflects the distribution among older adults of autobiographical memories that were judged to be especially vivid, as a function of the respondents' ages at the time the events occurred. The effect is not confined to vivid memories, however: It is also observed when adults are asked to recall "run-of-the-mill" autobiographical memories as well as when they are instructed to recall the first event that comes to mind in response to a cue word (e.g., ice cream; see Berntsen & Rubin, 2002, for a review). It is also observed when adults of different ages are asked to recall a specific event, such as the resignation of British Prime Minister Margaret Thatcher on November 22, 1990, for example (Cohen, Conway, & Maylor, 1994).

Why are events from the period of 10 to 30 years of age so well recalled? Rubin et al. (1998) argued that, because the effect is observed for semantic

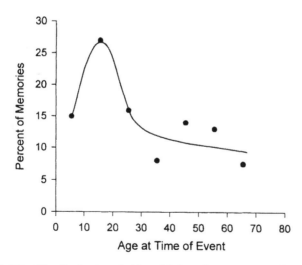

FIG. 2.3. The distribution of older adults' vivid memories as a function of their reported ages at the time the events occurred. From "Things Learned in Early Adulthood Are Remembered Best," by D. C. Rubin, T. A. Rahhal, and L. W. Poon, 1998, *Memory and Cognition, 26*, 3–19, Fig. 2. Copyright © 1998 by the Psychonomic Society. Reprinted with permission.

as well as episodic (and autobiographical) memory, explanation of it must extend beyond the domain of autobiographical memory. Indeed the effect is observed to extend even beyond memory: As reviewed by Rubin and his colleagues, adults *prefer* books, music, and films from the time they were 10 to 30 years of age. In addition, events from this period, both national and personal, are *judged to be of greater importance* relative to events from before or after this period.

At this point, there is no consensus on the explanation of the 10- to 30-year-old bump. Rubin et al. (1998) entertained three possible explanations for it, and Dorthe Berntsen and David Rubin (2002) introduced two others. One possible explanation suggested by Rubin and his colleagues is *cognitive* in nature: The bump occurs because, in contrast to the period of early childhood, late adolescence and early adulthood is a time of relative stability. Because life circumstances are changing less rapidly, relative to those in early childhood, it is cognitively "less expensive" to encode events (they are similar to experiences already in memory). In addition, the memories are retrieved frequently because events similar to those in memory are likely to be encountered. With time, as more and more similar events and memories for them accrue, the optimal conditions gradually fade, rendering events from age 30 and later less memorable.

A second explanation of the reminiscence bump, termed the *narrative/identity account*, is more social in nature. Late adolescence to early adulthood is the period during which adult identity is formed. It is during this time that individuals make decisions about life partners and occupations, the size of their families, religious commitments, and so forth. As they reflect on their lives, they remember the episodes that led to these choices. Each reference back to this period of identity formation essentially functions as a rehearsal trial, rendering events from this period more and more memorable (e.g., Fitzgerald, 1988). A similar, although distinct, possibility introduced by Berntsen and Rubin (2002) is that of the *life script*. Individuals may remember more events from adolescence and early adulthood because of cultural expectations that this is an especially important period of developmental change. By the life script account, better memory for this time of life is a product of social expectations and shared cultural norms.

A fourth explanation entertained by Rubin and his colleagues—the *biological/maturational account*—is that the period of 10 to 30 years of age is one of peak cognitive and neural efficiency and sensitivity. This may render the organism maximally fit to form lasting memories (Cohen et al., 1994, made a similar suggestion). Finally, Berntsen and Rubin (2002) speculated that psychological explanations such as those just reviewed may not be necessary to account for the bump. Rather, it may be the product of the *actual distribution of emotionally charged events across the life span*. In other words, individuals may remember more from the period of 10 to 30 years because this is the time of life when the most memorable events—those that are most affectively charged—occur with greatest frequency. Regardless of the explanation or combination of explanations, it is clear that the time in life at which an event occurred is related to how well it is recalled later in life.

## The Utility of Adults' Ratings

In the case of the so-called *reminiscence bump*, an objective measure—age at the time of the event—predicts the likelihood of later recall. I also reviewed relations between participants' subjective judgments of, for example, the distinctiveness of an event or the affective intensity of an event and the likelihood or completeness of subsequent recall of it. In addition to the characteristics discussed, there are any number of features of events that might predict later recall, including, for example, whether an objective record of the event exists (e.g., photographs, videotapes), whether the event was frequently recalled or rehearsed during the retention interval, the individual's role in the event (whether as participant or observer), and how much sensory information was encoded in the event representation. By and large, factors such as these have not been found to relate to adults' autobiographical memories (e.g., White, 2002). Indeed in my laboratory, in two separate samples of adult women and men who were asked to provide narrative accounts of recent life events, none of these factors, including retrospective reports of distinctiveness and affective intensity of events, was related to narrative content (Weigle & Bauer, 2000; West & Bauer, 1999; see also Abson & Rabbitt, 1988).

At first glance, it may seem odd that self-ratings of the qualities of one's memories bear such little relation to the memory content reported. It is, after all, *your* memory you are being asked to rate. Further consideration brings the lack of relation into perspective, however. As noted by Ulric Neisser and Lisa Libby (2000), asking adults to rate their own memories is a "paradoxical enterprise": If an individual has poor recall of an experience, then how much trust are we able to place in that individual's rating of her or his (poor) memory? In addition to this "memory introspection paradox," Douglas Herrmann (1982) discussed several other possible reasons for poor correspondence between individuals' ratings of their memories and their objective performance, including instability in self-reports that may be associated with motivational state and confidence in memory task performance. With these factors in mind, it is perhaps less surprising that adults' self-reports of the qualities of their own memories do not necessarily relate to the actual content reported. Because failures to find significant relations generally do not make their way into the literature, it is likely that we will never know such things as (a) the extent of the relation between ratings and recall, (b) how the relation might vary as a function of the nature of the event, and (c) how the relation might vary as a function of the period of life from which the event is drawn. More research on this topic is clearly called for, however, given the widespread use of memory questionnaires as measures of memory performance.

## Is Autobiographical Recall Accurate?

Throughout the history of research on autobiographical memory, the accuracy of adults' recall has been questioned. The issue plagues the literature because, in so many cases, there is no objective, public record of what *actually* occurred in the course of the event and, thus, no means to verify the memory report. Nor is there typically a record of the diary-type features that mark the personal significance of autobiographical memories. As discussed by William Brewer (1996), it is clear that individuals *believe* their autobiographical memories to be true. Moreover, judgments of confidence in one's memory are one of the few self-ratings that have been found to relate to memory accuracy (see Brewer, 1996, for a review; although see Neisser & Harsch, 1992; Schmolck, Buffalo, & Squire, 2000, for compelling exceptions). Yet just how accurate are adults' autobiographical memories?

One of the ways that the question of accuracy has been approached is to evaluate individuals' memories for national events, such as the bombing of Pearl Harbor (1941), the assassination of President John F. Kennedy (1963), or the September 11 terrorist attacks on the city of New York and the Pentagon (2001). Whereas some have argued that memories for such events are highly accurate, even photographic (or "flashbulb") accounts of what really happened (e.g., R. Brown & Kulik, 1977), others have suggested that memories of even these significant events are fraught with error. For example, Ulric Neisser and Nicole Harsch (1992) analyzed college students' memories of the explosion of the space shuttle *Challenger*. The shuttle was launched from Cape Canaveral, Florida (USA), on the morning of January 28, 1986. Within seconds of the launch, the craft exploded and all seven crew members were lost. The ill-fated mission had been widely publicized as the first to put a civilian in space: Christa McAuliffe, a school teacher, who had been selected to join the crew from among 10,000 entries for a competition. Live TV images of the event were seen by millions of people.

Neisser and Harsch's (1992) initial interview with their college-student participants was within 24 hours after the explosion of the space craft; the participants were interviewed again 2 to 3 years later. Neisser and Harsch found that as much as one quarter of the participants' later recall was in error. Schmolck et al. (2000) reported even higher rates of error and distortion in participants' recall of the circumstances surrounding the announcement of the verdict in the O. J. Simpson double-murder trial (a highly publicized event in the United States, the verdict of which was announced on October

3, 1995): 32 months after the event, the reports of 40% of the participants featured major distortions, relative to what they had reported 3 days after the event. Contrast the reports of participant M. G., for example, the first made 3 days after the verdict was announced and the second made 32 months later (from Schmolck et al., 2000):

*Three days after the verdict:*
I was in the Commuter Lounge at Revelle [College] and saw it on T.V. As 10:00 approached, more and more people came into the room. We kept having to turn up the volume, but it was kind of cool. Everyone was talking.

*Thirty-two months after the verdict:*
I first heard it while I was watching T.V. At home in my living room. My sister and father were with me. Doing nothing in particular, eating and watching how the news station was covering different groups of viewers just waiting to hear the verdict. I think that the focus was mostly on law students and their reactions to the verdict. (p. 41)

In contrast to the large percentage of participants who distorted their recall when tested after 32 months, Schmolck et al. (2000) reported high rates of accuracy after a delay of 15 months (different participants were tested after 15 months and after 32 months). Specifically, after 15 months, only roughly 1 in 10 participants (10.7%) featured major distortions in recall. Shorter retention intervals do not ensure accurate recall, however. For example, samples of Canadian (Smith et al., 2003) and Turkish (Tekcan, Ece, Gülgöz, & Er, 2003) respondents were interviewed within days of and again 6 months after the terrorist attacks of September 11, 2001. In both samples, there were significant declines in accuracy over the 6-month delay. Thus, even for distinctive events tested after relatively short delay intervals, memories are not necessarily accurate.

Although even for highly distinctive events of national significance there is no guarantee that memory will be totally accurate, there is nonetheless ample evidence of accurate memory of events from the past. For example, Marigold Linton (1975) reported very high levels of recognition of her daily diary entries, especially when recognition was supported by additional cueing. Similarly high levels of recollection of diary entries were reported by William Brewer (1988) and Willem Wagenaar (1994). An impressive example of the robustness of recall for a nationally significant event is available in a study by Tekcan and Peynircioğlu (2002). In this study, Turkish respondents were tested for recall of the events surrounding the death of Mustafa Kemal Atatürk, the founder and first president of the Republic of Turkey. At the time of Atatürk's death, the participants were at least 6 years of age. The test for recall of the event was conducted *58 years later*, when the participants were between 64 and 90 years of age. Although over 50 years had passed since Atatürk's death, almost three quarters (70%) of the participants accurately recalled autobiographically relevant details about it.

Finally, even when memory for some features of events seems fallible, it may be robust for other aspects of events. An interesting "dissociation" of this sort is apparent in the studies of recall of the September 11, 2001 attacks. As noted earlier, after 6 months, Canadian and Turkish respondents declined in accuracy of recall of the details of the events of the day, such as the timing of the attacks, the number of planes hijacked, and the crash locations. In contrast, over the same interval, the respondents maintained very high levels of recall of autobiographically relevant details, such as how they learned of the attacks, when they learned of them, and what they were doing when they heard about them (Smith et al., 2003; Tekcan et al., 2003). In short, although memory is at times fraught with error, at other times it is amazingly accurate. Moreover, it is important to keep in mind that, in the context of the study of autobiographical memory, even memory errors are interesting and important because they are part of the individual's life story or personal past. Indeed as noted at the beginning of this chapter, it is the event *as remembered* (not as it objectively happened) that forms the basis of autobiography (Wheeler, 2000).

## INDIVIDUAL AND GROUP DIFFERENCES IN ADULTS' AUTOBIOGRAPHICAL MEMORIES

Although for adults who have not suffered brain damage, autobiographical memory is virtually universal, there are individual differences. Whereas some of the differences are due to chance and other factors that we will never be able to adequately quantify, some sources of systematic differences have been identified. Here I discuss differences associated with the individual characteristic of personality traits, as well as the group difference of gender. I reserve for chapter 3 discussion of an especially active area of investigation—namely, gender and individual differences in the age of earliest autobiographical memory.

### Personality as a Source of Individual Differences

Individuals vary on a number of personality dimensions, some of which have been found to relate to autobiographical memory. For example, as discussed by Sven-Åke Christianson and Martin Safer (1996), in laboratory studies, individuals who suffer from clinical levels of depression have been found to recall roughly 10% more negative than positive stimuli (e.g., adjectives or sentences). In contrast, individuals who are not depressed recall about 8% more positive than negative stimuli. Similar effects have been found within the same individual. David Clark and John Teasdale (1982) reported that at times of the day when individuals with diurnal mood variation were less depressed, a larger percentage of the personal life events they recalled in response to specific cue words were positive than negative (51% vs. 37%, respectively). In contrast, at times of the day when the same individuals were more depressed, they recalled a greater percentage of negative relative to positive life events (52% vs. 38%, respectively).

Depression is also associated with difficulties retrieving *specific* memories. That is, when they are asked to retrieve memories of specific past events, individuals suffering from depression tend to retrieve generic memories instead. J. M. G. Williams (1996) reported the results of a study in which, even after receiving instructions to retrieve memories of one-time experiences, as well as examples of specific event memories, patients with depression retrieved fewer specific memories in response to cue words relative to nondepressed individuals. Although the patients were in the hospital at the time, the effect was not due to hospitalization because individuals who were hospitalized for reasons other than depression did not show the effect. As illustrated in Fig. 2.4, the difficulties that patients with depression had retrieving memories of specific, one-time experiences were especially pronounced for positive cue words (*happy, surprised, interested, successful,* and *safe*) relative to negative cue words (*clumsy, hurt, angry, lonely,* and *sorry*).

Individual differences in autobiographical memory have also been found to relate to an individual's *identity status,* in Eriksonian terms (Erikson, 1959,

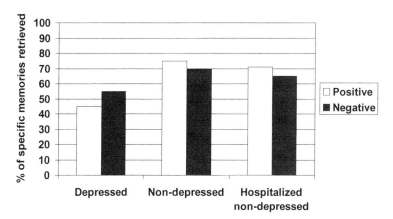

FIG. 2.4.   Percentage of specific (as opposed to general) memories retrieved in response to instructions to report memories of one-time experiences. Patients with depression retrieve a smaller percentage of specific memories relative to nondepressed individuals and individuals hospitalized for reasons other than depression. The effect was especially pronounced for positive cue words relative to negative cue words. Based on Williams (1996), Fig. 10.2; values are approximate.

1963). For Erik Erikson, an individual's identity is as much a social as a psychological construction that proceeds through a sequence of stages marked by characteristic conflicts. He considered the developmental period of adolescence and very early adulthood to be especially important because it was during this time that the individual began to feel a sense of her or his own unique identity. Erikson explicitly recognized that not all individuals resolve the challenge of formation of a personal identity in the same way. The result is that there are pronounced individual differences in identity status during this period of development. Some individuals have developed stable systems of values and commitments either as a result of periods of self-exploration (*achieved* identity status) or as a result of adoption of the value systems of parents or other authorities (*foreclosed* identity status). Other individuals have yet to achieve a stable identity either because they lack a system of commitments and values and yet are not actively exploring their identities (*diffuse* identity status) or they are still in the midst of an active struggle to achieve their identities (*moratorium* identity status; Marcia, 1966).

Greg Neimeyer and Margaret Rareshide (1991) hypothesized that, given the critical role of the self in autobiographical memory, individuals differing in their identity statuses might show different patterns of autobiographical recall. Specifically, Neimeyer and Rareshide suggested that because they have stable identities, individuals who are considered to have achieved or foreclosed identity statuses will have ready access to personal memories. In contrast, individuals who are less committed to an identity (i.e., individuals with diffuse or moratorium identity statuses) will have access to a smaller number of personal memories.

Consistent with their prediction, Neimeyer and Rareshide found that, in response to words cueing particular identity traits (e.g., *trustworthy*, *generous*, *courageous*, and *independent*), individuals with achieved and foreclosed identities recalled a greater number of personal memories relative to individuals with moratorium and diffuse identities. In addition, individuals with more committed identity statuses recalled their memories faster relative to individuals with less committed identity statuses (see also Neimeyer & Metzler, 1994). These studies suggest that differences in identity may contribute to individual differences in adults' autobiographical recall.

## Gender as a Source of Variability in Autobiographical Memory

Women and men alike talk about past experiences on a frequent basis. There are gender differences in autobiographical reports nonetheless. For example, as reviewed by Janine Buckner and Robyn Fivush (1998, 2000), women tend to be more accurate in dating their memories relative to men, women need less time to report their memories relative to men, and women tend to recall more events than do men. For the events that they recall, relative to men, women tend to provide narratives that are longer, more detailed, and more vivid (e.g., Bauer et al., 2003). One of the features that makes women's narratives more vivid is reference to the emotional states and reactions of the actors in events. That is, women tend to include more emotional content in their autobiographical narratives relative to men (Bauer et al., 2003; see Fivush, 1998, for discussion). There are also suggestions in the literature that emotion-laden memories are more readily available to women than to men. For instance, when they were asked to recall memories from their childhoods (defined as up to 14 years of age), women recalled more emotional memories than did men (Davis, 1999). The difference was unique to emotion-laden memories: Adult women and men did not differ in the number of nonemotional memories they recalled. Whether women's advantage in recall of emotional memories extends to events with both positive and negative valence is unclear: In a study by Fujita, Diener, and Sandvik (1991), women recalled both more happy and more unhappy events relative to men. Whereas the same effect was obtained in Study 1 of research reported by Seidlitz and Diener (1998), in Studies 2 and 3, women recalled more positive events than men, but gender differences in recall of negative events were less pronounced.

In a study in my laboratory, Leif Stennes, Jennifer Haight, and I asked adult women and men to provide written narratives describing recent life experiences (Bauer et al., 2003). We then examined the narratives to determine whether there were any gender differences in the ways that women and men described their internal states, such as how they felt during the event (conveyed through emotion terms such as *happy* and *sad*), what they were thinking during the event (conveyed through cognition terms such as *thinking* and *wondering*), and what they perceived during the event (conveyed through perception terms such as *see* and *hear*). We found that, relative to men, women used a larger number of words describing their emotional reactions to the events. In addition, women who used a larger number of words describing their emotional reactions also used a larger number words describing their cognitive and perceptual experiences. This pattern was not observed among men. For women, ratings of attributes such as their confidence in the details of the events on which they were reporting were not related to their use of internal states language in the narratives. For men, the more confident they were of the details of the events on which they reported and the more frequently they discussed the events, the fewer internal states terms they used to describe the events. These results tempt two conclusions. The first is that the more certain men are about what actually happened in an event, the less need they have to include information about how the event made them feel or think: Objective detail substitutes for subjective evaluation. The second tempting conclusion is that, as men talk about the times of their lives, they "strip" from their narratives mention of how the event influenced them cognitively and affectively. Alternatively, men may more frequently talk about events that have fewer internal states associated with them.

In contrast to findings of differential use of emotion terms in narratives, the women and men who participated in the study did not differ in their ratings of the personal significance of the events on which they reported, the uniqueness of the events, or the affective intensity of the events. Moreover, they did not differ in their confidence in the details of the events, the frequency with which the events had been discussed, or the visual versus propositional or "verbal" nature of the events. Nor did the gender groups differ in the perspective (first person—as if experiencing the event, versus third person—as if watching a movie of it) they had on the events on which they reported (Bauer et al., 2003). Thus, although women and men used differential amounts of emotion language, they did not use it to report on phenomenologically different types of events.

In addition to studies suggesting gender differences in the content of adults' autobiographical memories, as discussed by Janine Buckner and Robyn Fivush (2000), there are suggestions that women and men may engage in reminiscence for different reasons. Specifically, when asked why they engage in autobiographical reminiscing, women report that they do it for social reasons. That is, they indicate that they talk about the past to be intimate with another or to remember a loved one. In contrast, men report that they talk about the past to share an accomplishment, to feel good about themselves, or to take perspective on their progress in life. These differences in the reasons for autobiographical reminiscing may be related to differential orientation to interpersonal compared with agentic or individualistic themes (Buckner & Fivush, 2000). This issue is discussed again in chapters 3 and 9.

## SUMMARY

As for so many other concepts in psychology, there is no one single, accepted definition of *autobiographical* or *personal memory*. One feature on which scholars universally agree, however, is that autobiographical memories are about one's self. In addition, there is general (although not universal) agreement that autobiographical memories are of specific episodes or events, as opposed to general self-relevant facts or knowledge. In addition, retrieval of autobiographical memories is considered to involve awareness that one is reexperiencing an event that happened at some point in the past. In the taxonomy introduced in chapter 1 (Fig. 1.2), this complex of features places autobiographical memory squarely on the side of declarative memory, as opposed to nondeclarative memory. Most scholars maintain that, unlike other forms of declarative memory that may be expressed through nonverbal behavior (see chap. 4 for examples), autobiographical memories are expressed exclusively verbally. However, that does not imply that they are represented propositionally. On the contrary, mental imagery is considered to play an important role in autobiographical memory and may be the format in which many such memories are stored.

Autobiographical memories play an important role in the life of an individual. They not only are a principal means by which individuals share their lives with others, but they are a component of self-definition and are examined for their potential to explain current attitudes and behaviors. As such, although their source is a past event, they have an ongoing presence and influence on day-to-day life.

Whereas individuals certainly do not remember every event that happened to them, there are "bright spots" in autobiographical records. Events that are distinctive and that have intense emotion associated with them tend to be well remembered. There are also times in life from which individuals seem to have more memories. The period of adolescence through early adulthood is one for which there is especially dense representation of memories. Although we know some of the qualities of events that make them more memorable, and the life periods that seem to give rise to a larger number of memories, it is virtually impossible to predict what will and will not be remembered by an individual. In general, ratings of the features of events and of memories for them do not bear strong relations to later recall. In addition, there are both individual and gender differences in the quality and quantity of autobiographical memories.

In stark contrast to the density of memories from the period of adolescence through early adulthood, in the first 7 years of life, the population of recollections is sparse. These early years constitute a "black hole" in the space of memory. The phenomenon of adults' "amnesia" for events that occurred in the first several years of life is well documented. That does not mean it is well understood, however: The phenomenon represents one of the great mysteries in the field of memory in general and autobiographical memory in particular. Both because of the interest generated by the phenomenon and because explanation of it must figure prominently in any theory of the development of autobiographical memory, I devote the entirety of chapter 3 to discussion of childhood amnesia. In chapter 3, I document the phenomenon of the relative paucity of memories from early in life and begin discussion of the theories designed to explain it and the factors that might account for it.

# 3

# Infantile or Childhood Amnesia

*You are all familiar from actual experience with the peculiar* amnesia of childhood *to which we are subject. I mean that the first years of life, up to the age of five, six, or eight, have not left the same traces in memory as our later experiences. True, we come across individuals who can boast of continuous recollection from early infancy to the present time, but it is incomparably more common for the opposite, a blank in memory, to be found. In my opinion, this has not aroused sufficient surprise.*
—Sigmund Freud (1920/1935, pp. 177–178; emphasis in original;
from a series of lectures delivered
at the University of Vienna 1915–1917)

What is this "peculiar amnesia of childhood" that Sigmund Freud thought should arouse more surprise? It is precisely the amnesia introduced in chapter 2 as one of the "black holes" in adults' memories of the experiences of their lives—namely, *infantile amnesia* or *childhood amnesia*. In rough correspondence with Freud's description, adults have relatively continuous autobiographical histories from about the age of 7 years onward (with especially dense representation of memories from the second and third decades of life: the so-called *reminiscence bump* discussed in chap. 2). Prior to age 7, however, most adults suffer from an amnesic syndrome that has two phases. From the first phase—prior to age 3 years—adults have few, if any, memories. From the second phase—between the ages of 3 and 7 years—adults have a smaller number of memories than would be expected based on forgetting alone (see Fig. 2.1). In the literature, this two-part phenomenon is sometimes known as *infantile amnesia* and sometimes as *childhood amnesia*. In the balance of this volume, I use the term *childhood amnesia* to refer to both the initial period of most pronounced amnesia and the period marked by a smaller number of memories than would be expected.

From a theoretical standpoint, the peculiar amnesia of childhood is interesting and important because of its implications for our sense of self. Although we consider ourselves as continuous in space and time, there is a
point in development at which that continuity ends. That moment in time is
the "boundary" of childhood amnesia. Childhood amnesia thus presents itself
as apparent evidence of discontinuity in development. In this chapter, I provide a description of the phenomenon of childhood amnesia and review the
different categories of explanation for the phenomenon. I then begin evaluation of the adequacy of the explanations by first discussing some of the qualities of adults' earliest memories and then describing individual and group differences in the age of earliest memory and in the distribution of memories
from the preschool years. A major goal of the review is to determine the "fit"
between the phenomenon and each of the different theoretical accounts of
it. The chapter ends with a more explicit evaluation of the relative strengths
of the different categories of explanation for childhood amnesia. As becomes
apparent, a multicausal model is necessary to account for the patterns of observations, and it is toward such an account that this volume is directed.

## THE PHENOMENON OF CHILDHOOD AMNESIA

### Age of Earliest Memory

An invaluable review of the earliest days of research on the phenomenon of
childhood amnesia was published in 1941 by George and Martha Dudycha.
In their review, the Dudychas noted that, although she did not identify it as
such, the phenomenon of childhood amnesia was first reported by C. Miles
(1893). Miles used a questionnaire to gain information about the phenomenal experience of childhood. One of the questions included in the survey
was, "What is the earliest thing you are sure you can remember? How old
were you?" The average earliest memory of Miles' 89 respondents was age
3.04 years. Miles' initial report was followed by articles by Victor and Catherine Henri (1896, 1898), in which were published the results of a survey distributed through the professional journals *American Journal of Psychology*
(1895a) and *Psychological Review* (1895b). Dudycha and Dudycha credited
the Henris' study as the first to focus exclusively on early memories. It included 11 questions that queried not only the age of earliest memory, but its
phenomenal characteristics (e.g., its vividness, significance, etc.). Consistent
with the results obtained by Miles (1893), Henri and Henri (1896, 1898) reported that the earliest memory of the 118 respondents was age 3 years.
    Whereas Miles (1893) and Henri and Henri (1896, 1898) pioneered the
empirical study of memories from the first years of life, Sigmund Freud
(1905/1953) is credited with coining the term *infantile amnesia*. In his inter-

views with his adult patients, Freud noticed that few had memories from their early years. The memories that they did have were sketchy and incomplete. Freud termed this phenomenon *infantile amnesia*—". . . the peculiar amnesia which veils from most people (not from all) the first years of their childhood, usually the first six or eight years" (p. 581). Freud's interesting speculations about the sources of infantile amnesia are taken up later in the chapter. For now it is sufficient to note that, whereas earlier reports had identified age 3 as the average age of earliest memory, Freud noted the relative paucity of memories for the first 6 to 8 years of life.

In the years since Freud labeled childhood amnesia, there have been numerous studies of adults' memories of their childhoods. They have yielded one of the most robust findings in the memory literature—namely, that in Western culture, among adults, the average age of earliest verbalizable memory is 3 to 3½ years (individual and group differences in the average age of earliest memories are discussed later in the chapter). Indeed as illustrated in Table 3.1, the average age of earliest identifiable memory has remained quite stable for the 100-plus years since data on it were first reported.

One possible explanation for the apparent absence of memories among adults for events from prior to the age of 3 is that they have difficulty identifying their "earliest" memories. That is, whether responding to a survey or responding to a free-recall prompt, they must sift through a number of potential "earliest memories" to come up with their earliest. Confusion over whether Event 1 or Event 2 was the "earliest" could lead to a later estimate of the first event recalled. Although difficulties with identifying which among several potential candidate memories is the oldest is a possible explanation for the dating of earliest memory in the fourth year of life, it is not an adequate explanation. Similar estimates are obtained when individuals are

TABLE 3.1
Average Ages (in Years) of Earliest Identifiable Autobiographical
Memories for Women and Men, Women Only,
and Men Only From Representative Studies

|  |  | Participant Group | | |
| --- | --- | --- | --- | --- |
| *Study* | *Technique* | *Overall* | *Women* | *Men* |
| Miles (1893) | Survey | 3.04 | NA | NA |
| Potwin (1901) | Free recall | NA | 3.01 | 4.40 |
| Dudycha and Dudycha (1933b) | Survey | 3.58 | 3.50 | 3.67 |
| Waldfogel (1948) | Free recall | 3.50 | 3.23 | 3.64 |
| Kihlstrom and Harackiewicz (1982) | Survey | 3.24 | NA | NA |
| Howes, Siegel, and Brown (1993) | Free recall | NA | 3.07 | 3.40 |
| West and Bauer (1999) | Free recall | 3.33 | 3.33 | 3.33 |

*Note.* NA indicates that the data are not available.

asked to remember a specific event, the date of which is clearly known. Two examples of this research strategy make the point.

First, Karen Sheingold and Yvette Tenney (1982) asked female college students to provide accounts of the births of younger siblings. The respondents were between the ages of 1 year and 3 months and 17 years and 5 months at the time of their siblings' births. The researchers found that respondents who were younger than age 3 at the time of their siblings' births rarely reported remembering any details about the events. In contrast, respondents who had been age 4 or older at the time of their siblings' births were able to provide at least some details about them. Moreover, respondents who had been age 4 or older at the time of their siblings' births remembered about the same amount of detail about the events regardless of whether the births had been 3 years ago or 16 years ago.

Second, Eugene Winograd and William Killinger (1983) took an approach similar to Sheingold and Tenney (1982), but asked respondents not about the birth of a sibling, but about their recollections of the assassination of President John F. Kennedy in 1963. Although the types of events about which the respondents were to report were quite different (i.e., private birth of a sibling vs. a highly televised event of national significance), the findings were comparable. Individuals who had been younger than 3 in 1963 remembered little about the event, whereas individuals who had been 5 and older reported remembering the events surrounding the assassination. These studies make clear that the problem of dating early memories cannot account for the finding of age 3 as the average age of earliest identifiable memory: Even when the date of an event can be unequivocally located in time, individuals seem to have difficulty remembering events if they occurred before the age of 3 years.

## Distribution of Early Memories

The definition of *childhood amnesia* has two components. So far I have talked only about the first component—namely, the age of earliest memory. The second component of the definition is that, from the ages of 3 to 7 years, the number of memories that adults are able to retrieve is smaller than the number expected based on forgetting alone. What is meant by this and what is the status of evidence relevant to this component of the phenomenon?

As described by Scott Wetzler and John Sweeney (1986), normal forgetting is a linear function of the time since experience of an event. To use their example, imagine that an individual experiences 100 events per year and that, on average, each year after the event the individual forgets five events from the year. Hypothetically then, at age 20 years, the individual should recall 100 events from age 20, 95 events from age 19, 90 events from age 18, 80 events from age 16, 70 events from age 14, 60 events from age 12, 50

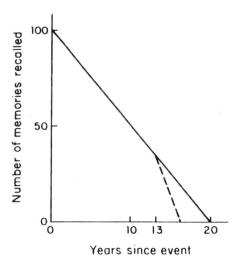

FIG. 3.1. The hypothetical distribution of autobiographical memories across the lifespan of a 20-year-old participant. The solid line represents a linear function of normal forgetting. The broken line represents the accelerated forgetting associated with childhood amnesia. From "Childhood Amnesia: An Empirical Demonstration," by S. E. Wetzler and J. A. Sweeney. In D. C. Rubin (Ed.), *Autobiographical Memory* (pp. 191–201, Fig. 11.1), 1986, New York: Cambridge University Press. Copyright © 1986 by Cambridge University Press. Reprinted with the permission of Cambridge University Press.

events from age 10, and so forth. Figure 3.1, reproduced from Wetzler and Sweeney's 1986 report, illustrates this function. If the number of events remembered were a strict function of time, then the solid black line should be observed. However, if there is differential loss of memories for events from the first years of life, then the broken line should be observed.

Are the empirical data a better fit to the solid black line or to the broken line? The weight of the evidence suggests that the broken line is a better fit to the data. The most compelling source of evidence that among adults there is an underrepresentation of memories from ages 3 to 7 is from studies employing the cue-word technique introduced in chapter 2: Respondents are asked to provide a memory related to each of a number of cue words (e.g., *ice cream*) and to estimate how old they were at the time of the event. This method has the advantage of yielding a large number of memories in a relatively brief space of time. For example, in one study, David Rubin (1982, Study 1) asked college students to provide memories in response to 125 cue words. Because the participants were not required to provide a narrative account of each event, Rubin was able to ask about such a large number of events, thus permitting him to plot the distribution of memories across the life span.

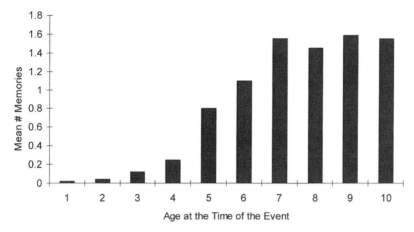

FIG. 3.2.   The distribution of autobiographical memories from the first 10
years of life generated in response to cue words. Based on Rubin and Schulkind
(1997), Fig. 1; values are approximate.

Based on data such as those provided by Rubin (1982), researchers have
created distributions of memories over the first decade of life. A sample distribution, derived from Rubin and Schulkind (1997), is illustrated in Fig. 3.2.
Both components of childhood amnesia are clearly apparent in the figure.
First, the 20-, 35-, and 70-year-old respondents reported few memories from
the period before age 3. Second, the number of memories reported increased
substantially from 3 to 7 years, at which point a flatter, more adultlike distribution was observed. This pattern has proved to be quite robust. In a review
of the literature published in the year 2000, David Rubin considered results
from 10 separate studies, which together included 10,118 memories up to age
7 and an additional 1,174 from the ages of 8 to 10. The distribution aggregated over all of the studies is depicted in Fig. 3.3. Moreover, Rubin (2000)
reported that the distribution of memories over the first decade of life is similar regardless of the specific method used to elicit the memories, the age of
the respondents at the time the memories were cued (i.e., in their 20s; in
their 30s, 40s, and 50s; and in their 60s and 70s), and the distribution is similar for females and males (I return to the issue of gender effects later in the
chapter). Thus, there is strong evidence for the second component of the
phenomenon of childhood amnesia.

## Summary

Whereas adults have robust and vivid memories from most of their lives,
they retrieve few if any memories of events that occurred in the first 3 years
of life. The relative paucity of early memories is not due to difficulties dating
events in memory: Even events with well-known times, such as the birth of a

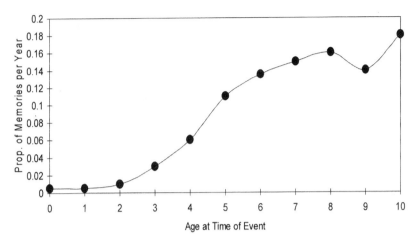

FIG. 3.3.   The distribution of autobiographical memories from early childhood
aggregated over 10 studies. Based on Rubin (2000), Fig. 1; values are approximate.

sibling, are not well recalled if they occurred prior to the age of 3. Between
the ages of 3 and 7, the number of memories adults retrieve is smaller than
the number that would be expected based on forgetting alone. Together
these features of adults' recall of early life events (or failure thereof) are indicative of so-called *childhood amnesia*. Both components of the amnesia are
robust and highly replicable across paradigms. Nevertheless, it is important
to keep in mind that both components of the phenomenon are based on retrospective accounts. That is, they are based on *adults'* recollections of their
childhoods. As seen in chapter 7, a different perspective on the development
of autobiographical memory is afforded by consideration of *preschoolers'* recall
of their pasts.

## THEORIES AS TO THE SOURCE
## OF CHILDHOOD AMNESIA

The empirical literature reviewed thus far makes clear that there is a real
phenomenon to be explained: Adults report having few memories of specific
events that happened from the time of their births to age 3. Adults remember an increasing number of experiences from the age of 3 through the preschool years, yet the number of memories from ages 3 to approximately 7 is
smaller than the number that would be expected based on forgetting alone.
Why do adults experience this relative paucity of memories from the first
years of life? In this section, I review the major categories of explanation that
have been advanced to account for childhood amnesia. For the most part,

critical evaluation of the explanations is reserved for later in the chapter, after more of the characteristics of adults' recollections of their childhoods have been explored.

## The "Hobbesean" Theory

The *least* formal theory as to the source of childhood amnesia to be considered is nicely illustrated in a cartoon from Calvin and Hobbes (by Bill Watterson). Calvin begins the exchange between the two characters:

Calvin:   You know what's weird? I don't remember much of anything until I was three years old. Half of my life is a complete blank! I must've been brainwashed! Good heavens, what kind of sicko would brainwash an infant?! And what did I know that someone wanted me to forget?? Boy, am I mysterious.

Hobbes:   I seem to recall you spent most of the time burping up.

The "explanation" offered by Hobbes for why Calvin cannot remember the events from his first years of life is that, in essence, nothing very memorable happened! Whereas there certainly is a range of "adventure" across individuals (with some individuals having more "colorful" early lives relative to others), this is not an especially viable candidate explanation. There is no doubt that young children have noteworthy experiences. Indeed one strategy for investigating adults' recall of early life events is to query them about distinctive, even life-changing experiences that were known to happen at specific times. For example, through surveys of undergraduate students, JoNell Usher and Ulric Neisser (1993) located 737 individuals who had experienced a sibling birth, family move, death of a family member, or hospitalization between the ages of 1 and 5. They asked the young adults whether they remembered these events. Although the events were clearly distinctive, the respondents did not remember details of sibling births or hospitalizations that occurred before the age of 2. They did not remember details of deaths in the family or family moves that occurred before the age of 3. Findings that even distinctive childhood events are not remembered by adults clearly invalidate the "Hobbesean" theory as to the source of childhood amnesia. We must admit then that the theory has more entertainment value than scientific merit.

## Freud's Explanation of Childhood Amnesia

In chapter 2, I mentioned the source of Freud's observations about childhood amnesia and made brief reference to part of his explanation. Freud noted that his patients rarely had memories of the first years of life. He commented on this observations in a 1905 lecture:

I believe we accept too indifferently the fact of infantile amnesia—that is, the failure of memory for the first years of our lives—and fail to find in it a strange riddle. We forget of what great intellectual accomplishments and of what complicated emotions a child of four years is capable. We really ought to wonder why the memory of later years has, as a rule, retained so little of these psychic processes, especially as we have every reason for assuming that these same forgotten childhood activities have not glided off without leaving a trace in the development of the person, but that they have left a definite influence for all future time. Yet, in spite of this unparalleled effectiveness they were forgotten! (1905/1953, p. 64)

Freud (1905/1953) further noted that memories of childhood that did exist often seemed ". . . strange or unintelligible" (p. 64). He placed little faith in them, remarking instead that they were "unreliable," yet in predictable ways. One notable characteristic was that they were not about the psychic struggles that Freud saw as the stuff of which mental life was made. Instead they had a bland, unimportant quality to them:

> . . . childhood memories . . . do not necessarily correspond to the important experiences of childhood years, nor even to those which must have seemed important from the child's point of view. They are often so commonplace and insignificant that we can only ask ourselves in astonishment why this particular detail has escaped oblivion. (1916/1966, p. 200)

From the perspective of a theory that emphasized dark and brooding psychic forces, especially in the early years of life, "underrepresentation" of what Freud viewed as significant experiences was, to him, suspicious.

Freud also was impressed by the observation that his patients often described their memories from the unrealistic third-person perspective. That is, rather than through the eyes of the beholder, the memories were described as from the perspective of a third party. Given that this was an impossible perspective for an autobiographical memory, Freud concluded that these memories were the result of reconstructive processes:

> In these scenes of childhood, whether they prove true or false, one usually sees his own childish person both in contour and dress. This circumstance must excite our wonder, for adults do not see their own persons in their recollections of later experiences. . . . Various sources force us to assume that the so-called earliest childhood recollections are not true memory traces but later elaborations of the same, elaborations which might have been subjected to the influences of many later psychic forces. (1905/1953, p. 65)

Together, Freud's observations that adults had few memories from early childhood, and that their existing memories were unrealistic in affect and perspective, motivated his *blockade* model and his description of *screen memo-*

*ries.* The relative paucity of early memories was, according to the blockade model, due to repression of inappropriate or disturbing content of early, often traumatic (due to their sexual nature) experiences. Events that were not repressed were altered to remove the offending content. In effect, he hypothesized that the negative emotion in these memories was screened off, leaving only the bland skeleton of a significant experience: ". . . through the processes . . . of condensation and more especially of displacement, what is important is replaced in memory by something else which appears unimportant. For this reason I have called these childhood memories 'screen memories' . . ." (Freud, 1916/1966, pp. 200–201).

## Different "Lenses" as an Explanation for Childhood Amnesia

A third type of explanation for childhood amnesia implicates differences in the way in which children view the world and the way in which adults view the world, both figuratively and literally. Although not a unified theory, the common element in these explanations is that there are different cognitive "lenses" for different life periods. By some accounts, the lenses differ in their reliance on language. Lacking language, young children encode memories visually or imaginally, but not linguistically. With the advent of language skills, exclusively nonverbal encoding gives way to primarily verbal encoding. As the system becomes more and more verbally saturated, it becomes increasingly difficult to gain access to memories encoded without language. As Ulric Neisser described it in a 1962 article, "Having learned speech, the child can no longer assimilate new—or old—situations as he once did, and will forget his infancy" (p. 66).

Whereas by some accounts cognitive lenses differ in their reliance on language, by other accounts different lenses are associated with different life periods, each of which has distinct hopes, fears, and challenges, for example. For instance, Martin Conway (1996) suggested that our individual autobiographical histories are broken into different life periods, "such as when I was in school, when I was at University, working for company X. . . ." Autobiographical history also may include childhood categories such as "first grade," "when I had Mrs. Z as my teacher," or "when I was friends with Y" (p. 68). Memories from different lifetime periods may differ from those from the current period—not only because of the passage of time, but because of the new "phase" of life, which may have concomitant changes in thinking or worldview.

There is also a more literal version of the "cognitive lenses" argument: Because children are physically smaller than adults, they actually experience events differently. A room that felt very large as a young child may, to an adult, feel small and cramped. The significant people in children's lives seem 10 feet tall, whereas as adults they are of normal size. The suggestion is that, as a consequence of these differences in physical perspective, cues that might be expected to trigger memories from the distant past (e.g., returning to one's childhood home) are ineffective at reinstating early memories (e.g., Campbell & Spear, 1972).

## Cognitive Development as an Explanation for Childhood Amnesia

Perhaps the largest category of explanation as to the source of childhood amnesia is that implicating general or specific cognitive developments that take place in early childhood. The strongest exemplar of this category of explanations is the suggestion that cognitive developments at the age of 3 make the storage and subsequent retrieval of memories for specific past events possible for the first time. To many, the name most readily associated with this perspective is Jean Piaget (e.g., 1952). Although Piaget is not well known for development of a specific theory of childhood amnesia, he provided a compelling explanation for it nonetheless: He maintained that, for the first 18 to 24 months of life, infants and children did not have the capacity for symbolic representation. Instead as discussed in more detail in chapter 4, they were thought to live in a sensorimotor or "here-and-now" world of physically present objects and entities that they could perceive with their senses and on which they could perform motor acts. Yet lacking symbolic capacity, they could not mentally re-present those entities in their absence. As a result, there was no mechanism for recall of past events (Piaget, 1952).

Piaget hypothesized that, by 18 to 24 months of age, children had constructed the capacity for mental representation. Why then did childhood amnesia extend to age 3 or 3½ years, fully 1 to 1½ years beyond that time? Piaget's (1962) explanation was that:

> There are no memories of early childhood for the excellent reason that at that stage there was no evocative mechanism capable of organising them. . . . The memory of the two or three year old child is still a medley of made-up stories and exact but chaotic reconstructions, organised memory developing only with the progress of intelligence as a whole. (p. 187)

In other words, Piaget suggested that, even once children had constructed the capacity to represent past events, they were still without the cognitive structures that would permit them to organize events along coherent dimensions that would make the events memorable. One of the most significant dimensions that Piaget suggested preschool-age children lacked was an understanding of temporal order. That is, he suggested that it was not until children approached the concrete operational period (at approximately 5 to 7 years of age) that they developed the ability to sequence events temporally.

Without a fundamental organizational device such as temporal order, it was no wonder that children lacked coherent memories for the events of their lives! Notice the difference between this category of explanation and that of different "lenses." The "different lenses" category of explanation suggests that the means by which early and later memories are stored are incompatible. In contrast, cognitive developmental theories suggest that, in the first years of life, children actually lack the means of storing memories for later recall. Even once the basic elements of the capacity are in place (i.e., symbolic capacity), children are thought to lack the mental organizational skills necessary to create a coherent life story.

Although Piaget's is the name most closely associated with the suggestion of qualitative changes in mental representational capacity, there are "traces" of this notion in virtually every developmental theory of information processing (e.g., Case, 1985; Fischer, 1980; Pascual-Leone, 1970). Regardless of whether they advanced specific theories of childhood amnesia, these perspectives provided ready explanations for the phenomenon in terms of limits on the number of "units" of information that could be processed. More specifically, they suggested that limits on cognitive capacity either prevented information from being encoded in an accessible format to begin with, or that limitations on retrieval mechanisms prevented it from being recalled at a later time. In most such theories, there was an implicit assumption, if not explicit statement, that changes in memory abilities were related to developments in the underlying neural structures that permit memory for specific past events. I reserve discussion of the neural changes that are implicated in memory development for chapter 6.

In addition to suggestions of global changes in cognition that make encoding, storage, and retrieval of memories possible after the age of 3, but not before age 3, there are also suggestions that specific conceptual changes play a role in the explanation of childhood amnesia. For example, Mark Howe and Mary Courage (1993, 1997a) advanced the hypothesis that the particular development of a cognitive sense of self plays a large role in the emergence of autobiographical memory. They noted the correspondence between the age from which some adults report their earliest memories—namely, 2 years (e.g., Usher & Neisser, 1993)—and developments in the sense of self that occur between 18 and 24 months. Prior to the end of the second year of life, infants may be aware that they are separate from the surrounding environment and the people in it, but they do not seem to have a concept of *me* as an individual with unique characteristics and features. In contrast, in the second half of the second year, children begin to show clear signs of a sense of self. For instance, they use their own features to recognize themselves in the mirror (as evidenced by self-directed touching when they see their reflection in the mirror, marred by a spot of rouge on their noses), they show evidence of self-consciousness (as suggested by coy smiling, for example), and they use their names to identify themselves in picture (see, e.g., Brooks-Gunn & Lewis, 1984, for a review). Howe and Courage viewed these signs of a concept of self as the cornerstone in the development of autobiographical memory: With the achievement of a cognitive sense of self, children have a device around which to organize their memories and thus can begin to construct a personal past. This and other conceptual changes that have been implicated in the explanation of childhood amnesia are discussed in more detail in chapter 8.

## The Sociocultural Perspective on Childhood Amnesia

The final category of explanation of childhood amnesia to be considered is the sociocultural account. This conceptualization emphasizes the interaction of several forces, including basic cognitive (and, specifically, memory) abilities, language, and social interaction in the construction of autobiographical memory. As two of its chief architects, Robyn Fivush and Katherine Nelson, explained it, adultlike autobiographical memory is the result of a prolonged process of establishment of a new memory ability on the foundation of episodic memory (e.g., Fivush, 1991b; Nelson, 1993a, 1993b; Nelson & Fivush, 2000, 2004). Unlike proponents of the cognitive-development perspective just described, in the sociocultural account, it is assumed that, from a young age, children are able to remember specific episodes and experiences. However, episodic memory abilities are considered only the "raw materials" of an autobiography: They are necessary, but not sufficient. Creation of enduring autobiographical memories depends on a number of additional elements, including a form for organizing and sharing memories and an appreciation of the significance of them. In this perspective, these elements are gained through the social process of joint reminiscing.

As discussed in more detail in chapters 7, 8, and 9, from early in development, children participate in the activity of sharing their own and others' memories. For young children who have limited verbal abilities, much of the work of recollecting a past experience falls to more verbally and narratively accomplished partners—typically the children's parents. Parents tell what happened in the course of an event; children participate by affirming the parents' contributions and by adding a bit of memory content here and there. Although early in the preschool years children are not the principal contributors to these conversations, through them they begin to learn how to talk about events from the past. Specifically, they begin to acquire the narrative form for telling another the *who, what, where, when, why*, and *how* of events. They also learn the important lesson of the quintessentially social function of talk about the past, which is to share your thoughts, feelings, reactions, and experiences with other people. Over the course of the preschool years, children internalize the narrative form as well as an appreciation of the social function of reminiscing. As the form becomes part of the child's own cognitive structures, it comes to serve as more than just a convenient means to convey a memory. In addition, it begins to function as a device around which memory representations are organized. As such, the internalized narrative form serves a basic mnemonic function that aids encoding, storage, and even retrieval of memories of past events.

As this discussion should make clear, in the sociocultural account, autobiographical memory is not only a personal construction, but also a social construction. As discussed in chapter 9, it is influenced by the immediate environment of a child's parents, as well as by the larger cultural milieu in which the child is raised. Families or cultures that place a high premium on talking about the past, and on the child's own experience of events, will likely promote more rapid development of structures for organizing autobiographical memories relative to families and cultures that place less emphasis on these aspects of experience. These variables interact with characteristics of the individual child, resulting in individual as well as group variation.

## Summary

Setting aside for the moment the "Hobbesean" account, there are four major categories of explanation for the phenomenon of childhood amnesia. The first serious account was that advanced by Sigmund Freud, who explained the "peculiar amnesia of childhood" in terms of repression and affective "screens." The second class of explanations invoked not screens, but "lenses," suggesting that children and adults view the world through different—and incompatible—cognitive spectacles. A major feature on which the lenses differ is their reliance on language: The cognitive world of the child is dominated by nonlinguistic representations, whereas the cognitive world of the adult is dominated by linguistic representations. From these two perspectives follow three expectations about the qualities of early memories relative to later memories. Derived from Freud's account are the expectations that the memories of childhood that would escape the veil of amnesia would be affectively bland (having been "cleansed" of unacceptable emotional content) and would be from a third-person perspective. Derived from the different cognitive lenses account is the expectation that the memories that survive childhood for later recall might be more visual (or less narrative) in nature, relative to memories from later life periods. In the next section, I review data on the qualities of early memories, with an eye toward evaluation of the extent to which they conform to these predictions. As becomes apparent, none of the expectations fares especially well.

The third and fourth families of explanations for childhood amnesia support predictions not so much about the qualities of early memories, but about patterns of development. Explanations in terms of cognitive development suggest that constraints on cognitive ability—in the form of limits on representational or organizational capacity or absence of a cognitive sense of self, for example—explain the relative paucity of memories from the first years of life. By such accounts, we would expect to see strong relations between developments in cognitive abilities and increases in autobiographical memories across the preschool and early school years. The sociocultural perspective also emphasizes developments in basic cognitive abilities as well as in language. In addition, there are expectations of different patterns of development as a function of socialization forces (both within the family and in the wider culture) to which children are subjected. From this perspective, different profiles of development would be expected for individuals and cultural groups living in different social environments. After reviewing the qualities of early memories as they bear on the first two categories of explanation, I review the data on individual and group differences in autobiographical memory, with the goal of assessing their fit with the predictions derived from the sociocultural model. Because of its large scope, the question of the role in autobiographical memory development played by age-related changes in cognition and language are reserved for subsequent chapters.

## QUALITIES OF EARLY MEMORIES

There are two ways to evaluate the qualities of early autobiographical memories. The first, an absolute approach, is to examine the reports and ratings that adults provide of their earliest experiences and characterize them along relevant dimensions (i.e., affective content, perspective, and visual vs. verbal content). The second, a relative approach, is to ask whether early and later memories differ on the relevant qualities. I take each approach in turn.

### An Absolute Approach

*Emotional Content.* Sigmund Freud's (1905/1953) theory of "screen" memories was based on the assumption that many early experiences are traumatic, and therefore tainted by negative emotion. As a protection against inappropriate and potentially ego-damaging content, the negative emotion in early memories was thought to be "screened" out. The result would be memories that were either devoid of emotion or memories in which negative affect had been replaced by positive emotion. The suggestion that early memories might be devoid of emotion or affectively neutral is not well supported by the literature. On the contrary, there is general agreement that many early memories are of events that engendered strong emotional reactions. For example, in their 1941 review of the literature, Dudycha and Dudycha reported that, in their own samples (Dudycha & Dudycha, 1933a, 1933b), only roughly 10% of early memories contained no emotion. More recent data (e.g., Howes, Siegel, & Brown, 1993; Kihlstrom & Harackiewicz, 1982) also indicate that emotion is well represented in the corpus of early memories.

Although it is clear that emotion is well represented in early memories, there is not consensus on the *nature* of the affective experiences that are remembered. Consistent with Freud's suggestion, in their 1941 review, George and Martha Dudycha reported that the literature at the time suggested ". . . better than two to one in favor of the recall of pleasant memories as against unpleasant ones" (p. 678). Some contemporary studies also indicate that early memories are more pleasant than unpleasant (e.g., Kihlstrom & Harackiewicz, 1982).

The literature also contains several studies indicating a preponderance of *negative* affect in early memories. Although Dudycha and Dudycha's (1941) review of the literature featured a number of studies that suggested more pleasant than unpleasant memories, their own research was not consistent with the overall trend. In one of their samples, 52% of early life events were associated with the negative emotions of fear, anger, sorrow, and disappointment (Dudycha & Dudycha, 1933a). In a second sample, 58% of early life events were associated with the negative emotions of fear, anger, pain, and shame and guilt (Dudycha & Dudycha, 1933b). In contrast, in the two samples, only 29% and 36% of early life events were associated with the positive emotions of joy, wonder, awe, and curiosity (Dudycha & Dudycha, 1933a, 1933b, respectively). Some more contemporary studies also have suggested a preponderance of negative emotional events in the corpus of early memories (e.g., Howes, Siegel, & Brown, 1993). For example, my colleagues and I found that, in their narrative descriptions of events that happened before the age of 7, adults included more than twice the number of negative emotion terms relative to positive emotion terms (Bauer et al., 2003). On balance, the empirical findings are not especially consistent with expectations derived from Freud's perspective: The events adults remember from early in their lives frequently have strong emotion attached to them and, in many studies, there is a preponderance of negative relative to positive emotion.

*First- Versus Third-Person Perspective.* A second expectation about the qualities of adults' memories of their childhoods is that, again due to reconstructive processes, they would be from the third-person as opposed to the first-person perspective. As discussed by Sheldon White and David Pillemer (1979), Freud (1899/1962) predicted that the majority of early memories should be in the third person. In the third-person perspective, the individual sees herself or himself moving through the event, as if watching a movie. Freud suggested that the unrealistic third-person view indicated the presence of a "screen" memory, from which inappropriate content had been censored, thereby altering the memory. Early data investigating perspective indicated that the majority of early memories are in the third person (Henri & Henri, 1896, 1898). However, more contemporary research suggests that early memories are more frequently from the first-person (64%) than from the third-person (33%) perspective (West & Bauer, 1999). Overall, as was the case with his perspective on the emotional qualities of early memories, the data are not especially consistent with Freud's suggestion on the perspective one should have on one's early memories: Both first- and third-person perspectives are well represented in the corpus of early memories.

*Visual or Imaginal Content.*    Perhaps because of the prominent role of imagery in adults' autobiographical memories (see chap. 2 for discussion), there has been a fair amount of speculation on the question of whether memories from early in life are rich in perceptual detail. Unfortunately, examination of adults' narratives and their ratings of their early memories has done little to resolve the question. On the one hand, consistent with the suggestion that early memories are encoded primarily through visual images (as opposed to linguistic symbols), there is evidence that early memories are rich in perceptual detail. For example, Miles (1893) described the memories she collected as heavily visual, as did Henri and Henri (1896, 1898). Contemporary research is consistent with these suggestions. Howes et al. (1993), for instance, reported that early memories contain a good deal of perceptual information, including color, spatial location, and image detail. Examination of narratives from participants in studies from my laboratory (Bauer et al., 2003; West & Bauer, 1999) suggests how such a conclusion might be reached:

> I was in Target with my mom and sister. It was a summer day. I asked my mom as we were checking out if I could have a pack of gum. She said "no," but I slipped it in my pocket anyway. We had a peach station wagon at the time and my sister and I were sitting in the back seat. I took out the pack of gum and my sister started whining "you didn't get me any gum!" Next thing you know my mom is taking me back into Target while I am crying madly. She made me tell the cashier what I had done. (Adult female, recalling her earliest memory, dated as age 3 years.)

> My sister and I were playing with a bunch of toys in our front yard. One toy we had was this rainbow-colored hoola-hoop with beads inside that rattled. We saw a group of older kids walking down our block toward us. We got scared and hid behind the fence that separated the front and back yards on the side of the house. I was scared that they'd steal our hoola-hoop. When we got back out front, the hoola-hoop was gone. (Adult male, recalling his earliest memory, dated as age 5 years.)

These examples contain a considerable amount of perceptual information. In her narrative, the adult female explicitly noted the store in which the event occurred, the time of year, the color of the car, where she and her sister were sitting in the car, as well as the gist of what was said during the episode. The adult male revealed where he and his sister were playing, details about the appearance of the toy with which they were playing, the direction of approach of the menacing older children, and where he and his sister took refuge from the older children. When one considers that several years had passed between the time of the events and the reports of them, the amount of detail provided in these sample narratives could be considered astounding.

Also represented in the literature is the suggestion that, in early memories, perceptual information, including visual detail, the vividness of the detail, and information about spatial arrangements, is underrepresented (e.g., Johnson, Foley, Suengas, & Raye, 1988). Once again, examination of narratives from participants in studies from my laboratory (Bauer et al., 2003; West & Bauer, 1999) suggests how such a conclusion might be reached:

> I was playing on a little ride-able toy car. I had been driving around the living room for a while. I looked down the stairs and took off. Down the stairs I went. I was fine but the car wasn't—it broke. (Adult male, recalling his earliest memory, dated as age 3 years.)

> I remember the first day of kindergarten and being sad because I was away from my mom. At the end of the day I got on the wrong bus and I started getting really scared when I realized this. By the time the driver's route was done, he had realized I was on the wrong bus and drove me home. I got off the bus, which is when I remember wearing my "St. Louis Park" orange t-shirt and ran home crying. (Adult female, recalling her earliest memory, dated as age 5 years.)

Although these narratives certainly are not devoid of detail, they make only passing reference to the physical settings of the events. That early memories may not be especially perceptually rich also is suggested by adults' ratings of their early memories. In the study from which the sample narratives were selected, adult women rated their early memories as only *moderately visual* (i.e., ratings of 2.5 on a 5-point scale; West & Bauer, 1999). Given the variability in reports of early life events, it is unlikely that examination of them will ever definitively address the question of whether early memories are "rich" in perceptual detail. It is clear that some are, whereas others are not. Additional light may be shed on the question by examining memories of early life events *as they compare to memories of later life events.*

## A Relative Approach

Examining the qualities of adults' memories of early life events is one approach to characterizing them. In isolation, however, this approach is limited because it provides no basis for comparison. That is, when we ask whether memories of early life events are positive or negative in tone, we learn something about the relative mix of affective valence, but we do not know whether the mix is unique to early life events or whether a similar balance is apparent in memories for later life events. Similarly, when we ask whether memories of early life events are "rich" in visual or perceptual features, we beg the question of "rich," relative to what? To learn whether memories of events from early in life have *unique* characteristics, we need to compare them to memories of events from later in life. In light of the attention that the phenomenon of childhood amnesia has received, there have been surprisingly few attempts to directly compare early and later memories. Indeed when Tiffany West Weigle and I looked into this question several years ago, we found no studies in which early and later memories from the same adult had been directly compared (West & Bauer, 1999). Accordingly, we conducted a within-subjects study of adults' written narrative accounts and subjective ratings of early memories (from before the age of 7) and later memories (from age 7 or later). We found surprisingly few differences in the narratives produced, although many differences in the subjective ratings.

The participants in the study that West and I conducted (West & Bauer, 1999) were college students ranging in age from 19 to 47 years, with a mean age of 24. Each participant was asked to provide written narratives of four memories from before the age of 7 and four memories from age 7 or later. They were also asked to rate each memory on a number of features, including distinctiveness, emotional intensity, and their confidence in the details of the event, for example. We then coded the memories for the presence or absence of a number of narrative elements, including imaginal properties (color and the presence of visual or other images) and emotion, as well as propositional properties (thoughts, words spoken, and narrative), locative information (including context and spatial information), and total categories, indicating the total number of categories of information represented in the narrative.

West and I found that the narratives from different life phases differed on few dimensions. Specifically, early and later memories contained different amounts, but not different types, of emotion. That is, narratives about later life events more frequently included emotion information (a finding consistent with Freud's [1899/1962] suggestion that early memories were devoid of emotion), but narratives from both life periods included both negative and positive emotion (with a preponderance of negative affect represented). Second, the percentage of later memories that the respondents indicated were from the first-person perspective was roughly comparable to the percentage of memories from early in life experienced as first person (82% and 64%, respectively). There was some suggestion in the data that, as predicted by "cognitive lenses" accounts of childhood amnesia, later memories were more narrative or propositional in nature relative to early memories, and early memories were more visual or imaginal relative to later memories. However, the findings were qualified by gender. For women only, reports of later memories were more narrative or propositional in nature relative to early memories, and reports of early and later memories did not differ in the amount of visual or imaginal information they contained. For men only, early memories were more visual or imaginal relative to later memories, and reports of early and later memories did not differ in the amount of narrative or propositional information they contained. Thus, even when they are evaluated relative to memories from later in life, reports of memories from early childhood do not seem to bear the marks expected by the Freudian or "different cognitive lenses" explanations of childhood amnesia.

It is interesting to note that, although the *contents* of women's and men's early and later memories were not strikingly dissimilar, both women and men rated their early and later memories as different on virtually every dimension. Specifically, respondents indicated that they were less confident of the details of their early memories, and that early memories had been discussed less frequently relative to later memories (women only; notice that less frequent discussion and, thus, less frequent rehearsal of early relative to late memories could contribute to lower confidence in the details of the older memories). In addition, respondents rated their early memories as less personally meaningful, less visual, less unique (women only), and less affectively intense than their later memories. Interestingly, participants' ratings of their memories did not predict the content that they provided. In other words, there were no systematic relations between ratings of confidence, uniqueness, or personal significance, for example, and the content provided in the written narratives. As discussed in chapter 2, this is not a unique finding (e.g., Abson & Rabbitt, 1988; Herrmann, 1982; Weigle & Bauer, 2000; White, 2002). The lack of relation between subjective ratings and objectively available content is an issue that merits conceptual and empirical attention: It seems that the two methods yield different pictures of the nature of memories and perhaps of differences between early and later memories in particular. Differences in subjective ratings may reflect implicit or folk theories about the nature of early autobiographical memories.

## Summary

In contrast to the empirical effort devoted to demonstration of the phenomenon of childhood amnesia, there has been surprisingly little attention paid to the characteristics of memories from the period obscured by childhood amnesia. Yet from the literature can be gleaned information relevant to the question of whether early and later memories differ on qualities predicted by two of the major categories of explanation of childhood amnesia. First, there is general agreement that early memories are of events that were affectively charged or intense; events with negative emotional tone are well represented in both early and later memories. Second, the majority of early memories are reported to be viewed from the first- as opposed to the third-person perspective. Third, rather than developmental differences, there seem to be individual, and perhaps even gender-related, differences in the visual or imaginal as opposed to narrative or propositional nature of early memories. In the next section, I bring the data on individual and group differences in reports of early autobiographical memories to bear on the possibility that significant socialization forces are at work in the offset of childhood amnesia.

## THE UNIVERSALITY OF CHILDHOOD AMNESIA

One of the features of childhood amnesia that makes it so compelling is that it is a universal phenomenon. That is, virtually every adult "suffers" from it to one extent or another. That does not mean that its form is identical across individuals, however. In this section, I consider variations in childhood amnesia through exploration of individual and group differences in the timing of its offset, in its density, and in the content of reports of early memories. The differences are interesting and important in their own right. They are also critical to consider as we evaluate theories as to the sources of childhood amnesia. For one thing, an adequate theory needs to account not only for the normative trend, but for individual and group differences as well. In addition, one of the major categories of explanation of the phenomenon of childhood amnesia—namely, the sociocultural account—explicitly predicts individual and group differences as a result of different socialization experiences. Patterns of variation consistent with those predicted by the sociocultural perspective would lend support to the account.

### Individual Differences

As already discussed, more than a century of research has revealed 3 to 3½ years as the average age of earliest memory. From the beginning of study of adults' early autobiographical memories, individual differences in the age of earliest memory have been apparent, however. For example, Victor and Catherine Henri based their 1896 and 1898 reports on 118 memories. In the corpus, there was one memory from the age of 6 months, two memories from the age of 8 months, and four memories from the age of 1 year. Thus, 6% of memories were from age 1 or younger. Thirty years later, George and Martha Dudycha (1933b) reported that, in their corpus of 233 memories, 10 memories (4% of the corpus) were accurately dated from the first year of life. In virtually all contemporary reports that provide information on variability, there are similar instances of a small number of memories from the first year of life. For example, 1 of 48 women respondents in West and Bauer (1999) dated her earliest memory from the age of 9 months.

An especially striking case of early memories is documented by the neurologist Aleksandr Luria in his 1968 book, *The Mind of a Mnemonist: A Little
Book About a Vast Memory*. In the book, Luria described the incredible mnemonic feats of a patient and long-time friend, know to the reader simply as
"S." Luria documents a number of striking features of S's memory, including
that he had recollections dating from his early infancy. Luria suggested that
the memories were never lost because S never developed the capacity for
". . . reshaping reminiscences into words, which is what happens to other of
us at a fairly early age" (p. 76; notice the similarity between Luria's explanation of S's preserved early memories and the "cognitive lenses" accounts described earlier). Whereas we might debate as to whether the excerpt that follows reflects a memory for a *specific* event, it is a report of experience
retained from infancy into adulthood:

> . . . I was very young then . . . not even a year old perhaps. . . . What comes to
> mind most clearly is the furniture in the room, not all of it, I can't remember
> that, but the corner of the room where my mother's bed and my cradle were
> . . . I remember that the wallpaper in the room was brown and the bed white
> . . . I can see my mother taking me in her arms, then she puts me down
> again. . . . (Luria, 1968, p. 77)

Whereas reports of memories for events that happened in the first year of
life are remarkable for their rarity, reports of memories from the second year of
life are not uncommon. Indeed in the contemporary literature, memories from
at least some respondents from age 2 are more the rule than the exception. As
an illustration, all 10 of the studies on which David Rubin based his 2000
analysis of the distribution of early childhood memories included some reports
of memories for events that occurred when the respondent was age 2. For
some types of events, if may even be more common to remember than to forget experiences from age 2. JoNell Usher and Ulric Neisser (1993) reported
that more than half of the respondents who at age 2 had experienced two particular events—namely, birth of a younger sibling and hospitalization (for
planned surgical procedures such as tonsillectomy, as opposed to for trauma or
critical illness)—were as young adults able to remember at least some things
about the events. For two other events—death of a family member and a family move—the majority of respondents were able to remember some details if
the events happened when they were 3 years of age, but not younger.[1]

---

[1]Usher and Neisser (1993) attributed the difference in their findings versus those of
Sheingold and Tenney (1982), who reported that the birth of a sibling was not remembered if it
occurred when the respondent was younger than age 3, to the fact that in Sheingold and Tenney,
respondents may have experienced retroactive interference: Memories of more recent sibling
births may have interfered with memories of earlier sibling births.

Just as there are differences in the *earliest* early memory (from as early as the first year of life), so are there differences in the *latest* early memory. An illustrative example is available in the research Stennes, Haight, and I conducted (Bauer et al., 2003). Of 48 women in the sample, the latest earliest memory was age 6; of 30 men, the latest earliest memory was age 5½. There are few developmental phenomena for which the age of onset is so variable. For example, consider one domain that is often cited as having considerable individual variability—early language development. Normally developing infants are observed to produce their first words sometime between 10 and 17 months (Bloom, 1998). Although this range is large indeed, it pales in comparison to the range in timing of adults' earliest memories, which in a single study varied from less than 1 year to 6 years!

In addition to differences in the age of earliest memory, there are *individual differences among adults in the* density *of early memories.* That is, some adults are able to recall many memories from their childhood years, whereas others remember only a few. For example, in the study Tiffany West and I conducted (West & Bauer, 1999), respondents were asked to describe four memories from before the age of 7. All 48 of the female respondents were able to identify four memories from the first 7 years of life, whereas 2 of 15 male respondents were unable to think of four memories from before the age of 7. To recollect four memories, these two men had to extend the window for "early memories" to age 10. Although the relevant measures are not available in the work that West and I conducted, others have reported relations between the density of recollections of early childhood and measures of intelligence (Rabbitt & McInnis, 1988; as discussed in Neisser & Libby, 2000). In summary, there is evidence of individual variation in the age of earliest memory as well as in the distribution of early memories. A major question to be explored in subsequent chapters is whether differences in cognitive development, early socialization, or both contribute to this variability.

## Group Differences

As outlined earlier, the sociocultural perspective suggests that the offset of childhood amnesia is associated with development of the capacity for autobiographical reminiscence. By this account, construction of an autobiographical history is as much a social as an individual accomplishment. Through their interactions with more skilled narrators, children learn what to encode about autobiographical experiences as well as how to tell autobiographical stories to others. As such, differences in the quality and quantity of interactions with conversational partners are expected to affect children's autobiographical competence. There are three literatures in which patterns of variation consistent with these expectations have been observed: gender effects, birth order effects, and cultural group effects. I discuss each in turn.

*Gender.*   Of all the possible sources of individual and group difference in the age of earliest memory one could contemplate, possible gender differences have received the most attention. A consistent finding is that women have memories from earlier in life than do men (see Table 3.1). Once again the trend is apparent as early as George and Martha Dudycha's 1941 review. They indicated average ages for earliest memories for women and men (respectively) as 3.01 and 4.40 years (Potwin, 1901), 3.40 and 3.60 years (Gordon, 1928), and 3.50 and 3.67 years (Dudycha & Dudycha, 1933b). Whether these differences would be statistically significant was not addressed in these early studies.

Reports of earlier memories for women than for men are frequent in the contemporary literature as well. In some cases, the differences are statistically reliable (e.g., Cowan & Davidson, 1984; Mullen, 1994, Study 2; Orlofsky & Frank, 1986; Waldfogel, 1948). In other cases, they are not (e.g., Mullen, 1994, Studies 1 and 3). In virtually every Western sample, however, the "advantage" of earlier memories (whether statistically significant or not) goes to women. Indeed I know of only one report of the average age of earliest memory being earlier for a sample of men relative to a sample of women (in a Western sample, that is: see *Culture* for intriguing exceptions). Specifically, in research by Qi Wang (2001), the average age of earliest memory was 3.45 years for American men, whereas it was 3.53 years for American women; the difference was not statistically significant. There is only one case of a "tie" in average age of earliest memory (3.33 years reported in West & Bauer, 1999). It is important to keep in mind that, although there is almost complete consistency in the *direction* of the advantage, and in many cases the differences are statistically significant, differences in the ages of earliest memories for women and men are often *small in magnitude*. The small magnitude of the effects is suggested in Fig. 3.4 from David Rubin's (2000) review of 10 separate studies of adults' memories from early childhood. It appears that females have more memories from the ages of 2 through 4, but then the advantage disappears.

Age of earliest memory is the most frequently considered potential difference between the gender groups, but it is not the only one: There are also some reports of differences in the length of women's and men's reports of early childhood events, in their affective qualities, and in the interpersonal themes represented in them. Women tend to provide longer, more detailed, and more vivid accounts of their early memories relative to men (Bauer et al., 2003; Friedman & Pines, 1991). Whereas women and men refer to emotion roughly equally in their narratives about early life events (Bauer et al., 2003), there are suggestions that they refer to different emotions. For instance, Dudycha and Dudycha (1933b) found the emotions of anger, shame, and guilt to be more common in the earliest memories of women relative to men. Nelson Cowan and George Davidson (1984) reported that women's

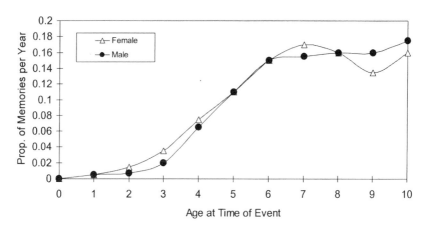

FIG. 3.4.    The distribution of autobiographical memories from early childhood separately for females (open triangles) and males (closed circles) aggregated over studies. Based on Rubin (2000), Fig. 3; values are approximate.

early emotional memories tended to concern attachment issues (i.e., concerns regarding security, approval, separation, and reunion), whereas those of men tended to concern competence issues (i.e., concerns regarding ability, performance, achievement, and identity). Similar patterns were reported by Avril Thorne (1995).

As discussed in detail in chapter 9, these intriguing gender differences in adults' recollections of their childhoods are consistent with sociocultural explanations of autobiographical memory development that emphasize differences in the socialization that girls and boys receive about how to talk about the past. Briefly, relative to their sons, parents talk with their daughters about the past more frequently and at greater length. Parents also emphasize emotional experience more with daughters than with sons, and they highlight the interpersonal aspects of experience with their daughters versus the individual aspects of experience with their sons. For example, in talking with their daughters, parents may emphasize how happy the girl was to play with her friends. In talking with their sons, parents may emphasize the sense of accomplishment that the boy derived from making an important goal in a sports competition. These patterns, and their possible implications for autobiographical memory development, are discussed in chapter 9.

**Birth Order.**    Although it has received significantly less research attention, relative to gender, birth order also has been found to be systematically related to age of earliest memory. A striking illustration of the effect is provided in Fig. 3.5 from research by Mary Mullen (1994). As is apparent from the figure, children who were born first had earlier memories than children

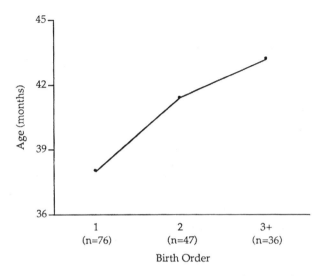

FIG. 3.5.   The average age of earliest autobiographical memory for participants who were first born (1), second born (2), and third or later born (3+).
Reprinted from *Cognition, 52*, M. K. Mullen, "Earliest Recollections of Childhood: A Demographic Analysis," 55–79, Fig. 3 (1994), with permission from
Elsevier.

who were later born. The effect was replicated in two subsequent samples,
also reported by Mullen (1994).

There also appear to be differences in the age of earliest memory as a
function of the number of children in the family and their spacing. In a sample of Chinese high school and college students, Qi Wang, Michelle Leichtman, and Sheldon White (1998) found that only children had earlier autobiographical memories relative to the oldest children in multichild families:
The ages of earliest autobiographical memories were 3.25 years and 3.98
years, respectively. Wang and her colleagues also noted a relation between
the spacing of births and the age of earliest memory. In their sample of 43
first-born children, the range of spacing between siblings was 1 to 8 years
(with an average of 4.4 years between births). First borns for whom there was
a larger difference in ages between themselves and their oldest siblings reported autobiographical memories from earlier in life relative to first borns
whose oldest siblings were more closely spaced. Effects of birth order, number
of siblings, and the spacing of siblings on adults' recollections of their childhoods are consistent with the sociocultural account elaborated in chapter 9.
Simply put, parents have more time and energy to devote to a first-born or
only child relative to later-born children. As a result, there is more opportunity for discussion of and reflection on past events and experiences, activities
that work to support autobiographical memory.

*Culture.* A final source of group-level differences in the age of earliest memory is the culture group of the respondent. To this point, almost all of the data I have discussed have been drawn from adults from Western societies, including Canada, Great Britain, and the United States. Recent studies with individuals from Eastern cultures make clear the limits to generalizability of the findings from Western culture. In 1994, Mary Mullen published a series of four studies in which she examined possible culture-group differences in age of earliest memory. In all four studies, she found systematic differences in the age of earliest memory for Whites compared with Asians living in the United States (some from various Asian cultures and some Asian Americans; Studies 1, 2, and 3), and Whites compared with Korean participants who grew up in Korea. In each case, the White samples had memories from earlier in life relative to the non-White samples. The differences were not only consistent, but, summarized in Table 3.2, were pronounced as well. The finding of later earliest memories from members of Asian cultural groups relative to Western cultural groups has been replicated by Qi Wang (2001), who found that, among American adults, the average age of earliest memory was 3.49 years, whereas that for Chinese adults was 3.96 years (a difference of half a year).

Research by Shelley MacDonald, Kimberly Uesiliana, and Harlene Hayne (2000) revealed patterns similar to those observed by Mullen (1994) and Wang (2001) and also extended the findings to different culture groups. MacDonald and her colleagues compared adults from three cultures: individuals of Maori or native New Zealand descent, individuals of European descent, and individuals of Asian descent (mostly Chinese). The average age of

TABLE 3.2
Average Ages (in Years) and Differences in Age (in Months)
of Earliest Memory for White Adults and Adults
From Asian Cultural Backgrounds

|  | Culture Group | | Difference (in months) |
|---|---|---|---|
|  | White | Asian | |
|  | (Average age of earliest memory, in years) | | |
| Mullen (1994) |  |  |  |
| Study 1 | 3.21 | 3.94 | 8.8 |
| Study 2 | 3.27 | 3.71 | 5.3 |
| Study 3 | 3.23 | 3.63 | 4.9 |
| Study 4 | 3.23 | 4.63 | 16.7 |

*Note.* In Studies 1, 2, and 3, the non-White respondents were individuals raised in various Asian cultures and living in the United States, as well as Asian Americans who grew up in the United States. In Study 4, the Asian respondents were Koreans who had grown up in Korea and were living in the United States at the time of the study. For Study 4, the age of earliest memory for the White respondents was the mean of that from Studies 1 to 3 (data from Mullen, 1994).

earliest memory differed for all three groups, with individuals of Maori descent having the earliest memories (with a mean of 2.72 years), individuals of European descent having the next earliest memories (with a mean of 3.58 years), and individuals of Asian descent have the latest earliest memories (with a mean of 4.82 years). The researchers did not find a gender difference in either their Maori or their European samples. However, in the Asian sample, women actually had substantially *later* memories relative to men (with means of 6.11 and 3.53 years, respectively). The effect was replicated in an independent sample of Chinese participants, albeit less dramatically (with means of 4.51 and 3.30 years for women and men, respectively). Notably, although the difference was not statistically significant, Mary Mullen (1994) observed later earliest memories for Korean women than Korean men (with means of 4.79 and 4.53 years, respectively; Study 4). A similar pattern was not obtained by Qi Wang (2001), however (with means of 3.73 and 4.07 years for Chinese women and men, respectively). Thus, it seems that in Western cultures the finding of earlier memories among women relative to men is common, whereas in some samples drawn from Eastern cultures the pattern may be reversed.

There are also cultural differences in the content of adult women's and men's reports of their early autobiographical experiences. Qi Wang (2001) asked 119 American and 137 Chinese undergraduate students to provide written narratives of their earliest childhood memories. In addition to the difference in age of earliest memory already mentioned, Wang found a number of other cultural differences. Specifically, relative to the Chinese respondents, the Americans provided longer memory narratives as measured by the total number of words and the number of propositions recorded. Their memories also more frequently were of a single event or specific memory, as opposed to a more general memory, relative to Chinese students (88% and 69%, respectively). American students more frequently commented on their own experiences and attitudes (42%) relative to Chinese students (23%). Americans also mentioned more emotions and feeling states in their narratives relative to Chinese. They also more frequently reflected an autonomous orientation in their narratives (i.e., reference to personal needs, preferences, personal evaluations, etc.) relative to Chinese. Conversely, American students mentioned family activities and practices less frequently relative to Chinese students (35% and 50%, respectively).

Findings of cultural group differences in the age and content of adults' earliest autobiographical recollections are consistent with the sociocultural account described earlier. As discussed in more detail in chapter 9, in this perspective, autobiographical memory is influenced by the immediate environment of a child's parents, as well as by the larger cultural milieu in which the child is raised. In cultures that place a high premium on talking about the past and on the child's own experiences, we would expect to see more rapid development of narrative structures for organizing autobiographical memories relative to families and cultures that place less emphasis on these aspects of experience. The expected result is culture-group differences in the offset of childhood amnesia, such as those just reviewed. The link is entirely plausible: As discussed in chapter 9, there are culture-group differences in a number of dimensions of narrative socialization. The differences are in the expected direction given the observed patterns.

## Summary

Although the phenomenon of childhood amnesia is virtually universal, there are individual and group differences in its expression. There is a striking range in the ages from which adults report having memories—from less than 1 year to as old as 6 years. There is also variability in the density of representation of early memories, with some individuals having a rich autobiographical repertoire from the early years and other individuals finding few memories to report. It is not uncommon to find that women report earlier memories relative to men. The effect is not found in all studies, however. Women tend to provide longer, more detailed, and more affectively "saturated" memory reports than men. Although possible effects of birth order have received proportionally little research attention, there are suggestions that first- and earlier-born children have earlier memories relative to later-born children. There is also a growing literature on culture-group differences in the domain of early autobiographical memory. Compared with adults from Asian cultures, adults from Western cultures tend to have earlier memories. They also provide longer narrative accounts that are more specific and self-focused. To date the question of whether the variance in early autobiographical memory accounted for by these sources of group difference is unique or overlapping has not been addressed. Finally, in each case, the patterns of differences across individuals and groups is consistent with a sociocultural explanation for the development of autobiographical memory.

## EVALUATION OF THEORIES AS TO THE SOURCE OF CHILDHOOD AMNESIA

Earlier in the chapter, I reviewed one humorous explanation for the phenomenon of childhood amnesia (that proferred by the cartoon character Hobbes) and four scholarly accounts. In this section, I use the findings of the qualities of adults' recollections of their childhoods and the patterns of individual and group differences in earliest memories to evaluate the viability of each of the candidate explanations.

## Freud's Explanation of Childhood Amnesia

Freud's explanation for childhood amnesia in terms of repression and affective "screens" was internally consistent with his larger theoretical framework. External to the theory, however, the explanation has not fared especially well. As discussed earlier in the chapter, more than a century of research on recollections of early childhood has made clear that adults do remember events from early in life; the average age of earliest autobiographical recollection is much earlier than Freud's suggestion of the offset of childhood amnesia at ages 7 to 8. It is the case that adults do not remember as many early experiences as they should, if only normal, adult rates of forgetting were in play, but they nevertheless have more memories from childhood than would be expected by Freud's model of repression. In addition, contrary to the suggestion that memories of early life events would be devoid of emotion or overwhelmingly positive, both traumatic and nontraumatic events from childhood are recalled. In some studies, memories of negative episodes actually outnumber positive episodes. This pattern is opposite that expected were recollections of early experiences "screens" behind which true memories of emotionally wrenching events were hidden. Finally, contrary to Freud's suggestion that early memories are primarily from the unrealistic third-person perspective, the bulk of early memories are from the first-person perspective. Today, Freud's suggestions of repression and screening of early memories generally are not considered viable candidate explanations for childhood amnesia.

## Different "Lenses" as an Explanation for Childhood Amnesia

Relative to Sigmund Freud's psychodynamic perspective, models that implicate different cognitive lenses as the explanation for childhood amnesia have been reasonably successful. By this perspective, different life periods are viewed through different—and sometimes incompatible—cognitive "lenses." By some accounts, the lenses differ in their reliance on language. By others, they differ in ways of thinking or worldview. Derived from such theories are expectations that (a) the representational formats of early and later memories are different, (b) early memories are not accessible later in life, and (c) memories from within a life period should be more readily accessible than memories across life periods.

In reviewing the characteristics of adults' earliest recollections, I directly evaluated only the first of these three expectations—namely, that the representational formats of early and later memories are different. I reviewed some evidence that early memories were more visual or imaginal in nature and that later memories were more narrative or propositional in nature. However, there were also exceptions to the pattern, as well as evidence that even as individuals become more proficient with language, visual images are still prominently featured in memory representations (see chap. 2). On balance, then, there is not a body of evidence that suggests that early memories are qualitatively different from later memories (although adults rate early and later memories as quantitatively different).

The second expectation derived from different cognitive "lenses" account—namely, that early memories are not accessible later in life—is reasonably well supported, albeit with negative evidence. Indeed the very phenomenon of childhood amnesia is one of later inaccessibility of early memories. As discussed more fully in chapter 10, there is little evidence that early, nonverbal memories later become accessible to be shared verbally. Although there is no direct evidence that developments in language actually *cause* early memories to become inaccessible, the fact that preverbal memories do not readily lend themselves to verbal description is consistent with suggestions of a basic incompatibility of the "processing systems" available to infants and young children, compared with those available to older children and adults. Alternative explanations for lack of verbal access to early memories are taken up in chapter 10.

Consistent with the third expectation of the hypothesis, there are suggestions that memories from *within* a life period are more readily accessible than memories *across* life periods. Illustrations of this phenomenon come from studies in which immigrants are asked to retrieve memories of events that took place either before or after they emigrated. For example, Robert Schrauf and David Rubin (1998) asked Spanish-English speakers who had emigrated to the United States as adults to retrieve memories in response to cue words presented in Spanish and English (words from the two languages were presented on different days) and to report the language in which the memories came to them. They found that the memories retrieved from the time before immigration more frequently were in Spanish than in English (82% vs. 18%, respectively) and, conversely, memories retrieved from the time after immigration more frequently were in English than in Spanish (65% vs. 35%, respectively). Thus, it seems that memories from within a life period are more accessible in the language of that period. Similar results were reported by Viorica Marian and Ulric Neisser (2000). They found that, among Russian immigrants, Russian cue words elicited more memories for events that had taken place in Russian, whereas English cue words elicited more memories for events that had taken place in English. In addition, on average, memories cued by Russian cue words were from earlier in life than memories cued by English cue words. On balance, accounts of childhood amnesia that rely on different cognitive "lenses" in different life periods as explanation for differential accessibility of memories within versus across life periods have fared relatively well.

## Cognitive Development as an Explanation for Childhood Amnesia

As noted earlier, a major category of explanations of childhood amnesia suggests that cognitive changes between infancy and the preschool years make possible the encoding, storage, and subsequent retrieval of autobiographical memories. By some accounts, "what develops" is a symbol system that permits children to retain memories in an accessible format, with subsequent developments in cognitive structures that permit memories to be retained in an organized manner. By other accounts, "what develops" is increased capacity (or more efficient use of existing capacity) that permits more effective encoding and subsequent retrieval of memories. Implicitly or explicitly, changes in capacity, efficiency, or both are linked with developments in the neural structures responsible for memory. By yet other accounts, "what develops" are more specific cognitive achievements, such as a cognitive sense of self, that provide a device around which a personal memory system can be organized.

A complete evaluation of the suggestion that cognitive and neurodevelopmental changes (be they general or specific) are the explanation for childhood amnesia is reserved for later chapters. For now it is sufficient to note that it is increasingly apparent that the capacity to store and retrieve memories for specific past events develops long before the age of 3 years. In addition, contrary to suggestions that early memories are disorganized, there is clear evidence that temporal organization is a device available to children from a young age. Nevertheless, there are cognitive and neural developments that take place throughout the first 3 years of life that no doubt contribute to developments in memory long after the capacity for recall first emerges. Moreover, developments continue throughout the preschool years and beyond. As such, whereas the "old version" of the story of qualitative change that made re-presentation of past events available for the first time at 18 to 24 months of age, and that posited further qualitative changes throughout the preschool years, no longer is viable, there is a "new and improved" version of the story that I take up in later chapters.

There is little doubt that specific cognitive developments, such as a sense of self, play a role in the "offset" of childhood amnesia. Autobiographical memories are about the self after all. Whereas there is virtually universal agreement that a sense of self is *necessary* for autobiographical memory to begin to develop, there is considerably less agreement on the suggestion that it is the linchpin or cornerstone achievement around which an autobiography is built. Perhaps most challenging for this explanation are observations (such as those reviewed earlier) of substantial individual variability among adults in the age of earliest memory and in the distribution of memories in the period obscured by childhood amnesia, and of group variability associated with gender, birth order, and culture. Given that mirror self-recognition and other indexes of self-consciousness virtually universally emerge by the end of the second year of life (Brooks-Gunn & Lewis, 1984), it is not clear that development of the construct indexed by behaviors such as these can serve as an account of the offset of childhood amnesia. In effect, emergence of a sense of self is necessary for autobiographical memory development, but it is doubtful that it will provide a sufficient explanation for childhood amnesia.

## The Sociocultural Perspective on Childhood Amnesia

The final category of explanation of childhood amnesia considered was the sociocultural account. By this conceptualization, autobiographical memories are the product of multiple interactive forces, including basic cognitive (and, specifically, memory) abilities and language. Largely through the process of joint reminiscing, these "raw materials" of an autobiography are shaped such that children construct a form for organizing and sharing memories and an appreciation of the significance of them. Differences in the characteristics of the family and culture group in which children engage in joint reminiscing interact with characteristics of the individual child, resulting in individual as well as group variation.

I reserve a thorough evaluation of the sociocultural explanation for the phenomenon of childhood amnesia for chapters 9 and 11. At this point, it is sufficient to note that the perspective has enjoyed considerable success as an account of the development of autobiographical memory. As seen in chapter 9, familial and cultural differences in early joint reminiscing are well documented, and there is evidence of relations between parental behavior in reminiscing contexts and children's concurrent and subsequent autobiographical narrative performance. In addition, it is seen that the patterns of differences in early joint reminiscing contexts as a function of gender and culture group map onto patterns of group and cultural differences in adults' narratives about their early childhoods. The literature is thus largely consistent with the tenets of the sociocultural perspective. More complete evaluations of the perspective and its implications are offered in later chapters.

### SUMMARY AND CONCLUSIONS

Our memories of our pasts serve as one of the most important sources of knowledge of who we are, where we have been, and even where we are going in the future. Whereas adults have a wealth of memories from later childhood and early adulthood in particular, there is a virtually universal paucity of memories from the first years of life. For over a century, there have been reports that the average age of earliest verbalizable memory among Western adults is age 3 to 3½. Adults report a larger and steadily increasing number of memories from the ages of 3 to 7. The number of events adults remember from the age of 7 onward is consistent with what would be expected based on adult rates of forgetting.

From a theoretical standpoint, the mystery of childhood amnesia is interesting and important because of its implications for our sense of self. For much of the space of our lives, we can construct a continuous timeline of events and experiences. The "boundary" of childhood amnesia represents a break in the otherwise continuous history. To more fully understand ourselves then, we must understand the paucity of memories from early in life. The phenomenon is also interesting and important from a practical standpoint. There are numerous clinical and forensic implications, for example. Moreover, theories of personality and psychopathology look to early experiences as an important source of adult attitudes and behaviors. For these analyses, it is crucial that we determine the nature of the "trace" that early experiences leave behind. Forensic concerns also compel research on memory for events during the period obscured by childhood amnesia. The veridicality and accessibility of memories of events from early in life are questions the answers to which can have profound consequences for childhood victims of crimes, as well as their perpetrators.

The fact that the phenomenon of childhood amnesia is almost universal does not mean that there are not individual and group differences in early memory. On the contrary, there is wide variation in the age of earliest memory, and there are differences as a function of gender, birth order, and culture group. Theories that hope to explain the relative lack among adults of memories of specific events from early in life must account not only for the age of earliest memory and distribution of early memories, but for these systematic sources of individual and group variability as well.

Two categories of explanation—namely, Sigmund Freud's psychodynamic theory and perspectives that emphasize different cognitive "lenses" at different points in development—account for the range of phenomena in the syndrome of childhood amnesia by appeal to processes that make early memories inaccessible later in life. Thus, by these accounts, memories for early life events are formed, but later functionally disappear. In contrast, the cognitive-developmental and sociocultural categories of explanation account for the range of phenomena by suggesting that autobiographical memory is a late development. In infancy and very early childhood, children lack the capacity to form autobiographical memories. It is only later in infancy and over the course of the preschool years that the necessary complex of skills becomes available and the new ability emerges. In chapter 4, I begin examination of the stronger of these two categories of hypotheses—namely, that infants and very young children are unable to form memories of specific past events. I do so through a review of the evidence of memory function in the first years of life. In subsequent chapters, I discuss changes in memory abilities over the course of the preschool years and beyond.

# II

## MEMORY IN INFANCY AND VERY EARLY CHILDHOOD

# 4

# Declarative Memory in the First Years of Life

*One shouldn't expect so much from memory; one shouldn't expect a film shot in the dark to develop new images. Of course not. Still, one can reproach a film shot in the daylight of one's life for missing frames.*
—Joseph Brodsky, from *Less Than One—Selected Essays* (1986, p. 492)

The subject of chapter 3 was the "remarkable amnesia of childhood ... the amnesia that veils our earliest youth from us and makes us strangers to it" (Freud, 1916/1966, p. 326). Although there are both individual and group differences in the ages of adults' earliest memories, most adults report having few (if any) memories from the first 3 years of life. The number of events from the balance of the preschool years that adults recollect seems to be smaller than would be expected based on the passage of time alone. In contrast, as reviewed in chapter 2, adults have rich autobiographies from later childhood and early adulthood, in particular.

What is the cause of the "remarkable amnesia of childhood"? In chapter 3, I outlined four categories of theories (excluding for the moment the comical "Hobbesean" account) that fall into two broad classes of explanation. Joseph Brodsky, recipient of the Nobel Prize in Literature (1987) and Poet Laureate of the United States (1991–1992), captured the essence of the classes in the excerpt that opens this chapter. By one class of accounts, early memories are "shot in the daylight," but we subsequently lose frames of them. In other words, memories of early life events are formed, but over time they are lost in whole or in part. Sigmund Freud, who gave the phenomenon of *childhood amnesia* its name, suggested precisely this process. According to Freud, memories of the first years of life are formed, but they are later blockaded from consciousness or so heavily screened to remove inappropriate psy-

chic content that they no longer represent the reality of the time. Whereas
the forces they hypothesize are substantially less dramatic, other theories also
account for childhood amnesia in terms of later *in*accessibility of memories
that were presumably accessible at one time (due to different cognitive
"lenses" at different points in time).

The second class of explanations suggests that, in essence, we take account of early experiences, but we do so on film that is "shot in the dark,"
with the result that no image is preserved. That is, in the early years of life,
we experience events, but accessible memories of them are not formed because a crucial ingredient for their registration is missing. In the case of film,
the necessary ingredient is light. In the parlance of cognitive-developmental
and sociocultural theories, the crucial missing ingredient is the fundamental
capacity to create lasting memories. By these accounts, the complex of skills
necessary to create autobiographical memories does not come together until
relatively late in the preschool years. Indeed until surprisingly recently, it was
widely believed that the period of infancy was one during which the young of
our species were unable to encode, store, and subsequently retrieve memories of the events they experienced and in which they participated. In other
words, it was thought that infants were unable to form declarative memories.
Moreover, it was thought that when children finally developed the capacity
to remember specific episodes, their memories were poorly organized and
generally unremarkable.

In this chapter, I evaluate the first portion of this strong hypothesis—that
regarding the cognitive (in)abilities of the human infant. Discussion of developments in basic cognitive abilities during the preschool years, as well as
other components of autobiographical memory suggested by the sociocultural
account, are reserved for chapters 7, 8, and 9. I first develop the traditional
cognitive-development hypothesis in more detail. I then describe methodological advances that made empirical test of it possible, and the resulting
data on developments in declarative memory in the first years of life. I conclude the chapter with discussion of some of the individual differences in declarative memory apparent in infancy and very early childhood. The individual differences not only affect the development and expression of declarative
memory in the first years of life, but likely influence the development of autobiographical memory as well.

## TRADITIONAL EXPECTATIONS REGARDING INFANTS' AND YOUNG CHILDREN'S ABILITIES TO RECALL THE PAST

The strong hypothesis that the capacity to form declarative memories was
not part of the repertoire of the human infant had a firm hold in psychology
for both conceptual and methodological reasons. In chapter 3, I described

one of the major theoretical bases for this perspective. That is, it was widely believed that infants lacked symbolic capacity, and thus could not mentally represent objects and events. For the first 18 to 24 months of life, infants were thought to live in a "here-and-now" world that included physically present entities, yet the entities had no past and no future. In other words, infants were described as living an "out-of-sight, out-of-mind" existence. As long as something was in front of them, they behaved in accord with its physical presence. However, as soon as something was out of sight, they acted as if it did not exist.

Compelling illustrations of the out-of-sight, out-of-mind "attitude" were provided in Jean Piaget's (1952, 1962) extensive observations of his own children. An example from his daughter, Lucienne, makes the point. At 8½ months of age, Lucienne was playing with a toy stork. Piaget took the toy and, in full view of Lucienne, hid it under a cover. As long as Piaget hid only a portion of the stork, Lucienne removed the cover and retrieved the toy. However, when Piaget hid the entire stork under the cover, Lucienne simply stared at Piaget or shifted her attention and began playing with a different toy. The change in attitude toward the stork was not for lack of interest in it—if Piaget then revealed the stork, Lucienne smiled and tried to grasp it. Nor was the "problem" the need to remove the cover: As long as a portion of the stork was visible, Lucienne easily moved the cover out of the way to get the toy. Piaget interpreted this assembly of behaviors as evidence that, when the toy was out of sight, it no longer existed for the infant. He suggested that the reason for this rather bizarre behavior was that infants lacked the symbolic means to represent information not available to the senses (i.e., to mentally re-present it). The lack of symbolic capacity not only affected infants' memories for toy storks, but had implications for infants' abilities to remember any of the experiences of their lives.

Throughout the 1970s and 1980s, many of the tenets attributed to Piagetian theory were challenged and found wanting (see, e.g., Gelman & Baillargeon, 1983, for a review of these developments). For instance, researchers found that preschool-age children were capable of solving problems that, based on Piagetian theory, they should not have been able to solve until the grade-school years. In addition, researchers began to find evidence that preschoolers not only were able to remember specific episodes, but that their memories were well organized. True, when preschool-age children were asked to remember lists of unrelated words or stories that were poorly organized (i.e., stories that had no especially logical beginning, middle, and end), their performance was far from "stellar." However, as shown by Jean Mandler and her colleagues (e.g., Mandler & DeForest, 1979; Mandler & Johnson, 1977), when the stories young children were asked to remember were well organized, they performed quite well. Moreover, as demonstrated by Katherine Nelson and her colleagues (K. Nelson, 1978, 1986; K. Nelson & Gruendel, 1981, 1986), when preschool-age children were asked to tell "what happens" in the course of everyday event and routines, they provided skeletal, yet nevertheless accurate and organized accounts. In response to the question of "what happens" when you bake cookies, for instance, a 3-year-old participant in Janet Gruendel's (1980) dissertation replied, "Well, you bake them and eat them" (K. Nelson & Gruendel, 1986, p. 27; developments in preschool-age children's recall memory are described in more detail in chap. 7).

Whereas many of the expectations derived from Piagetian theory were being challenged in the 1970s and 1980s, throughout much of that time, one of the strongest predictions went unexamined due to lack of suitable methodology. Specifically, the suggestion that infants were unable to recall past events remained out of reach of empirical test. In older children and adults, recall is examined primarily through verbal report. That is, we ask the 3-year-old child to tell us how to make cookies and she graciously obliges by telling us. For infants and children younger than age 3, however, this is not a viable alternative: The term *infant* is derived from the Latin *infantia*, meaning "inability to speak." Although there are enormous individual differences, most children do not begin producing even single words until late in the first year of life. They typically do not begin producing multiword utterances until the middle of the second year, and they do not become fluent speakers until the third year and beyond (Bloom, 1998). As they are gaining verbal fluency, children do not use language to talk about the past. Instead they use their emerging language skills to talk about ongoing events and routines. Thus, even as they are developing a tool for talking about the "there and then," they primarily use it to talk about the "here and now." It is not until the fourth year of life that most children become reliable partners in conversations about the past. Even then young children frequently require extensive prompts and considerable support from more skilled conversational partners to tell the stories of past events (K. Nelson, 1993a; see chaps. 7 and 8 for further discussion of developments in the ability to talk about the past).

The observations that infants are unable to talk at all, and that even once they begin to talk children are not especially facile at using language to retell past events, seemed wholly consistent with the suggestion that young children simply were unable to recall the past. This conclusion seemed further supported by the lack of memories among adults for events from the first 3 years of life (see chap. 3 for a review). These observations "conspired" to create the impression that age 3 marked the onset of the ability to remember. Yet is it reasonable to conclude that, because children cannot *verbally* recall, they lack the capacity to form, maintain, and subsequently retrieve accessible memories of past events? Although it is certainly more *convenient* to assess recall verbally, verbal expression is not a defining feature of declarative memory (Tulving & Markowitsch, 1998). As noted in chapter 1, even the criterion of conscious awareness may be met nonverbally (Köhler & Moscovitch, 1997). Indeed although there is general agreement that the specific type of declarative memory that is the subject of this volume—autobiographical memory—is necessarily verbal (e.g., Rubin, 1998), the argument is not universally accepted (e.g., Howe & Courage, 1993). Moreover, as noted in chapter 2, although autobiographical memories are expressed verbally, it is likely that nonverbal images are a critical aspect of their representation. As Jean Piaget (1952) persuasively argued, language is but one manifestation of symbolic capacity; imagery is another. In light of these considerations, exploration of the possibility of nonverbal yet declarative memories of past events is well justified.

In the next section of this chapter, I describe a nonverbal means to assess memory that has permitted test of the strong assumption that declarative memory is late to develop. As becomes apparent, use of the method with children in the first 3 years of life has provided unequivocal evidence that, although infants are not able to speak, they are nevertheless able to recall the past. The findings thus make clear that, in its strongest form, the hypothesis that memories from the first years of life are absent because no memories were formed cannot be true. What becomes equally clear, however, is that whereas infants and young children are able to recall the past, there are pronounced changes in recall ability throughout the period of transition from infancy to early childhood. As a consequence, it is not until late in the second year of life that recall of events over long delays is both reliable and robust.

## NONVERBAL MEASURES OF MEMORY

Evaluation of the conclusions that can and should not be drawn on the basis of nonverbal measures of memory demands that we keep in mind that memory is not pudding (chap. 1). Different nonverbal tasks likely measure different types of memory; not all of them measure declarative memory. It is clear that infants form memories that can be expressed nonverbally. For example, researchers have used infants' abilities to control the rate at which they suck on a pacifier to test memory in newborns. Mere hours after birth, infants distinguish between a novel story passage and one that their mothers had read aloud during the last weeks of pregnancy, as evidenced by different rates and intensities of sucking (DeCasper & Spence, 1986). Newborn infants also show that they remember by turning their heads first toward a sound and then, as the sound is heard over and over again, away from it. They exhibit this behavior even after a 24-hour delay, thus indicating that they remembered the original sound (Swain, Zelazo, & Clifton, 1993). Most of the experimental data on infants' memories are derived not from pacifiers or by causing heads to turn, however, but from three other techniques: *visual paired comparison* or *visual habituation, mobile conjugate reinforcement,* and *elicited imitation* or *deferred imitation.* The use of these techniques has provided a wealth of data on early memory development, broadly defined. For the first and second techniques, however, there are reasons to doubt whether the memories assessed are declarative. In contrast, there are excellent reasons to believe that imitation-based techniques tap declarative memory.

## Visual Paired Comparison and Habituation

The technique of *visual paired comparison* was introduced by Robert Fantz (1956). As reflected in the schematic diagram in Fig. 4.1, it involves exposing infants to pairs of pictures of a stimulus and then, after some period of familiarization, presenting the now "familiar" picture along with a different, novel picture and observing at what infants look. A variant of the technique, *visual habituation,* involves sequentially exposing infants to numerous pictures of a stimulus and then, after some criterion is reached (typically a 50% decrease in looking time), introducing a novel stimulus and noting any changes in the amount of time infants spend looking. In both techniques, differential

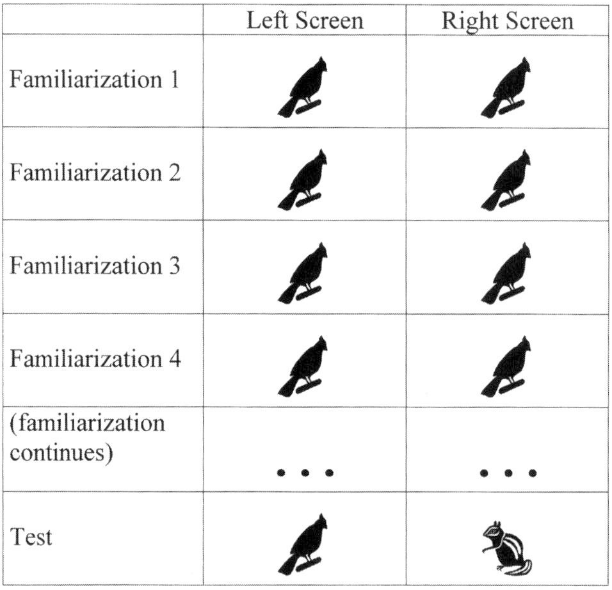

| | Left Screen | Right Screen |
|---|---|---|
| Familiarization 1 | | |
| Familiarization 2 | | |
| Familiarization 3 | | |
| Familiarization 4 | | |
| (familiarization continues) | • • • | • • • |
| Test | | |

FIG. 4.1. Schematic representation of the visual paired comparison procedure. The same picture is presented side-by-side, repeatedly, until the number of seconds participants spend looking at the picture decreases. The "familiar" picture is then paired with a picture of a novel stimulus, and the distribution of looking time to the old and new picture is measured.

division of attention, as evidenced by looking time to novel compared with familiar stimuli, is taken as evidence of memory. Typically, after short periods of familiarization infants prefer to look at familiar stimuli, whereas after longer periods of familiarization (or habituation) they spend more time looking at novel stimuli. The number of seconds of familiarization required to produce a novelty preference changes with age. For example, in research by Susan Rose and her colleagues, 3½-month-old infants required 30 seconds of exposure before exhibiting a preference for a novel stimulus, whereas 6½-month-old infants required only 15 seconds (Rose, Gottfried, Melloy-Carminar, & Bridger, 1982).

Changes in the distribution of looking time to familiar and novel stimuli typically are examined over relatively short spaces of time, with delays ranging from 0 seconds to a few minutes. However, these delays do not represent the upper limit on infant recognition memory. For example, 5-month-olds recognize face stimuli over a delay of 2 weeks (Fagan, 1973). Over longer retention intervals, the evidence for recognition changes. In research by Lorraine Bahrick and Jeffrey Pickens (1995), for instance, immediately after familiarization with a unique visual display, infants looked longer at a novel display. In contrast, after a delay of 3 months, they showed a reliable preference for the familiar display. In between, no preference was detected (i.e., the amount of looking to familiar and novel stimuli did not differ). Melanie Spence (1996) reported the same pattern for auditory recognition of familiar versus novel nursery rhymes.

The shifting distribution of attention to novel and familiar stimuli seen in these studies is taken as evidence of the differential status of mnemonic traces over time. The assumption is that, on the basis of a "fresh" memory trace (i.e., over a very short delay), infants need not spend time reprocessing familiar stimuli and, consequently, spend more time attending to novel stimuli. With increasing delay, as the memory trace begins to fade, infants distribute their attentional resources more evenly, encoding the novel stimulus and updating their memories for the familiar stimulus. After even longer delays, with yet further degradation of memory, infants devote the majority of attentional resources to reconstruction of the mnemonic trace for the once-familiar stimulus (Bahrick, Hernandez-Reif, & Pickens, 1997; Courage & Howe, 1998). In summary, the technique of paired comparison can be used to test infants' retention of particular stimuli; retention is demonstrated over both the short and long term. Depending on the circumstances of testing, recognition may be evidenced through greater attention to familiar stimuli or through greater attention to novel stimuli.

Whereas attentional preference techniques measure changes in infants' responses to previously encountered stimuli, it is unclear whether they measure the same type of recognition as evidenced when, for example, adults affirm or deny that they have seen a particular stimulus before. Jean Mandler

(1998) suggested that infant recognition memory experiments are actually more analogous to adult priming studies (such as introduced in chap. 1) than they are to adult recognition memory studies. She argued that the fact that the infant responds differentially to old and new stimuli indicates that information about the old stimulus has been stored, but it does not provide evidence that the infant was in any way aware of having experienced the stimulus before. The suggestion that awareness need not accompany primed responses is supported by findings that adults suffering from amnesia (such as patient H. M.) show normal priming even as they exhibit pronounced deficits in recognition memory (Warrington & Weiskrantz, 1974). Mandler acknowledged that changes in the distribution of infant attention as a result of prior exposure *may* be based on conscious recognition. However, because such recognition is not required to produce the response (McKee & Squire, 1993), it should not be assumed.

If it is not the result of conscious recognition, what is the source of a preference for novelty? Charles Nelson (1995, 1997) suggested that early novelty preferences may be responses to infrequently presented stimuli. Consistent with this suggestion, prior to 8 months of age, infants respond to novel stimuli based on the *frequency* with which they are presented, as opposed to their novelty per se (C. A. Nelson & Collins, 1991, 1992). At the neural level, changes in the distribution of looking as a function of increased familiarity may be driven by suppression effects (Snyder, 2001). As stimuli are repeated, and thereby become familiar, the population of neurons that fire in response to them shifts such that some of the cells begin to fire preferentially for that particular stimulus while other cells exhibit decreased rates of firing (the so-called *suppression effect*; in Li, Miller, & Desimone, 1993, approximately 33% of sampled cells exhibited decreased rates of firing). In other words, whereas originally a large population of neurons may fire in response to a stimulus, as the stimulus becomes familiar, the "responsibility" for firing in response to it is assumed by a smaller number of more "finely tuned" (more selective) neurons. As reflected in Fig. 4.2, on presentation of a new stimulus, the firing rates of previously suppressed neurons increase (at least temporarily until that stimulus too becomes "familiar"). Behaviorally, this could result in apparent "preference" for a novel stimulus. Critically, suppression effects occur even in anesthetized and awake, but passively fixated animals (E. K. Miller, Gochin, & Gross, 1991). This strongly implies that we need not invoke conscious awareness as an explanation for systematic behavior in infant looking-time studies.

## Mobile Conjugate Reinforcement

The second major technique used to test long-term retention in early infancy is *mobile conjugate reinforcement*. In this paradigm, an attractive mobile is attached to a stand and suspended above an infant's crib (or sling seat in the

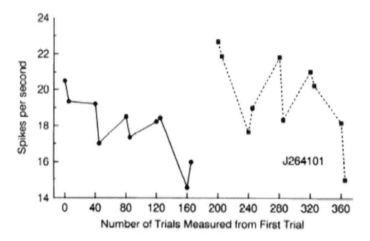

FIG. 4.2. Average responses of an individual neuron in the inferior temporal cortex to two sets of initially novel stimuli. Once the response of the neuron to the first set of stimuli declined (solid line), the second set was introduced. The response rebounded (dotted line) and then declined again as the new stimuli became familiar. From "The Representation of Stimulus Familiarity in Anterior Inferior Temporal Cortex," by L. Li, E. K. Miller, and R. Desimone, 1993, *Journal of Neurophysiology, 69,* 1918–1929, Fig. 5. Copyright © 1993 by The American Physiological Society. Used with permission.

case of older infants). For a 1- to 3-minute baseline period, the infant's leg is "tethered" to a second—empty—stand, via a ribbon. Researchers measure the rate at which the infant kicks. As depicted in Fig. 4.3, after the baseline phase, the ribbon is moved to the stand with the mobile. Now, as the infant kicks, the mobile moves (i.e., the infant's kicks are conjugated with the movement of the mobile). Over the course of a 3- to 9-minute acquisition period, infants learn the contingency between their own kicking and the movement of the mobile. Once the conditional response is acquired, a delay is imposed, after which the mobile is again suspended above the infant. As in the baseline phase, the infant's leg is attached to the "empty" stand (and thus, no contingency is in force). If the posttraining rate of kicking is greater than the rate of kicking in the procedurally identical baseline (i.e., before the infant experienced the contingency), then memory is inferred (e.g., Rovee-Collier & Gerhardstein, 1997).

The mobile conjugate reinforcement paradigm has been quite productive. With it researchers have learned that infants 2 months of age remember the mobile for 1 to 3 days and that by 6 months they remember for as many as 14 days (Hill, Borovsky, & Rovee-Collier, 1988). The length of time over which behavior toward the mobile is retained can be extended if infants are "reminded" of the mobile during the delay (Rovee-Collier, Sullivan, Enright,

FIG. 4.3. The configuration of a mobile conjugate reinforcement apparatus during the acquisition phase of testing. Because the infant's leg is tethered to the stand with the mobile, kicking movements of the infant's leg cause the mobile to move. During the baseline and test phases, the infant's leg is tethered to the empty stand (on the left), thereby removing the contingency. Photograph compliments of Carolyn Rovee-Collier, and used with permission.

Lucas, & Fagen, 1980). A number of other factors also affect the length of time over which the conditioned response can be retained, including the amount of training the infants receive, the distribution of training, and the affect they display during training (see Rovee-Collier & Gerhardstein, 1997; Rovee-Collier & Hayne, 2000, for reviews). One of the most striking characteristics of memory as evidenced by this paradigm is its specificity. For example, 2- and 3-month-old infants fail to recognize the training mobile if even a single element of it is changed (e.g., if one of the elements of a five-item mobile is changed). Even minor modifications in the design of the fabric that lines the crib (e.g., changing the shape of the figures on the liner from squares to circles) produce pronounced disruptions in performance (e.g., Borovsky & Rovee-Collier, 1990; Rovee-Collier, Schechter, Shyi, & Shields, 1992). Generalization from the stimulus or context associated with the learning episode to other similar stimuli occurs only as the details of the original stimulus are forgotten.

The very specificity of memory as demonstrated in the mobile conjugate reinforcement paradigm is one feature that has led to the suggestion that the type of memory measured by this technique is different from that assessed through verbal report and other declarative memory paradigms used with older children and adults. As discussed in chapter 1, a characteristic feature of declarative memory is its flexibility. In contrast, as noted by Jean Mandler (1998), the responses observed in the conjugate reinforcement paradigm show patterns of generalization, extinction, and reinstatement that are typical of operant conditioning paradigms (e.g., Campbell, 1984). This is one of the reasons that the memory demonstrated in the mobile conjugate reinforcement paradigm is thought to reflect nondeclarative learning, rather than declarative memory for a particular event or episode (e.g., Mandler, 1990b; C. A. Nelson, 1997; Schneider & Bjorklund, 1998; Squire, Knowlton, & Musen, 1993; although see Rovee-Collier, 1997, for a different view). (Another reason is speculation that the behavior relies on different neural structures than those responsible for declarative memory; C. A. Nelson, 1997; see chap. 5 for discussion of the neural structures implicated in declarative memory.)

## Elicited and Deferred Imitation

*Deferred Imitation* (imitation after a delay) was suggested by Jean Piaget (1952, 1962) as one of the hallmarks of the development of symbolic thought. Piaget described an incident in which, at the age of 16 months, his daughter Jacqueline observed a young cousin of hers display a temper tantrum. According to Piaget, Jacqueline had never before seen or engaged in a tantrum, and she watched it with great interest. A day later, in a different room of the house, when the young cousin was not present, Jacqueline stomped her little foot and flayed her arms about, in apparent deferred imitation of her cousin's behavior (Piaget, 1952). Piaget used this example as an illustration of Jacqueline's developing capacity for representational thought.

In the mid-1980s, Jean Mandler and I began to develop an imitation-based technique as a nonverbal test of mnemonic ability in infants and children throughout the first 3 years of life (e.g., Bauer & Mandler, 1989; Bauer & Shore, 1987). Simultaneously and independently, Andrew Meltzoff (1985, 1988a, 1988b, 1988c) was doing the same thing. The basic technique involves an adult using props to produce a single action or a multistep sequence of actions and then testing the infant's or young child's imitation of the model. In Fig. 4.4 is depicted an example sequence from my laboratory—"making a gong" by putting a support bar between two posts, hanging a metal plate from the bar, and hitting the plate with a mallet.

Across laboratories and studies, there are a number of procedural variations on the theme of the imitation task. One feature that differs across studies is whether imitation is deferred over a delay or whether immediate imitation is permitted. In *deferred imitation* paradigms, the opportunity to imitate comes only after a delay of minutes to months. By contrast, *elicited imitation* is a more generic term describing techniques in which infants or children may

FIG. 4.4. One version of the three-step sequence "make a gong" (materials are a wooden base with two posts, a wooden bar hinged to one of the posts, a square metal plate with a lip to fit over the bar, and a wooden mallet). The experimenter modeled folding the bar across the posts (to form a crosspiece), hanging the plate from the bar, and hitting the plate with the mallet (thereby causing it to ring).

be permitted to imitate actions or multistep sequences prior to imposition of a delay. There are other procedural variants as well. For example, in some cases, single object-specific actions are demonstrated as many as three times, in silence, followed by a time-limited response period signaled only by presentation of the object to the infant (e.g., Meltzoff, 1988a). In other cases, sequences varying in length from two to nine steps are demonstrated two times, with narration, followed by a child-controlled response period signaled by presentation of the objects to the infant, along with a verbal "reminder" of the sequences to be performed (e.g., Bauer, Hertsgaard, & Wewerka, 1995). Across these variations in methodology, imitation paradigms have reliably produced behaviors indicative of declarative memory. That is, learning is fast, and memories are both fallible and flexible. I review the evidence for each criterion in turn.

First, as noted in chapter 1, declarative memory is characterized as *fast*. Infants and young children rapidly form memories in imitation paradigms. Indeed numerous studies have revealed one-trial learning of modeled actions and action sequences (e.g., Bauer, 1992; Bauer & Hertsgaard, 1993; Mandler & McDonough, 1995; Meltzoff, 1988a, 1995). That is, infants observe as an action or action sequence is modeled for them and, on the basis of that single exposure, are able to reproduce it later. In most cases, the actions and sequences are novel to the infant or child. Sequences such as "making a gong," for example, are novel to infants and young children, based on parental report, and as measured by children's spontaneous interactions with the objects (prior to seeing the sequence modeled, children do not make gongs). In some cases, the modeled actions are actually rather bizarre! For instance, infants will imitate behaviors such as leaning over at the waist and tapping one's head on a pad that then lights up (Meltzoff, 1988a; it would be much more "efficient" to tap the pad with one's hand than one's head). Moreover, infants only watch as the to-be-imitated actions are modeled—they get to produce them only after modeling is complete. In some cases, the opportunity to produce the actions and sequences is deferred for days, weeks, and even months. Indeed production of events prior to imposition of a delay not only is not necessary for later reproduction, but it is not even reliably facilitative of later reproduction (e.g., Bauer et al., 1995; Carver & Bauer, 1999; Mandler & McDonough, 1995; Meltzoff, 1988a, 1988b, 1995). These conditions simply are not conducive to nondeclarative acquisition, which often requires multiple interactive learning trials to accomplish (Bachevalier, 1992; Knopman & Nissen, 1987; Mandler, 1990b; Meltzoff, 1990; Schacter & Moscovitch, 1984; Squire et al., 1993).

Second, declarative memory is characterized as *fallible*. The memories formed in imitation paradigms are vulnerable to storage and retrieval failures, and thus forgetting occurs. Although as reviewed later in this chapter, memory as tested via imitation can be long lasting, in some cases, forgetting sets in after as few as 24 to 48 hours (Bauer, Cheatham, Cary, & Van Abbema, 2002; Bauer, Van Abbema, & de Haan, 1999). Studies in which infants and very young children are tested over longer delay intervals (e.g., as many as 12 months; Bauer, Wenner, Dropik, & Wewerka, 2000) reveal a forgetting function quite similar to that observed in older children and even adults— namely, an initial steep decline in performance followed by a more shallow forgetting function (Rubin & Wenzel, 1996).

Third, declarative memory is characterized as *flexible*. The memories formed in imitation paradigms are not tied to specific materials or contexts. That is, memory can be demonstrated under conditions and in contexts different from those in which learning occurred. For instance, children have been shown to generalize their memories across changes in the size, shape, color, and/or material composition of the props used to model actions and sequences. That is, after seeing a gong made with the materials depicted in Fig. 4.4, they will make a gong using the materials depicted in Fig. 4.5 (Bauer & Dow, 1994; Bauer & Fivush, 1992; Lechuga, Marcos-Ruiz, & Bauer, 2001). Children also generalize imitation across changes in (a) the appearance of the room at the time of demonstration of modeled actions and at the time of memory test (e.g., they see the demonstration in a room decorated with large pink polka dots on the walls and then imitate the action in a plainly decorated room; Barnat, Klein, & Meltzoff, 1996; Klein & Meltzoff, 1999), (b) the setting for demonstration of the modeled actions and the test of memory for them (e.g., they see the demonstration in a day-care setting and then imitate it in their own homes; Hanna & Meltzoff, 1993; Klein & Meltzoff, 1999), and (c) the individual who demonstrated the actions and the individual who tested for memory for the actions (e.g., they see demonstration by a confederate peer and then imitate when tested by an adult experimenter; Hanna & Meltzoff, 1993). Infants are even able to use three-dimensional objects to produce events that they have only seen modeled on a TV screen (e.g., Meltzoff, 1988c).

It is also important to note that even as they show flexibility in their mnemonic responses, infants and young children exhibit memory for the original stimulus materials and locations (Barnat et al., 1996; Lechuga et al., 2001). This suggests that flexibility in memory is not born of forgetting. In research that Gina Dow and I conducted, for instance, in a forced-choice recognition task, 16- and 20-month-old children reliably selected the props used to enact event sequences (e.g., the materials depicted in Fig. 4.4), even when they were paired with props that could be used to produce structurally identical sequences (to continue the example, the materials depicted in Fig. 4.5).

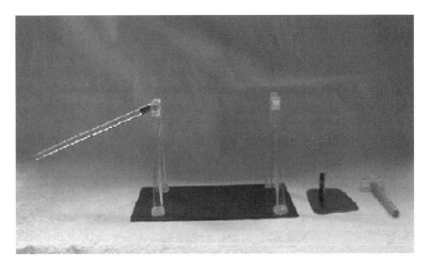

FIG. 4.5.   A different version of the three-step sequence "make a gong" (materials are a plastic base with two posts, a clear bar hinged to one of the posts, a rectangular metal plate with a hook to fit over the bar, and a plastic mallet). The actions modeled are the same as for the first version of "make a gong" depicted in Fig. 4.4.

In addition to being decontextualized, memories formed through observational learning share another characteristic of declarative memories—namely, they are *verbally accessible*. By necessity, evidence of verbal accessibility comes from children old enough to speak. As described in more detail in chapter 10, my colleagues and I analyzed the spontaneous verbalizations of children who, at the ages of 22 to 32 months, returned to the laboratory to be tested for memory of events to which they had been exposed 6 to 12 months earlier at the ages of 16 and 20 months. Both age groups provided verbal evidence of memory for events that they had imitated prior to imposition of the 6- to 12-month delays. The children who had been 20 months of age at the time of the events also provided mnemonic verbalizations about events they had only watched prior to the delays (Bauer, Kroupina, Schwade, Dropik, & Wewerka, 1998). The finding that children are subsequently able to talk about events experienced in the context of imitation paradigms is strong evidence that the memories formed are declarative in nature (i.e., only declarative memories are verbally accessible).

Ideally, the logical argument that performance in imitation paradigms is mediated by declarative memory processes would be complemented by direct evidence that populations known to have deficits in declarative memory also have difficulty with this task. In other words, it would be desirable to know whether, were he to be tested on an age-appropriate version of the task, Henry M. would be able to imitate either immediately or after a delay. To address this question, Laraine McDonough, Jean Mandler, Richard McKee, and Larry Squire (1995) tested adults with amnesia (i.e., individuals in whom declarative memory processes are impaired) and healthy control participants in a deferred-imitation task using multistep sequences. Whereas healthy adults performed well on the task, patients with amnesia did poorly. Indeed they performed no better than participants who had never seen the events demonstrated. Adolescents and young adults who, early in life, were rendered amnesic as a result of neural damage also exhibited deficits in performance on the task (Adlam, Vargha-Khadem, Mishkin, & de Haan, 2005). These findings strongly suggest that deferred imitation taps declarative memory.

Finally, deferred imitation taps recall memory, rather than recognition memory. The available props provide perceptual support for performance. For this reason, the task can be said to be one of cued recall (i.e., recall is cued by the perceptually available props). However, all recall is cued, either by an internal association or an external prompt or cue (Spear, 1978). In the case of multistep sequences, additional evidence that recall processes support performance comes from temporally ordered reproduction of modeled sequences. Consider that once an event sequence is modeled, no perceptual support for the order in which the actions are to be performed remains. To reproduce an ordered sequence, temporal order information must be encoded during presentation of the event sequence and subsequently retrieved from a representation of the event in the absence of ongoing perceptual support. In this requirement, the task is analogous to verbal report paradigms (Mandler, 1990b). Because it provides especially compelling evidence of recall, in this chapter, I pay special attention to infants' and children's abilities to recall the order in which events unfold.

## EXPLICIT MEMORY IN INFANCY AND VERY EARLY CHILDHOOD

Elicited and deferred imitation have been used to test infants as young as 6 months and children as old as 36 months of age. Because the same technique has been used across such a wide age span, we are afforded perspective on developments in recall memory from infancy throughout the period of transition to early childhood. The developmental picture that has emerged is one of relatively early competence in recall over the short term, developments in long-term ordered recall near the end of the first year of life, and consolidation of the ability over the course of the second year. I address each of these developments in turn.

### Recall in the First Year of Life

*Recall by 6-Month-Old Infants.* To date the youngest infants tested for imitation of actions or action sequences are 6-month-olds. Rachel Barr, Anne Dowden, and Harlene Hayne (1996) tested infants as young as 6 months of age for immediate and 24-hour delayed recall of the three-step sequence of pulling a mitten off a puppet's hand, shaking the mitten (which, at demonstration, contained a bell), and replacing the mitten on the puppet's hand (immediate and deferred imitation were tested in separate groups of infants). Barr and her colleagues found that two thirds (67%) of their 6-month-old participants imitated at least one action immediately after modeling. The same level of performance was observed after the 24-hour delay. These data thus provide evidence of immediate recall and recall over a brief delay in infants as young as 6 months.

Interestingly, what was not apparent in the research by Barr and her colleagues (Barr et al., 1996) was compelling evidence that the young infants recalled the *order* of the sequence. Although three actions were modeled in sequence (i.e., pull off, shake, and replace a mitten), only 17% and 25% of the infants produced more than one action when tested immediately and after the delay, respectively. Similarly, in a study by Rachael Collie and Harlene Hayne (1999; Experiment 1), 6-month-old infants were exposed to three target events, two of which required two steps to complete (for a total of five possible actions). When they were tested 24 hours later, few infants produced more than one of the five possible actions, and the authors reported no ordered reproduction of the action pairs. Moreover, among 6-month-old infants, recall is fragile and seems dependent on multiple experiences of to-be-remembered events. Specifically, in the research by Barr and her colleagues, among infants who received six exposures to the puppet sequence, two thirds reproduced at least one action after the 24-hour delay. In contrast, infants who saw the sequence demonstrated only three times (rather than six) performed no differently than naive control infants who had never seen the sequence modeled.

*Recall by 9- and 10-Month-Old Infants.*   By 9 months of age, developments in both the length of the delay that infants are able to tolerate and in recall of the order of event sequences are readily apparent. Some of the earliest work using the imitation paradigm was conducted by Andrew Meltzoff with 9-month-old infants as participants (e.g., Meltzoff, 1988b). He exposed infants to three novel, object-specific actions (e.g., depressing a recessed button in a box, causing it to "beep"). He tested the infants' abilities to reproduce the actions either immediately or after a 24-hour delay. Regardless of the delay, half of the infants produced zero or one of the target actions, whereas the other half produced two or all three of the actions.

Leslie Carver and I (Carver & Bauer, 1999) tested the limits of 9-month-olds' recall abilities by extending Meltzoff's (1988b) work in two ways. First, we increased the delay from 24 hours to 5 weeks. Such a radical increase in the delay period afforded us the opportunity to test 9-month-olds' recall over delays more similar to those used with older children (described in the next section), thereby providing a basis for comparison of levels of performance across a wider age span. Second, we tested infants' recall of novel two-step sequences as opposed to single actions. Using multistep sequences permitted us to test infants' abilities to encode, store, and retrieve information about temporal order, as well as the individual actions of events, and provides especially compelling evidence of recall.

Carver and I (Carver & Bauer, 1999) found that, in the sample as a whole, the 9-month-old infants showed evidence of recall of the individual actions of the two-step sequences. That is, after the 5-week delay, the infants produced more of the target actions of the sequences they had seen demonstrated 1 month earlier ("old" sequences) than of sequences that were new to them at the time of delayed-recall testing. Comparison of performance on old and new sequences is important because, over delays as long as 5 weeks, we may expect infants' problem-solving abilities to improve. Performance on new sequences tells us how much of infants' performance could be due to problem solving alone; if performance on old sequences is higher than performance on new sequences, the difference can be attributed to memory. Interestingly, as reflected

TABLE 4.1
The Percentage of 9-Month-Old Infants Exhibiting Ordered Recall
of Two-Step Sequences, From Three Independent Samples

| | Samples of 9-Month-Old Infants | | |
|---|---|---|---|
| | Carver and Bauer (1999) | Bauer, Wiebe, Carver, Waters, and Nelson (2003) | Bauer, Wiebe, Waters, and Bangston (2001) |
| Recalled temporal order | 45% | 46% | 43% |
| Did not recall temporal order | 55% | 54% | 57% |

in Table 4.1, roughly half of the infants showed evidence of temporally ordered recall memory after the 5-week delay, but the other half of the infants did not. As indicated in Table 4.1, this distribution has since been replicated in two independent samples of 9-month-olds (Bauer, Wiebe, Carver, Waters, & Nelson, 2003; Bauer, Wiebe, Waters, & Bangston, 2001).

The finding of ordered recall by approximately half of 9-month-old infants across three separate samples suggests that the distribution is not due to chance. Nor is it due to systematic differences in infants' participation in the task: On sequences new to them, the infants who do and do not exhibit ordered delayed recall do not differ. Thus, the infants are equally willing to participate in the task. Instead of attributing the findings to chance or to differences in infants' willingness to participate in the task, we interpret the findings as evidence of systematic individual differences in long-term declarative memory ability at 9 months of age.

There are at least two possible sources of individual differences in 9-month-old infants' delayed ordered recall. The first possible source is a stable characteristic of the infants. That is, it is possible that some infants are simply better mnemonists than others, and that the task of delayed ordered recall is especially diagnostic of memory ability. Such a finding would not be without precedent. Researchers have found infants' performance on visual paired comparison tasks in the first year of life to be related to later intelligence (the relations are moderate, yet significant; e.g., Fagan, 1984; Rose & Feldman, 1997). Perhaps in like fashion, individual differences in delayed ordered recall would be predictive of later intelligence or later memory abilities.

An alternative source of individual differences at 9 months of age is that we have sampled the groups of infants in different developmental states. In this scenario, the differences are reflective of differential *rates* of development within the population: Some infants have achieved a particular developmental milestone and others have not, but presumably will with time. In this case, there is no expectation of an enduring difference. By analogy, consider that there are large individual differences in the age at which infants take their first steps: Some infants take their first steps without support as early as 9 months of age, whereas others do not begin to walk until well into the second year of life (Bertenthal & Clifton, 1998). Age of first step is not to my knowledge related to later walking ability, however.

To begin to differentiate these possibilities, my colleagues and I conducted two types of studies: between and within subjects. In the first, Leslie Carver and I (Carver & Bauer, 2001) enrolled two groups of infants in a study of long-term ordered recall. One group of infants was enrolled at 9 months, and the other was enrolled at 10 months. The infants were exposed to the same two-step sequences. The infants were tested for recall of half of the sequences 1 month later and for the other half of the sequences 3 months later (different sequences were tested at each delay). The 9-month-olds showed evidence of memory for the temporal order of the sequences after 1 month, but not after 3 months. In contrast, the 10-month-olds showed evidence of memory for temporal order after both the 1- and 3-month delay intervals; there were few individual differences in the 10-month-olds' recall (Carver & Bauer, 2001). Thus, after only one additional month of development, (a) the length of time over which infants were able to remember increased from 1 month to 3 months, and (b) individual differences in long-term ordered recall diminished. Similar results have been reported by Jean Mandler and Laraine McDonough (1995). They found that infants 11 months of age at the time of experience of events were able to recall them 3 months later.

In the second study, my colleagues and I charted recall after 1 month longitudinally. In this research, infants were enrolled at the age of 9 months, at which time they were exposed to three 2-step sequences. One month later, the infants were tested for recall of the sequences. Within a few days of their first delayed-recall test, the infants, now 10 months of age, were exposed to three new 2-step sequences. They were tested for recall of those sequences 1 month later. At the first delayed-recall test, only 28% of the infants exhibited delayed ordered recall. In contrast, among the same infants, at the second delayed recall test, 80% showed evidence of delayed ordered recall (Bauer et al., 2006). Thus, after only 1 additional month of development, the capacity to retain temporal order information over a delay went from being an "exception" seen in only a subset of 9-month-olds to being the "rule" among 10-month-olds. This finding implies that, at 9 months of age, long-term ordered recall ability is not a stable individual difference. Overall, the data are more consistent with the suggestion that at 9 months of age some infants have crossed a developmental threshold that others have yet to cross. As becomes evident in later chapters, the timing of differences is consistent with what is known about the course of development of the neural structures that permit long-term explicit memory (see chap. 6).

Finally, it is important to note that whereas, relative to 6-month-olds, 9- and 10-month-olds are quite mnemonically proficient, there remains among the older infants a severe limitation on long-term recall. To ensure recall over the long term, infants of this young age seemingly require multiple experiences with sequences prior to imposition of a delay. In the research discussed thus far, the infants have been exposed to the event sequences at two or even three sessions (in all cases, however, imitation of the sequences was deferred). My colleagues and I have observed that 43% to 46% of the infants show ordered recall 1 month later. In contrast, if 9-month-old infants are exposed to to-be-remembered events at only a single session, only 7% to 14% of them evidence ordered recall after a 1-month delay (Bauer et al., 2001; Experiments 1 and 2, respectively). This apparent limitation on long-term recall ability does not undermine the argument that the infants are showing evidence of declarative memory. Declarative memory supports one-trial learning (i.e., declarative memory is characterized as "fast"; Squire et al., 1993), but does not *require* one-trial learning. Even for adults, in whom declarative memory processes are fully mature and intact, mastery of new material often requires more than one learning trial. Although 9-month-olds' apparent dependence on multiple experiences does not preclude formation of declarative memories, it may limit the opportunity for long-term maintenance and subsequence retrieval of *episodic* memories: memories for specific events that are located in a particular place at a particular time (Tulving, 1972; see chap. 1). As can be seen in the next section, this limitation is overcome during the second year of life.

## Recall in the Second Year of Life

Over the course of the second year, long-term recall ability becomes both reliable and robust. Whereas 9-month-olds' recall seems dependent on multiple experiences, by 13 months of age, children recall events they have experienced only once prior to imposition of a delay (Bauer et al., 1995). Multiple experiences nevertheless facilitate long-term recall regardless of age. With increasing age, children are also able to remember ever-longer sequences: 9- and 10-month-old infants are able to recall sequences two steps in length; by 24 months of age, children correctly recall sequences five steps in length (Bauer & Travis, 1993). Perhaps most notable, however, are *changes in the length of time over which children show evidence of ordered recall*. Whereas just under half of 9-month-old infants recall the order of multistep sequences after a 1-month delay, 100% of 20-month-old children exhibit ordered recall after 1 month. Strikingly, among children exposed to sequences at 20 months of age, well over half of the children still remember portions of the events 1 year later (Bauer et al., 2000).

The data on very long-term recall by 20-month-old children are from a study of memory development in the second and into the third year of life conducted in my laboratory (Bauer et al., 2000). Because of the large number of children involved in the study ($N = 360$), the large number of sessions in which they participated (1,440 sessions), and the length of time required to complete it (4½ years), the study earned the affectionate moniker of "Monster." Children were enrolled in the "Monster" study at the age of 13, 16, or 20 months. Of the 360 children who participated, 180 were 16-month-olds. To accommodate developments in the length of sequences that children of different ages can remember, all of the 20-month-olds and half of the 16-month-olds were tested on sequences four steps in length; all of the 13-month-olds and half of the 16-month-olds were tested on sequences three steps in length. The children returned for delayed recall testing after delays of either 1, 3, 6, 9, or 12 months (delay condition was a between-subjects manipulation). The result was a 20-cell design with 18 children per cell.

The children were exposed to six 3- or 4-step sequences at each of three sessions, spaced 1 week apart. As depicted in Table 4.2, at the first session, prior to demonstration or modeling by the experimenter, for each sequence in turn (designated A–F in the table), the children were given the event-related props for a child-controlled period of manipulation. The purpose of this premodeling phase was to determine whether the events were already within the children's behavioral repertoires. They were not, as evidenced by low levels of premodeling performance. The experimenter then modeled each sequence in turn, with accompanying narration of each step. After demonstration, the props were put away: The children were not permitted to imitate.

TABLE 4.2
Schematic of Research Design for the "Monster" Study (Bauer et al., 2000)

| Session | Testing Phase | | | |
| | Premodeling | Modeling | Imitation | Delayed Recall |
|---|---|---|---|---|
| 1 | A, B, C | A, B, C | | |
| | D, E, F | D, E, F | | |
| 2 | | A, B, C | | |
| | | D, E, F | | |
| 3 | | A, B, C | | |
| | | D, E, F | D, E, F | |
| Delay of 1, 3, 6, 9, or 12 months imposed | | | | |
| 4 | | | | A, B, C (watch) |
| | | | | D, E, F (imitate) |
| | | | | H, I, J (new) |

Note. Sessions 1, 2, and 3 each were spaced 1 week apart. Session 4 took place 1, 3, 6, 9, or 12 months after Session 3 (delay was a between-subjects manipulation). Unique letters indicate unique sequences. Sequences A, B, and C are designated "watch" sequences because infants only watched them demonstrated; infants were not permitted to imitate them prior to imposition of the delay. Sequences D, E, and F are designated "imitate" sequences because infants were permitted to imitate them one time prior to imposition of the delay. Sequences H, I, and J are designated "new" sequences because infants were not exposed to them prior to imposition of the delay.

One week later, at the second session, the children again watched as the experimenter modeled each sequence two times. Again no imitation was permitted. One week later, at the third session, the sequences were modeled again. For the first three sequences (in Table 4.2, Sequences A, B, and C), the children were not given the opportunity to imitate. The children were permitted to imitate each of the remaining three sequences (Sequences D, E, and F). Imitation was permitted both to provide an estimate of how well the children had learned the sequences, and to afford a test of whether the opportunity to imitate affects the length of delay over which events are remembered. As measured by imitation at Session 3, levels of learning of the sequences were high. For example, overall, the 20-month-olds produced 97% of the possible actions (four actions for each of three sequences) and 70% of all possible ordered pairs of actions (three ordered pairs for each of three sequences).

The children returned for a fourth session either 1, 3, 6, 9, or 12 months later, and we tested their recall of the sequences. At the delayed-recall session, the children were tested for recall of the three sequences that they had only watched (in Table 4.2, Sequences A, B, and C: "watch"), the three sequences they had imitated one time prior to the delay (Sequences D, E, and F: "imitate"), as well as on three new events as a within-subjects control (Sequences H, I, J: "new"). For all nine of the sequences, the children first experienced a period during which they were prompted only by the event-related props and a generic prompt. That is, the experimenter put the props in front of the children and said, "What can you do with that stuff?" After approximately 30 seconds, the experimenter further prompted the children by providing the verbal labels for the sequences that had been used to introduce them 1 to 12 months earlier. For example, the experimenter said, "You can use that stuff to make a gong. Show me how you make a gong." The verbal label was provided for sequences that the children had seen before (watch and imitate sequences) and for the new, control sequences.

In Fig. 4.6 are the percentages of children at each age at enrollment in the study who, at delayed testing, showed a pattern indicative of recall of the temporal order of the sequences. Specifically, they performed more pairs of actions in the modeled order on previously experienced than on new sequences (i.e., they showed higher levels of performance on watch and imitate sequences relative to new sequences). An asterisk indicates that the number of children with the pattern that indicates recall was greater than the number that would be expected by chance. Because the opportunity to imitate had only negligible effects on delayed-recall performance (see Bauer et al., 2000, for details of minor, isolated effects), the values in the figure are collapsed across the manipulation. In addition, because the patterns were the same for the two groups of 16-month-olds (those tested on three- and four-step sequences), in the figure are reflected the values for one group only—namely, the 16-month-olds tested on four-step sequences.

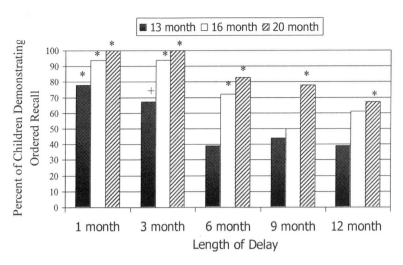

FIG. 4.6.   Results from the "Monster" study (Bauer et al., 2000). After intervals of 1, 3, 6, 9, or 12 months, 13- (filled bars), 16- (open bars), and 20-month-old (striped bars) children were tested for recall of six sequences to which they previously had been exposed, as well as on three new sequences as a within-subjects control. The values indicate the percentages of children of each age who performed at higher levels on previously experienced than on new, control sequences, thereby indicating recall. The values shown for 16-month-olds are for those tested with four-step sequences; the same pattern applied to the 16-month-olds tested on three-step sequences (see Bauer et al., 2000, for details). An asterisk indicates that the number of children exhibiting the pattern of ordered recall (i.e., higher level of performance on previously experienced than on new sequences) was reliably greater than chance; a cross indicates that the number exhibiting the pattern approached significance ($p < .10$). Because tied ranks are not included, identical percentages will not necessarily yield the same pattern of significance (i.e., 13-month-olds after 3 months and 20-month-olds after 12 months). Based on Bauer (2002).

For the children who were 13 months of age at the time of experience of the events, there was a relatively rapid decline in performance across the delays. After 6 months had passed, fewer than half of 13-month-olds showed evidence of ordered recall. In fact beyond 1 month, the number of 13-month-olds who performed at higher levels on previously experienced than on new event sequences was not greater than chance (although the value approached significance).

For the children who had been 16 months at the time of experience of the events, the percentage of children whose behavior indicated long-term ordered recall was reliably greater than chance in the 1-, 3-, and 6-month delay conditions, but not in the 9- and 12-month delay conditions. For children who had been 20 months of age at the time of exposure to the to-be-remembered events, even after 12 months, fully two thirds of the sample had higher levels of performance on previously experienced than on new event sequences. Moreover, for the 20-month-olds, in all of the delay conditions, the number of children showing evidence of recall was reliably greater than chance. Thus, for children who were 20 months at the time of exposure to the sequences, a large and significant proportion of the children performed at higher levels on old sequences than on new sequences.

The data in Fig. 4.6 are reflective of *increasing reliability in long-term ordered recall across the second year of life*. At the short delay interval of 1 month, across age groups, there were roughly comparable proportions of children who contribute to the "memory" effect: 78% of 13-month-olds, 94% of 16-month-olds, and 100% of 20-month-olds showed higher levels of performance on previously experienced than on new sequences (contrast these levels of performance with those of 9-month-olds tested after 1 month, fewer than 50% of whom exhibited ordered recall; Table 4.1). As delay interval increased, fewer children maintained the information they had learned about the events. The younger the children were at the time of experience of the events, the faster they "dropped out." For 13-month-olds, at 6 months and beyond, the chance of randomly selecting a child who would show temporally ordered recall was less than 50%. In contrast, even at the longest delay interval, a random selection among 20-month-olds would yield a roughly 70% chance that the child would show temporally ordered recall.

In addition to evidence of increasingly reliable recall, the "Monster" study provided evidence of *increasingly robust recall over the course of the second year*. Simply put, older children remembered more than younger children.[1] The age effects were apparent in children's ordered recall and in their production of the individual actions of the events. Moreover, age-related differences in the amount remembered were particularly apparent under the most challenging conditions. Specifically, when the children were prompted by the event-related props alone, age differences were observed in all delay conditions. When the children were prompted by the event-related props and by the verbal reminders of the sequences, age differences were observed only at the longer delay intervals of 9 and 12 months. Thus, age effects in how much information was retained over the long term were particularly apparent (a) when the children had less support for recall (i.e., when they were prompted by event-related props alone), and (b) at longer retention intervals.

---

[1]Examination of age-related differences in the amount remembered was conducted via analyses of covariance (ANCOVAs) in which we controlled for age-related differences in (a) children's initial learning of the sequences as measured by imitation at Session 3, and (b) children's problem-solving ability at the time of delayed-recall testing as measured by performance on new sequences. In evaluating age effects in *how much* is remembered, it is important to control for these two sources of variance: What we are trying to explain are age-related differences in long-term memory, not age-related differences in initial mastery or problem solving.

Together the data indicate that, over the second year of life, there are age-related increases in the reliability and robustness of long-term recall. The changes are highly suggestive of consolidation of long-term mnemonic function over this space of time. As is seen in chapter 6, developments in the neural structures responsible for explicit memory likely are a major contributor to these age-related changes.

## INDIVIDUAL AND GROUP DIFFERENCES IN THE EARLY DEVELOPMENT OF LONG-TERM RECALL

Whereas there are regular developments in long-term recall ability over the course of the first years of life, there is no "growth chart" type function for the length of time over which we expect children of specific ages to remember. First, the developmental progression that I have described is far from fixed. Indeed as discussed in chapter 6, it can be disrupted by biological and environmental factors. Second, there are many task differences that influence performance. As a result, the same child may appear to be a more or less competent mnemonist as a function of specific memory task on which the child is tested. Some of the factors that have been found to affect recall performance are discussed in chapter 7. Third, there are individual differences in children's performance throughout the period of transition from infancy to early childhood. For example, in the "Monster" study (Bauer et al., 2000), even among children in whom long-term recall ability was reliable and robust (20-month-olds), some children recalled all four possible actions of the sequences, whereas others recalled as few as one action. What accounts for such wide variation in performance? In the balance of this chapter, I address this question by examining potential sources of systematic individual differences in children's long-term recall performance.

## Children's Gender

For many, the first potential source of differences in early recall memory to come to mind is gender. The expectation of possible systematic differences in long-term recall memory performance as a function of children's gender stems from suggestions of faster maturation of girls relative to boys throughout infancy (e.g., Hutt, 1978; although see Reinisch, Rosenblum, Rubin, & Schulsinger, 1991). Although differential maturity provides a reasonable basis for expecting gender differences, few relations have been found.

One reason that few gender effects have been reported is that relatively few studies have tested for them. The lack of attention to possible gender effects is likely due to the fact that studies of early recall memory typically include small samples of children. For instance, a review of studies published from my own laboratory and from the laboratories of Harlene Hayne and Andrew Meltzoff (both of whom also employ imitation paradigms with children ages 2 years and younger) revealed sample sizes ranging from 8 to 32 participants per cell of the research designs; the most frequent sample size was 12 participants. To divide such small samples in half to examine gender differences is to invite null or, worse, spurious findings. Consistent with these possibilities, 18 of 22 studies that I reviewed from these laboratories conducted tests for possible gender effects and found none. In the four cases of positive findings (all from my laboratory), the results were inconsistent. Three of the four cases involved 9-month-olds—an age at which there is substantial variability in long-term recall ability. In two cases, the effect of gender favored boys (Bauer et al., 2001; Experiments 1 and 2); in one case, the effect favored girls (Carver & Bauer, 1999). In the fourth study (Bauer, Hertsgaard, Dropik, & Daly, 1998), 28-month-old children were challenged to reproduce lengthy sequences, the orders of which were arbitrary (accurate reproduction of this type of sequence is a late-developing skill; e.g., Wenner & Bauer, 1999). In this case, the advantage was for girls relative to boys.

What happens when larger samples are examined? Do consistent gender-related patterns emerge? We are able to address this question using the sample tested in the "Monster" study. The study featured a generous sample of 360 children—185 girls and 175 boys. The children were tested for long-term recall of multistep sequences after delays of 1 to 12 months. Examination of gender-related patterns of performance in the large sample thus affords a strong test of gender as a potential source of variability in young children's recall memory performance.

To examine potential effects of gender, Melissa Burch, Erica Kleinknecht, and I conducted separate analyses for the 20- and 16-month-olds tested on four-step event sequences, and for the 13- and 16-month-olds tested on three-step event sequences. When the children were prompted only by the event-related props, some isolated gender differences emerged. For example, 16- and 20-month-old girls tested for recall after 9 months had lower levels of performance than same-age boys. There were no reliable gender effects in the 1-, 3-, 6-, or 12-month delay conditions. For the children tested on three-step sequences, girls in the 6-month delay condition performed at higher levels relative to boys in the same condition. However, the effect was only apparent on the events that the children were permitted to imitate. Notably, once the verbal reminders of the events were provided, there were no gender-related effects either for the 16- and 20-month-olds or for the 13- and 16-month-olds (Bauer, Burch, & Kleinknecht, 2002).

The relative paucity of reports of gender differences in the literature on early recall memory, coupled with the lack of meaningful effects in a large-scale study, implies that gender is not a major source of variability in early recall memory performance. There are, however, two exceptions to this general statement. First, gender effects seem to be apparent at times of "transition." They were apparent at the "dawning" of the ability to engage in long-term temporally ordered recall (Bauer et al., 2001; Carver & Bauer, 1999) and at the dawning of the ability to accurately reproduce lengthy, arbitrarily ordered sequences (Bauer, Hertsgaard, et al., 1998). Second, in a large-scale study, gender effects were apparent under conditions of high cognitive demand (i.e., recall after a long delay) and lesser contextual support (i.e., in the absence of verbal reminders; Bauer et al., 2000).

## Children's Language

Another potential source of variability in early explicit memory is children's language. Despite the fact that elicited- and deferred-imitation tasks are nonverbal, children's own language facility might influence performance in several ways. First, in many studies (including all published studies from my laboratory), demonstration of to-be-remembered events is accompanied by verbal narration. Children's abilities to comprehend the language spoken to them is thus one potential source of variability. Second, even when narration is not provided (e.g., Meltzoff, 1985, 1988a, 1988b, 1995), language development is a possible source of variation because children with greater language skills potentially could verbally encode the events that they observe, thus providing themselves with additional retrieval cues. Indeed as is seen in chapter 10, the ability to "augment" nonverbal representations with language plays a role in the later verbal accessibility of memories likely encoded without the benefit of language. Nevertheless, systematic variation attributable to differences in children's language proficiency has rarely been examined.

The "Monster" study (Bauer et al., 2000) once again affords the opportunity to investigate the possibility that variability in language development accounts for systematic variance in long-term recall. Specifically, to match the children assigned to the different delay conditions (1–12 months), we used children's scores on the MacArthur–Bates Communicative Development Inventory for Toddlers (20-month-olds) and the MacArthur–Bates Communicative Development Inventory for Infants (13- and 16-month-olds; Fenson et al., 1994). The MacArthur–Bates inventories are well-normed, valid, parent-report instruments for assessing children's early communicative development. In the inventory for toddlers, parents are asked to indicate which of 680 words their children produce. In the inventory for infants, parents are asked to indicate with of 360 words they have heard their children produce and which of the words they think their children understand. Sample items

TABLE 4.3
Sample Items From Each of the 22 Semantic Categories Represented
in the MacArthur–Bates Communicative Development Inventories

| Semantic Category | Item |
| --- | --- |
| Sound effects and animal sounds | vroom, baa baa, meow |
| Animals | bunny, moose, pony |
| Vehicles | bus, stroller, truck |
| Toys | block, pen, present |
| Food and drink | cookie, pancake, raisin |
| Clothing | belt, jeans, sneaker |
| Body parts | cheek, head, toe |
| Small household items | basket, lamp, soap |
| Furniture and rooms | bed, porch, rocking chair |
| Outside things | flower, slide, stone |
| Places to go | beach, picnic, zoo |
| People | brother, lady, person |
| Games and routines | gonna get you!, hello, so big! |
| Action words | clap, look, think |
| Descriptive words | broken, little, sleepy |
| Words about time | before, night, yesterday |
| Pronouns | her, that, we |
| Question words | how, where, why |
| Prepositions and locations | around, down, there |
| Quantifiers and articles | a, every, some |
| Helping verbs | can, don't, were |
| Connecting words | because, but, then |

from each of the 22 semantic categories represented in the inventories are
provided in Table 4.3.

From the sample of 360 children, we had completed MacArthur–Bates inventories for 93% of the children (336 children). Children's reported productive vocabulary scores ranged from 0 to 651 words (across the 13- to 20-
month age range); their reported receptive vocabulary scores ranged from 11
to 393 words (across the 13- to 16-month age range). Although the sample
featured ample power and ample variability to permit detection of any systematic relations between children's language and children's recall memory
performance, no statistically significant relations were observed (Bauer,
Burch, & Kleinknecht, 2002). Thus, as measured in this large sample of children, neither reported productive nor receptive vocabulary was reliably related to recall memory performance.

## Children's Temperament

The final potential source of individual differences in recall to be considered
is temperament. What is temperament, and why might we expect it to be related to early recall memory? *Temperament* or *behavioral style* refers to pat-

terns of responding to environmental stimuli that seem to be inherent to the individual (e.g., Rothbart & Bates, 1998). Although there are many theories and operationalizations of the spectrum of behavioral patterns, there are three psychobiological dimensions of difference among children on which scholars seem to agree: positive affectivity or approach (e.g., response to an attractive toy), negative affectivity and inhibition (e.g., response to fear-provoking stimuli), and attention (i.e., orienting, and regulation and control).

It takes only a moment's reflection to think of several ways in which differences in positive and negative affectivity and attention might influence children's performance on imitation-based tests of recall memory. For example, children who are high in positive affect and approach might more readily engage in the task and, as a result, evidence better memory. In contrast, if memory is assessed in a novel laboratory context, children who characteristically experience a greater degree of fear or inhibition might be less likely to engage in the task and thus perform less well. Attention may play a role, in that infants and children whose attention may "wander" during demonstration of the event sequences may not adequately encode them, which would have negative consequences for recall.

Despite reasonably compelling motivation for examination of relations between temperament and early memory, there have been few such studies. Theodore Wachs, Judy Morrow, and Elizabeth Slabach (1990) examined relations between parent-reported temperament (assessed via the *Revised Infant Temperament Questionnaire*; Carey & McDevitt, 1978), home environment (assessed via the *Purdue Home Stimulation Inventory*), and recognition memory (assessed via novelty preference) in 3-month-old infants. They found relations between temperament and infants' performance on the recognition memory task. Specifically, infants who were rated by their parents as more adaptable, more positive in mood, and easier to manage were more consistent in their preference for novel stimuli. Relations between infant temperament (as described by their parents on the *Infant Behavior Questionnaire* [IBQ]; Rothbart, 1981) and visual recognition memory (measured via event-related potentials [ERPs]) also were reported by Megan Gunnar and Charles Nelson (1994). They found that 12-month-old infants whose parents reported that their infants expressed more positive affect showed more ERP activity during the visual recognition task. Thus, these findings suggest relations between recognition memory and positive affect in the first year of life.

There have also been a few studies of relations between early recall memory and children's temperament characteristics. In one such study, my colleagues and I found that high scores on the dimension of positive affect were correlated with 9-month-olds' ordered recall performance. As reviewed earlier in this chapter, among 9-month-olds, there are pronounced individual differences in ordered recall after a 1-month delay: Approximately half of 9-

month-olds demonstrate ordered recall and half do not. For the sample of infants tested in Bauer, Wiebe, et al. (2003), we asked the infants' parents to complete the IBQ as a measure of temperament. The group of infants who demonstrated ordered recall after 1 month differed from the group that did not on only one of the six subscales of the instrument (listed in Table 4.4, along with sample items from each subscale)—namely, *Smiling and Laughter* (result reported in Bauer, Burch, & Kleinknecht, 2002). Thus, as observed among 3- and 12-month-olds in recognition memory tasks (Wachs et al., 1990; Gunnar & Nelson, 1994, respectively), performance was correlated with positive affect.

TABLE 4.4
Items From the Subscales of the *Infant Behavior Questionnaire* (IBQ)
and *Toddler Behavior Assessment Questionnaire* (TBAQ)

| Subscale | Item |
|---|---|
| *Infant Behavior Questionnaire (IBQ)* | |
| Activity level | During feeding, how often did the baby: squirm or kick? wave his or her arms? |
| Distress to limitations | When having to wait for food or liquids during the last week, how often did the baby: show mild fussing? cry loudly? |
| Distress to novelty | When given a new food or liquid, how often did the baby: reject it by spitting it out? closing mouth? or not accept it no matter how many times offered? |
| Duration of orienting | How often during the last week did your baby: look at pictures in books and/or magazines for 5 minutes or longer at a time? play with one toy or object for 10 minutes or longer? |
| Smiling and laughter | When put into the bath water, how often did the baby: smile? laugh? |
| Soothability | Have you tried any of the following soothing techniques in the last 2 weeks? If so, how often did the method soothe the baby?: singing or talking, or showing the baby something to look at? |
| *Toddler Behavior Assessment Questionnaire (TBAQ)* | |
| Activity level | When playing inside the house or apartment, how often did your child: run through the house? climb over furniture? |
| Anger | When you removed something your child should not have been playing with, how often did she or he: scream? try to grab the object back? |
| Interest and persistence | While playing alone in a sandbox or playing with dolls, how often did your child: remain interested for 10 minutes or longer? remain interested for 30 minutes or longer? |
| Pleasure | When playing quietly with one of her or his favorite toys, how often did your child: smile? sound happy? |
| Social fear | When at the doctor's office or a clinic, how often did your child: cling or hold onto you and not want to let go? cry or struggle when the doctor tried to touch her or him? |

Among children in the second year of life, there has been only one examination of possible relations between recall memory and temperament. Once again the source of the data was the "Monster" study conducted in my laboratory (Bauer et al., 2000). Although the study was not designed to examine relations between temperament and memory, as a preliminary test of possible relations we obtained reports of temperament from some of the children's parents. We used the *Toddler Behavior Assessment Questionnaire* (TBAQ; Goldsmith, 1996), a parent-report instrument analogous to the IBQ used with infants. Sample items from each of the five subscales are provided in Table 4.4. Completed instruments were available for twenty-five 13-month-olds and twenty-eight 20-month-olds. We examined relations between children's observed long-term recall and their scores on each of the five subscales of the TBAQ (see Bauer, Burch, & Kleinknecht, 2002, for details).

Among the 13-month-olds, long-term recall was positively related with the *Pleasure* subscale of the TBAQ. The Pleasure subscale is the toddler analogue to the *Smiling and Laughter* subscale in the IBQ. The correlations indicate that higher levels of recall and, in particular, ordered recall were observed for children whose parents indicated that, for example, when seeing a familiar adult, their children expressed joy and babbled and talked. Importantly, children's scores on the *Pleasure* subscale were not related to their performance on the new, control sequences. Thus, the positive relations between *Pleasure* and performance after the delay are indicative of an effect on recall, as opposed to a more general influence on performance on the imitation task.

For the 20-month-olds, long-term recall was negatively related with the *Activity Level* subscale and positively related with the *Interest and Persistence* subscale of the TBAQ. Specifically, lower levels of recall were observed for children whose parents said that, for instance, their children like to play games that involve running, banging, and dumping out toys. In contrast, more robust recall was observed among children whose parents said that, for example, when playing with a detailed or complicated toy, their children explore the toy thoroughly. In the case of relations with the *Activity Level* subscale, similar patterns were observed on both old (watch and imitate) and new control sequences. In contrast, in the case of the *Interest and Persistence* subscale, the relations were specific to performance on the old sequences. Thus, children whose parents reported that their children have characteristically high levels of activity did less well on the imitation task more generally, whereas children whose parents reported that they have characteristically high levels of interest and persistence showed higher levels of recall memory.

The finding of different patterns of relations at 13 and 20 months is noteworthy. At the younger age, high levels of recall and, in particular, ordered recall were observed among infants whose parents reported that they find pleasure in new experiences. A similar pattern was observed among 9-

month-olds. Perhaps these infants embrace the novelty of the situation and the events, and their resulting focus of attention on the model affords them better recall. The consistent pattern of relations at 9 and 13 months indicates that, for children who are just "breaking into" the recall memory system, being a "happy camper" is a benefit. Whereas pleasure in novel situations facilitates memory for young infants, by 20 months, deriving pleasure from new experiences apparently no longer is sufficient to ensure high levels of recall. Instead, by 20 months, in order to remember, children need to be able to focus and regulate their attention to the specific properties of the materials and their manner of combination. Characteristically high levels of activity are not conducive to this "contemplative" attitude and thus were observed to be negatively related to successful mnemonic (and problem-solving, as in the case of new events) performance (Bauer, Burch, & Kleinknecht, 2002).

## Summary of Individual Differences in Early Recall Memory

Against a backdrop of systematic age-related increases in the reliability and robustness of long-term recall memory over the course of the first 2 years of life are individual differences in children's performance. Two of the most intuitively obvious potential sources of systematic variation in young children's recall performance—namely, children's gender and their levels of language development—appear to have little predictive utility. That is, even in a large sample that spanned most of the second year of life, gender was not found to relate to early recall memory in any substantial or systematic manner. Similarly, few relations between children's receptive or productive language have been observed.

In contrast to the lack of relations between children's gender and recall and their language and recall, intriguing relations between children's temperaments and their long-term recall memory abilities have emerged. At 9 and 13 months of age, at a time of high variability in the reliability and robustness of recall memory, performance is related to positive affect. Thus, being able to engage with new objects and people, and finding joy in the process, is associated with better memory. By 20 months of age, when long-term recall memory is more reliably observed and more robust, performance is no longer related to positive engagement in the task, but to the ability to regulate activity level, focus and control attention, and thereby maintain interest. Importantly, from a longitudinal sample, we have evidence that the dimensions of positive affect and attention are related. Specifically, children who had high *Pleasure* scores at 13 months of age had high *Interest and Persistence* scores at 24 months of age. The converse was not true: Scores on the *Interest and Persistence* subscale at 13 months were not significantly correlated with scores on the *Pleasure* subscale at 24 months (Bauer, Burch, & Kleinknecht, 2002). Thus, there seems to be an underlying continuity in the behavioral profile that affords some children an advantage in recall throughout the period of transition from infancy to early childhood.

It is likely more than coincidence that, over the period during which long-term recall ability seems to consolidate and become reliable, we see that the capacity to sustain interest and focus attention becomes important for acquiring and remembering new material (C. A. Nelson & Dukette, 1998). As reviewed by Mary Rothbart and Michael Posner (2001), developments in the ability to focus and sustain attention are thought to be related to changes in the limbic system (especially the hippocampus), the frontal cortex, and the connections between them. Over the course of the next two chapters (chaps. 5 and 6), it is seen that these same structures are implicated in declarative memory.

## SUMMARY AND CONCLUSIONS

For much of the history of research in cognitive development, the field was shaped by the assumption that infants and very young children lacked the capacity for declarative memory. The suggestion went untested until the 1980s, in large part, because we lacked an appropriate method. What was needed was a nonverbal analogue to verbal report. With the development of imitation-based techniques, the hypothesis of a period devoid of the capacity for recall memory has been tested and found wanting. It is now clear that the capacity to recall specific actions after a delay of 24 hours is available to 6-month-old infants. By the age of 9 months, recall of the individual actions of multistep sequences over delays as long as 5 weeks is observed; there are pronounced individual differences in ordered recall over the same delays. Moreover, in the first year, long-term recall ability is fragile: It seems dependent on multiple experiences of to-be-remembered events.

Over the course of the second year, the ability to recall the temporal order of sequences becomes both reliable and robust. In contrast to 9-month-olds, only roughly half of whom exhibit ordered recall after a 1-month delay, almost 80% of 13-month-olds and 100% of 20-month-olds show evidence of ordered recall over the same period. Whereas beyond 1 month children 13 months of age at the time of exposure to events exhibit a sharp forgetting function, 20-month-olds show a pattern of more "graceful degradation" in their performance. Differences in long-term recall between children earlier and later in the second year of life are especially apparent when children are tested under conditions of high cognitive demand, such as after a long delay or when they have fewer cues to recall.

At 9 months of age, individual differences in long-term recall ability are apparent in whether infants exhibit ordered recall; individual differences are the rule, rather than the exception. In contrast, during the second year of life, individual differences in whether children recall are the exception, not the rule. Nevertheless, individual differences in the *amount* that children recall are very much in evidence. Two of the most obvious potential sources of individual differences—children's gender and their language ability—have proved to be rather lackluster predictors of variation in long-term recall memory. Individual differences in the temperament characteristics of positive affectivity and control of attention are related to long-term memory performance, however. In subsequent chapters, I discuss the implications of these differences for later developments in autobiographical memory.

The data discussed in this chapter make clear that, in its strongest form, the hypothesis that memories from the first years of life are absent because no memories were formed cannot be true. Nevertheless, there are pronounced changes in declarative memory late in the first year and throughout the second year of life. What is responsible for the developmental changes in this foundational ability, and how might the changes be related to the development of autobiographical memory? In the 1990s, cognitive developmental scientists began to address the first of these questions by examining changes in the neural structures that support declarative memory. In this volume, I attempt to bring the insights we have gained to bear on the second question. Before we get there, however, we must do two things: examine the neural structures involved in declarative memory in the adult, and chronicle their development in the human infant. I pursue these agendas in chapters 5 and 6, respectively.

# 5

# The Neural Bases of
# Declarative Memory in Adults

*And I come to the fields and spacious palaces of my memory, where are the treasures of innumerable images, brought into it from things of all sorts perceived by the senses. There is stored up . . . those things which the sense hath come to . . . for thought to recall. . . . For even while I dwell in darkness and silence, in my memory I can produce colours, if I will. . . . So the other things, piled in and up by the other senses, I recall at my pleasure. Yea, I discern the breath of lilies from violets, though smelling nothing; and I prefer honey to sweet wine, smooth before rugged, at the time neither tasting nor handling, but remembering only.*

—Saint Aurelius Augustine, from
*The Confessions of Saint Augustine* (401 CE)

By what means is it possible to sample from "the fields and spacious palaces" of memory to "discern the breath of lilies from violets, though smelling nothing"? The question of how experiences from the past can be brought forth into the present has for centuries interested not only saints, but philosophers, scientists, practitioners, and the lay public alike. In previous chapters, I made passing references to the means by which this feat is accomplished. In the present chapter, we move beyond the metaphors of "fields and spacious palaces" to the more concrete reality of the true place of residence of memories—namely, the brain. Although the 21st-century version of the location in which memories reside is not as poetic as that of Augustine's time, the question of the origin and later reproduction of memories remains every bit as compelling: How is it that the roughly 1,500 grams (3½ pounds) of tissue that sits in the bony case atop our shoulders re-creates, in living color, the times of our lives once they are past? Although nearly two centuries have gone by since the time of Saint Augustine, we have not solved the entire mystery. Yet in the relatively recent history of modern brain science, we have made good progress. In this chapter, I provide a brief introduction to the major methods employed to investigate the neural bases of memory and then outline what we have learned using them. The present discussion is confined to function in the mature organism. Developmental issues are the subject of chapter 6.

## METHODS FOR STUDYING
## THE NEURAL BASES OF MEMORY

An early approach to studying relations between the brain and behavior (including memory) was to link patterns of variation in the surface of the skull with profiles of individual differences in abilities (Gall, 1835). The logic of this science of *phrenology* was that, as illustrated in Fig. 5.1, distinct psychological functions were localized within the cerebral cortex. Functions that were especially well developed were thought to produce bumps or bulges on the skull. Thus, an individual with a pronounced bump over

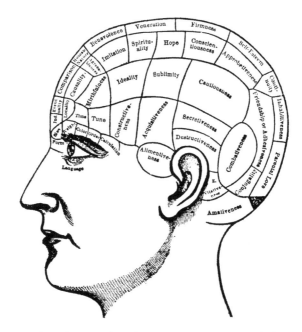

FIG. 5.1. Phrenology map from the early 1800s. Distinct psychological functions were thought to be controlled by specific areas of the brain that expanded as the functions developed, resulting in bumps or bulges on the skull. From E. R. Kandel, J. H. Schwartz, and T. M. Jessell, *Principles of Neural Science, Fourth Edition*, Fig. 1-1, p. 7, 2000, McGraw-Hill. Reproduced with permission of The McGraw-Hill Companies.

the cortical area responsible for "cautiousness" would exhibit a great deal of that characteristic.

Although Franz Joseph Gall's 19th-century science of phrenology correctly located cognitive function in the brain (as opposed to the Ancient Egyptians, who thought that human intelligence resided in the heart), it fell short of adequate, nonetheless. As soon as it became apparent that feeling the head from the outside was not going to be the way to learn about neural function, researchers faced the problem of how to peer inside a case that is made to prevent peering. The human brain is covered by five layers of scalp tissue, under which is the bony case of the cranium, under which lie three layers of protective tissue known as the meninges: the dura mater (the toughest outer layer), the arachnoid membrane, and the pia mater (the delicate inner layer). A variety of strategies for bypassing this armor and observing the human brain have been employed. In the present chapter, I focus on three of the most frequently used: (a) research with humans who have experienced brain damage or trauma resulting in memory impairments, (b) animal models of memory impairments, and (c) techniques for imaging the brain as it functions. Data from these three sources provide largely converging answers regarding the neural bases of declarative memory. Before proceeding with a description of the methods, however, it is important to identify the specific neural structures that will receive most of the attention in the discussion to follow.

## About What Part of the Brain Are We Talking?

Virtually the whole brain participates in cognition. Nevertheless, there is a degree of functional specialization of neural structures. Current conceptualizations suggest that the formation, maintenance, and subsequent retrieval of declarative memories depends on a multicomponent network involving structures in the parietal and frontal lobes, as well as in the temporal lobe. A lateral (side) view of the lobes is represented in Fig. 5.2, Panel A; the lateral–medial (side to middle) and dorsal–ventral (top to bottom) axes are illustrated in Panel B of the figure. As suggested by the case of patient Henry M. (introduced in chap. 1), structures in the temporal lobe play an especially critical role in establishing new memories. H. M. underwent a bilateral removal of large portions of his medial (interior) temporal lobes (see Fig. 1.1). The specific structures that were removed are represented in Fig. 5.3— namely, the hippocampus and surrounding areas, including a portion of the perirhinal cortex, the entire entorhinal cortex, and a portion of the parahippocampal cortex (Corkin et al., 1997; Scoville & Milner, 1957). One of the results of H. M.'s surgery was that he was rendered densely amnesic—he has great difficulty learning new facts and retaining information about world and personal events. The findings that removal of portions of H. M.'s medial

**A.**

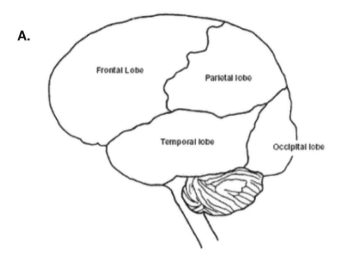

**B.** Lateral ←——— Medial ———→ Lateral

Dorsal

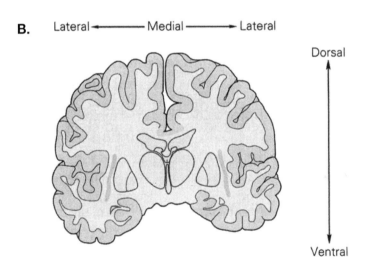

Ventral

FIG. 5.2.   Panel A: A lateral (toward the side) view of the four major lobes of the human brain (temporal, occipital, parietal, and frontal; the divide between the motor and sensory cortices is the boundary between the parietal and frontal lobes). Panel B: The lateral-to-medial (side to middle) and dorsal-to-ventral (top to bottom) axes of the human brain. Panel A from the Epilepsy Foundation (www.epilepsyfoundation.org); reproduced with permission of the Epilepsy Foundation. Panel B is from E. R. Kandel, J. H. Schwartz, and T. M. Jessell, *Principles of Neural Science, Fourth Edition*, Fig. 17-3, p. 321, 2000, McGraw-Hill. Reproduced with permission of The McGraw-Hill Companies.

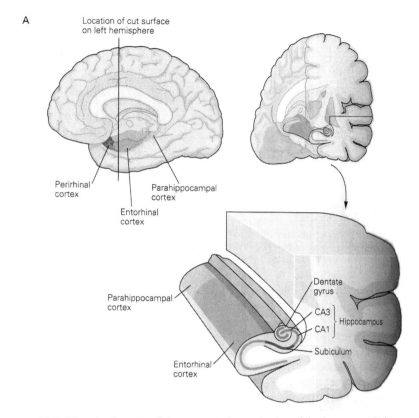

FIG. 5.3. A schematic of the anatomical organization of the human medial temporal structures. The perirhinal, entorhinal, and parahippocampal cortices can be seen in the medial view of the cerebral hemisphere (left side of figure). The ventral view (right side of figure) reveals the major components of the hippocampus. From E. R. Kandel, J. H. Schwartz, and T. M. Jessell, *Principles of Neural Science, Fourth Edition*, Fig. 62-5, p. 1232, 2000, McGraw-Hill. Reproduced with permission of The McGraw-Hill Companies.

temporal structures left him unable to form new memories, and that damage to other brain structures (e.g., the striatum) appears to leave declarative memory abilities virtually intact, were strong evidence of the role of the medial temporal structures in this fundamental cognitive process.

## Humans With Brain Damage or Trauma

As suggested by the reliance on the case of H. M. to describe mnemonic phenomena, one of the major methods of learning about the neural bases of memory is to examine relations between the behavior of individuals with brain damage and the sites of their lesions (e.g., Kleist, 1934; see chap. 1).

Although H. M. became amnesic, his ability to learn new motor skills, for example, has remained largely unaffected. The pattern of deficit and sparing in H. M. contributed to characterization of memory as declarative versus non-declarative. In the years since H. M. started teaching us lessons about memory and the brain, many other patients have lent their cognitive profiles to the cause. They have undergone extensive testing to determine as precisely as possible their areas of functional deficit and areas of sparing. For most of the history of this approach to studying relations between brain and behavior, however, certainty in identifying the specific brain structures affected by the trauma or disease came only with autopsy. Contemporary research still entails careful, detailed testing to determine areas of functional sparing and deficit. Fortunately, lesion sites can now be identified with relative certainty using neuroimaging techniques described later in this chapter.

By compiling data across patients with similar lesions, neuropsychologists and neuroscientists have been able to correlate the function of particular brain regions with particular cognitive processes. Although the approach has revealed a great deal about relations between structure and function, it is limited in some important ways. First, damage rarely is confined to one specific area of the brain. More commonly, patients have damage to multiple brain regions as well as to the connections among brain regions. In addition, the amount of damage varies across patients. This makes it difficult to know whether the behavioral profile is associated with the specific neural tissue that is compromised or with the amount of tissue damage. Most important, one can never draw a cause-and-effect relation. Because we rarely know what a patient's premorbid behavior looked like (except in cases of planned surgery, patients are not "patients" until they experience the trauma or disease that confers on them the status), we do not know whether the lesion actually affected their behavior (i.e., there is no "pretest" or baseline measure of premorbid function, only "posttest" measures are available).

In addition, even the mature brain is capable of a certain amount of recovery from trauma (i.e., brains are "plastic"). For obvious ethical reasons, the most direct evidence of neural plasticity comes from nonhuman as opposed to human animals. For example, Brian Leonard and his colleagues found that 1 year after surgical removal of the entorhinal cortex (see Fig. 5.3), the performance of operated monkeys had returned to normal levels following a period of pronounced deficit shortly after surgery. Postmortem examination revealed the likely basis for the recovery—new connections between the perirhinal cortex and the hippocampus, which bypassed the lesioned entorhinal cortex (Leonard, Amaral, Squire, & Zola-Morgan, 1995). The finding of such plasticity in adult animals is amazing in its own right. It is easy to appreciate how it can complicate interpretation of data based on the lesion approach, however, whether it be in human or nonhuman animals. For all of these reasons, it is extremely important to have converging evidence of relations between brain and behavior.

## Animal Models

One of the most productive sources of converging evidence of relations between neural structure and cognitive function in the human is an animal model of a cognitive deficit or syndrome. The most "popular" models for human memory are the nonhuman primate (frequently cynomolgus and rhesus monkeys) and the rat. In both cases, researchers can produce specific lesions that mimic those seen naturally in humans, in areas of the brain implicated in specific cognitive tasks. The animals can then be tested and resulting behavioral deficits can be identified. Because the lesions are experimentally induced, researchers can be certain of the premorbid condition of the animals, they can exert considerable control over the extent and location of the lesion, and they can verify lesion site with certainty at autopsy.

In the study of memory, animal models of human amnesia were established in the early 1980s by Larry Squire and his colleagues, and by Mortimer Mishkin and his colleagues (Mishkin, Spiegler, Saunders, & Malamut, 1982; Squire & Zola-Morgan, 1983). Establishing a nonhuman animal model of amnesia was especially important because, based on patient data alone, it was not clear what portions of the medial temporal lobe were implicated in declarative memory. In patient H. M., for example, in addition to the anterior (front) portion of the hippocampal formation, the medial temporal structure of the amygdala was damaged as well (see Corkin et al., 1997, for precise characterization of H. M.'s lesion). For many years, researchers could only speculate as to whether the amygdala itself was involved in the medial temporal memory system that was so obviously disrupted in H. M. Animal work permitted determination that, whereas the amygdala plays a modulatory role (Cahill & McGaugh, 1998; Sarter & Markowitsch, 1985), lesions to the amygdala alone do not produce deficits in declarative memory, yet they do impair memory for emotional components of events (e.g., Cahill, Babinsky, Markowitsch, & McGaugh, 1995; see discussion in a later section). Thus, animal models have permitted greater precision in determination of relations between structure and function relative to the study of human patient populations alone.

Whereas animal models provide invaluable information, this approach also has its limitations. Chief among them is that nonhuman animals are not human. If we really want to know how an intact human brain processes information, we must look to the intact human brain.

## Functional Neuroimaging

The capacity to obtain images of the functioning human brain has permitted enormous gains in identification of the neural structures involved in a variety of cognitive processes, including memory. There is literally an "alphabet soup" of brain imaging techniques, including CT (computerized tomography), DTI (diffusion-tensor imaging), EEG (electroencephalogram), EROS (event-related optical signal), ERP (event-related potentials), fMRI (functional magnetic resonance imaging), MRI (magnetic resonance imaging), MEG (magnetic encephalography), MRS (magnetic resonance spectroscopy), NIRS (near infrared spectroscopy), PET (positron emission tomography), and SPECT (single photon emission computed tomography). In most cases, these techniques do not actually provide direct images of brain activity. Instead they are indexes of brain function associated with cognitive task performance. As the brain works, for example, it uses oxygen and glucose. The technique of fMRI takes advantage of this fact by measuring oxygen-level-dependent changes in the magnetic properties of blood during cognitive task performance: Areas of brain showing the greatest changes in magnetic properties are those most active during the task. The technique of PET involves injection of a radioactive tracer immediately before the participant begins a cognitive task. As the task is performed, more blood flows to the most active areas of brain, resulting in a higher concentration of the tracer in those brain regions. The resulting distribution is what is imaged in a PET scan. Analogous principles underlie DTI and NIRS. In contrast, EEG, ERP, and MEG, for example, reflect neural activity in that they yield recordings of electrical oscillations (EEG and ERP) and magnetic activity (MEG) associated with the firing of populations of neurons. The activity is recorded by electrodes or sensors on the surface of the scalp.

The different imaging techniques have different strengths and weaknesses. PET and fMRI offer excellent spatial resolution, for example. That is, as suggested by Fig. 5.4, Panel A, they can be used to pinpoint the specific areas of the brain activated in a task. Their temporal resolution is poor, however: They are a summation of brain activity over minutes and seconds (respectively), as opposed to the milliseconds that it actually takes the brain to process a stimulus.

In contrast to PET and fMRI, ERP (for example) offers excellent temporal resolution: As reflected in Panel B of Fig. 5.4, one can track the brain's response to a specific stimulus, thereby determining, in milliseconds, such things as how long it takes to identify a stimulus as novel versus familiar, for instance. In contrast to its excellent temporal resolution, however, traditional, "low-density" ERP recordings (involving a small number of electrodes distributed across the scalp) offer poor spatial resolution because of what is known as the *inverse problem*. Electrical activity is recorded at the surface of the scalp. It is not generated there, however. Rather, the electrical current is derived from neurons in cerebral cortex and hippocampus and then conducted through extracellular space and up to the scalp. Because the signal is conducted through the volume of the brain, electrical activity recorded on the surface of the scalp cannot with confidence be "traced back" to the neural tissue just below it. For this reason, low-density ERP is not the method of

**A.**

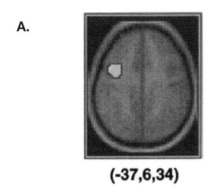

**(-37,6,34)**

**B.**

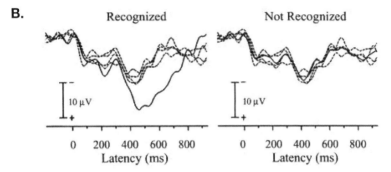

FIG. 5.4. Panel A: Specific (or focal) activation of the right anterior prefrontal region in the context of a memory retrieval task as detected by fMRI. Panel B: Event-related potential (ERP) waveforms at electrode site Pz in a pattern associated with recognition (on the left) and a pattern associated with lack of recognition (on the right). Panel A is reprinted from *Neuroimage, 7*, R. L. Buckner, W. Koutstaal, D. L. Schacter, A. M. Dale, M. Rotte, and B. R. Rosen, "Functional-Anatomic Study of Episodic Retrieval. II. Selective Averaging of Event-Related fMRI Trials to Test the Retrieval Success Hypothesis," 163–175, Fig. 5. Copyright © 1998, with permission from Elsevier; Panel B is from "The Role of Psychophysiology in Clinical Assessment: ERPs in the Evaluation of Memory," by J. J. B. Allen, 2002, *Psychophysiology, 39*, 261–280, Fig. 1. Copyright © 2002 by Cambridge University Press. Reprinted with the permission of Cambridge University Press.

choice for identifying the specific neural generators of a behavior. Greater spatial resolution can be achieved with what are known as "high-density" electrode arrays: "nets" of electrodes spaced closely together on the scalp (with interelectrode distances of no more than 2 to 3 centimeters). Finally, the techniques of MEG and NIRS offer high spatial and high temporal resolution, but they can be used to peer into only a few millimeters of cortical tissue: They cannot "go deep" into the brain. Thus, although neuroimaging techniques have much to offer, they too have their limitations.

## Reconciling Across Techniques

One of the impressions that one gets from reading both popular and scientific treatises on memory is that mnemonic processes are localized to specific parts of the brain. That is, images such as that in Fig. 5.4, Panel A, suggest that memory has a single source or rather small bits of neural tissue are involved in memory retrieval, for example. On the other hand, work with animal models has demonstrated that the degree of impairment on a task is proportional to the size of the lesion the animal sustained. This relation is nicely illustrated in Fig. 5.5 based on work by Stuart Zola and his colleagues. The figure is a representation of data from monkeys combined across a number of memory tasks. The different groups of animals experienced lesions of different portions of the medial temporal lobes. What is apparent is that memory is disrupted in proportion to the amount of tissue damaged, as well as the specific type of tissue damaged (Zola-Morgan, Squire, & Ramus, 1994; see also classic work by Lashley, 1950). Similarly, in adult humans, whereas some types of neural damage, such as to the medial temporal lobes, are associated with memory deficits, in only rare cases is task performance completely disrupted. More common is that the performance of a patient group is lower than performance of an intact control group. Figure 5.6 is a depiction of data from a task requiring selection of the photograph of a named famous person

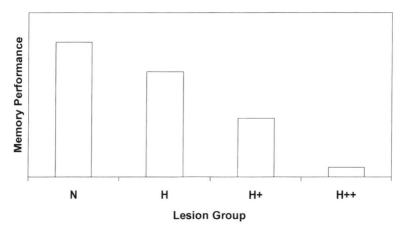

FIG. 5.5.   Schematic representation of average scores for monkeys with lesions of different extents across a number of different memory tasks: normal, healthy monkeys (N); monkeys with lesions confined to the hippocampal region (H); monkeys with lesions to the hippocampus as well as the adjacent entorhinal and parahippocampal cortices (H+); and monkeys with lesions to the hippocampus, entorhinal and parahippocampal cortices, with extension to the anterior entorhinal and perirhinal cortices (H++). Schematic representation based on Zola and Squire (2000), Fig. 30.2; relative levels of performance are approximate.

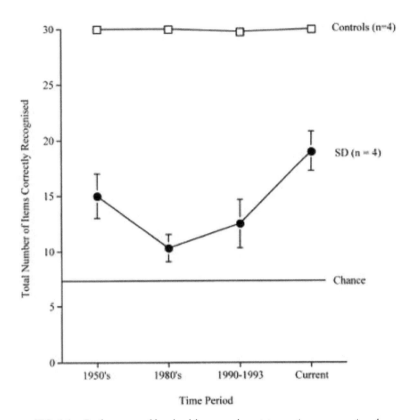

FIG. 5.6.   Performance of four healthy control participants (open squares) and four patients with semantic dementia (closed circles) on the recognition component of the *Famous Names Test*. Performance of the controls was at ceiling; performance of the patients was impaired relative to that of controls, yet still greater than would be expected by chance (i.e., 7.5 of 30 possible). Reprinted from *Neuropsychologia*, 36, J. R. Hodges and K. S. Graham, "A Reversal of the Temporal Gradient for Famous Person Knowledge in Semantic Dementia: Implications for the Neural Organisation of Long-Term Memory," 803–825, Fig. 2. Copyright © 1998, with permission from Elsevier.

(e.g., Sean Connery) from an array of four pictures. Whereas normal adults perform at ceiling (scoring 30 out of 30 possible), patients with temporal lobe amnesia perform less well, yet at a level that is reliably greater than chance (Hodges & Graham, 1998).

If, as suggested by PET and fMRI scans, performance on a task is supported by a specific bit of neural tissue, why should damage that extends beyond that spot of tissue be associated with additional decrements in performance? Moreover, why is it that damage to that tissue does not completely disrupt performance? In other words, why is it that the pictures we have of memory (literally—the fMRI scans) lead to one conclusion, yet behavioral data lead to another? There are several important features of the comparison across these sources of information that must be kept in mind. First, PET and fMRI scans that reveal activation in, for example, medial temporal structures are often of intact, healthy brains. In contrast, the behavioral data are from patients who have sustained damage to their brains or from animal models. A mature, intact brain may solve a problem differently than a damaged brain. This general caveat applies to any comparative approach—whether from intact to compromised systems, from nonhuman animals to human ones, or from mature brains to developing brains.

Second, it is also important to note that results from different neuroimaging techniques are not always concordant. For example, in studies investigating the role of medial temporal structures in encoding and retrieval (discussed in a subsequent section), Lepage, Habib, and Tulving's (1998) review of the literature using PET methodology suggested that anterior portions of the system (i.e., perirhinal cortex and the anterior portion of the hippocampus) are involved in encoding. Based on a review of the literature using fMRI methodology, Schacter and Wagner (1999) concluded just the opposite: Posterior portions of the medial temporal system (i.e., the parahippocampus and the posterior [back] portion of the hippocampal region) are involved in encoding! Such different conclusions were based, in part, on the use of different behavioral tasks in the two imaging environments (Schacter & Wagner, 1999). In two studies in which similar behavioral paradigms were used (i.e., encoding environmental scenes), PET and fMRI both revealed posterior activations during encoding (with PET: Maguire, Frackowiak, & Frith, 1996; Maguire, Frith, Burgess, Donnett, & O'Keefe, 1998; with fMRI: Aguirre, Detre, Alsop, & D'Esposito, 1996; Aguire & D'Esposito, 1997). Although the results of different techniques do not always concur, at the level of detail of this review, there is striking convergence both between and within each of the three major methods.

Third, for most of the three-dimensional imaging techniques (e.g., PET and fMRI), the brain regions involved in a task are identified through the *paired image* or *subtraction* method. That is, participants are scanned while they engage in a target task that involves the ability of interest (e.g., encoding or retrieval) and while they engage in a *reference task* that is thought to involve the same cognitive processes, save the one of interest. For example, in Kapur et al. (1996), participants studied words or visual patterns for later recall. In the reference task, they read words or merely looked at words. In Haxby et al. (1996), participants memorized faces, whereas in the reference task, they were asked to make perceptual matching judgments of the faces. Researchers then examine the pattern of activation in the target task and subtract from it the pattern of activation in the reference task. The difference is the activation that is thought associated with the specific cognitive process that differed across the tasks. Thus, many areas of the brain might be involved in the target task, but the small, specific part shown in the scan is that which is *unique* to that task or what is not shared by other, similar tasks. For this reason, it is more appropriate to conclude that different neural systems or networks involve different brain regions than to conclude that different brain regions perform different cognitive tasks.

Fourth, the roles or functions played by particular neural regions or structures may differ depending on the context in which they work. For this reason, "A full appreciation of the functional significance of activity within a brain region can only be gained by examining it in the context of interactions with other parts of the brain" (McIntosh, Nyberg, Bookstein, & Tulving, 1997, p. 327). The massive interaction of brain regions in the context of performance of a task is clearly illustrated in Fig. 5.7 in the form of functional network maps from research by Stefan Köhler and his colleagues (Köhler, McIntosh, Moscovitch, & Winocur, 1998). The figure reflects the

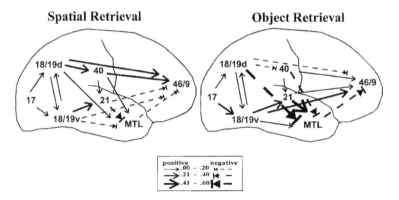

FIG. 5.7. Patterns of joint activations as measured by PET, across different brain regions as participants made recognition memory judgments. Excitatory co-activations are reflected in solid lines; inhibitory co-activations are reflected in dashed lines. The thicker the line, the stronger the co-activation. Different patterns of co-activation were observed in two different retrieval tasks. For example, in the spatial retrieval task interactions between the medial temporal region (MTL) and dorsally located posterior regions (areas 18/19d and 40) were positive in nature, whereas in the object retrieval task they were negative. Conversely, in the spatial retrieval task interactions between the medial temporal region (MTL) and the ventrally located posterior regions (areas 18/19v and 21) were negative in nature whereas in the object retrieval task they were positive. Reprinted from *Neuropsychologia, 36*, S. Köhler, M. Moscovitch, G. Winocur, S. Houle, and A. R. McIntosh, "Networks of Domain-Specific and General Regions Involved in Episodic Memory for Spatial Location and Object Identity," 129–142, Fig. 2. Copyright © 1998, with permission from Elsevier.

patterns of joint activations, as measured by PET, across different brain regions as participants made recognition memory judgments. In the "Spatial Retrieval" task, participants were required to identify which of two spatial configurations they had seen before; in the "Object Retrieval" task, they were required to identify which of two objects they had seen before. I present the functional network diagrams not for their details, but to make the point that multiple different regions of the brain work together to carry out the "event" of remembering. Moreover, the figure also helps make the point that the pattern of interaction among brain regions may be different for different tasks even when the tasks have a common feature, such as involving a recognition memory judgment. In addition, in an echo of the earlier caution regarding comparative approaches, patterns of interaction among brain regions may be different for different populations. For example, Eleanor Maguire (2001) found different patterns of connectivity among brain regions in an autobiographical memory task for healthy adults versus for a young man (Jon) who sustained hippocampal damage shortly after birth.

Finally, throughout this chapter, it is important to keep in mind that there are many phases to memory: Memories are *encoded*, *consolidated*, *stored*, and later *retrieved*. To talk about how the brain accomplishes an act of memory, we take the "event" and divide it into different phases. The result is that we highlight the role of a single structure during a single phase of what is a multiphase process accomplished by a network of structures. To maintain perspective on the process, we must remember that different neural structures may play especially crucial roles in some phases of memory, yet not be solely responsible for them.

## THE NEURAL BASES OF DECLARATIVE MEMORY, CIRCA 2005

Before launching into discussion of the neural bases of memory, I offer two caveats. First, I am painfully aware that because the field is moving so fast, between the time I write this chapter and the time this volume is published, what I have committed to the page already will be out of date. Second, even once the field gets all the details nailed down just right, there still will be an enormous gap in our knowledge of memory. The gap will stem from the fact that knowing exactly how experience is stored in the cells of the brain will *not* explain how Saint Augustine can, in his memory, "produce colours" or "discern the breath of lilies from violets, though smelling nothing." In other words, it will not tell us how the phenomenon of reexperience of an event in vivid, living color, as if it were happening in the moment, is accomplished. Description of the material causal reason for memory—the physical "stuff" that is necessary for a memory to be formed—is a description at one level only. That having been said, what do we know about the neural bases of memory at the time of the writing of this volume? Because the form of memory of greatest interest is declarative (as opposed to nondeclarative), I confine the discussion to declarative memory (see Schacter, Wagner, & Buckner, 2000, for a review of the neural bases of nondeclarative memory).

As already implied in the context of discussion of the patient H. M., declarative memory is thought to depend on particular neural structures. Whereas early theorizing about the neural bases of declarative memory emphasized medial temporal structures alone, current conceptualizations suggest that the formation, maintenance, and subsequent retrieval of declarative memories depend on a multicomponent network involving cortical structures (including posterior-parietal, anterior-prefrontal, and limbic-temporal association areas) as well as medial temporal structures (including the hippocampus, and entorhinal, perirhinal, and parahippocampal cortices; e.g., Eichenbaum & Cohen, 2001; Murray & Mishkin, 1998; Zola & Squire, 2000; see Figs. 5.2 and 5.3). The medial temporal structures may be considered "primary" in the sense that, without them, whether measured by recall or recognition, declarative memory is impaired (Moscovitch, 2000).

Briefly, it is thought that the formation of a declarative memory trace involves the multistep process illustrated schematically in Fig. 5.8. First, perceptual experience results in excitation across multiple brain regions distributed across the cortex. The different aspects of experience are brought together in various association cortices (e.g., prefrontal cortex, thus the name *association areas*), giving rise to conscious awareness of the experience. For information to remain in memory, it must be processed through the medial temporal structures which are thought to consolidate the distributed representation into a memory trace. Medial temporal structures are not the long-term storage sites for memories, however. Instead it is believed that memories are stored in the same cortical association areas that participated in initial registration of unified experience. One of the association cortices in particular—namely, prefrontal cortex—is implicated in retrieval of memories

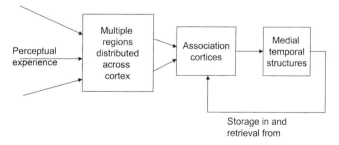

FIG. 5.8.   Schematic representation of the multistep process involved in declarative memory.

from long-term stores. In the sections to follow, I outline each of these steps in "how the brain builds a memory"—namely, encoding, consolidation, storage, and retrieval—in greater detail. Data from the three approaches introduced earlier—the study of humans with brain damage, animal models, and functional neuroimaging—are brought to bear to inform the question of the contribution to encoding, consolidation, storage, and retrieval made by each neural structure of the multicomponent network.

In this discussion of how the brain makes memories, it is important to be as precise as possible in terminology. Accordingly, I adopt Stuart Zola and Larry Squire's (2000) vocabulary. The term *hippocampus* (or *hippocampus proper*) refers to the cell fields of the hippocampus (CA3 and CA1) and the dentate gyrus (see Fig. 5.3). The term *hippocampal region* refers to the hippocampus plus the subiculum. The term *hippocampal formation* refers to the hippocampal region plus the entorhinal cortex. Finally, the term *medial temporal system* (or *medial temporal structures*) refers to the hippocampal formation plus the adjacent perirhinal and parahippocampal cortices.

## Encoding

Memory begins with encoding of experience into a memory trace. Encoding, in turn, begins with the initial registration of information in the brain. The whole of experience does not impinge on the brain at once in the same time and place, but is distributed across multiple cortical areas (Fig. 5.8). For example, fields in primary somatosensory cortex (see Fig. 5.9) register object- or event-related tactile information from the skin and proprioceptive inputs from the muscles and joints. Simultaneously, fields in primary visual cortex register the form, color, and motion of the object or event, and fields in primary auditory cortex respond to the various attributes of the sounds associated with the object or event. Inputs from these primary sensory cortices are projected to unimodal sensory association areas where they are integrated into whole percepts of what the object or event feels like, looks like, and sounds like, respectively. Unimodal sensory association areas, in turn, project to polymodal (also termed *multimodal*) posterior-parietal, anterior-prefrontal, and limbic-temporal association areas, where inputs from the different sense modalities are integrated.

Over the short term, information about a stimulus object or event is maintained in the cortical association areas. More than 30 years ago, Joaquin Fuster and Garret Alexander (1971) showed that, in monkeys, neurons in the dorsal prefrontal cortex (i.e., the back portion of prefrontal cortex) begin firing when a visual stimulus is presented. The neural activity is not involved only in the perception of the stimulus, however: If the stimulus is withdrawn, the neurons will continue to fire during a short delay interval (typically less than 30 sec). When the delay is over, the animal is able to make a correct

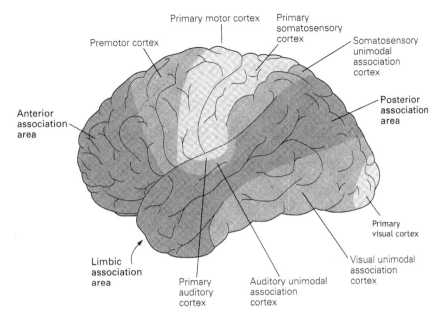

FIG. 5.9. Lateral view of the association areas of the human brain. From E. R. Kandel, J. H. Schwartz, and T. M. Jessell, *Principles of Neural Science, Fourth Edition*, Fig. 19-1, p. 350, 2000, McGraw-Hill. Reproduced with permission of The McGraw-Hill Companies.

look or reach to where the object or cue had been. Thus, the neurons "represent" the object in the brain even after the sensory stimulation is gone. In contrast, if during the delay period the neurons stop firing, the monkey in unable to locate the stimulus. Similar effects have been observed for neurons in posterior-parietal and inferior temporal association areas (reviewed in Eichenbaum & Cohen, 2001; Fuster, 1997).

The suggestion that association cortices are involved in encoding and short-term maintenance of information is further supported by lesion studies in nonhuman animals and humans, as well as results from neuroimaging studies. In both monkeys and humans, lesions in dorsolateral prefrontal cortex produce deficits in the short-term maintenance of information (monkeys: Goldman & Rosvold, 1970; Goldman, Rosvold, Vest, & Galkin, 1971; Petrides, 1995; humans: Butterworth, Cipolotti, & Warrington, 1996; Markowitsch et al., 1999; Shallice & Warrington, 1970). For example, they perform poorly on the delayed-response task, which requires that they remember over a brief delay in which of two locations a treat or object is hidden. Whereas on this task hippocampal lesions produce deficits after delays of 30 seconds or longer (Diamond, Zola-Morgan, & Squire, 1989), lesions of prefrontal cortex produce delays after only a few seconds (for review, see Diamond, 2001). Findings such as these are consistent with the suggestion that the association cortices play a role in short-term maintenance of information.

In both monkeys and humans, lesions in dorsolateral prefrontal cortex are associated with deficits in memory for temporal order in particular. In a study by Brenda Milner and Michael Petrides (1984), for example, patients with frontal lesions were shown a long series of pictures in rapid succession. On some trials, they were shown two of the pictures and asked to identify which had appeared more recently. The patients had difficulty on this temporal judgment task (see, e.g., Milner, McAndrews, & Leonard, 1990). Monkeys with dorsolateral prefrontal lesions exhibit similar deficits in working memory for temporal order (Petrides, 1995). Deficits in short-term maintenance of information have also been observed with lesions of the posterior-parietal association cortex. Patients with damage in the area where the left postero-inferior parietal lobe and the left temporal lobe meet (see Fig. 5.2) have deficits in short-term memory for sequences of phonemes: They may be able to remember only one or two spoken phonemes, compared with the normal span of approximately seven (e.g., McCarthy & Warrington, 1990; see also Eichenbaum & Cohen, 2001; Markowitsch, 2000, for additional examples and discussion).

Results from neuroimaging studies also implicate the association cortices in the initial registration of information. Indeed one of the most reliable findings from fMRI and PET work is that there is activation in left prefrontal cortex during memory encoding tasks (see Cabeza & Nyberg, 1997; Schacter et al., 2000, for reviews). Activation in these areas is observed when participants are asked to judge the meaning of words or learn unfamiliar faces or unfamiliar spatial locations, for example (e.g., Fletcher, Frith, & Rugg, 1997). Results such as these make clear that association cortices are involved in temporary registration of or transient storage of information.

## Consolidation

Given that the sites for long-term storage of event memories are the very association areas that are involved in initial registration of and encoding of experience, it seems that the story should end there: Information is received and maintained by the same neural structures. Although this sounds logical, there is strong evidence that, for information to "live on" in association areas over the long term, it must undergo additional processing subsequent to initial encoding. In other words, whereas distributed activity across the neocortex is the stuff of which immediate perceptual experience and temporary registration of experience is made, for an event to survive beyond the short term, it must be turned into a memory trace. The process is generally described as involving integration and stabilization of the various inputs from different cortical regions—tasks thought to be performed by medial temporal

structures. Whereas integration and stabilization processes begin on registration of a stimulus (and thus can appropriately be considered part of the encoding process), they do not end there. By some estimates, the process of stabilization of a memory trace, termed *consolidation*, continues for hours, days,
months, and even years.

As discussed by Howard Eichenbaum and Neal Cohen (2001), "*Memory
consolidation* is the name given to the hypothetical process(es) by which new
memories transition from an initially labile state to become permanently
fixed in long-term storage" (p. 344; italics original). Memories that are "fully"
consolidated are considered resistant to decay and associative interference,
although they are still vulnerable to retrieval failures (i.e., with time, they become increasingly difficult to retrieve). Eichenbaum and Cohen credit G.
Müller and A. Pilzecker (1900) with the original conceptualization of consolidation. They invoked it as an account of their observations of retroactive interference: Presentation of new material shortly after exposure to to-be-
remembered items resulted in decrements in memory for the earlier-learned
items. Observations such as these were interpreted to suggest that, until information is consolidated, it remains vulnerable to disruption.

*Evidence of Consolidation.*    There are two major types of evidence that
imply that memory traces undergo processing extending beyond initial encoding. Because I am not aware of any neuroimaging work that directly ad-
dresses consolidation processes, I present evidence of consolidation from humans with temporal lobe amnesia and animal models of amnesia. The first
source of evidence is the observation that humans suffering from temporal
lobe amnesia and animal models of amnesia are able to encode new experiences and maintain them over the very brief term (i.e., they have intact
short-term and working memory), but they are unable to remember them
over long delays (e.g., Squire, 1992; Squire & Zola-Morgan, 1991; Zola-
Morgan et al., 1986). Impaired storage is particularly pronounced for episodic (i.e., contextual) features of new events (e.g., Squire, 1986; Vargha-
Khadem et al., 1997). That is, patients with temporal lobe amnesia (such as
H. M.) have normal intelligence (as measured by IQ tests), normal short-
term memory (e.g., digit spans on par with normal control subjects), and normal nondeclarative memory (e.g., intact priming and procedural learning;
see subsequent section for discussion). However, they suffer from anterograde amnesia. Their impairments are readily apparent on both experimental
and standardized tests of memory, on which they perform well below healthy
control participants. They also show large discrepancies between their full-
scale measures of cognitive functioning and their memory test scores. As an
example, when tested in 1992, H. M.'s overall *Wechsler Adult Intelligence
Scale* (WAIS) score was 110 (a score of 100 is average). In contrast, he
scored only 73 on the subtest of the scale that tests memory in particular,

well below both his own overall intelligence score and that considered normal (i.e., a score of 100 is average; Corkin et al., 1997).

The pattern of impaired memory in the face of normal intelligence is not confined to patient H. M. In Table 5.1 are data from Jonathan Reed and Larry Squire (1998) on four patients with medial temporal lobe lesions. The patients all scored within the normal range on the Wechsler scale of intelligence. Nevertheless, they performed at levels below healthy control participants on a variety of declarative memory tasks, including diagram recall (reproducing a diagram after a 5- to 10-minute delay), recall and recognition of individual words presented on lists, and 24-hour delayed recognition of words and faces. In addition to demonstrating the pervasive deficits in formation of new memories apparent in patients with temporal lobe damage, the data also make clear that the deficits cannot be accounted for by problems with retrieval alone: Deficits are apparent on tests of recognition as well as recall, even though tests of recognition make lower retrieval demands relative to the demands of recall (i.e., in visual recognition, the material is perceptually available; the participant need only select the correct display). These observations imply that, for storage of new memories, something must intervene between encoding and long-term memory.

Research with animal models of temporal lobe amnesia has also yielded evidence of consolidation. Much of the work with nonhuman animals has been based on a task developed by Mortimer Mishkin (1978)—namely, trial-unique delayed nonmatching to sample (DNMS). In this task, the animal is shown a sample object (e.g., a cup; see Fig. 5.10); after a delay (ranging from a few seconds to several minutes), two objects are revealed—the sample object and a novel object (e.g., a chair). The animal's task is to select the nonmatch (i.e., the novel object). The objects are different on each trial. As reflected in Fig. 5.11, over brief delays of seconds to a minute, monkeys with

TABLE 5.1
*Wechsler Adult Intelligence Scale–Revised* (WAIS–R) Full-Scale IQ
and Anterograde Memory Test Performance for Four Patients With
Medial Temporal Lobe Amnesia and Eight Healthy Control Participants

| Patient | WAIS–R | Task | | | | |
|---|---|---|---|---|---|---|
| | | Diagram Recall | Word Recall (%) | Word Recognition (%) | Words (50) | Faces (50) |
| A. B. | 104 | 4 | 33 | 82.7 | 32 | 33 |
| L. J. | 98 | 3 | 40 | 84.7 | 33 | 29 |
| E. P. | 103 | 0 | 24 | 65.3 | 24 | 28 |
| G. T. | 92 | 0 | 20 | 70.0 | 27 | 27 |
| Controls | (100) | 20.6 | 71 | 97.0 | 41.1 | 38.1 |

*Note.* Controls ($N = 8$); WAIS–R scores are estimated based on population averages. Based on Reed and Squire (1998), Tables 1 and 2.

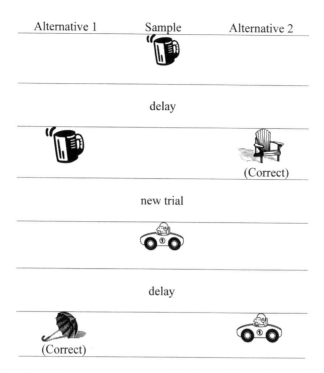

Alternative 1          Sample          Alternative 2

delay

(Correct)

new trial

delay

(Correct)

FIG. 5.10. Schematic representation of the phases of the trial-unique delayed nonmatching to sample (DNMS) task. A sample object is displayed, a delay is imposed, and then the sample object and a novel object are displayed. The correct response is to select the novel object. On the next trial, a different sample object is displayed, a delay is imposed, and then the second sample object and a completely novel object are displayed. The correct response is to select the novel object.

lesions to the hippocampal region perform normally on this task. However, when the delay stretches to 10 minutes, deficits become apparent (e.g., Alvarez, Zola-Morgan, & Squire, 1994). These patterns suggest that retention of information for more than a few minutes depends on processing mediated by hippocampal structures.

Also apparent from Fig. 5.11 is that the findings are similar whether lesions are ischemic (created by restriction of oxygen; Zola-Morgan, Squire, Rempel, Clower, & Amaral, 1992), produced by stereotaxic radiofrequency (current heats and destroys a specific area of tissue; Alvarez-Royo, Clower, & Zola-Morgan, 1991), or produced by neurotoxins such as ibotenic acid (which damages the target structures but spares adjacent white matter fibers; Murray & Mishkin, 1998; Zola, Squire, Teng, Stefanacci, & Clark, 2000). Whereas regardless of source, similar lesions produce parallel findings, as noted earlier and as illustrated in Fig. 5.5, the size of the lesion profoundly

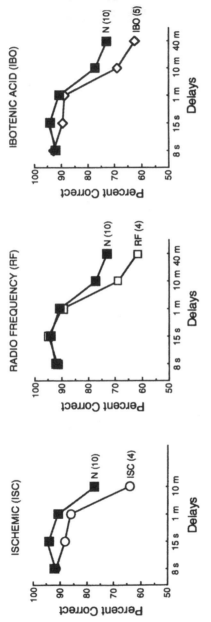

FIG. 5.11. Performance on the delayed nonmatching to sample (DNMS) task by normal, healthy monkeys (N [filled squares]) and monkeys with lesions limited to the hippocampal region (ISC [open circles], RF [open squares], and IBO [open triangles]). Regardless of the etiology of the lesion (whether due to ischemia [ISC], stereotaxic radiofrequency [RF], or ibotenic acid [IBO]), performance after brief delays is unimpaired. With increasing delay, impairments become obvious. From "The Medial Temporal Lobe and the Hippocampus," by S. M. Zola and L. R. Squire, 2000. From *The Oxford Handbook of Memory* (pp. 485–500, Fig. 30.3) by Endel Tulving and Fergus Craik, Copyright © 2000 by Endel Tulving and Fergus Craik. Used by permission of Oxford University Press, Inc., and the author.

affects the severity of the deficit. That is, the severity of impairment is related to the extent of damage to medial temporal structures (Zola-Morgan et al., 1994).

The second source of evidence of the hypothetical process of consolidation is the observation of *temporally graded retrograde amnesia*. That is, with damage to medial temporal lobe structures, memory for more recent events is impaired relative to memory for more remote events. In other words, the more recent information is, the more likely it will be lost to brain damage. Conversely, the older information is, the more likely it is to be preserved if the brain is damaged. Notice that this pattern is precisely the opposite of normal forgetting. Theodule Ribot (1881; English translation 1882) is credited with observation of this "law" of an inverse relation between the extent of memory loss and the recency of the event. As early as the turn of the last century, Burnham (1903; cited in Eichenbaum & Cohen, 2001) suggested that the cause of retrograde amnesia was interruption of the processing that normally occurs to integrate and stabilize a memory for long-term storage.

The phenomenon of temporally graded retrograde amnesia is well documented. Based on a review of the results of 247 studies, published in 61 articles, covering 694 patients with amnesia, with etiologies including Korsakoff's, Parkinson's, and Huntington's syndrome; closed head injury; encephalitis (inflammation of the brain); and lesions, infarctions (interruption of blood supply), and anoxia (interruption of oxygen supply), Alan Brown (2002) concluded that there was strong empirical support for the concept of temporally graded retrograde amnesia:

> ... amnesic patients show a consistent backward increase in memory performance for information acquired prior to the onset of their amnesic state. This evidence of graded RA [retrograde amnesia] is apparent in both absolute performance scores and in performance measured relative to controls. This trend is evident for more precisely defined (decades) as well as less precisely defined (life-stage) time periods. Furthermore, it is reliable across amnesias caused by Korsakoff's disease, neurodegenerative diseases, and acute head injury. (p. 417)

The pattern of temporally graded anterograde amnesia is illustrated in Fig. 5.12, from Brown's (2002) review. Included are data from patients whose amnesia was the result of Korsakoff's syndrome (introduced in chap. 1 with reference to Oliver Sacks', 1985, patient, Jimmie G.) and patients whose amnesia was acute due to lesion, infarction, or anoxia. Plotted in the figure are the percentages of items the patients remembered from different points in time, ranging from one to five decades from the onset of their amnesia. A nice feature of Brown's (2002) analysis is that he included two perspectives on the data. The patients' *absolute* performance reflects the percentage of items they remembered from each decade. Data on absolute performance can be difficult to interpret because it is impossible to equate the difficulty of items across decades.

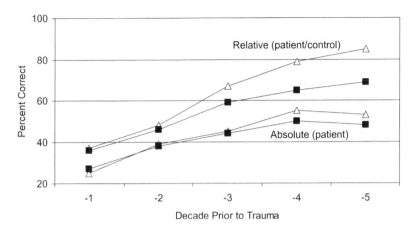

FIG. 5.12.   The percentage of items from each of five decades prior to trauma correctly remembered by patients with Korsakoff's syndrome (filled squares) and patients with acute hippocampal lesions (open triangles) expressed in absolute terms and relative terms (i.e., as a percentage of performance by healthy control participants). Based on Brown (2002), Fig. 4; values are approximate.

Consideration of patients' *relative* performance solves this problem: It reflects the percentage of correct items relative to the performance of healthy control participants. Any confounds due to item difficulty would be expected to influence patients and healthy participants in the same way. The finding that temporally graded retrograde amnesia is apparent by either analysis, across a range of patient groups, is strong support for the phenomenon.

In what should by now be a pattern familiar to the reader, there is evidence that the extent of temporally graded retrograde amnesia is influenced by the amount of tissue damage. For example, in the study mentioned earlier by Jonathan Reed and Larry Squire (1998; see Table 5.1), of the four patients, two (A. B. and L. J.) had lesions restricted to the hippocampal region, and the other two patients (E. P. and G. T.) had lesions that extended beyond the hippocampus to the temporal cortices. The patients were assessed on a battery of tasks, including tests of recall and recognition of vocabulary words that entered the lexicon at particular times (e.g., "astronaut" in the 1960s), public events (e.g., "Who killed John Lennon?"), and faces of famous people (e.g., Marilyn Monroe). The items were sampled from the decade of the time of test, as well as from the decades prior to the onset of anterograde amnesia. The retrograde amnesia of the patients with more extensive lesions (E. P. and G. T.) was more severe relative to that of the patients with more circumscribed lesions (A. B. and L. J.).

Reed and Squire (1998) also tested autobiographical memories from the recent and distant past. In the two patients with more focal damage (A. B. and L. J.), temporally graded amnesia for facts and nonautobiographical events extended back to the decade preceding the onset of anterograde amnesia. As suggested by inspection of Fig. 5.13, Panel A, there was no evidence of temporally graded retrograde amnesia for autobiographical memories. That is, the *Autobiographical Memory Interview* (AMI; introduced in chap. 2) scores for these two patients were roughly comparable to those of healthy control participants (see also Zola-Morgan et al., 1986). Reflected in Panel B of Fig. 5.13 are data from the two patients with more extensive temporal lobe damage. In one of the two patients (E. P.), evidence of temporally graded retrograde amnesia was apparent for autobiographical memories as

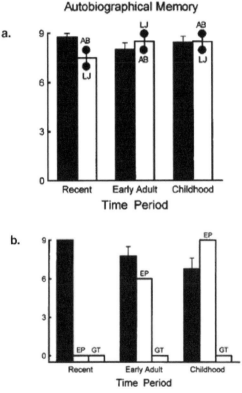

FIG. 5.13.    Panel A: Data from the *Autobiographical Memory Interview* (AMI) for patients A. B. and L. J. There is no evidence of temporally graded retrograde amnesia (i.e., there is no evidence of differential recall of recent and distant events). Panel B: Data from the AMI for patients E. P. and G. T. The data from patient E. P. suggest temporally graded retrograde amnesia: Recall of recent events is impaired relative to recall of more distant events. The amnesia of patient G. T. is dense and not temporally graded. From "Retrograde Amnesia for Facts and Events: Findings From Four New Cases," by J. M. Reed and L. R. Squire, 1998, *The Journal of Neuroscience, 18,* 3943–3954, Figs. 5 & 10. Copyright © 1998 by the Society for Neuroscience. Reprinted with permission.

well as facts. The amnesia of the other patient (G. T.) was dense and not temporally graded.

What is known about the extent of retrograde amnesia in patient H. M.? Initial observations of Henry M. suggested that his retrograde amnesia extended back 2 years prior to surgery, with more distant memories preserved (Scoville & Milner, 1957). More extensive subsequent study of H. M. by Suzanne Corkin and her colleagues (e.g., Corkin, 1984; Corkin, Cohen, & Sagar, 1983; Sagar, Cohen, Corkin, & Growdon, 1985) revealed that his amnesia extends to 11 years prior to his surgery in 1953. Although on experimental tests H. M.'s memory for events that occurred in the 1940s falls within the normal range, he does not remember the end of World War II or his graduation from high school in 1947 (yet he remembers the names of at least two girlfriends from his teenage years; Hilts, 1995). His memory for events from the 1950s is impaired relative to intact adults, and he is densely amnesic for events from the 1960s onward. H. M.'s pattern thus closely resembles that of Reed and Squire's (1998) patient, E. P. (Fig. 5.13, Panel B). In this regard, it is interesting to note that H. M.'s lesion spared portions of the hippocampus, and damage to the parahippocampal cortex is minimal (although the entorhinal cortex was lesioned; Corkin et al., 1997). Overall, the data from human patients suggest that the extent and time gradient of retrograde amnesia is dependent on both the amount and type of damage to the medial temporal lobe. In addition, findings that retrieval of old memories is impaired in time-dependent fashion are suggestive of a time-limited role for medial temporal structures in long-term memory. This issue is discussed in the next section on the process of consolidation.

Animal models of amnesia also provide strong evidence of temporally graded retrograde amnesia. In one study, for example, Jeansok Kim and Michael Fanselow (1992) conditioned rats to expect that, after hearing a tone, they would receive a shock to their feet. Animals indicate learning of the contingency between the tone and shock by freezing (i.e., inhibiting movement) at the sound of the tone. Between 1 and 28 days after the training, Kim and Fanselow produced in the animals hippocampal lesions and then tested them for retention of the conditioned response. As reflected in Fig. 5.14, healthy rats exhibited excellent retention of the conditioned response. When they were placed back into the training chamber, they froze. Their performance did not differ as a function of how long ago they had learned the tone–shock pairing. In contrast, rats in which hippocampal lesions had been produced showed temporally graded amnesia. When the surgery took place 1 day after training, the lesioned rats showed virtually no retention of the pairing: They did not freeze when put into the training chamber. When surgery took place 7 or 14 days after training, the lesioned rats showed some evidence of retention. When surgery took place 28 days after training, the performance of the rats with hippocampal lesions was indistinguishable from

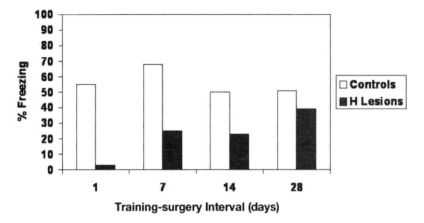

FIG. 5.14.    Percentage of time spent freezing in a contextual fear conditioning paradigm for healthy control rats (open bars) and rats with hippocampal lesions (filled bars) trained at different times prior to surgery. Based on Kim and Fanselow (1992); values are approximate.

control rats. Similar patterns across a variety of paradigms have been observed in rabbits, mice, and monkeys (see Eichenbaum & Cohen, 2001; Squire, 1992; Squire & Alvarez, 1995; for reviews).

Overall, the data on retrograde amnesia suggest that information stored in memory becomes increasingly resistant to forgetting over time. Data from humans suffering from amnesia and from animal models are consistent with Burnham's (1903) century-old suggestion that temporally graded retrograde amnesia is caused by a gradient of consolidation: Events from the distant past are better consolidated relative to events from the more recent past. Together the data on temporally graded retrograde amnesia and on anterograde amnesia provide strong support for the contention that memories undergo additional processing after encoding for some time after experience of an event. I now turn to a discussion of how memories might actually be "consolidated" for long-term storage and subsequent retrieval.

*The Process of Consolidation: A Systems Perspective.*    As implied by the association between impairments in the hypothetical process of consolidation and damage to medial temporal structures, it is thought that the medial temporal lobes, including the hippocampus, perirhinal, entorhinal, and parahippocampal cortices, do the work of binding into a single memory trace the distributed neocortical representation of an event (e.g., Kandel & Squire, 2000; Moscovitch, 1992; Zola-Morgan & Squire, 1990). The burden of the effort is shared with the cortical association areas that will be the ultimate repositories of long-term memories. As discussed by Alan Brown (2002) and Howard Eichenbaum and Neal Cohen (2001), there is general consensus that consolidation is accomplished in two stages. In the first stage, information is processed within the hippocampus and other medial temporal structures. The second stage involves an interplay between the medial temporal structures and cortical association areas through which representations are established within the association areas. I discuss each of these stages in turn.

The first stage of consolidation involves processing *within the medial temporal structures themselves*. Inputs from the unimodal and polymodal association areas (i.e., posterior-parietal, anterior-prefrontal, and limbic-temporal association areas; see Fig. 5.9) converge on perirhinal and parahippocampal structures in the medial temporal lobes. In Fig. 5.15 is a schematic representation

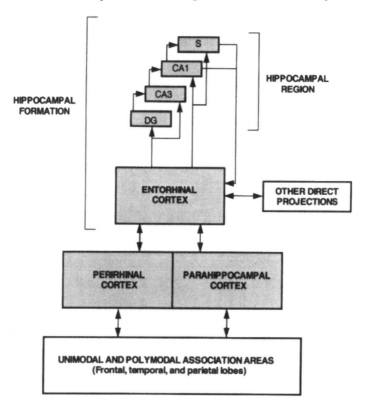

FIG. 5.15.   Schematic representation of the medial temporal lobe memory system. Although the connections are not pictured, the CA1 field of the hippocampus and the subiculum also receive direct projections from the perirhinal and parahippocampal cortices (Suzuki & Amaral, 1990). Only the entorhinal cortex projects to the dentate gyrus, however. From "Structure and Function of Declarative and Nondeclarative Memory Systems," by L. R. Squire and S. M. Zola, 1996, *Proceedings of the National Academy of Sciences, 93,* 13515–13522, Fig. 7. Copyright © 1996 National Academy of Sciences, U.S.A. Reprinted with permission.

of the inputs. Until the time of convergence, different inputs were processed by different association areas. It is in the perirhinal and parahippocampal cortices that they are brought together for the first time. Because the perirhinal and parahippocampal cortices receive projections from multiple cortical areas simultaneously, they are positioned to support encoding of relations or configurations of the stimuli that together represent an entire event. That processing is not, however, carried out by these structures themselves. Rather, they are thought to hold the isolated elements of experience in an "intermediate-term memory" on which the hippocampus proper operates. The information is held in the parahippocampal structures temporarily (over periods of at least several minutes), presumably as a result of prolonged firings of parahippocampal neurons (e.g., Suzuki, Miller, & Desimone, 1997; see Eichenbaum & Cohen, 2001, for discussion).

To be integrated and stabilized into a coherent memory trace, information must make its way into the hippocampus proper. It does so via the connecting link of the entorhinal cortex. Fully two thirds of the projections to the entorhinal cortex are from the perirhinal and parahippocampal cortices. The remaining one third are from the orbitofrontal, cingulate, and insular cortices; and the superior temporal gyrus (Eichenbaum & Cohen, 2001; Zola & Squire, 2000). Like the perirhinal and parahippocampal cortices, the entorhinal cortex operates as an intermediate-term memory store for information to be passed to the hippocampus. It projects stored information to the hippocampus proper, via the so-called *hippocampal trisynaptic circuit* (or "long route"; Andersen, Bliss, & Skrede, 1971) as well as directly (the "short route"). The long route entails projection of information from entorhinal cortex to the dentate gyrus of the hippocampus, from the dentate gyrus to the CA3 and CA1 fields of the hippocampus (a.k.a. Ammon's horn), from those fields to the subiculum, and from the subiculum back to the entorhinal cortex. The short route bypasses the dentate gyrus and the CA3 field and projects directly to CA1 and the subiculum. Although the precise functional significance of the two different routes is not known, there is speculation that long route processing may be involved in the storage of information and short route processing may be associated with memory retrieval (Gluck & Myers, 2001; some potential developmental implications of the different routes are discussed in chap. 6). Thus, the hippocampus "communicates" with the balance of the medial temporal structures via the entorhinal cortex. In turn the entorhinal cortex projects back to the perirhinal and parahippocampal cortices, which in turn project back to the very cortical areas that gave rise to the inputs (i.e., the association cortices).

The projections from the perirhinal and parahippocampal structures to the association cortices allow for the second stage of consolidation—namely, processing *between the medial temporal and cortical association areas*, the ultimate result of which is preservation of information in the cortical areas themselves. As described in the earlier section on *Encoding*, the association areas are involved in the initial registration of stimuli; they are also the eventual storage sites for long-term memories. The prevailing view is that, in the period between initial registration and eventual long-term storage, iterative processing in the medial temporal structures maintains the linkages between the distributed cortical representations that make up an entire event. As it does so, it strengthens the intracortical connections between the different elements of the event representation to the point that, eventually, they no longer require the activity of the medial temporal structures for their maintenance. It is at this point that memory traces are said to be independent of the medial temporal structures.

Evidence that the medial temporal structures are involved in the processes that lead to stabilization of memory traces comes not only from the studies of anterograde amnesia already reviewed, but from neuroimaging studies as well. For example, Martin Lepage, Reza Habib, and Endel Tulving (1998) analyzed 1,145 PET activations from 52 studies that imaged medial temporal lobe structures while participants were engaged in memory processing tasks. They noted activations in the hippocampal formation. Daniel Schacter and Anthony Wagner (1999) performed a similar analysis based on a sample of PET-based studies that largely, but not completely, overlapped with those sampled by Lepage and his colleagues, as well as a sample of studies using fMRI. They noted activations throughout the medial temporal system. Using event-related fMRI, Christopher Monk and his colleagues detected greater activation in the right hippocampus while human adults performed delayed matching-to-sample and delayed nonmatching-to-sample tasks relative to when they performed a perceptuomotor control task (Monk et al., 2002). Others have reported correlations between the amount of activation in the hippocampal formation and subsequent recall and recognition: The more activation at the time of experience of the event, the better the subsequent memory (e.g., Brewer, Zhao, Glover, & Gabrieli, 1998; Fernández et al., 1998; Wagner et al., 1998). In summary, both PET and fMRI studies indicate activity in the medial temporal structures during encoding and initial consolidation.

There is also evidence that the cortical areas participate in the consolidation process, as opposed to simply receiving fully processed memory representations. For example, Hans Markowitsch and his colleagues found a strong relation between the ability to remember newly acquired episodic and semantic memories and regional cerebral glucose metabolism in anterior and posterior association cortices. Specifically, lower metabolic levels as new information was being learned were associated with lower levels of memory (Markowitsch, Weber-Luxenburger, Ewald, Kessler, & Heiss, 1997). This implies that memories stored with less "energy" devoted to them subsequently were less well recalled.

Precisely how do activations in medial temporal and cortical structures work to "transform" temporary patterns of distributed activation into integrated long-term memory traces? Although there is not as yet a definitive answer to this question, the bulk of the data are consistent with the suggestion that the hippocampus works to encode specific conjunctions and relations among current stimuli (i.e., those that converge on and are held temporarily in the medial temporal cortices) and between current stimuli and those processed previously (i.e., between current stimuli and representations of stimuli and events already in long-term neocortical stores, contact with which is made through entorhinal cortex). Whether in the initial stage of processing the hippocampus provides an index, pointer, or address to the network of cortical connections that represent the memory (Teyler & Discenna, 1986), or whether it contains a complete, albeit "crude" or "gross" copy of the memory (Alvarez & Squire, 1994; McClelland et al., 1995), is a matter of disagreement. Regardless, the result of hippocampal processing is that the individual elements of experience represented in the medial temporal cortices become linked by association into a single event or episode; current episodes are associated with previous episodes on the basis of shared elements.

As Howard Eichenbaum and Neal Cohen (2001) described it, full relational processing likely ". . . comes about through multiple iterations of cortical input to the parahippocampal region and temporary storage there. This might be followed by hippocampus-mediated relational processing that adds to or restructures interconnections among the parahippocampal and the cortical representations" (pp. 342–343). With each iteration, both within- and between-episode connections are strengthened and elaborated. Eventually, as proposed by Donald Hebb as early as 1949, the simultaneous excitation or "synchronous convergence" (Fuster, 1997) causes connections to be forged: ". . . two cells or systems that are repeatedly active at the same time will tend to become associated, so that activity in one facilitates activity in the other" (Hebb, 1949, p. 60). Once the intracortical connections are "cemented," medial temporal activity is no longer necessary for the continued existence of the representation (Alvarez & Squire, 1994; McClelland et al., 1995).

The "and then a miracle occurs" flavor of the description just offered illustrates the chasm between explanation of the processes of the medial temporal and cortical structures at the level of the structures involved (the systems level) and explanation at the cellular and molecular levels. In the case of formation of connections between cells, the latter is necessary because it is at the level of plasticity in the cell that the connections are actually forged. Whereas a full description of the cascade of cellular and molecular changes that transpire at the birth of a memory is well beyond the scope of this volume, I offer an abstract of a description.

In brief, storage of explicit memories through medial temporal processing is thought to involve *long-term potentiation* (LTP). In the hippocampus, LTP is initiated when a high-frequency train of stimuli (known as a *tetanus*) is applied, with the result that the firing potential of either the presynaptic neuron (in the mossy fiber pathway that connects the dentate gyrus with the CA3 field) or both the pre- and postsynaptic neurons (in the Schaffer collateral pathway that connects the CA3 and CA1 fields) increases (see Fig. 5.16, Panel A). As illustrated in Fig. 5.16 (Panel B), the first phase of LTP (called *early LTP*) may last anywhere from 1 to 3 hours in a hippocampal slice. It is dependent on temporary changes in the activation of AMPA and NMDA receptors and the resulting flow of calcium ions. In effect it is a change in the *probability of transmitter release*. The second phase of LTP (called *late LTP*), which is initiated by multiple tetanuses, depends on new protein synthesis, which supports *structural changes that enhance functional connectivity*, including changes in the morphology and growth of new dendritic spines on postsynaptic neurons. As a result, late LTP can last for 24 hours or more (see Fig. 5.16, Panel B). Evidence that LTP is a means by which information is stabilized for long-term storage in the hippocampus comes from mice that have been genetically altered in such a way that late phase LTP is blocked (Kandel, Schwartz, & Jessell, 2000). Just like patient H. M., the animals have normal short-term memory, but they are unable to consolidate new learning into a stable long-term memory representation! Although there is still a long way to go to unite overt behavior to cellular and molecular events, clear progress is being made in identifying the actual mechanisms that instantiate Hebb's (1949) rule:

> When an axon of cell A ... excites a cell B and repeatedly or persistently takes part in firing it, some growth process or metabolic change takes place in one or both cells so that A's efficiency as one of the cells firing B is increased. (p. 62)

**Summary.**   In summary, intentional encoding of a stimulus involves anterior-prefrontal, posterior-parietal, and limbic-temporal association cortices. For maintenance of information beyond the bounds of a few seconds, medial temporal structures are involved as well. Whereas the medial temporal system participates in processing virtually from the beginning of encoding, its involvement in the integration and stabilization of memory traces for long-term storage extends well beyond the period of initial encoding. In the first of a two-phase process, memories are consolidated within the medial temporal structures. The second phase of consolidation involves a protracted period of interaction between medial temporal and cortical areas, during which the memory representation is established in neocortex. The process of consolidation may require days, weeks, and even years to complete. Indeed to the extent that new experiences make contact with memories of old ones,

A  Experimental setup

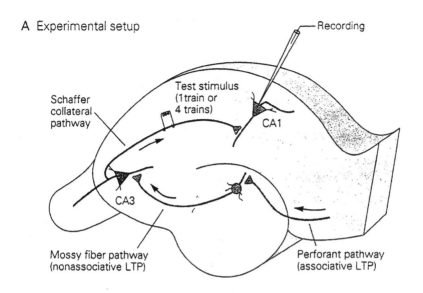

B  LTP in the hippocampus CA1 area

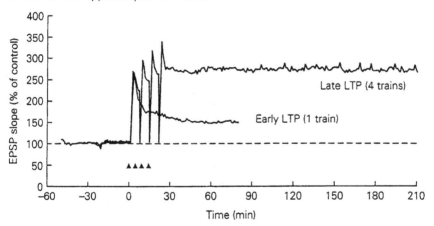

FIG. 5.16.    Panel A: Schematic representation of the procedure for inducing long-term potentiation (LTP) in the CA1 region of the hippocampus. Panel B: Early and late LTP of a cell in the CA1 region of the hippocampus. The graph is a plot of the rate of rise (a measure of synaptic efficacy) of the excitatory postsynaptic potentials in the cell as a function of time. A single stimulus (or tetanus) elicits early LTP, which lasts 2 to 3 hours. Late LTP is elicited by a train of four tetanuses, each separated by 10 minutes, and lasts 24 hours or more. From E. R. Kandel, J. H. Schwartz, and T. M. Jessell, *Principles of Neural Science, Fourth Edition*, Fig. 63-9, p. 1259, McGraw-Hill. Reproduced with permission of The McGraw-Hill Companies.

memory representations will continuously be activated and reactivated with the result that consolidation will continue virtually for a lifetime.

## Storage

As just reviewed, the second phase of consolidation involves establishing memory representations in cortical areas. This process is essential because the cortex, rather than the medial temporal lobes, is the long-term storage site for declarative memories. Whether once a memory representation is established in cortical areas the medial temporal structures continue to play a role in its storage is a matter of active debate. By some accounts, once the information has been distributed to cortical locations, the medial temporal lobe structures no longer have a role to play (e.g., Alvarez & Squire, 1994; Knowlton & Fanselow, 1998; McGaugh, 2000; Squire & Alvarez, 1995). By other accounts, medial temporal structures remain essential to maintenance and retrieval of the information no matter the age of the memory (e.g., Moscovitch & Nadel, 1998; Nadel & Moscovitch, 1997). The former view is more consistent with data from humans with amnesia and with animal models of amnesia, whereas the latter view may be seen as more consistent with the neuroimaging data on retrieval reviewed in the next section. Regardless of their position on whether the medial temporal structures continue to play a role in long-term memory, however, scholars agree that cortical areas are the main repositories of long-term memories.

The first suggestion that memories must be stored by structures other than those involved in their consolidation came from patients who had suffered lesions to the medial temporal system. Animal models of amnesia provided converging evidence for the suggestion. As just reviewed, individuals suffering from amnesia and animal models of the syndrome often exhibit temporally graded retrograde amnesia (see Fig. 5.12). Observations that organisms with medial temporal lobe damage have intact memories from the distant past, with impaired memory for more recent experiences, provide strong evidence that, after some period of time, medial temporal lobe structures are not where memories reside.

Neuroimaging studies provide another source of evidence of a time-limited role for medial temporal structures in memory storage. Karl Petersson, Christina Elfgren, and Martin Ingvar (1997) found that in humans, even within a short space of time, medial temporal lobe activation decreases as a function of repeated encoding and recall. Over the course of a 75-minute session, participants repeatedly copied abstract visuospatial designs and then later reproduced them from memory. As measured by PET relative to activation in the first two recall trials, activation during the last 2 (of 10) recall trials was lower. Conversely, patterns of effective connectivity across cortical areas (as measured by fMRI) have been shown to increase as a function of repeated performance of a task (Büchel, Coull, & Friston, 1999). Bontempi, Laurent-Demir, Destrade, and Jaffard (1999) showed that in mice, shortly after learning a spatial discrimination task, the hippocampal region was active as measured by regional metabolic activity. As the retention interval increased from 5 days to 25 days, hippocampal metabolic activity decreased.

There are also suggestions of reduced medial temporal involvement in memories from the remote relative to the more recent past. Frank Haist, Jane Bowden Gore, and Hui Mao (2001) tested 60- to 70-year-old participants for recognition of the faces of people who had been famous during different decades, ranging from the 1990s back to the 1940s. As measured by fMRI, there was more neural activity in the hippocampus in response to faces of people famous in the 1990s relative to faces of people famous in more remote decades. Evidence of a time-limited role for the hippocampus in long-term memory for autobiographical events has also been found. Martina Piefke and her colleagues (Piefke, Weiss, Zilles, Markowitsch, & Fink, 2003) asked adults to recall events from their childhoods (before the age of 10) and more recent events (within the last 5 years). They observed greater fMRI activations in the hippocampal region for the more recent relative to the more remote memories. Similar findings were reported by Kazuhisa Niki and Jing Luo (2002). They asked adults to recall places they had visited more than 7 years ago and places they had visited within 2 years. During fMRI scanning, the participants were asked to recall their experiences of visiting each of the locations. After the scan, they rated the level of detail recalled. Niki and Luo found greater left parahippocampal activation (with activation extending into the hippocampus proper) for recent relative to remote locations. The effect obtained when recent and remote locations recalled with many details were compared. However, when recent and remote locations recalled with few details were compared, the effect no longer obtained. These findings thus provide neuroimaging evidence of a time-limited role for the hippocampus in long-term memory.

In contrast to the results of Piefke and her colleagues (Piefke et al., 2003) and Niki and Luo (2002), a study by Eleanor Maguire and her colleagues (Maguire, Henson, Mummery, & Frith, 2001) suggested that the involvement of the hippocampus in autobiographical memory does not have a temporal gradient. In this study, participants were asked to judge the truthfulness of autobiographical events (e.g., "You did a tour of Concorde at Heathrow") and public events (e.g., "Windsor Castle was damaged by a fire"), sampled from different delays (ranging from a few weeks in the past to over 20 years in the past). During fMRI scanning, the participants were asked to judge the truthfulness of the statements (true:false ratio 3:1). Maguire and her colleagues found that activation in the ventrolateral prefrontal cortex, especially on the right, was uniquely related to the age of autobiographical memories, with more recent memories associated with more activation; no consistent change was apparent for public events. Hippo-campal activation was related to event type, but not to the age of the event: there was greater hippocampal activation for autobiographical than for public events; there was no evidence of sensitivity of the hippocampus to the age of the memory. The results thus suggest that the hippocampus is involved in autobiographical memory across the life span. Caution in interpretation of the results is warranted, however. In Niki and Luo (2002), only more de-tailed memories showed the time-related effect. As they pointed out, in Maguire et al. (2001), the truth value of an event could be established with-out recalling many details.

Regardless of whether medial temporal structures continue to play a role in memories, no matter their age (for additional discussion of this issue, see, e.g., Moscovitch & Nadel, 1998; Reed & Squire, 1998), there is agreement that cortical structures and, in particular, neocortical association areas are the pri-mary long-term storage sites. If declarative memories are eventually stored in neocortical association areas, then, as argued by Eric Kandel, James Schwartz, and Thomas Jessell (2000), ". . . damage to association cortex should destroy or impair recall of explicit knowledge acquired before the damage" (p. 1233). Indeed this is precisely what is observed. For example, individuals with lesions in limbic-temporal cortex show evidence of impaired receptive and expressive vocabulary, as well as impaired long-term memory for familiar objects and faces (e.g., Hodges & Patterson, 1995, 1996). In striking defiance of Ribot's law (1881; English translation 1882), such patients have been shown to have higher levels of recognition of names of famous people from the recent past relative to the remote past (Hodges & Graham, 1998). This pattern suggests that, as long as maintenance of the information is supported by intact medial temporal structures, the information is accessible. As the responsibility for storage is given over to cortical structures, however, accessibility is lost (see Mayes, 2000, for discussion). Similarly, individuals with lesions in anterior-prefrontal cortex show evidence of impaired long-term memory for specific past events and episodes. They have particular difficulty with episodic features such as the source of information acquired (Janowsky, Shimamura, & Squire, 1989) and the temporal order in which events unfolded (Shimamura, Janowsky, & Squire, 1990). Amnesia of this sort is of special interest for the topic of the present volume—autobiographical memory—because it makes it especially difficult to remember when and where a past event occurred, thereby robbing the individual of the sense of conscious recollection and reliv-ing of the past (Wheeler, 2000; see chap. 2).

The process of "passing the baton" from medial temporal to cortical struc-tures is illustrated in an elegant experiment by Kaori Takehara, Shigenori Kawahara, and Yutaka Kirino (2003). In one group of rats, they induced hippocampal lesions and observed the classic retrograde amnesia effect. That is, as illustrated in the left side of Fig. 5.17, rats lesioned 1 day after trace

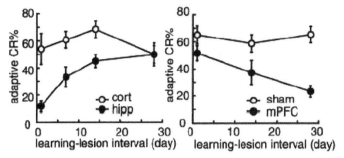

FIG. 5.17.    On the left side is reflected the percentage of adaptive conditioned responses in a trace eye-blink conditioning paradigm for rats with hippocampal lesions (filled circles) and rats with cortical control lesions (open circles). On the right side is reflected the performance of rats with lesions of the medial prefrontal cortex (filled circles) and rats with sham lesions (open circles) trained at different times prior to surgery. From "Time-Dependent Reorganization of the Brain Components Underlying Memory Retention in Trace Eyeblink Conditioning," by K. Takehara, S. Kawahara, and Y. Kirino, 2003, *The Journal of Neuroscience, 23*, 9897–9905, Fig. 5. Copyright © 2003 by the Society for Neuroscience. Reprinted with permission.

eye-blink conditioning (a form of conditioning that is dependent on the hippocampus) had impaired memory (relative to rats in a cortical lesion control group). With increasing delay between training and surgery, memory performance improved, such that when the lesion was induced 4 weeks after training, performance was unimpaired (the findings of Takehara et al.'s hippocampal lesion group are comparable to those of Kim & Fanselow, 1992, illustrated in Fig. 5.14). As illustrated in the right side of Fig. 5.17, over the same space of time that memories become independent of the hippocampus, they become dependent on association cortex: Whereas lesions to medial prefrontal cortex 1 day after trace eye-blink conditioning did not impair performance (relative to rats in a sham lesion control group), lesions induced 2 weeks and especially 4 weeks after training had pronounced effects. Conceptually similar results were obtained by Bontempi and his colleagues in their study of metabolic activity associated with spatial discrimination learning in mice (Bontempi et al., 1999). As noted earlier, over the course of 25 days after learning, the amount of activity in the hippocampal region decreased. Over the same period, there was an increase in metabolic activity in cortical areas, suggesting a time-dependent reorganization of the neural circuitry responsible for memory storage.

The transfer of responsibility (whether total or primary) for maintenance of memories over the long term from medial temporal structures to neocortex is a slow one. As just described, the period of consolidation may take days, weeks, months, and even years to accomplish. There is increasing speculation that the process works as it does to avoid "catastrophic interference"

(McCloskey & Cohen, 1989) with existing knowledge (Eichenbaum & Cohen, 2001; Gluck & Myers, 2001; Kandel et al., 2000; McClelland et al., 1995). When it comes to memory, the brain must do two things simultaneously: It must rapidly learn new material (which requires plasticity), but it must also maintain a storehouse of old material (which requires stability). Computer simulations have demonstrated that, within a single system, rapid learning leads to interference with existing knowledge (e.g., McCloskey & Cohen, 1989; Ratcliff, 1990). Thus, a system that can change rapidly to accept new inputs has difficulty maintaining old inputs. Conversely, a system that is good at maintaining old inputs has difficulty learning new things.

A compromise system is one that is actually made up of two subsystems: a fast-learning, limited-capacity subsystem, in which connections change rapidly; and a slow-learning, large-capacity subsystem, in which connections change gradually, but stability is maintained. Metaphorically, the hippocampus is the former and the neocortex is the latter (McClelland et al., 1995). In other words, medial temporal structures make possible the rapid learning of new information, but they are not designed for long-term storage. Cortical structures are designed for long-term storage, but are vulnerable to catastrophic interference. Catastrophic interference can be overcome by relatively slow addition of information. In the case of the human brain, the long process of consolidation permits new data to be stored in the neocortex without disrupting the neural circuits that represent already-stored information (Kandel et al., 2000). As stated by Niki and Luo (2002):

> The MTL [medial temporal lobe] can acquire information quickly, but consolidation is slow so that the neocortex can change in a more gradual way, incorporating into the representation not only the elements of one experience, but also the regularities of the environment that encompass many experiences. (p. 500)

Eventually long-term memories come to reside in the neocortex, from which they subsequently can be retrieved.

## Retrieval

The *raison d'être* for encoding, consolidation, and storage of declarative memories is so that they can be retrieved at some later point in time. But just what is "retrieval"? Joaquin Fuster (1997) suggested that retrieval is, in essence, a reactivation of the neural network that represents the event. Reactivation occurs because, "An internal or external stimulus, whose cortical representation is part of the network by prior association, will reactivate that representation and, again by association, the rest of the network" (Fuster, 1997, p. 455). What structures are involved in retrieval of information from long-term stores? As noted by Lepage et al. (1998), most cellular and molecular models of memory assume that encoding and retrieval processes are subserved by the same neural structures and even the same neurons. In other words, retrieval entails activation of the same circuits as were involved in encoding. We have seen that temporary registration of information during initial encoding involves the association cortices and that organization and integration of information for long-term storage involves medial temporal structures. Consistent with this perspective, there is general consensus that the polymodal association areas in general, and anterior-prefrontal association area in particular, are involved in retrieval of declarative memories. There is less agreement on the role of the medial temporal system in memory retrieval. I discuss the data for each component of the system in turn.

*Prefrontal and Other Association Cortices.*    Behavioral and neuroimaging data implicate prefrontal cortex in retrieval of memories from long-term stores. Specifically, damage to the prefrontal cortex disrupts long-term memory retrieval of both post- and premorbidly experienced facts and episodes. Deficits are especially apparent in free recall (as opposed to recognition), and for information about the temporal order of events and experiences and the specific source of experience (i.e., when and where a remembered item was encountered; e.g., Janowsky et al., 1989; Jetter, Poser, Freeman, & Markowitsch, 1986; Schacter, 1987; Squire, 1982, 1986). For example, patients with damage to prefrontal and temporal-polar regions often have profound retrograde amnesia for well-established semantic information, such as the definitions of words and facts that might be learned in school (e.g., Patterson & Hodges, 1995). The amnesia is apparent despite intact intelligence and, in some cases, the ability to learn new information (e.g., Kroll, Markowitsch, Knight, & von Cramon, 1997). Retrieval of temporal order information is also impaired. In research by Arthur Shimamura, Jeri Janowsky, and Larry Squire (1990), for instance, patients with prefrontal lesions were presented with a list of 15 words and then asked to reconstruct the order in which they occurred. As reflected in Fig. 5.18, the patients were able to recall and recognize the words, but were markedly impaired in memory for the sequential order of presentation of the items (see also, for e.g., Milner et al., 1990). Difficulties remembering the time and place of events may underlie suggestions that prefrontal cortex is especially involved in retrieval of autobiographical or personal memories (e.g., Barnett, Newman, Richardson, Thompson, & Upton, 2000; Markowitsch, 1995, 1996).

Prefrontal involvement in retrieval of episodic memories from long-term stores is also implied by neuroimaging studies (see Maguire, 2001; Nyberg, 1998, for reviews). For example, in PET results with normal adults, Endel Tulving and his colleagues (Tulving, Kapur, Craik, Moscovitch, & Houle, 1994) observed left-hemisphere prefrontal activation for episodic memory

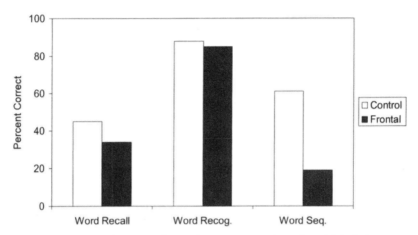

FIG. 5.18. Performance of control participants without frontal lobe lesions (open bars) and of frontal lobe patients (filled bars) in recalling words and recognizing words, and in reconstructing the sequential order of presentation of words. Based on Shimamura (1995); values are approximate.

encoding (discussed earlier) and right-hemispheric prefrontal activation for retrieval (see also Nyberg, Cabeza, & Tulving, 1996). Indeed increased activation in the right prefrontal cortex during memory retrieval has now been observed in several PET and fMRI studies (e.g., Buckner, Raichle, Miezin, & Petersen, 1996; Cabeza, McIntosh, Tulving, Nyberg, & Grady, 1997; Fletcher, Frith, & Rugg, 1997; Kapur et al., 1995; Nyberg et al., 1996). Recognition of deeply studied items is associated with increased activation (as measured by PET) in the prefrontal cortex (Rugg, Fletcher, Frith, Frackowiak, & Dolan, 1997). The findings generalize across many kinds of episodic retrieval tasks, including auditory and visual stimuli, and across recall and recognition. Further, consistent with results from patients with damage to prefrontal regions, there are suggestions of higher levels of activation (e.g., as measured by fMRI) of prefrontal structures in retrieval of events with more episodic detail, such as is present in autobiographical memories from the more recent past, compared with events with less episodic detail, such as is present in autobiographical memories from the more distant past (Maguire et al., 2001). Findings such as these suggest that memories with more episodic detail (e.g., temporal information) recruited more prefrontal resources.

   Although it is clear that the right prefrontal cortex is involved in episodic memory retrieval (indeed McIntosh et al., 1997, described it as the most reliable activation in imaging studies), there is some debate as to whether activations in prefrontal cortex are related to the *attempt* to remember or to *success* at retrieval (see Nyberg & Cabeza, 2000; Schacter et al., 2000, for discussion). That is, the results of some studies suggest that activation in the right prefrontal cortex (as measured by fMRI) is greater when recognition success is high relative to when it is low (e.g., Buckner, Koutstaal, Schacter, Wagner, & Rosen, 1998; see Rugg et al., 1996, 1997, for similar results using PET). Other studies suggest that the amount of prefrontal activation is unrelated to the success of memory retrieval: As long as participants are *attempting* retrieval, activation is observed (e.g., Nyberg et al., 1995; see also Kapur et al., 1995). Nyberg and Cabeza (2000) resolved this discrepancy by suggesting that some areas within the right prefrontal cortex are activated regardless of level of success in retrieval, whereas others may be activated in proportion to retrieval success.

Finally, whereas much of the "action" associated with retrieval seems to take place in the right prefrontal cortex, the posterior-parietal and limbic-temporal association areas are involved as well (reviewed in Nyberg & Cabeza, 2000; Schacter & Wagner, 1999). Indeed as discussed by Köhler, McIntosh, et al. (1998), distinct posterior cortical regions are activated as a function of the type of entity being retrieved. For example, PET studies have revealed activation in dorsal striate cortex when the retrieval target is a spatial location and in ventral extrastriate cortex when the retrieval target is a visually encoded object (Köhler, Moscovitch, Winocur, Houle, & McIntosh, 1998; see also Nyberg et al., 1995). Moreover, as discussed earlier in the chapter, cortical regions interact during memory retrieval (see Fig. 5.7 for an illustration). For instance, decreases in activation in lateral temporal regions have been observed in conjunction with increases in activation in the right prefrontal cortex, perhaps reflecting inhibition of task-irrelevant processing that might otherwise interfere with retrieval success (Nyberg & Cabeza, 2000).

*Medial Temporal Structures.*    Although there is consensus that prefrontal structures (as well as other association areas) play a role in memory retrieval, there is less consensus concerning the involvement of medial temporal structures. One perspective, derived from studies of patients with temporal lobe amnesia, is that the involvement of medial temporal structures in retrieval is not inevitable. The fact that patients with damage to medial temporal structures successfully retrieve old events (see Fig. 5.12) implies that the structures are not involved in retrieval of fully (or highly) consolidated memories. Consistent with this suggestion, studies of episodic retrieval often fail to document significant MRI activity in the medial temporal region (see Schacter et al., 2000, for a review).

On the other hand, there is a literature that suggests that medial temporal structures play a role in memory retrieval. I already referred to a review conducted by Martin Lepage, Reza Habib, and Endel Tulving (1998), in which they examined over 1,000 PET activations from 52 studies. They found that 94% of the activations that occurred in the posterior region of the medial temporal lobe (the hippocampus proper plus the posterior portion of the parahippocampal cortex) were associated with retrieval, as opposed to encoding conditions. Their analysis thus provides strong support for the suggestion that activation in the parahippocampal cortex is associated with retrieval. In this regard, it is interesting to note that patient H. M.'s lesion largely spared the posterior regions of the hippocampus and the parahippocampal cortex (Corkin et al., 1997). Lepage and his colleagues speculated that this may account for H. M.'s success in retrieving memories from his distant past.

How are we to reconcile the apparently conflicting findings regarding the participation of medial temporal structures in episodic memory retrieval? Clearly, the data from patients indicate that memories (at least remote ones) *can* be retrieved without an intact medial temporal lobe (even when posterior regions of the hippocampus are lesioned; e.g., Reed & Squire, 1998). This implies that participation of the medial temporal structures is not necessary for all retrievals—only for more recent ones. This observation may in fact bring resolution to some of the conflicting findings: The time scales are different. In most of the studies included in the analysis conducted by Lepage et al. (1998), for example, retrieval was minutes (not days, months, or years) after encoding. In these studies, it is entirely possible that the findings of medial temporal involvement in retrieval were due to the short intervals over which memories were tested: Given that little time had passed since encoding, consolidation processes were likely still underway.

Although the time scale might account for some of the variance, it does not explain the involvement of medial temporal structures in studies such as that conducted by Eleanor Maguire and her colleagues, in which participants were asked to retrieve memories from the distant past (Maguire et al., 2001). To reconcile these findings with those from the literature on human amnesia and animal models thereof, it may be necessary to recognize once again that the way a damaged brain accomplishes a task may be quite different from the way an intact brain performs the same task. In the absence of a medial temporal lobe, memories that are well consolidated (i.e., those from the distant past) can be retrieved. However, when the structures are intact, how well consolidated the memory is may not be a critical factor in determining whether medial temporal structures are involved. There are at least two reasons to make this suggestion. First, one role that the hippocampus plays is to relate new information with material already established in long-term memory (e.g., Eichenbaum & Cohen, 2001; Martin, Wiggs, Ungerleider, & Haxby, 1996). Because no two experiences are exactly alike, every task involves the processing of new information. This means that the hippocampus is involved in virtually all processing! (See Dolan & Fletcher, 1997; Fletcher, Frith, & Rugg, 1997; for similar arguments.)

The second reason to expect that, in the intact organism, medial temporal structures will be involved at the time of retrieval of a memory of an old event is that every act of retrieval is simultaneously an act of re-encoding of the information just retrieved (e.g., Buckner, Wheeler, & Sheridan, 2001; Markowitsch, 2000). Because the medial temporal structures are involved in encoding and consolidation, they will also be involved in memory retrieval because the latter entails the former. Thus, by implication, in the intact brain, medial temporal structures are going to be activated during the cognitive act of memory retrieval. Critically, the role that they play may not be in retrieval per se, but in *re-encoding* that accompanies retrieval in the healthy brain. Indeed there is considerable evidence that, on reactivation, memories—even those considered to have long since "consolidated"—return to a labile state and must actually undergo a period of reconsolidation to be restored (e.g., Debiec, LeDoux, & Nader, 2002; Nader, 2003).

## Consolidation Revisited

In addition to helping resolve the disparity in findings for patients suffering from amnesia and neuroimaging studies of the role of the medial temporal lobes in retrieval, the observation that every act of retrieval is an act of re-encoding (and reconsolidation) sets us on a productive path toward resolving the question of whether consolidation of memories is ever "complete" (Eichenbaum & Cohen, 2001). The research with patients with amnesia clearly indicates that there is a point in time at which further consolidation is not *necessary* to preserve a memory trace. However, in the healthy human, consolidation may continue for a lifetime because there are always new experiences to be integrated with old ones. That is, to the extent that there is overlap in representations, old memories will be reactivated by new ones as they are established. New and old experiences may overlap as a result of any number of elements in common across events, including the actors involved, the emotional states or reactions associated with the events, similarity in the locations of the events, and so forth. As a result of reactivations, old memories will be continually reshaped by new episodes and experiences. In a compromised system, however (a system with damaged or diseased medial temporal structures), new experiences are never integrated with old ones, resulting in a life story that is not "updated" to include new information. It is because he cannot update his memory that Henry M. does not know how old he is, that his hair has grayed, or how many years have passed since his surgery (see chap. 1).

### HOW SPECIFIC ARE THE NEURAL BASES
### OF DECLARATIVE MEMORY?

In chapter 1 of this volume, I argued that there is more than one type of memory, some of the major divisions of which are schematically represented in Fig. 1.2. The neural bases just reviewed were said to be that supporting one major memory system—namely, declarative memory. This claim raises two questions simultaneously, both concerning the specificity of the type of memory supported by the temporal-cortical network just described. First, does the network differentially support the different subtypes of declarative memory—namely, semantic and episodic memory? Second, does this network also support the other major type of memory—that characterized as nondeclarative? I approach each of these questions in turn. Although as just described declarative memory involves association cortices, medial temporal structures, and the connections between them, because the medial temporal structures are "primary" (Moscovitch, 2000), I focus on them in particular.

## Different Subtypes of Declarative Memory

The first question regarding the specificity of the neural bases of declarative memory is whether the temporal-cortical network differentially supports the different subtypes of declarative memory—semantic and episodic. Moreover, we might ask whether the neural structures that support episodic memory function differentially in support of recall of "run of the mill" episodic memories and more personal autobiographical ones. I address each of these questions in turn.

***Episodic and Semantic Memory.*** There are different perspectives on whether semantic and episodic memory are supported by common neural bases. To be clear, the debate is not about whether both subtypes of memory are declarative—among scholars who distinguish among memory systems, there is agreement that both semantic and episodic memory are declarative. Rather, the debate concerns whether semantic memory can function independently of episodic memory, or whether they depend on the same neural structures and thus suffer a common fate. The suggestion that semantic memory is independent of episodic memory stems from observations of so-called *double dissociations*.

As reviewed by John Hodges (2000), on the one side of the dissociation, patients with semantic dementia, associated with focal atrophy of the *lateral* temporal lobe (see Fig. 5.2), have been reported to have severely impaired semantic memory, but well-preserved episodic memory. In contrast, some patients with lesions to the hippocampus (a *medial* temporal structure; see Fig. 5.2) have severely impaired episodic memory, but seem to be able to learn new semantic facts. The most striking examples of the latter asymmetry are groups of patients described by Faraneh Vargha-Khadem and her colleagues (Gadian et al., 2000; Vargha-Khadem et al., 1997). In the 1997 publication, Vargha-Khadem and her colleagues reported data on the memory performance of three children who suffered hippocampal damage early in development (ranging from birth to age 9). In the 2000 publication, the researchers reported data on two of the original three children, as well as three additional children, all of whom experienced hippocampal lesions at or shortly after birth. Based on magnetic imaging data, the temporal cortices surrounding the hippocampus were observed to be intact in all of the children. Behaviorally, all of the children experienced severe disruption of episodic memory, as evidenced by inability to perform daily activities in a normal manner (e.g., they had way-finding difficulties, they were not well oriented as to date and time, and they could not provide reliable accounts of the events of the day), as well as performance on neuropsychological tests, the results of some of which are summarized in Table 5.2. In contrast, the children seemed to have normal semantic memory, as evidenced by intelligence tests scores within the normal range, and normative performance on spelling, basic reading, and reading comprehension tests (see Table 5.2). The results have been widely interpreted to suggest that the children had preserved semantic memory despite pronounced deficits in episodic memory.

The pattern of impairment and sparing in the patients studied by Vargha-Khadem and her colleagues (Gadian et al., 2000; Vargha-Khadem et al., 1997) led to the suggestion that episodic memory is dependent on the hippocampus (which in each child was severely compromised), whereas semantic memory can be supported not by the hippocampus proper, but by medial temporal cortices (which in each child remained intact). This interpretation was endorsed by Endel Tulving and Hans Markowitsch (1998), who suggested that episodic memory be considered a "unique extension" of semantic memory: Only episodic memories include the rich contextual elements that give rise to autonoetic (or self-knowing) awareness that what is being recalled is an experience from a previous point in time. In support of this argument, Mortimer Mishkin, Faraneh Vargha-Khadem, and David Gadian (1998) noted the position of the hippocampus at the highest level in the information-processing hierarchy (i.e., see Fig. 5.15; multimodal inputs converge as they reach the hippocampus). The fact that it is only in the hippocampus that all of the elements of experience come together is consistent with the suggestion that hippocampal processing results in the rich, detailed representations that are characteristic of episodic memory. In this conceptualization, semantic memories, which lack details of specific place and time, can if necessary (as a result of lesion or disease) be formed without the embellishments of the last station on the route.

In contrast to the perspective of independence of semantic memory from episodic memory, scholars such as Larry Squire and Stuart Zola (1998) maintained that both types of memory depend on the integrity of the medial temporal structures, including the hippocampus. They explicitly acknowledged the role of the medial temporal cortices as well as the hippocampus proper in supporting declarative memory, as evidenced by the fact that damage to any one component of the system results in deficits in performance and damage

## TABLE 5.2
Scores on "Episodic" and "Semantic" Memory Tasks for Five Patients Who Sustained Damage to Medial-Temporal Structures Early in Development and 35 Healthy Controls

| | Task | | | | | | | |
|---|---|---|---|---|---|---|---|---|
| | "Episodic" Memory Tasks | | | | | "Semantic" Memory Tasks | | |
| Case | Story Imm | Story Delayed | Geometric Imm | Geometric Delayed | Verbal IQ | Spelling | Basic Reading | Reading Comp. |
| Case 1 | 25.0 | 2.2 | 53.6 | 14.3 | 82 | 77 | 85 | 84 |
| Case 2 | 38.9 | 2.8 | 32.1 | 14.3 | 84 | 96 | 97 | 87 |
| Case 3 | 20.8 | 0 | 57.1 | 0 | 87 | 88 | 99 | 74 |
| Case 4 | 27.2 | 3.5 | 64.2 | 3.6 | 109 | 84 | 102 | 97 |
| Case 5 | 11.3 | 3.4 | 35.7 | 10.7 | 89 | 118 | 105 | 87 |
| Average | 24.6 | 2.4 | 48.5 | 10.7 | 90.2 | 92.6 | 97.6 | 85.8 |
| Controls | 41.4 | 32.3 | 82.2 | 77.8 | 101.1 | (100) | (100) | (100) |

*Note.* The "Story" and "Geometric" tasks were from the *Wechsler Memory Scale.* They require immediate recall and reproduction of stories and geometric designs, respectively, and recall and reproduction of stories and designs after delays of 90 minutes and 40 minutes, respectively. Verbal IQ was estimated from performance on the *Wechsler Intelligence Scale for Children–Third Edition.* Spelling, basic reading, and reading comprehension were tested with the *Wechsler Objective Reading Dimensions* test. Patients' scores on the spelling, basic reading, and reading comprehension tasks were compared to normative data. Based on Gadian et al. (2000), Tables 1 and 2.

to a combination of components produces larger deficits (e.g., Leonard et al., 1995). All of the medial temporal structures, including the hippocampus, are thought to contribute to semantic as well as episodic memory. In this perspective, the major source of difference between episodic and semantic memory stems not from involvement of the hippocampus in one but not the other (respectively), but from differential involvement of the frontal lobes in episodic memory: The frontal lobes are the source of the association of the content of an event with specific features that locate it in place and time. By this account, medial temporal lobe damage or disease is expected to result in deficits in both semantic and episodic memory; larger deficits in episodic relative to semantic memory would be associated with damage to the frontal lobes as well.

At present it is not clear that this controversy can be adequately addressed: There simply is not enough information about the functional role in declarative memory of each of the individual structures in the medial temporal system. Greater resolution can, however, be brought by closer evaluation of the argument for a "double dissociation" between semantic and episodic memory. On the one hand, although individuals with semantic dementia seem to have preserved episodic memory, John Hodges (2000) noted that it is selective: They have preserved autobiographical memory for events from the recent past, but impaired memory for events from the remote past (Graham & Hodges, 1997). Importantly, they show the same pattern in the semantic domain: Recently acquired semantic memories (i.e., the identities of people famous in the decade of the test) are preserved relative to more remotely acquired semantic memories (i.e., the identities of people famous in decades before the test; Hodges & Graham, 1998). A parsimonious explanation for this pattern is that, in the case of lateral temporal damage, intact medial temporal structures are able to mediate formation of new memories, both semantic and episodic. As the responsibility for storage is gradually given over to damaged cortical areas, memories are lost. The observation that patients with semantic dementia shown similar profiles for semantic and episodic content is consistent with the suggestion that the two types of declarative memory are representative of a single system that imparts to them a common fate.

There is also cause to reexamine (and perhaps reinterpret) the evidence from the cases of apparently preserved semantic memory in the face of impairments in episodic memory reported by Vargha-Khadem and her colleagues (Gadian et al., 2000; Vargha-Khadem et al., 1997). Evidence that the children (all of whom had hippocampal lesions that spared the temporal cortices surrounding the hippocampus) had impaired episodic memory is from neuropsychological tests (e.g., *Wechsler Memory Scale*; see Table 5.2) and, in the 1997 report, from the children's scores on 12 computerized, two-choice recognition tasks. The children's scores on the neuropsychological tests indicated severe impairments; the children performed less well than normal control children on 2 of the 12 experimental tasks. In contrast to the episodic memory tasks, all of which required that learning occur within a single trial, the sources of evidence of preserved semantic memory are the children's scores on general intelligence, as well as specific spelling, basic reading, and reading comprehension tests. On the spelling and basic reading tests, the children tended to score at or above the level predicted by their intelligence test scores; on the reading comprehension test, three of the five children had scores below those which would be expected by their intelligence test scores.

It is noteworthy that, of all the tests purported to assess semantic memory, only reading comprehension required new information to be encoded in a single trial. On this task, three of the five children had scores that were *lower* than expected by their intelligence test scores. The general intelligence, spelling, and basic reading tests, in contrast, all would permit the children to rely on knowledge and skills that would have been reinforced time and again in their many years at home and in school (the children were tested when they were 11–22 years of age). In this regard, it is important to keep in mind that humans and monkeys with lesions confined to the hippocampus proper are able to acquire new declarative knowledge. The object discrimination task is a good case in point.

In the object discrimination task, across several days of testing with multiple trials per day, participants learn which member of each pair of two objects is "correct" (one of the members of each pair is arbitrarily designated as the correct object or the object that will be rewarded). As reflected in Fig. 5.19, humans and monkeys with damage to the hippocampus perform less well on this task relative to healthy conspecifics (Fig. 5.19 reflects performance on the first three trials of each day's testing). What is equally apparent, however, is that humans and monkeys with hippocampal lesions nevertheless show *improved performance* on Day 2 relative to Day 1 and, in the case of monkeys, improved performance on Day 4 relative to Day 2 (human data: Squire, Zola-Morgan, & Chen, 1988; monkey data: Zola, Teng, Clark, et al., 1998). Thus, the hippocampus is essential for a normal rate of learning, yet learning can proceed, albeit more slowly, despite compromise to the hippocampus.

The presenting problems of the children tested by Vargha-Khadem and her colleagues suggest that the rate at which they acquired semantic knowledge was slow relative to their healthy peers: "Although all five children attended mainstream school, they were all struggling with memory and learning problems when they were referred to us for neuropsychological investigations" (Gadian et al., 2000, p. 503). The fact that the children nevertheless scored within the normal range on standardized tests indicates that they were able to acquire semantic knowledge. It is entirely likely that the

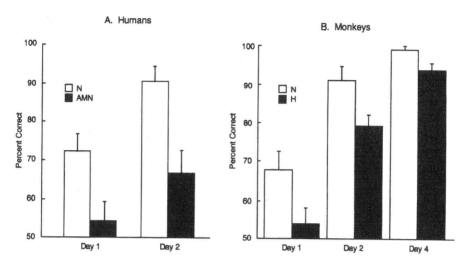

FIG. 5.19. Performance on the first three trials for each of 2 days of testing (humans) and 4 days of testing (monkeys) on an object discrimination task. For healthy humans and monkeys (open bars), the mean percent correct responses improved with each day of testing. Performance also improved for humans with medial temporal lesions and monkeys with lesions limited to the hippocampal region (filled bars). From "The Medial Temporal Lobe and the Hippocampus," by S. M. Zola and L. R. Squire, 2000. From *The Oxford Handbook of Memory* (pp. 485–500, Fig. 30.7) by Endel Tulving and Fergus Craik, Copyright © 2000 by Endel Tulving and Fergus Craik. Used by permission of Oxford University Press, Inc., and the author.

process by which they did so was not the single-trial learning that characterizes much of declarative knowledge acquisition, however. This suggests impaired semantic as well as episodic memory. On balance, the evidence of double dissociations in semantic and episodic memory is less compelling than it seemed at first glance. In contrast, evidence of common fate for the two subtypes of declarative memory remains strong (see Squire & Zola, 1998; Zola & Squire, 2000, for discussions).

*Episodic and Autobiographical Memory.* Although semantic and episodic memory are best viewed as relying on common medial temporal structures, they are not one-in-the-same type of declarative memory. Perhaps nowhere is the difference between episodic and semantic memory more apparent than when we consider the specific type of episodic memory that is the main subject of this volume—namely, autobiographical memory. When we compare the rich narrative memory of the new mother provided at the beginning of chapter 2 to the dispassionate claim that "the capital of North Carolina is Raleigh," we cannot help but believe that there is something different about the processes that formed these two different memories. Yet autobiographical memory falls under the rubric of episodic memory, the neural bases of which largely overlap with that of semantic memory (with prefrontal cortex playing a larger role in episodic relative to semantic memory). In this section, I consider whether, despite the large overlap in neural structures, there is nevertheless something that sets autobiographical memory apart not only from semantic memory, but also from "run-of-the-mill" episodic memory.

The case that autobiographical memory is different from semantic memory is easy to make: We need look no further than the distinction between semantic and episodic memory, only the latter of which includes information that locates the event in question in a specific place and specific time. Yet does autobiographical memory represent a distinct subtype of episodic memory? Endel Tulving (1972, 1983), the father of the semantic versus episodic distinction, did not distinguish different types of episodic memory. Indeed his definition of *episodic memory* implies the personal relevance that is the hallmark of autobiographical memory. Ironically, much of the work that has been done in the semantic–episodic tradition has used word lists and paired associates as stimuli—materials that hardly inspire the personal involvement that is part of the definition of *episodic memory*! Even research in which participants are asked to reflect on their states of awareness regarding words on study lists (Tulving, 1985b)—that is, to indicate whether they "remember" having encountered the word (as evidenced by memory for what they experienced at the time they studied the item) or merely "know" that they encountered the word (as evidenced by a general sense of familiarity with the item)—fails to capture the essence of autobiographical remembering. As discussed in chapter 2, autobiographical memories are infused with a sense of personal significance, relevance, or involvement. They go beyond the objective account of what happened in the course of an event to include the "... idiosyncratic perspectives, emotions, and thoughts of the person doing the remembering" (Wheeler, 2000, p. 597). Whereas making a "remember" versus a "know" judgment might meet the letter of the definition, it does not meet the spirit. The question of the moment is whether infusing a memory representation with the personal significance that is considered part and parcel of autobiographical memory requires a different type of neural processing relative to that required to construct a run of the mill episodic memory representation.

We have already noted some suggestions of differences when participants are asked to retrieve personal, autobiographical memories versus episodes in which they do not have a sense of personal involvement (e.g., Maguire et al., 2001). For example, Gereon Fink and his colleagues observed greater right prefrontal activations (as measured by PET) when participants were thinking about events they had actually experienced in the past (e.g., "When (I was) 15 (I) took part in a swimming marathon and succeeded to swim 10 miles") relative to when they were thinking about events that had happened to somebody else (Fink et al., 1996). Maguire and her colleagues noted different patterns of interaction among brain regions (as measured by fMRI) when participants are recalling public events (e.g., "Windsor Castle was damaged by a fire") as opposed to autobiographical experiences. Recall of autobiographical memories is characterized by an increase in connectivity between the parahippocampal cortex and the hippocampus; recall of public events is characterized by an increase in connectivity between the middle temporal gyrus and the temporal pole (Maguire, Mummery, & Büchel, 2000). Critically, in studies such as this, the *differences are in degree rather than kind.* That is, although there is *greater* activation associated with retrieval of autobiographical relative to nonautobiographical event memories, the same regions are activated in response to the two event types.

One possible source of greater activations in response to personally relevant events is their highly emotional character (Sarter & Markowitsch, 1985). Emotion plays a central role in autobiographical memory: Events that are "affectively charged," or have high levels of emotionality associated with them, either positive or negative, tend to be well recalled (e.g., Brewer, 1988; Thompson, 1998; Wagenaar, 1986; White, 2002; see chap. 2 for discussion). One of the means by which affect may influence the robustness of memory is by engaging different parts of the brain in processing of the event. For example, there is increasing evidence that the amygdala (a small, almond-shaped structure in the medial temporal lobe) plays a modulatory role in memory by regulating the processing of the emotional content of events (Cahill & McGaugh, 1998; Sarter & Markowitsch, 1985). Specifically, the amygdala is thought to aid in distinguishing the important elements of events (e.g., those associated with threat- or fear-provoking stimuli) from the less important ones; there typically is a strong relation between what is important and what produces strong emotion.

The suggestion that the amygdala plays a facilitating role in the encoding of the emotional content of experiences is supported by research by James McGaugh, Larry Cahill, and their colleagues. Using PET, they observed relations between the degree of activation of the amygdala while participants watched emotional film clips and their recall of the films 2 weeks later (Cahill et al., 1996). There is suggestive evidence that the arousal level of the stimuli modulates the amygdala response (Garavan, Pendergrass, Ross, Stein, & Risinger, 2001). The relation between amygdala activity and subsequent memory is more than correlational: Individuals in whom amygdala processing has been blocked by injection of a beta-adrenergic blocker show selective impairment of memory for the emotional elements of events (Cahill, Prins, Weber, & McGaugh, 1994).

The amygdala plays a role not only at the time of encoding, but also at the time of retrieval of event memories. Martina Piefke and her colleagues observed amygdala activations (as measured by fMRI) in response to recollection of personal memories. Activations when the participants were retrieving memories of events they had identified as positive were greater to those they had identified as negative (Piefke, Weiss, Zilles, Markowitsch, & Fink, 2003). Results such as these suggest that there may be a neural basis for why there is better memory for events that have a great deal of emotion associated with them. At the time of encoding, the amygdala likely plays a role in modulating the amount of emotional content that is encoded. It may also function to facilitate retrieval of memories of emotional events.

The question addressed in this section was whether, despite the large overlap in neural structures, there is nevertheless something that sets autobiographical memory apart from episodic memory for less personally relevant events. The two subtypes of memory seem to involve differential activation of medial temporal and frontal structures. In addition, the amygdala seems to be differentially involved in the encoding and retrieval of events with greater emotion attached to them. Whereas these quantitative differences are not sufficient to declare that these two subtypes of memory are representative of qualitatively different memory "systems," they are perhaps significant nonetheless: Quantitative changes can produce qualitative differences. It may be that, in the case of episodic and autobiographical memory, the quantitative difference in neural activation is what produces the qualitatively different sense associated with recall of autobiographical memories—namely, that the event is being relived, as opposed to simply "read off" from a generic knowledge store.

## Declarative and Nondeclarative Memory

The suggestion that there is more than one type of memory, and that the temporal-cortical network described in this chapter supports only one major type—declarative memory—requires evaluation of the possibility that the same network might also support nondeclarative memory. Although there is heterogeneity among the many different types of memory that are classified as nondeclarative, by definition they have one thing in common: They reflect changes in task performance as a function of previous experience that do not require conscious or intentional recollection of the experience (Graf & Schacter, 1985; Schacter, 1987). Virtually from the time of "discovery" of the memory deficits produced by H. M.'s lesioned medial temporal lobes, it has been apparent that his performance on a variety of tasks could be influenced by experience. For example, in chapter 1, I mentioned an early study in which it was demonstrated that H. M. could learn a new sensorimotor task (Milner et al., 1968). Specifically, H. M. learned to copy a geometric figure reflected in a mirror (see Fig. 5.20), making fewer and fewer errors as he gained more practice. H. M.'s performance improved each day, although he had no conscious recollection of ever having attempted the task before. This

**A.**

**B.**

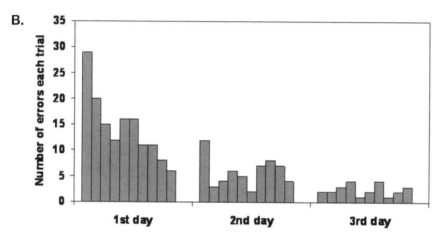

FIG. 5.20.    A representation of the mirror drawing test (Panel A) and H. M.'s performance on the test across 10 attempts on each of three successive days (Panel B). Photograph for Panel A by Jeanne Cowan, used with permission; Panel B based on Fig. 5.3 of Eichenbaum and Cohen (2001).

finding was a clear indication that not all types of memory are subserved by medial temporal structures, which in H. M. are severely compromised.

Since the initial identification of new sensorimotor learning in H. M., researchers have documented preserved function on a variety of other memory tasks in H. M. and in other patients with medial temporal lesions. It is now apparent that, despite compromised ability to acquire new semantic knowledge and encode new episodic memories, patients with medial temporal lobe lesions are able to learn skills and habits, they can be conditioned, and they show normal priming (see Eichenbaum & Cohen, 2001; Squire et al., 1993, for reviews).

Skill and habit learning are apparent in incremental improvement over trials in tasks such as mirror drawing, mirror reading, rotary pursuit, and serial reaction time. For example, patients with amnesia and healthy control participants show similar patterns and rates of improvement on a task requiring that they read lists of nonwords (i.e., words modified by letter substitutions that rendered them meaningless, but still pronounceable; e.g., *locapic, ganisper*). As reflected in the left side of Fig. 5.21, when the lists were made up of 100 *different* nonwords, reading speed did not improve over the course of 10 blocks of 10 trials each. In contrast, when the lists were comprised of blocks of 10 words that were *repeated* over trials, both groups of participants experienced decreases in reading speed (right side of figure; Musen & Squire, 1991). Patients with temporal lobe damage also show normal rates and patterns of acquisition and extinction of the conditioned response of blinking to a tone-light stimulus following paired presentation of the tone-light and a puff of air (e.g., Gabrieli et al., 1995). They also exhibit normal repetition priming. In this paradigm, participants study a list of words (*absent—in-*

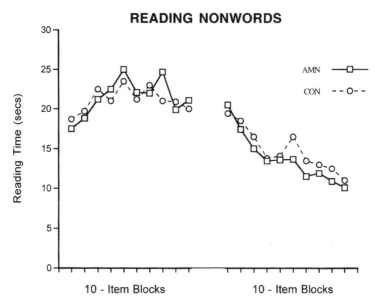

FIG. 5.21. Reading times (in seconds) for patients with amnesia (open squares) and healthy control participants (open circles) when reading lists of 100 different nonwords (on the left side of the figure) and lists comprised of 10 blocks of 10 words that repeated over trials (on the right side of the figure). From Squire (1992), Fig. 7.

*come—filly—discuss—elephant*). After a delay, they are asked to complete word stems that have more than one solution (e.g., the stem ELE_____ could be completed with the word *elephant* or *element*). Relative to participants who have not studied the list, both healthy controls and patients are more likely to complete the stem with a word from the study list (Graf, Squire, & Mandler, 1984).

As these examples illustrate, medial temporal lobe damage does not eliminate all forms of memory. It leaves intact performance on tasks on which memory is inferred by changes over trials in the speed or accuracy with which a response is executed, or by changes in the likelihood or tendency for a particular response to be produced. In contrast, it impairs performance on tasks that require the participant to intentionally reflect on past experience. For instance, when they are tested after word stem-completion tasks, such as administered by Peter Graf and his colleagues (Graf et al., 1984), healthy participants typically have high rates of both recall and recognition of the studied words. In contrast, recognition and especially recall are impaired among patients with medial temporal lesions. Similar dissociations in performance are apparent in animal models of amnesia (see Eichenbaum & Cohen, 2001; Squire, 1992, for reviews). The finding that performance on this variety of tasks is not impaired by medial temporal lobe lesions in humans or nonhuman animals makes clear that the nondeclarative form of memory that they reflect is not supported by the temporal-cortical network that underlies declarative memory. Instead it is likely supported by a number of different neural structures, including cerebellum in the case of some motor skill learning and conditioning paradigms, and extrastriate cortex in the case of priming.

## SUMMARY AND CONCLUSION

In this chapter, I described the neural structures thought to support declarative memory in the adult human. Declarative memory involves a distributed network of cortical and medial temporal structures. Primary, unimodal, and polymodal association cortices are involved in the initial encoding of the experiences of the organism. The information then must be consolidated for long-term storage. Consolidation is regarded as the province of the medial temporal structures. Over time the hippocampus is considered to "train up" the cortex to maintain the memory representation over the long term. Retrieval of memories from long-term storage sites is thought to involve the prefrontal cortex. Especially high demands on these structures are made when specific episodic features of events, such as the temporal order in which they occurred, must be retrieved. This may explain why retrieval of autobiographical memories seems to be particularly dependent on prefrontal structures.

The temporal-cortical network described in this chapter supports declarative, but not nondeclarative, memory. Although the network is specific to declarative memory, it is also general in that it permits both semantic and episodic memory. Moreover, although there is evidence that retrieval of personal or autobiographical memories makes greater demands on prefrontal structures relative to retrieval of impersonal episodic memories, there is no evidence that autobiographical memory recruits different neural structures. Having reviewed the temporal-cortical network that supports adult declarative memory, I now turn to discussion of its development in chapter 6.

# 6

# Development of the Neural Substrate for Declarative Memory

*The study of infant memory and its neurobiological bases is plagued by special methodological problems. Many of these difficulties arise from the fact that one studies organisms at a time when the underlying mechanisms responsible for their behavior are in a dynamic, fluctuating state. . . . Notwithstanding these difficulties, many facts are available to help us understand infantile amnesia, and it is possible, indeed profitable, to begin putting them together.*

—Lynn Nadel and Stuart Zola-Morgan (1984, pp. 147–150)

Lynn Nadel and Stuart Zola-Morgan were true pioneers when, in 1984, they challenged researchers of adult memory, neurobiology, and cognitive development to "begin putting . . . together" the "many facts" that each field had accumulated, with the goal of advancing our understanding of the ontogeny of human memory. Until that time, the study of the development of memory was largely separate from the study of memory in the adult. One reason was that, for much of the history of psychology, the prevailing view was of a profound discontinuity between the type of memory available to infants and very young children and that available to the adult. As discussed in chapter 4, until the 1980s, virtually universally, the dominant theories of cognitive development assumed that children younger than 3 years of age lacked the symbolic or representational capacity necessary to form accessible (i.e., declarative) memories. In contrast, adults were in full command of the facility.

In his preface to the edited volume in which Nadel and Zola-Morgan's chapter appeared, Morris Moscovitch (1984) identified another major reason for the relative isolation of the developmental and adult memory literatures. He placed much of the blame for the lack of contact on the vast differences in the methodologies used with infants and adults. As discussed in chapter 4, because infants are nonverbal, inferences about what they remembered were based on how long they looked or how hard they kicked. However, infants could not participate in the paradigm of choice for researchers of adult memory—namely, verbal report. Because the capacity to recall the past was linked with the capacity to talk, as far as inquiry into developments in declarative memory was concerned, infants and very young children seemed beyond the reaches of investigation.

Prior to the 1980s, the study of the ontogeny of human memory was isolated not only from the adult memory literature, but also from the literature on the neurobiology of memory. The lack of contact with the rapidly advancing field of neuroscience could be attributed to the fact that the respective domains ". . . typically seek answers to questions that lie at different points on a continuum of knowledge" (Nelson & Bloom, 1997), and that therefore require different levels of analysis. Whereas psychologists use observation to study behavioral indexes of memory, neuroscientists use chemical assays, and structural and functional images to study the behavior of molecules and cells. Some of the structural and functional imaging techniques were being applied to the study of neural systems in adults, but once again the developing human seemed beyond the reaches of investigation.

Since Nadel and Zola-Morgan's (1984) call for more integration across disparate fields, the circumstances of relative isolation of the study of human memory development from the study of adult memory and its neural underpinnings have changed. Methodological advances—such as the development of elicited and deferred imitation as nonverbal means of testing recall memory, increases in knowledge about human brain development, improvements in neuroimaging, and insights from theoretically interesting special populations—have made it possible to begin to articulate relations between developmental changes in the neural systems responsible for declarative memory and age-related changes in memory behavior. The result is that longstanding theories of a qualitative change in mnemonic function late in the second year of life have been put to empirical test. Contrary to assumptions derived from them, a now sizeable body of data indicates that the capacity for long-term recall is available by late in the first year of life. Nevertheless, as was apparent in chapter 4, over the course of the second year, there are pronounced changes in recall ability, such that by the end of the second year, the capacity for long-term recall is both reliable and robust.

What accounts for such rapid and profound change in declarative memory? In this chapter, I develop the argument that age-related changes in long-term recall are not the result of qualitative changes brought on by the dawning of a new capacity (e.g., the capacity to use symbols). Instead they can be attributed, in large part, to quantitative changes in the neural network that supports declarative memory. To develop this perspective, in chapter 5, I described the brain system responsible for declarative memory in adults. In this chapter, I discuss the system's course of development. The goal of the review is to address three questions. The first is whether the data on brain development "fit" with those on developments in behavior (reviewed in chap. 4). Relative fit between structural and functional changes at a general level is a necessary prerequisite for the next question, which is whether consideration of neurodevelopment can advance our understanding of "what develops?" in early memory. In other words, can it afford for us greater insight into the behavioral changes that are apparent? The third question returns to the theme of the volume as a whole: Does a neurodevelopmental perspective have anything to contribute to explanations of childhood amnesia? I maintain that the answer to all three questions is "yes."

## MULTIPLE MEMORY SYSTEMS
## IN THE HUMAN INFANT

The distinction between declarative and nondeclarative memory originally was derived from the adult cognitive and adult neuroscience literatures (see chaps. 1 and 5). As such, much of the work supporting the multiple memory systems view originally came from adult humans with amnesia and nonhuman animals. Some have argued that, because human infants are neither brain-damaged adults nor nonhuman animals, the distinction between different memory systems is not relevant to human developmental science (e.g., Rovee-Collier, 1997). Another caution in application of the multiple memory systems view to human cognitive development stems from use of the construct of conscious awareness as one of the criteria to differentiate declarative and nondeclarative forms of memory. As noted by Charles Nelson (1997) and Carolyn Rovee-Collier (1997), it is not clear how consciousness can be assessed in a nonverbal infant or nonhuman animal.

Although it is true that the distinction between memory systems originally was based on populations other than human infants, the source of the data does not present an insurmountable challenge to its application to the target population. A long tradition of comparative psychology suggests that "lessons" learned from one population can, with appropriate care, be applied to others. In addition, there is now a substantial body of work with intact human adults—using both behavioral and neuroimaging methods—that converges with the data from patients and animal models to suggest that there are indeed multiple systems of memory. Admittedly, it is a challenge to consider how to apply to preverbal children the criteria of consciousness. Critically, however, definitions of the construct do not require that it be expressed verbally. Indeed some scholars have specifically noted that conscious awareness may be expressed through nonverbal behavior (e.g., Köhler &

Moscovitch, 1997). Empirically, the concern about application of the criterion of *consciousness* has been addressed by designing tasks that bear other of the characteristic features of tests of declarative memory—such as requiring acquisition of novel behaviors on the basis of the single trial—and that produce behaviors that look quite different from those exhibited in nondeclarative memory paradigms—such as verbal access to the products of learning (see chap. 10).

It is fortunate that these challenges can be met because, for developmental scientists, the distinction between different types of memory is vitally important for two major reasons. First, as discussed by Jean Mandler (e.g., 2004), if we are to make progress in understanding cognitive development, we must be clear about the capacities we are studying. In essence, her argument is that if we do not know with what kind of knowledge we are dealing—whether it is nondeclarative in nature and thus inaccessible, or declarative in nature and thus accessible—we cannot begin to answer questions regarding the mechanisms by which the knowledge was acquired. In turn, unless we are clear about the nature of the knowledge being acquired, we cannot hope to address questions regarding the mechanisms of cognitive development more broadly. In the words of an argument from chapter 1—if we treat memory as pudding, we cannot hope to discover how it was made. It is only by recognizing that memory is an elephant that we will make progress in understanding why it takes the forms that it does. Thus, from a general theoretical perspective, it is important to specify what type of memory we are studying to constrain our theories of how it develops.

Second, the distinction between declarative and nondeclarative forms of memory is important developmentally because there is reason to believe that the neural structures that contribute to these different types of memory mature at different rates. Specifically, as reviewed by Charles Nelson (1995, 1997, 2000), there are reasons to believe that the structures that permit some of the different forms of nondeclarative memory are functional at an earlier age relative to those that permit declarative memory. For example, instrumental conditioning, such as observed in the mobile conjugate reinforcement paradigm (see Rovee-Collier & Hayne, 2000, for a review; see chap. 4 for a brief description of the task), likely depends largely on early developing cerebellum and certain deep nuclei of the brainstem. As discussed by Charles Nelson (1995, 1997), although development of the cerebellum lags behind that of the cortex early in gestation, it develops rapidly near the end of the prenatal period. During the first postnatal year, patterns of glucose utilization in the cerebellum closely approximate those of the adult (e.g., Chugani, 1994), and adultlike patterns of myelination are apparent by the third postnatal month (Barkovich, Kjos, Jackson, & Norman, 1988; see C. A. Nelson, 1995, 1997; C. A. Nelson & Webb, 2002, for discussion of the course of development of neural structures supporting other types of nondeclarative memory). In contrast, as is seen in the section to follow, the temporal-cortical network that supports declarative memory (described in chap. 5) has a slower, longer course of development. This contrast in rates of development makes clear that if we are to understand age-related changes in memory in neural terms, we need to chart neurodevelopmental changes in the specific structures under question. Our understanding of brain development should constrain our expectations regarding performance as well as inform our interpretation of data.

## DEVELOPMENT OF THE NEURAL NETWORK FOR DECLARATIVE MEMORY

In chapter 5, I reviewed the literature on the neural bases of declarative memory in the adult human. Relative to the large database amassed about the adult, in the human infant, little is known about the course of development of the neural structures that support declarative memory or about relations between their development and changes in memory functions. The state of affairs exists for a variety of reasons. First, as discussed in chapter 4, the human infant poses many challenges for scientific study. For memory researchers, one of the most serious issues is that, lacking the capacity for language, infants are unable to provide verbal reports of their memories. Researchers must rely instead on where and how long infants look, how vigorously they kick their legs, and their imitation of modeled actions, for example.

Second, much of the research that led to identification of multiple memory systems and their neural bases was made possible by traumas and diseases that happily are rare among the young of our species: Human infants do not frequently present with tumors, strokes, and closed head injuries. Those who do suffer neurological insults early in life often have more global lesions, making identification of the role played by specific neural structures difficult to establish (although see Gadian et al., 2000; Vargha-Khadem et al., 1997; discussed in chap. 5, for exceptions; additional exceptions are described later in this chapter).

Third, many of the neuroimaging techniques used with adults are not appropriate for infants. For example, PET requires injection of radioactive substances, rendering it inappropriate for normally developing infants and young children; and MRI and fMRI require that the participant remain motionless for long periods of time while being exposed to very strong magnetic fields. As a result, these neuroimaging techniques are not in wide use in research with infants and very young children (see Casey, Thomas, & McCandliss,

2001, for discussion of use of three-dimensional imaging techniques with older children).

Our relatively impoverished knowledge about the neurodevelopment of declarative memory can be largely attributed to this variety of limitations on methodology. To overcome them, researchers studying the anatomy and physiology of the developing brain have relied on animal models (e.g., Benes, 2001) and examination of prenatal and postnatal brains brought to autopsy (e.g., Seress, 2001). To study relations between brain and behavior, we use animal models of development (e.g., nonhuman primates; Bachevalier, 2001), behavioral tasks for which the neural bases in adults are known (e.g., delayed nonmatching to sample; Diamond, 2001), and noninvasive imaging techniques (e.g., event-related potentials [ERPs]; Nelson & Monk, 2001). Although each of these methods has limitations, and even their combination is less than fully satisfying, with the addition of each new piece of the puzzle, the picture emerging is sharpening every day.

## The Neural Bases of Declarative Memory

Chapter 5 featured a review of the multiple areas of the brain that together support declarative memory, including cortical association areas and medial temporal structures. An "abstract" of the argument is that formation of a declarative memory trace involves a multistep process that begins when perceptual experience produces excitation across multiple brain regions distributed across the cortex. Association cortices bring the information together, giving rise to conscious awareness of the experience. Medial temporal and neocortical structures are involved in the consolidation of the distributed representation into an enduring memory trace. The long-term storage sites of memory are the same cortical association areas that participated in initial registration of unified experience. Finally, retrieval of memories from long-term stores is thought to depend on the prefrontal cortex.

In the sections to follow, I describe what is known about development of the major components in this multicomponent network—the medial temporal structures and association cortices—with special emphasis on anterior-prefrontal association cortex. The description is an update and expansion of that provided in Carver and Bauer (2001). As Leslie Carver and I argued then (and as Charles Nelson argued in his 1995, 1997, and 2000 reviews), the evidence is consistent with the suggestion that, whereas some components of the temporal-cortical circuit develop early, it is only near the end of the first year of life that the entire network begins to function. It continues to develop for months and even years thereafter. After reviewing the evidence for these conclusions, I turn to an evaluation of the degree of "fit" between observed behavior (reviewed in chap. 4) and the course of neural development thought to contribute to it.

## Development of Medial Temporal Components

There are a number of indicators that, in the human, many of the medial temporal lobe components of the declarative memory system (see Fig. 6.1) develop early. First, the cells destined for most of the fields of the hippocampus (e.g., CA1 and CA3) are formed early in prenatal development. Specifically, as discussed by László Seress (2001), neurons in the entorhinal cortex (which is located in the parahippocampal region depicted in Fig. 6.1), the CA3 and CA1 fields of the hippocampus (a.k.a Ammon's horn; see insert of Fig. 6.1), and the subiculum are formed in the first half of gestation (Angevine, 1975; Rakic & Nowakowski, 1981) and virtually all have migrated prenatally. Indeed for most of the hippocampus, the last neurons are formed between the 20th and 24th week of gestation. By the 24th gesta-

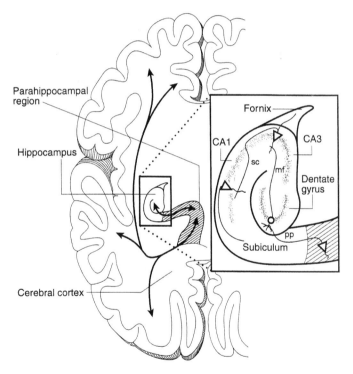

FIG. 6.1. A schematic diagram of the medial temporal lobe components of the declarative memory system. On the left is a horizontal section illustrating the major connective pathways between the hippocampus and the cortical areas. The inset (right side of diagram) indicates the major connections within the hippocampus. From *From Conditioning to Conscious Recollection: Memory Systems of the Brain* (Fig. 3.1), by Howard Eichenbaum and Neal J. Cohen. Copyright © 2001 by Oxford University Press, Inc. Used by permission of Oxford University Press and the author.

tional week, the cytoarchitecture (i.e., the size, shape, and organization of the cells) of most of the hippocampus is adultlike, and by 32 to 36 weeks gestation, immature cells no longer are apparent in the CA3 and CA1 fields (Arnold & Trojanowski, 1996). The neurons in most of the hippocampal formation also begin to connect early in development. Within the hippocampus, synapses are present as early as 15 weeks gestational age (Kostovic, Seress, Mrzljak, & Judas, 1989). Spine density and the number of synapses both increase rapidly after birth, with dendritic arborization at adult levels by approximately 6 postnatal months (Paldino & Purpura, 1979).

Studies of glucose utilization are consistent with the suggestion of relatively early development of most of the medial temporal lobe components of the declarative memory system. For example, PET studies show elevated levels of glucose utilization in temporal cortex by 3 months of age, followed by a gradual decrease to adult levels (Chugani, 1994; Chugani & Phelps, 1986). This rise and fall in glucose utilization corresponds to synapse overproduction and later pruning that has been observed in studies of the development of synapse formation (Huttenlocher, 1990, 2002). Although it is unclear exactly what elevated levels of glucose utilization mean, periods of high utilization coincide with periods of change in the behaviors supported by the region where the elevations are observed (Chugani, Phelps, & Mazziotta, 1987). This suggests that the increases may be related to the acquisition of new abilities. Conversely, decreases in utilization may be associated with regressive events (e.g., pruning of unused synaptic connections) implicated in eventual achievement of adult-level functioning.

In contrast to early proliferation, migration, and differentiation of most regions of the hippocampus, the course of development of the dentate gyrus of the hippocampus, an essential link in the trisynaptic circuit that connects the hippocampus with the balance of the temporal-cortical network that supports long-term declarative memory (see Fig. 5.15), is protracted. For instance, the pyramidal cell layers of the entorhinal cortex, the CA3 and CA1 fields of the hippocampus, and the subiculum, are adultlike by 23 to 25 weeks gestation. However, the granule cell layer in the dentate gyrus of the hippocampus only begins to form in the 13th to 14th week of gestation and continues to develop throughout the first postnatal year (Eckenhoff & Rakic, 1988; Seress, 1992). At birth the granule cell layer of the dentate gyrus includes only about 70% of the adult number of cells and has a volume that is 25% to 30% less than that of the adult (Seress, 1988; cited in Seress, 2001). This means that roughly 30% of granule cells proliferate, migrate, differentiate, and establish connections postnatally. Consistent with this suggestion, immature cells are apparent in the dentate gyrus as late as 8 postnatal months. By 12 to 15 postnatal months of age, immature cells no longer are apparent, and the general cytoarchitectonic features of the structure appear adultlike (Serres, 1992). Nevertheless, there is evidence that in the dentate gyrus of the hippocampus, neurogenesis continues throughout childhood and even into adulthood (Altman & Das, 1965; see Tanapat, Hastings, & Gould, 2001, for discussion).

Maximum synaptic density in the dentate gyrus also is delayed relative to that in the other regions of the hippocampus. In nonhuman primates, there is a period of rapid accumulation of synapses—or *synaptogenesis*—beginning the second or third postnatal month. Synaptic density reaches its peak in the fourth or fifth month; pruning to adult levels is not accomplished until 10 months of age. In the human, this time frame corresponds to roughly 8 to 12 months for the increase in synaptic density, 16 to 20 months for attainment of peak synaptic density, and 4 to 5 years for achievement of adult levels (Eckenhoff & Rakic, 1991; see Webb, Monk, & Nelson, 2001, for discussion; the approximate ratio of development in the nonhuman and human primate is 4 months to 1 month).

Although the functional significance of later development of the dentate gyrus is not clear, there is reason to speculate that it impacts behavior. As discussed in chapter 5, information from distributed regions of cortex converges on the entorhinal cortex via the perirhinal and parahippocampal cortices (see Fig. 5.15). From there it makes its way into the hippocampus in one of two ways: via the "long route" or the "short route." The long route (the *hippocampal trisynaptic circuit*) involves projections from entorhinal cortex to the dentate gyrus, from the dentate gyrus to Ammon's horn, from Ammon's horn to the subiculum, and from the subiculum back to the entorhinal cortex. The short route involves direct projections from the entorhinal cortex to the CA1 field of the hippocampus and the subiculum, thereby bypassing the dentate gyrus and CA3 field. These direct projections may be among the first cortico-cortical connections to be established in the human brain (Hevner & Kinney, 1996), and they likely support some forms of memory (C. A. Nelson, 1995; Seress, 2001; see later for discussion). However, based on data from rodents, there is reason to believe that adultlike behaviors such as spatial navigation are observed only once the full trisynaptic circuit is developed (Nadel & Willner, 1989). If at birth the granule cells of the rodent dentate gyrus are irradiated, normal function of the hippocampal formation is never attained (Czurkó, Czéh, Seress, Nadel, & Bures, 1997). Based on data such as these, it seems that the full trisynaptic circuit is critical for adultlike memory function (e.g., Seress, 2001). There is speculation that "long route" processing may be especially important for storage of new memories (in contrast to "short route" processing, which may be more closely associated with retrieval; Gluck & Myers, 2001). As such maturation of the dentate gyrus of the hippocampus may be a rate-limiting variable in the development of declarative memory early in life (Bauer, 2002, 2004; Bauer, Wiebe, et al., 2003; C. A. Nelson, 1995, 1997, 2000).

## Development of Association Cortices

In contrast to relatively early development of major portions of the medial temporal system, the association areas develop more slowly (Bachevalier, Brickson, & Hagger, 1993; Bachevalier & Mishkin, 1994). As discussed by Christopher Monk, Sara Webb, and Charles Nelson (2001), prenatally, neo-cortical neurons are formed later than hippocampal neurons (Arnold & Trojanowski, 1996), and neuroblasts migrating to the neocortex have a longer distance to travel relative to those migrating to the hippocampus (Nowakowski & Rakic, 1981). As a result, whereas by about 18 weeks gestation the hippocampus has begun to assume the "C"-shape characteristic of the adult, even at 20 weeks the cortex has divided into only three of the six layers of the mature brain. It is not until the seventh prenatal month that all six cortical layers are apparent.

Beginning about midgestation (i.e., 17–24 weeks), synaptogenesis begins in the cortex. Although different cortical areas mature at different rates, the phase of rapid accumulation of synapses begins almost simultaneously across all cortical areas (e.g., Bourgeois, Goldman-Rakic, & Rakic, 2000; Zecevic, 1998). What differs across areas are the times at which synaptogenesis ends and the times at which pruning of unused connections begins. The relative timing of synaptogenesis in two areas of cortex in the human—primary visual cortex and prefrontal cortex—is represented schematically in Fig. 6.2. In the human primary visual cortex, synaptogenesis ends between 8 and 12 postnatal months, and pruning begins at about 2 to 3 years. In contrast, in the prefrontal cortex, development takes a slower course. Synaptic density begins to increase dramatically at 8 postnatal months, peaks between 15 and 24 months, and pruning begins in later childhood (Huttenlocher, 1979; Huttenlocher & Dabholkar, 1997; see Bourgeois, 2001, for discussion). The postnatal months are marked by rapid dendritic growth in cortical Layers III and V until about 7½ months and 12 months, respectively. In Layer III, there is a marked increase in the length of the basal dendritic field between 7½ and 12 postnatal months of age. The dendrites continue to branch into early adulthood (Koenderink, Uylings, & Mrzljak, 1994). In Layer V, cell body size and the lengths of the dendrites increase until about 5 to 7 years of age (Koenderink & Uylings, 1995). In Layer II of some regions of dorsolateral prefrontal cortex, the process may continue until 12 to 15 years of age (see Benes, 2001, for discussion). Although the maximum density of synapses may be reached as early as 15 postnatal months, it is not until 24 months that synapses develop adult morphology (Huttenlocher, 1979).

Glucose utilization and blood flow studies also indicate that the frontal cortex matures relatively late (Chugani, Phelps, & Mazziotta, 1987). Blood flow and glucose utilization increase above adult levels by 8 to 12 and 13 to 14 months of age, respectively. These results, together with those of Peter

SYNAPTOGENESIS IN HUMAN CEREBRAL CORTEX

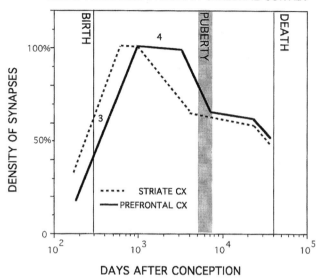

DAYS AFTER CONCEPTION

FIG. 6.2.   A schematic diagram of the relative timing of synaptogenesis in the primary visual cortex (broken line) and prefrontal cortex (solid line) of the human. From "Synaptogenesis in the Neocortex of the Newborn: The Ultimate Frontier for Individuation?", by J. P. Bourgeois. In C. A. Nelson and M. Luciana, *Handbook of Developmental Cognitive Neuroscience* (Fig. 2.3), The MIT Press, Publisher. Copyright © 2001 by Massachusetts Institute of Technology. Reprinted with permission.

Huttenlocher's data on synaptogenesis (Huttenlocher, 1994; Huttenlocher & Dabholkar, 1997), suggest that major developments in frontal lobe maturation may take place over the second half of the first year and continue into the second year of life and beyond. Other maturational changes in frontal cortex, such as myelination, continue into adolescence and early adulthood (e.g., Johnson, 1997; Schneider, Il'yasov, Hennig, & Martin, 2004). Adult levels of neurotransmitters such as acetylcholine and dopamine are not seen until 10 years of age and adulthood, respectively (discussed in Benes, 2001).

## Development of Connections

As important as the structures themselves are the connections between them. Indeed research by Fumihiko Yasuno and colleagues documented deficits in temporal order memory associated with disruption of the connections between the hippocampus and the frontal cortex in the absence of lesions in either of the structures themselves (Yasuno et al., 1999). Despite their obvious significance, less is known about the development of connections between structures in the brain relative to what is known about development of the structures themselves. Our knowledge of the connections between the specific structures involved in particular cognitive functions—such as the components of the declarative memory system—is even more impoverished.

With regard to connections in general, the relatively new technology of diffusion-tensor imaging (DTI) has revealed pronounced changes in the white matter (i.e., connective tissue) of the brain over the first years of life (see Watts, Liston, Niogi, & Uluğ, 2003, for an introduction to the technology in a pediatric context). The changes that take place from birth to 2 years are readily apparent in Fig. 6.3. The figure is of horizontal slices of the brain at three different levels (i.e., through the lower part of the temporal lobes, through roughly the middle of the brain, and near the top of the brain). What is revealed are dramatic changes in the volume of white matter from one time point to the next over the first 2 years of life. The changes are the result of increases in the number of connections between neurons and the progression of myelination of neuronal axons.

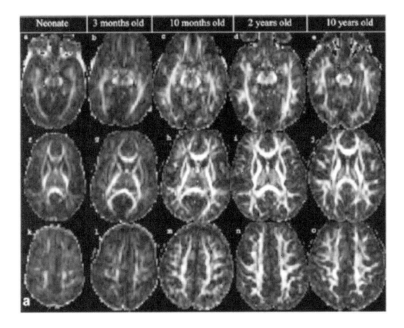

FIG. 6.3. Images of white matter tracts obtained via diffusion-tensor imaging (DTI) from five children ages 1 day to 10 years. The images are through the cerebral peduncle and temporal lobes (a–e), the basal ganglia (f–j), and centrum semiovale/corona radiata (k–o). From *Neuroradiology*, "Fast Quantitative Difusion-Tensor Imaging of Cerebral White Matter From the Neonatal Period to Adolescence," by J. F. Schneider, L. Il'yasov, J. Hennig, and E. Martin, Vol. 46, 258–266, Fig. 2a, 2004, copyright (2004), with permission of Springer and the author.

Whereas it is clear that connectivity increases with development, there is little information on age-related change within specific neural networks such as that implicated in declarative memory. As noted earlier, the "short route" that connects the entorhinal cortex directly with the CA1 region of the hippocampus and subiculum develops early. However, the "long route" that connects the entorhinal cortex to the hippocampus via the dentate gyrus is later to develop. Similarly, the connections from the neocortex to the entorhinal region develop later (Hevner & Kinney, 1996; Seress & Mrzljak, 1992).

Research with nonhuman primates suggests that the period corresponding to the end of the first year and the beginning of the second year of life in the human may be an important time for the development of connections between the cortical and medial temporal components of the declarative memory system. In monkeys, after about 3 months of age (corresponding to about 1 year in the human), lesioning of the connections between visual association areas and the medial temporal lobe structures produces pronounced deficits in performance on the delayed nonmatching to sample task (depicted in Fig. 5.10). In contrast, lesions inflicted prior to 3 months produce no loss of function. Preserved function is attributed to retention of otherwise transient projections between these regions that, in the healthy, mature adult, no longer exist (Webster, Ungerleider, & Bachevalier, 1991a, 1991b). These findings suggest that, during what corresponds to the first year of human life, connections between subcortical and cortical components of the declarative memory system are still undergoing developmental change (see Bachevalier et al., 1993; Bachevalier & Mishkin, 1994, for additional discussion). Christopher Monk, Sara Webb, and Charles Nelson (2001) speculated that the lack of stimulation from the neocortical regions to the hippocampus that would result from as-yet-undeveloped connections may contribute to the slow development of synapses in the hippocampus and, thus, declarative memory.

## Functional Maturity of the Temporal-Cortical Network

The network that supports declarative memory in the human can be expected to function as an integrated whole only once each of the components of the network, as well as the connections between them, has reached a level of functional maturity. What constitutes "functional maturity?" In other words, what neurodevelopmental events must transpire for the network to support behavior? Because so many aspects of the system are changing—cell body size, lengths of dendrites, levels of neurotransmitters, and more—there is no simple answer to this question. A reasonable candidate metric was suggested by Patricia Goldman-Rakic (1987). She argued that we should expect to see the emergence of what she termed the *signatory functions* (i.e., the characteristic functions) of a cortical area as the number of synapses in the region reaches it peak. Attainment of mature levels of function would coincide with the period of synapse elimination.

If we extend Goldman-Rakic's (1987) suggestion to the entire temporal-cortical network, we can predict the emergence of the signatory function of long-term declarative memory by late in the first year of life, with significant development over the course of the second year and continued development for years thereafter. Specifically, with the exception of the dentate gyrus of the hippocampus, the medial temporal components of the network would be expected to reach functional maturity between the second and sixth post-natal months (Paldino & Purpura, 1979). The cortical components of the network, and the connections both within the medial temporal lobe (i.e., those involving the dentate gyrus of the hippocampus) and between the cortex and the medial temporal components, would be expected to reach functional maturity late in the first year and over the course of the second year of life. The network would be expected to continue to develop, albeit less dramatically, for years thereafter. The time frame is based on increases in synaptogenesis from 8 to 20 months in the dentate gyrus (Eckenhoff & Rakic, 1991) and from 8 to 24 months in the prefrontal cortex (Huttenlocher, 1979; Huttenlocher & Dabholkar, 1997). The expectation of developmental changes for months and years thereafter stems from the schedule of protracted pruning both in the dentate gyrus (until 4 to 5 years; e.g., Eckenhoff & Rakic, 1991) and the prefrontal cortex (throughout adolescence; e.g., Huttenlocher & Dabholkar, 1997).

## RELATIONS BETWEEN BRAIN AND BEHAVIOR IN DEVELOPMENT

Having reviewed in chapter 5 the neural substrate of declarative memory, and thus far in this chapter its development, we are in a position to address the three questions raised in the introduction to this chapter: (a) Do the data on the course of brain development "fit" with those on developments in behavior (reviewed in chap. 4)? (b) Can consideration of neurodevelopment bring greater specificity to the question of "what develops?" in early memory development? (c) Does a neurodevelopmental perspective have anything to contribute to explanations of childhood amnesia? The balance of this chapter is given over to development of support for an affirmative answer to the first two questions discussed in this and the next section, respectively. The third is taken up over the course of the remaining chapters.

The first question is whether there is a fit between expectations for development based on consideration of the neurodevelopmental course and the behavioral data on memory. For now I focus on the first 3 years of life only; consideration of behavioral and neurodevelopmental changes in the preschool years and beyond is the focus of chapters 7 and 8. We saw in chapter 4 that, from early in life, infants exhibit memory as measured in visual paired comparison and habituation paradigms (in which memory is inferred from greater attention to a novel stimulus after repeated exposure to a different stimulus) and in the mobile conjugate reinforcement paradigm (in which memory is inferred from more robust kicking after acquisition of a contingency between kicking and movement of a mobile). Indeed these behaviors are apparent long before the end of the first year of life, and thus well before the temporal-cortical network is thought to begin to reach functional maturity. If these mnemonic behaviors were considered to rely on the temporal-cortical declarative memory network, their developmentally early appearance would represent a poor fit with the neurodevelopmental course just outlined. However, as discussed in chapter 4, this is not the case because neither of these types of behavior is considered to depend on this network (C. A. Nelson, 1995, 1997).

For visual paired comparison and habituation tasks, there is evidence that adult preference for novelty is dependent on medial temporal structures: Adults with bilateral damage to medial temporal structures fail to exhibit novelty preferences if the delay between familiarization and test is longer than a few seconds (e.g., McKee & Squire, 1993). However, as discussed in chapter 4, in the young infant, an apparent preference for novel stimuli may be a reflexive (Bachevalier, Hagger, & Mishkin, 1991) or an obligatory (C. A. Nelson, 1995, 1997; Nelson & Collins, 1991, 1992) response to stimuli that are presented infrequently; it need not signal conscious recognition. A plausible alternative basis for novelty "preference" in infants is repetition suppression at the neural level (Snyder, 2001). As discussed in chapter 4, as stimuli are repeated, and thereby become familiar, the population of neurons that fire in response to them becomes smaller and more specialized. On presentation of a new stimulus, the firing rates of previously suppressed neurons increase (see Fig. 4.2). Behaviorally, this could result in longer looking to the new stimulus. Repetition suppression is observed even after many intervening stimuli and after a delay; the mechanism is implicated in priming, a form of nondeclarative memory (Desimone, 1996); it is observed in animals that are anesthetized or awake, but passively fixating (Miller et al., 1991). For present purposes, the important point is that longer looking to a novel stimulus (i.e., "preference" for novelty) need not imply the function of the temporal-cortical network that supports declarative memory.

In the case of retention of the conditional kicking response in the mobile conjugate reinforcement paradigm, it is thought that acquisition of this type of instrumental behavior is mediated by the cerebellum, although recognition of the mobile may be mediated by the hippocampus (C. A. Nelson,

1995, 1997). Does participation of the hippocampus implicate the entire temporal-cortical network? Once again, the answer is likely no. A plausible neural circuit—one that involves the cerebellum and hippocampus, but not the balance of the temporal-cortical network—would begin with reception by visual areas of information specifying the mobile itself, and by primary and then secondary somatosensory cortex of proprioceptive information associated with kicking, received from receptors in the muscles and joints. Information from visual areas is projected to entorhinal cortex; information from secondary somatosensory cortex is projected to insular cortex, which in turn projects to entorhinal cortex (insular cortex is another of the sources of approximately one third of the projections to entorhinal cortex; Eichenbaum & Cohen, 2001; Kandel et al., 2000). From entorhinal cortex, information may be passed to the hippocampus via the early developing "short route." Consistent with this suggestion, in classical conditioning paradigms, activity in the CA1 region of the hippocampus increases as learning occurs (e.g., Woodruff-Pak, Logan, & Thompson, 1990). Hippocampal outputs could then influence cerebellar function via subcortical projections from the subiculum through the fornix, the major fiber bundle connecting the hippocampus with subcortical structures (Eichenbaum & Cohen, 2001). Although this proposal is highly speculative, it is a plausible route by which a conditioned foot-kick response could be mediated by other than the temporal-cortical network that underlies mature declarative memory.

In addition to evidence of memory as measured in visual paired comparison and habituation paradigms and the mobile conjugate reinforcement paradigm, in chapter 4 I also reviewed evidence of recall over a delay of 24 hours by 6-month-old infants as measured by deferred imitation (Barr et al., 1996; Collie & Hayne, 1999). Although apparent months before we expect to see functionally significant output from the temporal-cortical declarative memory network (i.e., near the end of the first year of life), this observation nevertheless is consistent with the proposed neurodevelopmental time frame. First, although the behavior spans a delay that clearly implies long-term memory, the length of the delay does not necessarily implicate participation of the full temporal-cortical network. Over delays of seconds to hours, activation of information may be maintained by intermediate-term stores in the parahippocampal region. It is only the later phases of consolidation that are thought to involve the full network (McGaugh, 2000). Although there is not consensus on the temporal parameters, there have been suggestions that information might be retained in intermediate-term stores over a period of as many as 24 hours (Marr, 1971). Critical to the present point is that there are candidate mechanisms by which memory representations might be maintained by the hippocampal formation alone, without requiring the interactive participation of the cortical components of the full declarative memory network.

Second, whereas two thirds of the 6-month-old infants in Barr et al. (1996) recalled at least one of the actions of the three-step sequence they were shown (taking a mitten off a puppet's hand, shaking the mitten, and replacing it on the puppet), only one quarter of the infants (three infants) showed evidence of memory for the temporal order of the actions (no information on ordered recall was provided in Collie & Hayne, 1999). Relational processing of the sort required to encode temporally ordered sequences is carried out by the hippocampus in cooperation with cortical and parahippocampal structures (e.g., Eichenbaum & Cohen, 2001). A circuit that does not yet support effective and efficient communication between the cortex and the relational processing center of the hippocampus (via intermediate-term stores in the parahippocampal region) would be expected to produce precisely this pattern. Indeed the profile is reminiscent of the "dissociation" between recall of content and recall of temporal order reported by Fumihiko Yasuno and colleagues (1999) in an adult patient in whom the integrity of the temporal-cortical network that supports declarative memory was undermined by damage to the tissue connecting the frontal lobes and the hippocampus. In the case of the human 6-month-olds who took part in the research of Rachel Barr and her colleagues, I attribute the low level of ordered recall not to neural damage, but to insufficient functional maturity of the neural network implicated in support of ordered recall. Individual differences in the rate of development, or perhaps chance shaking of the mitten of the puppet, would account for ordered recall by the three infants who demonstrated it.

With increases in the effectiveness and efficiency of communication between parahippocampal structures and the hippocampus, and thus the hippocampus and neocortex, we would expect to see increases in the reliability and robustness of recall in general, and in temporally ordered recall in particular. As reviewed in chapter 4, this is precisely what is observed. Near the end of the first year of life, coincident with increases in synaptogenesis in prefrontal cortex and the dentate gyrus of the hippocampus (e.g., Huttenlocher & Dabholkar, 1997; Eckenhoff & Rakic, 1991, respectively), infants show great strides in temporally ordered recall over long delays. Substantial development continues throughout the second year of life, coincident with the rise to peak of synaptogenesis and continued morphological development of synapses in these same regions. In general terms, then, the fit between expectations for development based on consideration of the neurodevelopmental course and the behavioral data on memory is a good one. In the next section, I move beyond general terms by using our understanding of neurodevelopment to inform the question of "what develops?" in early memory development. In other words, how do changes in medial temporal and other cortical brain regions, and the connections between them, produce the behavioral changes that characterize this important period of development in declarative memory?

## SPECIFYING "WHAT DEVELOPS?" IN EARLY DECLARATIVE MEMORY

By the analysis just provided, neurological changes are a rate-limiting variable in the development of long-term declarative memory. As the neural substrate develops, we see behavioral changes. Yet precisely how do changes in the medial temporal and cortical structures, and their interconnections, relate to changes in behavior? In other words, how do they relate to changes in memory representations? To address this question, we must once again consider "how the brain builds a memory" (chap. 5) and, thus, how the "recipe" for a memory might be affected by changes in the underlying neural structures. The argument I develop is that, of the candidate phases in building and retrieving a memory trace—encoding, consolidation, storage, and retrieval—changes in consolidation and storage processes (which, of course, are intimately intertwined) are largely responsible for developments in declarative memory late in the first year and throughout the second year of life (Bauer, 2004). I review each step of the recipe to evaluate the viability of this proposal.

Throughout the discussion to follow, it is important to keep in mind an important caveat: In human infants and young children, assessments of the phases in building and retrieving a memory trace will always be indirect and, unfortunately, imprecise. In adult humans, encoding processes can be monitored via fMRI or PET, for example. In nonhuman animals, electrodes implanted in the skull allow for monitoring of neuronal activity as information is being processed. In human infants and young children, none of these methods is viable. In these populations, we must assess encoding by examining behavior soon after learning and by manipulating variables that we expect to influence encoding (e.g., the amount of exposure), and observing their effects. Nor can we directly observe consolidation processes. Instead they must be inferred from disruptions in memory performance. Finally, storage and retrieval processes are notoriously difficult to assess for two reasons: (a) it is not always possible to determine whether the to-be-remembered material was encoded to begin with, and (b) when recall fails it is not a straightforward matter to determine whether it was the result of failed storage or failed retrieval. These states of affairs limit the certainty with which we can draw conclusions. We cannot, however, let them stop us from addressing the questions!

## Encoding

Association cortices are involved in the initial registration and temporary maintenance of experience (e.g., Fuster, 1997; Markowitsch, 2000). Prefrontal cortex in particular undergoes considerable postnatal development (see Benes, 2001; Bourgeois, 2001, for reviews). Presumably, at least in part as a result of these neurodevelopmental changes, over the first year of life, the amount of time it takes infants to encode stimuli decreases, and the length of time over which infants are able to retain stimuli in working memory increases. For example, as discussed in chapter 4, research by Susan Rose and her colleagues demonstrated that the number of seconds required to encode a stimulus (as evidenced by the amount of familiarization required to produce a novelty preference) decreases between 3½ and 6½ months of age (e.g., Rose et al., 1982).

There are also developmental changes in the amount of time infants are able to hold a stimulus in working memory. Adele Diamond (1985) demonstrated that at 7½ months of age, infants can tolerate a delay of only 2 seconds between hiding of a stimulus and the opportunity to search for it. By 12 months of age, the same infants can tolerate a delay of 10 seconds or more and still locate the stimulus (an average increase of about 2 seconds per month in the longitudinal sample; see Fig. 6.4). Age-related differences in encoding do not end at 1 year of age. Mark Howe and Mary Courage (1997b) found that, in the second year of life, relative to 15-month-olds, 12-month-olds required more trials to learn multistep sequences to a criterion of two errorless reproductions (achievement of this criterion indicates that the material was fully encoded). In turn, 15-month-olds were slower to learn the to-be-remembered material relative to 18-month-olds. Indeed across development, older children learn more rapidly than younger children (Howe & Brainerd, 1989).

Do apparent development changes in the proficiency with which information is encoded account for age-related changes in long-term declarative memory? Although age-related variation in encoding processes no doubt

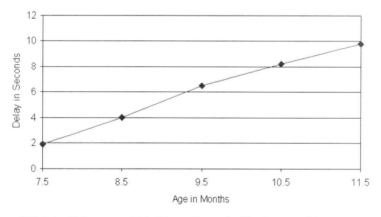

FIG. 6.4.   Delays over which 7½- to 12-month-old infants are able to maintain a stimulus in working memory, as measured by performance on the A not B task in a longitudinal sample. Based on Diamond (1985), Fig. 2; values are approximate.

plays a role in the explanation of age trends in long-term memory, there is clear evidence that encoding processes are not the *sole* source of age-related change: Even with the level of encoding controlled, older children remember more relative to younger children. For example, Howe and Courage (1997b) found that even after bringing children to a criterion of two correct reproductions of multistep sequences (thus ensuring encoding of the sequences), after a 3-month delay, 15-month-olds remembered more than 12-month-olds, and 18-month-olds remembered more than 15-month-olds.

Another source of data that changes in encoding processes alone do not explain developments in long-term recall is the "Monster" study conducted in my laboratory (introduced in chap. 4; Bauer et al., 2000). In this study, my colleagues and I examined recall by 13- to 20-month-old children over delay intervals ranging from 1 to 12 months. We found that, with levels of initial encoding of events (as measured by immediate recall) controlled statistically, the older children in the sample remembered more of the individual actions of events and more information about the temporal order of actions relative to the younger children. The results from the "Monster" study and from the study conducted by Howe and Courage (1997b) make clear that not all of the age-related differences in long-term recall can be attributed to developmental differences in encoding. What is more, data from the "Monster" study suggest that age-related differences may not even have an especially large role to play. That is, we found that only a small percentage of the developmental differences in long-term memory could be attributed to encoding: age-related differences in encoding allowed us to predict only 6% and 7% of the variability in long-term recall of the actions and temporal order of actions of the events after the delays, respectively (Bauer et al., 2000). Findings such as these suggest that we must look beyond encoding processes to explain developmental change in long-term declarative memory.

## Consolidation and Storage

Although separable phases in the life of a memory trace, I discuss consolidation and storage in tandem because, at the level of behavioral analysis available in the existing developmental data, these processes cannot be effectively separated (i.e., we cannot tell from behavior alone whether a memory trace is still being consolidated or has been successfully stored in neocortex). As reviewed in chapter 5, medial temporal structures are implicated in the processes by which new memories become "fixed" for long-term storage; cortical association areas are the presumed repositories for long-term memories (Eichenbaum & Cohen, 2001; Zola & Squire, 2000). In a fully mature, healthy adult, the changes in synaptic connectivity associated with consolidation of a memory trace continue for hours, weeks, and even months after experience of an event. As evidenced in the literature on retrograde amnesia (see chap. 5), memory traces are vulnerable throughout this period of time. For the developing organism, the road to a consolidated memory trace may be an even bumpier one relative to that traveled by the adult. Not only are some of the neural structures involved in the process themselves relatively undeveloped (i.e., the dentate gyrus and prefrontal cortex), but the connections between them are still being sculpted and thus are less than fully effective and efficient. As a result, even once children have successfully encoded an event, as evidenced by achievement of a criterion level of learning, for example, they remain vulnerable to forgetting. Younger children can be expected to be more vulnerable to forgetting relative to older children.

Empirical evaluation of the role of consolidation and storage processes in early declarative memory development is difficult. In the adult, the major sources of evidence of consolidation are the patterns of anterograde and retrograde amnesia associated with lesions to the medial temporal lobes. This is not a likely source of developmental data! Neither are there animal models of presumed developmental changes in consolidation processes. From my laboratory, there are two sources of data that are relevant to the discussion. First, my colleagues and I have collected imaging data in the form of event-related potentials (ERPs) that implicate consolidation and storage processes in the patterns of individual difference in memory after a 1-month delay by infants 9 months of age at the time of experience of multistep sequences (e.g., Bauer et al., 2001; Carver & Bauer, 1999). Second, there are behavioral indexes of age-related changes in consolidation and/or storage processes over the second year of life. I discuss each of these sources of data in turn.

*Electrophysiological Indexes of Memory Consolidation/Storage Processes.* In the first study of its kind, Leslie Carver, Charles Nelson, and I combined electrophysiological (event-related potential [ERP]) and behavioral (deferred imitation) measures to study long-term recognition and recall memory (respectively) in infants late in the first year of life (Carver, Bauer, & Nelson, 2000). We exposed 9-month-old infants to novel two-step sequences. To maximize the likelihood that the infants encoded the sequences, we provided them with three exposure sessions spaced 24 to 72 hours apart. One week after their last exposure session, using ERPs, we tested the infants' recognition memories for the props used to produce the sequences. As discussed in chapter 5, ERPs are recordings of electrical oscillations associated with excitatory and inhibitory postsynaptic potentials recorded by electrodes on the surface of the scalp. The recording apparatus is fetchingly modeled in Fig. 6.5. Because they are time locked to a particular stimulus, differences in the latency and amplitude of the electrical response to different classes of stimuli—familiar and novel, for example—can be interpreted as evidence of differential neural processing. To test recognition, we recorded infants' ERPs as they watched pictures of one of the sequences to which they had been exposed

FIG. 6.5.   A 9-month-old infant "modeling" a 32-channel electrode cap for recording of event-related potentials (ERPs). Photograph by Patricia J. Bauer.
Reprinted with permission.

and one new sequence. Finally, 1 month after the ERP session, we tested the
infants' long-term recall of the sequences (as described in chap. 4).

    After the 1-month delay, almost half (45%) of the 9-month-olds exhibited
ordered recall of the sequences, whereas the other half (55%) did not
(Carver & Bauer, 1999). As noted in chapter 4, this pattern has since been
replicated in two independent samples (Bauer, Wiebe, et al., 2003; Bauer et
al., 2001). Carver, Nelson, and I (Carver et al., 2000) made two groups of
the infants: those who exhibited ordered recall after the 1-month delay and
those who did not. Working backward, we then examined the ERP responses
of the infants in the two groups to the pictures of the familiar ("old") and
novel (new) stimuli presented after the 1-week delay. The infants who subsequently recalled the temporal order of the sequences exhibited recognition of
the stimuli after the 1-week delay: As reflected in the top portion of Fig. 6.6,
they responded differentially to the two classes of stimuli (old and new). In
contrast, the infants who did not go on to recall the sequences after the 1-
month delay did not show evidence of recognition of the stimuli after 1
week: Their ERP responses to the two classes of stimuli were indistinguishable (see the bottom portion of Fig. 6.6). Because all of the infants had been
exposed to the sequences three times, we were reasonably sure they had successfully encoded them (Bauer et al., 2001), and thus that the differences in

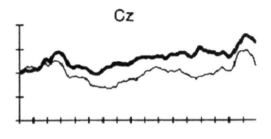

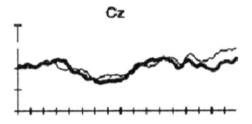

FIG. 6.6.    ERP responses from infants who did (top portion of figure) and did
not (bottom portion of figure) show evidence of temporally ordered recall after
a 1-month delay. Data from Carver, Bauer, and Nelson (2000).

recognition and subsequent recall memory were due to differences in retention (i.e., consolidation and/or storage). The conclusion is tentative, however, because no measure of encoding was available.

To more directly test the roles of encoding and consolidation/storage, my
colleagues and I conducted a second study in which, in addition to 1-week
delayed recognition and 1-month delayed recall (as in Carver et al., 2000),
we also assessed immediate recognition memory: If infants show evidence of
recognition immediately after exposure, we may assume that they encoded
the events (Bauer, Wiebe, et al., 2003). The design of the second study was
similar to that of the first, with the addition of the immediate ERP test; different old and new sequences were used as stimuli in the immediate and 1-
week delay recognition tests.

As reflected in Fig. 6.7, Panel A, at the immediate ERP test, regardless of
whether they subsequently recalled the events, the infants showed evidence
of recognition of the props used to produce the sequences: Their ERP responses were different to the old and new stimuli. This strongly implies that
the infants encoded the events prior to imposition of the delay. Nevertheless,
in a replication of the pattern observed in the first study (Carver et al.,
2000), 1 week later, at the delayed recognition test, the infants who would

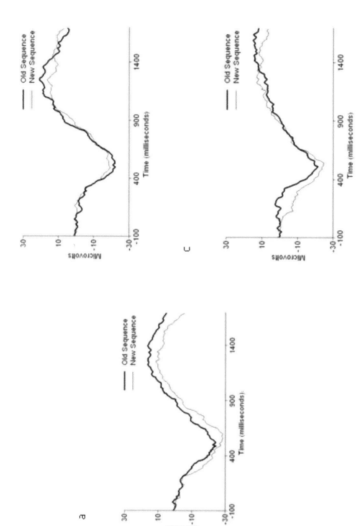

FIG. 6.7.   Panel A: ERP responses in an immediate recognition test. Panel B: ERP responses after a 1-week delay from infants who did not show evidence of ordered recall after 1 month. Panel C: ERP responses after a 1-week delay from infants who did show evidence of ordered recall after 1 month. From P. J. Bauer, S. A. Wiebe, L. J. Carver, J. M. Waters, and C. A. Nelson, "Developments in Long-Term Explicit Memory Late in the First Year of Life: Behavioral and Electrophysiological Indices," 2003, *Psychological Science, 14,* 629–635, Fig. 2. Copyright © 2003 by Blackwell Publishing Ltd. Reprinted with permission.

not go on to exhibit ordered recall failed to recognize the props, whereas infants who would go on to exhibit ordered recall did show evidence of recognition of them (see Fig. 6.7, Panels B and C, respectively). Moreover, the size
of the difference in delayed-recognition response to the old and new stimuli
(as measured by the size of the difference in latency to peak amplitude for old
and new stimuli) predicted children's recall performance 1 month later
(Bauer, Wiebe, et al., 2003). Thus, children who had stronger memory representations after a 1-week delay, as indexed by ERP, exhibited higher levels of
recall 1 month later, as indexed by deferred imitation. These data strongly
imply that, at 9 months of age, at the "dawning" of long-term declarative
memory, consolidation and/or storage processes are a source of individual
differences in mnemonic performance.

*Behavioral Indexes of Memory Consolidation/Storage Processes.*    The
work just described suggests that storage and/or consolidation processes are a
source of individual differences in 9-month-olds' long-term recognition and
recall. In the second year of life, there are behavioral suggestions of between-
age group differences in these processes over a shorter space of time, as well
as a replication of the finding among 9-month-olds that intermediate-term
consolidation and/or storage failure relates to recall over the long term. In
one experiment, my colleagues and I exposed children 16 and 20 months of
age to three-step sequences and tested for recall of them immediately and after a 24-hour delay. The immediate recall test served as a measure of encoding. As suggested by inspection of Fig. 6.8, over the delay, the younger chil-

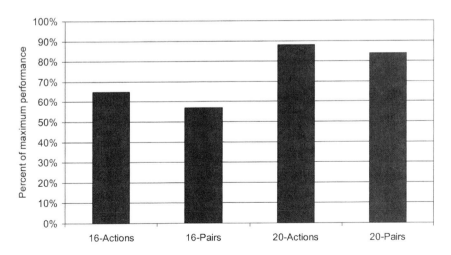

FIG. 6.8.   Percent of maximum possible performance of actions and pairs of
actions by 16- and 20-month-old children in a recall test administered after a
24-hour delay. Data from Bauer, Cheatham, Cary, and Van Abbema (2002).

dren forgot a substantial amount of what they had learned about the events: They produced only 65% of the target actions and only 57% of the ordered pairs of actions they had learned just 24 hours earlier. For the older children, the amount of forgetting over the 24-hour delay was not statistically reliable (Bauer, Cheatham, et al., 2002). Thus, whereas the younger children showed evidence of forgetting over the delay, the older children did not. It is not until 48 hours that children 20 months of age exhibit significant forgetting (Bauer et al., 1999). These observations suggest age-related differences in the vulnerability of memory traces during the initial period of consolidation.

In a different experiment also conducted by my colleagues Carol Cheatham, Mari Cary, Dana Van Abbema, and I, we tested whether the vulnerability of memory traces during the initial period of consolidation was related to the robustness of recall 1 month later. In this experiment, only 20-month-olds were tested. The children were exposed to three-step sequences and then tested for memory for some of the sequences immediately, some of the sequences after a 48-hour delay (a delay after which, based on Bauer et al., 1999, we expected to observe forgetting), and some of the sequences after a 1-month delay. Although the children exhibited high levels of initial encoding (as measured by immediate recall), they nevertheless exhibited significant forgetting after both 48 hours and 1 month. The robustness of memory 48 hours after exposure to the sequences was an important predictor of recall 1 month later. In contrast, individual differences in level of encoding (as measured by immediate recall) were not related to recall after 1 month (Bauer, Cheatham, et al., 2002). This effect is a conceptual replication of that observed with 9-month-olds in the study by Bauer, Wiebe, et al. (2003). In both cases, the amount of information lost to memory during the period of consolidation within days after exposure to the to-be-remembered events predicted how well the events would be remembered 1 month later.

The data just reviewed suggest that, even once children have successfully encoded an event, they remain vulnerable to forgetting. *Within age groups*, differences in vulnerability to intermediate-term forgetting (i.e., over the space of 48 hours and 1 week; Bauer, Cheatham, et al., 2002; Bauer, Wiebe, et al., 2003, respectively) are important predictors of long-term recall. *Between age groups*, younger children are more vulnerable to intermediate-term forgetting relative to older children. In the case of the data from the ERPs recorded from the 9-month-old infants, the source of intermediate-term forgetting can with relative confidence be attributed to consolidation and/or storage failure. First, ERPs obtained immediately after exposure to the events indicated that the sequences had been encoded. Second, the suggestion of consolidation and/or storage failure after 1 week was apparent on a measure of recognition—a task that makes low demands on retrieval processes, effectively eliminating them as a potential explanation for differences in later recall. The behavioral data are more ambiguous, however. It is possible that,

rather than to age-related differences in consolidation and/or storage processes, differences in performance by children 16 and 20 months of age should
be attributed to retrieval processes: After a delay, older children may appear
to remember more because the cues available to support recall are more effective for them relative to the younger children. I consider this issue in the
next section.

## Retrieval

Retrieval of memories from long-term storage sites is thought to depend on
prefrontal cortex (e.g., Markowitsch, 2000). As discussed earlier in this
chapter, prefrontal cortex undergoes a protracted period of postnatal development, making it a likely candidate source of age-related differences in
long-term recall. Indeed Connor Liston and Jerome Kagan (2002) implicated
changes in retrieval processes associated with developments in prefrontal
cortex as the explanation for their observation that children exposed to laboratory events at the ages of 17 and 24 months recalled them 4 months later,
whereas infants 9 months at the time of experience of the events did not.
    Although retrieval processes are a compelling candidate source of devel-
opmental differences in long-term recall, the available data are not on their
side. In fact there have been only two studies with children in the first years
of life that have yielded data that permit investigation of the relative contributions to long-term recall of consolidation and/or storage and retrieval
processes. In both cases, the results implicate consolidation and/or storage
rather than retrieval. A major reason for the relative lack of relevant empirical data was implied in the earlier discussion of consolidation and/or storage
processes: It is difficult to know whether a memory representation has lost its
integrity and become unavailable (consolidation/storage failure) or whether
the memory trace remains intact but has become inaccessible (retrieval failure; e.g., Tulving, 1983). Moreover, in many developmental studies, there is
an additional impediment to assessing the relative contributions of these
processes—in the form of uncontrolled differences in encoding. As discussed
in the section on encoding processes, older children learn more rapidly than
younger children. As a result, on the basis of a single experience or limited
number of experiences of an event, older children are likely to have encoded
the event more effectively. Determination of the relative contributions of
consolidation and/or storage and retrieval processes thus requires that encoding be controlled and memory be tested under conditions of high support
for retrieval. One study in which these conditions were met was Bauer,
Wiebe, et al. (2003). The results, which were described in the preceding section, clearly implicate consolidation and/or storage as opposed to retrieval.
    The other study that permits assessment of the relative contributions of
consolidation and/or storage processes and retrieval processes is the "Mon-

ster" study introduced in chapter 4 (Bauer et al., 2000). The study involved tests of recall of multistep sequences after delays of 1 to 12 months. Children 13 and 16 months at the time of enrollment in the study were tested on three-step sequences; children 16 and 20 months at the time of enrollment were tested on four-step sequences. In addition to providing data on children of multiple ages tested over several different delays, the study has three other features that make it an attractive source of data relevant to the question of interest. First, because immediate recall of half of the sequences was tested, measures of encoding are available.

Second, the children were given what amounted to multiple test trials, without intervening study trials, thereby providing multiple opportunities for retrieval. Specifically, children's recall was tested in a two-phase process. The children first were prompted by the props for the event, accompanied by a generic prompt: "What can you do with that stuff?" After approximately 30 seconds, the children then received an additional prompt in the form of a verbal reminder. For the sequence "make a gong," for example, children were told, "You can use that stuff to make a gong. Show me how you make a gong." The first phase can be considered the first test trial and the second phase a second test trial. As discussed by Mark Howe and his colleagues (e.g., Howe & Brainerd, 1989; Howe & O'Sullivan, 1997), the first test trial could be expected to initiate a retrieval attempt. If a memory trace remained and was at a reasonably high level of accessibility, the event would be re-called. In contrast, if a memory trace remained, but was relatively inaccessi-ble, the retrieval attempt would strengthen the trace and route to it, increas-ing accessibility on the second test trial. Conversely, lack of improvement in performance across test trials would imply that the trace is no longer avail-able and, thus, that storage failure had occurred. The fact that in the "Mon-ster" study the second test trial was further supported by additional retrieval cues in the form of verbal prompts makes it an especially strong test of whether a memory trace remained.

The third feature that makes the "Monster" study an attractive source of data is that immediately after the recall tests relearning was tested. That is, after the second test trial, the experimenter demonstrated each sequence once and allowed the children to imitate. Since the earliest days of labora-tory research on memory (i.e., Ebbinghaus, 1885), relearning has been used to distinguish between an intact but inaccessible memory trace and a trace that has disintegrated. Specifically, if the number of trials required to relearn a stimulus was smaller than the number required to learn it initially, savings in relearning were said to have occurred. Savings presumably accrue because the products of relearning are integrated with an existing (although not nec-essarily accessible) memory trace. Conversely, the absence of savings is at-tributed to storage failure: There is no residual trace on which to build. In developmental studies, age-related differences in relearning would suggest that the residual memory traces available to children of different ages are differentially intact.

To eliminate encoding processes as a potential source of developmental differences in long-term recall, in a re-analysis of the data from the "Monster" study (Bauer et al., 2000), I matched subsets of the children for levels of encoding (Bauer, 2005). That is, based on immediate recall performance, I created groups of 13- and 16-month-olds who exhibited identical levels of encoding and groups of 16- and 20-month-olds who exhibited identical levels of encoding. I then examined the amount of information the children forgot over the delays as measured by loss scores: the level of delayed recall minus the level of immediate recall (for each comparison, only the delay intervals over which both age groups exhibited recall were included in the analysis). As suggested by inspection of Fig. 6.9, for both age-group comparisons, although they were matched for levels of encoding, younger children exhibited more forgetting (i.e., had larger loss scores) relative to older children. The age effect was apparent on both test trials. Moreover, in both cases, for older children, levels of performance after the single relearning trial were as high as those at initial learning. In contrast, for younger children, performance after the relearning trial was lower than at initial learning (Bauer, 2005). Together the findings of age-related differential loss of information over time and of age effects in relearning strongly implicate storage processes, as opposed to retrieval processes, as the major source of age-related differences in delayed recall.

## Conclusion

I began this section with the question of how developments in the medial temporal and cortical structures, and their interconnections, relate to changes in behavior. Although throughout the period of transition from infancy to early childhood there are changes in encoding processes—and no doubt in retrieval processes as well—it seems that they are not the primary sources of age-related change in long-term recall memory at this time. Instead the available data implicate changes in the capacity to effectively consolidate and store memory representations as the primary source of development in early declarative memory.

The conclusion that changes in consolidation and/or storage processes are major contributors to age-related changes in long-term declarative memory not only is consistent with neurodevelopmental data, but also with predictions derived from the trace-integrity framework (Brainerd, Reyna, Howe, & Kingma, 1990) and the conceptually related fuzzy-trace theory (Brainerd & Reyna 1990). In these theoretical perspectives, the formation and loss of memories is characterized in the psychological terms of featural integration and disintegration. Integration of the different features that together make

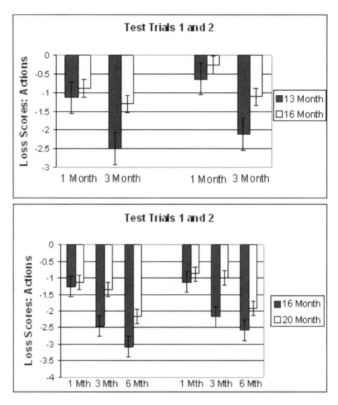

FIG. 6.9.  Mean loss scores (delayed recall minus immediate recall) for 13-
and 16-month-olds (filled and open bars, respectively) after 1- and 3-month
delays (top of figure) and for 16- and 20-month-olds (filled and open bars, respectively) after 1-, 3-, and 6-month delays (bottom of figure). Only those delay
intervals over which both age groups showed evidence of recall were included
in the analyses. From P. J. Bauer, "Developments in Declarative Memory: Decreasing Susceptibility to Storage Failure Over the Second Year of Life," 2005,
*Psychological Science, 16,* 41–47, Fig. 2. Copyright © 2005 by Blackwell Publishing Ltd. Reprinted with permission.

up an event produces a durable and distinctive mnemonic trace for it. The
process of integration begins, but does not end, with experience of the event;
it continues over time as the bonds that hold the elements of the trace together consolidate and stabilize. Memories remain strong as long as the
bonds are intact; they lose strength as the "glue" that holds the features together begins to dissolve. In this view, forgetting involves the loss of features
that lend to events their uniqueness and distinctiveness (in the parlance of
the conceptualization, *verbatim* features), leaving the "figure" of the event indistinguishable from the noise of the "background." The end result is a mem-

ory trace that cannot be retrieved. Thus, in this conceptualization, retrieval failure is a byproduct of storage failure.

Because the trace-integrity framework has its roots in cognitive science, rather than neuroscience, the neurological correlates of the implicated processes are in many cases not obvious. Nevertheless, the perspectives can be productively combined. In psychological terms, the work of the hippocampus is to bind together the features of an event that are distributed across the neocortex, converge on parahippocampal structures, and that together represent the event as a whole. In both psychological theory and neuroscience, the binding process takes time: Alterations in gene expression, protein synthesis, and growth of new synaptic connections that result in long-term memories are the neurological correlates of the "bonds" that in the trace-integrity framework consolidate and stabilize, and thereby come to hold the elements of the trace together. The verbatim features that in the trace-integrity framework make memories unique and distinctive may be viewed as the same features that impose particular burdens on prefrontal structures, such as temporal order information. The relational processing that binds the features of an event to one another takes place in a network involving components that are late to develop (i.e., dentate gyrus and prefrontal cortex). Indeed as discussed earlier, the structures and their connections continue to develop well beyond infancy. Consistent with functional consequences of continued development, Mark Howe and Julia O'Sullivan (1997) provided evidence that, although storage failure remains a significant source of forgetting throughout childhood, the rate at which information is lost from storage declines with age. Further discussion of this perspective, and of the possible neurodevelopmental correlates of observed age-related declines in storage failure rates across childhood, are provided in chapter 8.

## FURTHER IMPLICATIONS OF THE DEVELOPMENTAL SIGNIFICANCE OF CONSOLIDATION AND/OR STORAGE PROCESSES: DEVELOPMENT AT RISK

In discussing the neural bases of declarative memory in adults (chap. 5), much emphasis was placed on data from adults suffering from amnesia associated with lesion or disease in the medial temporal structures. Because human infants less frequently present with tumors, strokes, and closed head injuries, observations of the behavioral correlates of neural damage are not a major source of developmental data. One notable exception is the work by Faraneh Vargha-Khadem and her colleagues described in chapter 5 (Gadian et al., 2000; Vargha-Khadem et al., 1997). The researchers tested a small group of older children who in infancy or early childhood had experienced focal lesions to the hippocampus proper, resulting from temporary interruptions in the blood or oxygen supply to the brain. The children showed pronounced deficits in declarative memory.

In this section, I explore whether impairments in declarative memory are apparent in infancy and very early childhood as a result of a variety of insults that may be expected to affect medial temporal structures. By virtue of the fact that development of the neural substrate of long-term declarative memory is protracted, there is ample opportunity for it to be perturbed not only by lesions, but by other forces as well. Indeed scholars have proposed that the hippocampus, in particular, is open to postnatal environmental influence (e.g., Webb et al., 2001; Seress & Mrzljak, 1992). The hypothesized susceptibility of this neural structure, coupled with evidence that its major role—namely, consolidation and storage of memory traces—is a primary source of developmental change in the first years of life, suggests there may be developmental populations in whom consolidation and/or storage functions are compromised. In this section, I describe results from the study of children from three such populations: children born to mothers with diabetes, children born prior to term, and children from international orphanages. In each case, there is reason to suspect compromised medial temporal function. In each case, evidence of deficits in memory consolidation is apparent. By observing the development of declarative memory in populations for whom the construction process may be different from that typically observed, we gain insight into the factors that affect development more broadly.

## General Method

The data from each of the three target populations were collected in different studies. Nevertheless, across studies, my colleagues and I used common methods to evaluate declarative memory processes: In each study, using imitation-based techniques, the children were tested for immediate and 10-minute delayed recall of multistep sequences. Measures of immediate recall provide an opportunity to determine whether groups of children differ in encoding processes; measures of 10-minute delayed recall permit determination of whether groups of children differ in the formation of memory traces that would survive for long-term storage. Although 10 minutes may not seem a long time, my colleagues and I had three reasons to believe that performance after a 10-minute delay would be diagnostic of consolidation processes. First, adults suffering from medial temporal lobe amnesia exhibit deficits in performance on tasks such as diagram recall, in which they are required to reproduce a diagram from memory after a 5- to 10-minute delay (e.g., Reed & Squire, 1998). Second, as illustrated in Fig. 5.11, medial temporal lesions inflicted on nonhuman primates produce deficits in delayed nonmatching to sample performance after delays as brief as 10 minutes (e.g., Zola-Morgan et al., 1992). Third, in normally developing human children, recall after a 10-minute delay is correlated with recall after a 48-hour delay (Bauer et al., 1999). These observations suggest that performance after a 10-minute delay provides information as to the integrity of medial temporal function. In the case of work with children at risk, a brief delay is preferable because it permits all testing to take place in a single session. In addition, because the delay is so short, retrieval processes are relatively untaxed, thereby permitting evaluation of consolidation processes.

## Infants Born to Mothers With Diabetes

Maternal diabetes is relatively common: Approximately 3% to 10% of pregnancies are affected with abnormal glycemic (sugar) control, and 90% of those are diagnosed as gestational diabetes (Georgieff et al., 1990). Gestational diabetes occurs both when women who already have diabetes mellitus become pregnant and when otherwise healthy women develop blood sugar control problems during their pregnancies. Work with animal models has shown that infants of mothers with diabetes are exposed prenatally to chronic metabolic insults, including iron deficiency. It has been known for some time that deficiencies in iron are related to deficits in motor and cognitive function (see Georgieff & Rao, 2001, for a review). Whereas the motor impairments are reversible with iron replacement therapy, the cognitive impairments seem less amenable to treatment. As a result, even after iron levels have been restored, children who suffered iron deficiency prenatally may experience as much as a 10- to 12-point reduction in IQ as measured by tests such as the *Bayley Scales of Infant Development* (Lozoff, 1990).

As discussed by Michael Georgieff and Raghavendra Rao (2001), one possible reason for the persistent cognitive deficit associated with prenatal iron deficiency is that iron affects neurodevelopment. It is known that iron is essential for myelination (Larkin, Jarratt, & Rao, 1986). For reasons that are not clear at this time, the hippocampus is a region of the brain that is at particular risk for reductions in iron uptake (Erikson, Pinero, Connor, & Beard, 1997). This suggests that infants born to mothers with diabetes may be a population in whom medial temporal function is impaired.

As part of a larger, longitudinal study of the effects of prenatal iron deficiency, Charles Nelson and Michael Georgieff are following a group of infants born to mothers with diabetes. At 12 months of age, in collaboration with Tracy DeBoer and Sandi Wewerka, we tested the children for immediate and 10-minute delayed recall of two-step sequences (DeBoer, Wewerka, Bauer, Georgieff, & Nelson, in press). We tested the children again at 24 months of age, this time on four-step sequences (DeBoer, Wewerka, & Fong, 2003; the samples include many, although not all, of the same children). At both time points, we compared the children's performance to that of a group of children matched for age and gender; the children in the control group had not been prenatally iron deficient (verified by ferritin levels in umbilical cord blood). Depicted in Fig. 6.10 is the children's performance at 12 months of age (Panel A) and at 24 months of age (Panel B). At immediate testing, the performances of the children in the two groups did not differ at either age. That is, the number of actions of the sequences and the number of ordered pairs of actions that the children born to mothers with diabetes produced immediately after modeling did not differ from the numbers produced by the children who had not been born iron deficient.

Differences between the groups of children were apparent after the 10-minute delay. At 12 months of age, the children who had suffered prenatal iron deficiencies produced fewer pairs of actions in the target order relative

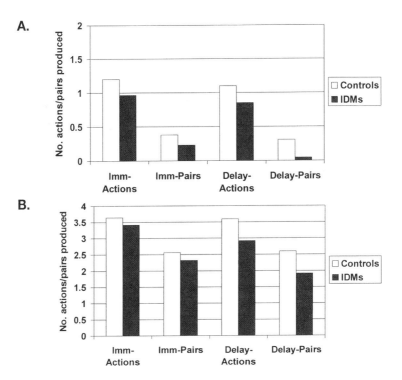

FIG. 6.10. Panel A: At 12 months of age, immediate recall and recall after a 10-minute delay of actions (maximum possible = 2.0) and ordered pairs of action (maximum possible = 1.0) by healthy, control children (open bars) and children born to mothers with gestational diabetes (infants of diabetic mothers: IDMs; filled bars). Panel B: At 24 months of age, immediate recall and recall after a 10-minute delay of actions (maximum possible = 4.0) and ordered pairs of action (maximum possible = 3.0) by healthy, control children (open bars) and children born to mothers with gestational diabetes (infants of diabetic mothers: IDMs; filled bars).

to the matched control children. The groups did not differ, however, in the number of actions of the sequences produced (DeBoer et al., in press). At 24 months of age, the children who had suffered prenatal iron deficiencies produced fewer actions as well as fewer ordered pairs of actions relative to the matched control children (DeBoer et al., 2003). Thus, both 1 year and 2 years from the time their iron stores were replenished, the children who had been prenatally deprived of iron showed signs of impaired declarative memory performance. Given that the children's encoding of the sequences was on par with that of the non-iron-deficient control children (as measured by immediate recall performance), the most likely source of the decrement over the 10-minute delay was compromised initial consolidation. Critically, the long-term impact of these early differences in declarative memory is not known: With additional development, children born with prenatal iron deficiency may "catch up" to their non-iron-deficient peers.

## Infants Born Prior to Term, but Otherwise at Low Risk

Most infants are born after 38 to 40 weeks of gestation. However, a number are born preterm (i.e., at less than or equal to 37 weeks gestation). There is an extensive literature documenting poor cognitive outcomes for preterm infants with medical risk factors (e.g., infants who had very low birth weight or experienced intraventricular hemorrhages). The patient, Jon, tested by Vargha-Khadem and her colleagues, is a case in point. Jon was born at 26 weeks gestation, weighing only 940 grams. He suffered breathing problems that required intubation (i.e., insertion of a tube into his lungs). Whereas normal breathing was established within an hour of his birth, at the age of 3 weeks, his condition deteriorated and he required intubation and ventilation for 1 week (Gadian et al., 2000). Jon suffers pronounced declarative memory impairments (see chap. 5 for discussion). Because prematurity strikes disproportionally among populations who receive poor prenatal care (although this apparently was not the case with Jon), preterm infants are often at social risk as well as medical risk (e.g., there is a high rate of preterm birth among young, single mothers of low socioeconomic status). Relatively less is known about the later developmental status of infants who survive prematurity sustaining no measurable neurological damage and with few to no social risk factors. These infants are of considerable theoretical interest because they provide a potential "experimental" model for investigating the relative importance of maturational and experiential factors in the development of cognitive abilities (e.g., Jiang, 1995; Matthews, Ellis, & Nelson, 1996; van Hof-van Duin, Heersema, Groenendaal, Baerts, & Fetter, 1992).

Mounting evidence that experience plays a crucial role in shaping normative brain development suggests that the atypical timing and nature of postnatal experience in preterm infants may have lasting consequences for subsequent brain and behavioral development. As an example, in the domain of visual perception, visual acuity and visual form perception are not affected in healthy preterms (Seigal, 1994; van Hof-van Duin et al., 1992), but visuospatial processing is compromised even into the school age (Foreman, Fielder, Minshell, Hurrion, & Sergienko, 1997). This differential sensitivity of different aspects of visual processing to the effects of prematurity is argued to be due to the differences in timing of development of the dorsal visual pathway (spatial or "where" pathway) and ventral visual pathway (object or "what" pathway) that render them differentially sensitive to postnatal experience. Similarly, later and more slowly developing memory systems may be most vulnerable to variations in postnatal experience.

To determine whether preterm birth, in the absence of known medical and social risk factors, is associated with deficits in declarative memory function, Michelle de Haan, Michael Georgieff, Charles Nelson, and I tested two populations of children born prior to term and compared their performance to a group of full-term children (de Haan, Bauer, Georgieff, & Nelson, 2000). As reflected in Table 6.1, the medical criteria for inclusion in the sample were stringent and effectively eliminated children at medical risk. In addition, all children were from two-parent households, all parents had at least a high school education, and average household incomes were in the range of $65,000 to $75,000 per year.

The sample was evenly divided into three groups: infants born at term (i.e., greater than 37 weeks gestation), infants born preterm but physiologically mature (i.e., 35–37 weeks gestation), and infants born preterm and physiologically immature (i.e., 27–34 weeks gestation). Although they are born early, physiologically mature infants are prepared for extrauterine life. For example, they are able to feed orally, they rarely have respiratory distress syndrome, and they can thermoregulate. In contrast, physiologically immature infants are not prepared for life outside the uterus. They have uncoordinated sucking and swallowing and so must be fed through a gastric tube, and they cannot thermoregulate, necessitating that they be kept in an incubator. All three groups of children were tested for immediate and 10-minute de-

TABLE 6.1
Medical Criteria for Inclusion in de Haan et al. (2000)

1. Appropriate size for gestational age
2. No pregnancy complications
3. Normal labor and delivery
4. Uncomplicated neonatal course (e.g., no seizures, hyperbilirubemia)
5. No Grade III or IV intraventricular hemorrhage (IVH)
6. Normal eye exam at 4 months corrected age
7. Ventilation for < 24 hrs

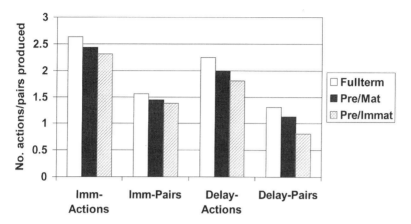

FIG. 6.11. Immediate recall and recall after a 10-minute delay of actions (maximum possible = 3.0) and pairs of actions (maximum possible = 2.0) by full term, control infants (open bars), infants born prior to term but physiologically mature (Pre/Mat; filled bars), and infants born prior to term and physiologically immature (Pre/Immat; hatched bars).

layed recall of three-step sequences. At the time of testing, the children had a mean age of 19 months (corrected for preterm birth, such that the actual postnatal ages of the three groups of children were 19.8, 20.5, and 21.8 months, for the full-term, preterm but physiologically mature, and preterm and physiologically immature, infants, respectively).

The pattern of performance was similar to that observed for the children born to mothers with diabetes, just described. Specifically, as reflected in Fig. 6.11, on the measure of immediate recall performance, the groups did not differ either in their levels of production of the individual actions of the sequences or in their levels of ordered recall. Thus, each of the groups of children showed the ability to encode the events. In contrast, children's abilities to maintain the event-related information over the 10-minute delay differed across groups. The children who had been born at term performed at higher levels relative to children born preterm and physiologically immature; infants born preterm but physiologically mature performed at an intermediate level.[1] This pattern was observed although, at the time of test, the children who had been born prior to term and physiologically immature were 2 months older than the children who had been born at term.

[1]The pattern of results reported in this chapter differs somewhat from that reported in de Haan et al. (2000). In the full report, the analyses were based on the children's performance on sequences that varied in their temporal relations (see chap. 7). For present purposes, to facilitate comparison across the other special populations, all of which were tested on only one sequence type—namely, sequences constrained by enabling relations—I included the data for only that sequence type.

The group difference in children's 10-minute delayed recall is unlikely to be the result of complicating medical or social factors typically found in samples of high-risk preterm infants. Instead it seems that preterm birth has a primary effect on development of declarative memory. By depriving infants of the "expected environment" for the last weeks of gestation, preterm birth may compromise the development of the declarative memory system. As argued in the context of discussion of the data from infants born to mothers with diabetes, given the absence of group differences in encoding of the sequences (as measured by immediate recall performance), the most likely source of the decrement over the 10-minute delay was compromised initial consolidation. As I noted in discussion of the performance of children with prenatal iron deficiency, we simply do not know whether, with additional development, early differences in performance will resolve.

## Infants Adopted From International Orphanages

There are a number of reasons to expect the possibility of compromised hippocampal development in children who spent their early months in an institutional environment. Perhaps chief among them is deprivation, both cognitive and social. Thankfully, at the end of the 20th century, conditions in most orphanages (almost all of which are in the developing world and Eastern Europe) are significantly better than those observed under the Ceaucescu regime in Romania (which fell in the early 1990s; see the 1998 report by Michael Rutter and the English and Romanian Adoptees study team, for a description), for example. Nevertheless, relative to the "expected" environment, institutions invariably fall short. Even when adequate nutrition and health care are available, children rarely are provided with levels of stimulation and support sufficient to ensure normative development. Ratios of children to staff are often high, the staff frequently turns over, and, due to concerns about transmission of disease, children are given few toys to manipulate and explore (see Gunnar, 2001, for discussion). These conditions virtually ensure that children receive suboptimal levels of social and cognitive interaction. As a consequence, institutionalized children frequently exhibit sensorimotor, cognitive, and language delays. The longer children remain institutionalized, the more pronounced the effects (see Gunnar, 2001, for a review).

Animal models of early deprivation provide some insight into one potential source of cognitive delay—namely, compromised hippocampal function. For example, primates deprived of normal rearing conditions exhibit elevated levels of glucocorticoids in response to stressors (e.g., Higley, Suomi, & Linnoila, 1992). High levels of glucocorticoids are not healthy for hippocampal neurons. In addition, there are suggestions that the licking and grooming that rodent mothers provide to their pups support the development of the hippocampus (Caldji et al., 1998). Removal of this source of stimulation results in levels of hippocampal cell death as much as 50% higher than normal (Zhang, Xing, Levine, Post, & Smith, 1997). The combination of these effects could be profound indeed: Infants deprived of socioemotional support and stimulation could be expected to mount exaggerated responses to stressors, leading to cell death in a hippocampus that already has fewer than the expected number of neurons. Coupled with a lack of cognitive stimulation, compromised hippocampal function seems likely.

To determine whether early deprivation is associated with deficits in declarative memory function, Maria Kroupina, Megan Gunnar, Dana Johnson, and I tested a group of children adopted into Minnesota (USA) from orphanages in China and Russia. The children were recruited through the International Adoption Clinic in Minneapolis, Minnesota (directed by Dr. Dana Johnson). The children were adopted between the ages of 4 and 18 months. On average, they were tested 8 months postadoption. Most of the children were around 20 months at the time of the test. The younger children were tested on two-step sequences, whereas the older children were tested on three-step sequences. The children's performance on immediate and 10-minute deferred imitation tasks was compared to that of a group of home-reared children matched to the orphanage-reared children on age and gender (although not on race and ethnicity: the home-reared children were all Whites raised in the upper midwest of the United States). The children were also administered the *Bayley Scales of Infant Development* as a measure of general intellectual development (Kroupina, Bauer, Gunnar, & Johnson, 2004).

In what should by now be a pattern familiar to the reader, on the test of immediate recall, the home-reared children and the children adopted from orphanages did not differ from one another (see Fig. 6.12; the data are presented in proportions because sequences of different lengths were used in the sample). Thus, the ability to encode the events was intact in the institutionally reared children. Whereas the 10-minute delay had no observable effect on the performance of the home-reared children (i.e., immediate and 10-minute delayed recall did not differ), for the children who spent their early months in institutional care, the 10-minute delay produced a decrement in performance. The resulting difference between the groups remained even after children's Bayley scores were taken into account. Thus, as many as 8 months after adoption out of an impoverished environment into what, by comparison, would be described as an "enriched" environment, children who spent their first months of life in institutional care exhibited decrements in delayed recall. Given that they exhibited adequate encoding of sequences in the immediate recall condition, the most likely source of the decrement was compromised initial consolidation. Again follow-up research is necessary to

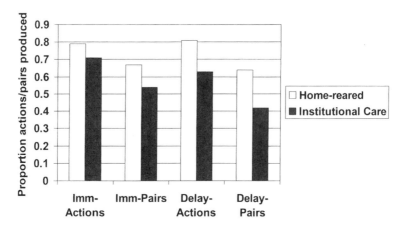

FIG. 6.12.   Immediate recall and recall after a 10-minute delay of actions and pairs of actions (expressed in proportions) by home-reared, control children (open bars) and children who spent their first months of life in institutional care (filled bars).

determine whether, over time, these apparent deficits in long-term declarative memory performance will resolve.

## Summary

The neural structures implicated in long-term declarative memory develop well into the postnatal period. As such there is ample opportunity for the structures that support declarative memory to be perturbed by postnatal as well as prenatal factors. Because of the role that the medial temporal structures play in consolidation of declarative memories for long-term storage, and because consolidation processes have proved to be a significant source of age-related differences in long-term memory in the first years of life, my colleagues and I explored three populations of children in whom we had reason to believe the medial temporal structures might have been compromised: infants born to mothers with diabetes, infants born prior to term, and infants adopted into homes in the United States after having spent their early months of life in institutional care. We found evidence of compromised 10-minute delayed recall performance in all three of the populations. In all three of the populations, we were able to eliminate encoding processes as a major source of differences in performance. The data from these populations provide further support for the suggestion that age-related developments in consolidation processes are a major contributor to increases in the reliability and robustness of long-term declarative memory in the first years of life. The changes are likely related to developments in the structures underlying declarative memory.

## CONCLUSIONS AND IMPLICATIONS

In this chapter, I traced the development of the neural structures implicated in long-term declarative memory. At both a general level (i.e., in terms of the timing of developmental changes) and a specific level (i.e., in terms of the functional changes one would expect given the structural changes), the neurodevelopmental and behavioral data are a good match for one another. Based on the analysis and the available data, there is excellent reason to believe that the capacity for long-term declarative memory is newly emergent near the end of the first year of life. At that time, it is fragile (i.e., dependent on multiple experiences) and not especially reliable (i.e., it is observed in only a subset of the population). Over the course of the second year of life, long-term recall memory becomes both reliable and robust. There are strong suggestions that the behavioral changes are due to improvements in consolidation and/or storage processes associated with developments in medial temporal and cortical structures, and the connections between them. Consistent with this suggestion is evidence of deficits in initial consolidation of memory representations in populations of young children with suspected compromised hippocampal development.

As discussed in the opening of this chapter, these data make clear that, in its strongest form, the hypothesis that among adults memories from the first years of life are absent because no memories were formed cannot be true. Infants and young children form declarative memories. By the middle to the end of the second year of life, they retain them over long delays. Although the data demonstrate that even very young children form declarative memories, they are rather silent regarding the specific type of declarative memory that is the main subject of this volume—autobiographical memory. Indeed none of the evidence reviewed thus far indicates that infants and very young children have the capacity to form autobiographical memories. That is, there is no evidence of personal involvement in events such as making a gong, there is no evidence that when the children reproduce the events they experience "autonoetic awareness" or a reliving of the earlier episode of the event, and there is no evidence that the memories they form in the first years of life live on beyond infancy. These elements are implicated in autobiographical memory. When do we see evidence of their emergence? As becomes apparent in chapter 7, these features of autobiographical memory are readily observed in preschoolers' recall of the experiences of their lives.

# III

# AUTOBIOGRAPHICAL MEMORY IN CHILDHOOD

# 7

## Event and Autobiographical Memory in the Preschool Years

*Interviewer:*  I also heard that you got to do something really, really fun. You went to Wisconsin to the Dells water park. Can you tell me about that?

*Child:*  Well there's this big bucket of water that rings a bell and then dumps all the water and a lot of kids come running. Even I did too and my sister and other kids. And there's, um, this tube you can go down with your mom—your mom or your dad—[or] by yourself. And me and my dad went on it and my mom and it like flips you over. . . . It just like um, like it tips you up one side and down and up and in.

*Interviewer:*  That sounds like a lot of fun. What else did you do there?

*Child:*  Well they had a slide . . . that shoots you down [and] there's these other slides that like once when I went on the slide on my tummy I—I hurt my knee. But another one that's littler I rode on that one on my tummy and my feet were first and it was fast.

*Interviewer:*  Wow. That does sound like fun. What else?

*Child:*  Umm, we um, slept in a hotel there. And me and my sister had to share a bed and some had bunk beds, but we didn't get a bunk bed.

*Interviewer:*  Oh that's too bad. Maybe next time.

When you read the words of the 4½-year-old girl that open this chapter, it is hard to imagine that until the 1980s a widely accepted explanation for the absence of memories among adults for the first years of life was that, during that time, accessible or declarative memories simply were not formed. It was further thought that even once a rudimentary capacity to remember past events developed in late infancy and very early childhood, children's memories were fragile, unorganized, and, as a result, destined to be short-lived. This 4½-year-old's recollection of her trip to a water park—recounted to an

interviewer in my laboratory—casts significant doubt on both of these assumptions. Her account of the unique experience is detailed and organized
so as to convey to the listener the range of activities in which she participated, and even her mild disappointment at being denied the opportunity to
sleep in a bunk bed.

The data reviewed in chapter 4 made clear that the absence of memories
from the first years of life cannot be attributed to very young children's inability to form them. As measured nonverbally (using imitation-based techniques), the capacity to remember the past emerges in the first year and, by
the end of the second year, is both reliable and robust. Moreover, mention
has already been made of somewhat older children's ability to report on everyday "goings on," such as going to preschool and making cookies. Yet in
neither of these literatures do the demonstrations or reports bear the marks
of autobiographical or personal memories. That is, as far as we know, they
are not rich in perceptual detail about the context in which the event occurred, nor are they laden with affect, either positive or negative. Importantly, neither are they recollections of events and experiences that were especially personally significant for the child. Making a gong is fun, true, but
we may hope that it is not a "high point" of a child's life! Similarly, knowing
what happens when you make cookies is not the same as remembering a specific episode of cookie baking that happened at a particular place, at a particular time. What this means is that, although we now know that infants and
young children can remember, thus far the data I have used to document
their mnemonic abilities have told us little about the development of autobiographical or personal memory in particular. For that we must look to children's reports of the unique times of their lives.

Given the long-standing interest in the phenomenon of childhood amnesia, it is ironic that for almost a century theories as to the source of the amnesia were advanced without reference to data from children! That is,
throughout most of the history of research on adults' recollections of childhood (scientific study of which was begun by C. Miles in 1893; see chap. 3),
nobody bothered to actually ask children such as our 4½-year-old narrator
whether they remember the past. Thus, a critical ingredient in evaluation of
candidate explanations for childhood amnesia was missing. This situation
now has been remedied. In this chapter, I review the literature on children's
memories for events that occurred during the period for which adults have
fewer memories than would be expected based on adult rates of forgetting
alone (i.e., ages 3–7 years). As is seen, it is during this time that children begin to share autobiographical memories: Our narrator's account of her trip to
a water park is a case in point. Before going there, we need to step back a
moment, further into the childhood of the scientific study of memory in children, to see how we got from incompetence, to baking cookies, to the earliest
autobiographical memories.

## EARLY RESEARCH ON MEMORY
## IN THE PRESCHOOL YEARS

### The Scientific Study of Memory in Childhood

The scientific study of memory in children had a delayed onset relative to that in adults. Moreover, in adults, research on autobiographical memory (Galton, 1880) and controlled studies of episodic memory (Calkins, 1894; Ebbinghaus, 1885) proceeded in parallel (at least in the beginning). In contrast, in children, research on autobiographical memory was late to begin relative to that on episodic and semantic memory. Indeed research on children's recall of personal experiences was virtually nonexistent until the 1980s. Both of these situations were signs of the times. As described by Willard Hartup, Ann Johnson, and Richard Weinberg (2001), the early history of the study of child development focused primarily on motor and physical development and on children's affective development. In the United States, much of the research took place in what were known as "Institutes of Child Welfare," one of which was at the University of Minnesota. Pioneers such as Richard Scammon and Edith Boyd studied changes in height and weight in the fetus through adolescence (e.g., Scammon & Boyd, 1932). Florence Goodenough spent hours observing young children's affective states and eventually concluded that expressions of anger peaked in the second year of life and waned thereafter (i.e., the "terrible twos"). With the exception of Josephine Foster (1928), who conducted one of the earliest studies of memory for prose material by preschool-age children, relatively less attention was focused on specific cognitive developments such as memory. Instead much of the early work on cognition concerned the development of general intellectual ability (e.g., Goodenough's study of developmental differences in performance on the *Draw-a-Man* test, published in 1926), as well as reasoning and problem-solving skills (e.g., Heidbreder, 1928).

In the late 1950s and early 1960s, the world of cognitive developmental psychology changed dramatically. The impetus for change was the translation of Jean Piaget's writings from French into English and their broad dissemination to educators and researchers. Research into cognitive development in general took on new life. Although it was not a primary focus, research on memory development became common. The perspective that guided the research was that memory changed as a function of changes in Piagetian operational structures (Inhelder & Piaget, 1958). With regard to memories of events, the important point is that there was an expectation that memories would be poorly organized. The basis for this expectation was the suggestion that, until roughly 5 to 7 years of age, children were not able to create ordered series of elements. A classic problem with which they were presented was seriation. Given a set of sticks of different heights, such as depicted in Fig. 7.1 (Panel A) and the instruction to put them in serial order, adults and older children created ordered arrangements from the shortest to the longest or vice versa (Panel B). In contrast, children in the so-called *preoperational period* (i.e., ages 3–7) made arrangements that were unorganized. At best they might order the sticks on one end, but ignore the other end (Panel C); at worst they made pictures with the sticks (Panel D), seemingly oblivious to the task they were assigned.

Critically, the problem children seemed to have with sticks extended to other cognitive content as well. Consider this pair of premises: "Mary is shorter than George. George is shorter than Susan." To an older child or adult, the answer to the question "Who is shorter, Mary or Susan?" is obvious: Mary. However, to the preoperational child, there was nothing obvious at all. They insisted that without seeing Mary and Susan they could not possibly answer the question! For the purpose of this volume, the most important corollary was that neither could children order a sequence of events. Piaget (1926, 1969) reported that, in retelling fairy tales, children as old as 7 years of age made errors in temporal sequencing. He attributed their failure to reconstruct the temporal order of the tales to the lack of reversible thought. The expectation was that, during the preschool years, children developed *operational* structures that support organization along spatial and

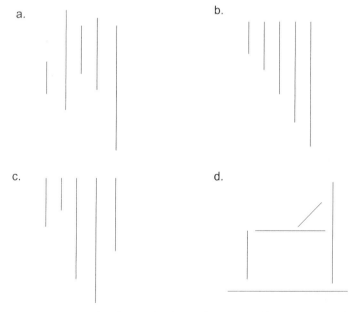

FIG. 7.1.   Series of sticks unordered (Panel A), ordered by an adult or older child (Panel B), ordered by a child attending to only one end (Panel C), and no order, but a "picture" instead (Panel D).

temporal dimensions. As they do so, they develop the capacity to tell a story from beginning, to middle, to end.

With the rise of influence of information-processing theories in the 1960s and 1970s, the focus of research in memory changed. Rather than on improvements in memory over time as a function of changes in operational structures, attention was paid to developmental improvements in memory as a result of hypothesized changes in the efficiency of encoding, storage, and retrieval processes that permit access to memories of events from the past. Throughout this period, focus was not on autobiographical memory, however, but rather on episodic and semantic memory. The reason was simple: In all of psychology, researchers studied things that could be controlled, and personal memories could not be controlled. Thus, in adult cognitive psychology laboratories, participants in research studied lists of words and were asked to recall them later. The major interest was in how properties of the to-be-remembered materials, study conditions, activities during the retention interval, and so forth influenced memory. To evaluate the determinants of memory, researchers needed to have control over the materials and the behavior of the participants during the retention interval. Such control was not possible in the domain of autobiographical memory, where the researcher could not even be certain of what actually happened in the event, much less what the participant had done with the material during the retention interval!

Just as in the adult literature, in which the focus was on memory for material over which the experimenter had virtually complete control, so it was in the literature on memory development. A prototypical memory experiment from the 1960s and 1970s was to give children of different ages lists of words or pictures to study and remember. For example, in a classic study, John Flavell and his colleagues gave picture lists to children 5, 7, and 10 years of age. They found that the youngest children did little to help themselves remember (i.e., they did not employ memory strategies) and in fact remembered few pictures, whereas the oldest children verbally rehearsed the materials and, presumably as a consequence, remembered more (Flavell, Beach, Chinsky, 1966; see Schneider & Bjorklund, 1998, for a review). This general pattern was so robust that it became the "recipe" for a successful experiment: include preschool-age and older children, thereby virtually assuring yourself of a nice picture of developmental change that could be reported in the literature. The trend was apparent in studies of memory for stories as well as pictures. Whereas it seemed that 3-year-olds could not remember stories in the right order if their lives depended on it, by age 7 children were competent storytellers. Although nobody talked about autobiographical memory at the time, the pattern of results was quite compatible with the findings of childhood amnesia: It seemed that preschool-age children simply lacked the skills to remember the past.

## Initiating Research on Children's Memories
## of Personally Relevant Material

Several "events" happened in the late 1970s and early 1980s that changed
the direction of research on children's memory and, eventually, contributed
to the study of autobiographical memory in children. Although not chrono-
logically first, the first contribution to the "movement" actually happened in
the adult literature, but its effects were felt in the developmental community
as well. In 1982, one of the fathers of cognitive psychology, Ulric Neisser,
published a brief essay entitled, *Memory: What Are The Important Questions?*
In it he bemoaned that, "If X is an interesting or socially significant aspect of
memory, then psychologists have hardly ever studied X" (Neisser, 1982, p.
4). In the essay, he called for a more ecological approach in psychology—one
that would recognize the organism *and its natural environment* as a valid unit
of study. He argued that the most challenging questions for memory researchers are not how structured sets of materials are learned and remembered in the laboratory, but how real people apply their own past experiences
to interpret the present and anticipate the future. After all, this is the stuff
that constitutes cognition. Neisser's 1982 observations had an impact. Within the space of a few years, researchers interested in "everyday memory," of
which autobiographical memory certainly was one sort, came out of the
woodwork, and the area has been bathed in light since then (see Pillemer,
1998, for a discussion of the increasing legitimacy of autobiographical memory research during the 1980s).

   Ulric Neisser's (1982) words fell on receptive ears in the developmental
community. Beginning in the mid-1970s, rumblings and dissatisfactions with
Piagetian theory were being heard across the land. A major reason was empirical: In many instances, researchers tested for competencies that Piaget indicated should be late to develop and found that, when the question was
asked in the "right" way, they were early to develop (see Gelman & Baillargeon, 1983, for a review). Jean Mandler and her colleagues (e.g., Mandler &
DeForest, 1979; Mandler & Johnson, 1977), had already found that the
"right" way to test whether children could remember stories was to present
them with "good" as opposed to "bad" ones. She noted that the stories Piaget
had used were typically poorly organized: They did not conform to the canonical structure of a beginning, logically unfolding middle, and clear end.
No wonder children's recall was all jumbled up—so were the stories they
were asked to remember! When children were presented with well-formed
stories, their recall was qualitatively (if not quantitatively) similar to that of
adults.

   Another "right" way to test children's mnemonic competence was to ask
them to remember material from a familiar, as opposed to an unfamiliar, domain. One of the most compelling illustrations of the difference familiarity

can make was Michelene Chi's (1978) demonstration of the radically different perspectives one gets on children's mnemonic competence when one tested in a familiar versus an unfamiliar domain. Chi conducted two tests of the memory abilities of children and adults. In one test, the participants were required to remember chess positions; in the other, they were required to remember random strings of digits. What made the study unique was that the children in the study (who had an average age of 10½ years) were more knowledgeable about chess relative to the adults. Chi's results are summarized in Fig. 7.2. She found that, in the domain of strings of digits, as was expected the adults outperformed the children. However, in the domain of chess, the children outperformed the adults. Based on these and similar results from other studies, Chi concluded that knowledge of a domain was an important determinant of memory performance.

Lessons on the importance of the structure of materials and familiarity with them were combined in another influential research program. First at Yale University and then at the City University of New York, Katherine Nelson and her colleagues began testing preschoolers' mnemonic competence in well-structured domains with which the children were highly familiar. Rather than asking about standard laboratory lists of furniture, clothing items, and vegetables (the stuff of which memory research in the 1960s and early 1970s was made), they asked, "What happens when you make cookies?" and "What happens when you go to McDonald's?" (K. Nelson, 1978; K. Nelson & Gruendel, 1981). Like Mandler and Chi, Nelson and her colleagues found unsuspected competence in these domains. Not only could the children remember the components of the events (putting unbaked cookies in the oven, ordering food, eating food, etc.), but they reported the components in the

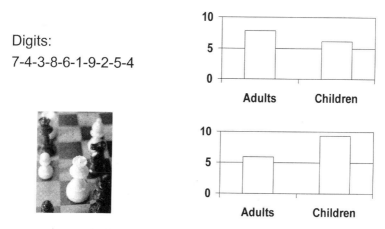

FIG. 7.2. Levels of memory performance for strings of digits and for chess positions by adults and by children with expertise in chess. Based on Chi (1978).

temporal order in which they occur. Moreover, in their reports, the children captured the most important aspects of the events (that you get to eat the cookies when they are finished baking!), thereby demonstrating that their perspective on them was more adultlike than expected.

Although none of these events focused attention on children's autobiographical memories per se, they were instrumental in initiating inquiry into the domain. Neisser's (1982) call to study "things that matter" brought legitimacy to research on personal memories in the adult cognitive literature. At the same time, discoveries of mnemonic competence (as opposed to incompetence) in very young children raised the possibility that, in addition to stories, chess pieces, and what you do at fast-food restaurants, children might remember some of the unique, personally meaningful events of their lives. In crucial ways then, although these developments were not about autobiographical memory, they were instrumental in getting the study of autobiographical memory in childhood off the ground.

## WHAT DO CHILDREN REMEMBER ABOUT CHILDHOOD EVENTS?

Today, we recognize the question of what children remember about childhood events as critical to evaluation of theories of the source of childhood amnesia. However, as just discussed, as recently as 1980, researchers who asked children what they remember (and expected a coherent answer!) were true pioneers. After reviewing some of the early evidence of preschoolers' competence in recalling previously experienced events, I discuss some of the more recent data indicating that preschoolers remember the unique experiences of their lives.

### Initiating the Study of Preschoolers' Mnemonic Competence

An early collection of research on children's memories for "things that matter" was published in 1980 under the simple title *Children's Memory* (Perlmutter, 1980). In her own contribution to the edited volume, Marion Perlmutter and her collaborator Christine Todd (Todd & Perlmutter, 1980) described the results of a naturalistic study of preschoolers' memories. They visited the homes of children ages 3 to 4 and, in the context of relatively unstructured play with the children, posed memory questions such as, "Have you ever been to the zoo?" and "What did you do at school today?" (p. 73). They found that even the youngest children, some of whom had relatively limited language abilities, nevertheless were able to respond to these requests for reports on past events. In some cases, the reports were relatively sparse and nonspecific such as, "Sometimes I go to the bakery" (p. 74). In other cases, however, the children responded with detailed accounts of specific experiences. For example, one 3-year-old told her "playmate" about a movie she had seen 2 weeks prior to the session: "And I saw movie too. It was Sleeping Beauty. And there was a icky witch . . . I was so tired I had even been sleeped in Mom's lap" (p. 74). In this example, the child used the correct verb tense (". . . I *saw* movie . . .") and provided many of the familiar narrative elements of *who, what, where, when, why,* and *how*.

Whereas Todd and Perlmutter (1980) found many instances of memory for events that the children experienced in the past, they nevertheless reported some apparent limitations on young children's memories for naturally occurring events. First, the 3- and 4-year-olds provided about the same number of "memory units" per event discussed (a "memory unit" is a unique piece of information about an event, such as what happened, to whom, or when; the average numbers of memory units for 3- and 4-year-olds were 10.4 and 11.0, respectively). However, the interviewer had to work harder to elicit the information from the younger children. That is, the younger children responded to the interviewer's questions with fewer unique pieces of information relative to the older children (the average numbers of memory units were 7.6 and 9.6, respectively). Thus, the younger the child, the more questions the interviewer had to pose to get the same amount of information. Second, the children tended to require relatively specific questions to provide memory reports. For example, when the interviewer simply asked, "What did you do today?", the children rarely responded with an informative report. Specific questions such as, "What did you put on your Christmas tree?", were more successful at eliciting detailed reports of specific events. Third, even with relatively specific prompts and probes, most of the memories that the children provided were from the recent past. That is, almost half of the events that the children recalled had occurred in the past month. In contrast, only a few (3%) of the events had occurred more than 12 months in the past. It is noteworthy that, although few of the events recalled were from the distant past, those that were recalled after such a long delay were as accurate as those from the more recent past as judged by the children's mothers.

As already noted, other pioneers in the study of young children's memories for naturally occurring events were Katherine Nelson and her colleagues. Their studies of young children's recall of routine events demonstrated not only that children remembered past experiences, but that, like adults, their representations of the past were coherent, organized knowledge structures that children use to keep track of the past and also to anticipate what will happen in the future. Nelson's early work was influenced by Roger Schank and Robert Abelson's (1977) script model. Schank and Abelson posited cognitive structures termed *scripts* that guide adults' actions in familiar situations. For example, most adults have a script for what happens at a fast-food restaurant. When we enter a restaurant and find a counter, behind which is mounted a menu board, we know that we should approach the counter to order. We can also anticipate that we will be asked to pay for our order before we receive it and that, at the end of the meal, we should bus our own tables. We "know" that we should behave in this way even if we have never visited the particular restaurant location before, and even if we have never frequented that particular restaurant chain before. We know not only the elements of the event, but the order in which the actions should be carried out. Scripts also tell us what *not* to expect: It is our fast-food restaurant script that would cause us to be surprised if, on driving up to a fast-food restaurant, a tuxedo-clad valet offered to park our car.

In the mid-1970s, Katherine Nelson and her colleague Janice Gruendel set out to determine whether young children also seem to be guided by scripts for what to do (K. Nelson & Gruendel, 1981, 1986). As Nelson described it in a 1997 chapter:

> Our research design was simple: We asked 3- and 4-year-old children to tell us what happened when they engaged in some everyday routines. Following Abelson and Schank's lead that adults have prototypical restaurant scripts, one of our first script questions was 'what happens when you go to MacDonald's.' . . . Even the 3-year-olds turned out to be extraordinarily good at this, and produced the first systematic evidence that 3- and 4-year-olds could reliably order an extended sequence of actions according to its temporal and causal relations. (p. 3)

On average, the children mentioned 11 different acts in the McDonald's "event," and they agreed on 82% of them. K. Nelson and Gruendel (1986) interpreted the fact that all of the children mentioned the act of eating as evidence that they appreciated the central goal of the event. In addition, the children's temporal ordering of the 11 acts was virtually flawless (with only the act of paying commonly being mentioned out of order). Moreover, Nelson and her colleagues found that children did not require multiple experiences of events to show evidence of having formed a scriptlike representation. For example, Robyn Fivush (1984) interviewed kindergarten children after only a single day of school. Although the children had experienced the school-day routine just once, they nevertheless appeared to have general representations of it, as suggested by this response from one of the participants to the question, "What happens when you go to school?":

> Play. Say hello to the teacher and then you do reading or something. You can do anything you want to . . . clean up and then you play some more and then clean up and then play some more and then clean up. And then you go to the gym or playground. And then you go home. Have your lunch and go home.

TABLE 7.1
Percentage of Use of Present and Past Tense in Response to General
Questions ("what happens") and Specific Questions ("what happened")

| | Question Type | |
|---|---|---|
| Tense Use | General | Specific |
| Present | 86% | 26% |
| Past | 14% | 74% |

Note.   Based on K. Nelson and Gruendel (1986), Table 2.7.


You go out the school and you ride on the bus or train and go home. . . .
(Fivush & Slackman, 1986, p. 78)


Although young children seem to form generalized memories of the
events of their lives, K. Nelson and Gruendel (1986) demonstrated that they
also distinguish between *what happens* (in general) and *what happened* (in particular). They interviewed 3- and 5-year-old children about "What *happens*
when you have snack at camp?" and "What *happened* when you had snack at
camp yesterday?" (The children were attending a summer day camp at the
time.) As illustrated in Table 7.1, the children clearly differentiated between
the general question and the specific question. When asked the general
question, they responded in the timeless present tense (e.g., "We *have* cookies"); when asked the specific question, they responded in the past tense
(e.g., "We *had* grape juice"). Whereas at least under some circumstances,
children can separate a specific instance from general experience, as discussed by Robyn Fivush (1997), Judith Hudson (1986), and Katherine Nelson and Robyn Fivush (2000), "blurring" of repeated episodes of a similar
kind is also apparent and may figure prominently in forgetting of specific past
events. This possibility is discussed more in a later section.

## Preschoolers' Recall of Specific Past Events

Reports of mnemonic competence such as those provided by Todd and
Perlmutter (1980) and K. Nelson and Gruendel (1981) stimulated further research on children's recall of events. Whereas some of the research continued the focus on memory for routine or repeated events (e.g., Farrar &
Goodman, 1990; Hudson, 1990a; see also Fivush, 1997; Hudson, Fivush, &
Kuebli, 1992, for reviews), other studies focused on children's recall of
unique episodes. Because recall of unique episodes relates most directly to
the issue of development of autobiographical memory, I focus on that research in particular.

An early and influential study of young children's recall of specific past events was conducted by Robyn Fivush and her colleagues (Fivush, Gray, & Fromhoff, 1987). In the study, 2½- to 3-year-old children were interviewed about events that had occurred within the past 3 months and about events that had occurred more than 3 months ago. A striking finding of the study was that all 10 of the children in the sample were able to recall specific events from the past. Moreover, all of the children recalled at least one event that had happened 6 or more months in the past. The passage of time did not ravage these young children's event memories: The children reported the same amount of information about events that had taken place more than 3 months ago (an average of 12.30 memory units) as they did about events that had taken place within 3 months (an average of 12.89 memory units). Thus, this study convincingly demonstrated that children quite young at the time of experience of specific, unique events remember them over long periods of time.

Additional evidence of young children's mnemonic prowess comes from a study by Nina Hamond and Robyn Fivush (1991). The design of the study is illustrated in Table 7.2, Panel A. The researchers examined children's recall of an event that they had experienced at the age of 36 months or 48 months; they interviewed the children either 6 months later or 18 months later. The design permitted the researchers to examine children's long-term recall as a function of the children's age at the time of the experience and as a function of the amount of time that had elapsed since the experience. Another attractive feature of the study is that all of the children experienced the same event—a trip to DisneyWorld.

The researchers began the interviews with general, open-ended questions such as, "Can you tell me about DisneyWorld?" As the children appeared to

TABLE 7.2
Study Design (Panel A) and Representative Findings
(Panel B) From Hamond and Fivush (1991)

| Age at Event | Retention Interval | | Across Intervals |
|---|---|---|---|
| | 6 months | 18 months | |
| Panel A | Age at Interview | | |
| 36 months | 42 months | 54 months | |
| 48 months | 54 months | 66 months | |
| Panel B | Amount Remembered (in Information Units) | | |
| 36 months | 33 | 42 | 37.5 |
| 48 months | 49 | 44 | 46.5 |
| Across ages | 41 | 43 | |

*Note.* Panel B is based on Hamond and Fivush (1991), Table 1.

run out of things to say, the interviewer asked a series of specific questions such as, "Who went with you?", "What did you see at DisneyWorld?", and "Did you buy anything at DisneyWorld?" There were a number of surprises in the data. First, as can be seen in Table 7.2, Panel B, the length of time that had elapsed since the trip to DisneyWorld was not significantly related to the amount of information that the children remembered about the event. That is, whether the children had experienced the event 6 months previously or 18 months previously, the amount recalled did not differ. Second, there was not a statistically reliable difference in the number of units of information provided by the older and younger children: The amount of information reported by children who were only 36 months of age when they visited DisneyWorld was not different from the amount reported by children who were a full year older. The age groups did differ, however, in how *elaborate* their reports were. The younger children tended to earn their "memory points" by providing the minimum required response to a question, whereas the older children tended to elaborate their responses a bit more. For example, when asked, "What did you see at DisneyWorld?", younger children tended to reply "Dumbos," whereas older children tended to reply "big Dumbos." Although it is possible that some of the impressive amount of information recalled by these young children was derived from general knowledge of DisneyWorld, the children could not have relied on general knowledge to answer questions such as, "Who went with you?", "Where did you stay?", "What did you like/dislike about it?", and "Did anything bad happen at DisneyWorld?"

The results of studies such as those conducted by Fivush et al. (1987) and Hamond and Fivush (1991) indicate that, even over long delays, the memories of 2- to 4-year-old children remain relatively robust. Other studies have also found retention of events over long delays (e.g., Hudson & Nelson, 1986). For example, Judith Hudson and Robyn Fivush (1991) reported the results of a study of long-term recall by children 5 years of age at the time of experience of a distinctive field trip to an archaeology museum. During the visit, the children heard a brief history of the museum and were provided information about what archaeologists do and how they conduct their work, after which the children were permitted to dig for "artifacts" in a large sandbox. They then made clay models of the artifacts they found. Throughout the trip, one of the investigators took pictures of the activities, thereby creating a record of the event.

The children were interviewed about their museum experience four times: the same day (immediate recall), 6 weeks later, 1 year later, and 6 years later (when the children were 11 years of age). Over time the children tended to recall fewer of the features of the experience (nine features recalled immediately vs. only three recalled 6 years later). However, for the features that were remembered, the children provided the same number of elaborations on the feature across the delay intervals. Thus, if they remembered a feature of the event, they were able to describe it in as much detail 6 years later as they had used to described it virtually immediately after the experience. Interestingly, the children tended to forget the more typical aspects of the experience (e.g., walking to the museum, going up the stairs, and talking to the guide), but to remember the distinctive features of the field trip (i.e., digging in the sandbox for "artifacts" using archaeological tools and making clay models of the artifacts). These aspects of the experience were well remembered immediately and after the short delays, as well as after the long delay of 6 years. Thus, for these children, there was substantial consistency in recall of the more distinctive features of the event even after a delay of several years. I have more to say about the role of distinctive features in recall in the next section.

## AGE-RELATED CHANGES IN PRESCHOOLERS' RECALL OF SPECIFIC PAST EVENTS

We have just seen that children as young as 2½ years of age are able to provide verbal reports of events they experienced in the past. This demonstrates that *within* the period of life eventually obscured by childhood amnesia, children form and retain memories of unique experiences. Critically, in terms of childhood amnesia, unlike the first years of life, this period is not totally devoid of memories. Rather, from this period, adults retrieve a smaller number of memories than would be expected based on adult rates of forgetting alone; the number of memories retrieved from age 3 to age 7 steadily increases, when an adult distribution of memories is assumed (see Fig. 2.1). The steady increase in memories from childhood accessible in adulthood implies that there might be age-related changes in memory throughout the preschool years. In addition, discussion of developmental changes in the neural bases of memory in chapter 6 also provides reason to expect age-related changes in this period: Although critical developments that permit the formation of explicit memories take place in the first 2 years of life, there is continued change throughout the preschool period (and beyond; neural developments in the preschool years are discussed in chap. 8). Indeed, although they were not emphasized in the last section, during this age period, there are age-related changes in children's memories. Some of the most salient changes are apparent in the excerpts in Table 7.3 from the same young girl—Patty—at 3½ and 6 years of age (Fivush & Haden, 1997). As illustrated by Patty's narratives, over the preschool years, children provide more and more information in response to cues for retrieval, they report more information and more detailed information about events, and they report more distinctive information. In this section, I describe these changes in more detail. In the section to follow, I discuss continuities against this backdrop of change.

TABLE 7.3
Samples From a Young Narrator at 3½ and 6 Years of Age

---

"Patty" at Age 3½ Years

Child: We saw—we saw the clown riding on a—in a train.
Interviewer: You saw a clown riding in a train? Wow! What else?
Child: And there was a lots of clowns that at the circus.... And lots of Indians at the circus.
Interviewer: ... What else happened?
Child: And there was lots of music goin' on there, too. And they squirt fire at the clowns.
Interviewer: ... Wow, that sounds like fun. What else happened at the circus?
Child: Um ... there was too much music on and they play lots of music and when the circus is over we went to get some food at the food place.

"Patty" at Age 6 Years

Child: Well, when we went to Epcot Center I saw, we saw the fireworks.... And we went to this Chinese restaurant.... At Epcot, they had all these different country restaurants and we went to the Chinese.... But I got the baby back ribs.
Interviewer: You got baby back ribs at the Chinese restaurant?
Child: Yeah. I didn't know they'd be in Chinese. I thought they'd be in English ... Cause I like English ones. But instead they were in Chinese.
Interviewer: The ribs were in Chinese. You didn't like those kind?
Child: Yeah. But the dessert was okay.... Except the honey.

---

*Note.* Based on Fivush and Haden (1997).

## Age-Related Changes in How Long Children Remember

Taking our cues from the literature on memory development in the first 2 years of life, we might expect to see increases in the length of time over which preschool-age children show evidence of remembering. In infancy, whereas 9-month-olds remember for 1 month, but not 3 months, by 20 months of age, a substantial proportion of children exhibit recall after as many as 12 months.

Although it seems logical that increases in the length of time over which children are able to recall also might occur in the preschool years, *over the delays examined to date*, there are not especially noteworthy developments in this regard. For example, in the study by Hamond and Fivush (1991), even after an 18-month delay, children 3 and 4 years of age remembered their trips to DisneyWorld (see Table 7.2). Nor is long-term recall restricted to special events such as trips to DisneyWorld. In the research by Robyn Fivush, Jacquelyn Gray, and Fayne Fromhoff (1987) mentioned earlier in the chapter, children as young as 2½ years of age were interviewed about naturally occurring events sampled from their lives. The events included trips to amusement parks, but also events such as birthday parties, recreational activities, and medical visits, for example. As already noted, all 10 of the children in the sample were able to remember at least one event that had happened more than 6 months in the past. This time frame is roughly consistent with that derived from young children's nonverbal recall of events, such as demonstrated in the "Monster" study described in chapter 4 (i.e., Bauer et al., 2000). Evidence that, by 1½ to 2½ years of age, children are able to remember events for as much as a full year suggests that, by that age, the long-term recall memory system is well established. Additional research is necessary to determine whether, as delays stretch from months to years, age-related differences in how long memories are stored and remain accessible begin to emerge. Reasons to expect that they might are discussed in chapter 8. In chapter 11, I examine the possible contribution to childhood amnesia of differences in the length of time children are able to remember events relative to the length of time adults are able to remember.

## Age-Related Changes in Dependence on External Cues to Recall

Although even young children are able to recall over the long term, there are suggestions in the literature that their recall is more dependent on external cues and reminders relative to that of older children. For example, in the study by Hamond and Fivush's (1991) of children's reports of trips to DisneyWorld, only about one quarter (22%) of the children's recall was spontaneous. The balance of the information was elicited in response to direct questions. Although the effect was not substantial, the younger children produced less information spontaneously (19%) relative to the older children (25%). Thus, whereas an older child's response to a question like "What did you do at DisneyWorld?" might be "We rode fun rides," a younger child might simply respond "rides." If the interviewer wanted more information about the rides, such as whether they were fun, she would need to ask, "Was it fun?", in response to which the younger child would likely respond "Yes." The net effect is that, to get information about what was done and how the child felt about it, the interviewer must provide more prompts and probes to the younger, relative to the older, child.

Discussion of possible reasons for younger children's seemingly greater reliance on external prompts and cues, relative to older children, is reserved for chapter 8. For now it is important to note at least two potential consequences of it. The first is that memories of events from early in life may be *less frequently and less effectively reinstated in memory* relative to events from later in life. It is clear that long-term retention is facilitated by reinstatement. Indeed the very process of consolidation of a memory trace involves repeated co-activation of associative links between and among the elements that together represent an event (see chap. 5). The links in a memory network are strengthened each time they are activated, either by another experience of the same or a highly similar event or by overlap in a subset of the features from a different event. If younger children are less autonomous in this process—if they are dependent on outside cueing for reinstatement—then the elements of their memory representations are likely to be less frequently co-activated and, as a result, will not continue to strengthen over time.

The second potential consequence of young children's reliance on external prompts and cues is *less consistency in what is retrieved about an event*. As discussed by Robyn Fivush and Nina Hamond (1990), if elements of an event are remembered as a function of cueing, then if the cues are the same on each retrieval attempt, the same elements will be retrieved on each trial. However, if the cues are different on each retrieval attempt, then different elements will be retrieved on each trial. The result would be a low level of consistency in recall from trial to trial. A study conducted by Fivush and Hamond (1990) provided data consistent with this suggestion. They asked mothers of 2½-year-olds to talk with their children about a number of novel events from the past (e.g., the first airplane trip, going to the beach, etc.). Six weeks later, an individual who was previously unknown to the child interviewed the child about the same events. A striking finding from this research was that three quarters (76%) of the information that the children reported at the second interview was new and different relative to what the children had provided at the first interview. Nevertheless, the information was judged by the children's mothers to be accurate.

Some of the children in Fivush and Hamond's (1990) research were interviewed once again, 14 months after the second interview, when they were approximately 4 years of age. The third interview was conducted by yet a different person. In addition to asking the children about some of the events they had talked about 14 months previously ("old" events), the interviewer also asked the children about a number of events that had occurred within the past year ("new" events). As illustrated in Fig. 7.3, despite that more than a year had passed since the children had experienced the old events (the children's mothers verified that the events had not been reexperienced), the children recalled them quite well. In fact the number of units of information that the children reported about the old events at the age of 4 did not differ from the number of units of information they had reported at the age of 2½. What is more, the amount of information that the children provided about the old events was comparable to the amount reported about the new events. Thus, by the standard metric of the number of items reported, the children exhibited virtually no forgetting of the events over the 14-month delay. Moreover, three quarters (74%) of the information that the 4-year-old children provided about the old events had not been reported at either of the previous interviews (yet was accurate as judged by the children's mothers). The observed inconsistency in young children's recall contrasts with the con-

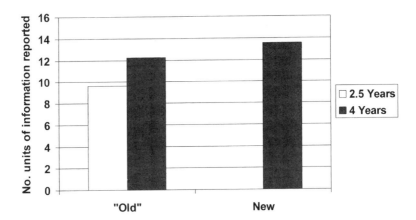

FIG. 7.3. The number of units of information reported by 2½-year-old children (open bar) and 4-year-old children (filled bars) about old events (events experienced at approximately 2½ years of age) and new events (events experienced within a year of the 4-year interview). Data from Fivush and Hamond (1990).

sistency seen in adults (McCloskey, Wible, & Cohen, 1988). Critically, over time, it may contribute to instability of the memory trace:

> Because they are not providing their own retrieval cues, they are not recalling a stable set of remembered information about any given event during any given recall trial. Thus, these early memories will tend to become more fragmented and therefore more difficult to recall later in development. (Fivush & Hamond, 1990, p. 245)

The end result may be that children preserve a small, stable core of features that is called up each time they talk about an event, but that the less stable "fringe" around the core eventually becomes inaccessible.

One final point to be made about developmental changes in reliance in external cues to recall is that, *regardless of age, we are dependent on cueing to ensure retrieval of memories from long-term stores.* Indeed in chapter 5, *retrieval* was defined as re-activation of the neural network representing the event put into motion by "an internal or external stimulus, whose cortical representation is part of the network by prior association, will reactivate that representation and, again by association, the rest of the network" (Fuster, 1997, p. 455). In other words, retrieval of memory representations is initiated by cues. An illustrative example of the power of external cueing is available in the data from a study already described—namely, the museum study conducted by Judith Hudson and Robyn Fivush (1991).

Although the children in Hudson and Fivush's (1991) museum study remembered much about the event over the 6-year interval, there was a striking difference in the accessibility of the memories over time. Six weeks after the trip to the museum, all of the children indicated that they remembered the field trip in response to the open-ended question, "What happened at the Jewish Museum?" Indeed more than half (61%) of the information the children reported was provided in response to this invitation. In contrast, 1 year later, only one child indicated memory in response to this general prompt, and only a small amount (5%) of the information children reported was provided in response to the open-ended prompt. Six years later, one child indicated memory in response to the general prompt, and only 8% of information was provided in response to this prompt. In contrast, photographs of the event were as effective 6 years after the field trip as they had been 6 weeks after it. When aided by photographs, 11 of the 13 children exhibited memory for the trip even after 6 years. The impressive level of memory cannot be attributed to children simply talking about the pictures: The photographs did not depict the features counted as evidence of memory. Thus, these findings indicate impressive recall. They also clearly demonstrate the importance of the "right" retrieval cue.

Finally, dependence on external cues does not lessen in adulthood: Levels of cued recall are consistently higher than levels of free recall (see Koriat, 2000, for discussion of the role of cueing in memory retrieval in adults). For present purposes, the important point is that younger children differ from older children (and adults) not in their *dependence* on external cues to aid retrieval of a memory representation, but in the *amount of information that they seemingly retrieve in response to any given cue.*

## Age-Related Changes in *How Much* Children Remember (or Report)

Younger children provide less information spontaneously and less information per cue relative to older children. Even with cueing, younger children provide less elaborate memory reports. The research on children's recall of their trip to DisneyWorld conducted by Nina Hamond and Robyn Fivush (1991) is an example of this pattern. Whereas older children respond to a question such as, "What did you see at DisneyWorld?" by replying "big Dumbos," younger children tend to reply simply "Dumbos." The result is that older children provide more features in their reports. From 3½ to 6 years of age, the increase in narrative length is dramatic as illustrated in research by Robyn Fivush and Catherine Haden (1997): The length of children's narratives increased from about 10 propositions at 3½ years of age to an average of 23 propositions by 6 years of age. It is a basic fact of information processing that more elaborated memory traces are more resistant to forgetting. As implied by the discussion of the relative absence of age-related changes in the length of time over which children remember, we do not necessarily see the effects of differential length or elaboration of memory reports *within* the period eventually obscured by childhood amnesia. However, it is yet to be seen whether they will have longer-term implications. I consider this possibility in chapter 10.

In evaluating the significance of the observation that children provide less information about past events relative to older children, it is important to keep in mind that a verbal report is not the equivalent of a memory. When a child reports three pieces of information about a past event, we know that she remembered at least that much. It is entirely possible that she remembered more, however. The suggestion that verbal reports may underestimate the richness of the memories of young children, in particular, was illustrated in the example from Fivush and Hamond's (1990) work provided earlier: When they were interviewed after a 6-week delay, three quarters of the information that 2½-year-old children provided about past events was new relative to the first interview, yet was accurate nonetheless. Data such as these compel the conclusion that, in any given interview, children likely are providing only a portion of what they remember. It is likely that the younger the child, the smaller the proportion (see Mandler, 1990a, for further discussion of this point).

## Age-Related Changes in *What* Children Report

With age, children not only report more information in their narratives, but they include different types of information. In autobiographical narratives, older children and adults focus on what is unique or distinctive about an experience. What is worth sharing is what was different about today's trip to the grocery store, compared with all other trips, or how different the tomatoes of Italy taste relative to those from the grocery in North Carolina. In contrast, young children seem to comment on what is *common* across experiences or what is routine. Some of the earliest indications of this tendency were reported by Katherine Nelson (1984, 1989) based on the "Emily monologues." Emily, the young child of a friend of the Nelson family, had a tendency to talk to herself while in her crib before going to sleep. Her extremely cooperative parents agreed to tape several months of Emily's "monologues," beginning at 21 months. Although Emily was free to talk about anything she wanted to, she did not talk about distinctive events, such as the birth of her new baby brother. Instead she seemed to focus on routine events, such as going shopping at a store called Child World:

> Daddy said buy diapers for Stevie and Emmy . . . on Saturday go Child World
> buy diaper for Emmy and diaper for the baby and then buy something for the

Emmy . . . and that diaper for anybody. And buy moon that day at Child Word and buy coats. . . . (K. Nelson, 1984, p. 117)

A similar tendency to select routine events as the topic of conversation was reported by Christine Todd and Marion Perlmutter (1980). They found that roughly half of the past events recorded during their study were initiated by the children. Of the child-nominated events, two thirds (66%) concerned routine, as opposed to novel, experiences.

The tendency to focus on routine or common features continues into the early preschool years. For example, in the study by Fivush and Hamond (1990), in response to the interviewer's invitation to talk about going camping, after providing the interviewer with the distinctive information that the family had slept in a tent, a 2½-year-old child went on to report on the more typical features of the camping experience:

Interviewer: You slept in a tent? Wow, that sounds like a lot of fun.
Child: And then we waked up and eat dinner. First we eat dinner, then go to bed, and then wake up and eat breakfast.
Interviewer: What else did you do when you went camping? What did you do when you got up, after you at breakfast?
Child: Umm, in the night, and went to sleep. (p. 231)

In the study from which this excerpt was taken, almost half (48%) of the information that the children reported was judged to be distinctive, implying that the other half was not. Given that many of the events that young children experience are "firsts" (e.g., first camping trip, first airplane ride, first visit to the dentist), to understand them, children may focus on what the novel experience has in common with previous experiences. That is, they may attend to features that overlap with more familiar events, thereby assimilating new events to their general knowledge and events that are more familiar to them. This pattern changes over time. In the study by Fivush and Hamond (1990), for example, whereas 2½-year-olds reported roughly comparable proportions of typical and distinctive information, at the age of 4 years, they reported about three times more distinctive information than typical information.

What are the potential consequences of focus on the features that different events have in common as opposed to what makes them unique? One likely consequence is that, relative to older children, *younger children's event memories may lack distinctive features and become generalized.* There is strong evidence that, over the course of repeated experiences of the same or a highly similar event, event memories become generalized and schematized. For example, Robyn Fivush and Elizabeth Slackman (1986) discussed how individual children's reports of the same feature of a repeated event

changed over time. From the second day of school to the 10th week, children's reports of what happens on arriving at kindergarten become increasingly "efficient":

Day 2:      We play with the blocks over there, and the puppet thing over
            there, and we could paint.
Week 2:    And then we could start playing.
Week 10:  We can play.

The "efficiency" derived from generalization or schematization of an event
memory likely has costs as well as benefits. As the typical features of the
event are abstracted, the episodic quality of the memory for each individual
experience of the event is lost. The end result is a highly stable, but very generic, representation of what typically happens, as opposed to "what happened one time" (see Hudson, 1986, for additional discussion). Even when
events differ from one another, if children focus on what is common across
experience (as opposed to what is unique and different), then the same out-
come is to be expected. In effect, the event of camping gets "fused" into the
daily routine of eating and sleeping. As it does, the distinctive feature of
sleeping in a tent may fade into the background and be lost.

## CONTINUITIES IN RECALL OF PAST EVENTS

Against the backdrop of age-related changes in the apparent dependence of
children on external cues to recall, and in how much and what type of information children report about past events, there are also aspects of children's
recall that remain the same across the preschool years. Indeed the continuities extend beyond the preschool years in both directions in developmental
time. There are three factors in particular that have been shown to have pronounced influences on recall, seemingly regardless of age: (a) the role of the
participant in events, (b) the structure of events, and (c) familiarity with or
repeated experience of events. I discuss each of these factors in turn.

### Effects of the Role of the Child

Children and adults alike experience events in one of two ways: as participants or observers. Not surprisingly, it has been found that children's recall
of events is better when they are active participants in them relative to when
they are only bystanders. For example, Tamar Murachver and her colleagues
examined the recall of 5- and 6-year-old children who experienced a novel
"pirate" event, which involved dressing up in a pirate costume, making a pirate map, winning a key, and finding and opening a treasure chest (Mu-

rachver, Pipe, Gordon, Owens, & Fivush, 1996). One group of children experienced the event directly by enacting it, another group experienced the event indirectly by watching another child enact the event, and yet another group of children only listened to a story about the event. When the children were interviewed several days after the experience, children who actively participated in the event recalled more about it; the effects of direct experience were more pronounced in children's verbal recall than in behavioral reenactment. Even after they had heard the story three times, recall by the children in the least participatory group did not match that of the most active participants.

In a similar vein, Lynne Baker-Ward, Thomas Hess, and Dorothy Flannagan (1990) found that children as old as 10 years of age had higher levels of recall of activities they themselves had performed up to 1 month earlier relative to activities they had witnessed another child perform (i.e., in the two conditions, the children recalled 55% and 43% of the available information, respectively). Leslie Rudy and Gail Goodman (1991) did not find an effect of active participation on the *amount* that children recalled after a 10- to 12-day delay, but they did find an effect on children's resistance to suggestive questioning. Four- and 7-year-old children who participated in a novel event involving a set of games (e.g., Simon Says, thumb wrestling) were more resistant to misleading questions relative to the children who only watched the event. Findings such as these indicate that active participation in events strengthens the memory representations that children form of them.

Active participation in events also facilitates recognition and recall in infancy and early childhood, at least over short delays. For example, Louise Hertsgaard, Sandi Wewerka, and I found that, after a 1-month delay, 15-month-old children had high levels of recall of event sequences. As reflected in Fig. 7.4, children who were permitted to imitate the events prior to imposition of the delay exhibited small, yet reliably greater, levels of performance relative to children who only watched the events modeled (i.e., children for whom the opportunity to imitate was deferred for 1 month; Bauer et al., 1995). We have observed similar effects in the first year of life: 9-month-olds who are permitted to imitate prior to imposition of a 1-month delay have higher levels of ordered recall relative to infants who only watch (Lukowski et al., 2005). Over longer delays, the effects of active participation seem to be less apparent. Andrew Meltzoff (1995) found that, after 2 and 4 months, recall was comparable for children who were and were not allowed to imitate prior to imposition of the delays. Similarly, in the "Monster" study from my laboratory (Bauer et al., 2000), we found that recall after delay intervals of as many as 12 months was comparable for events that children had been and had not been allowed to imitate one time prior to imposition of the delays. Thus, for both younger and older children, over the short term (i.e., days to weeks), active participation in events facilitates recall. Over the long term

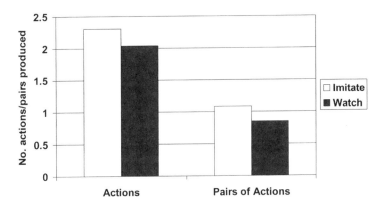

FIG. 7.4.   Number of actions (maximum possible of 3.0) and number of ordered pairs of actions (maximum possible of 2.0) produced after a 1-month delay by 15-month-old children who were allowed to imitate prior to imposition
of the delay (open bars) and by same-age children who only watched the events
prior to imposition of the delay (filled bars; imitation was deferred for 1 month).
Based on Bauer et al. (1995).

(i.e., as weeks stretch to months), for younger children at least, the effects
seem to dissipate. Because older children have been tested only over shorter
intervals, it is not know whether, with increased delay, effects of active participation on older children's recall also would diminish.

## Effects of Event Structure and Children's Comprehension of It

In their landmark work on scripts, Roger Schank and Robert Abelson (1977)
noted that, from the standpoint of learning and memory, not all events are
created equal. For some events, we seem to create "strong" scripts, whereas
for others our scripts are "weak." The difference between the two is the nature of the temporal connections inherent in them. Strong scripts are constrained by "giant causal chains" (Schank & Abelson, 1977) that dictate the
order in which actions in the event happen. For example, if you want to get
to your table in a restaurant, you must first go through the door (unless, of
course, you are dining *al fresco*). As such, going through the door *enables* you
to get to your table. Strong scripts provide a good basis for memory for the
order in which events unfolded, as well as for prediction of their order in the
future. In contrast, weak scripts are less temporally constrained. The elements of such events can occur in variable orders. My own "Saturday errands" script is weak in this regard: On any given Saturday, I have a number
of errands I must run, such as getting money from the ATM, stopping at the
hardware store, shopping for groceries, mailing a package at the post office,

and so forth. For the most part, the order in which I execute these errands is arbitrary and, consequently, highly variable. As a result, my memory for the order in which I ran my many errands on any given Saturday is likely to be quite poor.

One of the most robust findings in the literature on event memory is that, seemingly across the life span, people are better able to remember events with causal or enabling relations in them (i.e., analogous to strong scripts) relative to events that lack such relations and, thus, are arbitrarily ordered (i.e., analogous to weak scripts). In adults, the influence of event structure is often tested in the context of story-recall tasks, in which one version of the story contains many enabling relations and a different version of the same story contains few enabling relations. Adults consistently demonstrate better recall of the more constrained versions of the text (e.g., Fletcher, Briggs, & Linzie, 1997; Trabasso, van den Broek, & Suh, 1989). The advantage in re-call is apparent both in the number of elements of the story that adults recall and in their memory for the order of the actions of the story.

Similar strategies have been used to evaluate children's sensitivity to event structure. For example, in research by Tom Trabasso, Paul van den Broek, and their colleagues, children were presented with stories containing either few or many enabling relations (e.g., Trabasso, Secco, & van den

### TABLE 7.4
#### Sample Text Containing More and Less Strongly Related Story Elements

1. There once was a boy named Jimmy
2. who wanted to buy a bike.
3. He called a bike store to ask for prices.
4. He counted his money.
5. The money was not enough for a bike.
6. He put his piggy bank back on the top shelf of his closet
7. and covered it with clothes.
8. Jimmy wanted to get some money
9. so he asked his mother for some.
10. His mother said, "No, you should earn your own."
11. Jimmy decided to get a paper route.
12. He called the newspaper agency
13. and asked about a route.
14. The secretary told him to come in.
15. Jimmy talked to the manager
16. and got his job.
17. He worked very hard on his job
18. and earned a lot of tips.
19. Pretty soon he had earned $200.
20. He went to the bike store
21. and bought a beautiful bike.
22. He was the happiest kid in town.

*Note.* Based on van den Broek (1997), Table 12.1.

Broek, 1984). To illustrate, consider Paul van den Broek's story of Jimmy, presented in Table 7.4 (van den Broek, 1989). Some of the elements in the story are strongly related to others: The fact that Jimmy wanted to buy a bike (Statement 2) is related to counting his money (Statement 4), as well as to his trip to the bike store (Statement 20). Other elements of the story have few relations: The fact that Jimmy covered his piggy bank with his clothes (Statement 7) is not especially consequential. As illustrated in Fig. 7.5, both 6- and 10-year-olds had better recall of elements of the story that had many causal antecedents and consequents: The more connections an element had, the more frequently it was recalled (see van den Broek, 1997, for a review).

Effects of event structure are also apparent in children's reenactments of events and in their elicited and deferred imitation of event sequences. Robyn Fivush, Janet Kuebli, and Patricia Clubb (1992) presented to 3- and 5-year-old children two events that the children were later asked to reenact. One of the events was constrained by enabling relations, whereas the other was not. After a single experience of the events, both age groups had higher levels of recall (both verbal and behavioral) of the event with enabling relations relative to the event that lacked enabling relations. Even after four experiences

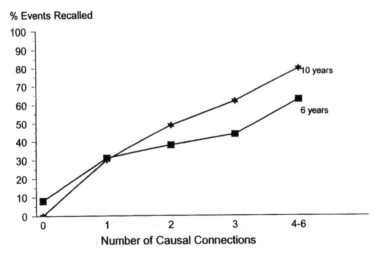

FIG. 7.5.    Levels of recall of elements of a story by 6- and 10-year-old children as a function of the number of causal connections (i.e., causal antecedents and consequents) with other elements of the story. From "Discovering the Cement of the Universe: The Development of Event Comprehension From Childhood to Adulthood," by P. van den Broek. In *Developmental Spans in Event Representation and Comprehension: Bridging Fictional and Actual Events* (pp. 321–342), Fig. 12.1, edited by P. van den Broek, P. J. Bauer, and T. Bourg, 1997, Mahwah, NJ: Lawrence Erlbaum Associates. Copyright © 1997 by Lawrence Erlbaum Associates. Reprinted with permission of Lawrence Erlbaum Associates and the author.

of the events (with the arbitrarily ordered event presented in the same order each time), the children still had superior recall of the event with enabling relations. Similar effects have been observed across different kinds of to-be-remembered materials and by different laboratories (e.g., Hudson & Nelson, 1986; Ratner, Smith, & Dion, 1986; Slackman & Nelson, 1984).

Even infants and very young children have better recall of events structured by enabling relations. In several studies, young children's recall of novel events containing enabling relations has been contrasted with that of novel arbitrarily ordered events. Events such as "make a rattle" (pictured in Fig. 7.6, Panel A) are constrained by enabling relations: To make a rattle of two halves of a barrel and a ball requires that the ball be put into one barrel half before covering it with the other half; to avoid losing the ball, the barrels

a.

b.

FIG. 7.6.   Panel A: Materials for the sequence "make a rattle," which is constrained by enabling relations. Panel B: Materials for the sequence "make a party hat," which is arbitrarily ordered.

must be fitted together before shaking. In contrast, events such as "make a party hat" (pictured in Fig. 7.6, Panel B) are arbitrarily ordered: The order in which decorative elements of the "hat" (i.e., balloon top, sticker, and band) are added does not matter to the final product.

Children's ordered recall of events with enabling relations consistently is greater than that of events that are arbitrarily ordered. The advantage is apparent at both immediate testing (e.g., Bauer, 1992; Bauer & Thal, 1990; Bauer & Travis, 1993) and delayed testing (e.g., Barr & Hayne, 1996; Bauer & Dow, 1994; Bauer & Hertsgaard, 1993; Bauer et al., 1995; Bauer & Mandler, 1989; Mandler & McDonough, 1995). Also, just as in the research by Fivush et al. (1992) with older children, it is apparent even after several experiences of arbitrarily ordered events in an invariant temporal order (Bauer & Travis, 1993; see Bauer, 1992, 1995; Bauer & Travis, 1993, for a discussion of the means by which enabling relations in events may influence ordered recall). Whereas 9- to 11-month-old infants accurately recall multistep sequences constrained by enabling relations (e.g., Carver & Bauer, 1999; Mandler & McDonough, 1995), it is not until 20 to 28 months that children reproduce arbitrarily ordered sequences in the correct temporal order (Bauer, Hertsgaard, et al., 1998; Wenner & Bauer, 1999). Finally, the robust facilitating effect of enabling relations in events cannot be attributed to the problem-solving abilities of young children: Control conditions make clear that children who have not seen the target events modeled do not "figure out" how to produce them (e.g., Bauer, 1992; Bauer et al., 1995). Thus, across an impressively wide age range, there is evidence that event memory is influenced by the nature of the temporal relations inherent in events.

Children's understanding of the causal and temporal relations inherent in events seems to have effects that extend beyond the laboratory. For example, David Pillemer (1992) reported the results of a study in which he examined 3½- and 4½-year-old children's memories for an unexpected fire alarm in their preschool. The alarm was set off by popcorn burning in the basement of the school. When the alarm sounded, the children were evacuated from the building and instructed to go to the playground. The firefighters arrived and turned off the alarm. On their return to the classroom, the teachers and students talked together about the fire alarm, including what had set off the alarm. Two weeks after the incident, Pillemer interviewed the children about the event. The children were first asked an open-ended question ("What happened when you heard the fire alarm?") and then were asked a series of direct questions. Pillemer reported that most of the children provided at least some information in response to the open-ended question, and all of the children were able to answer at least some of the questions correctly. The younger children made more errors, however. For example, whereas nearly all (94%) of the older children correctly said that they were inside the building when the fire alarm sounded, about half (55%) of the younger children responded that they were *outside* at the time of the alarm. The errors may have been related to the younger children's apparently poorer understanding of the event itself. Only a third of the younger children, in contrast to three quarters of the older children, described a sense of urgency in leaving the building. In addition, almost half (44%) of the older children, but only a few (8%) of the younger children, mentioned the cause of the alarm spontaneously.

The age-related differences in the children's performance were even more pronounced over the long term. Six years after the fire alarm, when the children were 9½ and 10½ years of age, David Pillemer and his colleagues Martha Picariello and Jenzi Pruett tracked down 25 of the original children (11 from the younger classroom and 14 from the older classroom) to find out whether they still remembered the fire alarm. They found striking age differences. Fifty-seven percent of the children who had been 4½ years at the time of the experience were able to provide either a full or at least a fragmentary narrative about the event, whereas only 18% of the children who had been 3½ at the time of the experience were able to do so. In addition, nearly all (86%) of the older children, but only half (54%) of the younger children, correctly identified the classroom they had been in at the time the alarm sounded (Pillemer, Picariello, & Pruett, 1994). The authors concluded that, for the children who showed higher levels of recall after the long delay, ". . . causal reasoning at time 1 may have served as an organizing principle for thinking about the event, for imposing temporal order on the sequence of events, and for constructing a story-like narrative memory" (p. 103). Age-related differences in children's comprehension of events have been implicated as a determinants of long-term recall by other researchers as well (e.g., Peterson & Whalen, 2001; Warren & Swartwood, 1992).

## Effects of Familiarity With and Repeated Experience of Events

A third major factor that has been shown to influence recall of events is familiarity with the event or repeated experience of it. It is clear from the data reviewed earlier in this chapter that children need not experience events multiple times to recall them: Even after long delays, children are able to recall events they experienced only once (e.g., a trip to DisneyWorld; Hamond & Fivush, 1991). Nevertheless, some aspects of recall of the past are facilitated by repeated experience of or familiarity with events. For example, Robyn Fivush (1984) found that the amount of information children provided in response to the question "What happens when you go to school?" increased from 7 acts on the second day of school to 12 acts by the 10th week of school (see also Hudson, 1986, 1990a, for evidence of increases in the amount of information provided as a function of repeated experience).

With repeated experience, children also provide more temporally complex narratives. Whereas even in Fivush's (1984) first interview the children's reports were temporally organized, over time children mentioned more conditionals in their reports: "I do my handwriting. *If I have time*, I do art project" (Fivush, 1984, p. 1709; italics added; see also Hudson, 1990a).

From experimental contexts, there is evidence that the length of time children remember events increases as a function of repeated experience. For instance, Robyn Fivush and Nina Hamond (1989) gave 2- and 2½-year-old children either one or two experiences with laboratory events. After a 3-month delay, the children who had experienced the events two times recalled more about them relative to the children who had experienced the events only once. Moreover, children with repeated experience recalled as much after the 3-month retention interval as they had after only 2 weeks.

Similar facilitating effects of repeated experience have been observed in children in the second year of life. For children ages 13 and 15 months, repeated experience is not necessary for recall of events over the short term: After 1 week, children of this age recall both the individual actions and the temporal order of actions of novel events experienced only once (Bauer & Hertsgaard, 1993; Bauer et al., 1995). Nevertheless, particularly over the longer term, repeated experience clearly facilitates recall. As illustrated in Fig. 7.7, for events experienced only once, relative to performance after a 1-week delay, performance after 1 month falls off precipitously. In contrast, events experienced three times before imposition of a 1-month delay are well recalled. Notably, recall after 1 month of events experienced three times is comparable to that after 1 week of events experienced only once (Bauer et al., 1995).

Judith Hudson and her colleagues have shown that events need not be reexperienced in their entirety for recall to be facilitated. Simply showing children a subset of events (i.e., three of an original six experienced) facilitates memory for the entire set (Sheffield & Hudson, 1994). Effects such as these cannot be attributed to confounding factors such as an increased likelihood of children spontaneously generating the target sequences as a result of greater comfort with the testing situation or familiarity with the props. Gina Dow and I (Bauer & Dow, 1994) demonstrated that children who are given repeated experience with the setting, experimenter, and props, but who are not exposed to the modeled events, produce no more actions and sequences at their second testing than they do at their first. Thus, the facilitating effects of repeated experience accrue only with exposure to the target events.

The examples just provided are of enhanced recall as a function of repeated experience of events. However, repeated experience is a double-edged sword. In the case of events that are virtually identical at each experience, the effects of repeated experience are positive. Yet in life outside the laboratory, events are never the same from experience to experience: There

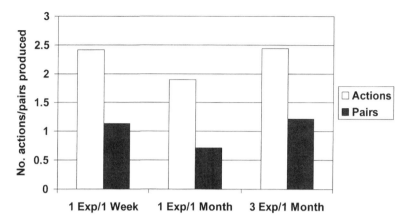

FIG. 7.7. Number of actions (open bars; maximum possible of 3.0) and number of ordered pairs of actions (filled bars; maximum possible of 2.0) produced by three groups of 13- to 15-month-old children: children who experienced events once and were tested after a 1-week delay (1 Exp/1 Week), children who experienced events once and were tested after a 1-month delay (1 Exp/1 Month), and children who experienced events three times and were tested after a 1-month delay (3 Exp/1 Month). Based on Bauer et al. (1995).

are always variations. Research both inside and outside the laboratory has made clear that memories for events that are experienced multiple times, each time with slight variations, simultaneously become more robust and less distinctive. In neural terms, increases in the robustness of memories presumably accrue as a result of consolidation (see chap. 5); in psychological terms, they presumably are the result of schematization. By precisely the same processes, however, the distinctive features of events are lost as typical features are extracted and come to represent a generic version of "what usually happens" in the course of the event (see Hudson, 1986, 1990a). I provided an example of the loss of distinctive features earlier in the chapter. Over the course of 10 weeks, kindergartners omitted the specific details of one-time experiences and substituted timeless, but extremely generic, information (Fivush, 1984; Fivush & Slackman, 1986). That is, on the second day of kindergarten, children noted that, on arrival at school: "We play with the blocks over there, and the puppet thing over there, and we could paint." By the 10th week of school, the same prompt yielded a response such as "We can play."

It is possible that age-related differences in how thoroughly children "commit" to a generalized or schematized event representation could be a determinant of long-term recall. M. Jeffrey Farrar and Gail Goodman (1990) conducted a study in which 4- and 7-year-old children participated in a play activity on each of four occasions. The second occasion differed from the other three in some details of the way the activities unfolded during the session. After the four experiences, the children were asked to recall what happened in the course of the event. The 7-year-olds were able to describe both what usually happened and what happened on the one, unique occasion. In contrast, the 4-year-olds had a well-formed "script" for the event, but poor recall of the single, unique episode.

Findings such as Farrar and Goodman's (1990) make clear that repeated experiences of the same or highly similar events can interfere with memory for any single episode. The potential for interference may be greater for younger relative to older children (see Hudson et al., 1992, for further discussion). As discussed earlier, younger children seem to encode fewer distinctive features of events relative to older children. As experience with highly similar events accrues, even the few distinctive features may be lost in what is common across the experiences. Consideration of the consequences of repeated experience in conjunction with those of event structure paints an even bleaker picture. If children have only one experience of an event, they run the risk of not understanding it—a condition that can be remedied by multiple experiences of the same or similar events. However, with multiple experiences comes the risk that common elements will swamp unique details and the details will be lost from memory.

## SUMMARY AND CONCLUSIONS

Until roughly the last two decades of the 20th century, there was a widespread belief that young children could not remember the times of their lives. The assumption was derived from theories of cognitive development in children and seemed to be "confirmed" by the inability of adults to remember much if anything from their early years. A number of "events" conspired to change the perspective, including a movement toward testing memory in meaningful contexts. When they were asked about events that mattered to them—such as making cookies and going to McDonald's—even 3-year-olds revealed substantial mnemonic competence. Of critical significance for the topic of autobiographical memory in particular was the finding that children remembered not only "what happens" in everyday events and routines, but "what happened" in the course of specific events and episodes. With this discovery, the study of developments in autobiographical memory—as opposed to the study of the absence of childhood memories among adults—began.

Interviews with preschool-age children about unique events such as going to DisneyWorld revealed that memories could be long lasting and quite detailed. Moreover, studies revealed continuities in the factors that affect memory. Across impressively wide developmental spans, active participation in events, temporal constraints in events, and familiarity or repeated experience of events were found to facilitate recall. In light of expectations of qualitative changes in memory functions derived from traditional theories, these continuities were unexpected indeed.

Throughout the preschool years, there are also changes in children's recall of the past. Specifically, relative to younger preschoolers, older preschoolers require fewer prompts and probes to reveal their memories. In part as a consequence, there are changes in how much information children report about events. Indeed the lengths of children's narratives more than double between the ages of 3 and 6 years. There are also changes in the type of information children report about events and experiences. Whereas early in the preschool years they seem to focus on what is common across experiences, by the end of the period they focus instead on what is distinctive. The net effect of these changes in that, by the time they enter school, children are competent tellers of the tales of the unique experiences of their lives.

Describing developmental change is an essential step in understanding its causes. In times past, developments such as these might have been attributed to changes in the operational structures available to younger relative to older children. With development of information-processing theories and the rise of the computer metaphor of the mind, explanations shifted from operational structures to functional processes: Changes in memory were described in terms of increases in the efficiency with which information is encoded, stored, and later retrieved. With increases in our understanding of the neural bases of memory, the possibility of grounding these processes in neural structures is on the horizon. In the next chapter, I take up the question of "what develops?" in memory development in the preschool years. In addition to changes in processes and the neural structures that support them, I consider changes in conceptual understanding and changes in the mode of expression of autobiographical memory—namely, the memory narrative.

# 8

# "What Develops" in Preschoolers' Recall of Specific Past Events?

> *A constant question with [my father] was, "I wonder what is the cause of*
> *so-and-so," or, again putting it directly to me, "Can you tell the cause of*
> *this?"*
>
> —Herbert Spencer, from *An Autobiography*
> (1904; cited in *Random House Webster's Quotationary*,
> Leonard Roy Frank, Ed. New York: Random House, p. 104)

As outlined in chapter 7, over the course of the preschool years, there are changes in children's recall of specific past events. With increasing age, children provide more information in response to cues for retrieval, they report more information and more detailed information about events, and the information they report is more distinctive. In this chapter, I take up the question posed by the father of the English philosopher, Herbert Spencer. I ask, "what is the cause" of this? What is responsible for these changes? Whereas the senior Mr. Spencer seems to have been interested in "*the* cause" of various phenomena, in the domain of autobiographical memory, there is no single cause or single source of developmental change. Rather, as Elizabeth Bates (1979) said of the capacity to understand and use linguistic and nonlinguistic symbols, autobiographical memory is a "collage" constituted of different parts. Each of the parts makes a contribution to the whole, and each has its own course of development.

One source of developmental change in autobiographical memory in the preschool years is the same as that implicated in the period of infancy—namely, improvements in the efficacy and efficiency of the basic processes of encoding, consolidation, storage, and retrieval of memories. These changes affect the strength and integrity of memory representations themselves, as well as the accessibility of them. There is every reason to believe (although surprisingly little data to test the suggestion) that improvements in the basic mnemonic processes are linked with age-related changes in the neural structures of declarative memory, development of which continues throughout the preschool years and beyond.

Although improvements in the basic mnemonic processes no doubt have a large role to play in the changes in memory for specific past events observed throughout the preschool years, they alone do not explain developments in autobiographical or personal memory. As outlined in chapter 3, theories that emphasize cognitive advances as explanations for childhood amnesia suggest that, in addition to changes in basic mnemonic processes, developments in the conceptual domain of self, for example, also contribute to the emergence of autobiographical memory and, thus, the "offset" of childhood amnesia. Developmental changes in the understanding of temporal concepts and autonoetic awareness (and awareness of the sources of knowledge representations more generally) also have been implicated in autobiographical memory development. Sociocultural accounts of the development of autobiographical memory (also introduced in chap. 3) go further still. They suggest that basic mnemonic skills and specific conceptual developments are, in essence, the "cake" of autobiographical memory. The "icing" on the cake is the narrative skill that permits the sharing of personal memories with others. Thus, in the preschool years, there are a minimum of three sources of age-related change in memory for specific past events in general and autobiographical memory in particular: changes in basic mnemonic processes, developments in specific conceptual domains, and advances in narrative skills. I discuss each of these sources of developmental change in turn.

## DEVELOPMENTAL CHANGES IN BASIC MNEMONIC PROCESSES

In chapter 5, I reviewed the neural structures involved in encoding, consolidation, storage, and retrieval of long-term declarative memories. In chapter 6, I discussed the early course of development of the structures and associated changes in behavior. By way of brief review, cortical association areas are involved in the initial encoding of event memories; medial temporal structures are involved in the processes whereby memory traces are stabilized for long-term storage in cortical areas; prefrontal cortex in particular is involved in retrieval of memories from long-term stores (see Fig. 5.8). Whereas most of the medial temporal structures mature early, the dentate gyrus of the hippocampus matures later, as do prefrontal cortex and the connections between the elements of the temporal-cortical network. The entire network is thought to reach functional maturity late in the first year and throughout the second year of life (see chap. 6 for elaboration). Consistent with this time frame, there is a dramatic increase in the reliability and robustness of long-term declarative memory during this age period (see chap. 4).

The changes in the neural network that make long-term declarative memory possible are profound indeed. However, they are not the end of the story of brain development: Changes in the neural structures implicated in declarative memory in general, and episodic memory in particular, continue for years beyond infancy. Within the medial temporal system, early developmental changes result in a steep increase in the volume of the hippocampus throughout the second or third year of life. There are more gradual increases in hippocampal volume throughout childhood and into adolescence (e.g., Pfluger et al., 1999; Utsunomiya, Takano, Okazaki, & Mistudome, 1999). Within the dentate gyrus of the hippocampus, as many as 30% of the granule cells proliferate, migrate, differentiate, and establish connections postnatally. Whereas much of the work is accomplished by the second year of life, there is evidence that neurogenesis continues throughout childhood and even into adulthood (Altman & Das, 1965; see Tanapat et al., 2001, for discussion). Functional maturity of the structure is expected to be reached by 16 to 20 months of age, coincident with the rise to peak number of synapses. Full maturity—associated with achievement of the adult number of synapses—is delayed until at least 4 to 5 years of age (Eckenhoff & Rakic, 1991; see Webb et al., 2001, for discussion). Moreover, myelination in the hippocampal region continues throughout childhood and adolescence (Arnold & Trojanowski, 1996; Benes, Turtle, Khan, & Farol, 1994; Schneider, Il'yasov, Hennig, & Martin, 2004).

There are also continued developments in the prefrontal cortex. For example, in some prefrontal cortical layers, there are changes in the size of cells and the lengths and branching of dendrites (Koenderink et al., 1994; see Benes, 2001, for discussion). Whereas synaptic density in the prefrontal cortex begins to increase dramatically at 8 postnatal months, it does not peak until 15 to 24 months. It is only at the end of this time period that the adult morphology of synapses is apparent (Huttenlocher, 1979; Huttenlocher & Dabholkar, 1997). The subtractive events associated with full maturity of the structure are delayed even further: Pruning of synapses to adult levels does not begin until late childhood (Huttenlocher, 1979; Huttenlocher & Dabholkar, 1997; see Bourgeois, 2001, for discussion). As a result of pruning and other regressive events (i.e., loss of neurons and axonal branches), the thickness of the cortical mantle itself begins to decline in adolescence (e.g., Giedd et al., 1999; see Van Petten, 2004, for discussion). The reduction in gray matter volume in the frontal cortex is depicted in Fig. 8.1, Panel A, based on structural MRI data from children ages 7 to 16 years (Sowell, Delis, Stiles, & Jernigan, 2001). Coincident with decreases in gray matter volume are increases in white matter volume associated with greater connectivity between

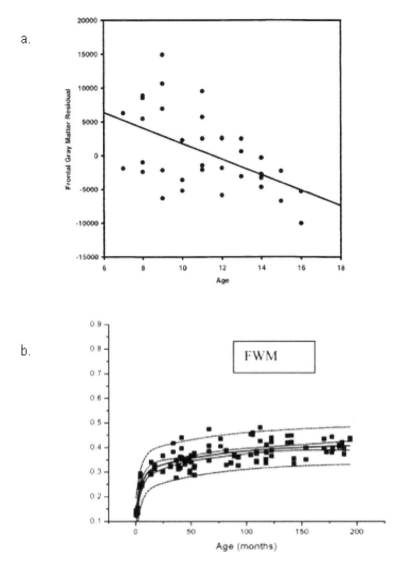

FIG. 8.1.    Panel A: Reduction in frontal gray matter volume from ages 7 to 16 years as measured by structural magnetic resonance imaging (MRI). Panel B: Increase in frontal white matter (FWM) volume from ages 1 day to 16 years as measured by diffusion-tensor imaging (DTI). Panel A is from "Improved Memory Functioning and Frontal Lobe Maturation Between Childhood and Adolescence: A Structural MRI Study," by E. R. Sowell, D. Delis, J. Stiles, and T. L. Jernigan, 2001, *Journal of International Neuropsychological Society, 7,* 312–322, Fig. 3A, copyright © 2001 by Cambridge University Press. Reprinted with permission. Panel B is a portion of Fig. 1 from *Neuroradiology,* "Fast Quantitative Difusion-Tensor Imaging of Cerebral White Matter From the Neonatal Period to Adolescence," by J. F. L. Schneider, K. A. Il'yasov, J. Hennig, and E. Martin, Vol. 46, 258–266, 2004, copyright © 2004, with permission of Springer and the author.

brain regions and with myelination processes that continue well into adolescence (e.g., Johnson, 1997; Schneider et al., 2004). The steady increase is apparent in Fig. 8.1, Panel B, based on diffusion-tensor imaging (DTI) data from children 1 day of age to 16 years of age (Schneider et al., 2004). Finally, it is not until adolescence that neurotransmitters such as acetylcholine reach adult levels (discussed in Benes, 2001).

This brief review makes clear that, well beyond infancy, there is continued development in the neural structures that support long-term declarative memory. Perhaps because of the trend toward focus on *early* brain development (i.e., development within the first 3 years of life), in the domain of memory, the potential functional significance of these postinfancy changes has gone largely unexplored. Yet there are strong conceptual reasons to believe that the neural developments have functional consequences: Throughout phylogeny as well as ontogeny, changes in structure are associated with changes in function. There is also empirical support for a link at a general level at least. For example, Elizabeth Sowell and her colleagues (Sowell et al., 2001) reported relations between structural changes in the medial temporal and frontal regions, as measured by MRI, and performance on behavioral tests of memory. Specifically, children with structurally more mature medial temporal lobe regions performed at higher levels on spatial memory tasks. Children with structurally more mature frontal cortices performed at higher levels on verbal as well as spatial memory tasks. Thus, in general terms at least, neurodevelopmental changes in the preschool years and beyond are associated with functional changes in memory. I now turn to examination of more specific relations between neural developments and age-related changes in the basic mnemonic processes of encoding, consolidation and storage, and retrieval.

## Encoding

Developmental changes in prefrontal cortex in particular can be expected to contribute to age-related changes in the efficiency with which preschool-age children encode information for subsequent consolidation and storage. For example, there are changes in short-term memory span as measured by tests such as memory for digits or words. Whereas children 2 years of age are only able to hold about two units of information in mind (i.e., two words or digits), by the ages of 5 and 7, they can remember four and five units, respectively. Over the course of the preschool years, children become more effective at keeping task-irrelevant thoughts out of short-term memory, thereby reducing the amount of potentially interfering "cognitive clutter" that otherwise would limit capacity. For example, they get better at remembering items they are instructed to remember (e.g., "Pay attention to the objects outlined in red") and at ignoring items that are presented as distracters (e.g., pictures of objects outlined in blue). In addition, although the most pronounced changes in the use of memory strategies are apparent in the school years, even in the preschool years, there are developmental increases in the use of rehearsal as a means to maintain the accessibility of to-be-remembered material over time (see Bjorklund & Douglas, 1997; Schneider & Bjorklund, 1998, for reviews). The net result of these changes is that children become increasingly adept not only at maintaining information in temporary registration, but also at initiating the type of organizational processing that promotes consolidation of it.

Although there is sound rationale for expecting that developmental changes in encoding over the course of the preschool years might contribute to age-related changes in long-term recall over the same period, there are actually few studies that can be brought to bear to evaluate the hypothesized relation. One reason for the paucity of relevant data is that researchers interested in long-term memory frequently either have not measured initial encoding (i.e., memory is tested only well after the event), or levels of encoding have not been considered in interpretation of the findings (i.e., immediate memory may be tested, but the impact of age-related differences in initial learning is not evaluated). Indeed in the autobiographical memory literature, I know of no studies in which the role of age-related differences in encoding has been systematically evaluated.

Whereas there do not seem to be studies in which the possibility of age-related differences in encoding has been evaluated for its potential impact on long-term recall, there are some experimental studies in which encoding has been eliminated from the equation by bringing children of different ages to the same level of encoding, by requiring them to reach a criterion level of learning. Most such studies have been conducted with school-age children (i.e., 7- to 11-year-olds; e.g., Brainerd & Reyna, 1995), or with very young children (i.e., 12- to 18-month-olds; Howe & Courage, 1997, reviewed in chap. 6), as opposed to preschoolers. We saw in chapter 6 that with levels of learning taken into account in this way, age-related differences in infants' and very young children's long-term memory are still apparent (Howe & Courage, 1997; see also Bauer, 2005; Bauer et al., 2000, for the same result when level of encoding is controlled by matching and when it is controlled statistically, respectively). As reviewed by Mark Howe and Julia O'Sullivan (1997), the same result is obtained with school-age children and, based on a much smaller data base, with preschool-age children as well. Although the number of studies with preschoolers is small, given evidence that age-related differences in encoding processes are not the major source of developmental change in long-term declarative memory either in infancy or in the school years, it is reasonably safe to assume that neither are they the most significant source of age-related differences in the intervening preschool years. Thus, we must look to sources other than encoding for explanation of age-related differences in long-term memory.

## Consolidation and Storage

Changes in the processes by which memory representations are consolidated and distributed to long-term memory stores can be expected throughout the preschool years, in association with neurodevelopmental changes within the medial temporal and prefrontal structures themselves, as well as the connections between them. As noted in chapter 6, evaluating the developmental implications of hypothesized age-related changes in consolidation and/or storage processes is difficult. There are few opportunities to observe patterns of retrograde amnesia in child patients (thank goodness), and there are no "early childhood" or "adolescent" animal models of the processes. Although as they have been in the infancy period, neuroimaging techniques such as event-related potentials (ERPs) could be brought to bear on the question (Bauer, Wiebe, et al., 2003; Carver et al., 2000), I know of no such studies with preschool-age children. The only data then are behavioral. As discussed in chapter 6, unfortunately, interpretation of behavioral data often is complicated by an inability to separate the contributions of the basic mnemonic processes. On the basis of a single test, it is difficult, if not impossible, to know whether a memory representation remains intact but is inaccessible given the cues provided (retrieval failure) or whether the trace has lost its integrity (consolidation/storage failure; Tulving, 1983). Moreover, as noted in the section on encoding, in developmental research, an additional complication is the likelihood of age-related differences in encoding. The result is that there are few research traditions that yield data that can productively be applied to the question of whether hypothesized age-related differences in consolidation and/or storage processes contribute to age-related differences in the robustness of long-term recall.

The laboratories of Charles Brainerd, Mark Howe, and Valerie Reyna have produced a series of studies designed to permit evaluation of the relative contributions of different basic mnemonic processes. Their work is conducted in the context of the trace-integrity framework (Brainerd et al., 1990) and conceptually related fuzzy-trace theory (Brainerd & Reyna 1990). In studies in these traditions, to eliminate encoding differences as a source of age-related effects, participants are brought to a criterion level of learning prior to imposition of a delay. In addition, to permit evaluation of the contributions of consolidation and/or storage processes versus retrieval processes, participants are provided multiple test trials without intervening study trials. As discussed in chapter 6, it is assumed that, if performance improves over test trials, at least a residual memory trace must have remained even if the participant failed to retrieve it on an earlier trial (retrieval failure). If, however, performance does not change over test trials, it is likely that the memory trace has disintegrated (storage failure; although see Howe & O'Sullivan, 1997, for multiple nuances of this argument).

As noted earlier in evaluation of the role of encoding processes, most studies in the trace-integrity framework and fuzzy-trace theory traditions have been conducted with school-age children; the number of studies conducted with preschoolers is much smaller. In one such study, 4- and 6-year-old children learned and then recalled eight-item picture lists (Howe, 1995). In this study, as in virtually every other study conducted within this tradition (see Howe & O'Sullivan, 1997, for a review), consolidation and/or storage failure was the strongest predictor of age-related differences in children's recall. That is, statistical estimates of how much information was lost from storage were more important in predicting later recall than were estimates of how much information was stored, but could not be effectively retrieved. Between 4 and 6 years of age, storage failure rates declined (as they do throughout childhood), suggesting that these processes are a source of developmental change.

## Retrieval

Retrieval of memories from long-term storage sites is thought to depend on a neural structure that undergoes an extremely long course of postnatal development—namely, prefrontal cortex (e.g., Markowitsch, 2000). Because they would be expected to change slowly as a consequence, retrieval processes seem to provide a ready answer to the question "what develops?" in memory during the preschool years. The results of research from the trace-integrity framework and fuzzy-trace theory traditions stand in apparent contradiction of this expectation, however. As reviewed in Howe and O'Sullivan (1997), for example, research designed to evaluate the contributions of consolidation and/or storage versus retrieval processes reveals that, whereas consolidation and/or storage failure rates decline throughout childhood, retrieval failure rates remain at relatively constant levels. The apparent lack of change in retrieval failure rates throughout childhood undermines the suggestion that retrieval processes are a major source of developmental change during this period.

If changes in retrieval processes are not a major source of age-related changes in long-term recall in childhood, then why do retrieval cues make such an enormous difference in young children's performance on tests of long-term recall? Also why do younger children seem to be more dependent on external retrieval cues relative to older children? The answers to these questions may lie in recognition that the presence or absence of retrieval cues makes an enormous difference *regardless of age*. Even at our peak of mnemonic competence, we are dependent on cues to retrieval. Indeed it seems that all recall is cued, be it by an external prompt or an internal association (Spear, 1978). Thus, as noted in chapter 7, the developmental phenomenon is not that with increasing age, children gain independence from cueing. Rather, with increasing age, children provide more information per cue. The change in "rate of return" from external prompts and probes may imply that cues "spread" further (or faster) for older children relative to younger children. That is, it is possible that in older children a given cue activates more associated elements (or activates associated elements more quickly) relative to the number activated in a younger child. Of course an alternative possibility is that the "spread per cue" does not change with age, but that older children simply report more of the co-activated elements relative to younger children. In other words, in both cases, the cue "What did you see there?" may activate the object—"Dumbos"—and the attribute— "big"—but only the older children mention the attribute.

Another distinct possibility is that, with age, children are able to benefit from a wider and wider array of cues. Judith Hudson documented developmental differences in young children's sensitivity to different types of external reminders of past events. Specifically, at 18 months of age, exposure to a videotape of another child performing laboratory events, such as "make a gong" (Fig. 4.4), facilitates children's memories for the events, but exposure to still photographs of the same activity does not. At 24 months, exposure to still photographs of activities facilitates memory, but simply hearing the event described does not. By the age of 3 years, a verbal description of an event is sufficient to reinstate memory for it (Hudson, 1991, 1993; Hudson & Sheffield, 1998). In a similar vein, my colleagues and I found that whether they encountered them in the laboratory in which they had been used, or at home, the props used to produce sequences such as "make a gong" facilitated 3-year-old children's verbal memories for events they had experienced at the age of 20 months. In contrast, still photographs of the event-related props did not support verbally accessible memories of the events at age 3 years (Bauer et al., 2004). These specific examples are of apparent changes in the sensitivity to different types of external cues by children during the period of transition from infancy to early childhood. Across the preschool period, change may come in the form of differential sensitivity to different types of verbal cues to recall. If this is the case (and I know of no research that has directly tested the possibility), then more cues may be necessary to obtain the same amount of information from younger relative to older children because for younger children some of the cues simply will not be effective aids to retrieval.

If, regardless of age, we are dependent on cueing to recall, then could it be that the pronounced changes in prefrontal cortex that led to postulation of retrieval processes as a major source of developmental change actually have nothing to do with memory development in childhood? Although possible, this is highly unlikely! More reasonable is the conclusion that developmental changes in prefrontal cortex play a role, but that their role is different than that previously assumed. Rather than affecting profound changes in retrieval processes, developments in prefrontal structures may exert large effects on consolidation and/or storage processes. As discussed in chapter 5, consolidation is an interactive process between medial temporal and cortical structures. As a result, changes in cortical structures may be every bit as important to developments in consolidation processes as are changes in medial temporal structures. Moreover, the ultimate storage sites for long-term memories are the association cortices. Prefrontal cortex is thought to play an especially significant role in storage of information about the *where* and *when* of events and experiences, the very features that locate autobiographical memories in specific place and time. Thus, developmental changes in prefrontal cortex may play their primary role in supporting more efficient consolidation and more effective storage; their role in improving retrieval processes may be secondary.

## DEVELOPMENTAL CHANGES IN SPECIFIC CONCEPTUAL DOMAINS

Changes in basic mnemonic processes associated with brain development are not the only source of developmental change in the preschool years. There is reason to expect that developments in a number of conceptual domains also contribute to age-related changes in memories of specific past events in general and autobiographical memories in particular. As discussed in chapter 3, one concept in particular has been suggested to play a causal role in the development of autobiographical memory—namely, development of a cognitive sense of self (Howe & Courage, 1993, 1997). Developments in understanding temporal concepts and the emergence of autonoetic awareness (and emerging understanding of the sources of mental representations more generally) are also thought to play important roles in autobiographical memory development. I discuss each in turn.

### Developments in Self-Concept

As noted in chapter 2, the one defining feature of autobiographical memory is that it concerns memories about one's self. A concept of "self" is thus a necessary ingredient for an autobiographical memory. Historically, there has been much discussion in the literature of the concept of self. The list of scholars who have worked to define the concept is a veritable "whose who" of philosophy and psychology, including John Bowlby (1969), Sigmund Freud (1915/1959), William James (1892/1961), George Mead (1934), and Jean Piaget (1954). Emerging from the efforts of these and other scholars is a fundamental distinction between a subjective sense of "I" as an entity with thoughts and feelings and an objective sense of "me" as an entity with features and characteristics that make one different and separate from others. Together these senses of self comprise one's "self-concept." It is reasonable to assume that developments in the self-concept may be linked to developments in autobiographical memory.

A comprehensive review of the vast literature on development of the self-concept would be well beyond the scope of this volume (see Moore & Lemmon, 2001, for a collection of relevant papers). For present purposes, it is sufficient to note that the "I" and the "me" are thought to develop in tandem over the first 2 years of life (although further developments may occur beyond at 2 years). As discussed in chapter 3, in the second half of the second year of life, they coalesce into a self-system that scholars such as Mark Howe and Mary Courage (1993, 1997) view as sufficient to serve as an organizer for experiences as relevant to the self. In making this argument, Howe and Courage noted the correspondence between the age from which some adults report their earliest memories—namely, 2 years (e.g., Usher & Neisser, 1993)—and developments in the sense of self that occur between 18 and 24 months. As discussed in chapter 3, the developments are signaled by the ability to recognize one's self in a mirror, for example (see, e.g., Brooks-Gunn & Lewis, 1984, for a review). Mirror self-recognition is apparent when, on seeing in a mirror a reflection of themselves with a spot of rouge on their noses (unobtrusively placed there earlier in the test session), children touch their own noses rather than the "nose in the mirror." Awareness that the reflection belongs to themselves is taken as evidence that children have a concept of self. The concept is thought to be a sufficient device around which to organize memories, and thus to begin to construct a personal past (Howe & Courage, 1993, 1997).

At least two laboratories have provided evidence consistent with the suggestion that the self-concept available to children by the end of the second year of life is related to developments in memory. Specifically, Mark Howe (2003) reported that 15- to 23-month-old children who exhibited recognition of themselves in a mirror had more robust event memories relative to children who did not exhibit mirror self-recognition. In a longitudinal study of children tested at 19, 25, and 32 months of age, Keryn Harley and Elaine Reese (1999) found that children who were earlier to recognize themselves in the mirror (assessed at the 19-month time point) made faster progress in independent autobiographical memory reports (assessed at the 25- and 32-month time points) relative to children who were later to evidence mirror self-recognition.

The well-established finding that by the age of 2 years children are able to recognize themselves, and the more recent findings of relations between this important development and autobiographical memory, are significant indeed. Like most complex concepts, that of *self* has more than one facet, however. As depicted in Table 8.1, emerging from the literature are at least three

TABLE 8.1
Multiple Aspects of the Self-Concept

| Aspect of the Self-Concept | Description |
| --- | --- |
| Physical self | Recognition of one's own physical features as depicted in a mirror or photograph, for example |
| Temporally extended self | Understanding that the self extends backward and forward in time |
| Psychological self | Appreciation of one's psychological qualities and attributes |
| Evaluative or subjective self | Perspective on one's internal states, such as emotions, cognitions, and perceptions |

aspects of the self that seem to emerge after the "physical self"—namely, temporally extended self, psychological self, and evaluative or subjective self. Each of these aspects of the self can be expected—and indeed has been found—to relate to further developments in autobiographical memory.

*Temporally Extended Self.* There are relations between developments in children's understanding of what Katherine Nelson (1989) referred to as *self in time* and Daniel Povinelli (1995) termed the *temporally extended self* and achievements in autobiographical narrative production. These scholars pointed out that, although by 18 to 24 months of age children are able to identify themselves in the mirror, they do not yet appreciate that the *self extends backward and forward in time*. To test this concept empirically, Povinelli and his colleagues played a simple game with 2- to 4-year-old children in the course of which they patted the children on the head. Unbeknownst to the children at the time, during one of the pats on the head, the experimenter "marked" the child's head by placing a large, brightly colored sticker on it. The entire game was videotaped. After a 3-minute delay, the child was shown the videotape on which both the marking event and the sticker-bedecked child were clearly apparent.

In contrast to 4-year-olds, three quarters of whom quickly searched for the sticker on their heads, none of the 2-year-olds and only one quarter of the 3-year-olds searched for the sticker (Povinelli, Landau, & Perilloux, 1996). The younger children were able to identify themselves on the image. What they did not seem to be able to do, however, was make the connection between "past self," as evident on the video, and "present self." Additional support for this interpretation was provided in a follow-up study in which 2- and 3-year-old children were shown *live* video images of themselves. When no delay was involved, the majority (62%) of the children searched for the sticker on their heads (Povinelli, 2001).

The implications for autobiography of an understanding of self as extending backward in time are obvious: For a past event to be relevant to the present self, the rememberer must realize that the self who is remembering is the same as the self who experienced the event in the past (e.g., McCormack & Hoerl, 2001). As such, organization of memories of the past around a concept of self is greatly facilitated by an understanding that the present self and the past self are one in the same. Melissa Welch-Ross (2001) reported the results of research in which she tested this suggestion empirically. She examined delayed video self-recognition and contributions to mother–child autobiographical memory conversations in 36-month-old children. She found that children who performed well on the delayed video self-recognition task also tended to exhibit good recall. Thus, 3-year-old children who behaved as if they recognized the relation between past self and present self (as evidenced by reaching for the sticker on their heads) made more contributions to the autobiographical memory conversations relative to children who did not show evidence of appreciation of themselves existing over time.

*Psychological Self.*    Another aspect of the self that develops only after children demonstrate mirror self-recognition and that has been found to be related to developments in autobiographical memory is *appreciation of one's psychological qualities and attributes*. Just as the physical aspect of the self continues over time, so too does the psychological aspect of the self: Our attitudes and dispositions remain relatively consistent over time. One consequence of consistency in psychological attributes and dispositions is temporal coherence. If yesterday I was favorably disposed toward the color purple, chances are that I will find the color purple pleasing today as well. Another consequence of consistency over time is construct coherence. As argued by Melissa Welch-Ross (2001), as children make connections between their impressions and behaviors at Times 1 and 2, their senses of how they typically interpret the world and how they typically behave in it will be strengthened. The result should be a more coherent view of one's psychological self. In turn, a more coherent view of one's psychological self should serve as a stable core around which to organize autobiographical experiences.

Welch-Ross (2001) explored the possibility of relations between consistency in psychological self and autobiographical memory using data from a study in which she and her colleagues asked 3½- to 4½-year-old children and their mothers to participate in autobiographical memory conversations (Welch-Ross, Fasig, & Farrar, 1999). In addition, the children completed the *Children's Self-View Questionnaire* (Eder, 1990). The questionnaire measures 10 dispositional constructs such as aggression, harm avoidance, social anxiety, and social closeness. Children complete the questionnaire by endorsing one of two positions stated by a puppet. They are asked to choose, for example, between the statements that "I like to tease people" and "I don't like to tease people." Children high in consistency on a given construct are those who endorse multiple items in the same direction, such as "I don't like to tease people" and "I don't ever try to push in front of people in line." Children low in consistency were those who endorsed items in the opposite direction: "I don't like to tease people" and "I try to push in front of people in line." The children in Welch-Ross' sample varied in the degree to which they displayed a consistent self-view. Although there were not *direct* relations between consistency of self-view scores and children's recall, she found that children with higher consistency scores derived more benefit from the support that their conversational partners provided in the context of conversations about the past. This and other "conditional" relations are just some of the evidence that cognitive developments alone do not explain age-related changes in autobiographical memory. Further discussion of this point is reserved for chapter 9.

*Subjective Perspective.*    The third aspect of the self that is later to develop (relative to recognition of one's physical features) and that has been found to relate to developments in autobiographical memory is an evaluative or subjective perspective on events—that is, a *perspective on how the event made the experiencer think or feel*. As discussed by Robyn Fivush (2001), whereas episodic memory representations include the *objective* details of what happened, when, and to whom, autobiographical memories are ". . . representations of what happened *to me*" (p. 36; italics in original). The personal ownership that is part and parcel of this type of memory implies a subjective perspective that Fivush (2001) viewed as ". . . the critical component of transforming episodic memories into autobiographical memories" (p. 37). A subjective perspective is apparent when the memory report includes information about the internal states of the narrator, such as references to emotions and cognitions. For example, when a child's narrative includes statements such as "I was *angry* at my brother" or "I *didn't want* to go to the party" (Fivush, 2001, p. 39), it conveys the child's own perspective on the event, one that may or may not be shared by others. It is this subjective perspective that provides the explanation for why the event was funny or sad and, thus, of significance to one's self.

Empirical support for the suggestion that a subjective perspective is related to developments in autobiographical memory comes from research reported by Melissa Welch-Ross (2001). She asked mothers and their 36-month-old children to participate in conversations about past events and asked the children's mothers to complete the *Self-Development Questionnaire* (Stipek, Gralinski, & Kopp, 1990). Included in the questionnaire are items designed to capture an evaluative perspective on the part of the child. For example, mothers were asked to report whether their children used general evaluative terms about themselves or others (e.g., "I'm nice" and "bad dog," respectively), and whether they used evaluative descriptive terms such as "sticky hands." Welch-Ross found that the Evaluative Perspective index derived from the *Self-Development Questionnaire* was related to children's auto-biographical reports: Children with a greater subjective perspective made more contributions to autobiographical memory conversations. However, the relation was found only for children whose mothers exhibited a particular "style" of conversation, discussion of which is reserved for chapter 9.

## Developments in Temporal Concepts

One of the features of autobiographical memories is that they are of specific events that happened at a specific time. This implies that developments in the ability to locate events and experiences in time would contribute to de-velopments in autobiographical memory.

Evidence of age-related changes in infants' abilities to locate events in time was discussed in chapter 4. As early as 9 months of age, a large subset of infants remember the temporal order in which multistep sequences unfold (as tested by elicited and deferred imitation). By 20 months of age, this abil-ity is both reliable and robust. Nevertheless, there are subsequent develop-mental changes that can be expected to contribute to children's abilities to locate events in time. One source of change is in children's abilities to se-quence events at the local level. As discussed in chapter 7, if sequences are constrained by enabling relations, even 9- to 11-month-old infants are able to reproduce them accurately (e.g., Bauer & Mandler, 1992; Carver & Bauer, 1999). In contrast, if sequences lack enabling relations and instead are arbitrarily ordered, it is not until they are almost 2 years of age that chil-dren reliably reproduce them (e.g., Bauer & Thal, 1990; Bauer, Hertsgaard, et al., 1998; Wenner & Bauer, 1999). Children continue to have difficulty sequencing arbitrarily ordered events throughout the preschool years (e.g., Ratner, Smith, & Padgett, 1990). Moreover, children's abilities to accurately sequence events that are logically ordered depend on their comprehension of the structure of the events. As demonstrated in the fire alarm study con-ducted by David Pillemer and his colleagues (discussed in chap. 7), children who did not appreciate the significance of the fire alarm—that it signals cause for evacuation of the building—incorrectly indicated that the alarm went off *after* they had left the building, as opposed to *before* they left the building. Thus, at the local level, we can expect better and better organiza-tion of events with age.

There are also changes in understanding of the temporal properties of events at a more "global" level. They too may be expected to contribute to children's abilities to locate events in place and time. As noted by Teresa McCormack and Christoph Hoerl (2001), the early sequencing abilities dem-onstrated in the context of elicited and deferred imitation, for example, make clear that, *within an event*, children know that Action 1 happened be-fore Action 2. What is not apparent in such studies, however, is an appreciation of *when the entire event occurred* relative to when another entire event occurred. In other words, what is not apparent is *precise temporal location of the event.* Katherine Nelson and Robyn Fivush (2004) suggested that it is only when children begin marking events as having happened "on my birthday," "at Halloween," or "last winter" that we have evidence that they are conceiving of the event as having happened at a particular time. Such markings not only establish that the event happened at a time different from the present, but they permit construction of a time line or organized historical record of when events occurred relative to one another: "my birthday" comes after "Halloween." As discussed by K. Nelson and Fivush (2004), this is a relatively late achievement, as suggested by the observation that consistent use of such markers is not apparent until children are 4 to 5 years of age.

Although it is clear that children's understanding of temporal order at a more global level develops over the course of the preschool years (e.g., Friedman, 1992; Friedman & Kemp, 1998), and although there is a clear logical argument that such developments might relate to age-related changes in autobiographical memory (McCormack & Hoerl, 2001; K. Nelson & Fivush, 2004), there is not a body of data relating the two domains. Clearly, systematic empirical research on the relation is required. Also missing from the literature are studies examining children's abilities to locate memories in a particular place and of how the ability to do so is related to autobiographical memory.

## Developments in Autonoetic Awareness

Autobiographical memory entails a sense of conscious awareness that one is reexperiencing an event that happened at some point in one's own past. This specific type of awareness, termed *autonoetic* or *self-knowing*, has been associated with memory from the time of William James (1890). Indeed for James, "Memory requires more than the mere dating of a fact in the past. It must be dated in *my* past . . . I must think that I directly experienced its occurrence" (p. 612). At the most fundamental level, this component is a requirement that the individual be aware—consciously—that she or he is recalling a past event. This feature thus clearly distinguishes autobiographical memories from implicit or nondeclarative memories (see chaps. 1 and 5). In the case of nondeclarative memory, the individual is not aware of the source of influence on her or his behavior. For example, after having studied a list of words that contained the word *elephant*, individuals are more likely to accurately complete the word fragment "e l _ p _ _ n t" although they are not necessarily able to explain why.

Yet the feature of autonoetic awareness does more than differentiate autobiographical memories from nondeclarative memories: It infuses autobiographical recollections with a sense that one is reliving the event, yet knowing that the event is from the past. As noted by Mark Wheeler (2000), this feature means that autobiographical remembering is closely related to higher order cognitive functions other than memory, including introspecting about present experiences and imagining the future. What these experiences have in common with memory is that they require that one change the focus of attention from activities ongoing in the immediate sensory environment to internal, mental activities of reflection on the past or present or anticipation of the future. In each case, the experiencer maintains the perspective that the source of the cognition is something other than immediate experience. In the case of memory, the source of the representation is a past event.

In children, the ability to engage in cognitive acts that signal autonoetic awareness is not readily apparent until they are 4 to 6 years of age. It is at this age that children show evidence of the ability to identify the sources of their knowledge. For instance, it is not until 4 to 6 years of age that children (a) seem to know what sense organ to use to find out the properties of an object (e.g., that one uses one's eyes, not one's hands, to determine color; O'Neill, Astington, & Flavell, 1992), (b) accurately identify the source of learning of newly acquired words versus words that they have known for a long time (e.g., Taylor, Esbensen, & Bennett, 1994), and (c) distinguish true knowledge from a lucky guess (Sodian & Wimmer, 1987).

There is some evidence that developments in the ability to identify the sources of knowledge are related to improvements in recall. For instance, 3- and 5-year-old children who successfully distinguish a lucky guess from true knowledge have been shown to have higher levels of free recall of items on a list relative to same-age peers who fail to make the distinction (Perner & Ruffman, 1995). In addition, children who understand what senses can be used to gain what types of information (e.g., that eyes can determine color, but only hands can determine weight; O'Neill et al., 1992) show an advantage in recall for pictures directly experienced relative to pictures seen only on video, whereas children who fail to evidence such knowledge do not (Perner, 2001). Although correlational, results such as these are consistent with the suggestion that conscious appreciation that the source of a representation is a past event may contribute to autobiographical memory development.

## DEVELOPMENT CHANGES
## IN NARRATIVE SKILLS

The third source of age-related differences in long-term recall over the course of the preschool years is in children's abilities to *report* what they remember. Early in development, children do not have the capacity to describe their memories verbally. As discussed in chapter 4, prior to development of language skills, we must use nonverbal means of testing memory, such as elicited and deferred imitation. It is unlikely that age-related differences in children's abilities to participate in these paradigms are a major source of developmental differences in performance. First, researchers using these techniques take great pains to make certain that children in the target age range are able to perform the actions of the sequences. Second, the degree of challenge of the to-be-remembered events is closely matched to children's abilities (e.g., at 9 months of age, children are tested on two-step sequences; by 24 months of age, they are tested on four- and five-step sequences; e.g., Carver & Bauer, 1999; Bauer & Travis, 1993, respectively). In the case of a verbal paradigm, however, there is reason to believe that the children's verbal abilities could themselves be a source of age-related changes in performance. Throughout the preschool years, there are developments in the basic elements of successful communication (e.g., vocabulary, grammar), as well as developments in the narrative form used to convey stories of past events. I discuss each of these sources of developmental change in turn, with special emphasis on age-related changes in narrative production.

## Basic Elements of Language

Briefly, over the course of the first 4 years of life, most normally developing children go from being strictly nonverbal to using most of the adult forms of grammar. Although there are individual differences, children typically utter their first words sometime between 9 and 15 months of age. On average, by roughly 18 months, they have 50 words in their vocabularies. From this age until first grade, children are estimated to learn 5.5 words per day; by the fifth grade, they understand approximately 40,000 words (Anglin, 1993). Often coincident with the milestone of 50 words, children begin producing simple multiword forms such as "more juice." The first elements of grammar (e.g., morphological markings) are apparent by 30 months of age. By age 4 years, all but the more intricate grammatical forms (e.g., passive constructions) are apparent (in English, that is; there is considerable cross-linguistic variability in grammatical development; see Bloom, 1998; Maratsos, 1998, for reviews). Acquiring the structures of complex sentences and forms continues well into the school years (e.g., Dale, 1976). With developments in the basic elements of language, children are able to convey the contents of their memories more effectively and efficiently.

## Narrative Production

It is no surprise that, as soon as children begin acquiring the basic elements of language, they recruit them in their efforts to communicate. Much (although certainly not all) of early language use is instrumental: Children are undoubtedly trying to *accomplish* something when they utter "more juice."

Whereas children refer to events in the here-and-now as soon as they have words, it is sometime before they use language to refer to the there-and-then. There is an even longer course of development of narrative conventions for telling a story that informs the listener regarding the *who, what, where, when, why,* and *how* of personal experience.

Children begin using past-tense forms by the middle of the second year of life. As discussed by Katherine Nelson and Robyn Fivush (2000), at this young age, the forms typically are used to refer to events from the very recent past (e.g., K. Nelson, 1989; Sachs, 1983) or for routine, "scripted" activities. Indeed during the first 2 years of life, children do not use their language to tell "what happened" in an event already past. They do, however, participate in memory conversations by answering questions posed by adult partners. Essentially, the adult partner tells what happened and asks the child to affirm or deny the events (Eisenberg, 1985). As such, the adult is providing the content as well as the structure of the conversation. For example, the adult might say, "We had ice-cream, didn't we?", and the child would participate by responding "Yes!"

By about 24 months of age, children begin to contribute to memory conversations by providing mnemonic content. At this age, when parents ask their children "What did we have?", they can expect an answer: "Ice-cream!" Children do not, however, go on to elaborate their responses. If the adult wants to know the flavor of the ice cream, for example, she or he must ask that specific question. Thus, the structure of the conversation is provided by the adult, and the burden for keeping the conversation going is born by the adult.

Beginning at around age 3 years, children become fuller participants in memory conversations. Whereas at this age most memory conversations are still initiated by parents, children do bring up past events as potential topics of conversations (K. Nelson & Fivush, 2000). Some children are able to tell complete, albeit brief, stories about past events (e.g., Fivush et al., 1987). More commonly, they participate by providing content-filled responses to inquiries from their parents, as well as some elaborations. An excerpt from a conversation between a 3-year-old girl and her parent that took place in my laboratory illustrates these characteristics well:

Parent:  Do you remember when, um, when we went in our car and we saw some donkeys out our car window? Who was in the car with us?

Child:   *I don't know.*

Parent:  Was Sandy in the car?

Child:   *(nods head in agreement)*

Parent:  Who else was in the car?

Child:   *Dada.*

Parent:  Was it snowing outside that day or was it hot?
Child:   *Cold.*
Parent:  It was cold?
Child:   *And the reindeers, and dada reindeer not there.*
Parent:  A reindeer? Remember those donkeys that came up to our car
         window? They . . .
Child:   *Yeah. It runned closer to you.*
Parent:  But we didn't open our window, did we?
Child:   *No, we don't.*

In this exchange, the parent orients the child to the event by asking the child to recall the context (who was there, whether it was winter or summer). After a few conversational turns, the child provides the information that she saw reindeers (actually donkeys) and that the "dada" reindeer was not there. After a bit more information from her parent, the child contributes the "punch line" of the story, which is that the donkeys "runned closer" to the family car. Although the child's contributions to this conversation lack the quality of a narrative that she would tell on her own, they reflect considerable development in the ability to share past experience.

Developments in narrative continue throughout the balance of the preschool years and beyond. To examine this development, Robyn Fivush and Catherine Haden (1997) followed a group of children longitudinally from 3½ to almost 6 years. This period encompasses the transition from full participation in memory conversations to independent narrative competence. To examine this transition, at each of four time points (3½, 4, 5, and 6 years of age), they collected personal narratives from the children. Throughout the study, Fivush and Haden observed developmental changes in the use of various narrative devices, as well as in the coherence of children's past-event narratives.

At 3½ years of age, children only infrequently oriented the listener to the time and place of an event (*when* and *where*), introduced the characters involved (*who*), and established the background for the experience. By age 6 years, inclusion of these devices was common. Even at the first time point, the children typically stated what actions occurred in the course of the event (*what*); it was not until 6 years of age that children included conditional actions with any frequency (e.g., "*When it turned red light*, we stopped"; p. 186). There was surprisingly little change in the use of evaluations across the period. That is, across the age period of the study, children used about the same number of intensifiers, qualifiers, and internal evaluations. Finally, over the period of the study, the children's narratives were increasingly cohesive. Even at the beginning of the study, the children used simple temporal and causal connections to link the actions of their narratives (e.g., *then, before, after*; and *because, so, in order to*; respectively). As reflected in Fig. 8.2, their use of these devices did not change substantially over time. In contrast, the number of descriptive words the children used, and thus, the amount of elaboration and detail they provided, increased dramatically between 3½ and 6 years.

These developments in narrative skill have profound consequences for the accounts that children provide about past events. For one thing, as a result of these developments, older children tell better stories than younger children: The stories they tell are more complete, easier to follow, and more engaging. In fact older children tell better stories than younger children even when the event happened long ago. In other words, at least in part as a result of increases in narrative competence, children actually report *more* information when they are interviewed about an event after a

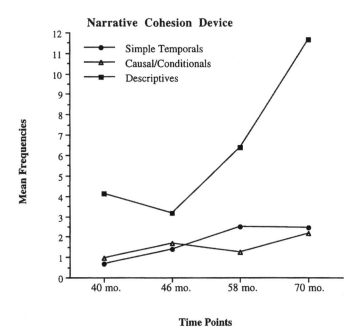

FIG. 8.2.  Mean frequency of use of simple temporal connections (filled circles), causal and conditional connections (open triangles), and descriptive words (filled squares), in a longitudinal sample tested at the ages of 3½ years (40 months), 4 years (46 months), 5 years (58 months), and 6 years (70 months). From "Narrating and Representing Experience: Preschoolers' Developing Autobiographical Accounts," by R. Fivush and C. A. Haden. In P. van den Broek, P. J. Bauer, and T. Bourg (Eds.), *Developmental Spans in Event Representation and Comprehension: Bridging Fictional and Actual Events* (pp. 169–198, Fig. 7.2), 1997, Mahwah, NJ: Lawrence Erlbaum Associates. Copyright © 1997 by Lawrence Erlbaum Associates. Reprinted with permission of Lawrence Erlbaum Associates and the author.

long delay relative to the amount of information provided when they were younger. This trend is, of course, precisely the opposite of the typical decline in recall over time.

The work of Lorraine Bahrick, Robyn Fivush, Janat Parker, and their colleagues provides a striking example of the phenomenon. In 1992, Hurricane Andrew, a Class IV hurricane, devastated portions of southern Florida. Within 6 months of the storm, the researchers interviewed 3- and 4-year-old children about the hurricane (Bahrick, Parker, Merritt, & Fivush, 1998). Six years later, when the children were 9 and 10 years of age, they interviewed the children again. Perhaps not surprisingly, given the nature and extent of the event, all of the children remembered the hurricane at the second interview. Unexpectedly, the children's reports about the hurricane were *twice as long* at the second interview as they had been at the first. Whereas at the first interview the children had reported an average of 57 propositions, 6 years after the storm they reported an average of 117 propositions (Fivush, Sales, Goldberg, Bahrick, & Parker, 2004). The increased length of the reports after 6 years could not be attributed to acquisition of more general knowledge about hurricanes or other storms in the time between interviews: Overwhelmingly, the new information was specific details about the experiences of the children's families, as opposed to general information about storms. These remarkable findings reinforce two important messages. First, they suggest that children, perhaps especially young ones, remember more about events than they convey in their verbal reports. Second, because we have no reason to believe that the children's actual memories of the hurricane improved with time, the findings remind us not to equate verbal reports of events with the memories themselves.

## Why the Development of Narrative Skills Is Important to Autobiographical Memory

Given that in the preschool years and beyond the primary means of expressing memories is through language, it is obvious why changes in narrative skill are important to autobiographical memory: Without them, how would you convey to others the events of your life? Yet many scholars view narrative skills as much more than a convenient vehicle for sharing past experiences. Indeed by some accounts, a well-formed narrative provides not merely the "icing" on the cake, but the organizational "glue" that holds together the bits and pieces of stored experience that together make up an event memory. Encoding an event along the dimensions of a narrative provides a "frame" for organization. Thus, a well-internalized frame not only guides the telling of a story, but its encoding, storage, and retrieval as well. In this regard, the narrative frame functions as the "script" for mnemonic representation of the events of our lives.

A canonical narrative includes a number of elements. Using the journalistic shorthand, it specifies the *who*, *what*, *where*, *when*, *why*, and *how* of an event or experience. Although easy to say, this is actually a tall order. The narratives of young children often do not identify who is performing the actions (Peterson, 1990). In response to a question such as "Tell me about the last time you went to the beach," it is not uncommon for a young preschooler to launch right in with "She picked up shells," seemingly without so much as a thought that who "she" is might not be obvious to the listener. Yet even the egocentric response of this young narrator conveys *what* happened in the course of the event: Shells were picked up. Indeed the most basic personal narratives typically include at least one action (e.g., Miller & Sperry, 1988). In this example, the *where* was provided by the questioner: at the beach. This is fortunate given that only about one third of 2-year-old children's narratives include orientation to place (Peterson, 1990). *When* locates the event in a particular time and, in this example, is also provided by the questioner: the *last time* you went to the beach. Again this is fortunate given that 2- to 3-year-olds rarely locate events in a particular time (Peterson, 1990). With age, children more frequently include important orienting information (i.e., the *who*, *where*, and *when*), and also use a greater variety of orienting devices (e.g., Peterson & McCabe, 1983). For example, whereas younger children tend to introduce characters by name only, older children provide descriptions of the characters.

*Why* an event unfolded the way it did is an element of the causal structure discussed in chapter 7. In the example in the preceding paragraph, the motivation for picking up shells can only be assumed. Over the course of the preschool years, children make the *why* of events more explicit by incorporating into their narratives more causal and conditional temporal devices (e.g., Fivush & Haden, 1997). Finally, in the context of autobiographical narrative, *how* conveys the "texture" of events by noting the attitudes, interests, and responses of the participants in the event, as well as adjectives, adverbs, and modifiers that paint a vivid picture of the experience. From a young age, children include in their narratives intensifiers (e.g., "It was *so* fun"), qualifiers (e.g., "I didn't like the cake *but the icing was okay*"), and internal evaluations (e.g., "I was *scared*"; e.g., Fivush & Haden, 1997; see also Miller & Sperry, 1988; Peterson & McCabe, 1983). The amount of descriptive detail provided increases dramatically over the course of the preschool years. In the study by Fivush and Haden (1997) just described, for example, children went from using approximately 4 descriptive terms per event at 3½ years to using 12 such terms per event at 6 years (see Fig. 8.2). The result is a much more elaborate narrative that brings both the storyteller and the listener to the brink of reliving the experience.

The elements of a narrative do more than provide the listener with the information she or he needs to understand the event. Critically, the narrative structure also provides a handy tool for differentiating one event from another, as well as for creating associative links between events. Even highly similar events or experiences differ from one another in a number of ways. What makes one experience different from another is that *who* was there is different, *what* was done is different, or *how* the experience felt is different. When each of these elements is encoded with some specificity, they set different experiences apart from one another. At the same time, they provide the opportunity for linking one experience with another. When you encode "shells," you are reminded of other episodes of your life that involved shells. When you encode "fun," you are reminded of other episodes that were fun (and perhaps of some that were decidedly "not fun"). When you encode the participants, you are reminded of other episodes that involved those participants, and so forth. The point is that each of these elements has the potential to provide the distinctions that make one event stand out from another in memory, as well as the commonalities that link experiences with one another. As such, development of the canonical narrative form not only provides a means of telling others a good story, but of encoding and consolidating events in a way that simultaneously preserves their uniqueness and integrates them with other memories in long-term stores. We may expect then that both developmental and individual differences in narrative skill will be systematically related to variability in autobiographical memory.

## SUMMARY AND CONCLUSIONS

In this chapter, I provided three answers to the question "what develops?" in children's recall of specific past events in general and autobiographical experiences in particular. One contributor to developmental change is improvement in the efficiency of the basic mnemonic processes of encoding, consolidation, storage, and retrieval. These improvements likely are the result of neural developments throughout the preschool period (and beyond). Another source of age-related differences in children's recall of past events is development in a number of conceptual domains. Specifically, there are theoretical reasons to expect that changes in the self-concept, in concepts that permit location of events in time (and in place), and in understanding of the sources of knowledge all may contribute to event and autobiographical memory. The available empirical literature, although not large, is largely consistent with theoretical expectations. Finally, developments in children's narrative skills were considered as a third source of age-related change in event and autobiographical memory. Clearly, advances in narrative skill make for better stories about past events. They are more than just a "convenience" for communicating stories to others, however: They also provide a framework for structuring experience by facilitating encoding, consolidation, storage, and retrieval of the distinctive features that make events memorable over the long term.

The sources of age-related change in autobiographical memory development are interesting and important in their own right. They are also relevant to evaluation of the candidate explanations for childhood amnesia outlined in chapter 3. Identification of changes in basic mnemonic processes clearly bears on suggestions derived from theories that emphasize cognitive developments between infancy and the preschool years as responsible for the emergence of autobiographical memory and the "offset" of childhood amnesia. Cognitive explanations are further supported by findings that developments in the conceptual domains of self, time, and understanding of the sources of one's cognitions are linked with changes in event memory and memory for autobiographical experiences. The third suggestion of "what develops"—namely, narrative skills—relates to cognitive accounts as well: After all, narrative skills are a cognitive (and linguistic) achievement.

From the perspective of the final category of explanation for childhood amnesia introduced in chapter 3—namely, sociocultural accounts—cognitive (and linguistic) achievements are necessary, but not sufficient, explanations for the emergence of autobiographical memory. In this conceptualization, autobiographical memory is the product of multiple interactive forces, including basic cognitive (and specifically, memory) abilities, language, and importantly, social interaction. It is largely through social interaction in general, and the process of joint reminiscing in particular, that the "raw materials" of an autobiography are shaped. In the language of the introduction to this chapter, in this perspective, neither the cake (basic mnemonic skills and specific conceptual developments) nor the icing on it (narrative skills) is a strictly cognitive (or linguistic) achievement. Rather, the complex confection is as much a social as a cognitive creation, "baked" as it is in the context of the family and larger society within which autobiographical experiences are had and in which memories of them are formed and shared. By this account, to understand developments in autobiographical memory, we must consider the processes by which memory skills are socialized in the context of the family and wider culture. These processes are the subjects of chapter 9.

# 9

# The Context of Autobiographical Memory Development

*The destiny of human individuals . . . is to enter into a cultural environment,
complete with all the social institutions, symbolic forms, artifacts, activities,
interpersonal scripts, rules, expectations, technologies, fashions, moral stric-
tures, and so on. Not least of these are the languages of the groups within
which participatory interactions take place. These languages . . . become the
vehicle of enculturation as well as the content and structure of internal representations and the tools of complex thinking. Thus to a large extent in the
course of human childhood, between about 2 and 6 years of age, language
and the surrounding culture take over the human mind.*
—Katherine Nelson (1996, p. 325)

In the excerpt that opens this chapter, Katherine Nelson (1996) made clear
that children do not develop in a vacuum. This basic fact of life has far-
reaching implications; autobiographical memory development is well within
its reach. Indeed this simple fact of life is the starting point of sociocultural
perspectives on the development of autobiographical memory. As outlined in
chapter 8, there are many "raw materials" for autobiographical memory, perhaps the most fundamental of which is the ability to encode, consolidate,
store, and later retrieve representations of specific past events. Recognition
of the relevance of events for one's self, location of events in time (and in
place), and awareness that the origins of recollective experiences are episodes from the past are additional essential contributors. Yet as Katherine
Nelson's words imply, these ingredients alone are not the "stuff" of which autobiographical memories are made. Nor are they autonomous developments.
Creation of internal representations—of which autobiographical memories
are one type—depends on a number of additional elements gained in specific

sociocultural contexts. Those contexts leave their marks on the developing child, essentially "taking over" the young mind.

From early in development, children participate in the activity of verbally sharing with others of their culture the experiences of their lives. As described in chapter 8, early on, much of the work of recollecting past experiences falls to more accomplished conversational partners, typically the children's parents. Yet even before they become principal contributors to these conversations, children begin to learn from the activity the "art" of talking about events from the past. By listening and contributing to narratives, they learn what features to include in them (i.e., the *who, what, where, when, why,* and *how* of events). Over time the form becomes more than a format for reporting on events: It functions as a means to organize memory representations as well. Reminiscing also imparts the important lesson that the purpose of talking about the past is to share your thoughts, feelings, reactions, and experiences with others. Thus, by participating in conversations, children come to appreciate the social function of reminiscing.

As this discussion should make clear, in the sociocultural perspective, autobiographical memory is as much a social as a personal construction. It is thought to be influenced by the immediate environment of the family, as well as by the larger cultural milieu in which the child is raised. The suggestion is that families and cultures that seem to place a high premium on talking about the past, and on the child's own experiences, provide a rich context for the development of structures for organizing autobiographical memories and for sharing them with others. As a result, the development of autobiographical memory is facilitated. Of course the features of the familial and cultural environment are always "channeled" through the child. Thus, the characteristics of the individual child will interact with those of the surrounding contexts. The result will be group as well as individual differences in autobiographical memory and its expression. To the extent that the resulting differences match those seen when adults recollect childhood experiences, the approach will have succeeded in providing not only an account of the development of autobiographical memory in childhood, but a productive perspective on childhood amnesia as well.

In the balance of this chapter, I take a number of steps to elaborate the sociocultural approach to the study of autobiographical memory development. The first step is to describe the "proximal" narrative context in which autobiographical memory develops—namely, that of the family. As becomes apparent, parents seem to adopt different "styles" in the conversations about past events that they have with their young children. The second step is to determine whether the differences in parental styles have implications for children's development, both in the domain of narrative skills and in the pace and progress of change in related conceptual domains (i.e., concepts of self, time, and the source of knowledge). The third step is to examine possible variations in the processes of development that might be associated with characteristics of individual children. The fourth step is to describe the "distal" context in which autobiographical memory develops—that of the larger culture in which the child is raised. Throughout, major questions are whether there is evidence that the social contexts in which children are raised seem to "matter" for autobiographical memory development, and whether the observed patterns are consistent with those apparent in adults' recollections of their childhoods.

## FAMILIAL INFLUENCES ON NARRATIVE SOCIALIZATION AND CONCEPTUAL DEVELOPMENT

Even monologues—such as those produced by Emily in her crib (K. Nelson, 1989; see chap. 7 for discussion)—are influenced by the social context in which children experience the events of their lives. The importance of the context for getting narrative ability off the ground is readily apparent when the early course of autobiographical narrative production is considered. As discussed in chapter 8 (see also Fivush, Haden, & Reese, 1996), before the age of 2 years, children rarely reminisce spontaneously. Instead the events of the past are mentioned by a conversational partner who invites the child to contribute to the conversation by either affirming or repeating the information provided by the adult. Between 2 and 3 years of age, children begin to contribute content to memory conversations, but they are still dependent on their dialogue partners for moving the conversation along. It is only in the fourth year of life that children begin to bear the burden of both structuring and filling in the content of conversations about past events.

The description just offered focused on the changing nature of the child's contributions to conversations about past events. Of course the role of the adult partner in the conversation is also changing. Indeed the sequence illustrates a process of adult supporting or "scaffolding" of a task that at first is too difficult to be accomplished by the child alone. Since the mid-1980s, it has been apparent that parents differ in the way they scaffold their children's developing narrative skills. Moreover, it is increasingly obvious that variability among parents is systematically related to individual differences in children's narrative skill development. In the subsection to follow, I characterize the major dimensions of difference observed among parents. I consider some of the implications of stylistic differences for children's autobiographical narrative development in the subsection thereafter.

## Parental "Styles" of Conversation

One of the earliest descriptions of differences in parents' narrative "style" in the context of conversations about past events was provided by Susan Engel (1986). Engel noted that when they talked with their children about the past, some mothers tended to have short conversations with few embellishments. These *practical rememberers* tended to approach the conversation as a task to be accomplished—namely, to get their children to remember a particular event or aspect of it. Other mothers engaged in long conversations in which they described events in elaborate detail. Engel identified this group of mothers as *reminiscers*. She suggested that mothers using the reminiscing style seemed to approach the conversation as an opportunity to share a memory with their children and, in the process, co-construct the past.

Observations similar to those made by Susan Engel (1986) have since been made by several different research groups (e.g., Bauer & Burch, 2004; Fivush & Fromhoff, 1988; Haden, Ornstein, Eckerman, & Didow, 2001; Hudson, 1990b; McCabe & Peterson, 1991; Reese, Haden, & Fivush, 1993). Although a variety of labels have been used to capture the differences, there is consensus that parents generally exhibit one of two styles that vary in terms of the apparent goals for reminiscing and in terms of the parents' contributions to conversations. Parents who frequently engage in conversations about the past, provide rich descriptive information about previous experiences, and invite their children to "join in" on the construction of stories about the past are said to use an *elaborative* style. In contrast, parents who provide fewer details about past experiences and instead pose specific questions to their children are said to use a *low-elaborative* or *repetitive* style. In Table 9.1 are two examples from conversations recorded in my laboratory that help illustrate the difference, as well as why the low-elaborative style is also described as "repetitive." In both cases, the conversations are between mothers and their 3-year-old children.

Parents exhibiting a more *elaborative* style, such as illustrated in Conversation 1, seem to have a "social" goal for reminiscing. That is, they do not seem to be trying to get their children to remember specific pieces of information. Rather, the goal seems to be to engage the child in conversation. In the first example, the mother opens the conversation by mentioning a specific event. When the child fails to respond, the mother provides additional information. She then expands on the child's minimal reply and, in the next turn, provides some descriptive information to flesh out the story ("Oh and it was so soft"). In the next exchange, the child volunteers some new information ("And they got away") that the mother affirms on her next turn. Across the conversation, the mother contributes a lot of detail, as well as a range of narrative elements. Indeed in this brief exchange, she manages to hit almost all of the highlights of the canonical narrative form. Information is provided

TABLE 9.1

Examples of Conversations Between Mothers and Their 3-Year-Old Children Illustrating Elaborative and Low-Elaborative Parental Styles

| | |
|---|---|
| Conversation 1 (Elaborative style) | |
| Mother: | Say, [child's name], what was at Lauren's house a long time ago at her birthday party? |
| Child: | (no response) |
| Mother: | What did you hold—they were so tiny—at Lauren's house? Remember? |
| Child: | A baby. |
| Mother: | A baby kitty. |
| Child: | Yeah, a baby kitty. |
| Mother: | That's right. Oh and it was so soft. How many kitties did she have? |
| Child: | Um, five. |
| Mother: | Uh-huh. That's right. |
| Child: | And they got away. |
| Mother: | And they got away from you. Yeah. |
| Conversation 2 (Low-elaborative style) | |
| Mother: | [child's name], do you remember going to Sandy's house and playing at her house? |
| Child: | (nods in agreement) |
| Mother: | Did they have some kids at her house? |
| Child: | Yeah. |
| Mother: | What kinds of kids were at her house? |
| Child: | David. |
| Mother: | David. Was he the only child that was at her house? |
| Child: | (nods in agreement) |
| Mother: | What other kids were at her house? |

about *who* (the child himself), *what* (held kitties), *where* (at Lauren's house), *when* (a long time ago), and *how* (the kitties were soft)—the only element missing is *why*. Although not apparent from this brief excerpt, the elaborative style is characterized by more lengthy conversations relative to the low-elaborative style.

Parents exhibiting a less elaborative or *low-elaborative* style, such as illustrated in Conversation 2, seem to have a "cognitive" goal for reminiscing. They seem to be testing their children's memories for specific aspects of events. This flavor comes through in Conversation 2 in the form of the mother's repetition of the question of who was at Sandy's house. One result of the tendency to repeat old information, rather than make unique contributions, is that parents exhibiting the low-elaborative style tend to provide few details and, thus, few narrative elements in a conversation. Conversations involving parents using this style also tend to be shorter relative to conversations involving parents using the elaborative style.

Stylistic differences are robust and extend beyond the context of mother–child conversations about past events. For example, although much of the research on stylistic differences in early autobiographic contexts has been with mothers, the limited research done with fathers indicates that they too exhibit stylistic differences (Haden, Haine, & Fivush, 1997). Whereas both mothers and fathers become more elaborative as their children get older and more narratively skilled, levels of elaboration nevertheless are correlated over time (Reese, Haden, & Fivush, 1993). In addition, mothers at least show similar patterns with multiple children in the family (Haden, 1998; K. Lewis, 1999; the relevant studies with fathers have not yet been done). Stylistic differences also extend beyond the context of conversations to imitation-based paradigms. Melissa Burch and I observed mothers as they attempted to teach and then test their children's recall of four-, five-, and six-step sequences such as "make a rattle" (see Fig. 7.6). The mothers provided more elaborations on the most difficult sequences (i.e., the longest ones), yet mothers who provided the highest numbers of elaborations on the six-step sequences were also the most elaborative on the simpler, four-step sequences (Bauer & Burch, 2004). Findings such as these make clear that differences in adults' behavior in mnemonic contexts involving their children are the rule, rather than the exception.

## Relations Between Parental Style and Autobiographical Memory Development

Differences in the ways parents approach and contribute to conversations about past events with their children are interesting in their own right. They are more than that, however: Parental stylistic differences have been found to have implications for children's autobiographical narrative development. There is a small body of evidence that they relate to conceptual developments as well. Each is discussed in turn.

*Relations With Narrative Development.* Both concurrently and over time, children of parents using a more elaborative style report more about past events than children of parents using a less elaborative style (e.g., Bauer & Burch, 2004; Fivush, 1991b; Fivush & Fromhoff, 1988; Peterson & McCabe, 1994). Both of these patterns are nicely illustrated in a longitudinal study conducted by Elaine Reese, Catherine Haden, and Robyn Fivush (1993; see also Fivush, Haden, & Adam, 1995; Fivush, Haden, & Reese, 1996; Haden et al., 1997; Reese, Haden, & Fivush, 1996, for analyses from the same longitudinal sample). The study was based on 24 families enrolled when the target children were 3½ years of age. The families were seen again when the children were 4, 5, and 6 years of age. By the end of the study, 19 families remained in the sample.

As reflected in Fig. 9.1, Reese et al. (1993) observed concurrent relations between maternal elaborations and children's memory responses at all four time points. The correlations were strong, ranging from .59 to .85. Thus, at

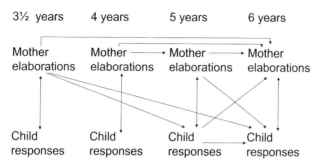

FIG. 9.1.   Concurrent and cross-lagged relations between maternal elaborations and children's memory responses in a longitudinal sample at four time
points. Based on Reese et al. (1993), Fig. 5.

each session, the more elaborations mothers provided, the more memory
contributions their children made. Concurrent relations between maternal
elaborations and children's participation in memory interviews have been observed in samples of children as young as 19 months of age (Farrant & Reese,
2000) and 2 to 2½ years of age (Hudson, 1990b). In addition, in my laboratory, Melissa Burch and I observed concurrent relations between maternal
verbal elaborations and 24-month-old children's performance in an imitation-based task. Children of mothers who produced more elaborations were
more engaged in the task, as measured by production of the target actions of
the four-, five-, and six-step sequences on which they were tested (Bauer &
Burch, 2004). Thus, the effects of maternal elaboration extend beyond verbal paradigms to nonverbal measures of children's memory performance in
controlled laboratory tasks.

Also apparent in the data from Reese et al. (1993) are "long-distance" relations between maternal verbal behavior and children's memory contributions (i.e., relations over time). Specifically, mothers who used more elaborations when their children were 3½ years of age had children who at 5 and 6
years of age made more memory contributions. Maternal elaborations at the
5-year time point were related to children's memory contributions at the 6-
year time point. Largely absent from the data were relations (a) within children across time (e.g., children's memory responses at 3½ years were not related to children's memory responses at 4 years), and (b) between children's
behavior at earlier time points and mothers' behavior at later time points
(e.g., children memory responses at 3½ years were not related to mother
elaborations at 4 years). In both cases, the only such relations were observed
between the 5- and 6-year time points. The entire pattern is consistent with
suggestions that the process of autobiographical narrative development is
one of social construction, with more experienced partners scaffolding the
performance of their younger collaborators. Keryn Harley and Elaine Reese
(1999) have since extended this pattern of findings to mother–child dyads

enrolled at 19 months of age and followed longitudinally until 32 months of age. These results imply that scaffolding begins well before children begin making independent contributions to memory conversations.

If it is through conversations about past events that children internalize the canonical narrative form for organizing and expressing their memories, then we should see evidence that the skills they acquire extend beyond the context of mother–child conversations, and that the skills remain with the children with the passage of time. There is evidence in support of both predictions. Evidence that the skills extend beyond the context of mother–child conversations comes from relations between maternal use of particular narrative devices in the context of mother–child conversations and children's performance in independent narrative tasks. For instance, Melissa Burch and I found that mothers' use of *associations* (i.e., relating the event being discussed to other, similar events from the child's past) when talking with their children about past events was related to 3-year-old children's abilities to talk with an experimenter about laboratory events (such as *making a rattle* and *making a party hat*; see Fig. 7.6) they had experienced months earlier (Bauer & Burch, 2004). Research by Keryn Harley and Elaine Reese (1999) suggested that these effects may be observed only after children become truly active participants in memory conversations, however. Prior to that time (i.e., before about 32 months of age), the effects of maternal style do not appear to generalize to children's independent memory contributions. This finding illustrates the need for additional research on early mother–child conversational interactions and their consequences for children's independent performance.

Evidence that the skills children are acquiring not only extend beyond the context, but also persist over time, is suggested by a number of studies. For example, Carole Peterson and Allyssa McCabe (1992) followed two children and their mothers for an 18-month period, beginning when the children were 27 months of age. Both mothers were highly elaborative, yet one mother emphasized contextual information to a greater extent. That is, she asked a large number of *who*, *where*, and *when* questions. Between 27 and 44 months, her child came to incorporate a lot of contextual information into her independent narratives. The other mother tended to emphasize temporal information, and, over time, her children's independent narratives were better organized. In a similar vein, Robyn Fivush (1991b) found that mothers differed in the amount of orienting and evaluative information they provided in conversations with their 2½- to 3-year-old children. Twelve months later, children whose mothers had emphasized these types of content included more orientations and evaluations in their independent narratives.

The relations just discussed between maternal style at an earlier point in time and children's later independent narratives are relatively specific: Narrative devices that mothers used when their children were younger were especially prominent in children's narratives as they grew older. This raises the question of whether children are acquiring a narrative *form* for organizing their reports or specific *content* to be inserted into the form. That is, are children learning a narrative structure or are they learning a specific narrative? If the influence is on *what* children say, then there would be no reason to expect effects of maternal style to extend beyond events that mothers and children have "rehearsed" together. We have already seen that there are relations between maternal style variables and children's independent narrative production. Moreover, even when mothers and children have talked about a specific event, there is little evidence that maternal narrative content is incorporated into children's subsequent independent reports. In a direct test of this possibility, Robyn Fivush, Catherine Haden, and Elaine Reese (1996) evaluated the amount of information from a previous mother–child interview that children included in an independent narrative. They found that children repeated only 10% of the information that their mothers had provided in a previous interview. These patterns are inconsistent with the suggestion that children are learning a particular narrative and instead suggest that they are developing a general narrative structure. In Judith Hudson's (1990b) words, children ". . . are learning *how* to remember, not *what* to remember" (p. 194).

Finally, it is important to note that, whereas little of the specific content that mothers provide as they reminisce with their children appears in the children's subsequent independent narratives, there are relations between the content of conversation *as events are experienced* and children's subsequent recall. In separate studies, Catherine Haden and her colleagues (Haden et al., 2001) and Minda Tessler and Katherine Nelson (1994) found that what might be referred to as a *dual focus* on objects or activities by mothers and their children has a profound effect on later recall. Specifically, objects or activities that were labeled and discussed by *both* mothers and their children as they experience an event—so-called *jointly encoded* items— were better remembered relative to items not jointly encoded. In the work by Haden and her colleagues, 3 weeks after experience of a novel event, $3\frac{1}{2}$- year-old children recalled nearly half (45%) of all jointly encoded items. In contrast, they recalled only a quarter of items that were handled by both mothers and children but labeled only by the mother, or handled by both mothers and children but not labeled at all. Recall of items that were handled by both mothers and children but labeled only by the children was too low even to be analyzed.

Similar effects were reported by Tessler and Nelson (1994). They found that the only elements of a museum visit that 3-year-old children recalled after a 1-week delay were those that the mothers and children had talked about during the event. Thus, clearly language works to highlight elements of experience at the time of encoding. It seems to aid children in identifying what is important about the event and thus what they might want to include in a subsequent narrative about it. It does not, however, provide children with the specific content of what to say about the event.

*Relations With Conceptual Development.* The body of evidence relevant to the question of relations between parental styles of conversation and children's narrative development is sizeable. As just reviewed, it paints a consistent picture suggesting that, over time, the narrative environment has implications for the narratives that children themselves produce. The literature that bears on relations between parents' approaches to reminiscing and developments in the concepts that have been implicated in autobiographical memory development is substantially smaller and "spottier"—many of the relevant questions have yet to be asked. Nevertheless, there are some suggestions of relations between the narrative environment in which children are raised and conceptual developments in the domains of self and understanding of the sources of knowledge. To my knowledge, there is not a literature testing relations between parental style and development in children's understanding of temporal concepts.

As noted in chapter 8, there are relations between developments in the self-concept and event and autobiographical memory. One source of evidence was from a study by Keryn Harley and Elaine Reese (1999), in which it was found that children who were earlier to recognize themselves in the mirror (assessed at 19 months) made faster progress in independent autobiographical memory reports (assessed at 25 and 32 months) relative to children who were later to evidence mirror self-recognition. Critically, the relation was not uniform. As depicted in Fig. 9.2, the children who made the greatest progress in independent autobiographical narrative between 25 and 32 months were children who were both early to recognize themselves in the mirror *and* who had mothers classified as *high elaborators*. This finding suggests that there is more than one "pathway" into autobiographical memory. Notice in Fig. 9.2 that, at 25 months of age, the children who made the largest number of independent memory elaborations were those who, relative to their peers, were *late* to evidence mirror self-recognition (but whose mothers were highly elaborative).

Another aspect of the self-concept discussed in chapter 8 concerned the subjective or evaluative perspective. As noted in chapter 8, a subjective perspective is evident when children use evaluative terms to describe themselves or others, such as "I'm nice" and "bad dog" (respectively). Melissa Welch-Ross (2001) found that an evaluative perspective (as measured by the Evaluative Perspective index of the *Self-Development Questionnaire*; Stipek, Gralinski, & Kopp, 1990) was related to children's autobiographical reports: Children with a greater subjective perspective made more contributions to autobiographical memory conversations. However, as reflected in Table 9.2, the relation was only apparent for children of mothers classified as using a

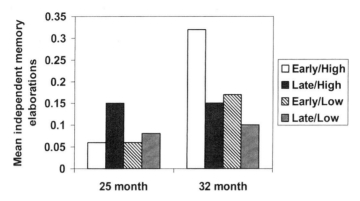

FIG. 9.2.    Children's independent memory elaborations at 25 and 32 months of age as a function of mirror self-recognition status (i.e., did [early recognizers] or did not [late recognizers] exhibit mirror self-recognition at 19 months) and maternal narrative style (i.e., high elaborator or low elaborator). Based on Harley & Reese (1999), Fig. 3; values are approximate.

TABLE 9.2
Contributions to Mother–Child Memory Conversations
by 3-Year-Old Children as a Function of the Child's
Evaluative Perspective and the Mother's Narrative Style

|  | Child's Level of Evaluative Perspective | | |
|---|---|---|---|
| Maternal Style | High | Medium | Low |
| High elaborative | 2.47 | .90 | .61 |
| Low elaborative | .61 | .71 | .57 |

*Note.*    Based on Welch-Ross (2001), Table 6.1. The index of children's contributions was the ratio of child memory responses to conversational placeholders.

highly elaborative maternal style. That is, relative to their peers with lower scores on the evaluative self-awareness measure, children with higher scores made more contributions to the autobiographical conversations, but only if their mothers used a high-elaborative style. For children of mothers classified as using a low-elaborative style, the level of evaluative self-awareness was un-related to children's mnemonic contributions. This finding illustrates the in-terplay between the child's subjective perspective and the narrative environ-ment in which autobiography is practiced.

Relations between parental narrative style and an evaluative self or sub-jective perspective are also observed over time. Specifically, children whose mothers used a number of evaluative terms in autobiographical memory conversations when the children were 3½ years of age used a larger number of such terms when they were 6 years of age (Fivush, 2001; Haden et al., 1997). Maternal behavior at 3½ years predicted children's behavior at 6 years even after differences in children's own use of evaluations at 40 months, and both children's and mothers' use of evaluations at 70 months had been taken into account.

Finally, there has been only a little research on how maternal narrative style relates to developments in children's understanding of the representational nature of mind. In the one study of which I am aware, Melissa Welch-Ross (1997) found that maternal elaborations were positively related to 3½- to 4½-year-old children's scores on tasks designed to assess their understanding of mind; these scores were negatively related to maternal repetitions. In other words, children who did well on the tasks had mothers who used a larger number of elaborations and a smaller number of repetitions.

Whereas there has been little research on the familial variable of maternal narrative style on children's understanding of the representational nature of mind, there has been more research on possible relations with other familial variables—notably, family size and constellation. For example, research by Josef Perner and his colleagues revealed associations between the number of siblings a child has and performance on false-belief tasks (i.e., tasks in which children are required to reconcile their initial [erroneous] impressions with the true state of affairs; e.g., Perner, Ruffman, & Leekam, 1994): Children with siblings perform better on such tasks relative to children without siblings. This finding suggests that mental-states understanding is facilitated by sibling interaction. This suggestion is supported by evidence that the quality of sibling interactions before age 3 years predicts false-belief task performance at age 4 (Dunn, Brown, Slomkowski, Tesla, & Youngblade, 1991).

Research by Charlie Lewis and his colleagues revealed that differences in false-belief task performance can be explained in part by the number of adult kin and the number of older children (other than siblings) with whom children interact on a regular basis (C. Lewis, Freeman, Kyriakidou, Maridaki-Kassotaki, & Berridge, 1996). Lewis and his colleagues also brought greater specificity to the "sibling effect" identified by Perner et al. (1994). They provided strong evidence that it is not simply a sibling effect, but an *older* sibling effect. As reflected in Table 9.3, the number of older siblings a 3- to 5-year-old child has is strongly related to her or his success on false-belief tasks. Children who were first born, and thus had no older siblings, had the lowest rates of success on the entire complement of false-belief tasks administered to them. Children who were third or later born, and thus had at least two older siblings, had the highest rates of success.

## Children Affect Their Own Socialization

The manner in which adults structure and participate in conversations about past events with their children clearly relates to the development of children's skills in producing autobiographical narratives, both collaboratively

TABLE 9.3
The Percentage of Children Who Performed Well
on False-Belief Tasks as a Function of Birth Order

| | Birth Order | | |
| --- | --- | --- | --- |
| Experiment | First Born | Second Born | Third or Later Born |
| Experiment 1 | 50% | 76% | 95% |
| Experiment 2 | 16% | 40% | 72% |

Note. More challenging versions of the questions were posed to the children in Experiment 2 relative to Experiment 1, which accounts for the lower level of success in the second experiment. Data from C. Lewis et al. (1996).

and independently. But are adults the only important influences on children's narratives? In other words, are characteristics of the adult all that matter, or do children differ in ways that also influence the course of development of their own autobiographical skills? In keeping with the tradition in cognitive psychology of focusing on group trends, relatively little attention has been paid to how the process of socialization might differ as a function of characteristics of the children being socialized. In this section, I discuss the research dealing with three characteristics of children that have been explored for their implications for the socialization of autobiographical narrative, namely, children's gender, language, and temperament. I also examine one characteristic of the parent–child dyad: attachment history. Although there is a small body of evidence that parental style differences also relate to conceptual developments associated with autobiographical memory, the possibility that characteristics of children themselves might influence their own development in these domains is not discussed due to lack of relevant data.

*Children's Gender.* As was the case in the earlier discussion of memory development in the first years of life (chap. 4), one of the first candidate sources of variability to come to mind is gender. Whereas gender bears little relation with children's nonverbal recall, it seems to be an important factor in narrative skill development. That is, there are differences in the behavior of parents and in the behavior of children as a function of gender of the child (but not as a function of the gender of the parent).

In the context of autobiographical memory narratives, gender was considered potentially important in part because of differences in adult women's and adult men's autobiographical narratives, discussed in chapter 2. Briefly, when they talk about past events, relative to men, women tend to produce narratives that are longer, more detailed, and more vivid. One of most salient differences between the narratives of women and men is the way emotion is represented. Women report talking about emotions more frequently than do men (Allen & Hamsher, 1974), and memories about emotional experiences seem to be more readily accessible to women than to men (Davis, 1999). Leif Stennes, Jennifer Haight, and I found that, in their autobiographical narratives about events from the age of 7 and later, adult women include more emotion words than do men (Bauer, Stennes, & Haight, 2003). The differences were observed even though women and men reported that the events they were recalling were equally personally significant, equally unique, and equally emotionally intense. Women and men also did not differ in their ratings of their confidence in the details of the events or the frequency with which the events had been discussed. These findings suggest that features of the events themselves will not explain the observed gender differences in adults' autobiographical narratives. Instead we must look to other factors to help explain them. Given evidence that autobiographical narrative skills are subject to socialization, researchers have been motivated to determine whether parents talk with their daughters differently than they talk with their sons, and whether the patterns might help explain differences in adulthood.

On the one hand, there is evidence that girls and boys are differentially socialized in the context of conversations about past events. As reviewed by Robyn Fivush (1998), for example, there are documented gender-related differences in the themes that parents select to talk about with their children, in the amount of elaboration they provide in conversations with their children, and in the types of emotion terms that they use. On the other hand, in the context of conversations about past events, the differences tend to be small, and they are not entirely consistent across studies. Moreover, many, although not all, of the findings are from the same group of children—namely, the longitudinal sample followed by Robyn Fivush and her colleagues from 3½ to 6 years. This is the same sample that has been the source of much of the data on differences in autobiographical narrative development associated with a more or less elaborative style used by children's parents (e.g., Reese et al., 1993).

As just noted, the themes of conversation about past events that parents initiate with their children differ as a function of the children's gender. However, they do not seem to differ as a function of parents' gender. For example, Janine Buckner and Robyn Fivush (2000) analyzed the 3½- and 6-year time points from the longitudinal sample, both of which included both mother–child and father–child conversations. They found that, for conversations with their daughters, both mothers and fathers elected to talk about events with social or relational themes (Buckner & Fivush, 2000; see also Fivush, 1993; Fivush & Kuebli, 1997). Over time, with girls, a high percentage (57%) of the themes of conversation were social or interpersonal in nature, compared with a smaller percentage (33%) for boys. In conversations with their daughters, parents tended to talk about people's roles in the emotional experience. The topic might be how happy the child was that she was playing with a favorite friend, for instance.

With sons, parents tended to focus more on autonomous themes that emphasized the individual state of the child: two thirds of conversations with boys emphasized autonomous themes (Buckner & Fivush, 2000; see also Fivush, Brotman, Buckner, & Goodman, 2000). In this type of event, the topic might be how happy the child was that he successfully completed a difficult task. Thus, in this sample, both mothers and fathers tended to emphasize social-relational themes with their daughters and individual-autonomous themes with their sons. The effect may not extend to discussions of events that are negative in tone, however. In a study based on a different sample of children, Fivush and her colleagues found that when dyads were asked to talk about events during which the children felt sad, angry, or fearful, the majority of conversations involving both girls and boys concerned social-relational themes (i.e., 69% and 62% of the conversations with girls and boys, respectively; Fivush, Berlin, McDermott Sales, Mennuti-Washburn, & Cassidy, 2003).

Whereas the extent to which parents talk about different themes with their daughters and their sons may be affected by the emotional valence or content of the events, there is a consistent finding that parents are more elaborative in conversations about past events with their daughters than with their sons (Fivush, 1998). This effect has been observed with children 3½ to 4 years of age (Fivush, Berlin, et al., 2003). It has also been observed longitudinally across the preschool years. As reported by Fivush (1998), over the 3½- to 6-year period of observation of her longitudinal sample, mothers and fathers were more elaborative with their daughters (averaging roughly 22 elaborations per event) than with their sons (averaging roughly 18 elaborations per event). Parents also more frequently confirmed the participation of their daughters in the conversations relative to their sons. These findings suggest that, compared with boys, girls receive more reinforcement for participating in conversations about past events and the conversations in which they engage are more detailed and elaborate.

Differences associated with the gender of the child with whom parents are reminiscing are also apparent in the emotional content of conversations about past events. Susan Adams, Janet Kuebli, Patricia Boyle, and Robyn Fivush (1995) reported that, across the 3½- to 6-year time points, parents used both a greater number and a greater variety of emotion words with their daughters than with their sons. The pattern is indicated in Table 9.4. In a separate sample of 2½-year-olds and their mothers, however, this trend was not apparent and in fact, was even reversed (i.e., mothers used a nominally larger number and variety of emotion words with sons than with daughters; Fivush & Kuebli, 1997). Whether the different patterns are the result of the different ages sampled or differences in the samples themselves cannot be determined from the existing data.

When they are left to their own designs to select events, mothers tend to talk about different emotions with their preschool-age daughters and sons.

TABLE 9.4
Mean Number and Variety of Emotion Words Mothers and Fathers
Used With Daughters and Sons at 3½ and 6 Years of Age

| Time Point/Child Gender | Number | | Variety | |
|---|---|---|---|---|
| | Mothers | Fathers | Mothers | Fathers |
| 3½ years | | | | |
| With daughters | 8.2 | 9.0 | 6.4 | 5.9 |
| With sons | 6.0 | 3.3 | 4.0 | 2.9 |
| 6 years | | | | |
| With daughters | 16.5 | 13.2 | 10.2 | 9.2 |
| With sons | 7.2 | 11.0 | 4.7 | 5.8 |

Note.   Based on Adams et al. (1995), Table 1.

For instance, Fivush and Kuebli (1997) found that the emotion of sadness was more frequently talked about with daughters than with sons (i.e., across 20 girls, sadness was mentioned 28 times; across 20 boys, sadness was mentioned 10 times). The emotion of anger was more frequently talked about with sons than with daughters (i.e., across 20 boys, anger was mentioned 14 times; across 20 girls, anger was mentioned 4 times; Fivush & Kuebli, 1997; data abstracted from Table 10.2). For the emotion of sadness, the pattern persisted over time and was still apparent at age 6 years.

Differential attention to the emotion of sadness with daughters and sons is also apparent when mothers are specifically asked to talk about events in which their preschool-age children felt sad or angry. In conversations about these targeted emotions, mothers spend more time talking about sadness with their daughters and more time talking about anger with their sons (as measured by the number of conversational turns that mothers and children exchange; Fivush, 1991a; this effect was not observed in Fivush, Berlin, et al., 2003, however). Mothers did not differ in the amount of time they spent talking with their daughters and sons about events in which their children were scared or happy. Together these findings suggest that both mothers and fathers discuss emotional aspects of past events differently with daughters and sons.

The "lessons" about narrative in general and emotion language in particular offered by their parents are not lost on preschool-age children. For instance, Janine Buckner and Robyn Fivush (1998) found that 7½-year-old girls tend to produce longer, more coherent, and more detailed narratives than boys of the same age. In addition, relative to the boys', more of the girls' narratives were social in their theme (i.e., 71% and 88% of narrative were social in nature, respectively). Girls and boys also differ in use of emotion language in their autobiographical narratives. As discussed by Janet Kuebli, Susan Butler, and Robyn Fivush (1995), in the longitudinal sample that was the source of much of the data described in this section, across the 3½- 5-, and 6-year time points, both the number and variety of emotion words used by girls increased (depicted in Fig. 9.3). For boys, in contrast, neither number nor variety increased.

The trends just described result in a striking gender difference. As suggested by Fig. 9.3, whereas at 3½ years of age, the girls and boys in Kuebli et al. (1995) sample did not differ in the number or variety of emotion words used, by the time the children were 6 years of age, girls were producing both a greater number and a larger variety of emotion words relative to boys. Janine Buckner and Robyn Fivush (1998) reported that this pattern was still apparent at 7½ years of age (based on a sample that included 14 children from the longitudinal sample analyzed in the study by Kuebli et al., 1995). Over the course of the preschool years then, girls come to pepper their autobiographical narratives with emotion, whereas boys do not increase in their emotional expressiveness. This pattern is reflected in adults' autobiographical narratives about events from their childhoods. As discussed at the beginning of this section, when adult women were asked to reminisce about events from the age of 7 years and later, they included in their narratives more emotion terms relative to men. In their narratives about events from before the age of 7, however, there was no difference in the amount of emotion language represented (Bauer, Stennes, & Haight, 2003). This time frame corresponds quite closely with the observations in Kuebli et al. (1995) and Buckner and Fivush (1998) of gender differences in emotional expression by the age of 6 to 7½ years.

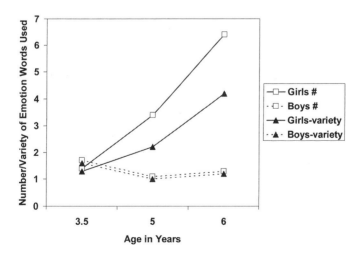

FIG. 9.3.    The number (open squares) and variety (closed triangles) of emotion words used by girls (solid lines) and boys (broken lines) in a longitudinal sample at 3½, 5, and 6 years of age. Based on Kuebli et al. (1995), Table 2.

*Children's Language.* There has been relatively little work on the question of whether differences in children's language abilities relate to the process of socialization into the canonical autobiographical narrative form. Yet as discussed by Kate Farrant and Elaine Reese (2000), children's language abilities, perhaps especially early in autobiographical memory development, may play an important role in children's socialization. For example, children who are more participatory may be expected to engender greater parental responsiveness. Also children who have greater receptive language skills may be expected to benefit more from the language input they receive. Consistent with these possibilities, Farrant and Reese found that both children's expressive language abilities and their receptive language abilities were related to maternal reminiscing style concurrently as well as over the period of 19 to 40 months. Harley and Reese (1999) reported that the relations were especially strong for children who were later to demonstrate recognition of themselves in the mirror.

Melissa Burch and I also found relations between children's vocabulary development and characteristics of maternal style. In this study, mothers were asked to teach four- to six-step sequences to their 24-month-old children and then test their memories for them immediately and after a 1-week delay. We found that on the shortest sequences, mothers who reported that their children had larger productive vocabularies produced more elaborations as they demonstrated the sequences. On the longest sequences, there were no relations between children's language abilities and the degree of maternal elaboration (Bauer & Burch, 2004). Burch and I interpreted this changing pattern as a function of sequence length as a maternal response to the increased demands of the task: As sequence length increased, mothers provided a larger number of elaborations. Thus, they seemed to respond to the "situational" factor of their children's needs for more scaffolding and support, and less to the "dispositional" factor of whether, under typical circumstances, their children demonstrate proficiency with language: They increased their levels of verbal elaboration regardless of the characteristics of their children. Although far from definitive, these two studies of relations between young children's language abilities and maternal verbal behavior are suggestive. They should serve to motivate additional research with children early in the socialization process, as well as with children throughout the preschool years.

*Children's Temperament.* The possibility that individual differences in children's temperaments might play a role in the process of socialization into the canonical autobiographical narrative form is just beginning to be examined. As discussed in chapter 4, temperament or behavioral style refers to typical patterns of responding to environmental stimuli (e.g., Gunnar, 1990; Rothbart & Bates, 1998). In her 1999 paper, Kristina Lewis speculated that differences in children's temperaments might contribute to differences in the process of autobiographical narrative socialization. She noted a study by Cheryl Slomkowski, Keith Nelson, Judy Dunn, and Robert Plomin (1992), in which the researchers found relations between sociability at age 2 years and language production and comprehension skills at age 3 years, as well as receptive language skills at 7 years. Slomkowski and her colleagues suggested that highly sociable children might engage their parents in more interactions and thereby facilitate their own vocabulary development.

K. Lewis (1999) reasoned that if highly sociable children are eliciting more social interaction from their parents (as suggested by Slomkowski et al., 1992), they might also encourage a more elaborative style of maternal conversation. Conversely, children who have difficulty regulating their attention or level of activity might elicit a higher level of regulatory speech, perhaps manifesting itself in more repetitions of maternal questions. Lewis examined these possibilities in samples of 3- and 5-year-old children and their parents. She found that children rated by their parents as more sociable and active received fewer repetitions and evaluations and proportionally more elaborations. Lewis interpreted these effects to suggest that mothers of less active children may perceive the need to engage them in the task by using evaluations and repetitions of their utterances. On the other hand, children perceived to be more sociable may be viewed as good conversational partners: In the preschool years, readiness to participate in conversation is likely a major component of what gets termed "sociability."

Melissa Burch and I observed similar findings in the sample of 24-month-old children whose mothers tested them on four- to six-step sequences (Bauer & Burch, 2004). Specifically, we found that on the easier four-step sequences, mothers who rated their children as high on the Interest and Persistence subscale of the *Toddler Behavior Assessment Questionnaire* (TBAQ) were especially verbally engaged with their children, as measured by higher rates of production of elaborations, repetitions, and affirmations. Thus, children who were perceived as typically showing evidence of interest and persistence received in the elicited-imitation context more verbal scaffolding. In contrast to K. Lewis' (1999) observations with older children, maternal verbal behavior was unrelated to scores on the Activity Level subscale of the TBAQ. As we observed in the case of the earlier discussion of children's language abilities, on the more difficult six-step sequences, mothers responded more to the situation of greater challenge than to their children's characteristics: They increased their levels of verbal elaboration regardless of the characteristics of their children. As a result, on the more difficult sequences, few relations with children's temperament were apparent. Again, although far from definitive, these two studies of relations between children's temperament characteristics and maternal behavior in conversations about past events are suggestive. They should serve to motivate additional research with children early in the socialization process, as well as with children throughout the preschool years.

*The Attachment History of the Dyad.* The final variable to be considered as potentially related to the process of socialization of autobiographical narrative is not a characteristic of the child herself or himself, but a feature of the parent–child dyad—namely, their attachment history. Robyn Fivush and Anjali Vasudeva (2002) developed the argument that, given the social purpose of reminiscing, other aspects of the socioemotional relationship between the adult and child might be related to their "style" of co-construction of the events of their lives. This expectation is derived, in part, from the observation that mothers seem to have different goals as they reminisce with their children. As discussed in an earlier section of this chapter, mothers who are less elaborative in their style appear as if they have a more pragmatic purpose: to get their children to remember specific pieces of information. Mothers who are more elaborative in their style appear to have the goal of engaging their children in conversation for the sake of sharing. The goals of engagement and sharing of experience not only are facilitated by a strong interpersonal relationship, but actually emerge from it. That is, it is the strong socioemotional connection that motivates one to share to begin with.

The concept of mother–child attachment has a long and distinguished history, and I do not hope to give it an adequate review in this chapter (for reviews, see Cassidy & Shaver, 1999; Sroufe, 1979). For present purposes, it is sufficient to note that parents and their children differ in the "quality" of their attachment relationship. Most mothers are sensitive to their children's needs and respond to their infants signals in timely and appropriate manners. Their infants are likely to develop secure attachments that keep them in proximity to their mothers, yet permit them to move beyond her to explore the world and gain a measure of independence from the caregiver, apparently confident in the knowledge that, on return, mother not only will be there, but be welcoming. Other mothers exhibit less sensitivity to their infants' signals and needs. They might respond less contingently or not at all, presumably engendering in their infants a sense that the caregiver cannot be counted on. Their infants are more likely to develop an insecure attachment that is less successful in promoting developmentally appropriate levels of dependence and independence. Infant members of these dyads may signal the insecure nature of their attachment by exhibiting behaviors that are avoidant or dismissive of, or ambivalent toward, the caregiver. Some authors suggest that the fruits of early attachment relationships are preserved well beyond infancy, as evidenced by relations with adult romantic relationships (Roisman, Madsen, Henninghausen, Sroufe, & Collins, 2001; although others have noted a lack of consistency over time; e.g., M. Lewis, Feiring, & Rosenthal, 2000).

The suggestion that the mother–child attachment relationship might be related to the style of reminiscing in the dyad is supported by a body of research within the attachment tradition. For example, dyads with a secure attachment relationship have been described as engaging in more open communication relative to dyads with less secure relationships (e.g., Bretherton, 1990). In addition, children who are classified as securely attached exhibit more sophisticated narrative skills in tasks in which they are asked to complete a story with a socioemotional theme (e.g., Waters, Rodriguez, & Ridgeway, 1998). Discussions of emotional and evaluative aspects of events may be especially influenced by the attachment relationship, given that they involve a measure of interpretation of the internal states of others. I have already considered findings of individual differences in the extent to which parents and children talk about emotions (e.g., Adams et al., 1995). These differences seem to have long-term consequences, in that parents who talk more about emotions when their children are young have children who include more emotion language in their later narratives (e.g., Kuebli et al., 1995).

Although there is compelling motivation and rationale for investigating possible relations between the attachment relationship and maternal style of reminiscing, there have been few empirical studies. Robyn Fivush and Anjali Vasudeva (2002) examined the possibility of a relation in a sample of mothers and their 4-year-old children. The dyads engaged in joint reminiscing about two shared events from the past and also participated in a joint laboratory activity involving making an art collage. From these phases of the session, the researchers derived measures of maternal and child narrative contributions (elaborations and repetition of utterances, and use of emotion terms) and maternal and child warmth, respectively. Mothers also completed the *Attachment Behavior Q-set* (Waters, 1987), a measure of the attachment relationship. Fivush and Vasudeva found a significant relation between attachment status and maternal elaborations: Mothers who indicated a more secure attachment relationship with their children were more elaborative in the memory conversation context. The relation was apparent for both mother–daughter and mother–son dyads. In addition, the researchers found that mothers who used a high proportion of emotion terms had children who produced a large number of memory elaborations. Separate analyses for girls and boys revealed this relation only among mother–daughter dyads, however. This study thus provides intriguing suggestions of relations between attachment security and maternal style, and, for girls only, relations between maternal use of emotion terms and children's memory elaborations. As argued by the authors, the pattern as a whole suggests that children in securely attached dyads are more likely to engage in elaborative parent–child reminiscing, which in turn promotes development of skills for autobiographical narrative production.

Rhiannon Newcombe and Elaine Reese (2003) conducted a longitudinal investigation of possible relations between maternal reminiscing style and children's narrative development as a function of the security of the attachment relationship. The sample is the same as that introduced in the earlier discussion of relations between maternal style and children's language development (Farrant & Reese, 2000; Harley & Reese, 1999). The families were enrolled in the study when the children were 19 months of age. They were followed longitudinally with observations at 25, 32, 40, and 51 months. At the last session, the mothers completed the *Attachment Behavior Q-set*. Q-set responses were then used to divide the sample into children who were rated as securely attached and children who were insecurely attached.

Newcombe and Reese (2003) found that mothers in dyads classified as securely attached increased their use of evaluations over the course of the study, whereas mothers in insecurely attached dyads did not. Across the time points of the study (i.e., from 25–51 months), children in securely attached dyads produced more evaluations than did children in insecurely attached dyads. In addition, beginning when children were 25 months of age, there were both concurrent and cross-lagged relations between mothers' and children's use of evaluations in the context of conversations about past events. That is, mothers who used more evaluations tended to have children who also used more evaluations both at the same session and at later sessions. These results suggest that the development of aspects of a child's narrative competence are influenced by the quality of the socioemotional relationship between the mother and her child. Together with the findings of Fivush and Vasudeva (2002), they compel additional research on relations between attachment history and the process of socialization of autobiographical narrative.

## Style Only or Substance Too?

An important caveat relevant to the work on influences of the narrative context on developments in the domain of autobiographical memory is that it is not clear whether stylistic differences relate to memory per se or whether they relate to the *reporting* of memories. That is, it is apparent that over time children whose parents use a more elaborative style come to produce longer memory reports, include more sophisticated narrative devices, and include more evaluative comments. Each of these features contributes to a more "colorful" narrative. However, as I and others have discussed (e.g., Bauer, 1993; Mandler, 1990a), a more detailed narrative account is not the same as a more detailed memory representation. Individuals who produce shorter, less dramatic accounts of their experiences may well have memory representations that are every bit as detailed, integrated, and coherent as individuals who produce more dramatic ones: The difference may be in the public story, rather than in the private memory representation. This consideration does not make the study of social influences on narrative development any less interesting or important. Yet it is desirable that it be kept in mind as we consider the mechanisms of autobiographical memory development.

## CULTURAL INFLUENCES ON NARRATIVE SOCIALIZATION AND CONCEPTUAL DEVELOPMENT

The work reviewed thus far in this chapter strongly suggests that the social context in which children practice the skills for narrative construction matters for their later autobiographical narrative performance. There are also suggestions that the social context matters for the development of concepts related to autobiographical memory, such as the concept of self. Until now I have, by default, defined the social context in terms of the middle-class, White samples that have been involved in most of the research on the socialization of autobiographical skills. That context is not the only setting in which development occurs, however. Indeed it is not even a majority context. Given that value systems and traditions vary across social contexts, there are reasons to expect cross-cultural differences in the narrative models provided to children and perhaps also in the goals for parent–child reminiscing. In this section, I review the small yet rapidly growing body of data on cultural differences in early narrative socialization. I then review the still smaller literature that bears on the possibility that cultural differences might relate to conceptual development, with specific focus on the self-concept.

### Cultural Influences on Narrative Socialization

The motivation for examination of possible culture group influences on narrative socialization came from both the developmental and adult autobiographical memory literatures. From the developmental literature came the findings just described of systematic relations between parental styles and children's narrative development. The possibility of differences in parental styles as a function of culture was a logical extension of the theoretical approach underlying much of this work (e.g., K. Nelson, 1993b). The adult autobiographical memory literature provided another impetus for examination of possible culture group influences. As reviewed in chapter 3, research by Mary Mullen (1994) revealed striking differences in the age of earliest reportable autobiographical memory for European-Americans compared with Asian Americans and Koreans living in America (see also Wang, 2001). Mullen found that, on average, the age of earliest memory for European-Americans was 6 months earlier than that of Asian Americans and fully 16 months earlier than the earliest reportable autobiographical memory for Koreans. The finding of later earliest memories from members of Asian cultural groups has since been replicated by Shelley MacDonald, Kimberly Uesiliana, and Harlene Hayne (2000). Both Mullen and MacDonald and her colleagues speculated that one source of the effect is a different pattern of socialization in the art of talking about the personal past. As described by Mullen (1994):

> The difference between Asians and Caucasians may reflect two very different sets of socialization goals: one in which conformity to norms of social behavior is highly valued and dwelling on one's own subjective experiences is maladaptive, and one in which adults actively encourage children to elaboratively narrativize their personal experiences as part of a process of developing a sense of individuality and self-expression that is valued in the culture. (pp. 76–77)

To conclude that differences in adults' autobiographical memories from early childhood are influenced by differences in socialization, it would be necessary to show that the differences are apparent in early parent–child interaction. To begin to test this hypothesis, Mary Mullen and Soonhyung Yi (1995) collected and analyzed naturally occurring conversations between American and Korean mothers and their 3-year-old children. They found that Korean dyads engaged in talk about the past less frequently than American dyads. In addition, the conversations of the Korean dyads included fewer details than those of American dyads (see also Choi, 1992, for comparison of Korean and Canadian mothers). These differences in talk about the past are reminiscent of differences in mothers who exhibit an elaborative compared with a low-elaborative style: Dyads in which the mother exhibits an elaborative style tend to have longer conversations that include more narrative content.

To determine whether mother–child conversations about the past also differ in other of the features that distinguish the elaborative from the low-elaborative maternal style, Qi Wang, Michelle Leichtman, and Katharine Davies (2000) collected memory narratives from American mothers and their children and from Chinese mothers and their children. In both culture groups, the children ranged in age from 3 to 4 years. The samples included comparable numbers of girls and boys, and the children were well matched for their levels of language development as measured by the average length of the utterances they produced. The dyads were observed in their homes in the United States and China, respectively, by an experimenter from the same native country as the dyad. Each dyad was asked to talk about two events from the recent past (i.e., that had taken place within the past month). Under these circumstances, Wang et al. did not replicate Mullen and Yi's (1995) finding of less detailed conversations by Asian dyads relative to American dyads: The culture groups did not differ in the number of conversational turns they took or in the level of detail of the conversations. Nor did the mothers from the two groups differ in the number of elaborations they produced. However, American mothers did produce fewer repetitions and more evaluations when talking with their children relative to Chinese mothers, and American children produced more elaborations than Chinese children. Moreover, Wang and her colleagues found that, relative to Chinese dyads, American dyads had a greater tendency to follow an elaboration with an elaboration. Thus, American mothers tended to elaborate on their children's contributions, and American children tended to elaborate on their mothers' contributions in a truly co-constructive manner. This tendency was less prominent among the Chinese dyads.

In addition to differences in the language variables that have come to typify the elaborative and low-elaborative styles, Wang et al. (2000) also found differences in the conversation themes of the Chinese and American dyads. Specifically, relative to American dyads, when talking about past events, Chinese mothers and their children both produced more didactic talk. That is, they included more statements and questions about moral standards, social norms, and expectations for behavior relative to American mothers and their children. For example, Chinese mothers asked questions such as, "What *should* people do when crossing the street?", and children expressed prohibitions such as, "It's *wrong* to kill birds." In contrast, relative to Chinese dyads, American mothers and their children included more talk about autonomy: They included more statements and questions about personal needs or preferences and personal judgements and opinions relative to Chinese dyads. For instance, American mothers made statements such as, "Bear *wanted* to get that big cake," and children expressed opinions such as, "*I think* pandas are lazy" (Wang et al., 2000, p. 163; italics added). The asymmetry in the themes of conversations is reflective of the more interdependent orientation of Chinese culture and more independent orientation of American culture (e.g., Markus & Kitayama, 1991).

In the larger literature on stylistic differences in mother–child conversations about past events, there are relations between maternal style and children's narrative production not only in the context of shared conversations, but in children's independent memory narratives as well. Indeed for cross-cultural differences in narrative socialization to prove to be a major source of differences in adults' memories of their childhoods, such effects would be a necessary condition. Is there evidence of differences in the independent narratives produced by children from Asian and American cultures?

To address this question, Jessica Jungsook Han, Michelle Leichtman, and Qi Wang (1998) asked samples of Korean, Chinese, and American 4- and 6-year-old children to talk with an experimenter about recent personally experienced events. As reflected in Table 9.5, whether measured by the number of words produced, the number of propositions produced, the ratio of words to propositions (an index of the level of detail provided in each proposition),

TABLE 9.5
Measures of Narrative Production for Samples of 4- and 6-Year-Old
Children From the United States, Korea, and China

| Culture Group | Measure (Across Age Groups) | | | | |
|---|---|---|---|---|---|
| | Number of Words | Number of Propositions | Ratio of Words to Propositions | Temporal Markers | Descriptive Terms |
| American | 248 | 35 | 6.78 | 13 | 16 |
| Korean | 93 | 17 | 5.40 | 4 | 4 |
| Chinese | 215 | 36 | 5.89 | 14 | 7 |

Note. Based on Han et al. (1998), Tables 1, 2, and 3.

the number of temporal markers produced (a measure of narrative cohesion), or the number of descriptive terms produced, American children had longer and more detailed narratives relative to Korean children. Their narratives also included more details that distinguished the specific episode under discussion from other, potentially similar events. As measured by words, propositions, and temporal markers, Chinese children's narratives were more comparable to those of American children. However, Chinese children's narratives were less detailed and less specific than those of American children: Their ratios of words per proposition, the number of descriptive terms included in their narratives, and the level of specificity of their narratives were more comparable to the Korean children. American children also included in their narratives more information about their own and others' internal states (e.g., cognition terms, statements of preference, evaluations, emotion terms) relative to Chinese and Korean children. In addition, whereas children in all three culture groups frequently mentioned themselves in their narratives, American children had the highest proportion of references to themselves relative to others. Finally, gender differences were observed in the American sample only: American girls produced more words, more words per proposition, more temporal markers, more descriptive terms, and more internal states terms relative to American boys.

Together the results of Han et al. (1998) paint a picture of American children (and especially American girls) producing autobiographical narratives that are longer, more detailed, more specific, and more "personal" (both in terms of mention of self and mention of internal states) relative to children from China and Korea. The pattern is consistent with expectations derived from the finding that, in their conversations about past events, American mothers and their children are more elaborative and more focused on autonomous themes relative to Chinese mothers and their children (Wang et al., 2000), and Korean mothers and their children have less frequent and less detailed conversations about the past relative to American dyads (Mullen & Yi, 1995).

It is tempting to relate the findings of differences in early reminiscing in American compared with Asian cultures to the variation observed in studies of adults' recollections of their childhoods (e.g., Mullen, 1994; Wang, 2001). As discussed by Han and her colleagues, "It is distinctly possible that the more elaborated content of American children's narratives, as compared with those of Asian children, contributes to the earlier first memories found in American adult populations" (Han et al., 1998, p. 710). Similarly, it is possible that the rich narrative tradition of the native New Zealand Maori culture relates to the finding that adults of Maori descent have memories from earlier in life (MacDonald et al., 2000; see chap. 3, this volume). These patterns seem to license the conclusion that the culture in which a child is raised has long-term consequences for autobiographical memory development. However, only prospective research will tell: Only studies that track the "fate" of memories from childhood to adulthood can address the possibility that events that were more elaboratively encoded in the preschool years are more accessible to recollection in the adult years.

## Cultural Influences on Conceptual Development

The possibility of culture group differences in development in the conceptual domains that have been associated with autobiographical memory—self-concept, temporal understanding, and understanding of the origins of knowledge—is only beginning to be explored. Indeed at this point in the literature, only the most suggestive target for socialization—namely, the self-concept—has been examined for possible culture group effects. Within the larger self-concept, the most likely component of the self to be affected by cultural group differences is the evaluative self or the subjective perspective. This expectation is derived from the fact that cultural group does not seem to have a pronounced effect on recognition of the physical self. Even in a culture in which infants have no exposure to mirrors—Bedouin families—infants show a typical pattern and rate of mirror self-recognition (Priel & De Schonen, 1986). In contrast, research by Michelle Leichtman and Qi Wang and their colleagues has revealed a number of aspects of parent–child conversational style in Asian culture groups that could be expected to impact the development of a subjective perspective. For instance, Leichtman and Wang found that when Chinese mothers and their children talk about the past, they make fewer mentions of the child relative to mothers and children from the United States. Instead of focusing on children's preferences and feelings, they tend to emphasize social norms and appropriate conduct. Perhaps not coincidentally, in conversations about the past, children from Asian cultures refer to themselves less frequently and provide fewer personal evaluations (Han et al., 1998; Wang et al., 2000).

## THE CHILD, THE FAMILY,
## AND THE CULTURE WORK TOGETHER

To say that characteristics of the child herself or himself, characteristics of the familial context, and characteristics of the cultural context each relates to the rate and course of development of autobiographical memory is only part of the story: The factors also work together to impact autobiographical memory development. A perfect illustration of the multiple sources of influence is consideration of gender and its relations to autobiographical memory development. As described in chapter 4, early on in development, there are no measurable differences in declarative memory between girls and boys. By the time they are 6 years of age, however, American girls' and boys' autobiographical narratives differ on a number of dimensions. For example, girls produce longer and more detailed narratives relative to boys, girls use both a greater number and greater variety of emotion words relative to boys, and girls make more evaluative statements relative to boys. Importantly, these differences are not apparent in Asian cultures. Why? In Western cultures, at least, girls are perceived to be more social and more verbal relative to boys. Perhaps as a consequence, they are treated to more elaborative parental conversational styles, as well as more evaluative conversation relative to boys. These differences are not apparent in Asian cultures, in which, in general, there is less focus on the individual child and the child's subjective experience of events.

Gender is not the only example of the interactions of forces that ultimately contribute to differences in autobiographical memory. Earlier in the chapter, I mentioned findings of Melissa Welch-Ross (2001) that levels of evaluative perspective and self-awareness only mattered for children of mothers using a high-elaborative style. For children of mothers using a less elaborative style, level of evaluative self-awareness had no implications for their contributions to autobiographical memory conversations (see Table 9.2). Similarly, as is apparent in Fig. 9.4, Welch-Ross found that whether children passed the test of appreciation of the temporally extended self (i.e., delayed video self-recognition) mattered only for children of mothers using a high-elaborative style. For children of mothers using a less elaborative style, whether the child passed the test of temporally extended self had no implications for his or her contributions to autobiographical memory conversations.

In the examples just provided, relations between autobiographical memory and some conceptual variables (i.e., evaluative perspective on the self and temporally extended self) were only observed for children whose mothers were more elaborative in style. There are also examples of cases in which relations between autobiographical memory and maternal narrative style are observed only for children who have achieved certain conceptual "milestones." For instance, Welch-Ross (2001) explored the possibility of relations

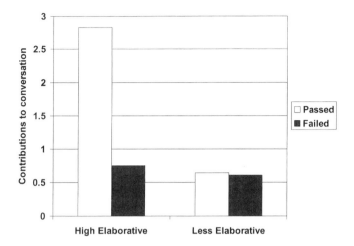

FIG. 9.4.   Three-year-old children's contributions to mother–child conversations (as measured by the ratio of child memory responses to conversational placeholders) as a function of (a) performance on the delayed video self-recognition test of temporally extended self, and (b) maternal conversational style. Based on Welch-Ross (2001), Table 6.2.

between consistency in psychological self and autobiographical memory in 3½- and 4½-year-old children. Children high in consistency on a given construct were those who, on the *Children's Self-View Questionnaire* (Eder, 1990), endorsed multiple items in the same direction such as, "I don't like to tease people" and "I don't ever try to push in front of people in line." She found that the beneficial effects of an elaborative maternal style were especially apparent for children with a more consistent psychological self-view. That is, children whose mothers used an elaborative style made more contributions to autobiographical memory conversations, but only if they had higher consistency scores. Exposure to an elaborative style did not have beneficial effects for children with lower consistency scores. Keryn Harley and Elaine Reese (1999) reported a similar pattern with the more basic test of mirror self-recognition: Maternal style had the most pronounced effects for children who were early to recognize themselves in the mirror. For children who were late to recognize themselves in the mirror, effects of maternal style were less readily apparent (see Fig. 9.2).

    The major point of this discussion of multiple effects that interact with one another is to illustrate the multicausal nature of developments in autobiographical memory. There is no one factor that "causes" autobiographical memory to emerge or that "explains" its development. Instead a number of factors work together to determine the rate and course of development of memories that exhibit the features that we recognize as "autobiographical." This is not a novel argument: Katherine Nelson and Robyn Fivush (2004) outlined a multicausal theory of autobiographical memory development from a sociocultural perspective. Consistent with the analysis I provided, K. Nelson and Fivush emphasized the many factors that contribute to the emergence of autobiographical memory, including aspects of self development, developments in basic mnemonic abilities, age-related changes in narrative structure and content, and developments in children's understanding of mental concepts and the representational nature of mind. Perspectives such as that provided by K. Nelson and Fivush and that which I provide in this chapter differ from many other current conceptualizations of autobiographical memory development, in that they explicitly recognize the multiple, interactive elements that constitute autobiographical memory and, thus, that contribute to its development.

## SUMMARY AND CONCLUSIONS

Characteristics of the narrative contexts in which children are engaged in conversations about past events bear strong relations with the types of verbal reports that children produce. Both concurrently and over time, children exposed to a more elaborative style report more about events, their narratives are more coherently organized, and their narratives are more "alive" with intensifiers and qualifiers that convey the narrator's perspective on the event. In addition to a form that helps them organize, remember, and subsequently retrieve stories of previous life events, it seems that children are also developing an "attitude" toward remembering based on the social context in which they engage in reminiscence. Parents who approach autobiographical reminiscing as an opportunity for sharing and social interaction have children who (seemingly) come to view it in that way as well. In contrast, parents who approach autobiographical reminiscing as a test to see what their children remember about or have learned from the past have children who (seemingly) come to view remembering as something that one does on demand, but which is not valued in and of itself (K. Nelson & Fivush, 2004).

Presumably at least in part as a function of the contexts in which they reminisce, by the end of the preschool years, children exhibit pronounced individual differences in narrative skill even when they are well matched on the "basic building blocks" of vocabulary and syntax. Some of the individual differences are associated with children's gender; there is some suggestive evidence of effects of children's language, their temperaments, and the quality of attachment to their primary caregivers. There is also increasing evidence of culture group differences in the ways that children structure their own independent autobiographical narratives. Finally, there is a small body of evidence to suggest that the contexts of the family and the wider culture influence the development of concepts linked to autobiographical memory, including, most prominently, the self.

Two major questions raised at the beginning of this chapter were whether the social contexts in which children are raised seem to "matter" for autobiographical memory development and whether the observed patterns of sociocultural influence are consistent with the profiles of autobiographical memory exhibited by adults as they recollect their childhoods. With both of the questions answered in the affirmative, it seems that we should be well on our way to an account of autobiographical memory development and an explanation of childhood amnesia. There is one more ingredient that remains to be added, however: We must examine the "fates" of autobiographical memories as children make the two transitions that identify the boundaries of childhood amnesia. The first transition is that from infancy to early childhood: What happens to early memories such that, by adults, they are not accessible for recollection? The second transition is that from the preschool to the school years, when an adultlike distribution of autobiographical memories is assumed to emerge: What happens to memories of events from the preschool years such that, by adults, the number of memories retrieved from this period is smaller than the number expected based on forgetting alone? These questions are the focus of the next chapter.

# IV

## THE "FATES"
## OF EARLY MEMORIES

# 10

# Crossing the Great Divides of Childhood Amnesia

*Intuitively, early recollections are interesting (because) ... despite the wealth of experiences which young children have, their autobiographical records are typically quite fragmentary before age seven, and the earliest memory is rarely dated before age three.*
—Kihlstrom and Harackiewicz (1982, p. 134)

John Kihlstrom and Judith Harackiewicz's (1982) observations about children's autobiographical records should by now sound quite familiar. Indeed in this single statement, the authors captured both components of the phenomenon of childhood amnesia. The most "famous" component of the amnesia is the relative paucity among adults of verbally accessible memories from the first 3 years of life. The second and less frequently discussed component is the smaller than expected number of memories from the ages of roughly 3 to 7 or 8 years (the pattern is captured in the schematic presented in Fig. 2.1). What is striking about Kihlstrom and Harackiewicz's observation is not their comment on both components of childhood amnesia, however, but that they made it in reference to *children's* autobiographical records, not adults'. Interestingly, the article in which their statement appeared was written before research on children's recall of the experiences of their lives had gotten underway in earnest (as discussed in chap. 7, systematic studies of children's recall of specific past events began to appear in the mid- to late 1980s). Moreover, it was made without reference to any research with children!—the authors provided no citation for the source of their observations, and not 1 of the 37 references in the article was of research focused on the memories of human children (although some research on the ontogeny of memory in nonhuman animals was cited).

Informed by the results of productive years of research on children's recollections of the times of their young lives, it might seem that Kihlstrom and

Harackiewicz (1982) were mistaken in their extension to children of the *adult* phenomenon of childhood amnesia. As reviewed in chapters 4 and 6, even in the first 3 years of life, infants and young children are able to recall the past as evidenced by their nonverbal behavior. The review provided in chapter 7 made clear that preschool-age children remember and talk about the events of their young lives. In chapters 8 and 9, I considered some of the possible sources of age-related changes in autobiographical memory and the individual and cultural differences that are typical of early autobiographical reports. Taken as a whole, the data provide a compelling story of considerable autobiographical competence by the end of the preschool years. With hindsight then, it may seem patently obvious that Kihlstrom and Harackiewicz were mistaken in their suggestions that children's earliest memories are rarely dated before age 3 years, and that until the age of 7 years children's autobiographical records are fragmentary.

Were Kihlstrom and Harackiewicz (1982) mistaken, or did their comments simply lack empirical support? In the years that have passed since 1982, there has accrued a large literature on developments in memory during the period eventually obscured by childhood amnesia. However, there stand only a few studies of the fates of early memories as children make the two transitions that mark the "inflection points" in the childhood amnesia curve—namely, the transition from infancy to early childhood and the transition from preschool to later childhood. As a result, although we have ample evidence that children under 3 years of age can remember events, we have little data on whether those early memories cross the "great divide" that seems to separate the period of infancy from that of the preschool years. Similarly, although we have ample evidence that preschoolers remember the events of their lives, we have little data on whether their memories cross the "great divide" that seems to separate the period of the preschool years from that of middle and later childhood (and adulthood). Moreover, we have little data with which to evaluate the implicit assumption of many theories of childhood amnesia—that an adultlike distribution of autobiographical memories is achieved at roughly 7 to 8 years of age (i.e., that the number of events adults remember from ages 7–8 and later is the number that would be expected based on forgetting alone). In this chapter, I address these issues by using extensions of the research on infants' and very young children's nonverbal recall of events and of the research on preschoolers' verbal recall of autobiographical events, respectively.

## CROSSING THE FIRST "GREAT DIVIDE": INFANCY TO EARLY CHILDHOOD

The most salient component of the phenomenon of childhood amnesia is the relative paucity among adults of verbally accessible memories from the first 2 to 4 years of life. Although as discussed in chapter 3 there are both individual and group differences in the age of earliest memory among adults, for well over a century the average age of earliest memory among samples of Western adults has been age 3½ years. Among adults from some Eastern cultures (e.g., Korea), the average age of earliest memory is several months later. I already discussed the most common explanation for this "remarkable amnesia of childhood" (Freud, 1916/1966, p. 326)—that the first 3 years of life are devoid of memories because infants and very young children lack the capacity to form them. This explanation was not born of a failure to notice that infants and young children learn and otherwise benefit from past experience. They learn to walk, recognize familiar faces, feed themselves, and many more things. Nor was it born of a failure to notice that specific experiences might leave their marks on infants' and young children's minds. For example, early attachment relationships have long been thought to influence later social relationships (e.g., Bowlby, 1969).

Rather than of a failure to take note of the effects of early experience, the suggestion that infants lacked the capacity to form lasting memories was born of the assumption that the types of memories that children formed were not accessible to verbal report. As a result, distinctive, even traumatic, experiences would go if not gently, then nonverbally, into that good night. Classically, this impression stemmed from theoretical assumptions about the nature of mental representation in infancy (e.g., Piaget, 1952). In more recent history, it stemmed from a striking lack of evidence of "translation" of early, nonverbal memories into verbal form. Not only are there few reported positive observations of children once equipped with language using it to describe their early memories, but there are negative observations. One such negative observation comes from a case study of a little girl named Audrey.

In 1995, Theodore Gaensbauer and his colleagues published a case study of 4-year-old Audrey who, at the age of 12½ months, witnessed the violent death of her mother caused by the explosion of a letter bomb (Gaensbauer, Chatoor, Drell, Siegel, & Zeanah, 1995). As described by Gaensbauer and his colleagues, in the years after the traumatic loss, Audrey experienced a number of symptoms that eventually culminated in her referral for psychological evaluation. Virtually immediately after the incident, Audrey began to experience disturbed sleep, including frequent night wakings and recurrent nightmares. She had intense screaming episodes that, over time, decreased in frequency, yet recurred at times of stress. She was quite fearful of loud noises, such as cars backfiring, as well as other stimuli thought to remind her of the trauma (e.g., Santa Claus presumably because of his red clothing). Audrey also experienced eating disturbances and exhibited angry, disruptive, and resistant behavior. Her symptoms, preceded as they had been by an apparently normal course of development prior to the event of her mother's death, seem relatively clearly to be related to the violent episode and traumatic loss. Moreover, although she did not verbalize it, in the course of an evaluation at the age of 4 years, Audrey expressed memory for the event, nonverbally: She engaged in what both the evaluator and her adopted mother interpreted as a behavioral reenactment of the violent episode that she had witnessed at the age of 12½ months.

This case is a prime example of the apparent inaccessibility of early memories to later verbal report. It was relatively obvious that Audrey remembered the episode of her mother's violent death, but the form in which Audrey retained the experience was far from clear. Did Audrey remember the episode in the traditional sense of the term (i.e., entailing conscious access) or did the experience leave its indelible mark only on her unconscious mind? Conceptually related to the question of the nature or form of memory representations are questions about the later verbal accessibility of early memories: Audrey behaviorally reenacted, yet did not verbally report on, her previous experience. The fact that she did not talk about the event was consistent with the assumption that children of her young age at the time of the experience were not able to form declarative memories. Indeed the assumption that very young children did not yet have available to them declarative memory capacity resolved the issue of the apparent lack of verbal accessibility of early memories. Only conscious, declarative memories can be expressed through language; because young children lacked declarative memories, they had no content to express. Consistent with this perspective, Gaensbauer and his colleagues interpreted Audrey's behavioral reenactment as evidence of nondeclarative, but not of declarative, memory for the traumatic event of her mother's death (Gaensbauer et al., 1995).

Today, the assumption that children as young as Audrey are not able to form memories of events that they subsequently can recall no longer is tenable. As described in chapter 4, it is now clear that, by late in the first year of life, infants are able to recall events over delays of several weeks. By the end of the second year, they tolerate delays of several months. Although evidence of continuity in basic mnemonic processes now abounds, there remains a striking discontinuity in the form of mnemonic *expression*: Young children rely exclusively on nonverbal expression, whereas older children and adults use language to convey the contents of their memories. This difference may sound trivial—of course older children are able to provide verbal reports of their past experiences: They have command of the verbal medium. However, the difference in mode of expression of early compared with later memories persists even once children have become well integrated into the language community. Audrey's is an illustrative case in point. Whereas she had experienced some speech delay, at the time of evaluation at the age of 4 years, her language use was appropriate for her age (Gaensbauer et al., 1995). Nevertheless, although questioned relatively directly, she failed to use language to express her memory for the traumatic event.

The relevance of the question of later verbal accessibility of early memories for explanations of childhood amnesia should be clear: If children do not have verbal access to their early memories, we should not be surprised that adults do not either. Despite the obvious significance of this question, there have been few studies specifically designed to address it. More common are case studies such as Audrey's. Another such case study is Katherine Nelson's (1989, 1993a) of Emily and her crib monologues. Nelson analyzed Emily's crib monologues for a number of months beginning at the age of 21 months. Although Emily routinely made reference to past events, she tended to confine her comments to events that had occurred no more than a few days or weeks ago. Indeed K. Nelson (1993a) noted that the oldest event of which Emily spoke was from 3 months in the past. Based on this observation, Nelson speculated that, although some of Emily's early memories were verbally accessible at the time and for weeks after the event, they would not be retained over the long term. Some larger scale studies of the ability of older children to provide verbal reports of their early memories seem to bear out this prediction. After discussing some illustrative examples, I turn to consideration of the conditions for later verbal access to early memories, and some studies suggesting that when they are met children *are* able to talk about events from their early lives.

## Suggestions That Early Memories Later Are Verbally *In*accessible

An example of a study providing a negative response to the question of whether early memories later are accessible to verbal report is one conducted by Carole Peterson and Regina Rideout (1998). In this research, Peterson and Rideout interviewed children about trips to the emergency room necessitated by accidents that resulted in broken bones, burns, and cuts that required suturing, for example. Given their traumatic nature, we might expect such events to be highly memorable. The accidents occurred when the children were 13 to 34 months of age; the interviews were conducted in the children's homes shortly thereafter, and again 6 months, 12 months, and 18 or 24 months later. A qualitative description of the children's performance at each interview is provided in Table 10.1. As can be seen in the upper third of the table (2-year narrators), children who were 26 months or older at the time of the experience provided verbal reports at all delays. Indeed even 2 years later, all but one of the children was able to provide a narrative account of the experience (indicated with "PA" or "FA" in the table). This finding of well-preserved verbal recall in children 2 years of age at the time of an experience is consistent with research on children's memories for nontraumatic

TABLE 10.1
Children's Long-Term Verbal Recall of Medical Emergencies
as a Function of Their Age at the Time of the Experience

| Group | Age (months) | 6 months | 12 months | 18/24 months |
|---|---|---|---|---|
| 2-year narrators | 26 | PA | PA | PA |
| | 26 | ID | — | FA |
| | 28 | PA | FA | PA |
| | 30 | ID | FA | PA |
| | 32 | ID | ID | FA |
| | 32 | PA | ID | FA |
| | 32 | ID | FA | FA |
| | 32 | ID | ID | No |
| | 32 | ID | No | PA |
| | 33 | PA | PA | FA |
| | 33 | FA | — | FA |
| | 34 | FA | FA | FA |
| Older toddlers | 20 | ID | No | — |
| | 21 | ID | ID | ID |
| | 21 | PA | PA | No |
| | 22 | PA | PA | PA |
| | 23 | ID | — | PA |
| | 23 | No | No | No |
| | 23 | ID | No | ID |
| | 23 | ID | ID | ID |
| | 24 | No | ID | — |
| | 24 | ID | No | — |
| | 25 | PA | ID | FA |
| | 25 | No | No | — |
| Young toddlers | 13 | No | No | No |
| | 13 | No | ID | ID |
| | 14 | No | PA | ID |
| | 16 | No | ? | ID |
| | 16 | ID | No | No |
| | 17 | No | No | — |
| | 17 | ID | No | — |
| | 17 | No | No | No |
| | 18 | ID | PA | — |
| | 18 | No | No | — |
| | 18 | ID | No | — |
| | 18 | No | No | No |

*Note.* Based on Peterson and Rideout (1998), Table 4. The interviews were analyzed to determine whether children included information about (a) what was injured, (b) how the injury occurred, and (c) the major medical treatment (PA or FA for partial or full account, respectively). ID indicates isolated details only. Dashes indicate that no interview was conducted. The question mark indicates that the child provided information in response to parental prompting, rather than independently.

events summarized in chapter 7 (e.g., Fivush et al., 1987). Thus, it is clear that children who are relatively proficient at language at the time of their experiences are able to use language to talk about them later.

Interestingly, although the children who were injured between 20 and 25 months were not able to describe their experiences at the time, they were able to provide verbal reports 6 months later. As reflected in the middle portion of Table 10.1 (Older toddlers), 3 of the 12 children in this group provided a partial account, and another 6 children provided isolated details (what Peterson & Rideout, 1998, termed *spot* recall). One year after the events, six children retained at least some verbal access to their memories, but four children's memories were less accessible after the additional delay (i.e., their recall changed from *isolated details* to *no* or from *partial account* to *isolated details*). Eighteen months after the experiences, only one child provided a narrative that included all of the major elements of the experience (i.e., what was injured, how the injury occurred, and the major medical treatment). Finally, as reflected in the bottom portion of Table 10.1 (Young toddlers), among the children who were 13 to 18 months at the time of their injuries, none was able to provide a complete verbal account of the experience, even though at the later interviews they had the requisite language ability to do so. Peterson and Rideout attributed the youngest children's difficulty verbally describing their experiences to unavailability of a verbal means of encoding at the time of the events: They were not able to use language to represent the event in memory.

Another study suggesting limited verbal accessibility of preverbal memories was conducted by Gabrielle Simcock and Harlene Hayne (2002). When children were 27, 33, or 39 months of age, Simcock and Hayne visited the children's homes and played with them using a unique "Magic Shrinking Machine." Full-sized toys were placed into the machine and smaller, yet otherwise identical versions of the toys emerged from it. As one might expect, the children found this event quite interesting, leading to the expectation that they might form strong memories of it.

Separate groups of children were visited in their homes 6 months and 12 months after experiencing the shrinking machine and were asked, "What were the names of the toys?" and "How did we make the magic machine work?" (Simcock & Hayne, 2002, p. 226). For their reports, the children were first supported only by verbal prompts from the experimenter and then by a photograph of the "Magic Shrinking Machine." Although between exposure to the unique event and test of verbally accessible memory for it the children had acquired most of the language necessary to describe the operation of the machine (as indicated by independent assessments of productive vocabulary), the researchers reported that in no case did a child verbally provide information about the event that was not part of her or his productive vocabulary at the time of the experience of it. Once again it seemed that if children did not use language to represent the event in memory at the time of experience of it, it was not later accessible to verbal report. Together the results of Peterson and Rideout (1998) and Simcock and Hayne (2002) suggest quite limited verbal accessibility of early memories, even once children have the language to describe them (see Myers, Perris, & Speaker, 1994, for similar findings).

## Mapping Words to Their (Past Event) Referents

Studies such as those conducted by Peterson and Rideout (1998) and Simcock and Hayne (2002) seem to provide a ready explanation for why so few events from early in life are carried forward across the great divide of the transition from nonverbal to primarily verbal expression of memory. They suggest that if language is not used to encode events, then language cannot later be used to describe them. Indeed findings such as these have led to skepticism regarding the nature of early, preverbal memories. For example, in their 1989 review of the literature on autobiographical memory and the phenomenon of childhood amnesia, David Pillemer and Sheldon White used the apparent fact of later verbal inaccessibility of early memories to argue that early memories are qualitatively different from later, conscious memories. They suggested that if they were qualitatively similar, then early memories ". . . should become verbally expressible when the child has the ability to reconstrue preverbal events in narrative form" (Pillemer & White, 1989, p. 321; see also K. Nelson & Ross, 1980; Pillemer, 1998). In the absence of such evidence, early memories are described as indicative of the function of a "behavioral memory system" that in some cases supports ". . . early memory images (that) are persistent enough to influence feelings and behaviors after months or years" (Pillemer, 1998, p. 115), but which is nondeclarative, rather than declarative. This argument is, in effect, a modern version of the suggestion that older children's (and adults') inability to recall the events of their lives (verbally) is evidence that the capacity for declarative memory is late to develop.

   Before accepting either the argument that early memories later are verbally inaccessible or that later verbal inaccessibility would imply that early memories are nondeclarative or behavioral, it is important to consider the relation between memory for a past event and language. For children who are verbal at the time of an experience, the marriage of memory and language comes naturally because the event can be encoded verbally. No special conditions must be present to permit children to talk about their memories. However, for children who are not verbal at the time of an experience, the marriage of language and event memory must be "arranged." Studies such as those conducted by Peterson and Rideout (1998) and Simcock and Hayne (2002) suggest that the arrangement does not come easily. One potential im-

pediment to the union would stem from incompatibility of the representational formats of language and memory. Of course, this is the roadblock implied by arguments that early memories are exclusively behavioral or
nondeclarative as opposed to declarative (e.g., Pillemer, 1998). Another
source of impediment is not incompatibility of representational formats, but
lack of communication between otherwise compatible ones. Whatever else
they are, preverbal memories are not linguistic or propositional. As a consequence, for preverbal memories to be expressed using language, words must
be "mapped onto" them. The fact that this problem is so obviously solved in
the case of acquisition of words for concrete objects makes its apparent insolubility in the domain of memory all the more striking.

In the world of concrete objects, new linguistic tokens are mapped onto
previously acquired meanings with apparent ease. For example, as schematically illustrated in Fig. 10.1 (top row), before they comprehend or produce
the word *cup*, children may construct a concept of a cup as a type of container, especially useful for liquid. With increased linguistic competence, the
child can benefit from adult labeling of the object to map language to it.
That is, an adult can point to the object and utter the sound string "C-U-P"
and the child can readily connect the two. Voilà!—the word is mapped to
the referent, and a preverbal concept has become accessible to linguistic expression. I think scholars have this process in mind when they make the prediction that, assuming a memory is declarative, once language is acquired it
should be easily applied to the preverbal memory. A moment's reflection
makes clear, however, that when the referent is a past event, voilà!—conditions almost never occur. By definition, past events happened *in the past* and
are not perceptually available in the present. When children experience an
event (such as making a gong) prior to the time they have the language to
describe it (Fig. 10.1, middle row), they create a nonverbal memory representation (not unlike the preverbal concept). At some later point in time, the
child may acquire the linguistic competence to comprehend and even produce language to describe the event, but unlike the physical cup and the
word *cup*, the referent (the *past* event) and the language (*gong*) are never
available simultaneously. As a result, there is no opportunity to map the language onto the prelinguistic representation. The only way to "infuse" a
preverbal memory representation with language is to get the representation
of the past event *reinstated* in memory at a time of greater language competence relative to that at the time of original experience (Fig. 10.1, bottom
row).

This analysis puts the burden for ensuring later verbal accessibility of early
memories not on language available at the time of encoding, but on reinstatement of memory at a time when language is available to describe the experience. Herein lies another possible impediment to later verbal descriptions of early memories: The conditions that work to ensure reinstatement of

| Preverbal Experience | | Increased Linguistic Competence | | Mapping of Words to Referents |
|---|---|---|---|---|
| concept or event | language to describe it | concept or event | language to describe it | verbally accessible or inaccessible |
|  | NA |  | "cup" | verbally accessible |
|  | NA |  | "gong" | not verbally accessible |
|  | NA |  | "gong" | verbally accessible |

*Note.* NA = not available.

FIG. 10.1. Schematic representation of the conditions for mapping words to their referents. For concrete objects (top row of figure), even if the concept was acquired prior to language production or comprehension, words can be successfully mapped to their referents because they can be made available simultaneously. In the case of events experienced prior to the onset of language (middle row of figure), because the event happened in the past, words to refer to the event and the event itself never are available simultaneously. As a result, word/referent mapping is unsuccessful. However, if an event from the past can be effectively reinstated in memory (bottom row of figure), then the mapping can occur.

memories encoded verbally—namely, verbal cues—are less effective in reinstating preverbal memories. As discussed in chapter 7, for children younger than 3 years of age, verbal prompts alone are not especially effective retrieval cues (Hudson, 1991, 1993). It is well documented that a retrieval cue is effective only if it overlaps with information stored in memory (e.g., Tulving & Thomson, 1973). Because preverbal memories were encoded without the benefits of language, language is not effective in retrieving them.

Unfortunately, in many studies of children's memories for events from early in life, verbal cues are all that are provided. In the study by Peterson and Rideout (1998), for example, children were interviewed in their homes about events that had occurred in the emergency room; the interviews were conducted without the aid of any but verbal prompts and cues. Similarly, in the study by Simcock and Hayne (2002), although both the experience of the "Magic Shrinking Machine" and the memory interview took place in the children's homes, during the interview children were supported only by the experimenter's verbal prompts and a photograph of the machine. It may well be that the failure to observe verbally accessible memories under these conditions was not due to the nature of the memory representation or to the lack of availability of language at the time of encoding, but to failure to effectively reinstate the event memory given the cues provided. If this is the case, under conditions of more effective reinstatement of memory, we should observe that words and their referents can be mapped onto one another.

## Early Memories Can Be Verbally Described Under the "Right" Conditions

As just discussed, because preverbal memories were encoded without the benefits of language, language is not effective in reinstating them. However, once language is available, if the event can be reinstated by some other means (e.g., reexperience of the original context), then there is opportunity to redescribe the event into language or augment the nonverbal memory representation with language. As a result, a memory that was originally encoded nonverbally could become available for verbal expression. My colleagues and I have observed precisely this result in my laboratory. The studies are beginning to provide a coherent picture of the conditions under which we may expect to observe early memories surviving to cross the great divide that seemingly separates preverbal and verbal memories.

*Verbal Descriptions of Early Memories.*   In contrast to studies suggesting limited verbal accessibility of early memories, the results of research from my laboratory indicate that, at least under certain circumstances, early memories later are accessible to verbal report. In these studies, subsets of children who participated in the "Monster" study introduced in chapter 4 (Bauer et al., 2000) were tested to determine whether, in addition to nonverbal recall, the children might also show verbal recall of the events. As described in chapter 4, the children were enrolled in the "Monster" study at the ages of 13, 16, or 20 months, at which time they were exposed to novel multistep sequences. The children were permitted to imitate half of the sequences one time; the other half of the sequences were tested in deferred fashion (i.e., imitation was permitted only after imposition of a delay). The children were tested for recall of the sequences after intervals of either 1, 3, 6, 9, or 12 months.

As summarized in chapter 4 (see Fig. 4.6), the majority of 13-month-olds showed nonverbal evidence of recall of the sequences for 1 to 3 months; the majority of 16- and 20-month-olds showed nonverbal evidence of recall for 6 and 12 months, respectively. What was not mentioned in chapter 4 is that, at the time of their nonverbal delayed-recall tests, some of the children spontaneously talked about the events. For example, while sitting at the testing table, they labeled or described an event (e.g., on seeing the props to make the gong, they commented that it "makes a loud noise") or they requested or commented on an as yet unseen prop or event (e.g., "Can I see the bell?"). My colleagues and I characterized the spontaneous verbalizations of a subset of the 16- and 20-month-olds as either indicative of memory or not indicative of memory. Both age groups displayed verbal memory of events that they had been permitted to imitate prior to imposition of the delays. That is, they provided more verbalizations classified as *mnemonic* (i.e., indicative of memory) in response to events they had imitated before than in response to events that were new to them at the time of the recall test (coders were unaware of which events the children had seen before and which were new to them). The children who had been 20 months of age at the time of experience of the events also provided verbal evidence of memory of the events that they had only watched (Bauer, Kroupina, et al., 1998; see also Bauer & Wewerka, 1995, for similar results).

Perhaps even more striking than spontaneous verbal recall by some of the children is the finding that the children who had been the oldest at the time of enrollment in the study—namely, children who had been 20 months of age—were able to talk about the events after an additional delay averaging 11 months (Bauer, Kroupina, et al., 1998). For this study, the children returned to the laboratory when they were 3 years of age. Because most 3-year-olds can be expected to participate in verbal interviews, during the 3-year visit, we explicitly asked the children to describe the events they had experienced when they were 16 or 20 months of age. For each event in turn, we put the props on the table and asked the children to "Tell me what this was called" and "Tell me what we did with this." The children who had been enrolled at 20 months provided verbal evidence of memory at age 3 years. For example, in response to the experimenter's request to tell her what the sequence "Popper" was called (i.e., pull a plunger out of a tube, insert a ball into the tube, and push the plunger in, causing the ball to "pop" out), a 39-month-old child replied, "I remember that. It's a popper." The experimenter then asked the child to tell her how to make a popper. The child replied, "You put the ball in and then you pop it." The experimenter then asked for more detail and the child provided, "Well, you pull the handle. You pull that handle and then it pops." Not only is this an accurate description of how the "popper" works, but it is a virtually complete description.

In contrast to the children originally enrolled in the study at age 20 months, the children who had been enrolled at 16 months did not provide verbal evidence of memory at age 3 years. Jennifer Wenner, Maria Kroupina, and I tested for replication of these results in an independent sample of children drawn from the same larger study. Once again children who had been 20 months of age at the time of first experience of the novel laboratory events provided verbal evidence of memory of them at age 3 years. In contrast, children who had been 13 and 16 months of age at the time of experience of the events provided no verbal evidence of memory at age 3 years (Bauer, Wenner, & Kroupina, 2002).

*Circumstances of Later Verbal Accessibility.*    In the studies from my laboratory that I have described thus far, the children were tested in the same room, with the same props as they had experienced at the time of encoding of the events. For many, although not all, of the children, the experimenter also was the same. Thus, the contexts of the earlier and later testing experiences were highly similar. The overlap of contexts may play an important role in later verbal access to early memories because, as noted earlier, retrieval cues are most effective when they overlap with information stored in memory (e.g., Tulving & Thomson, 1973). This raises the question of whether such a high degree of contextual support is *necessary* to support later verbal access to early memories.

To address the question of the role of contextual support for later verbal recall, my colleagues and I (Bauer et al., 2004) compared the later verbal accessibility of early memories in two groups of children: children tested in the laboratory and supported by the props originally used to enact the events (as in Bauer, Kroupina, et al., 1998; Bauer, Wenner, & Kroupina, 2002) and children tested in their homes and supported by color photographs of the event-related props (as in Simcock & Hayne, 2002). In the context of the laboratory, we observed a replication of the results of prior related research—namely, verbally accessible memories at least among children who had been 20 months at the time of exposure to the events. In contrast, when two potentially important elements of context—that is, the familiar laboratory setting and the familiar event-related props—were removed, children did not show verbal evidence of recall. In a separate experiment, we tested a group of children in their homes, supported by the event-related props, rather than by photographs. Although they were tested out of the context in which they originally experienced the events, the children provided verbal evidence of recall of the events (Bauer et al., 2004).

The results of this line of research make clear that, under a range of circumstances, children are able to provide verbal reports of events experienced early in life. First, children provide verbal evidence of memory when they are tested in the laboratory with event-related props or in their homes with event-related props. They do not provide verbal evidence of memory when recall is tested in the home with color photographs of event-related props. This pattern indicates that three-dimensional props are effective aids to retrieval, even when they are encountered outside of their typical context, whereas color photographs that represent events are not effective retrieval cues for 3-year-old children being asked to recall an event experienced several months in the past. It is possible that the low efficacy of photographs as aids to retrieval after long delays accounts at least in part for Simcock and Hayne's (2002) findings of limited verbal accessibility of memories by children exposed to a unique "Magic Shrinking Machine" at 27 to 39 months of age: The children were aided in their retrieval only by the experimenter's questions and a photograph of the machine.

Second, verbal evidence of memory at age 3 years is apparent only among children who experienced events at 20 months of age. Children who had been 13 or 16 months of age at the time of experience of the events did not provide verbal evidence of memory. This pattern is consistent with that observed by Carole Peterson and Regina Rideout (1998), who found that children who were 18 months of age and younger at the time of experience of a medical emergency were unable to talk about the event when interviewed many months later. Thus, it seems that, across studies, there is emerging a general pattern of failed verbal recall by children younger than 20 months at the time of experience. The only apparent exception to the pattern is the study by Bauer, Kroupina, et al. (1998), in which, at 22 to 28 months, children who were 16 months of age at the time of experience of events spontaneously talked about events they had been permitted to imitate. However, they did not maintain verbally accessible representations of the events over the long term: When interviewed about the events at age 3, the children were not able to describe them verbally. Thus, it seems that, whereas with high levels of contextual support children younger than 20 months at the time of experience of events may be able to describe them after short delays, even with high levels of contextual support they do not maintain verbally accessible representations of the events over the long term.

A third factor that likely influences later verbal accessibility of early memories is the nature of the to-be-remembered event itself. In the "Magic Shrinking Machine" research by Simcock and Hayne (2002), children did not verbally recall events experienced briefly at 27 to 39 months of age. This negative finding stands in sharp contrast to those from the children in studies such as those conducted by Peterson and Rideout (1998) and Hamond and Fivush (1991). In the study by Peterson and Rideout, children who were 26 months of age or older at the time of their medical emergencies were able to describe the experiences as much as 2 years later. In the study by Hamond and Fivush, children verbally recalled a unique event (a trip to Disney-World) that they experienced as early as age 2½.

I suggest that the different "fates" of memories in these studies be attributed to the nature of the events experienced in each. In Peterson and Rideout's (1998) study, the experiences were unique, highly personally meaningful, and perhaps even traumatic (i.e., broken bones, cuts requiring sutures, treatments for burns, etc.). In Hamond and Fivush's (1991) study, the trip to DisneyWorld was unique and likely of personal significance to the children. These events also were long in duration, and families likely "kept them alive" through conversations about them for days, weeks, and perhaps months afterward. In contrast, in Simcock and Hayne's (2002) study, the event was engaging and fun for the children, but perhaps it was not especially personally meaningful. These features may have rendered the experience of playing with a "Magic Shrinking Machine" relatively unmemorable and, consequently, less accessible to verbal recall after a long delay.

Whereas the factors just described bring some consistency to the small literature on the later verbal accessibility of early memories, there remains one apparent contradiction. Peterson and Rideout (1998) reported that there was seemingly "transient" verbal accessibility of memories for experiences that occurred when children were between 20 and 25 months of age (see Table 10.1), whereas in my laboratory my colleagues and I have found reliable long-term accessibility of memories for events experienced at 20 months of age. Although there has not yet been a direct test of the suggestion, it is likely that the difference in the reliability of long-term verbal accessibility for children 20 to 25 months of age can be attributed to the fact that in the research from my laboratory, children were reexposed to the event sequences at approximately 26 months of age (i.e., when their nonverbal recall was tested). In Peterson and Rideout's study, the children were interviewed about their experiences 6 months later (at approximately 26–31 months of age). However, the verbal interview may not have effectively reinstated the event memory. As discussed by Judith Hudson (1991, 1993), *verbal* means of reinstating event memories probably are not effective until children are at least 3 years of age. In contrast, *nonverbal* means of reinstatement are effective from as young as 9 months of age (e.g., Bauer et al., 2001). The importance of the reinstating experience is brought home by the results of analyses in which we examined the predictors of later verbal accessibility of early memories, discussed next.

*Predicting Verbal Expression of Memory at Age 3 Years.* The traditional perspective on later verbal accessibility of early memories makes the assumption that language at the time of experience of an event is the single most important predictor of later verbal accessibility. The literature reviewed thus far has not allowed for a strong test of this assumption due to a combination of factors. First, there are relatively few studies of later verbal test of recall of events experienced in the first years of life. Second, the tests that exist tend to be based on small samples of children. For example, in the work from my laboratory, sample sizes have ranged from only 10 to 15 children per age at the time of experience of events. Third, in some of the research, independent measures of children's language at the time the events were experienced, at the time of tests for recall, or both, are not available (Peterson & Rideout, 1998). Fourth, independent measures of the children's memory for the event are rarely considered (Peterson & Rideout, 1998). As a result, it is not clear whether verbal memory is poor because the test is verbal or because children did not adequately encode the events to begin with. This combination of factors makes it difficult to establish the unique contributions of the range of potential predictors of later verbal accessibility of early memories.

Carol Cheatham and I addressed this deficiency in the literature by examining a sample of 97 children, all drawn from the "Monster" study (Cheatham & Bauer, 2005). In this study, we wanted to provide a test of whether the fate of early memories, as measured by later verbal recall, is different if events are encoded before versus after the age of 18 months (a suggestion derived from Peterson & Rideout, 1998, as well as from the studies from my laboratory discussed thus far). For this reason, we included children who were 16 months of age at the time of enrollment in the parent study and children who were 20 months of age. Fortunately, we were able to examine a number of possible predictor variables, including several not examined in previous relevant studies. As reflected in Table 10.2, we included variables from the time of initial experience of the events, variables from the time of the first (spontaneous) delayed recall test, as well as variables from the second (elicited) delayed recall test.

As already noted, traditionally variables from the time of first experience of events have been considered to be the most important in determining later verbal access to early memories. To test this suggestion, Cheatham and I conducted an initial analysis in which we examined only the variables from the time of first experience of the events—namely, children's ages and their language abilities at the time of enrollment. Only age was related to later verbal expression of memory; its relation was not especially strong, however (i.e., it accounted for only 8% of the variance). Language at the time of experience of the events was not related to later verbal expression, even weakly (Cheatham & Bauer, 2005).

The finding that neither age nor language at the time of encoding of the events is a powerful contributor to later verbal expression of memory was further suggested by the results of analyses in which we considered the full set of possible determinants listed in Table 10.2. With the full set of variables under consideration, neither of the variables from the time of initial experience of the events emerged as important to children's verbal recall at age 3. Instead we found that the most important contributors to later verbal expression of memory were (in order of importance): (a) children's spontaneous verbal expression of memory at 17 to 32 months, and (b) children's age at the first delayed-recall test. In effect, what contributed to verbal recall at age 3 was a previous opportunity to invoke the memory representation (i.e.,

TABLE 10.2
Possible Predictors of Later Verbal Recall From the Time
of Initial Experience of Events, the First Delayed-Recall Test,
and the Second Delayed-Recall Test

| Variable | Provides a Measure of: |
|---|---|
| From Initial Experience | |
| 1. Age (16–20 months) | NA |
| 2. Language | Verbal encoding ability at the time of experience (MacArthur-Bates Communicative Development Inventory) |
| From Delayed-Recall Test 1 (spontaneous) | |
| 3. Age (17–32 months) | NA |
| 4. Language | Verbal ability at the time of spontaneous verbal report (as measured by total talk during the session) |
| 5. Delay between exposure and test | Passage of time between exposure and test (1–12 months) |
| 6. Nonverbal memory | Independent assessment of memory trace strength (number of actions and pairs of actions of events produced) |
| 7. Verbal memory | Assessment of spontaneous verbal expression |
| From Delayed-Recall Test 2 (elicited) | |
| 8. Age (36–42 months) | NA |
| 9. Language | Verbal ability at the time of elicited verbal report (as measured by total talk during the session) |

Note.   Based on Cheatham and Bauer (2005). NA = not applicable.

the first delayed-recall test) and augment it with a verbal description of the event (as indexed by spontaneous verbal expression of memory).

The finding that spontaneous verbal expression of memory at ages 17 to 32 months was important to elicited verbal expression of memory at age 3 years leads to the question of what is important for *spontaneous* verbal expression of memory. To answer this question, Cheatham and I (Cheatham & Bauer, 2005) conducted additional analyses in which we considered only Variables 1 through 6 in Table 10.2. Only language at the time spontaneous verbal expression of memory was tested proved to be an important contributor to it.

The full pattern of results from this study suggests a cascade effect. First, verbal ability at the time of reinstatement of the event memory permits verbal "augmentation" of a primarily nonverbal memory trace. Second, reencoding of the event memory using language keeps the memory "alive" in verbally accessible form over a subsequent delay averaging 12½ months (and ranging from 6–21.4 months). The conclusion that language played little role in the original memory representation is suggested by the fact that language at the time of encoding was not related to either spontaneous or later elicited verbal expression of memory. In contrast, children who were more verbal at the time the memory representation was reinstated (at the first delayed-recall test) used their language to talk about the events. It was their spontaneous verbal expressions of memory at ages 17 to 32 months that predicted subsequent verbal expression of memory at ages 36 to 42 months. This pattern of findings suggests that our traditional conceptualizations of the factors influencing later verbal accessibility of early memories are sorely in need of revision. Moreover, it indicates that a simple explanation of childhood amnesia in terms of inaccessibility of early memories to later verbal report will not be adequate.

## Why So Few Memories "Make the Crossing"

Given that, at least under some circumstances, children are able to talk about events that were likely to have been encoded primarily nonverbally, why do so few memories apparently "make the crossing" of the great divide between infant memory and childhood memory? To address this question, we must again consider the conditions under which we see verbal children successfully engage in conversations about pre- and early verbal memories.

*Apparent Constraints on Later Verbal Accessibility of Early Memories.* With high levels of contextual support, children who were younger than 20 months at the time they experienced events may be able to report on the events after some months have passed. However, even with high levels of contextual support, they are unlikely to be able to report on the events after a lengthy delay. In light of the relation between language ability at the time of memory reinstatement and later verbal recall (Cheatham & Bauer, 2005), we may speculate that, for such young children, a major impediment to long-term preservation of a verbally accessible memory is insufficient verbal augmentation of the memory representation at the time of reinstatement. In effect, very young children experience a Catch 22. Unless the delay between experience and test is long, by the time of test, children will not have gained sufficient verbal fluency to augment their nonverbal memory representations. Thus, they retrieve memories, but they still do not have sufficient command of language to adequately supplement their representations with language. However, if the delay is long enough to permit adequate language, it likely will be too long to permit effective reinstatement of the memory: Fewer than 50% of 13-month-olds remember for longer than 3 months; a significant number of 16-month-olds remember for 6 months, but not longer (Bauer et al., 2000). Language cannot supplement what does not exist!

For children near the end of the second year of life at the time of experience of events, contextual reinstatement is not necessary to elicit verbal reports even after long delays: Even when they were tested in their homes, children who were 20 months of age at the time of original experience of events provided verbal evidence of memory at age 3. Photographs alone may not be effective retrieval aids, however (Bauer et al., 2004). This implies that the conditions under which early memories can be retrieved are limited. Strong contextual support may be necessary for successful retrieval. Moreover, in the absence of an effective reinstating experience at some point in the retention interval, verbal accessibility may not be maintained over the long term.

For children 2 years of age and older at the time of experience of a unique event, the limiting factor on long-term verbal accessibility may be the nature of the event itself. If the event is sufficiently unique or personally meaningful, it may be verbally accessible for months after experience. If the event is more mundane, it may not be verbally accessible even if tested after only a few months.

***Implications of the Constraints.***   This analysis begins to make clear why so few early memories cross the "bridge" between the preverbal past and the verbal present. If language is not available at the time of encoding of an event, it must be added to an exclusively or primarily nonverbal memory representation. Language can be added, but only if the memory representation can be effectively reinstated at a time of availability of language sufficient to describe the event. If a child is very young at the time of experience of the event, then she or he will likely experience a long delay before sufficient language is available. Unfortunately, time is the enemy of a memory representation, perhaps especially one stored in a neural system that is still "under construction"—the brain of the young child is still undergoing significant development (see chap. 6 for discussion). Also, the conditions under which reinstatement is successful seem to be more restricted for younger children relative to older children. Language itself is not especially effective (Hudson, 1991, 1993); it seems that neither are pictures at least when they are presented out of context (Bauer et al., 2004).

Although there are many ways that the system can fail, it is increasingly clear that, under certain circumstances, such as when strong physical cues are available, early memories can be retrieved even after long delays. Once retrieved, children can use their newly developed language skills to augment their primarily nonverbal representations with language. Those representations can survive into early childhood, permitting verbal reports of events experienced early in life. However, this "just right" combination of conditions may be rare indeed. Its improbability may account in part for the relative paucity of verbally accessible memories from the earliest years of life.

In addition to making clear why so few memories cross the great divide separating preverbal infancy and verbal early childhood, this analysis also suggests that the fact that memories typically fail to make the crossing is not the result of pronounced discontinuities in memory development. That is, there is no evidence of a *qualitative* change in the nature of representation: Preverbal memories are not fundamentally incompatible with "postverbal" memories. Rather under typical circumstances, memories from early in life fail to cross the bridge between the preverbal past and the verbal present because, by the time the narrative skills necessary to talk about the past are available, the experiences are long since forgotten. Indeed even if storage failure is not complete, linguistic reminders may not aid retrieval because language is not a particularly effective cue for pre- and early verbal memories. This analysis takes some of the "romance" out of the phenomenon of the later verbal inaccessibility of most early memories. Simultaneously, however, it resolves some of the mystery of the wide range in age of earliest memory, with some adults reporting recall of events from the age of 2 years (e.g., Usher & Neisser, 1993). If we recognize that with the right combination of circumstances early memories can survive to be described by the older child and even the adult, then we need not view these early recollections as special exceptions to a rule of fundamental incompatibility of early and later memory.

## THE SECOND "GREAT DIVIDE": PRESCHOOL TO MIDDLE CHILDHOOD

The most salient component of the phenomenon of childhood amnesia is the relative paucity among adults of verbally accessible memories from the first 2 to 4 years of life. An equally important component of the phenomenon is that, among adults, the number of memories of events that occurred from the ages of 3 to 7 years is smaller than the number that would be expected by forgetting alone (see Fig. 2.1). Whereas the rarity of combination of just the right circumstances for later verbal accessibility of early memories helps account for the first component of the phenomenon, it does not help to explain this second component. Moreover, just as there are individual differences in the age of earliest memory (ranging from 2–6 years; e.g., West & Bauer, 1999), so are there individual differences in the "density" of early memories (Weigle & Bauer, 2000): Some adults find it easy to report several memories from before the age of 7 years, whereas others seemingly have few events from which to sample. To understand this component of childhood amnesia, it is necessary to track the fate of memories from the preschool years as children make the transition across the "great divide" that separates the preschool and early childhood years.

Despite the obvious significance of research that examines older children's recall of events that occurred between the ages of 3 and 7 years, there is actually little work relevant to the question. On the one hand, research on

adults' recollections of their childhoods—which is the source of the observation of the smaller than expected number of memories from ages 3 to 7—is,
by definition, with adults. On the other hand, most of the developmental
work on autobiographical memory has been conducted with children in the
preschool years to determine whether they remember. Because this work
made clear that preschool-age children do have autobiographical memories,
there was little motivation to explore the question in older children: The basic ability was mapped out; work with older children could be expected to reveal further developments in narrative ability, but little additional light
would be shed on autobiographical memory per se.

From the standpoint of research on the phenomenon of childhood amnesia, at least two factors have conspired to maintain the focus on questions
other than the fate of memories from the preschool years. First, the literature
documenting that children in the preschool years have memories is relatively
new, having originated as recently as the mid-1980s. Second, questions regarding what happens to memories from the preschool years as preschoolers
develop into older children and older children develop into adults are best
addressed through prospective, longitudinal methods. Longitudinal research
is expensive to conduct and extremely time-consuming. The result is that
there is only a small body of work that bears on the question of when in development the adultlike distribution of memories is observed. I begin the review of the small literature with work examining older children's recollections of salient events from their early childhood years. I then turn to the
small body of work that permits examination of the distribution of memories
from early childhood.

## Remembering Salient Childhood Events

One of the earliest studies of older children's memories for salient childhood
events was conducted by Karen Sheingold and Yvette Tenney (1982). They
interviewed adults and older children about the birth of a younger sibling. In
chapter 3, I reviewed the results of the work with adults. Briefly, Sheingold
and Tenney found that virtually none of the college-age participants in their
study remembered any details about the birth of a sibling if they were younger than 3 years of age at the time of the birth. In fact most of the adults who
had siblings born before the age of 3 could not answer any of the 20 questions posed to them, which are reproduced in Table 10.3. In contrast, as depicted in Fig. 10.2, for births that occurred when the participant was 3 years
of age or older (range 3–17 years), high levels of recall were observed. Indeed
for participants who had been at least 3 years of age at the time of their siblings' births, there was no relation between the number of questions answered and the amount of time that had elapsed since the birth. Thus,
among young adults, Sheingold and Tenney observed a sharp "boundary" at

## TABLE 10.3
### Questions of the Details of a Sibling's Birth Posed
### by Sheingold and Tenney (1982)

1. Who told you that your mother was leaving to go to the hospital?
2. What were you doing when you were told that she was leaving?
3. What time of day was it when she left to go to the hospital?
4. Who went with her? Did you go?
5. Who took care of you right after your mother left to go to the hospital?
6. What did you do right after your mother left?
7. How did you find out that the baby was a boy or girl?
8. Who took care of you while your mother was in the hospital?
9. What things did you do with that person while your mother was in the hospital?
10. Did you visit your mother while she was in the hospital?
11. Did you talk to your mother on the telephone while she was in the hospital?
12. How long did she stay in the hospital?
13. Who picked your mother and the baby up?
14. What day of the week did they come home?
15. What time of day was it?
16. What did you do when your mother and the baby arrived at home?
17. What was the baby wearing when you first saw it?
18. What presents did the baby get?
19. Did you get any presents at that time?
20. How did you find out that your mother was going to have a baby?

*Note.* Based on Sheingold and Tenney (1982), Table 19-1.

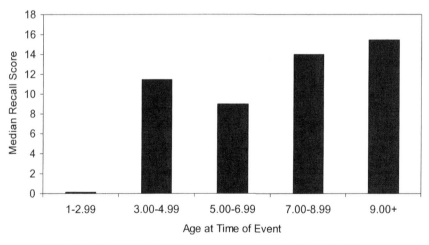

FIG. 10.2. Levels of recall of the events surrounding the birth of a sibling as a function of the participants' ages at the time of the siblings' births. Based on Sheingold and Tenney (1982), Fig. 19.1; values are approximate.

age 3. After 3 years, however, memory was intact regardless of how many years had passed since the event.

Sheingold and Tenney (1982) also interviewed children who had experienced the birth of a sibling when they were between 3 and 4 years of age (none of the child participants had siblings who were born when the participants were younger than age 3). At the time of the interviews, the children were in three age groups, with average ages of 4 years, 8 years, and 12 years. Although different amounts of time had elapsed between the siblings' births and the interviews, and some of the children had crossed out of the period eventually obscured by childhood amnesia, all three age groups remembered a great deal about the event. Indeed the number of questions answered correctly did not differ across the groups: 4- and 8-year-olds answered roughly 14 questions correctly (of 20 questions asked) and 12-year-olds answered roughly 12 questions correctly. Sheingold and Tenney interpreted their results as indicative of extremely well-preserved memory for a salient event that occurred at the age of 3 to 4 years. They suggested that ". . . the impact of development is on initial encoding—that is, on the amount of information initially taken in—rather than on later transformations of the information" (Sheingold & Tenney, 1982, pp. 210–211). Thus, these data provided no hints as to the processes that might account for the smaller than expected number of memories among adults for events from ages 3 to 7: If the event was salient, it appears that it should be recalled regardless of the passage of time.

Additional evidence of well-preserved memories for an event from the preschool years comes from a study conducted by Judith Hudson and Robyn Fivush (1991). As discussed in chapter 7, these investigators arranged a special trip to a museum of archeology for a classroom of 5-year-olds. Fully 6 years after the trip, when the children were 11 years old, the investigators questioned 13 of the original 18 participants about their memories of the event. When aided by the generic prompt, "Can you tell me what happened when you went to the Jewish Museum?", only one child reported remembering the trip. However, when they were given more specific reminders, including pictures of some aspects of the event, 11 of the 13 children provided accurate reports. As reflected in Fig. 10.3, the children recalled fewer of the acts of the experience after 6 years relative to when they were interviewed about the field trip immediately, 6 weeks, and 1 year after it (labeled *Acts* in Fig. 10.3). However, for the elements that they did remember, the 11-year-old children provided as many elaborations and descriptions of the actions as they had at the earlier interviews. Thus, the information that was recalled was reported in as much detail as it had been 5 to 6 years earlier. The children's high levels of recall cannot be attributed entirely to the pictures themselves because the children typically included elements of the event that were not depicted in the pictures. For example, when shown a picture of

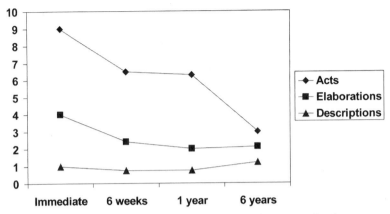

FIG. 10.3. Mean levels of recall of the acts (diamonds) associated with a special trip to a museum, and mean number of elaborations (squares) and descriptions (triangles) of the acts produced at each of four interviews: immediately after the field trip (1), 6 weeks later (2), 1 year later (3), and 6 years later (4). From "As Time Goes By: Sixth Graders Remember a Kindergarten Experience," by J. A. Hudson and R. Fivush, *Applied Cognitive Psychology*, 5, 347–360, Fig. 1, 1991. © John Wiley & Sons Limited. Reproduced with permission.

children digging in a sandbox (a mock archeological pit), the children advised that, "We were digging for artifacts," which was not apparent in the picture.

The literature also contains a number of reports of quite robust memories by older children for traumatic events experienced in the preschool years. In general, the studies reveal better later memory for events among children who were older at the time of their experiences relative to children who were younger. For example, Jodi Quas and her colleagues (Quas et al., 1999) assessed the memories of children 3 to 13 years of age for a painful catheterization procedure they had experienced between the ages of 2 and 6 years. Children who were older at the time of the procedure provided clearer evidence of recall of it. In contrast to the older children's detailed reports, the reports of the younger children were vague or even lacking altogether. In fact none of the children who had been 2 years of age at the time of the procedure demonstrated clear memory for it later, whereas most of the children who had been at least 4 years old at the time of the procedure remembered it. A similar pattern of results was observed by Carole Peterson and Nikki Whalen (2001), who interviewed children 7 to 18 years of age about injuries incurred 5 years previously, when they were 2 to 13 years of age.

Another illustration of a relation between age at the time of the event and later memory is provided by David Pillemer and his colleagues, Martha Picariello, and Jenzi Pruett (Pillemer et al., 1994). As discussed in chapter 7, Pillemer and his colleagues took advantage of an unexpected preschool fire alarm to study the durability of memories from early childhood. At the ages of 3½ or 4½ years, children experienced a fire alarm triggered by burning popcorn that led to a school evacuation. Six years after the fire alarm, when the children were 9½ and 10½ years old, Pillemer and his colleagues interviewed the children to determine what, if anything, they remembered about the event. Over half of the children who had been 4½ years of age at the time of the incident were able to provide at least a partial narrative account of the experience after the long delay. In contrast, fewer than 20% of the children who had been only 3½ years of age at the time of the incident were able to provide a narrative description of it.

These studies paint a relatively consistent picture of patterns of recall by older children of events experienced during the preschool years. First, even when they are interviewed as much as 6 years after a salient childhood event, children of at least 3 years of age at the time of the event are able to recall it. Second, when children of more than one age at the time of the experience are included in a study, there is a general pattern of better later recall by the children who were older at the time of the event relative to children who were younger. This finding is consistent with expectations derived from the literature on adults' recall of early childhood events: Among adults, more events are remembered from later in the preschool years than from early in the preschool years. Third, although it is not apparent in each of the studies I have reviewed, there are suggestions that memories become less accessible over time (e.g., Hudson & Fivush, 1991). That is, with the passage of time, children are more dependent on prompts and cues to recall events.

Two exceptions to this general pattern are the study by Sheingold and Tenney (1982), discussed earlier in this section, and the study by Fivush et al. (2004), discussed in chapter 8. In Sheingold and Tenney's study of children's recall of the birth of a younger sibling, there appeared to be no loss of information about the event even when children were interviewed almost a decade after the sibling birth. Similarly, in their follow-up to an earlier study of 3- and 4-year-old children's recall of Hurricane Andrew, a Class IV hurricane that devastated portions of southern Florida in 1992, Fivush and her colleagues found that 6 years after the hurricane, the children—now 9 and 10 years of age—actually reported *more* information about the storm than they had when they were originally interviewed within months after it.

It is interesting to speculate about the possible sources of the different effects in the studies of children's memories for siblings births and a hurricane, compared with those in which children's memories for museum trips, catheterization procedures, and fire alarms were studied. In the cases of sibling births and the hurricane, there are daily reminders of the event in the form of the sibling (who does not go away . . .) and changes in lifestyle after the storm (e.g., many families were forced to relocate) or possible losses resulting from it. In contrast, trips to museums, diagnostic medical procedures, and fire alarms carry no day-to-day reminders of their occurrence. As a result, memories for those experiences likely are not reinstated with the frequency of memories for more life-changing events. Importantly, even for events with less impact on children, although children may forget information about the event over time, that which they do remember is reported with detail (Hudson & Fivush, 1991) and accuracy. For example, Quas and her colleagues (Quas et al., 1999) found that longer delays between a catheterization procedure and the test for memory for it were associated with lower levels of recall, yet there was no decrease in the accuracy of the information provided. Thus, whereas for at least some, and perhaps for most, salient childhood events, children forget some information over time, but that which they do remember tends to be detailed and accurate.

## The Distribution of Memories in the School Years

Studies of older children's recall of salient childhood events provide proof that some childhood memories survive the period eventually obscured by childhood amnesia. This of course is no surprise: Unless we were to assume that adults' memories of their preschool years were pure confabulations, we would fully expect to find that children remember at least some events as well. What remains to be explored is the *distribution* of memories from early childhood. Among adults, the preschool years yield fewer memories than would be expected based on forgetting alone. Is the same pattern apparent in childhood? If so, when does the adult distribution of autobiographical memories become apparent? These questions can only be addressed by examining a corpus of early memories, and tracking them over time, to see how many are retained into the later school years. Likely because the field is not very old to begin with, and because prospective research takes a long time and is expensive to conduct, there are few relevant data sets. In fact I know of precisely two. I discuss each in turn.

*Eight-Year-Olds' Memories of Childhood.* The first relevant data were reported by Robyn Fivush and April Schwarzmueller (1998). In this study, 8-year-old children were interviewed about events they had experienced as many as 5 years in the past. The children and their parents had taken part in a longitudinal study of memory. At the ages of 3½, 4, 5, and 6 years, with one of their parents or with an experimenter, the children talked about a number of unique experiences, such as going to amusement parks, first airplane rides, and the like. The results of these early interviews were reported in a number of the studies reviewed in chapters 7, 8, and 9 (e.g., Haden et al., 1997; Reese, Haden, & Fivush, 1993, 1996). In a follow-up to the original study, when the children were 8 years of age, Fivush and Schwarzmueller interviewed 16 of the original sample of 24 children. They asked the children about four to six events they had recalled previously. At the earlier visits the children had talked about the events with their mothers, their fathers, an experimenter, or with some combination thereof, whereas at age 8 years the interviews were conducted by an experimenter with whom the children were not previously acquainted.

In total, the 8-year-old children were asked about 68 events, and they recalled 58 of them (85%). This very high rate of recall was observed even though the experimenters followed a strict protocol in which they provided relatively few specific cues about the events, and some of the events had not been included in an interview protocol since the children were 3½ and 4 years of age. Moreover, as reflected in Table 10.4, the children recalled as much about the events at age 8 as they had at their earlier interviews. That is, the number of propositions they reported about the events at 8 years did not differ from the number they reported the first time they talked about the events. Children's later recall did not differ significantly as a function of their conversational partner the first time they talked about the events, or whether the events had been included in only one or two previous interviews (no events were queried at more than two previous interviews). Neither were there relations between the amount reported at age 8 years and children's mothers' estimates of the frequency with which the events had been discussed in the home. The lack of relation may be due to the fact that mothers estimated high rates of rehearsal for almost all of the events.

The findings from Fivush and Schwarzmueller's (1998) study indicate that as children "exit" the period typically obscured by childhood amnesia, they nevertheless exhibit high rates of recall of events experienced 2 to 5 years previously. Thus, they suggest that at least at age 8 distinctive events that children had talked about at some point in the past remain highly verbally accessible. As such the data reveal nothing akin to the adultlike distribution of memories from the preschool years. Nor can the patterns be attributed to reconstructive processes that might permit children to generate, rather than

TABLE 10.4

Amount Recalled (as Measured by Propositions) About Events Originally Reported at 3½, 4, 5, or 6 Years of Age and Again at the Age of 8 Years

| Events Originally Reported at | Number of Propositions Reported | |
|---|---|---|
| | At Original Interview | At Age 8 Years |
| 3½ years | 10.61 | 9.57 |
| 4 years | 11.08 | 11.78 |
| 5 years | 9.67 | 9.40 |
| 6 years | 18.52 | 16.80 |

Note.   Based on Fivush and Schwarzmueller (1998), Table 3.

remember, activities associated with their early experiences, such as a trip to SeaWorld. A reconstruction of an event would not be expected to include detailed information such as, "We were sitting way high up and when Shamu jumped he splashed and we got all wet" (Fivush & Schwarzmueller, 1998, p. 468). As noted by the authors, the fact that the children's accounts were vivid and personalized suggests that they were based on memories for specific past events—events that had taken place during the period of time that in adults is obscured (although not made opaque) by childhood amnesia.

*Seven- to Nine-Year-Olds' Memories of Childhood.*   The second study that was explicitly designed to address the question of the later accessibility of memories from the preschool years was conducted in my laboratory. The sample was a subset of the children who, as infants, had participated in the "Monster" study (Bauer et al., 2000). As noted earlier in this chapter, we invited some of the children who participated in that study to return to the laboratory at the age of 3 years. One purpose of the return visit was to test whether the children could talk about the laboratory events they had experienced as infants. Another purpose was to gather autobiographical reports from the children.

After the 3-year-old children had been interviewed about the prop-supported events that they had first experienced at the ages of 13, 16, or 20 months, my colleagues and I asked the children and their parents (typically mothers) to sit together and talk about as many as six events that had happened in the past few months. As in studies such as that by Fivush and Schwarzmueller (1998), we asked the parents to select events that were relatively unique, such as the child's first airplane ride. Consistent with the research reviewed in chapters 7, 8, and 9, the children were able to talk about their experiences. These early reports provided the "raw materials" for our follow-up study conducted years later.

When the children were of school age, Dana Van Abbema and I (Van Abbema & Bauer, 2005) invited 47 of them back to the laboratory for yet another memory interview. At the follow-up, 13 of the children were 7 years of age, 19 of the children were 8 years of age, and 15 of the children were 9 years of age. All of the children were interviewed about the events by an experimenter. The experimenter began the interview with a probe that introduced the event, such as, "Tell me about the time you went to Texas." As the interview continued, the interviewer provided additional cues about the event, derived from the original interviews at age 3 (e.g., "When you went to Texas, you stayed at the beach").

In addition to events from the distant past, we also asked the children to report on two events from the more recent past—within 1 to 6 months. Inclusion of events from the more recent past, along with events from the distant past, provides an opportunity not available in any of the other studies of school-age children's recall of events—namely, to conduct a direct comparison of children's narratives about events experienced at different points in developmental time. In studies such as that by Fivush and Schwarzmueller (1998), for example, the claim that children show little forgetting is based both on the number of events that they remember and the amount of information they report (see also Sheingold & Tenney, 1982). However, in the space of time between interviews at ages 3 years and 7 to 9 years, children's narrative abilities develop dramatically (see chap. 8 for a review). If memory stays the same and narrative length increases, one might expect an actual *increase* in the amount of information reported (such as observed in the follow-up to the Hurricane Andrew study conducted by Fivush et al., 2003). In contrast, the finding that the same amount of information was reported at two points in time (e.g., Fivush & Schwarzmueller, 1998) raises the possibility that some forgetting had occurred, but that the values remained the same because of increases in narrative ability. This possibility can be evaluated by comparing the amount of information provided about events from the recent and distant past.

After interviewing the 7- to 9-year-old children about events from age 3 and events from the more recent past, using the same criteria as adopted in the study by Fivush and Schwarzmueller (1998), Van Abbema and I determined whether the children remembered the events. Specifically, children who provided at least two unique pieces of information about the event (i.e., information not contained in the original probe or subsequent prompts) were considered to have remembered the event. The analyses of children's recall of the events from the distant past (from the age of 3) revealed a striking pattern. Whereas the 7-year-olds remembered 60% of the events, the 8- and 9-year-olds remembered only 36% and 34% of the events, respectively. The results are not in keeping with the idea of a "graceful degradation" that occurs over time. Instead they are suggestive of a "childhood amnesia component" to autobiographical memory—whereas children within the period eventually obscured by childhood amnesia remembered most of the events, children of ages presumed to have a more adultlike distribution of memories—namely 8- and 9-year-olds—remembered barely more than one third of the events.

In a now-familiar pattern, Van Abbema and I found that if the children remembered the events at all, their reports of them were both qualitatively and quantitatively similar to the reports they had provided at the time of the original interview at age 3. That is, as reflected in Table 10.5, Panel A, the children provided the same number of content elements for the events at the two points in time, and they included a similar breadth of narrative elements (i.e., the *who, what, where, when, why,* and *how* of the events) in their reports. In addition, for events from the distant past, there were not differences across the three age groups. Thus, if an event was remembered,

TABLE 10.5
Mean Frequencies for Total Content Provided and Breadth
of Narrative Reports at Age 3 Years and at the Age of 7, 8, or 9 Years

|  | *Age at the First and Second Interviews* | | | | | |
|---|---|---|---|---|---|---|
|  | *3 years* | *7 years* | *3 years* | *8 years* | *3 years* | *9 years* |
| Panel A: Distant events |  |  |  |  |  |  |
| Total content | 9.65 | 9.99 | 8.90 | 10.06 | 6.67 | 16.33 |
| Breadth | 2.94 | 3.28 | 3.01 | 3.34 | 2.70 | 3.78 |
| Panel B: Recent events |  |  |  |  |  |  |
| Total content | — | 16.08 | — | 30.96 | — | 39.44 |
| Breadth | — | 3.75 | — | 4.50 | — | 4.44 |

*Note.* Data from Van Abbema and Bauer (2005).

the amount of information reported about it was the same regardless of how many years had passed since the event. The absence of age differences in the length of the reports was not due to lack of development of narrative skills over the time. As reflected in Table 10.5, Panel B, on the more recent events, Van Abbema and I observed the age-related change in narrative that one would expect—namely, older children provided both more detailed and more complete accounts of the events from the recent past relative to younger children.

Direct comparison of children's reports of events from the recent and distant past also was quite interesting (compare Table 10.5, Panels A and B). The children provided substantially more content in their reports of the more recent relative to the distant events. Their narrative accounts of the more recent events were also more complete than their accounts of the more distant events. Both effects were larger among the older relative to the younger children (Van Abbema & Bauer, 2005). By these metrics then, children did exhibit forgetting of the events from the distant past: Their narrative accounts of them were neither as detailed nor as complete as those from the more recent past. This finding, coupled with the age-related decline in the number of events remembered, suggests that "childhood amnesia" is not solely an adult phenomenon, but is observed in children beginning as early as 7 years of age.

*Across-Study Comparison.* The findings from the studies by Fivush and Schwarzmueller (1998) and Van Abbema and Bauer (2005) are in some ways consistent and in other ways inconsistent with one another. Most notably, both studies provided evidence that when school-age children remember events from their childhoods, they remember them in considerable detail even after an extended period of time. Indeed the amount of information the children provided about the events when they were of school age did not differ from the amount of information they provided near the time the events occurred.

The studies differ, however, in their implications for when an adultlike distribution of early memories becomes apparent. The findings from the study by Fivush and Schwarzmueller (1998) have been interpreted to suggest that children retain robust memories for events from the preschool years. Not only did the children remember 85% of the events they had talked about at the earlier interviews, but the amount of information recalled shortly after the events and at age 8 years did not differ. In contrast, the findings from the study that Van Abbema and I conducted (Van Abbema & Bauer, 2005) imply that by the time children were 7 to 9 years of age, they had forgotten many of the events from the preschool years. There was greater forgetting among the 8- and 9-year-olds (64% and 66% of events forgotten, respectively) relative to the 7-year-olds (40% of events forgotten). Moreover, comparison of children's levels of recall of events experienced in the recent compared with the distant past implied that details of the more distant events had been forgotten even when the event itself was recalled. As noted, Van Abbema and I interpret these findings as evidence that "childhood amnesia" begins to set in when children are as young as age 7.

One possible reason for the differences between the two studies is the number of times the events were formally queried. In the study by Fivush and Schwarzmueller (1998), almost one quarter (22%) of the events discussed at age 8 had been talked about with two different conversational partners, either in the same session or across different sessions. In contrast, in the study by Van Abbema and Bauer (2005), the children participated in only one previous recall session. This difference alone likely does not account for the different results between the studies, yet we should be mindful of the potential impact of multiple formal interviews about a past event.

A second possible reason for the differences between the two studies is that they differed in the amount of time over which recall was tested. In the study by Fivush and Schwarzmueller (1998), 8-year-old children were questioned about events that had happened in the months prior to interviews that took place when the children were approximately 3½, 4, 5, or 6 years of age. Thus, as reflected on the left side of Fig. 10.4, as few as 26 months and a maximum of 56 months had passed since the children were first interviewed about the events. In contrast, as reflected on the right side of Fig. 10.4, in the study that Van Abbema and I conducted (Van Abbema & Bauer, 2005), a minimum average of 50 months and a maximum average of 74 months had passed since the children had been interviewed about the events (as in the study by Fivush and Schwarzmueller, the events took place some months before the first interview). Although Fivush and Schwarzmueller did not evaluate the trend formally, in their study the children remembered a smaller percentage of events from the more distant past (events first queried 50 and 56

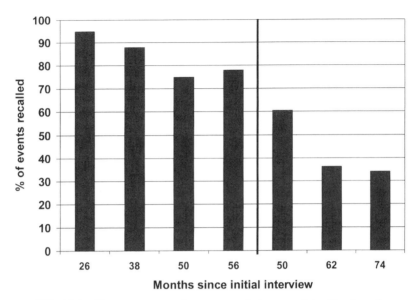

FIG. 10.4. The percentage of events recalled reported in Fivush and Schwarzmueller (1998; left side of figure) and in Van Abbema and Bauer (2005; right side of figure) as a function of the length of time (in months) since the initial interview about the event.

months previously) than from the more recent past (events first queried 26 and 38 months previously). Thus, as suggested by inspection of Fig. 10.4, whereas the absolute levels of event recall were higher in the Fivush and Schwarzmueller study, relative to the Van Abbema and Bauer study, it seems that the same trend was apparent—namely, lower levels of recall as the amount of time since experience of the events increased. When considered in this light, both studies of the distribution of school-age children's recall of events from the preschool years suggest the beginnings of an adultlike distribution of memory.

## Predicting Later Recall of Early Life Events

Because there have been only a few studies of older children's recall of early life events, we know relatively little about the predictors of "survival" of memories for early experiences across the "great divide" of preschool to middle childhood. One obvious predictor that is implicated in several of the studies reviewed in this chapter is the age of the child at the time of the event: The older children were at the time of the experience of the event, the greater the likelihood that they recalled the event in middle childhood. Of course age is only a proxy variable. That is, when we invoke age as an explanation, we are actually implicating a wide range of developments and changes that occur with age. As described in chapter 8, throughout the preschool years, there are developments in the brain structures that support declarative memory. As a result, there are age-related improvements in the basic mnemonic processes of encoding, consolidation, storage, and retrieval of event memories. Older children also have more world knowledge, permitting them greater understanding of the causes and consequences of the events of their lives. Greater comprehension in turn contributes to higher levels of recall. In addition, older children seem to encode more distinctive features of events relative to younger children. Distinctive features permit experiences to "stand out" against the backdrop of routine events, rendering specific episodes more memorable.

A second factor implicated in later recall of experiences from early in life is reinstatement of memory for the event during the retention interval. For example, Fivush and Schwarzmueller (1998) speculated that one of the reasons for such high levels of preservation of event memories into middle childhood was that the events had been frequently talked about at the time they were experienced. The researchers suggested that conversations about the events permitted children to create well-organized narratives that supported long-term retention. Earlier I speculated that frequent reinstatement may help preserve memories of life-changing events, such as the birth of a sibling, a hurricane, or a tornado. Because the consequences of such events persist over time, memories for the events themselves may be frequently reinstated, contributing to high levels of recall even after long delays.

A third potential contributor to preservation of memories for early life events into middle childhood is a factor shown to have both concurrent and predictive relations with children's recall during the preschool years—namely, maternal style. In chapter 9, I described two different styles of conversation about past events. Some parents provide a great deal of detail when talking about past events with their children, they engage their children in conversation, and they follow their children's conversational leads. In contrast to this so-called *elaborative* style, other parents provide less detail, talk about the past less frequently, and attempt to get their children to recall specific features of events, instead of co-constructing narrative about them. If the child fails to recall the feature, the parent simply repeats the question, leading to characterization of this style as *repetitive* or *low-elaborative*. As discussed in chapter 9, during the preschool period, children with parents who use a more elaborative style of conversation report more about past events. Thus, within the period eventually obscured by childhood amnesia, there are clear relations between the conversational style of the parent and children's autobiographical narratives. Do similar relations obtain as children cross the boundary between the preschool years and middle childhood? In other words, do effects of parental conversational style persist across the second "great divide"?

At present there are only two data sets that can be brought to bear on the question of whether there are "long-distance" relations between conversational style variables and children's later recall of early life events. One of the data sets is that which has provided much of the grist for the parental style mill—namely, that from the laboratory of Robyn Fivush. In most of the published reports from this data set, Fivush and her colleagues have presented data from the 3½-, 4-, 5-, and 6-year observations. In their 1998 report, Fivush and Schwarzmueller presented data from a subset (16) of the children who were tested again at 8 years of age. Earlier in this chapter, I discussed data obtained when the children were interviewed by an experimenter. In addition to the experimenter–child interviews, at the 8-year session, Fivush and her colleagues asked the children and their mothers to talk about some of the events from the previous sessions. As they had at earlier time points, the researchers observed that mothers who were more elaborative had children who made more contributions to the conversations. Critically, they also observed "long-distance" relations. That is, mothers who were more elaborative when their children were 3½ years of age had children who made more contributions to the conversations when they were 8 years of age (R. Fivush, personal communication, 2003). This finding is theoretically significant because it indicates a relation between maternal behavior from the preschool years and the behavior of the offspring in the middle childhood years.

The data just described provide evidence of relations between maternal verbal behavior in the context of mother–child conversations at age 3½ years and children's behavior in the same collaborative context at 8 years. Do characteristics of maternal style in the preschool years also relate to children's later *independent* narratives about early life events? Although the results are still preliminary, data from my laboratory suggest that they do. As described earlier in this chapter, the children who participated in the research Van Abbema and I conducted (Van Abbema & Bauer, 2005) provided independent narratives at the ages of 7, 8, or 9 years. The events about which the children were queried in middle childhood were discussed in the context of mother–child conversations at the age of 3. To determine whether maternal style when children were 3 years of age was related to children's reports in the preschool years (in the collaborative context), in middle childhood (in the independent context), or both, we coded the maternal contributions at 3 years for variables associated with the elaborative style.

At 3 years of age, the expected pattern of relations was obtained. That is, children whose mothers produced more elaborations made more contributions to the conversations. Critically, we found that even over the longest interval (i.e., for 9-year-olds, the oldest children in the sample), maternal elaborations in the context of collaborative conversations at age 3 were strongly related to both the diversity of content and the breadth of narrative content of the children's independent memory narratives. Whereas these results are preliminary and the relation is correlational (not causal), the pattern suggests that exposure to an elaborative conversational style early in the preschool years has lasting effects that work to increase the amount that older children remember about early life experiences.

## SUMMARY AND CONCLUSIONS

In this chapter, I reviewed the results of studies that bear on the fate of memories as they cross the great divides of the transition from infancy to early childhood and the transition from the preschool to the early school years. In both cases, there are surprisingly few studies that bear directly on the questions. Few studies have been designed to determine whether events from the first years of life—events likely encoded without the benefit of language—survive the transition to the preschool years and a verbal mode of expression. Even fewer studies have been designed to address the question of whether older children remember events from early in the preschool years.

Although the results of studies of the later verbal accessibility of early memories are mixed, there is clear evidence that under some circumstances children are able to talk about events that likely were encoded primarily nonverbally. Children who were younger than 20 months of age at the time of experience of events may be able to report on the event after some months have passed. However, even with high levels of contextual support, they are unlikely to verbally describe the event after a lengthy delay. In effect, such young children experience a Catch 22: If the delay between experience of the event and test for it is long enough to ensure language proficiency at the time of test, it is likely too long for a memory representation to survive given the relative fragility of memory traces in very young children. This does not mean that language at the time of experience of an event is the major determinant of later verbal accessibility of an early memory, however. Children who were as young as 20 months of age at the time of experience of events are able to provide verbal reports even after long delays. Importantly, later verbal accessibility seems to be dependent on an effective reinstating experience at some point in the retention interval. When children 26 months of age and older experience a unique event, the limiting factor on long-term verbal accessibility may be the nature of the event itself: Events that are sufficiently unique or personally meaningful may be verbally accessible for months after they are experienced.

Whereas it is now apparent that there are some conditions under which events experienced in the first years of life can survive to be described later in the preschool years, the right combination of conditions may be rare indeed. It is likely that this fact accounts for the relative paucity of verbally accessible memories from the earliest years of life. This implies that we need not invoke qualitative changes in the nature of mnemonic representation to account for the first component of childhood amnesia. Instead we may look to a combination of factors that together conspire to render early life experiences unavailable for later verbal description.

In contrast to the literature on the later verbal accessibility of early memories, the literature that bears on the second "great divide"—that between the preschool and the early school years—is relatively consistent: Children are able to remember into the school years events that took place in early childhood. Salient life events such as the birth of a sibling or a natural disaster are well recalled by children as young as 3 years of age at the time they occurred. Nevertheless, children who were older at the time of their experiences have better memory for them relative to children who were younger at the time they experienced the events. Age-related differences in the robustness of memory are likely related to developmental changes in basic memory processes, better comprehension of events by older children, and greater likelihood of encoding the distinctive and thus memorable features of events by older relative to younger children. Although some events from early in life are remembered into middle childhood, with increasing age and thus increasing delay since the events occurred, children begin to exhibit forgetting. Because there are only a few studies that permit address of the question, it remains unclear when the adultlike forgetting function becomes apparent. What is increasingly obvious, however, is that the phenomenon of childhood amnesia extends beyond adulthood to later childhood: Even as children, we begin to forget events from early in our lives.

# 11

# The Shifting Balance of Remembering and Forgetting

*The progress we have made in the study of memory has not been attributable as much to striking new discoveries than to a gradual elimination of wrong and unfruitful ideas.*

—Tulving (1983, p. 4)

Over the course of 10 chapters, I have reviewed much of the empirical, scientific literature that bears on the question of how we remember the times of their lives. The "times of our lives" have been defined as autobiographical memories or memories of specific past events that are relevant or significant to one's self. The story I have told has included "chapters" on how we begin to remember and on the shape that remembering takes in the healthy adult. I have approached the phenomenon of autobiographical memory and its development from different levels of analysis, ranging from the neural structures that are implicated in the act of remembering to cultural variations in autobiography in children and adults. I also have introduced multiple different explanations that have been offered to account for one of the most enigmatic "black holes" in adults' memories—namely, the phenomenon of childhood amnesia. In this final chapter, I bring together the different strands of the story. The aim is to provide a conceptualization of the development of autobiographical memory that acknowledges the multiple factors that contribute to it, and that provides a reasonable account of both the normative trends that are apparent as well as the individual and group differences.

## THE "WHAT" AND "WHEN"
## OF AUTOBIOGRAPHICAL MEMORY

At the beginning of this volume, I argued that memory is like an elephant, not a pudding. Because there are different types of memory (just as there are different parts to an elephant), and because the conclusions one draws about memory depend on which type is being sampled (the tail of the elephant is like a rope, whereas the tusk of an elephant is like a spear), if we are to make progress in describing memory—and certainly if we are to make progress in explaining it—we must be clear about what "it" is. This is true when we are attempting to explain autobiographical memory in the adult. It is even more important when we are attempting to explain the development of autobiographical memory. If we are not clear about what "it" is, how can we know of what we are tracing the development?

## Defining Autobiographical Memory

Although the need for agreement on what—exactly—constitutes an *autobiographical memory* is clear, we actually lack a straightforward definition of the construct. Logical concepts such as a square, for example, can be defined by features that are individually necessary and jointly sufficient: A square is any closed figure with four sides of equal length at 90-degree angles to one another. In contrast, autobiographical memory is a "family resemblance" category: It is defined primarily in terms of characteristic features rather than necessary ones (Rosch & Mervis, 1975). As discussed in chapter 2, the one exception is the strict requirement that autobiographical memories are about one's self. But just as the single feature of "closed figure" does not uniquely identify a square (circles too are closed figures), the single feature of "relevant to one's self" is not sufficient to identify a memory as "autobiographical." Individuals have many memories that are self-relevant, but that are not considered to be autobiographical memories. One's memories of one's name, date of birth, height, weight, shoe size, and the like are obvious examples. Rather than by the feature of self-relevance alone, autobiographical memory is identified by a number of features that are characteristic, yet not defining.

In addition to the "defining" feature that they be about one's self, autobiographical memories tend to be of *specific events or episodes*. That is, the prototypical autobiographical memory is of an experience that happened at a particular place, at a particular time. Although there is general agreement on this feature of autobiographical memory, agreement is not universal. Nora Newcombe and her colleagues (Lie & Newcombe, 1999; Newcombe & Fox, 1994), for example, argued that recurrent experiences that are salient to the self and that can be expected to influence later behavior also should be considered autobiographical. By this expanded definition, memories such as,

"Every Sunday I used to go to church and then visit my grandmother" and "When I was in first grade I had only one friend to play with. I remember her face even now, after 20 years" (Lie & Newcombe, 1999, p. 102) would be included, rather than excluded, from the category of autobiographical memory.

A second characteristic feature is that retrieval of an autobiographical memory *involves awareness that one is reexperiencing an event that happened in the past.* Although long a part of the definition of what today is characterized as episodic memory (of which autobiographical memory is a subtype; e.g., Tulving, 1972, 1983), only relatively recently has this feature of autobiographical memory received much attention. Whereas awareness of prior experience plays a prominent role in some theories of the development of autobiographical memory (e.g., Perner, 2000), in others it does not (e.g., Howe & Courage, 1993, 1997).

A third characteristic feature of autobiographical memories is that they are *expressed verbally.* This feature is taken for granted in most discussions of autobiographical memory in adults. In the developmental literature, however, there is some disagreement on this point, with many scholars explicitly noting verbal accessibility as a feature (e.g., K. Nelson & Fivush, 2000; Pillemer & White, 1989), and others explicitly arguing that autobiographical memories can be expressed nonverbally (e.g., Howe & Courage, 1993, 1997). Additional characteristics that either appear in the literature or are alluded to include the suggestions that autobiographical memories should be *long lasting* (K. Nelson, 1993a) and *veridical* (Brewer, 1996).

## Autobiographical Memory as an "Early" Versus a "Late" Development

For developmental scientists, the lack of a singular, agreed-on definition that identifies a memory as "autobiographical" is more than an inconvenience that requires that we each say what we mean when we undertake to discuss autobiographical memory development. More than that, it leads to unproductive arguments about when the capacity to form such memories emerges. An illustrative example is provided in the contrast of two influential perspectives on the development of autobiographical memory.

Resting heavily on the one "defining" feature that autobiographical memories are relevant to the self, Mark Howe and Mary Courage (1993, 1997) have developed the argument that autobiographical memory emerges at about 18 to 24 months of age, coincident with a "cognitive self" around which to organize experience (see chaps. 3 and 8 for discussion). The suggestion that children have a concept of self by 18 to 24 months of age is supported by a number of developments, including achievement of mirror self-recognition, correct identification of the self in a "peer lineup" (i.e., children selecting their own pictures from among pictures of same-age and same-sex peers), and appropriate use of the pronouns *I* and *me*. Howe and Courage noted that, coincident with these developments in self-understanding, children begin talking about events that happened in the past. Whereas at first the "narratives" are simple (e.g., "I fell down") and make reference to events from the recent past, by the time children are 2½ years of age, they talk about events from the distant past as well (see chap. 7 for examples). As further support for the contention that autobiographical memory is apparent by the time children are 2 to 2½ years of age, Howe and Courage noted that, although among adults the average age of earliest autobiographical memory is 3½ years, many adults report memories from the age of 2 years (e.g., Usher & Neisser, 1993).

In contrast to the more "liberal" perspective of Howe and Courage (1993, 1997), Josef Perner (1991, 2000, 2001) suggested that autobiographical memory does not emerge until late in the preschool years, at roughly 4 to 6 years of age, when children develop the ability to identify the sources of their own cognitions. He arrived at this conclusion based on a definition that emphasizes the characteristic feature of autobiographical memory as involving *autonoetic awareness* (or self-knowing awareness). Autonoetic awareness of a past event implies not only that we remember the event in question, but that we *know that we are remembering* the event. In other words, it requires awareness that the event occurred in the past and, thus, that the source of our knowledge of the event is past experience. Perner argued that children are not capable of episodic memory until age 4 to 6 because, until that time, they lack the prerequisite concepts (see discussion in chap. 8). That is, it is not until the end of the preschool years that children have the capacity to identify the source or origin of their knowledge and, thus, the capacity to know that the source of a memory is a prior experience. Until that time, they are not able to form autobiographical memories.

Confronted with the argument that children require autonoetic awareness for autobiographical memories and, thus, that the early memories they identify as autobiographical cannot be, Howe and Courage (1997) argued that, ". . . despite the growth of interest in the experiential aspect of autobiographical remembering (the autonoetic component), it is not clear that such an experience is critical to the establishment of autobiographical memory" and ". . . the existence of personalized memories is not contingent on such experiencing" (p. 508). Conversely, confronted with the argument that children much younger than 4 to 6 years of age remember past events and, thus, that his estimate is overly conservative, Perner (2000) argued that memories before the age of 4 lack qualities of memories from children ages 4 to 6 and older. The most significant deficiency of memories from before the age of 4 years is that they lack evidence that the event is ". . . remembered *as* an experienced event . . ." (p. 306; italics in original). Prior to the development of this insight, ". . . children (may) have knowledge of past events, and perhaps mental reruns of these experiences, but no genuine episodic memories (proper memories / remembrances in James' sense), because they cannot appreciate their mental experiences as re-experiences of, and originating in, their original experiences" (Perner, 2001, p. 197). In essence, these contrasting perspectives are locked in a battle of definition, with Team 1 arguing that the "rules" suggested by Team 2 are not appropriate (i.e., that autonoetic awareness is not a defining feature of autobiographical memory) and Team 2 arguing that the evidence provided by Team 1 is not "genuine" (i.e., that early memories do not qualify as "proper" autobiographical memories). Although I have highlighted one particular rivalry, Teams 1 and 2 do not constitute the entire league: Similar arguments that turn on the definition of autobiographical memory are made in many places in the literature.

## SUCCESSIVE APPROXIMATIONS OF MEMORIES THAT ARE "AUTOBIOGRAPHICAL"

How are we as a field to extricate ourselves from the unproductive argument over when autobiographical memory first emerges? Short of an autocratic edict that declares that from this day forward autobiographical memory will be defined in a particular way, we will not "fix" the problems created by a "characteristic features" definition. Instead of trying to fix the definition, following the wise advice of my graduate advisor, Cecilia Shore, I recommend that we "feature" it ("If you can't fix it, feature it": C. Shore, personal communication, many times over, between 1981–1985). That is, instead of arguing over what constitutes a "real" autobiographical memory, I suggest we use the fact that many of the features of autobiographical memories are characteristic to better understand "what develops." As William Brewer (1996) noted in the conclusion of his article "What Is Recollective Memory?", autobiographical memory is a "mental natural kind" (p. 60). In making this point, Brewer highlighted the correlated features of autobiographical memories. That is, he pointed out that certain features—such as personal significance and location of an event in a particular place and time—seem to co-occur in autobiographical memories, just as the features of hair (or fur) and bearing of live young co-occur in certain types of animals (mammals). Another implication of viewing the category of autobiographical memory as a "natural kind"—an implication not emphasized by Brewer—is recognition that some exemplars have many or even all of the features that are characteristic of members of the category, whereas other exemplars have few of them. Those with many of the features are viewed as prototypical; those with fewer of the features are seen as atypical yet are nevertheless accepted as members of the category: An ostrich is a bird even though, unlike a robin, it is not an especially "good" bird.

Extension of this principle to the domain of autobiographical memory permits identification of "prototypical" and "nonprototypical" autobiographical

TABLE 11.1
Features of "Prototypical" and "Nonprototypical"
Autobiographical Memories

| Variable | Feature | |
| --- | --- | --- |
| | Prototypical | Nonprototypical |
| Relevance to self | Highly self-relevant and integrated with larger self-concept | Personal significance is less clear or perspective on the recollection is less individualized |
| Location in place and time | Unique episode with distinct spatial and temporal location | Recurrent event or event that is less specifically located in place and time |
| Mode of expression | Expressed verbally in context of joint reminiscence | Expressed nonverbally or goes unspoken |
| Phenomenological experience | Retrieval of the representation is accompanied by a sense of "reliving" the event | Recollection is less vivid or source of the representation is unclear |

memories. As reflected in Table 11.1, prototypical autobiographical memories are of events with clear personal relevance and significance. They are of specific past events that can be located in a particular place and time. They are expressed verbally, and retrieval of them is accompanied by a "reliving" of the experience as an event from the past. Less prototypical autobiographical memories lack one or more of these characteristic features. They may be of recurrent events (Lie & Newcombe, 1999), they may not be shared verbally (Bauer, 1993), or they may be less vivid or less phenomenological recollections (Howe & Courage, 1993, 1997). Framed in this way, we may view the early autobiographical memories identified by scholars such as Howe and Courage (1993, 1997) as less prototypical exemplars of the category and the later autobiographical memories identified by scholars such as Perner (2000, 2001) as more prototypical exemplars. This changes the question from "When do autobiographical memories first become apparent?" to "What changes such that with development, autobiographical memories become more prototypical?" Addressing the latter question requires consideration of the course of development of each of the major features of autobiographical memories. Because each of the features has been discussed in previous chapters, I review them only briefly in turn.

## Autobiographical Memories Are of Events of Significance to the Self

As already noted, if autobiographical memory has a defining feature, it is that the memories are about one's self. A concept of *self* is then a necessary ingredient for an autobiographical memory. Moreover, it is logical to assume that developments in the self-concept may be linked to developments in autobiographical memory. Consistent with this assumption, children's first references to themselves in past events occur at about the same point in developmental time as developments in, for example, mirror self-recognition. In addition, developments in the two arenas are related. That is, in the second half of the second year of life, children who exhibit mirror self-recognition have more robust event memories (Howe, 2003), and they make faster progress in independent autobiographical reports (Harley & Reese, 1999) relative to children who do not yet exhibit self-recognition. The children who experience the greatest increase in independent autobiographical narrative competence are those who are *both* early to recognize themselves in the mirror *and* who have mothers classified as "high elaborators" (Harley & Reese, 1999; depicted in Fig. 9.2).

Attainment of mirror self-recognition is an early indicator of children's appreciation of the concept of self. Over the course of the preschool years, there are at least three further developments, each of which has been found to be related to autobiographical narrative competence. Specifically, there are developments in (a) the temporally extended self or "self in time," (b) the subjective or evaluative self, and (c) the coherence of the self-construct (see chap. 8). Research by Melissa Welch-Ross (2001) suggests relations between children's autobiographical memory development and each of these later developing aspects of the self-concept. For example, in the preschool years, the children who make the most contributions to mother–child autobiographical memory conversations are those who seem to appreciate the relation between past self and present self (i.e., a temporally extended self) and those who have a more evaluative perspective. A more consistent self-view seems to afford children a greater benefit from maternal elaborations: Children whose mothers use an elaborative style make more contributions to autobiographical memory conversations, but only if they have higher consistency scores.

In summary, what we see over the course of the first years of life are developments in multiple aspects of the self, each of which can be expected to play a role in making autobiographical memories more and more prototypical. A basic sense of self as a physical being separate from others provides an essential core concept around which memories of relevance to the self can be organized. Whereas this early achievement is necessary, it is reasonable to expect that further developments in the self-concept would contribute to the texture and richness that makes for "good" autobiographical memories. Recognition of continuity of self over time, both in physical features and psychological characteristics, makes possible establishment of a history of experiences of significance to the self. The implications of this development for autobiography are obvious: For a past event to be relevant to the present self, the rememberer must realize that the self who is remembering is the same as the self who experienced the event in the past (McCormack & Hoerl, 2001). In other words, it makes experiences from the past relevant to the present in a way that an ahistorical, stuck-in-the-present self-concept simply cannot.

An increasingly subjective perspective on experience also facilitates inclusion of events in an autobiographical record: Experiences are not just objective events that played out, but are events that influenced the self in one way or another. The personal significance of the events is conveyed, in particular, by references to the emotional and cognitive states of the experiencer. Such references indicate the sense of personal ownership that is so characteristic of autobiographical memories. A subjective perspective also facilitates development of an autobiography that is unique to the individual even when the record is based on experiences that were shared. With the recognition that one's perspective is unique, one's own interpretation of an event takes on increased significance: Only the self is the repository of one's experiences. Moreover, to the extent that events are entered into the autobiographical record as a result of a deliberate act, these developmental changes also could be expected to contribute to the ability to determine for one's self the experiences that are self-relevant and, thus, important to remember. Together these developments in the self-concept make more and more aspects of more and more events relevant to the self. The net effect of this process is that, with development, memories become more and more prototypical on the dimension of self-relevance.

## Autobiographical Memories Are of Specific Past Events

One of the characteristic features of autobiographical memories is that they are of specific events that happened at a specific place at a specific time. This implies that memories of recurring events and memories that cannot be located in a particular place or a particular time are less prototypical. Are there developmental changes in children's memories such that children become increasingly able to remember events that they experienced only once, and to remember them in detail such that they can be located in place and time?

By the second half of the first year of life, infants show evidence of the ability to form and retain memories of events that are unique and have details of time and place associated with them, as evidenced by their performance on elicited and deferred imitation tasks (see chaps. 4 and 6). By the end of the second year, recall is both reliable and robust. Because the actions and sequences on which infants and young children are tested are novel to them, their behavior provides evidence that they are able to remember unique events. Moreover, because infants and children recall sequences in the correct temporal order, there is evidence that they remember *when* events occurred. It is also apparent that young children remember specific features of events, such as the objects used to produce multistep sequences: Children as young as 16 months of age (the youngest children tested on such a task) reliably select the correct objects from arrays, including objects that are different from, yet perceptually similar to, those used to produce event sequences (Bauer & Dow, 1994). These behaviors make clear that by the end of the second year of life, children have the "raw materials" to form and retain memories of specific events that happened at a particular place at a particular time.

Whereas infants and very young children display impressive mnemonic competence, their abilities are limited in at least two important ways: Both of the limitations are overcome in the preschool years. With the developmental changes, there no doubt is an increase in the number of memories that are prototypical on the dimension of specific time and place. The first apparent limitation of infants' and young children's event memories that would make for fewer typical autobiographical memories is that, *based on a single experience*, the amount of time over which memories can be retained may be limited. For children in the first year of life, multiple experiences seem necessary to ensure recall as measured by deferred imitation. At 6 months of age, infants show evidence of recall if they have six exposures, but not if they have only three (Barr, Dowden, & Hayne, 1996). At 9 months of age, infants exhibit recall if they have three exposures, but not if they have only one or two (Bauer et al., 2001). In the second year, it is clear that, over delays of weeks to a few months, multiple experiences are no longer necessary: 1- to 2-year-olds recall multistep sequences after 6 weeks (Bauer & Shore, 1987), and they recall single object-specific actions after 2 and 4 months (Meltzoff, 1995). However, whether multiple experiences are necessary to support recall over substantially longer delays is not know: Studies in which long delays have been imposed tend to feature multiple experiences with events prior to imposition of the delays (e.g., Bauer et al., 2000).

By 3 years of age, children remember unique events for long periods of time, as shown, for example, by their ability to remember trips to DisneyWorld after a year and a half (Hamond & Fivush, 1991). In these cases, however, there typically is considerable "rehearsal" of the event at least immediately after it, which may be crucial to keeping the memory alive for a long period. Also children's recall of such experiences after long delays is heavily dependent on the support and scaffolding provided by their conversational partners. In short, as a result of the conditions under which recall over long delays has been tested, we simply do not have good data on developmental changes in young children's abilities to remember single instances of novel events over extended periods of time. We certainly may expect them given that, as discussed in chapters 6 and 8, there are developmental changes in memory storage processes across the preschool years. They can be expected to contribute to the ability to remember a single instance and, thus, to memory for unique episodes.

The second source of developmental change that would make for more prototypical autobiographical memories is an increase in the ability to locate events in a particular time and place. By 9 months of age, a large subset of infants remember the temporal order in which events unfold. By 20 months of age, this ability is both reliable and robust. Nevertheless, there are subsequent developmental changes that would contribute to children's abilities to locate events in time. At the "local" level, there are age-related improvements in children's abilities to sequence arbitrarily ordered events. The result is better and better organization of events with age. At the "global" level, there are age-related increases in children's abilities to locate events in time relative to one another. For example, with age, children make increasing use of temporal markers such as *yesterday* and *last summer* (K. Nelson & Fivush, 2004). Markings such as these make clear that the event happened at a time different from the present. They also begin to serve as a timeline along which records of events can be ordered.

In summary, over the course of the first years of life are developments in children's abilities to remember unique events and in their abilities to locate events as having happened at a particular time. The developments can be expected to play a role in making autobiographical memories more and more prototypical. If in infancy and very early childhood memory for event sequences taught in the laboratory is dependent on multiple experiences (as the existing data suggest), then it would be extremely difficult for early memories to meet the characteristic feature of "unique" or "one-time" experiences. With development, however, children evidence increasing ability to retain over the long term memories of unique experiences. As a consequence, over the course of the preschool years, children have more and more memories of events that happened only once. Also over the course of the preschool years, children gain conceptual and linguistic tools that are critical for locating events in time and relative to one another. As more and more unique events are located as having occurred at particular points in time, more and more memories will bear the marks of prototypicality on this important dimension.

## Autobiographical Memories Are Expressed Verbally

Almost universally, scholars agree that autobiographical memories are expressed verbally. Indeed it is not clear how at least one of the other characteristic features of autobiographical memories—autonoetic awareness—could be evidenced nonverbally. Given that the mode of expression is verbal, it is reasonable to assume that developments in the ability to convey thoughts and feelings verbally and to use language to tell coherent narratives about the past will contribute to an increase in the representation of memories that bear the marks of autobiography.

In chapter 8, I provided a brief review of some of the literature on the influences on autobiographical narrative of developments in language per se. Clearly they play a part because children who have larger vocabularies, more sophisticated syntax, and so forth, will find it easier to report on their experiences. Consistent with this suggestion, Keryn Harley and Elaine Reese (1999) found productive vocabulary at 19 months of age to be related both to children's contributions in mother–child conversations about the past at 19, 25, and 32 months of age and to children's contributions in conversations with an experimenter at 25 months of age. Thus, at a young age, differences in vocabulary production are related to differences in children's autobiographical narratives. Later in the preschool years, rather than productive language, receptive language (as measured by instruments such as the *Test of Early Language Development*, for example) has been found to be related to children's recall in a laboratory context (e.g., Walkenfeld, 2000; cited in K. Nelson & Fivush, 2004).

With increasing age, developmental changes in children's narrative skills take on greater significance as a contributor to children's abilities to report on the events of their lives. As discussed in chapters 7 and 8, over the course of the preschool years, children's participation in conversations about past events changes dramatically. Children take on increasingly active roles in conversations, they provide more of the elements of a "good" narrative (i.e., the *who*, *what*, *where*, *when*, *why*, and *how* of events), and they provide more descriptive details and more evaluative information, thereby adding texture to their narratives. A more complete narrative not only makes for a "better story" for the listener, but also provides the story teller with a structure for organizing memory representations, differentiating events from one another, and creating associative links between events. Thus, it works to facilitate encoding and consolidation of event memories in a way that simultaneously preserves their uniqueness and integrates them with other memories in long-term stores, thereby strengthening their representation. Finally, just as a narrative frame can be expected to aid organization by functioning as an implicit guide for what elements are to be encoded, so it may aid memory retrieval.

What are the implications of changes in narrative skills for increases in the representation of "prototypical" autobiographical memories with age? In the case of the self-concept, it was possible to address this question empirically by asking whether developments in the self-concept are related to developments in autobiographical narrative production. Similarly, although not all of the relevant components have been investigated, it was possible to consider how developments in children's abilities to remember unique events and to locate them in time would be related to developments in autobiographical memory narratives. In the case of changes in narrative skill, a similar analysis is complicated by the fact that it is largely through developmental changes in narrative that we assess developmental changes in autobiography. As such, developments in autobiographical narrative skills must be accompanied by developments in narrative skills more generally. The converse is not necessarily true, however: Children could display narrative skills in the context of story recall or story production, for example, that are not "translated" into the domain of autobiographical memory. In fact there is evidence of precisely this asymmetrical pattern in the cross-cultural autobiographical memory literature.

As part of a larger study, Jessica Hungsook Han, Michelle Leichtman, and Qi Wang (1998) obtained autobiographical narratives from American and Korean 4- and 6-year-old children and also asked them to recall and answer specific questions about a story presented in slide show format. They found two patterns suggestive of asymmetrical application of narrative skills. First, in the autobiographical memory narratives, there were culture group differences in the specificity of children's answers to questions: American children indicated more specific memories relative to Korean children (see chap. 9). The culture effect was not apparent in children's answers to questions about the slide show, however. Second, in the autobiographical narratives, gender effects were apparent in the American sample: American girls produced longer narratives and included more descriptive terms and temporal markers relative to boys. Gender differences were not apparent in the Korean children's autobiographical narratives. There were no gender effects for either culture group on the story recall and question tasks. Thus, there were neither culture group nor gender effects in children's *general* narrative competence (as assessed by the story tasks). When that competence was applied to autobiographical memory, effects emerged. Results such as these make clear that, although autobiographical memory reports are dependent on developments in narrative skills more broadly, only some of the differences in the "prototypicality" of autobiographical reports can be accounted for by differences in narrative competence.

## Retrieval of Autobiographical Memories Is Accompanied by Autonoetic Awareness

The final "feature" of prototypical autobiographical memories is that retrieval of them is accompanied by autonoetic awareness: a sense of awareness that the event recollected is one that happened in the past. This component infuses autobiographical recollections with a sense that one is reliving the event, yet knowing that the event is from the past. As discussed earlier in this chapter (and in chap. 8), in children the ability to engage in cognitive acts that signal autonoetic awareness is not readily apparent until ages 4 to 6.

It is at this age that children show evidence of the ability to identify the sources of their knowledge. Relative to their peers with apparently lower levels of understanding of the sources of their knowledge, children who are more accomplished show higher levels of free recall of items on a list (Perner & Ruffman, 1995) and of pictures directly experienced relative to pictures seen only on video (Perner, 2001).

Aside from satisfying a definitional "requirement" that retrieval of episodic and, thus, autobiographical memories be accompanied by autonoetic awareness (Tulving, 1985a), how might this metacognitive development contribute to increased frequency of "prototypical" autobiographical memories? Except in the laboratory and on the pages of scholarly publications, there is little explicit discussion of whether retrieval of a memory is accompanied by awareness that the event happened in the past. More frequent are declarations of the richness or vividness of a memory of a past event ("I can see it as clearly now as I did then")—characteristics that would contribute to a sense of reliving the experience. However, indications that memories are rich in the details that would contribute to the sense of reliving the experience are apparent even in young children's narratives in the form of intensifiers ("Cause she was *very* naughty"), qualifiers ("I *didn't like* her videotape"), elements of suspense ("And *you know what?*"; examples from Fivush & Haden, 1997, Table 7.2, p. 186), and even repetition of the dialogue spoken in the event (". . . I said, 'I hope my Nintendo my Super Nintendo is still here.' "; Ackil et al., 2003). Moreover, such vivid memories are not unique to recollections of specific past events, as illustrated by the quotation earlier in the chapter from an individual recalling a recurrent experience from childhood: "When I was in first grade I had only one friend to play with. *I remember her face even now*, after 20 years" (Lie & Newcombe, 1999, p. 102; italics added). In what way then might the metacognitive achievement of understanding the source of experience be associated with increases in the number of prototypical autobiographical memories?

There are at least three ways in which understanding the source of experience might contribute to increases in the number of prototypical autobiographical memories in the corpus. First, it would be expected to *aid in location of an event in space and time*, thereby contributing to the specificity of memories (as discussed earlier in this section). Second, understanding that the source of a current cognition is a past event would *aid in the realization that, to share the event memory with another, the narrator must provide the listener with orientation to the circumstances of the past*. That is, because the event is not ongoing, the listener must be "cued in" to the specifics of the event, such as who was there, where it took place, and even what happened in the course of the event. The understanding thus could be expected to lead children to include in their reports more of the elements that make for a full narrative account, including the all-important elements that signal a subjective perspective on the event

(Fivush, 2001). Consistent with this suggestion, Melissa Welch-Ross (1997) found that, in mother–child conversations about past events, relative to 3½- to 4½-year-olds who performed at lower levels on understanding of knowledge tasks, preschoolers who performed at higher levels were more likely to respond to their mothers' questions by providing information about the event that had not already been introduced into the conversation.

Third, understanding that the self—and thus others too—have mental representations of events from the past may *foster the subjective or evaluative perspective* and thereby autobiographical memory. As children come to appreciate that the sources of their cognitions are representations, and that others too have representations, both of which are internal and unique to the individuals, they can begin to construct unique, personal perspectives on events. It is this perspective that would lead children to begin to include in their autobiographical narratives information about how a given event made them think or feel, as well as to inquire as to how the same event made others think and feel. The resulting conversations are opportunities for further refinement of one's own perspective, as well as elements of the experience the subjective impressions of which are shared by different individuals. Over time the practice of reflecting on one's evaluation of an event would be expected to foster further development of the self-concept, in that children have the opportunity to reflect on the continuities (as well as discontinuities) in their own and others' reactions to events and experiences (e.g., Fivush, 2001; Welch-Ross et al., 1999). In a variety of ways, then, both directly and indirectly, conscious appreciation that the source of a representation is a past event may contribute to increases in the representation of prototypical autobiographical memories in the corpus.

## Summary and Implications

Over the course of the first years of life, there are developments in each of the "features" of autobiographical memories. Specifically, with age, memories are increasingly unique to and more personally significant for individuals, they are more adequately located in place and time, they are expressed using more narrative elements as well as more eloquent arrangements of the elements, and they are more readily explicitly recognized as arising from past experience. The result is that, over the same space of time, memories change from having the "bare minimum" requirements (i.e., that the memory be declarative and that it be referenced to one's self) to having all of the features that characterize adults' autobiographical recollections. During the period in between, it seems profitable to maintain the perspective that autobiographical reports are a "mental natural kind" (Brewer, 1996), allowing for variety among the exemplars of the category, such that some are better representatives than others.

What is to be gained by viewing some memories as ostriches—as "not especially good" exemplars—yet exemplars nonetheless? As discussed at the beginning of this section, one advantage is that this perspective frees the field from the bounds of unproductive arguments over when "proper" autobiographical memory emerges. It replaces that focus with one that aims to elucidate the factors that contribute to ever more prototypical autobiographical memories.

Another advantage of admitting less prototypical exemplars into the "autobiographical" category is that, by considering these less typical members, we stand to learn more about the category itself. Take, for example, the new perspective on autobiographical memory afforded by consideration of recurring events as "autobiographical." Most of the events of our lives are not unique, one-time-only experiences. As such the stories of our lives are not stories of novelty. Instead they are stories of regularities, punctuated by especially funny, sad, or poignant episodes. A case could even be made that the strength of the fabric of our lives is derived not from the single experiences that researchers probe in studies of autobiographical memory, but from recurrent events from which were extracted the lessons by which we live. By excluding from consideration as "autobiographical" any event that is not absolutely unique, we eliminate many of the events that shape us and define who we are and how we relate to others. Eunhui Lie and Nora Newcombe (1999) extended this argument further, arguing that the range of experiences considered relevant to the study of autobiographical memory development should be enlarged to include, for example, memory for one's preschool classmates. By moving beyond the category of "events," we stand to learn whether the patterns of remembering and forgetting for experiences that can be encoded linguistically (specific past events) and for material that is less effectively encoded linguistically (faces) are the same or different.

Important perspective is also gained by examining the feature of verbal expression. It is critical to remember that whereas autobiographical reports are *conveyed* exclusively verbally, the representations that underlie them are not themselves narrative or even verbal. When we think about a past event, it does not come to us as a script of a play. Rather it comes as a series of images that we then describe. Indeed as discussed in chapter 2, nonverbal images are regarded as a central component of autobiographical memories. A narrative frame may aid encoding and retrieval, but it is not the format in which memory is stored. When we keep this in mind, it is easier to also remember that memories may be autobiographical, yet not verbal. This happens when memories are never shared; it happens when aspects of memories defy translation into language (Bauer, 1993). The emphasis should be on *potentially* verbally accessible, as opposed to verbal per se. That is, to be autobiographical, a memory must be encoded in a format that is *accessible* to language, but it need not be symbolic.

Regardless of the perspective one takes on the question of whether it is beneficial to consider as "autobiographical" memories that seem to possess less than the full complement of characteristic features, it is clear that, by the end of the preschool years, children "have" autobiographical memories that are qualitatively similar to those of adults. Critically, the changes in the features that contribute to prototypical autobiographical memories do not occur in isolation. To understand the dynamics of the system, it is important to think not only about the individual features that are undergoing developmental change, but about the contexts in which they are doing so. Characteristics of the child, as well as both the proximal (familial) and distal (cultural) environments in which the child operates, impact the developmental process. It is to these characteristics and contexts that I now turn.

## INDIVIDUAL AND CONTEXTUAL EFFECTS ON DEVELOPMENTS IN AUTOBIOGRAPHICAL MEMORY

The environments in which the skills for autobiographical memory develop are not uniform. Instead individual children with individual differences live, breathe, and behave in different families that are embedded within different cultures. Each of these sources can be expected to influence the course of development of autobiographical memory and the features that are characteristic of it. Because I reviewed many of the differences in previous chapters, I discuss them relatively briefly here, with emphasis on the ways in which they might be expected to impact the "prototypicality" of early autobiographical memories.

### Characteristics of the Child

There are numerous sources of individual differences to consider in the evaluation of how characteristics of the child who is doing the remembering might affect the features of her or his autobiographical memories. In terms of the most basic element of the self-concept—mirror self-recognition—there are substantial individual differences. In the research by Harley and Reese (1999), for example, at 19 months of age, only roughly half of the children passed the task (i.e., on seeing a spot of rouge on their noses, they touched their noses), whereas the other half did not. Even by the end of the second year, as many as one quarter of children do not provide evidence of the mark-directed behavior indicative of self-recognition (reviewed in Howe & Courage, 1997). A similar range of behavior is apparent on tasks designed to assess the temporally extended self (Povinelli, 1995). That is, at 3 years of age, one quarter of children already show evidence of recognition that the past and present selves are one in the same. A full year later, three quarters of children show this evidence, but one quarter still do not. There are also substantial individual differences in the extent to which an evaluative or subjective perspective is apparent in children's narratives. For instance, over the course of the preschool years, some children display an ever-increasing number and variety of emotion terms, whereas other children exhibit less change on these dimensions (e.g., Adams et al., 1995). Each of these individual differences can be expected to relate to the extent to which children reference events as relevant to the self and, thus, to the prototypicality of early autobiographical memories.

Individual differences across children are also apparent in the ability to remember specific past events, as well as locate events in time. By the end of the second year of life 100% of children evidence memory for multistep sequences over a delay of 1 month, yet some children evidence more robust memories relative to others. In the "Monster" study from my laboratory (Bauer et al., 2000), for example, some children recalled all possible target actions of the sequences with which they were presented, whereas others recalled as few as one action; some children showed perfect temporally ordered recall, whereas others revealed no evidence of ordered recall (Bauer, Burch, & Kleinknecht, 2002). Individual differences are not apparent only in infancy and very early childhood, but also in the later preschool and early school years. For instance, Carolyn Jones and Margaret-Ellen Pipe (2002) reported a range in 5- to 7-year-old children's recall across delays as long as 6 months. Individual differences were apparent in children's free recall, in their cued recall, and in the accuracy of their responses to specific questions. There are also individual differences in children's acquisition of temporal and relational concepts that have been argued to aid in location of events in time and in relation to one another (K. Nelson & Fivush, 2004). Each of these sources of individual differences can be expected to contribute to variation in the extent to which early autobiographical memory reports appear "prototypical" of their class.

Children also differ in the third feature of autobiographical memory—namely, verbal expression. Variation in vocabulary size could affect verbal expression of memory, in particular, by permitting children with larger vocabularies to encode their experiences with just the right words. The child who can verbally encode conditionals and probabilities is more likely to maintain separate representations of different versions of the same or highly similar events. Because the narrative form is thought to affect not only the encoding, but also the storage and subsequent retrieval of event memories, differences among children in their levels of narrative sophistication can be expected to influence not only the autobiographical *reports* that children provide, but the underlying event representations as well (K. Nelson & Fivush, 2004).

Finally, there are individual differences in children's understanding of a variety of cognitive concepts that are hypothesized to relate to autonoetic awareness and, thus, autobiographical memory. For example, in a study by Charlie Lewis and his colleagues, the majority (58%) of 3- to 3½-year-olds passed the "deceptive box" false-belief task (i.e., a task in which children are required to reconcile their initial [erroneous] impressions of what is in an unopened box with the actual contents once they are revealed). Although older children more frequently succeeded on the task (as they do on others like it), even at 4½ to 5 years of age, one out of four children failed (Lewis et al., 1996). Even once children have mastered preschool versions of "theory of mind" tasks, there are individual differences in the construct when measured by more challenging assessments, such as tasks that require that children select arguments that would persuade individuals who hold different beliefs, for example (Bartsch & London, 2000). In short, there are a number of individual differences among children that can be expected to contribute to variability in the "prototypicality" of their early autobiographical memory reports.

## Characteristics of the "Proximal" (Familial) Environment

Individual children with individual differences do not operate alone to construct autobiographical memories: They accomplish the development in the context of home environments that themselves are variable. With regard to development of the self-concept, family demographic variables such as maternal education, socioeconomic status (SES), birth order, and number of siblings have not been found to be associated with systematic variability in the onset of mark-directed behavior (Lewis & Brooks-Gunn, 1979). Whether such variables affect development of the temporally extended self, the psychological coherence of the self, or the development of an evaluative self has not been systematically explored. There is evidence that another familial variable—namely, parental narrative style—has effects on the development of an evaluative self or subjective perspective. For instance, children whose mothers used a number of evaluative terms in autobiographical memory conversations when the children were 3½ years of age used a larger number of such terms when they were 6 years of age (Fivush, 2001; Haden et al., 1997). Frequency of use of evaluations may be related to a characteristic of the dyad—namely, securing of attachment (Fivush & Vasudeva, 2002). Attachment security is relevant in that trust is required to be able to share one's thoughts and feelings, and especially to disagree on perceptions of how an event made you feel and even what happened in the course of the event. The necessary trust is there for securely attached dyads, but may not be there for insecurely attached dyads. We might expect then that the narrative style to which children are exposed and the security of their attachment relationships would contribute to variation in the "prototypicality" of early autobiographical memory reports.

As I discussed at length in chapter 9, the family environment—in the form of parental narrative style—also has substantial and significant effects on children's verbal reports. Children exposed to a more elaborative style report more about events both concurrently and over time. It seems that they are internalizing a narrative form that helps them organize, remember, and subsequently retrieve stories of previous life events. Children also presumably are acquiring an "attitude" toward remembering. Autobiographical reminiscing comes to be viewed either as an opportunity for sharing and social interaction or as a "test" that one takes on demand, but that does not have any value in and of itself (K. Nelson & Fivush, 2004). Once again these differences may relate to variation in the "prototypicality" of early autobiographical memory reports: The narratives of children exposed to an elaborative narrative style bear more of the features of prototypical autobiographical memories.

The family environment also has been found to have implications for developments in children's understanding of the representational nature of mind. For example, as discussed in chapter 9, Josef Perner and his colleagues found associations between the number of siblings a child has and performance on false-belief tasks (e.g., Perner et al., 1994). Further research by Charlie Lewis and his colleagues refined the relation: It seems that the critical factor is the number of *older* siblings a child has (see Table 9.3). Children who are first born, and thus have no older siblings, have the lowest rates of success on tests of the representational nature of mind; children who are later born have higher rates of success (Lewis et al., 1996). Interestingly, the direction of this effect undermines the suggestion of a causal role for mental concepts in autobiographical memory development (e.g., Perner, 2001): It is difficult to reconcile with the finding that among adults first-born children have earlier memories relative to later-born children (see Fig. 3.6). Later achievement of representational understanding by first-born children, relative to later-born children, would predict precisely the opposite pattern. As stated earlier, the larger point is that there are numerous differences among the families in which children live as they develop the skills for autobiographical reminiscing. There are compelling reasons to believe that some of the differences will impact the prototypicality of early autobiographical memories.

## Characteristics of the "Distal" (Cultural) Environment

Just as important as differences in the child who is doing the remembering and in the familial environment in which memory for the event is being shaped are differences in the larger cultural milieu of experience. As reviewed in chapter 9, clear examples of apparent influences of culture on autobiographical memory development are provided by the work of Michelle Leichtman and Qi Wang and their colleagues on contrasts between children from Eastern and Western culture groups. Briefly, the early autobiographical memory reports of children from Asian cultures include fewer references to themselves and fewer personal evaluations relative to reports from children in the United States. In addition, the autobiographical memory reports of children from Asian cultures tend to feature generic as opposed to specific events, and they are shorter and less detailed relative to those provided by children in the United States (Han et al., 1998; Wang et al., 2000). Thus, on at least three of the features that make autobiographical narratives prototypically "autobiographical"—significance to the self, specificity in place and time, and verbal expression—the early narratives of children from Asian cultures may be viewed as less prototypical relative to the narratives of children from the United States.

## IF CHILDREN'S MEMORIES GET BETTER, WHY DO ADULTS' SEEM TO GET WORSE?

The analysis provided in this chapter presents a major paradox: If, over the course of the preschool years, memories of the times of our lives increasingly take on the features that we view as characteristic of autobiographical memories, why then as adults do we have so few personal memories from this period of time? In other words, if everything "just gets better and better," why is it that for adults it seems to get worse? Addressing this question requires that we consider both the rate at which autobiographical memories are formed and the rate at which they are forgotten. Joint consideration of the two components provides a reasonable approximation of an adequate address of the paradox: Although prototypical autobiographical memories are formed at a faster and faster clip over the course of the preschool years, they are also forgotten at an accelerated rate relative to the rate of forgetting in later childhood and adulthood. The result is that, of early childhood, adults have a smaller number of memories than would be expected based on adult rates of forgetting.

### The Rate at Which Memories Are Formed

The evidence that, over the course of the preschool years, children form more and more autobiographical memories is incontrovertible. Even among scholars who argue that the capacity for "true" or "proper" autobiographical memory does not emerge until relatively late (e.g., Perner, 2001), there is recognition that, by the end of the preschool years, children encode and store memories of specific past events that are relevant to themselves, retrieval of which is accompanied by recognition that the event representation is based on a past experience.

Yet long before they pass tasks thought to index the capacity for autonoetic awareness, children show evidence of autobiographical memory. As early as they are able to use past-tense markers, children refer to past events of relevance to themselves. As they gain in narrative sophistication, children's stories become more complete and coherent. Children's narratives about past events also take on more and more elements of drama, and they contain an increasing amount of evidence of the significance of the event for the child. Stories are told not only about routine events, but about unique experiences that happened at a particular place, at a particular time. Some events—although certainly not all—are remembered for months and even years. Whereas prior to 4 to 6 years of age children do not pass tasks that permit researchers to say that they are aware of the sources of their representations, children's narratives certainly contain evidence of vivid recollections of events from the past: They include elements that provide a sense of the intensity of experience, elements of suspense, and information about the internal states of the participants, for example (e.g., Ackil et al., 2003; Fivush & Haden, 1997). In summary, over the course of the preschool years, children's stories about the times of their lives bear more and more of the marks of typical autobiographical reports. As a result, children exhibit an increasing number of memories that are recognized as "autobiographical."

## The Rate at Which Memories Are Forgotten

Given that over the course of the preschool years children are not only accumulating memories of past experiences but the memories increasingly resemble prototypical autobiographical memories, why is it that the number of memories from the first several years of life on which adults are able to report is smaller than the number expected based on forgetting alone? I suggest that the answer to this question is that the number of accessible memories is *not* smaller than the number expected based on forgetting alone, *if we recognize that the rate of forgetting in childhood is faster than the rate in adulthood*. In other words, the key to the riddle lies in the standard for the "number of memories that would be expected based on forgetting alone." At present, the standard is based on the rate of forgetting *in adults*. It is application of an adult standard to the period of early childhood that creates the impression of an accelerated rate of forgetting of events from the early years of life and, thus, the enigma of childhood amnesia.

Consider that in their oft-cited empirical demonstration of the phenomenon of childhood amnesia, Scott Wetzler and John Sweeney (1986) used data from research conducted by David Rubin (1982, Experiment 1), in which Rubin asked young adults to locate in time personal memories associated with a large number of different cue words (e.g., *ice cream*; see chap. 2 for discussion of the cue-word technique). To the data, Wetzler and Sweeney applied a "normal forgetting criterion" (p. 197) based on a power function that in many investigations (e.g., Crovitz & Schiffman, 1974; Rubin et al., 1986) has been shown to capture the distribution of memories across the lifespan (and which, in the study by Rubin & Wenzel, 1996, was shown to provide a superior fit to autobiographical memory data relative to linear, hyperbolic, exponential, and logarithmic functions).[1] Critically, they derived the power function based on memories from age 8 until adulthood. They then fitted that function to data from birth to age 6 (they excluded age 7 because it is considered the "inflection point" for childhood amnesia). The resulting data plot is reproduced in Fig. 11.1. It depicts the frequency of memories from 1 hour ago to 18 years ago (the participants in Rubin's study were college students). The number of memories from 16 and 17 years ago is off the function, implying accelerated forgetting for the childhood years. Two other experiments analyzed in the same way (Crovitz & Schiffman, 1974; Rubin, 1982, Experiment 2) revealed accelerated forgetting of memories from ages 6 and below. However, it is largely on Wetzler and Sweeney's (1986) analysis that contemporary scholars rely when they identify the parameters of childhood amnesia.

What are the consequences of using an adult standard to determine the rate of forgetting that is to be expected over time? Among those who have bothered to ask the question (e.g., Wetzler & Sweeney, 1986, did not discuss the issue), the answer has been that the consequences should be negligible. Application of the adult standard to data from early childhood has been considered acceptable because of a widely held assumption that the rate of forgetting is a constant across the lifespan. For example, David Rubin and Amy Wenzel (1996) argued that, because many researchers have reported no age differences in the retention function (citing Fajnsztejn-Pollack, 1973; Hulicka & Weiss, 1965; Morrison, Haith, & Kagan, 1980; Rubin et al., 1986; Wickelgren, 1975) or only small differences (citing Giambra & Arenberg, 1993), ". . . retention . . . is not affected by age over the range of ages tested . . ." (p. 738). Yet much of the research they cited was carried out with adults (Giambra & Arenberg, 1993; Hulicka & Weiss, 1965; Rubin et al., 1986) or older children (i.e., 8- to 10-year-olds; Wickelgren, 1975). Thus, "the range of ages tested" did not include early childhood. The research that was conducted with young children (Fajnsztejn-Pollack, 1973; Morrison et

---

[1]As discussed by Rubin and Wenzel (1996), the power function was introduced by Wickelgren (1974, 1975) to describe the retention function derived from mathematical models of memory. It implies that equal ratios of time ($t_1/t_2 = t_3/t_4$) will result in equal ratios of recall (recall$_1$/recall$_2$ = recall$_3$/recall$_4$).

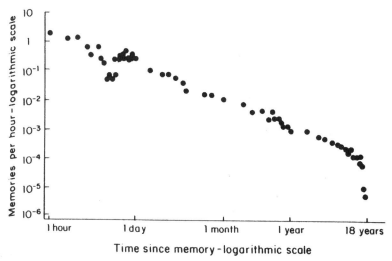

FIG. 11.1.   The average number of memories retrieved in response to cue words as a function of the time elapsed since the event. The function that created the line was based on memories from age 8 until adulthood. The function was then fitted to data from birth to 6 years. The data for the function are from Rubin (1982); the function itself was created by Wetzler and Sweeney (1986). From "Childhood Amnesia: An Empirical Demonstration," by S. E. Wetzler and J. A. Sweeney, in D. C. Rubin (Ed.), *Autobiographical Memory* (pp. 191–201, Fig. 11.2), 1986, New York: Cambridge University Press. Copyright © 1986 by Cambridge University Press. Reprinted with the permission of Cambridge University Press.

al., 1980) assessed recognition memory, rather than recall memory, yet recognition measures are notoriously insensitive to age-related differences (e.g., Brainerd et al., 1990).

In contrast to the suggestion that the rate of forgetting is age invariant, there is evidence that when measures of recall rather than recognition are used, the retention function is *not* the same across the lifespan. That is, although from a relatively young age children are able to retain memories over long periods of time, younger children nevertheless exhibit faster rates of forgetting relative to older children. Differential rates of forgetting are apparent in infancy and very early childhood (chaps. 4 and 6), as well as in the preschool years (chaps. 8 and 10). They are apparent even when the variability associated with initial learning or encoding of events is considered (by controlling it statistically, by matching, or via a criterion design). This suggests that even if developmental differences in the rate of forgetting are not a factor among older children and adults, in the early years of life—those most affected by childhood amnesia—they likely are a major factor.

Rather than negligible, I suggest that the consequences of using an adult standard to determine the rate of forgetting of memories from early in life that is to be expected over time are profound. In fact I suggest that were we to apply an early childhood rate of forgetting, rather than an adult rate of forgetting, we would find that the number of memories from the childhood years that are retained by adults is not smaller than expected. In other words, if we were to apply age-appropriate criteria, we likely would find that the observation of an ". . . accelerated (rate of) forgetting over and above normal forgetting . . ." (Wetzler & Sweeney, 1986, p. 194) would disappear, and the number of memories from early in life would be exactly as predicted.

Unfortunately, at this time, the hypothesis just advanced cannot be put to empirical test because we do not know what the "age-appropriate" criterion rate of forgetting should be. Studies in which it is theoretically possible to evaluate potential age-related differences in the forgetting function over childhood—independent of age-related differences in encoding—tend to test children's recall of materials that are not especially personally relevant and the delays imposed tend to be short. For example, in a study by Charles Brainerd and his colleagues (Brainerd et al., 1990), 7- and 11-year-olds were asked to recall 16-item lists of pictures or words after a 2-week interval. Conversely, in studies in which the delays are long and the events are personally significant, there is no control over encoding differences. In research by Jodi Quas and her colleagues (Quas et al., 1999; chap. 9), for instance, children who were older at the time of a painful and embarrassing catheterization procedure provided more detailed reports of the experience after long delays relative to children who were younger at the time of the procedure. Whereas this effect is *suggestive* of age-related differences in forgetting rates, it also could be due to likely differences in encoding of the event by children who were only 2 years of age relative to children 6 years of age at the time the procedure was performed.

To test this hypothesis, we need data from children of different ages, tested after the same, long retention intervals for memories of personally significant events, the elements of which were encoded to begin with. I expect that we would see that within the period of childhood, memories formed at age 8 years and older would be forgotten at a slower rate relative to memories formed at the ages of 4 and 6 years, for example. A study to provide precisely these types of data is currently ongoing in my laboratory. Until the data from this study and others like it are available, or until we have available data from cue-word type procedures executed with children as opposed to only adults, we will not know whether a different, yet equally "normal" forgetting function would provide a better fit for the data from ages 6 and younger. All that we know at this point is that the power function that fits retrospective data collected from adults for life events from age 8 years onward does not fit the data from age 6 and younger.

This analysis begs the question of why we would expect the rate of forgetting in early childhood to be faster than the rate of forgetting in later childhood and adulthood. There are two related reasons why we should predict exactly this effect. First, there are *neurodevelopmental changes that make memories formed in early childhood more vulnerable to consolidation and storage failures relative to memories formed later in life.* As described in chapter 5, declarative memory relies on a multicomponent neural network for the encoding, consolidation, storage, and subsequent retrieval of memories. As described in chapters 6 and 8, some of the components of the network develop early, permitting retention of small amounts of information over short periods of time. However, the processes that permit the integration and consolidation of memory representations for long-term storage develop more slowly. Aspects of the medial temporal structures implicated in these processes undergo pronounced development between 8 and 20 months after birth. There is continued development of these structures and the processes they support throughout the preschool years and beyond. The prefrontal structures implicated in the consolidation, storage, and subsequent retrieval of memories also develop slowly. They too exhibit pronounced changes in the second year of life, with continued development well beyond the preschool years. As a result, we should expect age-related neurodevelopmental changes to affect declarative memory processes throughout early childhood. Whereas the developmental changes in the prefrontal structures that permit more effective and efficient retrieval get the most "media play" (e.g., Liston & Kagan, 2002), there is, in fact, substantial evidence that developmental changes in memory consolidation and storage processes are primary (e.g., Bauer, 2002, 2005; Brainerd et al., 1990; Howe & O'Sullivan, 1997). The reason is simple: A memory representation must be effectively consolidated and stored if it is to be retrieved later.

The second reason that we should expect the rate of forgetting in early childhood to be faster than the rate of forgetting in later childhood and adulthood is that *the memory representations that younger children have available for consolidation and storage contain fewer of the features that ensure long-term retention* relative to memory representations from later in life. As discussed throughout this chapter, the memories that the young child is asking her or his immature brain to consolidate and store contain fewer of the features that typify autobiographical memories: (a) the "self" to which they are referenced is not as stable and coherent a construct as it will be later in development; (b) relative to later memories, early memories tend to contain fewer distinctive features and are less specifically located in space and time; (c) younger children likely encode fewer of the elements that make for a good narrative relative to older children, thereby denying themselves an effective retrieval tool; and (d) early memory representations can be expected to contain fewer "hints" as to their origin in events from the past relative to those encoded with a more mature understanding of the representational nature of the human mind. Given that in early childhood we have less than optimal processes operating on less than optimal raw materials, we should expect—rather than be surprised by—output, the quality of which simply is not as high as that in later childhood and adulthood, when we have more optimal processes operating on more optimal materials.

## The "Cross-Over" of Two Functions

The net effect of this analysis is a model suggesting that, among adults, we see an increase in autobiographical memories dating from around ages 4 to 6 years because, as depicted in Fig. 11.2, this is the point at which the functions of memory formation and forgetting of memories "cross over." Prior to the age of 4, the rate at which memories are lost is faster than the rate at which memories are gained; after the age of 6 years, the rate at which memories are formed is faster than the rate at which memories are lost. Considering the adult phenomenon of childhood amnesia to be a result of the cross-over of two functions—the rate of formation of autobiographical memories and the rate of forgetting—has several advantages. One advantage is that it does not require that we invoke special mechanisms or pronounced developmental changes to account either for the increase in autobiographical memories at ages 4 to 6, or for the relative paucity of autobiographical memories from the first years of life. That is, we need not invoke a later developmental change, such as the dawning of autonoetic awareness, that comes on line at 4 to 6 years of age and "jump starts" the autobiographical memory system. The system has been "up and running" for some time. We begin to see substantial evidence of it at the end of the preschool years because by that

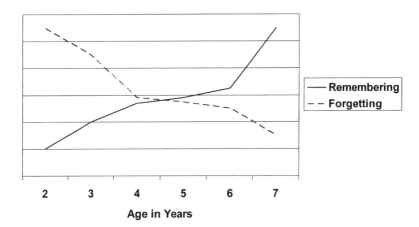

FIG. 11.2.  Schematic representation of the cross-over in the preschool years of the functions of remembering (the rate of which increases with age; solid line) and forgetting (the rate of which decreases with age; broken line). The period of intersection between ages 4 and 6 is recognized as the "dawning" of autobiographical memory and the "offset" of childhood amnesia.

time the rate of memory formation has outstripped the rate of forgetting. Nor do we need to invoke a mechanism such as "repression," for example, to explain why early memories that we know were formed (based on studies with preschoolers) are later inaccessible—they are lost to normal (for the age period) forgetting. The results of a study Dana Van Abbema and I conducted (Van Abbema & Bauer, 2005; described in chap. 10 of this volume) suggest that adultlike forgetting of memories from the early preschool years begins to become apparent as early as 8 to 9 years of age.

Another advantage of the conceptualization in terms of a cross-over of two functions is that it makes it easy to see how "pushing around" one or the other (or both) functions results in individual and group differences. As depicted in Fig. 11.3, there are several different possibilities. For example, two individuals who as children had the same rate of forgetting (see Fig. 11.3, Panels A and B) may nevertheless have vastly different "offsets" of childhood amnesia as a function of differences in the slopes of change in the remembering function. Children in a family and cultural environment that places a premium on narrative and that encourages reflection on the meanings of events and their significance for the child—as in the Maori culture in New Zealand (MacDonald et al., 2000)—may have autobiographical memories from early in the preschool years (Panel A). In contrast, children in a family and cultural environment that uses a less elaborative style and does not encourage reflection on the self—as in some Asian cultures (Wang et al., 2000)—may have autobiographical memories from later in the preschool years (Panel B).

Individual differences could also result from differences in the slopes of forgetting functions. That is, individuals whose rates of increase in the formation of autobiographical memories are the same (Fig. 11.3, Panels C and D) could nevertheless experience a different course of development of autobiographical memory because of differences in the rate at which memories are forgotten. Variability in the forgetting function no doubt is associated with a variety of factors, including different rates of maturational change in the neural structures that subserve declarative memory and associated differences in the basic mnemonic processes of encoding, consolidation, storage, and retrieval. As such the conceptualization provides a ready account of individual and cultural differences: They result from differences in the "quality" of the autobiographical memories that are formed during the period and from the likelihood of survival of the memories over time.

## FINAL REMARKS

The pages of this volume have covered a lot of territory. The discussion has ranged from the manner in which cells in the different fields of the hippocampus and surrounding cortices communicate with one another to stabilize

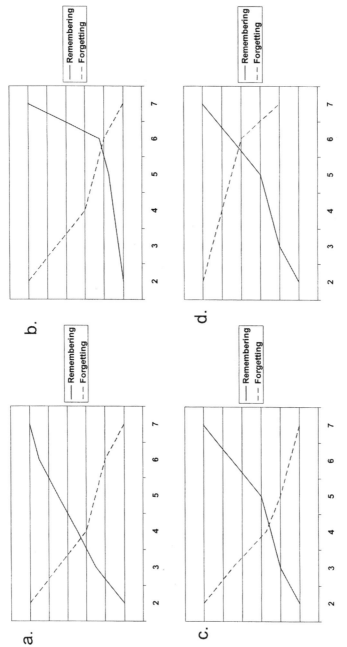

FIG. 11.3. Schematic representations of variation in the cross-over point of remembering (solid lines) and forgetting (broken lines). Panels A and B indicate the same forgetting function with different remembering functions. Panels C and D indicate the same remembering function with different forgetting functions.

and consolidate memory representations for long-term storage, to the manner in which cultural mores and traditions influence the narrative practices of parents and their children and the possible implications of those practices for the autobiographical memories of individuals from different culture groups. From the broad range of issues covered, there are three points about autobiographical memory that to me are especially salient. It is with brief discussion of these three points that I close the volume.

First, autobiographical memory is with us virtually for our lifetimes. Whereas the first 2 years of life—prior to the development of long-term declarative memory abilities and even a rudimentary sense of self as an individual—are likely devoid of autobiographical memories, they are our companions from that time forward. Early in development, we represent the times of our lives clumsily, without much specificity or personality, and without much longevity. We represent them nonetheless. With development, autobiographical memory changes from an ugly duckling into a beautiful swan. It brings along with it a perspective on the events of our lives that is personal and unique. Also with age develops the capacity to share the experiences of our lives with others, through narratives that tell not only what happened to whom, but why things happened, and how they impacted the individuals involved in and thus touched by the events. There is significant pressure for autobiographical memory to develop because of the critical social function it serves: It is by sharing memories with others that we share ourselves. Our autobiographical memories also provide us with explanations for our current and future behaviors in terms of our past experiences. It is also through our autobiographies that we define ourselves. Nowhere is this more apparent than in the poignant story of Oliver Sacks' (1985) patient, Jimmie G., who, because he had lost the capacity to form new autobiographical memories, had essentially lost himself in time (chap. 2).

Second, unless they have sustained brain damage or insult, all members of the species share the capacity for autobiographical memory; yet there are substantial individual and group differences in it. The differences are apparent in childhood and adulthood, as well as in adults' recollections of their childhoods. Some of the most salient differences are associated with gender, parental narrative style, and culture. The fact that the differences are systematic is consistent with the suggestion that they are the products of a large number of factors that interact as they shape the development and expression of autobiographical memory. The undeniable truth that a large number of factors contribute to the development of autobiographical memory makes clear that no single-causal model will ever succeed in explaining its development. Rather, because autobiographical memory and its course of development are multiply determined, models that aspire to explain it need to be multifaceted. Moreover, because the factors that contribute to autobiographical memory and its development operate at multiple levels (from neurons to culture), no single level of analysis will suffice: Neither an explanation at the level of neural systems, nor an explanation at a metacognitive level, nor an explanation at the cultural level will be sufficient; all will be necessary.

Finally and critically, the story of the development of autobiographical memory and the story of the phenomenon of childhood amnesia are not one in the same. For much of the history of the field of psychology—in between the time the phenomenon of childhood amnesia was "discovered" and the end of the 20th century—the onset of autobiographical memory was defined, almost by default, as the offset of childhood amnesia. Yet autobiographical memory develops in childhood, whereas childhood amnesia is experienced by adults. There are any number of reasons that adults might not remember their early childhoods. Only one of the reasons is that they lack autobiographical memories from that period. We must be especially cautious about making the equation between the development of autobiographical memory and the offset of childhood amnesia because it leads to the erroneous assumption that, at the end of the preschool years, autobiographical memory changes qualitatively. This contributes to models that explain the acceleration of memories beginning at 4 to 6 years of age in terms of something that is, in effect, "turned on" to permit their rapid formation. A candidate mechanism is the development of autonoetic awareness, for example. With the flip of the "autonoetic switch," remembering can begin. Alternatively, it contributes to models which acknowledge that autobiographical memories are formed prior to ages 4 to 6, but that at roughly that time something happens to make them inaccessible, thereby accounting for the accelerated forgetting of early memories observed among adults. Candidate mechanisms include repression, development of different representational formats that render previous formats inaccessible, and changes in worldview.

In this chapter, I have argued that a more profitable approach is to view the change in distribution of memories near the end of the preschool years in terms of a "crossing over" of the two complementary functions of remembering and forgetting. Early in the preschool years, forgetting outstrips remembering; by later in the preschool years, remembering begins to outstrip forgetting. Because the rate of forgetting of events from early childhood is more rapid than that from later childhood and adulthood, if one looks back from the perspective of adults' lenses, it appears that something has happened to accelerate forgetting. However, if one looks forward from the perspective afforded by developmental lenses, one sees that what has happened is that the rate of forgetting has begun to approach the rate in adulthood. What this perspective lacks in glamour and mystery it makes up for by permitting us to see the continuity of autobiographical memory that may otherwise be obscured. Continuity is itself a precious commodity. In the words of D. Ewen Cameron (1963):

Intelligence may be the pride—the towering distinction of man; emotion gives colour and force to his actions; but memory is the bastion of his being. Without memory, there is no personal identity, there is no continuity to the days of his life. Memory provides the raw material for designs both small and great. Thus, governed and enriched by memory, all the enterprises of man go forward. (p. 325)

# Glossary

**Anterograde amnesia:** The inability to form new declarative or explicit memories.

**Autobiographical memory** (a.k.a. Personal memory): A type of memory seemingly specialized for encoding, storage, and retrieval of the events and experiences that make up one's life story or personal past.

**Autonoetic awareness:** A form of conscious awareness that one is re-experiencing an event that happened in the past.

**Childhood amnesia** (a.k.a. Infantile amnesia): The relative paucity among adults of verbally accessible memories from the first years of life.

**Consolidation:** A hypothetical process whereby inputs from different cortical regions are integrated and stabilized for long-term storage; the associated processes are thought to take place in the hippocampus and may continue for hours, days, months, and even years after experience of an event.

**Declarative memory:** A form of memory specialized for rapid acquisition of new information such as names, dates, places, and events; retrieval of representations is accompanied by conscious awareness; though the concepts are not isomorphic, largely overlapping with the construct of explicit memory.

**Deferred imitation:** A nonverbal measure of memory in which props are used by an adult to produce individual actions or multistep sequences that participants (typically infants and young children) later (i.e., after some delay) are invited to imitate (*see also* Elicited imitation).

**Double dissociations:** An asymmetric pattern of impairment and sparing such that, in one patient population with damage to one neural structure or network of structures, performance is impaired on Task 1 and spared on Task 2, whereas in another patient populations with damage to different neural structures, performance is spared on Task 1 and impaired on Task 2; such dissociations are taken as especially compelling evidence that different processes are supported by different neural structures.

**Elicited imitation:** A nonverbal measure in which props are used by an adult to produce individual actions or multistep sequences that participants are invited to imitate either immediately, after some delay, or both (*see also* Deferred imitation).

**Encoding:** The initial stage of processing in establishing an internal representation based on information received from distributed cortical regions.

**Entorhinal cortex:** A structure in the medial temporal lobe; it is both the main input to and output from the hippocampus.

**Episodic memory:** Supports retention of information about unique events; contrasted with semantic memory, which supports retention of general knowledge.

**Explicit memory:** A form of memory specialized for rapid acquisition of new information such as names, dates, places, and events; retrieval of representations is accompanied by conscious awareness; though the concepts are not isomorphic, largely overlapping with the construct of declarative memory.

**Frontal lobe:** One of the four major lobes of the brain named for its position at the front of the cortex; principal functions include motor control and coordination, executive functions, and involvement in memory encoding and retrieval processes.

**Hippocampal formation:** The hippocampus proper (i.e., the cell fields and the dentate gyrus of the hippocampus), the subiculum, and the entorhinal cortex.

**Hippocampal region:** The hippocampus proper (i.e., the cell fields and the dentate gyrus of the hippocampus) and the subiculum.

**Hippocampal trisynaptic circuit** (a.k.a. Long route): A circuit by which information is projected from the entorhinal cortex to the dentate gyrus of the hippocampus, from the dentate gyrus to the CA3 and CA1 fields of the hippocampus (a.k.a. Ammon's horn), from the cell fields to the subiculum, and from the subiculum back to the entorhinal cortex.

**Hippocampus or hippocampus proper:** The cell fields (i.e., CA1 and CA3 fields; a.k.a. Ammon's horn) and the dentate gyrus.

**Implicit memory:** A heterogeneous collection of types of information storage the defining feature of which is that the effects of prior experience are reflected in changes in task performance that do not require conscious or intentional recollection of the experience; though the concepts are not isomorphic, largely overlapping with the construct of nondeclarative or procedural memory.

**Infantile amnesia** (a.k.a. Childhood amnesia): The relative paucity among adults of verbally accessible memories from the first years of life.

**Long-term potentiation** (LTP): An increase in the magnitude of responsiveness of a presynaptic neuron (nonassociative LTP) or pre- and postsynaptic neurons (associative LTP) in response to previous stimulations; hypothesized to serve as a cellular or molecular basis for storage of information in memory.

**Medial temporal lobe structures or system:** The hippocampus proper (i.e., the cell fields and the dentate gyrus of the hippocampus), the subiculum, the entorhinal cortex, and the perirhinal and parahippocampal cortices.

**Mobile conjugate reinforcement:** A technique in which infants first acquire and then are tested for memory for the contingent movement of a mobile tethered to their legs such that as they kick the mobile moves.

**Multimodal association cortex** (a.k.a. Polymodal association cortex): A region of cortex in which information from the individual sense modalities (e.g., vision, audition) is brought together and integrated into a single percept; three such cortices are posterior-parietal, anterior-prefrontal, and limbic-temporal.

**Nondeclarative memory:** A heterogeneous collection of types of information storage, the defining feature of which is that the effects of prior experience are reflected in changes in task performance that do not require conscious or intentional recollection of the experience; though the concepts are not isomorphic, largely overlapping with the construct of implicit or procedural memory.

**Occipital lobe:** One of the four major lobes of the brain; primarily involved in processing of visual information.

**Parahippocampal cortex:** A posterior medial temporal lobe structure that receives inputs from uni- and polymodal association areas and projects the information to the entorhinal cortex; thought to be involved in temporary storage of information during the initial phases of consolidation into a long-term memory trace.

**Parietal lobe:** One of the four major lobes of the brain; primarily involved in processing of sensory information.

**Perirhinal cortex:** An anterior medial temporal lobe structure that receives inputs from uni- and polymodal association areas and projects the information to the entorhinal cortex; thought to be involved in temporary storage of information during the initial phases of consolidation into a long-term memory trace.

**Personal memory** (a.k.a. Autobiographical memory): A type of memory seemingly specialized for encoding, storage, and retrieval of the events and experiences that make up one's life story or personal past.

**Phrenology:** 19th-century attempt to link patterns of variation in the surface of the skull with profiles of individual differences in abilities (most closely associated with Franz Joseph Gall).

**Polymodal association cortex** (a.k.a. Multimodal association cortex): A region of cortex in which information from the individual sense modalities (e.g., vision, audition) is brought together and integrated into a single percept; three such cortices are posterior-parietal, anterior-prefrontal, and limbic-temporal.

**Prefrontal cortex:** Region of the frontal lobe implicated in executive functions, in memory for temporal order information, and in retrieval of declarative or explicit memories.

**Primary cortex:** Region of cortex responsible for registration of information from a single sense modality (i.e., primary somatosensory cortex, primary visual cortex, and primary auditory cortex); different fields within primary cortical regions are specialized for receipt of different types of information within their respective modalities (e.g., fields in primary visual cortex register the form, color, or motion of an object or event); inputs are subsequently projected to unimodal association cortices.

**Priming:** Strengthening of a behavioral response to a stimulus following prior exposure to the stimulus; the respondent need not be aware of the link between the magnitude of the response and prior exposure to the stimulus.

**Procedural memory:** A heterogeneous collection of types of information storage, the defining feature of which is that the effects of prior experience are reflected in changes in task performance that do not require conscious or intentional recollection of the experience; though the concepts are not isomorphic, largely overlapping with the construct of implicit or nondeclarative memory.

**Retrieval:** The process of bringing to awareness of a stored memory representation; thought to be, in essence, a reactivation of the neural network that represents the original experience which occurs as a result of an internal or external stimulus.

**Retrograde amnesia:** Impaired memory for events and experiences from the past.

**Semantic memory:** Supports retention of general knowledge; contrasted with episodic memory, which supports retention of information about unique events.

**Storage:** Establishing memory representations in cortical areas, the long-term storage sites for declarative memories.

**Synaptogenesis:** Rapid accumulation of synapses.

**Temperament:** Typical patterns of responding to environmental stimuli that seem to be inherent to the individual.

**Temporal lobe:** One of the four major lobes of the brain; principal functions include hearing, memory, and, in humans, speech and language processing.

**Temporally graded retrograde amnesia:** Impairment in memory for past events in a time-dependent fashion, such that memory for more recent events is impaired relative to memory for more remote events.

**Unimodal association cortex:** Region of cortex responsible for integration into whole percepts of information from a given primary sensory cortex; inputs are subsequently projected to polymodal (or multimodal) association cortices.

**Visual habituation:** Nonverbal technique for measuring memory in which the organism is sequentially exposed to numerous pictures of a stimulus and then, after some criterion is reached (typically a 50% decrease in looking time), is introduced to a novel stimulus; differential division of attention, as evidenced by looking time to novel compared with familiar stimuli, is taken as evidence of memory (*see also* Visual paired comparison).

**Visual paired comparison:** Nonverbal technique for measuring memory, in which the organism is exposed to pairs of pictures of a stimulus and then, after some period of familiarization, is presented the now "familiar" picture along with a different, novel picture; differential division of attention, as evidenced by looking time to novel compared with familiar stimuli, is taken as evidence of memory (*see also* Visual habituation).

# References

Abson, V., & Rabbitt, P. (1988). What do self rating questionnaires tell us about changes in competence in old age? In M. M. Gruneberg, P. E. Morris, & R. N. Sykes (Eds.), *Practical aspects of memory: Current research and issues* (pp. 186–191). Chichester: Wiley.

Ackil, J. K., Van Abbema, D. L., & Bauer, P. J. (2003). After the storm: Enduring differences in mother–child recollections of traumatic and nontraumatic events. *Journal of Experimental Child Psychology, 84,* 286–309.

Adams, S., Kuebli, J., Boyle, P. A., & Fivush, R. (1995). Gender differences in parent–child conversations about past emotions: A longitudinal investigation. *Sex Roles, 33,* 309–323.

Adlam, A.-L. R., Vargha-Khadem, F., Mishkin, M., & de Haan, M. (2005). Deferred imitation of action sequences in developmental amnesia. *Journal of Cognitive Neuroscience, 17,* 240–248.

Aguirre, G. K., & D'Esposito, M. (1997). Environmental knowledge is subserved by separable dorsal/ventral neural areas. *Journal of Neuroscience, 17,* 2513–2518.

Aguirre, G. K., Detre, J. A., Alsop, D. C., & D'Esposito, M. (1996). The parahippocampus subserves topographic learning in man. *Cerebral Cortex, 16,* 823–829.

Allen, J. G., & Hamsher, J. H. (1974). The development and validation of a test of emotional styles. *Journal of Counseling and Clinical Psychology, 42,* 663–668.

Allen, J. J. B. (2002). The role of psychophysiology in clinical assessment: ERPs in the evaluation of memory. *Psychophysiology, 39,* 261–280.

Altman, J., & Das, G. D. (1965). Autoradiographic and histological evidence of postnatal hippocampal neurogenesis in rats. *Journal of Comparative Neurology, 124,* 319–335.

Alvarez, P., & Squire, L. R. (1994). Memory consolidation and the medial temporal lobe: A simple network model. *Proceedings of the National Academy of Sciences, 91,* 7041–7045.

Alvarez, P., Zola-Morgan, S., & Squire, L. R. (1994). The animal model of human amnesia: Long-term memory impaired and short-term memory intact. *Proceedings of the National Academy of Sciences, 91,* 5637–5641.

Alvarez-Royo, P., Clower, R. P., & Zola-Morgan, S. (1991). Stereotaxic lesions of the hippocampus in monkeys: Determination of surgical coordinates and analysis of lesions using magnetic resonance imaging. *Journal of Neuroscience Methods, 38,* 223–232.

384

Andersen, P., Bliss, T. V., & Skrede, K. K. (1971). Unit analysis of hippocampal population spikes. *Experimental Brain Research, 13,* 208–221.

Angevine, J. B. (1975). Development of the hippocampal formation. In R. L. Isaacson & K. H. Pribram (Eds.), *The hippocampus* (pp. 61–90). New York: Plenum.

Anglin, J. (1993). Vocabulary development: A morphological analysis. *Monographs of the Society for Research in Child Development, 58*(10, Serial No. 238).

Arnold, S. E., & Trojanowski, J. Q. (1996). Human fetal hippocampal development: I. Cytoarchitecture, myeloarchitecture, and neuronal morphologic features. *Journal of Comparative Neurology, 367,* 274–292.

Augustine, A. (~401 CE). *The confessions of Saint Augustine.* Book X, Chapter VIII (E. B. Pusey, Trans.). Grand Rapids, MI: Christian Classics Ethereal Library.

Bachevalier, J. (1992). Cortical versus limbic immaturity: Relationship to infantile amnesia. In M. R. Gunnar & C. A. Nelson (Eds.), *Developmental behavioral neuroscience: The Minnesota Symposia on Child Psychology* (Vol. 24, pp. 129–153). Hillsdale, NJ: Lawrence Erlbaum Associates.

Bachevalier, J. (2001). Neural bases of memory development: Insights from neuropsychological studies in primates. In C. A. Nelson & M. Luciana (Eds.), *Handbook of developmental cognitive neuroscience* (pp. 365–379). Cambridge, MA: MIT Press.

Bachevalier, J., Brickson, M., & Hagger, C. (1993). Limbic-dependent recognition memory in monkeys develops early in infancy. *NeuroReport, 4,* 77–80.

Bachevalier, J., Hagger, C., & Mishkin, M. (1991). Functional maturation of the occipitotemporal pathway in infant rhesus monkeys. In N. A. Lassen, D. H. Ingvar, M. E. Raichle, & L. Friberg (Eds.), *Alfred Benzon symposium No. 31: Brain work and mental activity, quantitative studies with radioactive tracers* (pp. 231–240). Copenhagen, Denmark: Munksgaard.

Bachevalier, J., & Mishkin, M. (1994). Effects of selective neonatal temporal lobe lesions on visual recognition memory in rhesus monkeys. *Journal of Neuroscience, 14,* 2128–2139.

Bahrick, H. P. (2000). Long-term maintenance of knowledge. In E. Tulving & F. I. M. Craik (Eds.), *The Oxford handbook of memory* (pp. 347–362). New York: Oxford University Press.

Bahrick, L. E., Hernandez-Reif, M., & Pickens, J. N. (1997). The effect of retrieval cues on visual preferences and memory in infancy: Evidence for a four-phase attention function. *Journal of Experimental Child Psychology, 67,* 1–20.

Bahrick, L. E., Parker, J., Merritt, K., & Fivush, R. (1998). Children's memory for Hurricane Andrew. *Journal of Experimental Psychology: Applied, 4,* 308–331.

Bahrick, L. E., & Pickens, J. N. (1995). Infant memory for object motion across a period of three months: Implications for a four-phase attention function. *Journal of Experimental Child Psychology, 59,* 343–371.

Baker-Ward, L., Hess, T. M., & Flannagan, D. A. (1990). The effects of involvement on children's memory for events. *Cognitive Development, 5,* 55–69.

Barclay, C. R., & DeCooke, P. A. (1988). Ordinary everyday memories: Some of the things of which selves are made. In U. Neisser & E. Winograd (Eds.), *Remembering reconsidered: Ecological and traditional approaches to the study of memory* (pp. 91–125). Cambridge, UK: Cambridge University Press.

Barkovich, A. J., Kjos, B. O., Jackson, D. E., & Norman, D. (1988). Normal maturation of the neonatal and infant brain: Mr imaging at 1.5 T. *Neuroradiology, 166,* 173–180.

Barnat, S. B., Klein, P. J., & Meltzoff, A. N. (1996). Deferred imitation across changes in context and object: Memory and generalization in 14-month-old children. *Infant Behavior and Development, 19,* 241–251.

Barnett, M. P., Newman, H. W., Richardson, J. T. E., Thompson, P., & Upton, D. (2000). The constituent structure of autobiographical memory: Autobiographical fluency in people with chronic epilepsy. *Memory, 8,* 413–424.

Barr, R., Dowden, A., & Hayne, H. (1996). Developmental change in deferred imitation by 6- to 24-month-old infants. *Infant Behavior and Development, 19,* 159–170.

Barr, R., & Hayne, H. (1996). The effect of event structure on imitation in infancy: Practice makes perfect? *Infant Behavior and Development, 19,* 253–257.

Bartsch, K., & London, K. (2000). Children's use of mental state information in selecting persuasive arguments. *Developmental Psychology, 36,* 352–365.

Bates, E. (1979). *The emergence of symbols.* New York: Academic Press.

Bauer, P. J. (1992). Holding it all together: How enabling relations facilitate young children's event recall. *Cognitive Development, 7,* 1–28.

Bauer, P. J. (1993). Identifying subsystems of autobiographical memory: Commentary on Nelson. In C. A. Nelson (Ed.), *The Minnesota symposium on child psychology: Vol. 26. Memory and affect in development* (pp. 25–37). Hillsdale, NJ: Lawrence Erlbaum Associates.

Bauer, P. J. (1995). Recalling the past: From infancy to early childhood. *Annals of Child Development, 11,* 25–71.

Bauer, P. J. (2002). Long-term recall memory: Behavioral and neuro-developmental changes in the first 2 years of life. *Current Directions in Psychological Science, 11,* 137–141.

Bauer, P. J. (2004). Getting explicit memory off the ground: Steps toward construction of a neuro-developmental account of changes in the first two years of life. *Developmental Review, 24,* 347–373.

Bauer, P. J. (2005). Developments in declarative memory: Decreasing susceptibility to storage failure over the second year of life. *Psychological Science, 16,* 41–47.

Bauer, P. J., & Burch, M. M. (2004). Developments in early memory: Multiple mediators of foundational processes. In J. Lucariello, J. A. Hudson, R. Fivush, & P. J. Bauer (Eds.), *Development of the mediated mind: Culture and cognitive development. Essays in honor of Katherine Nelson* (pp. 101–125). Mahwah, NJ: Lawrence Erlbaum Associates.

Bauer, P. J., Burch, M. M., & Kleinknecht, E. E. (2002). Developments in early recall memory: Normative trends and individual differences. In R. Kail (Ed.), *Advances in child development and behavior* (pp. 103–152). San Diego, CA: Academic Press.

Bauer, P. J., Cheatham, C. L., Cary, M. S., & Van Abbema, D. L. (2002). Short-term forgetting: Charting its course and its implications for long-term remembering. In S. P. Shohov (Ed.), *Advances in psychology research* (Vol. 9, pp. 53–74). Huntington, NY: Nova Science Publishers.

Bauer, P. J., & Dow, G. A. A. (1994). Episodic memory in 16- and 20-month-old children: Specifics are generalized, but not forgotten. *Developmental Psychology, 30,* 403–417.

Bauer, P. J., & Fivush, R. (1992). Constructing event representations: Building on a foundation of variation and enabling relations. *Cognitive Development, 7,* 381–401.

Bauer, P. J., & Hertsgaard, L. A. (1993). Increasing steps in recall of events: Factors facilitating immediate and long-term memory in 13.5- and 16.5-month-old children. *Child Development, 64,* 1204–1223.

Bauer, P. J., Hertsgaard, L. A., Dropik, P., & Daly, B. P. (1998). When even arbitrary order becomes important: Developments in reliable temporal sequencing of arbitrarily ordered events. *Memory, 6,* 165–198.

Bauer, P. J., Hertsgaard, L. A., & Wewerka, S. S. (1995). Effects of experience and reminding on long-term recall in infancy: Remembering not to forget. *Journal of Experimental Child Psychology, 59,* 260–298.

Bauer, P. J., Kroupina, M. G., Schwade, J. A., Dropik, P. L., & Wewerka, S. S. (1998). If memory serves, will language? Later verbal accessibility of early memories. *Development and Psychopathology, 10,* 655–679.

Bauer, P. J., & Mandler, J. M. (1989). One thing follows another: Effects of temporal structure on one- to two-year-olds' recall of events. *Developmental Psychology, 25,* 197–206.

Bauer, P. J., & Shore, C. M. (1987). Making a memorable event: Effects of familiarity and organization on young children's recall of action sequences. *Cognitive Development, 2,* 327–338.

Bauer, P. J., Stennes, L., & Haight, J. C. (2003). Representation of the inner self in autobiography: Women's and men's use of internal states language in personal narratives. *Memory, 11,* 27–42.

Bauer, P. J., & Thal, D. J. (1990). Scripts or scraps: Reconsidering the development of sequential understanding. *Journal of Experimental Child Psychology, 50,* 287–304.

Bauer, P. J., & Travis, L. L. (1993). The fabric of an event: Different sources of temporal invariance differentially affect 24-month-olds' recall. *Cognitive Development, 8,* 319–341.

Bauer, P. J., Van Abbema, D. L., & de Haan, M. (1999). In for the short haul: Immediate and short-term remembering and forgetting by 20-month-old children. *Infant Behavior and Development, 22,* 321–343.

Bauer, P. J., Van Abbema, D. L., Wiebe, S. A., Cary, M. S., Phill, C., & Burch, M. M. (2004). Props, not pictures, are worth a thousand words: Verbal accessibility of early memories under different conditions of contextual support. *Applied Cognitive Psychology, 18,* 373–392.

Bauer, P. J., Wenner, J. A., Dropik, P. L., & Wewerka, S. S. (2000). Parameters of remembering and forgetting in the transition from infancy to early childhood. *Monographs of the Society for Research in Child Development, 65*(4, Serial No. 263).

Bauer, P. J., Wenner, J. A., & Kroupina, M. G. (2002). Making the past present: Later verbal accessibility of early memories. *Journal of Cognition and Development, 3,* 21–47.

Bauer, P. J., & Wewerka, S. S. (1995). One- to two-year-olds' recall of past events: The more expressed, the more impressed. *Journal of Experimental Child Psychology, 59,* 475–496.

Bauer, P. J., & Wewerka, S. S. (1997). Saying is revealing: Verbal expression of event memory in the transition from infancy to early childhood. In P. van den Broek, P. J. Bauer, & T. Bourg (Eds.), *Developmental spans in event representation and comprehension: Bridging fictional and actual events* (pp. 139–168). Mahwah, NJ: Lawrence Erlbaum Associates.

Bauer, P. J., Wiebe, S. A., Carver, L. J., Lukowski, A. F., Haight, J. C., Waters, J. M., & Nelson, C. A. (2006). Electrophysiological indices of encoding and behavioral indices of recall: Examining relations and developmental change late in the first year of life. *Developmental Neuropsychology, 29,* 293–320.

Bauer, P. J., Wiebe, S. A., Carver, L. J., Waters, J. M., & Nelson, C. A. (2003). Developments in long-term explicit memory late in the first year of life: Behavioral and electrophysiological indices. *Psychological Science, 14,* 629–635.

Bauer, P. J., Wiebe, S. A., Waters, J. M., & Bangston, S. K. (2001). Reexposure breeds recall: Effects of experience on 9-month-olds' ordered recall. *Journal of Experimental Child Psychology, 80,* 174–200.

Benes, F. M. (2001). The development of prefrontal cortex: The maturation of neurotransmitter systems and their interaction. In C. A. Nelson & M. Luciana (Eds.), *Handbook of developmental cognitive neuroscience* (pp. 79–92). Cambridge, MA: MIT Press.

Benes, F. M., Turtle, M., Khan, Y., & Farol, P. (1994). Myelination of a key relay zone in the hippocampal formation occurs in the human brain during childhood, adolescence, and adulthood. *Archives of General Psychiatry, 51,* 477–484.

Berntsen, D., & Rubin, D. C. (2002). Emotionally charged autobiographical memories across the life span: The recall of happy, sad, traumatic, and involuntary memories. *Psychology and Aging, 17,* 636–652.

Bertenthal, B. I., & Clifton, R. K. (1998). Perception and action. In W. Damon (Editor-in-Chief) & D. Kuhn & R. S. Siegler (Vol. Eds.), *Handbook of child psychology: Vol. 2. Cognition, perception, and language* (5th ed., pp. 51–102). New York: Wiley.

Bjorklund, D. F., & Douglas, R. N. (1997). The development of memory strategies. In N. Cowan (Ed.), *The development of memory in childhood* (pp. 201–246). Hove East Sussex, UK: Psychology Press.

Bloom, L. (1998). Language acquisition in its developmental context. In W. Damon (Editor-in-Chief) & D. Kuhn & R. S. Siegler (Vol. Eds.), *Handbook of child psychology: Vol. 2. Cognition, perception, and language* (5th ed., pp. 309–370). New York: Wiley.

Bontempi, B., Laurent-Demir, C., Destrade, C., & Jaffard, R. (1999). Time-dependent reorganization of brain circuitry underlying long-term memory storage. *Nature, 400,* 671–675.

Borovsky, D., & Rovee-Collier, C. (1990). Contextual constraints on memory retrieval at six months. *Child Development, 61,* 1569–1583.

Bourgeois, J.-P. (2001). Synaptogenesis in the neocortex of the newborn: The ultimate frontier for individuation? In C. A. Nelson & M. Luciana (Eds.), *Handbook of developmental cognitive neuroscience* (pp. 23–34). Cambridge, MA: MIT Press.

Bourgeois, J.-P., Goldman-Rakic, P. S., & Rakic, P. (2000). Formation, elimination and stabilization of synapses in the primate cerebral cortex. In M. Gazzaniga (Ed.), *The new cognitive neurosciences* (pp. 45–53). Cambridge, MA: MIT Press.

Bowlby, J. (1969). *Attachment and loss* (Vol. 1). New York: Basic Books.

Brainerd, C. J., & Reyna, V. F. (1990). Gist is the grist: Fuzzy-trace theory and the new intuitionism. *Developmental Review, 10,* 3–47.

Brainerd, C. J., & Reyna, V. F. (1995). Learning rate, learning opportunities, and the development of forgetting. *Developmental Psychology, 31,* 251–262.

Brainerd, C. J., Reyna, V. F., Howe, M. L., & Kingma, J. (1990). The development of forgetting and reminiscence. *Monographs of the Society for Research in Child Development, 55*(3–4, Serial No. 222).

Bretherton, I. (1990). Open communication and internal working models: Their role in the development of attachment relationships. In R. A. Thompson (Ed.), *Nebraska symposium on motivation: Vol. 36. Socioemotional development* (pp. 59–113). Lincoln: University of Nebraska Press.

Brewer, J. B., Zhao, Z., Glover, G. H., & Gabrieli, J. D. E. (1998). Making memories: Brain activity that predicts whether visual experiences will be remembered or forgotten. *Science, 281,* 1185–1187.

Brewer, W. F. (1986). What is autobiographical memory? In D. C. Rubin (Ed.), *Autobiographical memory* (pp. 25–49). New York: Cambridge University Press.

Brewer, W. F. (1988). Memory for randomly sampled autobiographical events. In U. Neisser & E. Winograd (Eds.), *Remembering reconsidered: Ecological and traditional approaches to the study of memory* (pp. 21–90). Cambridge, UK: Cambridge University Press.

Brewer, W. F. (1996). What is recollective memory? In D. C. Rubin (Ed.), *Remembering our past: Studies in autobiographical memory* (pp. 19–66). Cambridge, UK: Cambridge University Press.

Brodsky, J. (1986). *Less than one—Selected essays.* New York: Farrar Straus Giroux.

Brooks-Gunn, J., & Lewis, M. (1984). The development of early visual self-recognition. *Developmental Review, 4,* 215–239.

Brown, A. S. (2002). Consolidation theory and retrograde amnesia in humans. *Psychonomic Bulletin and Review, 9,* 403–425.

Brown, R., & Kulik, J. (1977). Flashbulb memories. *Cognition, 5,* 73–99.

Büchel, C., Coull, J. T., & Friston, K. J. (1999). The predictive value of changes in effective connectivity for human learning. *Science, 283,* 1538–1541.

Buckner, J. P., & Fivush, R. (1998). Gender and self in children's autobiographical narratives. *Applied Cognitive Psychology, 12,* 407–429.

Buckner, J. P., & Fivush, R. (2000). Gendered themes in family reminiscing. *Memory, 8,* 401–412.

Buckner, R. L., Koutstaal, W., Schacter, D. L., Dale, A. M., Rotte, M., & Rosen, B. R. (1998). Functional-anatomic study of episodic retrieval: II. Selective averaging of event-related fMRI trials to test the retrieval success hypothesis. *Neuroimage, 7,* 163–175.

Buckner, R. L., Koutstaal, W., Schacter, D. L., Wagner, A. D., & Rosen, B. R. (1998). Functional-anatomic study of episodic retrieval using fMRI: I. Retrieval effort versus retrieval success. *Neuroimage, 7,* 151–162.

Buckner, R. L., Raichle, M. E., Miezin, F. M., & Petersen, S. E. (1996). Functional anatomic studies of memory retrieval for auditory words and visual pictures. *Journal of Neuroscience, 16,* 6219–6235.

Buckner, R. L., Wheeler, M. E., & Sheridan, M. A. (2001). Encoding processes during retrieval tasks. *Journal of Cognitive Neuroscience, 13,* 406–415.

Burnham, W. M. (1903). Retroactive amnesia: Illustrative cases and a tentative explanation. *American Journal of Psychology, 14,* 382–396.

Butterworth, B., Cipolotti, L., & Warrington, E. K. (1996). Short-term memory impairment and arithmetical ability. *Quarterly Journal of Experimental Psychology, 49A,* 251–262.

Cabeza, R., McIntosh, A. R., Tulving, E., Nyberg, L., & Grady, C. L. (1997). Age-related differences in effective neural connectivity during encoding and recall. *NeuroReport, 8,* 3479–3483.

Cabeza, R., & Nyberg, L. (1997). Imaging cognition: An empirical review of PET studies with normal subjects. *Journal of Cognitive Neuroscience, 9,* 1–26.

Cahill, L., Babinsky, R., Markowitsch, J. H., & McGaugh, J. L. (1995). Involvement of the amygdaloid complex in emotional memory. *Nature, 377,* 295–296.

Cahill, L., Haier, R. J., Fallon, J., Alkire, M. T., Tang, C., Keator, D., Wu, J., & McGaugh, J. L. (1996). Amygdala activity at encoding correlated with long-term, free recall of emotional information. *Proceedings of the National Academy of Sciences, 93,* 8016–8021.

Cahill, L., & McGaugh, J. L. (1998). Mechanisms of emotional arousal and lasting declarative memory. *Trends in Neuroscience, 21,* 294–298.

Cahill, L., Prins, B., Weber, M., & McGaugh, J. L. (1994). β-Adrenergic activation and memory for emotional events. *Nature, 371,* 702–704.

Caldji, C., Tannenbaum, B., Sharma, S., Francis, D., Plotsky, P. M, & Meaney, M. J. (1998). Maternal care during infancy regulates the development of neural systems mediating the expression of fearfulness in the rat. *Proceedings of the National Academy of Sciences, 95,* 5340–5445.

Calkins, M. W. (1894). Association. *Psychological Review, 1,* 476–483.

Cameron, D. E. (1963). The processes of remembering. *British Journal of Psychiatry, 109,* 325–340.

Campbell, B. A. (1984). Reflections on the ontogeny of learning and memory. In R. Kail & N. E. Spear (Eds.), *Comparative perspectives on the development of memory.* Hillsdale, NJ: Lawrence Erlbaum Associates.

Campbell, B. A., & Spear, N. E. (1972). Ontogeny of memory. *Psychological Review, 79,* 215–236.

Carey, W. B., & McDevitt, S. C. (1978). Stability and change in individual temperament diagnoses from infancy to early childhood. *Journal of the American Academy of Child Psychiatry, 17,* 331–337.

Carroll, L. (1982). *Through the looking glass and what Alice found there.* In *The complete illustrated works of Lewis Carroll.* New York: Crown Publishers. (Original work published 1872)

Carver, L. J., & Bauer, P. J. (1999). When the event is more than the sum of its parts: Nine-month-olds' long-term ordered recall. *Memory, 7,* 147–174.

Carver, L. J., & Bauer, P. J. (2001). The dawning of a past: The emergence of long-term explicit memory in infancy. *Journal of Experimental Psychology: General, 130,* 726–745.

Carver, L. J., Bauer, P. J., & Nelson, C. A. (2000). Associations between infant brain activity and recall memory. *Developmental Science, 3,* 234–246.

Case, R. (1985). *Intellectual development: A systematic reinterpretation.* New York: Academic Press.

Casey, B. J., Thomas, K. M., & McCandliss, B. (2001). Applications of magnetic resonance imaging to the study of development. In C. A. Nelson & M. Luciana (Eds.), *Handbook of developmental cognitive neuroscience* (pp. 137–147). Cambridge, MA: MIT Press.

Cassidy, J., & Shaver, P. R. (1999). *Handbook of attachment: Theory, research and clinical applications.* New York: Guilford.

Cheatham, C. L., & Bauer, P. J. (2005). Construction of a more coherent story: Prior verbal recall predicts later verbal accessibility of early memories. *Memory, 13,* 516–532.

Chi, M. T. H. (1978). Knowledge structures and memory development. In R. S. Siegler (Ed.), *Children's thinking: What develops?* (pp. 73–95). Hillsdale, NJ: Lawrence Erlbaum Associates.

Choi, S. H. (1992). Communicative socialization processes: Korea and Canada. In S. Iwasaki, Y. Kashima, & L. Leung (Eds.), *Innovations in cross-cultural psychology* (pp. 103–122). Amsterdam: Swets & Zeitlinger.

Christianson, S.-Å., & Loftus, E. F. (1990). Some characteristics of people's traumatic memories. *Bulletin of the Psychonomic Society, 28,* 195–198.

Christianson, S.-Å., & Safer, M. A. (1996). Emotional events and emotions in autobiographical memories. In D. C. Rubin (Ed.), *Remembering our past: Studies in autobiographical memory* (pp. 218–243). New York: Cambridge University Press.

Chugani, H. T. (1994). Development of regional blood glucose metabolism in relation to behavior and plasticity. In G. Dawson & K. Fischer (Eds.), *Human behavior and the developing brain* (pp. 153–175). New York: Guilford.

Chugani, H. T., & Phelps, M. E. (1986). Maturational changes in cerebral function determined by 18FDG positron emission tomography. *Science, 231,* 840–843.

Chugani, H. T., Phelps, M., & Mazziotta, J. (1987). Positron emission tomography study of human brain functional development. *Annals of Neurology, 22,* 487–497.

Clark, D. M., & Teasdale, J. D. (1982). Diurnal variation in clinical depression and accessibility of memories of positive and negative experiences. *Journal of Abnormal Psychology, 91,* 87–95.

Cohen, G., Conway, M. A., & Maylor, E. A. (1994). Flashbulb memories in older adults. *Psychology and Aging, 9,* 454–463.

Collie, R., & Hayne, H. (1999). Deferred imitation by 6- and 9-month-old infants: More evidence of declarative memory. *Developmental Psychobiology, 35,* 83–90.

Conway, M. A. (1996). Autobiographical knowledge and autobiographical memories. In D. C. Rubin (Ed.), *Remembering our past: Studies in autobiographical memory* (pp. 67–93). New York: Cambridge University Press.

Corkin, S. (1984). Lasting consequences of bilateral medial temporal lobectomy: Clinical course and experimental findings in H. M. *Seminars in Neurology, 4,* 249–259.

Corkin, S. (2002). What's new with the amnesic patient H. M.? *Nature Reviews, 3,* 153–160.

Corkin, S., Amaral, D. G., González, R. G., Johnson, K. A., & Hyman, B. T. (1997). H. M.'s medial temporal lobe lesion: Findings from magnetic resonance imaging. *The Journal of Neuroscience, 17,* 3964–3979.

Corkin, S., Cohen, N. J., & Sagar, H. J. (1983). Memory for remote personal and public events after bilateral medial temporal lobectomy. *Society for Neuroscience Abstracts, 9,* 28.

Courage, M. L., & Howe, M. L. (1998). The ebb and flow of infant attentional preferences: Evidence for long-term recognition memory in 3-month-olds. *Journal of Experimental Child Psychology, 70,* 26–53.

Cowan, N., & Davidson, G. (1984). Salient childhood memories. *The Journal of Genetic Psychology, 145,* 101–107.

Crovitz, J. F., & Quina-Holland, K. (1976). Proportion of episodic memories from early childhood by years of age. *Bulletin of the Psychonomic Society, 7,* 61–62.

Crovitz, J. F., & Schiffman, H. (1974). Frequency of episodic memories as a function of their age. *Bulletin of the Psychonomic Society, 4,* 517–518.

Csikszentmihalyi, M., Larson, R., & Prescott, S. (1977). The ecology of adolescent activity and experience. *Journal of Youth and Adolescence, 6,* 281–294.

Czurkó, A., Czéh, B., Seress, L., Nadel, L., & Bures, J. (1997). Severe spatial navigation deficit in the Morris water maze after single high dose of neonatal X-ray irradiation in the rat. *Proceedings of the National Academy of Sciences, 94,* 2766–2771.

Dale, P. S. (1976). *Language development: Structure and function* (2nd ed.). New York: Holt, Rinehart & Winston.

Davis, P. J. (1999). Gender differences in autobiographical memory for childhood emotional experiences. *Journal of Personality and Social Psychology, 76,* 498–510.

Debiec, J., LeDoux, J. E., & Nader, K. (2002). Cellular and systems reconsolidation in the hippo-campus. *Neuron, 36*, 527–538.

DeBoer, T., Wewerka, S., Bauer, P. J., Georgieff, M. K., & Nelson, C. A. (in press). Explicit memory performance in infants of diabetic mothers at 1 year of age. *Developmental Medicine and Child Neurology.*

DeBoer, T. L., Wewerka, S. S., & Fong, S. S. (2003, April). *Elicited imitation as a tool to investigate the impact of abnormal prenatal environments on memory development.* Paper presented at the 70th biennial meeting of the Society for Research in Child Development, Tampa, FL.

DeCasper, A. J., & Spence, M. J. (1986). Prenatal maternal speech influences newborns' percep-tions of speech sounds. *Infant Behavior and Development, 9*, 133–150.

de Haan, M., Bauer, P. J., Georgieff, M. K., & Nelson, C. A. (2000). Explicit memory in low-risk infants aged 19 months born between 27 and 42 weeks of gestation. *Developmental Medicine and Child Neurology, 42*, 304–312.

Desimone, R. (1996). Neural mechanisms for visual memory and their role in attention. *Proceed-ings of the National Academy of Sciences, 93*, 13494–13499.

Diamond, A. (1985). Development of the ability to use recall to guide action, as indicated by in-fants' performance on A not B. *Child Development, 56*, 868–883.

Diamond, A. (2001). A model system for studying the role of dopamine in the prefrontal cortex during early development in humans: Early and continuously treated phenylketonuria. In C. A. Nelson & M. Luciana (Eds.), *Handbook of developmental cognitive neuroscience* (pp. 433–472). Cambridge, MA: MIT Press.

Diamond, A., Zola-Morgan, S., & Squire, L. R. (1989). Successful performance by monkeys with lesions of the hippocampal formation on A-not-B and object retrieval, two tasks that mark developmental changes in human infants. *Behavioral Neuroscience, 103*, 526–537.

Dolan, R. J., & Fletcher, P. C. (1997). Dissociating prefrontal and hippocampal function in epi-sodic memory encoding. *Nature, 388*, 582–585.

Dudycha, G. J., & Dudycha, M. M. (1933a). Adolescents' memories of preschool experiences. *Journal of Genetic Psychology, 42*, 468–480.

Dudycha, G. J., & Dudycha, M. M. (1933b). Some factors and characteristics of childhood mem-ories. *Child Development, 4*, 265–278.

Dudycha, G. J., & Dudycha, M. M. (1941). Childhood memories: A review of the literature. *Psy-chological Bulletin, 36*, 668–682.

Dunn, J., Brown, J., Slomkowski, C., Tesla, C., & Youngblade, L. (1991). Young children's un-derstanding of other people's feelings and beliefs: Individual differences and their antece-dents. *Child Development, 62*, 1352–1366.

Ebbinghaus, H. (1885). *On memory* (H. A. Ruger & C. E. Bussenius, Trans.). New York: Teachers' College, 1913. Paperback edition, New York: Dover, 1964.

Eckenhoff, M. F., & Rakic, P. (1988). Nature and fate of proliferative cells in the hippocampal dentate gyrus during the life span of the rhesus monkey. *Journal of Neuroscience, 8*, 2729–2747.

Eckenhoff, M. F., & Rakic, P. (1991). A quantitative analysis of synaptogenesis in the molecular layer of the dentate gyrus in the rhesus monkey. *Developmental Brain Research, 64*, 129–135.

Eder, R. A. (1990). Uncovering young children's psychological selves: Individual and develop-mental differences. *Child Development, 61*, 849–863.

Eichenbaum, H., & Cohen, N. J. (2001). *From conditioning to conscious recollection: Memory sys-tems of the brain.* New York: Oxford University Press.

Eisenberg, A. (1985). Learning to describe past experience in conversation. *Discourse Processes, 8*, 177–204.

Engel, S. (1986). *Learning to reminisce: A developmental study of how young children talk about the past.* Unpublished doctoral dissertation, City University of New York Graduate Center.

Erikson, E. H. (1959). *Identity and the life cycle.* New York: International Universities Press.

Erikson, E. H. (1963). *Childhood and society.* New York: Norton.

Erikson, K. M., Pinero, D. J., Connor, J. R., & Beard, J. L. (1997). Regional brain iron, ferritin, and transferrin concentrations during iron deficiency and iron repletion in developing rats. *Journal of Nutrition, 127,* 2030–2038.

Fagan, J. F. (1973). Infants' delayed recognition memory and forgetting. *Journal of Experimental Child Psychology, 16,* 425–450.

Fagan, J. F. (1984). The intelligent infant: Theoretical implications. *Intelligence, 8,* 1–9.

Fajnsztejn-Pollack, G. (1973). A developmental study of the decay rate in long term memory. *Journal of Experimental Child Psychology, 16,* 225–235.

Fantz, R. L. (1956). A method for studying early visual development. *Perceptual and Motor Skills, 6,* 13–15.

Farrant, K., & Reese, E. (2000). Maternal style and children's participation in reminiscing: Stepping stones in children's autobiographical memory development. *Journal of Cognition and Development, 1,* 193–225.

Farrar, M. J., & Goodman, G. S. (1990). Developmental differences in the relation between scripts and episodic memory: Do they exist? In R. Fivush & J. A. Hudson (Eds.), *Knowing and remembering in young children* (pp. 30–64). New York: Cambridge University Press.

Fenson, L., Dale, P. S., Reznick, J. S., Bates, E., Thal, D. J., & Pethick, S. J. (1994). Variability in early communicative development. *Monographs of the Society for Research in Child Development, 59*(5).

Fernández, G., Weyerts, H., Schrader-Bölsche, M., Tendolkar, I., Smid, H. G. O. M., Tempelmann, C., Hinrichs, H., Scheich, H., Egler, C. E., Mangun, G. R., & Heinze, H.-J. (1998). Successful verbal encoding into episodic memory engages the posterior hippocampus: A parametrically analyzed functional magnetic resonance imaging study. *The Journal of Neuroscience, 18,* 1841–1847.

Fink, G. R., Markowitsch, H. J., Reinkemeier, M., Bruckbauer, T., Kessler, J., & Heiss, W. D. (1996). Cerebral representation of one's own past: Neural networks involved in autobiographical memory. *The Journal of Neuroscience, 16,* 4275–4282.

Fischer, K. W. (1980). A theory of cognitive development: The control and construction of hierarchies of skills. *Psychological Review, 87,* 477–531.

Fitzgerald, J. M. (1988). Vivid memories and the reminiscence phenomenon: The role of a self narrative. *Human Development, 31,* 261–273.

Fitzgerald, J. M. (1992). Autobiographical memory and conceptualizations of the self. In M. A. Conway, D. C. Rubin, H. Spinnler, & W. A. Wagenaar (Eds.), *Theoretical perspectives on autobiographical memory* (pp. 99–114). Dordrecht, The Netherlands: Kluwer Academic.

Fivush, R. (1984). Learning about school: The development of kindergartners' school scripts. *Child Development, 55,* 1697–1709.

Fivush, R. (1991a). Gender and emotion in mother–child conversations about the past. *Journal of Narrative and Life History, 1,* 325–341.

Fivush, R. (1991b). The social construction of personal narratives. *Merrill-Palmer Quarterly, 37,* 59–82.

Fivush, R. (1993). Emotional content of parent–child conversations about the past. In C. A. Nelson (Ed.), *The Minnesota symposium on child psychology: Vol. 26. Memory and affect in development* (pp. 39–77). Hillsdale, NJ: Lawrence Erlbaum Associates.

Fivush, R. (1997). Event memory in early childhood. In N. Cowan (Ed.), *The development of memory in childhood* (pp. 139–161). Hove East Sussex: Psychology Press.

Fivush, R. (1998). Gendered narratives: Elaboration, structure, and emotion in parent–child reminiscing across the preschool years. In C. P. Thompson, D. J. Herrmann, D. Bruce, J. D. Read, D. G. Payne, & M. P. Toglia (Eds.), *Autobiographical memory: Theoretical and applied perspectives* (pp. 79–103). Mahwah, NJ: Lawrence Erlbaum Associates.

Fivush, R. (2001). Owning experience: Developing subjective perspective in autobiographical narratives. In C. Moore & K. Lemmon (Eds.), *The self in time: Developmental perspectives* (pp. 35–52). Mahwah, NJ: Lawrence Erlbaum Associates.

Fivush, R., Berlin, L. J., McDermott Sales, J., Mennuti-Washburn, J., & Cassidy, J. (2003). Functions of parent–child reminiscing about emotionally negative events. *Memory, 11*, 179–192.

Fivush, R., Brotman, M. A., Buckner, J. P., & Goodman, S. H. (2000). Gender differences in parent–child emotion narratives. *Sex Roles, 42*, 233–253.

Fivush, R., Edwards, V. J., & Mennuti-Washburn, J. (2003). Narratives of 9/11: Relations among personal involvement, narrative content and memory for the emotional impact over time. *Applied Cognitive Psychology, 17*, 1099–1111.

Fivush, R., & Fromhoff, F. (1988). Style and structure in mother–child conversations about the past. *Discourse Processes, 11*, 337–355.

Fivush, R., Gray, J. T., & Fromhoff, F. A. (1987). Two-year-olds talk about the past. *Cognitive Development, 2*, 393–409.

Fivush, R., & Haden, C. A. (1997). Narrating and representing experience: Preschoolers' developing autobiographical accounts. In P. van den Broek, P. J. Bauer, & T. Bourg (Eds.), *Developmental spans in event representation and comprehension: Bridging fictional and actual events* (pp. 169–198). Mahwah, NJ: Lawrence Erlbaum Associates.

Fivush, R., Haden, C., & Adams, S. (1995). Structure and coherence of preschoolers' personal narratives over time: Implications for childhood amnesia. *Journal of Experimental Child Psychology, 60*, 32–56.

Fivush, R., Haden, C., & Reese, E. (1996). Remembering, recounting, and reminiscing: The development of autobiographical memory in social context. In D. C. Rubin (Ed.), *Remembering our past: Studies in autobiographical memory* (pp. 341–359). New York: Cambridge University Press.

Fivush, R., & Hamond, N. R. (1989). Time and again: Effects of repetition and retention interval on 2-year-olds' event recall. *Journal of Experimental Child Psychology, 47*, 259–273.

Fivush, R., & Hamond, N. R. (1990). Autobiographical memory across the preschool years: Toward reconceptualizing childhood amnesia. In R. Fivush & J. A. Hudson (Eds.), *Knowing and remembering in young children* (pp. 223–248). New York: Cambridge University Press.

Fivush, R., & Kuebli, J. (1997). Making everyday events emotional: The construal of emotion in parent–child conversations about the past. In N. L. Stein, P. A. Ornstein, B. Tversky, & C. Brainerd (Eds.), *Memory for everyday and emotional events* (pp. 239–266). Mahwah, NJ: Lawrence Erlbaum Associates.

Fivush, R., Kuebli, J., & Clubb, P. A. (1992). The structure of events and event representations: Developmental analysis. *Child Development, 63*, 188–201.

Fivush, R., Sales, J. M., Goldberg, A., Bahrick, L., & Parker, J. F. (2004). Weathering the storm: Children's long-term recall of Hurricane Andrew. *Memory, 12*, 104–118.

Fivush, R., & Schwarzmueller, A. (1998). Children remember childhood: Implications for childhood amnesia. *Applied Cognitive Psychology, 12*, 455–473.

Fivush, R., & Slackman, E. (1986). The acquisition and development of scripts. In K. Nelson (Ed.), *Event knowledge: Structure and function in development* (pp. 71–96). Hillsdale, NJ: Lawrence Erlbaum Associates.

Fivush, R., & Vasudeva, A. (2002). Remembering to relate: Socioemotional correlates of mother–child reminiscing. *Journal of Cognition and Development, 3*, 73–90.

Flavell, J. H., Beach, D. R., & Chinsky, J. H. (1966). Spontaneous verbal rehearsal in a memory task as a function of age. *Child Development, 37*, 283–299.

Fletcher, C. R., Briggs, A., & Linzie, B. (1997). Understanding the causal structure of narrative events. In P. van den Broek, P. J. Bauer, & T. Bourg (Eds.), *Developmental spans in event representation and comprehension: Bridging fictional and actual events* (pp. 343–360). Mahwah, NJ: Lawrence Erlbaum Associates.

Fletcher, P. C., Frith, C. D., & Rugg, M. D. (1997). The functional neuroanatomy of episodic memory. *Trends in Neuroscience, 20*, 213–218.

Foreman, N., Fielder, A., Minshell, C., Hurrion, E., & Sergienko, E. (1997). Visual search, perception, and visual-motor skill in "healthy" children born 27–32 weeks' gestation. *Journal of Experimental Child Psychology, 64*, 27–41.

Foster, J. C. (1928). Verbal memory in the preschool child. *Journal of Genetic Psychology, 35*, 26–44.

Frank, L. R. (Ed.). (2001). *Random House Webster's Quotationary.* New York: Random House.

Freud, S. (1899/1962). *The standard edition of the complete works of Sigmund Freud* (Vol. 3) (J. Sprachey, Trans.). Toronto: Hogarth.

Freud, S. (1905/1953). Childhood and concealing memories. In A. A. Brill (Trans. & Ed.), *The basic writings of Sigmund Freud* (pp. 62–68). New York: The Modern Library.

Freud, S. (1915/1959). Instincts and their vicissitudes. *Collected Papers.* New York: Basic Books.

Freud, S. (1916/1966). The archaic features and infantilism of dreams. In J. Strachey (Trans. & Ed.), *Introductory lectures on psychoanalysis* (pp. 199–212). New York: Norton.

Freud, S. (1920/1935). *A general introduction to psycho-analysis* (J. Riviere, Trans.). Garden City, NY: Garden City Publishing.

Friedman, A., & Pines, A. (1991). Sex differences in gender-related childhood memories. *Sex Roles, 25*, 25–32.

Friedman, W. J. (1992). Children's time memory: The development of a differentiated past. *Cognitive Development, 7*, 171–188.

Friedman, W. J., & Kemp, S. (1998). The effects of elapsed time and retrieval on young children's judgments of the temporal distances of past events. *Cognitive Development, 13*, 335–367.

Fujita, F., Diener, E., & Sandvik, E. (1991). Gender differences in negative affect and well-being: The case for emotional intensity. *Journal of Personality and Social Psychology, 61*, 427–434.

Fuster, J. M. (1997). Network memory. *Trends in Neuroscience, 20*, 451–459.

Fuster, J. M., & Alexander, G. E. (1971). Neuron activity related to short-term memory. *Science, 173*, 652–654.

Gabrieli, J. D. E., Carrillo, M. C., Cermak, L. S., McGlinchey-Berroth, R., Gluck, M., & Disterhoft, J. F. (1995). Intact delay-eyeblink classical conditioning in amnesia. *Behavioral Neuroscience, 109*, 819–827.

Gadian, D. G., Aicardi, J., Watkins, K. E., Porter, D. A., Mishkin, M., & Vargha-Khadem, F. (2000). Developmental amnesia associated with hear hypoxic-ischaemic injury. *Brain, 123*, 499–507.

Gaensbauer, T., Chatoor, I., Drell, M., Siegel, D., & Zeanah, C. H. (1995). Traumatic loss in a one-year-old girl. *Journal of the American Academy of Child and Adolescent Psychiatry, 34*, 520–528.

Gall, F. J. (1835). *The influence of the brain on the form of the head* (W. Lewis, Trans.). Boston: Marsh, Capen & Lyon.

Galton, F. (1879). Psychometric experiments. *Brain, 2*, 149–162.

Galton, F. (1880). Statistics of mental imagery. *Mind, 5*, 301–318.

Garavan, H., Pendergrass, J. C., Ross, T. J., Stein, E. A., & Risinger, R. C. (2001). Amygdala response to both positively and negatively valenced stimuli. *NeuroReport, 12*, 2779–2783.

Gelman, R., & Baillargeon, R. (1983). A review of some Piagetian concepts. In J. H. Flavell & E. M. Markman (Eds.), *Handbook of child psychology: Vol. III. Cognitive development* (pp. 167–230). New York: Wiley.

Georgieff, M. K., Landon, M. B., Mills, M. M., Hedlund, B. E., Faassen, A. E., Schmidt, R. L., Ophoven, J. J., & Widness, J. A. (1990). Abnormal iron distribution in infants of diabetic mothers: Spectrum and maternal antecedents. *Journal of Pediatrics, 117*, 455–461.

Georgieff, M. K., & Rao, R. (2001). The role of nutrition in cognitive development. In C. A. Nelson & M. Luciana (Eds.), *Handbook of developmental cognitive neuroscience* (pp. 491–504). Cambridge, MA: MIT Press.

Giambra, L. M., & Arenberg, D. (1993). Adult aging in forgetting sentences. *Psychology and Aging, 8,* 451–462.

Giedd, J. N., Blumenthal, J., Jeffries, N. O., Castellanos, F. X., Liu, H., & Zijdenbos, A., Paus, T., Evans, A. C., & Rapoport, J. L. (1999). Brain development during childhood and adolescence: A longitudinal MRI study. *Nature Neuroscience, 2,* 861–863.

Gluck, M. A., & Myers, C. E. (2001). *Gateway to memory: An introduction to neural network modeling of the hippocampus and learning.* Cambridge, MA: MIT Press.

Goldman, P. S., & Rosvold, H. E. (1970). Localization of function within the dorso-lateral prefrontal cortex of the rhesus monkey. *Experimental Neurology, 27,* 291–304.

Goldman, P. S., Rosvold, H. E., Vest, B., & Galkin, T. W. (1971). Analysis of the delayed alternation deficit produced by dorsolateral prefrontal lesions in the rhesus monkey. *Journal of Comparative Physiology and Psychology, 77,* 212–220.

Goldman-Rakic, P. S. (1987). Circuitry of primate prefrontal cortex and regulation of behavior by representational memory. In F. Plum (Ed.), *Handbook of physiology, the nervous system, higher functions of the brain* (Vol. 5, pp. 373–417). Bethesda, MD: American Physiological Society.

Goldsmith, H. H. (1996). Studying temperament via construction of the toddler behavior assessment questionnaire. *Child Development, 67,* 218–235.

Goodenough, F. L. (1926). *Measurement of intelligence by drawings.* Yonkers-on-Hudson, NY: World Book.

Goodenough, F. L. (1931). Anger in young children. *Institute of Child Welfare Monograph Series, No. 9.* Minneapolis: University of Minnesota Press.

Gordon, K. (1928). A study of early memories. *Journal Delinquent, 12,* 129–132.

Graf, P., & Schacter, D. L. (1985). Implicit and explicit memory for new associations in normal subjects and amnesic patients. *Journal of Experimental Psychology: Learning, Memory, and Cognition, 11,* 501–518.

Graf, P., Squire, L. R., & Mandler, G. (1984). The information that amnesic patients do not forget. *Journal of Experimental Psychology: Learning, Memory, and Cognition, 10,* 164–178.

Graham, K. S., & Hodges, J. R. (1997). Differentiating the roles of the hippocampal system and the neocortex in long-term memory storage: Evidence from the study of semantic dementia and Alzheimer's disease. *Neuropsychology, 11,* 77–89.

Gruendel, J. M. (1980). *Scripts and stories: A study of children's event narratives.* Unpublished doctoral dissertation, Yale University.

Gunnar, M. R. (1990). The psychobiology of infant temperament. In J. Colombo & J. Fagan (Eds.), *Individual differences in infancy: Reliability, stability, prediction.* Hillsdale, NJ: Lawrence Erlbaum Associates.

Gunnar, M. R. (2001). Effects of early deprivation: Findings from orphanage-reared infants and children. In C. A. Nelson & M. Luciana (Eds.), *Handbook of developmental cognitive neuroscience* (pp. 617–629). Cambridge, MA: MIT Press.

Gunnar, M. R., & Nelson, C. A. (1994). Event-related potentials in year-old infants predict negative emotionality and hormonal responses to separation. *Child Development, 65,* 80–94.

Haden, C. A. (1998). Reminiscing with different children: Relating maternal stylistic consistency and sibling similarity in talk about the past. *Developmental Psychology, 34,* 99–114.

Haden, C. A., Haine, R., & Fivush, R. (1997). Development narrative structure in parent–child conversations about the past. *Developmental Psychology, 33,* 295–307.

Haden, C. A., Ornstein, P. A., Eckerman, C. O., & Didow, S. M. (2001). Mother–child conversational interactions as events unfold: Linkages to subsequent remembering. *Child Development, 72,* 1016–1031.

Haist, F., Gore, J. B., & Mao, H. (2001). Consolidation of human memory over decades revealed by functional magnetic resonance imaging. *Nature Neuroscience, 4,* 1139–1145.

Hamond, N. R., & Fivush, R. (1991). Memories of Mickey Mouse: Young children recount their trip to Disneyworld. *Cognitive Development, 6,* 433–448.

Han, J. J., Leichtman, M. D., & Wang, Q. (1998). Autobiographical memory in Korean, Chinese, and American children. *Developmental Psychology, 34*, 701–713.

Hanna, E., & Meltzoff, A. N. (1993). Peer imitation by toddlers in laboratory, home, and daycare contexts: Implications for social learning and memory. *Developmental Psychology, 29*, 702–710.

Harley, K., & Reese, E. (1999). Origins of autobiographical memory. *Developmental Psychology, 35*, 1338–1348.

Hartup, W. W., Johnson, A., & Weinberg, R. A. (2001). *The Institute of Child Development: Pioneering in Science and Application 1925–2000.* Minneapolis: University of Minnesota Printing Services.

Haxby, J., Ungerleider, L., Horwitz, B., Maisog, J., Rappaport, S., & Grady, C. (1996). Face encoding and recognition in the human brain. *Proceedings of the National Academy of Sciences, 93*, 922–927.

Hebb, D. O. (1949). *The organization of behavior.* New York: Wiley.

Heidbreder, E. F. (1928). Problem solving in children and adults. *Journal of Genetic Psychology, 35*, 522–545.

Henri, V., & Henri, C. (1895a). On our earliest recollections of childhood. *American Journal of Psychology, 7*, 303–304.

Henri, V., & Henri, C. (1895b). On our earliest recollections of childhood. *Psychological Review, 2*, 215–216.

Henri, V., & Henri, C. (1896). Enquete sur les premiers souvenirs de l'enfance. *Annee Psychology, 3*, 184–198.

Henri, V., & Henri, C. (1898). Earliest recollections. *Popular Science Monthly, 53*, 108–115.

Herrmann, D. J. (1982). Know thy memory: The use of questionnaires to assess and study memory. *Psychological Bulletin, 92*, 434–452.

Hevner, R. F., & Kinney, H. C. (1996). Reciprocal entorhinal-hippocampal connections established by human fetal midgestation. *Journal of Comparative Neurology, 372*, 384–394.

Higley, L. D., Suomi, S. J., & Linnoila, M. (1992). A longitudinal study of CSF monoamine metabolite and plasma cortisol concentrations in young rhesus monkeys: Effects of early experience, age, sex, and stress on continuity of individual differences. *Biological Psychiatry, 32*, 127–145.

Hill, W. L., Borovsky, D., & Rovee-Collier, C. (1988). Continuities in infant memory development. *Developmental Psychobiology, 21*, 43–62.

Hilts, P. J. (1995). *Memory's ghost—The strange tale of Mr. M. and the nature of memory.* New York: Simon & Schuster.

Hodges, J. R. (2000). Memory in the dementias. In E. Tulving & F. I. M. Craik (Eds.), *The Oxford handbook of memory* (pp. 441–459). New York: Oxford University Press.

Hodges, J. R., & Graham, K. S. (1998). A reversal of the temporal gradient for famous person knowledge in semantic dementia: Implications for the neural organisation of long-term memory. *Neuropsychologia, 36*, 803–825.

Hodges, J. R., & Patterson, K. (1995). Is semantic memory consistently impaired early in the course of Alzheimer's disease? Neuroanatomical and diagnostic implications. *Neuropsychologia, 33*, 441–459.

Hodges, J. R., & Patterson, K. (1996). Non-fluent progressive aphasia and semantic dementia: A comparative neuropsychological study. *Journal of the International Neuropsychological Society, 2*, 511–525.

Holmes, D. S. (1970). Differential change in affective intensity and the forgetting of unpleasant personal experiences. *Journal of Personality and Social Psychology, 3*, 234–239.

Howe, M. L. (1995). Interference effects in young children's long-term retention. *Developmental Psychology, 31*, 579–596.

Howe, M. L. (2003). Memories from the cradle. *Current Directions in Psychological Science, 12*, 62–65.

Howe, M. L., & Brainerd, C. J. (1989). Development of children's long-term retention. *Developmental Review, 9*, 301–340.

Howe, M. L., & Courage, M. L. (1993). On resolving the enigma of infantile amnesia. *Psychological Bulletin, 113*, 305–326.

Howe, M. L., & Courage, M. L. (1997a). The emergence and early development of autobiographical memory. *Psychological Review, 104*, 499–523.

Howe, M. L., & Courage, M. L. (1997b). Independent paths in the development of infant learning and forgetting. *Journal of Experimental Child Psychology, 67*, 131–163.

Howe, M. L., & O'Sullivan, J. T. (1997). What children's memories tell us about recalling our childhoods: A review of storage and retrieval processes in the development of long-term retention. *Developmental Review, 17*, 148–204.

Howes, M., Siegel, M., & Brown, F. (1993). Early childhood memories: Accuracy and affect. *Cognition, 47*, 95–119.

Hudson, J. A. (1986). Memories are made of this: General event knowledge and the development of autobiographical memory. In K. Nelson (Ed.), *Event knowledge: Structure and function in development* (pp. 97–118). Hillsdale, NJ: Lawrence Erlbaum Associates.

Hudson, J. A. (1990a). Constructive processing in children's event memory. *Developmental Psychology, 26*, 180–187.

Hudson, J. A. (1990b). The emergence of autobiographical memory in mother–child conversation. In R. Fivush & J. A. Hudson (Eds.), *Knowing and remembering in young children* (pp. 166–196). Cambridge, MA: Cambridge University Press.

Hudson, J. A. (1991). Learning to reminisce: A case study. *Journal of Narrative and Life History, 1*, 295–324.

Hudson, J. A. (1993). Reminiscing with mothers and others: Autobiographical memory in young two-year-olds. *Journal of Narrative and Life History, 3*, 1–32.

Hudson, J. A., & Fivush, R. (1991). As time goes by: Sixth graders remember a kindergarten experience. *Applied Cognitive Psychology, 5*, 347–360.

Hudson, J. A., Fivush, R., & Kuebli, J. (1992). Scripts and episodes: The development of event memory. *Applied Cognitive Psychology, 6*, 483–505.

Hudson, J. A., & Nelson, K. (1986). Repeated encounters of a similar kind: Effects of familiarity on children's autobiographical memory. *Cognitive Development, 1*, 253–271.

Hudson, J. A., & Sheffield, E. G. (1998). Déjà vu all over again: Effects of reenactment on toddlers' event memory. *Child Development, 69*, 51–67.

Hulicka, I. M., & Weiss, R. L. (1965). Age differences in retention as a function of learning. *Journal of Consulting Psychology, 29*, 125–129.

Hutt, C. (1978). Biological bases of psychological sex differences. *American Journal of Diseases in Children, 132*, 170–177.

Huttenlocher, P. R. (1979). Synaptic density in human frontal cortex: Developmental changes and effects of aging. *Brain Research, 163*, 195–205.

Huttenlocher, P. R. (1990). Morphometric study of human cerebral cortex development. *Neuropsychologia, 28*, 517–527.

Huttenlocher, P. R. (1994). Synaptogenesis, synapse elimination, & neural plasticity in human cerebral cortex. In C. A. Nelson (Ed.), *The Minnesota symposium on child psychology: Vol. 27. Threats to optimal development: Integrating biological, psychological, and social risk factors* (pp. 35–54). Hillsdale, NJ: Lawrence Erlbaum Associates.

Huttenlocher, P. R. (2002). *Neural plasticity: The effects of environment on the development of the cerebral cortex.* Cambridge, MA: Harvard University Press.

Huttenlocher, P. R., & Dabholkar, A. S. (1997). Regional differences in synaptogenesis in human cerebral cortex. *Journal of Comparative Neurology, 387*, 167–178.

Inhelder, B., & Piaget, J. (1958). *The growth of logical thinking from childhood to adolescence.* New York: Basic Books.

James, W. (1890). *Principles of psychology.* Cambridge, MA: Harvard University Press.

James, W. (1892/1961). *Psychology: The briefer course*. New York: Harper.

Janowsky, J. S., Shimamura, A. P., & Squire, L. R. (1989). Source memory impairment in patients with frontal lobe lesions. *Neuropsychologia, 27*, 1043–1056.

Jetter, W., Poser, U., Freeman, R. B., & Markowitsch, H. J. (1986). A verbal long term memory deficit in frontal lobe damaged patients. *Cortex, 22*, 229–242.

Jiang, Z. D. (1995). Maturation of the auditory brainstem in low risk-preterm infants: A comparison with age-matched full term infants up to 6 years. *Early Human Development, 42*, 49–65.

Johnson, M. H. (1997). *Developmental cognitive neuroscience*. Oxford, England: Blackwell.

Johnson, M. K., Foley, M. A., Suengas, A. G., & Raye, C. L. (1988). Phenomenal characteristics of memories for perceived and imagined autobiographical events. *Journal of Experimental Psychology: General, 117*, 371–376.

Jones, C. H., & Pipe, M.-E. (2002). How quickly do children forget events? A systematic study of children's event reports as a function of delay. *Applied Cognitive Psychology, 16*, 755–768.

Kagan, J. (1972). A psychologist's account at mid-career. In T. S. Krawiec (Ed.), *The psychologists* (Vol. 1, pp. 137–165). New York: Oxford University Press.

Kandel, E. R., Schwartz, J. H., & Jessell, T. M. (2000). *Principles of neural science* (4th ed.). New York: McGraw-Hill.

Kandel, E. R., & Squire, L. R. (2000). Neuroscience: Breaking down scientific barriers to the study of brain and mind. *Science, 290*, 1113–1120.

Kapur, S., Craik, F. I. M., Jones, C., Brown, G. M., Houle, S., & Tulving, E. (1995). Functional role of the prefrontal cortex in memory retrieval: A PET study. *NeuroReport, 6*, 1880–1884.

Kapur, S., Tulving, E., Cabeza, R., McIntosh, A. R., Houle, S., & Craik, F. I. M. (1996). The neural correlates of intentional learning of verbal materials: A PET study in humans. *Cognitive Brain Research, 4*, 243–249.

Kihlstrom, J. F., & Harackiewicz, J. M. (1982). The earliest recollection: A new survey. *Journal of Personality, 50*, 134–148.

Kim, J. J., & Fanselow, M. S. (1992). Modality-specific retrograde amnesia of fear. *Science, 256*, 675–677.

Klein, P. J., & Meltzoff, A. N. (1999). Long-term memory, forgetting, and deferred imitation in 12-month-old infants. *Developmental Science, 2*, 102–113.

Kleist, K. (1934). Kriegsverletzungen des Gehirns in inhrer Bedeutung fur die Hirnlokalisation and Hirnpathologie. In K. Bonhoeffer (Ed.), *Handbuch der Aerztlichen Erfahrungen im Weltkriege 1914/1918: Vol. 4. Geistes- und Nervenkrankheiten* (pp. 343–1360). Leipzig: Barth.

Knopman, D. S., & Nissen, M. J. (1987). Implicit learning in patients with probable Alzheimer's disease. *Neurology, 5*, 784–788.

Knowlton, B. J., & Fanselow, M. S. (1998). The hippocampus, consolidation and on-line memory. *Current Opinion in Neurobiology, 8*, 293–296.

Koenderink, M. J. T., & Uylings, H. B. M. (1995). Postnatal maturation of layer V pyramidal neurons in the human prefrontal cortex. A quantitative Golgi analysis. *Brain Research, 678*, 233–243.

Koenderink, M. J. T., Uylings, H. B. M., & Mrzljak, L. (1994). Postnatal maturation of the layer III pyramidal neurons in the human prefrontal cortex: A quantitative Golgi study. *Brain Research, 653*, 173–182.

Köhler, S., McIntosh, A. R., Moscovitch, M., & Winocur, G. (1998). Functional interactions between the medial temporal lobes and posterior neocortex related to episodic memory retrieval. *Cerebral Cortex, 8*, 451–461.

Köhler, S., & Moscovitch, M. (1997). Unconscious visual processing in neuropsychological syndromes: A survey of the literature and evaluation of models of consciousness. In M. D. Rugg (Ed.), *Cognitive neuroscience* (pp. 305–373). London: UCL Press.

Köhler, S., Moscovitch, M., Winocur, G., Houle, S., & McIntosh, A. R. (1998). Networks of domain-specific and general regions involved in episodic memory for spatial location and object identity. *Neuropsychologia, 36*, 129–142.

Kopelman, M. D., Wilson, B. A., & Baddeley, A. D. (1989). The autobiographical memory interview: A new assessment of autobiographical and personal semantic memory in amnesic patients. *Journal of Clinical and Experimental Neuropsychology, 5,* 724–744.

Kopelman, M. D., Wilson, B. A., & Baddeley, A. D. (1990). *The Autobiographical Memory Interview.* Thurston, Suffolk, England: Thames Valley Test Company.

Koriat, A. (2000). Control processes in remembering. In E. Tulving & F. I. M. Craik (Eds.), *The Oxford handbook of memory* (pp. 333–346). New York: Oxford University Press.

Kostovic, I., Seress, L., Mrzljak, L., & Judas, M. (1989). Early onset of synapse formation in the human hippocampus: A correlation with Nissl-Golgi architectonics in 15- and 16.5-week-old fetuses. *Neuroscience, 30,* 105–116.

Kroll, N. E. A., Markowitsch, H. J., Knight, R. T., & von Cramon, D. Y. (1997). Retrieval of old memories: The temporofrontal hypothesis. *Brain, 120,* 1377–1399.

Kroupina, M. G., Bauer, P. J., Gunnar, M., & Johnson, D. (2004). *Explicit memory in post-institutionalized toddlers.* Manuscript in review.

Kuebli, J., Butler, S., & Fivush, R. (1995). Mother–child talk about past emotions: Relations of maternal language and child gender over time. *Cognition and Emotion, 9,* 265–283.

Larkin, E. C., Jarratt, B. A., & Rao, G. A. (1986). Reduction of relative levels of nervonic to lignoceric acid in the brain of rat pups due to iron deficiency. *Nutrition Research, 6,* 309–314.

Larsen, S. F. (1992). Personal context in autobiographical and narrative memories. In M. A. Conway, D. C. Rubin, H. Spinnler, & W. A. Wagenaar (Eds.), *Theoretical perspectives on autobiographical memory* (pp. 53–71). NATO ASI Series D: Behavioural and Social Sciences, Vol. 65. Dordrecht, The Netherlands: Kluwer Academic.

Larsen, S. F. (1998). What is it like to remember: On phenomenal qualities of memory. In C. P. Thompson, D. J. Hermann, D. Bruce, J. D. Read, D. G. Payne, & M. P. Toglia (Eds.), *Autobiographical memory: Theoretical and applied perspectives* (pp. 163–190). Mahwah, NJ: Lawrence Erlbaum Associates.

Lashley, K. S. (1950). In search of the engram. Symposia. *Society for Experimental Biology, 4,* 454–482.

Lechuga, M. T., Marcos-Ruiz, R., & Bauer, P. J. (2001). Episodic recall of specifics and generalisation coexist in 25-month-old children. *Memory, 9,* 117–132.

Leonard, B. W., Amaral, D. G., Squire, L. R., & Zola-Morgan, S. (1995). Transient memory impairment in monkeys with bilateral lesions of the entorhinal cortex. *The Journal of Neuroscience, 15,* 5637–5659.

Lepage, M., Habib, R., & Tulving, E. (1998). Hippocampal PET activations of memory encoding and retrieval: The HIPER model. *Hippocampus, 8,* 313–322.

Levine, B., Svoboda, E., Hay, J. F., Winocur, G., & Moscovitch, M. (2002). Aging and autobiographical memory: Dissociating episodic from semantic retrieval. *Psychology and Aging, 17,* 677–689.

Lewis, C., Freeman, N. H., Kyriakidou, C., Maridaki-Kassotaki, K., & Berridge, D. M. (1996). Social influences on false belief assess: Specific sibling influences or general apprenticeship? *Child Development, 67,* 2930–2947.

Lewis, K. D. (1999). Maternal style in reminiscing: Relations to child individual differences. *Cognitive Development, 14,* 381–399.

Lewis, M., & Brooks-Gunn, J. (1979). *Social cognition and the acquisition of self.* New York: Plenum.

Lewis, M., Feirinig, C., & Rosenthal, S. (2000). Attachment over time. *Child Development, 71,* 707–720.

Li, L., Miller, E. K., & Desimone, R. (1993). The representation of stimulus familiarity in anterior inferior temporal cortex. *Journal of Neurophysiology, 69,* 1918–1929.

Lie, E., & Newcombe, N. S. (1999). Elementary school children's explicit and implicit memory for faces of preschool classmates. *Developmental Psychology, 35,* 102–112.

Linton, M. (1975). Memory for real-world events. In D. A. Norman & D. E. Rumelhart (Eds.), *Explorations in cognition* (pp. 376–404). San Francisco, CA: Freeman.

Linton, M. (1978). Real world memory after six years: An *in vivo* study of very long term memory. In M. M. Gruneberg, P. E. Morris, & R. N. Sykes (Eds.), *Practical aspects of memory* (pp. 69–76). London: Academic Press.

Linton, M. (1982). Transformations of memory in everyday life. In U. Neisser (Ed.), *Memory observed: Remembering in natural contexts* (pp. 77–91). San Francisco, CA: Freeman.

Liston, C., & Kagan, J. (2002). Memory enhancement in early childhood. *Nature, 419,* 896.

Lockhart, R. S. (2000). Methods of memory research. In E. Tulving & F. I. M. Craik (Eds.), *The Oxford handbook of memory* (pp. 45–57). New York: Oxford University Press.

Lozoff, B. (1990). Has iron deficiency been shown to cause altered behavior in infants? In J. Dobbing (Ed.), *Brain, behavior and iron in the infant diet* (pp. 107–131). London: Springer-Verlag.

Lukowski, A. F., Wiebe, S. A., Haight, J. C., DeBoer, T., Nelson, C. A., & Bauer, P. J. (2005). Forming a stable memory representation in the first year of life: Why imitation is more than child's play. *Developmental Science, 8,* 279–298.

Luria, A. R. (1968). *The mind of a mnemonist: A little book about a vast memory* (L. Solotaroff, Trans.). Cambridge, MA: Harvard University Press.

MacDonald, S., Uesiliana, K., & Hayne, H. (2000). Cross-cultural and gender differences in childhood amnesia. *Memory, 8,* 365–376.

Maguire, E. A. (2001). Neuroimaging studies of autobiographical event memory. *Philosophical Transactions Royal Society of London, 356,* 1441–1451.

Maguire, E. A., Frackowiak, R. S. J., & Frith, C. D. (1996). Learning to find your way: A role for the human hippocampal formation. *Proceedings of the Royal Society of London Series, 263,* 1745–1750.

Maguire, E. A., Frith, C. D., Burgess, N., Donnett, J. G., & O'Keefe, J. (1998). Knowing where things are: Parahippocampal involvement in encoding object locations in virtual large-scale space. *Journal of Cognitive Neuroscience, 10,* 61–76.

Maguire, E. A., Henson, R. N. A., Mummery, C. J., & Frith, C. D. (2001). Activity in prefrontal cortex, not hippocampus, varies parametrically with the increasing remoteness of memories. *NeuroReport, 12,* 441–444.

Maguire, E. A., Mummery, C. J., & Büchel, C. (2000). Patterns of hippocampal-cortical interaction dissociate temporal lobe memory subsystems. *Hippocampus, 10,* 475–482.

Mandler, J. M. (1990a). Recall and its verbal expression. In R. Fivush & J. A. Hudson (Eds.), *Knowing and remembering in young children* (pp. 317–330). New York: Cambridge University Press.

Mandler, J. M. (1990b). Recall of events by preverbal children. In A. Diamond (Ed.), *The development and neural bases of higher cognitive functions* (pp. 485–516). New York: New York Academy of Science.

Mandler, J. M. (1998). Representation. In W. Damon (Editor-in-Chief) & D. Kuhn & R. S. Siegler (Vol. Eds.), *Handbook of child psychology: Vol. 2. Cognition, perception, and language* (5th ed., pp. 255–308). New York: Wiley.

Mandler, J. M. (2004). Two kinds of knowledge acquisition. In J. M. Lucariello, J. A. Hudson, R. Fivush, & P. J. Bauer (Eds.), *Development of the mediated mind: Culture and cognitive development. Essays in honor of Katherine Nelson* (pp. 13–32). Mahwah, NJ: Lawrence Erlbaum Associates.

Mandler, J. M., & DeForest, M. (1979). Is there more than one way to recall a story? *Child Development, 50,* 886–889.

Mandler, J. M., & Johnson, N. S. (1977). Remembrance of things parsed: Story structure and recall. *Cognitive Psychology, 9,* 111–151.

Mandler, J. M., & McDonough, L. (1995). Long-term recall of event sequences in infancy. *Journal of Experimental Child Psychology, 59,* 457–474.

Maratsos, M. (1998). The acquisition of grammar. In W. Damon (Editor-in-Chief) & D. Kuhn & R. S. Siegler (Vol. Eds.), *Handbook of child psychology: Vol. 2. Cognition, perception, and language* (5th ed., pp. 421–466). New York: Wiley.

Marcia, J. E. (1966). Development and validation of ego identity status. *Journal of Personality and Social Psychology, 3,* 551–558.

Marian, V., & Neisser, U. (2000). Language-dependent recall of autobiographical memories. *Journal of Experimental Psychology: General, 129,* 361–368.

Markowitsch, H. J. (1995). Which brain regions are critically involved in the retrieval of old episodic memory? *Brain Research Reviews, 21,* 117–127.

Markowitsch, H. J. (1996). Organic and psychogenic retrograde amnesia: Two sides of the same coin? *Neurocase, 2,* 357–371.

Markowitsch, H. J. (2000). Neuroanatomy of memory. In E. Tulving & F. I. M. Craik (Eds.), *The Oxford handbook of memory* (pp. 465–484). New York: Oxford University Press.

Markowitsch, H. J., Kalbe, E., Kessler, J., von Stockhausen, H.-M., Ghaemi, M., & Heiss, W.-D. (1999). Short-term memory deficit after focal parietal damage. *Journal of Clinical and Experimental Neuropsychology, 21,* 784–797.

Markowitsch, H. J., Weber-Luxenburger, G., Ewald, K., Kessler, J., & Heiss, W.-D. (1997). Patients with heart attacks are not valid models for medial temporal lobe amnesia: A neuropsychological and FDG-PET study with consequences for memory research. *European Journal of Neurology, 4,* 178–184.

Markus, H. R., & Kitayama, S. (1991). Culture and the self: Implications for cognition, emotion, and motivation. *Psychological Review, 98,* 224–253.

Marr, D. (1971). Simply memory: A theory for archicortex. *Philosophical Transactions of the Royal Society of London, Series B, 262,* 23–81.

Martin, A., Wiggs, C., Ungerleider, L., & Haxby, J. C. (1996). Neural correlates of category-specific knowledge. *Nature, 379,* 649–652.

Matthews, A., Ellis, A. E., & Nelson, C. A. (1996). Development of preterm and full-term infant ability on AB, recall memory, transparent barrier detour, and means-end. *Child Development, 67,* 2658–2676.

Mayes, A. R. (2000). Selective memory disorders. In E. Tulving & F. I. M. Craik (Eds.), *The Oxford handbook of memory* (pp. 427–440). New York: Oxford University Press.

McCabe, A., & Peterson, C. (1991). Getting the story: A longitudinal study of parental styles in eliciting narratives and developing narrative skill. In A. McCabe & C. Peterson (Eds.), *Developing narrative structure* (pp. 217–253). Hillsdale, NJ: Lawrence Erlbaum Associates.

McCarthy, R. A., & Warrington, E. K. (1990). *Cognitive neuropsychology.* San Diego, CA: Academic Press.

McClelland, J. L., McNaughton, B. L., & O'Reilly, R. C. (1995). Why there are complementary learning systems in the hippocampus and neocortex: Insights from the successes and failures of connectionist models of learning and memory. *Psychological Review, 102,* 419–457.

McCloskey, M., & Cohen, N. J. (1989). Catastrophic interference in connectionist networks: The sequential learning problem. In G. H. Bower (Ed.), *The psychology of learning and motivation* (Vol. 24, pp. 109–165). New York: Academic Press.

McCloskey, M., Wible, C. G., & Cohen, N. J. (1988). Is there a special flashbulb memory mechanism? *Journal of Experimental Psychology: General, 117,* 171–181.

McCormack, T., & Hoerl, C. (2001). The child in time: Temporal concepts and self-consciousness in the development of episodic memory. In C. Moore & K. Lemmon (Eds.), *The self in time: Developmental perspectives* (pp. 203–227). Mahwah, NJ: Lawrence Erlbaum Associates.

McDonough, L., Mandler, J. M., McKee, R. D., & Squire, L. R. (1995). The deferred imitation task as a nonverbal measure of declarative memory. *Proceedings of the National Academy of Sciences, 92,* 7580–7584.

McGaugh, J. L. (2000). Memory—A century of consolidation. *Science, 287,* 248–251.

McIntosh, A. R., Nyberg, L., Bookstein, F. L., & Tulving, E. (1997). Differential functional connectivity of prefrontal and medial temporal cortices during episodic memory retrieval. *Human Brain Mapping, 5,* 323–327.

McKee, R. D., & Squire, L. R. (1993). On the development of declarative memory. *Journal of Experimental Psychology: Learning, Memory, and Cognition, 19,* 397–404.

Mead, G. H. (1934). *Mind, self, and society.* Chicago, IL: University of Chicago Press.

Meltzoff, A. N. (1985). Immediate and deferred imitation in fourteen- and twenty-four-month-old infants. *Child Development, 56,* 62–72.

Meltzoff, A. N. (1988a). Infant imitation after a 1-week delay: Long-term memory for novel acts and multiple stimuli. *Developmental Psychology, 24,* 470–476.

Meltzoff, A. N. (1988b). Infant imitation and memory: Nine-month-olds in immediate and deferred tests. *Child Development, 59,* 217–225.

Meltzoff, A. N. (1988c). Imitation of televised models by infants. *Child Development, 59,* 1221–1229.

Meltzoff, A. N. (1990). The implications of cross-modal matching and imitation for the development of representation and memory in infants. In A. Diamond (Ed.), *The development and neural bases of higher cognitive functions* (pp. 1–35). New York: New York Academy of Science.

Meltzoff, A. N. (1995). What infant memory tells us about infantile amnesia: Long-term recall and deferred imitation. *Journal of Experimental Child Psychology, 59,* 497–515.

Miles, C. (1893). A study of individual psychology. *American Journal of Psychology, 6,* 534–558.

Miller, E. K., Gochin, P. M., & Gross, C. G. (1991). Habituation-like decrease in the responses of neurons in inferior temporal cortex of the macaque. *Visual Neuroscience, 7,* 357–362.

Miller, P., & Sperry, L. L. (1988). Early talk about the past: The origins of conversational stories of personal experience. *Journal of Child Language, 15,* 293–315.

Milner, B. M., Corkin, S., & Teuber, H. L. (1968). Further analysis of the hippocampal amnesic syndrome: 14-year followup study of H. M. *Neuropsychologia, 6,* 215–234.

Milner, B. M., McAndrews, P., & Leonard, G. (1990). Frontal lobes and memory for the temporal order of recent events. *Cold Springs Harbor Symposium on Quantitative Biology, 55,* 987–994.

Milner, B. M., & Petrides, M. (1984). Behavioural effects of frontal-lobe lesions in man. *Trends in Neuroscience, 7,* 403–407.

Mishkin, M. (1978). Memory in monkeys severely impaired by combined but not by separate removal of amygdala and hippocampus. *Nature, 273,* 297–298.

Mishkin, M., & Petri, H. L. (1984). Memories and habits: Some implications for the analysis of learning and retention. In L. Squire & N. Butters (Eds.), *Neuropsychology of memory* (pp. 287–296). New York: Guilford.

Mishkin, M., Spiegler, B. J., Saunders, R. C., & Malamut, B. J. (1982). An animal model of global amnesia. In S. Corkin, K. L. Davis, J. H. Growdon, E. J. Usdin, & R. J. Wurtman (Eds.), *Toward a treatment of Alzheimer's disease* (pp. 235–247). New York: Raven.

Mishkin, M., Vargha-Khadem, F., & Gadian, D. G. (1998). Amnesia and the organization of the hippocampal system. *Hippocampus, 8,* 212–216.

Monk, C. S., Webb, S. J., & Nelson, C. A. (2001). Prenatal neurobiological development: Molecular mechanisms and anatomical change. *Developmental Neuropsychology, 19,* 211–236.

Monk, C. S., Zhuang, J., Curtis, W. J., Ofenloch, I.-T., Tottenham, N., Nelson, C. A., & Hu, X. (2002). Human hippocampal activation in the delayed matching- and nonmatching-to-sample memory tasks: An event-related functional MRI approach. *Behavioral Neuroscience, 116,* 716–721.

Moore, C., & Lemmon, K. (Eds.). (2001). *The self in time: Developmental perspectives.* Mahwah, NJ: Lawrence Erlbaum Associates.

Morrison, F. J., Haith, M. M., & Kagan, J. (1980). Age trends in recognition memory for pictures: The effects of delay and testing procedure. *Bulletin of the Psychonomic Society, 16,* 480–483.

Moscovitch, M. (1984). Preface. In M. Moscovitch (Ed.), *Infant memory: Its relation to normal and pathological memory in humans and other animals* (pp. ix–x). New York: Plenum.

Moscovitch, M. (1992). Memory and working-with-memory: A component process model based on modules and central systems. *Journal of Cognitive Neuroscience, 4*, 257–266.

Moscovitch, M. (2000). Theories of memory and consciousness. In E. Tulving & F. I. M. Craik (Eds.), *The Oxford handbook of memory* (pp. 609–625). New York: Oxford University Press.

Moscovitch, M., & Nadel, L. (1998). Consolidation and the hippocampal complex revisited: In defense of the multiple-trace model. *Current Opinion in Neurobiology, 8*, 297–300.

Mullen, M. K. (1994). Earliest recollections of childhood: A demographic analysis. *Cognition, 52*, 55–79.

Mullen, M. K., & Yi, S. (1995). The cultural context of talk about the past: Implications for the development of autobiographical memory. *Cognitive Development, 10*, 407–419.

Müller, G. E., & Pilzecker, A. (1900). Experimentalle Beitrage zur Lehre vom Gedachtnis. *Zeitschrift fur Psychologie, 1*, 1–300.

Murachver, T., Pipe, M. E., Gordon, R., Owens, J. L., & Fivush, R. (1996). Do, show, and tell: Children's event memories acquired through direct experience, observation, and stories. *Child Development, 67*, 3029–3044.

Murray, E. A., & Mishkin, M. (1998). Object recognition and location memory in monkeys with excitotoxic lesions of the amygdala and hippocampus. *Journal of Neuroscience, 18*, 6568–6582.

Musen, G., & Squire, L. R. (1991). Normal acquisition of novel verbal information in amnesia. *Journal of Experimental Psychology: Learning, Memory, and Cognition, 17*, 1095–1104.

Myers, N. A., Perris, E. E., & Speaker, C. J. (1994). Fifty months of memory: A longitudinal study in early childhood. *Memory, 2*, 383–415.

Nadel, L., & Moscovitch, M. (1997). Memory consolidation, retrograde amnesia and the hippocampal complex. *Current Opinion in Neurobiology, 7*, 217–227.

Nadel, L., & Willner, J. (1989). Some implications of postnatal maturation of the hippocampus. In V. Chan-Palay & C. Köhler (Eds.), *The hippocampus—New vistas* (pp. 17–31). New York: Alan R. Liss.

Nadel, L., & Zola-Morgan, S. (1984). Infantile amnesia: A neurobiological perspective. In M. Moscovitch (Ed.), *Infant memory: Its relation to normal and pathological memory in humans and other animals* (pp. 145–172). New York: Plenum.

Nader, K. (2003). Memory traces unbound. *Trends in Neuroscience, 26*, 65–72.

Neimeyer, G. J., & Metzler, A. E. (1994). Personal identity and autobiographical recall. In U. Neisser & R. Fivush (Eds.), *The remembering self: Construction and accuracy in the self-narrative* (pp. 105–135). New York: Cambridge University Press.

Neimeyer, G. J., & Rareshide, M. B. (1991). Personal memories and personal identity: The impact of ego identity development on autobiographical memory recall. *Journal of Personality and Social Psychology, 60*, 562–569.

Neisser, U. (1962). Cultural and cognitive discontinuity. In T. E. Gladwin & W. Sturtevant (Eds.), *Anthropology and human behavior* (pp. 54–71). Washington, DC: Anthropological Society of Washington DC.

Neisser, U. (1982). Memory: What are the important questions? In U. Neisser (Ed.), *Memory observed: Remembering in natural contexts* (pp. 3–19). New York: W.H. Freeman.

Neisser, U., & Harsch, N. (1992). Phantom flashbulbs: False recollections of hearing the news about *Challenger*. In E. Winograd & U. Neisser (Eds.), *Affect and accuracy in recall: Studies of "flashbulb" memories* (pp. 9–31). New York: Cambridge University Press.

Neisser, U., & Libby, L. K. (2000). Remembering life experiences. In E. Tulving & F. I. M. Craik (Eds.), *The Oxford handbook of memory* (pp. 315–332). New York: Oxford University Press.

Nelson, C. A. (1995). The ontogeny of human memory: A cognitive neuroscience perspective. *Developmental Psychology, 31*, 723–738.

Nelson, C. A. (1997). The neurobiological basis of early memory development. In N. Cowan (Ed.), *The development of memory in childhood* (pp. 41–82). Hove, East Sussex: Psychology Press.

Nelson, C. A. (2000). Neural plasticity and human development: The role of early experience in sculpting memory systems. *Developmental Science, 3,* 115–136.

Nelson, C. A., & Bloom, F. E. (1997). Child development and neuroscience. *Child Development, 68,* 970–987.

Nelson, C. A., & Collins, P. F. (1991). Event-related potential and looking time analysis of infants' responses to familiar and novel events: Implications for visual recognition memory. *Developmental Psychology, 27,* 50–58.

Nelson, C. A., & Collins, P. F. (1992). Neural and behavioral correlates of recognition memory in 4- and 8-month-old infants. *Brain and Cognition, 19,* 105–121.

Nelson, C. A., & Dukette, D. (1998). A cognitive neuroscience perspective on the relation between attention and memory development. In J. E. Richards (Ed.), *Cognitive neuroscience of attention: A developmental perspective* (pp. 327–362). Mahwah, NJ: Lawrence Erlbaum Associates.

Nelson, C. A., & Monk, C. S. (2001). The use of event-related potentials in the study of cognitive development. In C. A. Nelson & M. Luciana (Eds.), *Handbook of developmental cognitive neuroscience* (pp. 125–136). Cambridge, MA: MIT Press.

Nelson, C. A., & Webb, S. J. (2002). A cognitive neuroscience perspective on early memory development. In M. de Haan & M. H. Johnson (Eds.), *The cognitive neuroscience of development* (pp. 99–125). London: Psychology Press.

Nelson, K. (1978). How young children represent knowledge of their world in and out of language. In R. S. Siegler (Ed.), *Children's thinking: What develops?* (pp. 255–273). Hillsdale, NJ: Lawrence Erlbaum Associates.

Nelson, K. (1984). The transition from infant to child memory. In M. Moscovitch (Ed.), *Infant memory: Its relation to normal and pathological memory in humans and other animals* (pp. 103–130). New York: Plenum.

Nelson, K. (1986). *Event knowledge: Structure and function in development.* Hillsdale, NJ: Lawrence Erlbaum Associates.

Nelson, K. (1989). *Narratives from the crib.* Cambridge, MA: Harvard University Press.

Nelson, K. (1993a). Events, narratives, memory: What develops? In C. A. Nelson (Ed.), *The Minnesota symposium on child psychology: Vol. 26. Memory and affect in development* (pp. 1–24). Hillsdale, NJ: Lawrence Erlbaum Associates.

Nelson, K. (1993b). The psychological and social origins of autobiographical memory. *Psychological Science, 4,* 7–14.

Nelson, K. (1996). *Language in cognitive development: The emergence of the mediated mind.* New York: Cambridge University Press.

Nelson, K. (1997). Event representations then, now, and next. In P. van den Broek, P. J. Bauer, & T. Bourg (Eds.), *Developmental spans in event representation and comprehension: Bridging fictional and actual events* (pp. 1–26). Mahwah, NJ: Lawrence Erlbaum Associates.

Nelson, K., & Fivush, R. (2000). Socialization of memory. In E. Tulving & F. I. M. Craik (Eds.), *The Oxford handbook of memory* (pp. 283–295). New York: Oxford University Press.

Nelson, K., & Fivush, R. (2004). The emergence of autobiographical memory: A social cultural developmental theory. *Psychological Review, 111,* 486–511.

Nelson, K., & Gruendel, J. (1981). Generalized event representations: Basic building blocks of cognitive development. In M. E. Lamb & A. L. Brown (Eds.), *Advances in developmental psychology* (Vol. 1, pp. 131–158). Hillsdale, NJ: Lawrence Erlbaum Associates.

Nelson, K., & Gruendel, J. (1986). Children's scripts. In K. Nelson (Ed.), *Event knowledge: Structure and function in development* (pp. 21–46). Hillsdale, NJ: Lawrence Erlbaum Associates.

Nelson, K., & Ross, G. (1980). The generalities and specifics of long-term memory in infants and young children. In M. Perlmutter (Ed.), *New directions in child development—Children's memory* (pp. 87–101). San Francisco: Jossey-Bass.

Newcombe, N., & Fox, N. (1994). Infantile amnesia: Through a glass darkly. *Child Development, 65*, 31–40.

Newcombe, R., & Reese, E. (2003). *Reflections on a shared past: Attachment security and mother–child reminiscing.* Paper presented at the 70th biennial meeting of the Society for Research in Child Development, Tampa, FL.

Niki, K., & Luo, J. (2002). An fMRI study on the time-limited role of the medial temporal lobe in long-term topographical autobiographical memory. *Journal of Cognitive Neuroscience, 14*, 500–507.

Nowakowski, R. S., & Rakic, P. (1981). The site of origin and route and rate of migration of neurons to the hippocampal region of the rhesus monkey. *Journal of Comparative Neurology, 196*, 129–154.

Nyberg, L. (1998). Mapping episodic memory. *Behavioral Brain Research, 90*, 107–114.

Nyberg, L., & Cabeza, R. (2000). Brain imaging of memory. In E. Tulving & F. I. M. Craik (Eds.), *The Oxford handbook of memory* (pp. 501–519). New York: Oxford University Press.

Nyberg, L., Cabeza, R., & Tulving, E. (1996). PET studies of encoding and retrieval: The HERA model. *Psychonomic Bulletin and Review, 3*, 135–148.

Nyberg, L., McIntosh, A. R., Cabeza, R., Nilsson, L.-G., Houle, S., Habib, R., & Tulving, E. (1996). Network analysis of positron emission tomography regional cerebral blood flow data: Ensemble inhibition during episodic memory retrieval. *Journal of Neuroscience, 16*, 3753–3759.

Nyberg, L., Tulving, E., Habib, R., Nilsson, L.-G., Kapur, S., Houle, S., & McIntosh, A. R. (1995). Functional brain maps of retrieval mode and recovery of episodic information. *NeuroReport, 7*, 249–252.

O'Neill, D. K., Astington, J. W., & Flavell, J. H. (1992). Young children's understanding of the role that sensory experiences play in knowledge acquisition. *Child Development, 63*, 474–490.

Orlofsky, J., & Frank, M. (1986). Personality structure as viewed through early memories and identity status in college men and women. *Journal of Personality and Social Psychology, 50*, 580–586.

Paldino, A., & Purpura, D. (1979). Quantitative analysis of the spatial distribution of axonal and dendritic terminals of hippocampal pyramidal neurons in immature human brain. *Experimental Neurology, 64*, 604–619.

Pascual-Leone, J. (1970). A mathematical model for the transition rule in Piaget's developmental stages. *Acta Psychologica, 32*, 301–345.

Patterson, K., & Hodges, J. R. (1995). Disorders of semantic memory. In A. D. Baddeley, B. A. Wilson, & F. N. Watts (Eds.), *Handbook of memory disorders* (pp. 167–187). Chichester, UK: Wiley.

Perlmutter, M. (Ed.). (1980). *New directions for child development: Children's memory.* San Francisco, CA: Jossey-Bass.

Perner, J. (1991). *Understanding the representational mind.* Cambridge, MA: MIT Press.

Perner, J. (2000). Memory and theory of mind. In E. Tulving & F. I. M. Craik (Eds.), *The Oxford handbook of memory* (pp. 297–312). New York: Oxford University Press.

Perner, J. (2001). Episodic memory: Essential distinctions and developmental implications. In C. Moore & K. Lemmon (Eds.), *The self in time: Developmental perspectives* (pp. 181–202). Mahwah, NJ: Lawrence Erlbaum Associates.

Perner, J., & Ruffman, T. (1995). Episodic memory and autonoetic consciousness: Developmental evidence and a theory of childhood amnesia. *Journal of Experimental Child Psychology, 59*, 516–548.

Perner, J., Ruffman, T., & Leekam, S. R. (1994). Theory of mind is contagious: You can catch it from your sibs. *Child Development, 65*, 1228–1238.

Peterson, C. (1990). The who, when and where of early narratives. *Journal of Child Language, 17,* 433–455.

Peterson, C., & McCabe, A. (1983). *Developmental psycholinguistics: Three ways of looking at a child's narrative.* New York: Plenum.

Peterson, C., & McCabe, A. (1992). Parental styles of narrative elicitation: Effect on children's narrative structure and content. *First Language, 12,* 299–321.

Peterson, C., & McCabe, A. (1994). A social interactionist account of developing decontextualized narrative skill. *Developmental Psychology, 30,* 937–948.

Peterson, C., & Rideout, R. (1998). Memory for medical emergencies experienced by 1- and 2-year-olds. *Developmental Psychology, 34,* 1059–1072.

Peterson, C., & Whalen, N. (2001). Five years later: Children's memory for medical emergencies. *Applied Cognitive Psychology, 15,* S7–S24.

Petersson, K. M., Elfgren, C., & Ingvar, M. (1997). A dynamic role of the medial temporal lobe during retrieval of declarative memory in man. *Neuroimage, 6,* 1–11.

Petrides, M. (1995). Impairments on nonspatial self-ordered and externally ordered working memory tasks after lesions of the mid-dorsal part of the lateral frontal cortex in monkeys. *The Journal of Neuroscience, 15,* 359–375.

Pezdek, K. (2003). Event memory and autobiographical memory for the events of September 11, 2001. *Applied Cognitive Psychology, 17,* 1033–1045.

Pfluger, T., Weil, S., Wies, S., Vollmar, C., Heiss, D., Egger, J., Scheck, R., & Hahn, K. (1999). Normative volumetric data of the developing hippocampus in children based on magnetic resonance imaging. *Epilepsia, 40,* 414–423.

Piefke, M., Weiss, P. H., Zilles, K., Markowitsch, H. J., & Fink, G. R. (2003). Differential remoteness and emotional tone modulate the neural correlates of autobiographical memory. *Brain, 126,* 650–668.

Piaget, J. (1926). *The language and thought of the child.* New York: Harcourt, Brace.

Piaget, J. (1952). *The origins of intelligence in children.* New York: International Universities Press.

Piaget, J. (1954). *The construction of reality in the child.* New York: Basic Books.

Piaget, J. (1962). *Play, dreams and imitation in childhood.* New York: W. W. Norton.

Piaget, J. (1969). *The child's conception of time.* London: Routledge & Kegan Paul.

Piefke, M., Weiss, P. H., Zilles, K., Markowitsch, H. J., & Fink, G. R. (2003). Differential remoteness and emotional tone modulate the neural correlates of autobiographical memory. *Brain, 126,* 650–668.

Pillemer, D. B. (1992). Remembering personal circumstances: A functional analysis. In E. Winograd & U. Neisser (Eds.), *Affect and accuracy in recall: Studies of "flashbulb" memories* (pp. 236–264). New York: Cambridge University Press.

Pillemer, D. B. (1998). *Momentous events, vivid memories: How unforgettable moments help us understand the meaning of our lives.* Cambridge, MA: Harvard University Press.

Pillemer, D. B., Picariello, M. L., Law, A. B., & Reichman, J. S. (1996). Memories of college: The importance of specific educational episodes. In D. C. Rubin (Ed.), *Remember our past* (pp. 318–337). Cambridge, UK: Cambridge University Press.

Pillemer, D. B., Picariello, M. L., & Pruett, J. C. (1994). Very long-term memories of a salient preschool event. *Applied Cognitive Psychology, 8,* 95–106.

Pillemer, D. B., & White, S. H. (1989). Childhood events recalled by children and adults. In H. W. Reese (Ed.), *Advances in child development and behavior* (Vol. 21, pp. 297–340). Orlando, FL: Academic Press.

Plato. (~354 BCE). *Collected works of Plato* (Vol. 5) (E. Grassi, Ed.). Hamburg, Germany: Rowohlt.

Potwin, E. B. (1901). Study of early memories. *Psychological Review, 8,* 596–601.

Povinelli, D. J. (1995). The unduplicated self. In P. Rochat (Ed.), *The self in early infancy* (pp. 161–192). Amsterdam: Elsevier.

Povinelli, D. J. (2001). The self: Elevated in consciousness and extended in time. In C. Moore & K. Lemmon (Eds.), *The self in time: Developmental perspectives* (pp. 75–95). Mahwah, NJ: Lawrence Erlbaum Associates.

Povinelli, D. J., Landau, K. R., & Perilloux, H. K. (1996). Self-recognition in young children using delayed versus live feedback: Evidence of a developmental asynchrony. *Child Development, 67,* 1540–1554.

Priel, B., & De Schonen, S. (1986). Self-recognition: A study of a population without mirrors. *Journal of Experimental Child Psychology, 41,* 237–250.

Quas, J. A., Goodman, G. S., Bibrose, S., Pipe, M.-E., Craw, S., & Ablin, D. S. (1999). Emotion and memory: Children's long-term remembering, forgetting, and suggestibility. *Journal of Experimental Child Psychology, 72,* 235–270.

Rabbitt, P., & McInnis, L. (1988). Do clever old people have earlier and richer first memories? *Psychology and Aging, 3,* 338–341.

Rakic, P., & Nowakowski, R. S. (1981). The time of origin of neurons in the hippocampal region of the rhesus monkey. *Journal of Comparative Neurology, 196,* 99–128.

Ratcliff, R. (1990). Connectionist models of recognition memory: Constraints imposed by learning and forgetting functions. *Psychological Review, 97,* 285–308.

Ratner, H. H., Smith, B. S., & Dion, S. A. (1986). Development of memory for events. *Journal of Experimental Child Psychology, 41,* 411–428.

Ratner, H. H., Smith, B. S., & Padgett, R. J. (1990). Children's organization of events and event memories. In R. Fivush & J. A. Hudson (Eds.), *Knowing and remembering in young children* (pp. 65–93). New York: Cambridge University Press.

Reed, J. M., & Squire, L. R. (1998). Retrograde amnesia for facts and events: Findings from four new cases. *The Journal of Neuroscience, 18,* 3943–3954.

Reese, E., & Brown, N. (2000). Reminiscing and recounting in the preschool years. *Applied Cognitive Psychology, 14,* 1–17.

Reese, E., & Fivush, R. (1993). Parental styles of talking about the past. *Developmental Psychology, 29,* 596–606.

Reese, E., Haden, C. A., & Fivush, R. (1993). Mother–child conversations about the past: Relationships of style and memory over time. *Cognitive Development, 8,* 403–430.

Reese, E., Haden, C., & Fivush, R. (1996). Mothers, fathers, daughters, sons: Gender differences in reminiscing. *Research on Language and Social Interaction, 29,* 27–56.

Reinisch, J. M., Rosenblum, L. A., Rubin, D. B., & Schulsinger, M. F. (1991). Sex differences in developmental milestones during the first year of life. *Journal of Psychology and Human Sexuality, 4,* 19.

Reisberg, D., Heuer, F., McLean, J., & O'Shaughnessy, M. (1988). The quantity, not the quality, of affect predicts memory vividness. *Bulletin of the Psychonomic Society, 26,* 100–103.

Ribot, T. (1881). *Les maladies de la memoire* [Diseases of memory]. Paris: Germer Baillere.

Ribot, T. (1882). *Diseases of memory.* New York: D. Appleton.

Roediger, H. L., & Blaxton, T. A. (1987). Effects of varying modality, surface features, and retention interval on priming in word-fragment completion. *Memory & Cognition, 15,* 379–388.

Roediger, H. L., Rajaram, S., & Srinivas, K. (1990). Specifying criteria for postulating memory systems. *Annals of the New York Academy of Sciences, 608,* 572–589.

Roisman, G. I., Madsen, S. D., Henninghausen, K. H., Sroufe, L. A., & Collins, W. A. (2001). The coherence of dyadic behavior across parent–child and romantic relationships as mediated by the internalized representation of experience. *Attachment & Human Development, 3,* 156–172.

Rosch, E. H., & Mervis, C. B. (1975). Family resemblances: Studies in the internal structure of categories. *Cognitive Psychology, 7,* 573–605.

Rose, S. A., & Feldman, J. F. (1997). Memory and speed: Their role in the relation of infant information processing to later IQ. *Child Development, 68,* 630–641.

Rose, S. A., Gottfried, A. W., Melloy-Carminar, P., & Bridger, W. H. (1982). Familiarity and novelty preferences in infant recognition memory: Implications for information processing. *Developmental Psychology, 18*, 704–713.

Rothbart, M. K. (1981). Measurement of temperament in infancy. *Child Development, 52*, 569–578.

Rothbart, M. K., & Bates, J. E. (1998). Temperament. In W. Damon (Editor-in-Chief) & W. S. E. Damon & N. V. E. Eisenberg (Vol. Eds.), *Handbook of child psychology: Vol. 3. Social, emotional and personality development* (5th ed., pp. 105–176). New York: Wiley.

Rothbart, M. K., & Posner, M. I. (2001). Mechanism and variation in the development of attentional networks. In C. A. Nelson & M. Luciana (Eds.), *Handbook of developmental cognitive neuroscience* (pp. 353–363). Cambridge, MA: MIT Press.

Rovee-Collier, C. (1997). Dissociations in infant memory: Rethinking the development of implicit and explicit memory. *Psychological Review, 104*, 467–498.

Rovee-Collier, C., & Gerhardstein, P. (1997). The development of infant memory. In N. Cowan (Ed.), *The development of memory in childhood* (pp. 5–39). Hove, East Sussex: Psychology Press.

Rovee-Collier, C., & Hayne, H. (2000). Memory in infancy and early childhood. In E. Tulving & F. I. M. Craik (Eds.), *The Oxford handbook of memory* (pp. 267–282). New York: Oxford University Press.

Rovee-Collier, C., Schechter, A., Shyi, G., & Shields, P. (1992). Perceptual identification of contextual attributes and infant memory retrieval. *Developmental Psychology, 28*, 307–318.

Rovee-Collier, C., Sullivan, M. W., Enright, M. K., Lucas, D., & Fagen, J. W. (1980). Reactivation of infant memory. *Science, 208*, 1159–1161.

Rubin, D. C. (1982). On the retention function for autobiographical memory. *Journal of Verbal Learning and Verbal Behavior, 21*, 21–38.

Rubin, D. C. (1998). Beginnings of a theory of autobiographical remembering. In C. P. Thompson, D. J. Herrmann, D. Bruce, J. D. Read, D. G. Payne, & M. P. Toglia (Eds.), *Autobiographical memory: Theoretical and applied perspectives* (pp. 47–67). Mahwah, NJ: Lawrence Erlbaum Associates.

Rubin, D. C. (2000). The distribution of early childhood memories. *Memory, 8*, 265–269.

Rubin, D. C., & Kozin, M. (1984). Vivid memories. *Cognition, 16*, 81–95.

Rubin, D. C., Rahhal, T. A., & Poon, L. W. (1998). Things learned in early adulthood are remembered best. *Memory and Cognition, 26*, 3–19.

Rubin, D. C., & Schulkind, M. D. (1997). The distribution of important and word-cued autobiographical memories in 20-, 35-, and 70-year-old adults. *Psychology and Aging, 12*, 524–535.

Rubin, D. C., & Wenzel, A. E. (1996). One hundred years of forgetting: A quantitative description of retention. *Psychological Review, 103*, 734–760.

Rubin, D. C., Wetzler, S. E., & Nebes, R. D. (1986). Autobiographical memory across the adult lifespan. In D. C. Rubin (Ed.), *Autobiographical memory* (pp. 202–221). Cambridge: Cambridge University Press.

Rudy, L., & Goodman, G. S. (1991). Effects of participation on children's reports: Implications for children's testimony. *Developmental Psychology, 27*, 527–538.

Rugg, M. D., Fletcher, P. C., Frith, C. D., Frackowiak, R. S. J., & Dolan, R. J. (1996). Differential activation of the prefrontal cortex in successful and unsuccessful memory retrieval. *Brain, 119*, 2073–2083.

Rugg, M. D., Fletcher, P. C., Frith, C. D., Frackowiak, R. S. J., & Dolan, R. J. (1997). Brain regions supporting intentional and incidental memory: A PET study. *NeuroReport, 8*, 1283–1287.

Rutter, M., & the English and Romanian Adoptees (ERP) study team. (1998). Developmental catch-up, and deficit, following adoption after severe global early privation. *Journal of Child Psychology and Psychiatry, 39*, 465–476.

Sachs, J. (1983). Talking about the there and then: The emergence of displaced reference in parent–child discourse. In K. Nelson (Ed.), *Children's language* (Vol. 4, pp. 1–28). Hillsdale, NJ: Lawrence Erlbaum Associates.

Sacks, O. (1985). *The man who mistook his wife for a hat.* New York: HarperCollins.

Sagar, H. H., Cohen, N. J., Corkin, S., & Growdon, J. H. (1985). Dissociations among processes in remote memory. In D. S. Olton, E. Gamzu, & S. Corkin (Eds.), *Memory dysfunctions* (pp. 533–535). New York: New York Academy of Science.

Sarter, M., & Markowitsch, H. J. (1985). The amygdala's role in human mnemonic processing. *Cortex, 21*, 7–24.

Scammon, R., & Boyd, E. (1932). Measurement and analysis of human growth. *White House conference on child health and protection. Report of the Committee on Growth and Development. Part IV. Appraisement of the child. Section II. Physical Status* (pp. 233–244). New York: Century.

Schacter, D. L. (1987). Implicit memory: History and current status. *Journal of Experimental Psychology: Learning, Memory, and Cognition, 13*, 501–518.

Schacter, D. L., & Moscovitch, M. (1984). Infants, amnesics, and dissociable memory systems. In M. Moscovitch (Ed.), *Infant memory: Its relation to normal and pathological memory in humans and other animals* (pp. 173–216). New York: Plenum.

Schacter, D. L., & Tulving, E. (1994). What are the memory systems of 1994? In D. L. Schacter & E. Tulving (Eds.), *Memory systems* (pp. 1–38). Cambridge, MA: MIT Press.

Schacter, D. L., & Wagner, A. D. (1999). Medial temporal lobe activations in fMRI and PET studies of episodic encoding and retrieval. *Hippocampus, 9*, 7–24.

Schacter, D. L., Wagner, A. D., & Buckner, R. L. (2000). Memory systems of 1999. In E. Tulving & F. I. M. Craik (Eds.), *The Oxford handbook of memory* (pp. 627–643). New York: Oxford University Press.

Schank, R. C., & Abelson, R. P. (1977). *Scripts, plans, goals and understanding.* Hillsdale, NJ: Lawrence Erlbaum Associates.

Schmolck, H., Buffalo, E. A., & Squire, L. R. (2000). Memory distortions develop over time: Recollections of the O. J. Simpson trial verdict after 15 and 32 months. *Psychological Science, 11*, 39–45.

Schneider, J. F. L., Il'yasov, K. A., Hennig, J., & Martin, E. (2004). Fast quantitative difusiontensor imaging of cerebral white matter from the neonatal period to adolescence. *Neuroradiology, 46*, 258–266.

Schneider, W., & Bjorklund, D. F. (1998). Memory. In W. Damon (Editor-in-Chief) & D. Kuhn & R. S. Siegler (Vol. Eds.), *Handbook of child psychology: Vol. 2. Cognition, perception, and language* (5th ed., pp. 467–521). New York: Wiley.

Schrauf, R. W., & Rubin, D. C. (1998). Bilingual autobiographical memory in older adult immigrants: A test of cognitive explanations of the reminiscence bump and the linguistic encoding of memories. *Journal of Memory and Language, 39*, 437–457.

Scoville, W. B., & Milner, B. (1957). Loss of recent memory after bilateral hippocampal lesions. *Journal of Neurological and Neurosurgical Psychiatry, 20*, 11–12.

Seidlitz, L., & Diener, E. (1998). Sex differences in the recall of affective experiences. *Journal of Personality and Social Psychology, 74*, 262–271.

Seigal, L. S. (1994). The long-term prognosis of pre-term infants: Conceptual, methodological and ethical issues. *Human Nature, 5*, 103–126.

Seress, L. (1988). Interspecies comparison of the hippocampal formation shows increased emphasis on the region superior in the Ammon's horn of the human brain. *Journal Hirnforsch, 29*, 335–340.

Seress, L. (1992). Morphological variability and developmental aspects of monkey and human granule cells: Differences between the rodent and primate dentate gyrus. *Epilepsy Research, 7*(Suppl.), 3–28.

Seress, L. (2001). Morphological changes of the human hippocampal formation from mid-gestation to early childhood. In C. A. Nelson & M. Luciana (Eds.), *Handbook of developmental cognitive neuroscience* (pp. 45–58). Cambridge, MA: MIT Press.

Seress, L., & Mrzljak, L. (1992). Postnatal development of mossy cells in the human dentate gyrus: A light microscopic Golgi study. *Hippocampus, 2*, 127–142.

Shallice, T., & Warrington, E. K. (1970). Independent functioning of verbal memory stores: A neuropsychological study. *Quarterly Journal of Experimental Psychology, 22*, 261–273.

Sheffield, E., & Hudson, J. A. (1994). Reactivation of toddlers' event memory. *Memory, 2*, 447–465.

Sheingold, K., & Tenney, Y. J. (1982). Memory for a salient childhood event. In U. Neisser (Ed.), *Memory observed: Remembering in natural contexts* (pp. 201–212). New York: W.H. Freeman.

Shimamura, A. P. (1995). Memory and frontal lobe function. In M. S. Gazzaniga (Ed.), *The cognitive neurosciences* (pp. 803–813). Cambridge, MA: MIT Press.

Shimamura, A. P., Janowsky, J. S., & Squire, L. R. (1990). Memory for the temporal order of events in patients with frontal lobe lesions and amnesic patients. *Neuropsychologia, 28*, 803–813.

Simcock, G., & Hayne, H. (2002). Breaking the barrier? Children fail to translate their preverbal memories into language. *Psychological Science, 13*, 225–231.

Slackman, E. A., & Nelson, K. (1984). Acquisition of an unfamiliar script in story form by young children. *Child Development, 55*, 329–340.

Slomkowski, C. L., Nelson, K., Dunn, J., & Plomin, R. (1992). Temperament and language: Relations from toddlerhood to middle childhood. *Developmental Psychology, 28*, 1090–1095.

Smith, M. C., Bibi, U., & Sheard, D. E. (2003). Evidence for the differential impact of time and emotion on personal and event memories for September 11, 2001. *Applied Cognitive Psychology, 17*, 1047–1055.

Snyder, K. (2001). *Novelty preferences reconsidered: A developmental cognitive neuroscience perspective*. Unpublished manuscript.

Sodian, B., & Wimmer, H. (1987). Children's understanding of inference as a source of knowledge. *Child Development, 58*, 424–433.

Sowell, E. R., Delis, D., Stiles, J., & Jernigan, T. L. (2001). Improved memory functioning and frontal lobe maturation between childhood and adolescence: A structural MRI study. *Journal of International Neuropsychological Society, 7*, 312–322.

Spear, N. E. (1978). *The processing of memories: Forgetting and retention*. Hillsdale, NJ: Lawrence Erlbaum Associates.

Spence, M. J. (1996). Young infants' long-term auditory memory: Evidence for changes in preferences as a function of delay. *Developmental Psychobiology, 29*, 685–695.

Squire, L. R. (1982). The neuropsychology of human memory. *Annual Review of Neuroscience, 5*, 241–273.

Squire, L. R. (1986). Mechanisms of memory. *Science, 232*, 1612–1619.

Squire, L. R. (1987). *Memory and brain*. New York: Oxford University Press.

Squire, L. R. (1992). Memory and the hippocampus: A synthesis from findings with rats, monkeys, and humans. *Psychological Review, 99*, 195–231.

Squire, L. R., & Alvarez, P. (1995). Retrograde amnesia and memory consolidation: A neurobiological perspective. *Current Opinion in Neurobiology, 5*, 169–177.

Squire, L. R., Knowlton, B., & Musen, G. (1993). The structure and organization of memory. *Annual Review of Psychology, 44*, 453–495.

Squire, L. R., & Zola, S. M. (1996). Structure and function of declarative and nondeclarative memory systems. *Proceedings of the National Academy of Sciences, 93*, 13515–13522.

Squire, L. R., & Zola, S. M. (1998). Episodic memory, semantic memory, and amnesia. *Hippocampus, 8*, 205–211.

Squire, L. R., & Zola-Morgan, S. (1983). The neurology of memory: The case for correspondence between the findings for human and nonhuman primate. In J. A. Deutsch (Ed.), *The physiological basis of memory* (pp. 199–268). New York: Academic Press.

Squire, L. R., & Zola-Morgan, S. (1991). The medial temporal lobe memory system. *Science, 253,* 1380–1386.

Squire, L. R., Zola-Morgan, S., & Chen, K. (1988). Human amnesia and animal models of amnesia: Performance of amnesic patients on tests designed for the monkey. *Behavioral Neuroscience, 102,* 210–221.

Sroufe, L. A. (1979). The coherence of individual development: Early care, attachment, and subsequent developmental issues. *American Psychologist, 34,* 834–841.

Stipek, D., Gralinski, J. H., & Kopp, C. B. (1990). Self-concept development in the toddler years. *Developmental Psychology, 26,* 972–977.

Suzuki, W., & Amaral, D. G. (1990). Cortical inputs to the CA1 field of the monkey hippocampus originate from the perirhinal and parahippocampal cortex but not from area TE. *Neuroscience Letters, 115,* 43–48.

Suzuki, W. A., Miller, E. A., & Desimone, R. (1997). Object and place memory in the macaque entorhinal cortex. *Journal of Neurophysiology, 78,* 1062–1081.

Swain, I. U., Zelazo, P. R., & Clifton, R. K. (1993). Newborn infants' memory for speech sounds retained over 24 hours. *Developmental Psychology, 29,* 312–323.

Takehara, K., Kawahara, S., & Kirino, Y. (2003). Time-dependent reorganization of the brain components underlying memory retention in trace eyeblink conditioning. *The Journal of Neuroscience, 23,* 9897–9905.

Tanapat, P., Hastings, N. B., & Gould, E. (2001). Adult neurogenesis in the hippocampal formation. In C. A. Nelson & M. Luciana (Eds.), *Handbook of developmental cognitive neuroscience* (pp. 93–105). Cambridge, MA: MIT Press.

Taylor, M., Esbensen, B., & Bennett, R. T. (1994). Children's understanding of knowledge acquisition: The tendency for children to report they have always known what they have just learned. *Child Development, 65,* 1581–1604.

Tekcan, A. İ., Ece, B., Gülgöz, S., & Er, N. (2003). Autobiographical and event memory for 9/11: Changes across one year. *Applied Cognitive Psychology, 17,* 1057–1066.

Tekcan, A. İ., & Peynircioğlu, Z. F. (2002). Effects of age on flashbulb memories. *Psychology and Aging, 17,* 416–422.

Tessler, M., & Nelson, K. (1994). Making memories: The influence of joint encoding on later recall by young children. *Consciousness and Cognition, 3,* 307–326.

Teyler, T. J., & Discenna, P. (1986). The hippocampal memory indexing theory. *Behavioral Neuroscience, 100,* 147–154.

Thompson, C. P. (1998). The bounty of everyday memory. In C. P. Thompson, D. J. Hermann, D. Bruce, J. D. Read, D. G. Payne, & M. P. Toglia (Eds.), *Autobiographical memory: Theoretical and applied perspectives* (pp. 29–44). Mahwah, NJ: Lawrence Erlbaum Associates.

Thorne, A. (1995). Developmental truths in memories of childhood and adolescence. *Journal of Personality, 63,* 139–163.

Todd, C. M., & Perlmutter, M. (1980). Reality recalled by preschool children. In M. Perlmutter (Ed.), *New directions for child development: Children's memory* (pp. 69–85). San Francisco, CA: Jossey-Bass.

Trabasso, T., Secco, T., & van den Broek, P. W. (1984). Causal cohesion and story coherence. In H. Mandl, N. L. Stein, & T. Trabasso (Eds.), *Learning and comprehension of text* (pp. 83–111). Hillsdale, NJ: Lawrence Erlbaum Associates.

Trabasso, T., van den Broek, P. W., & Suh, S. Y. (1989). Logical necessity and transitivity relations in stories. *Discourse Processes, 12,* 1–25.

Tulving, E. (1972). Episodic and semantic memory. In E. Tulving & W. Donaldson (Eds.), *Organization of memory* (pp. 381–403). New York: Academic Press.

Tulving, E. (1983). *Elements of episodic memory.* Oxford: Oxford University Press.

Tulving, E. (1985a). How many memory systems are there? *American Psychologist, 40*, 385–398.

Tulving, E. (1985b). Memory and consciousness. *Canadian Psychology, 26*, 1–12.

Tulving, E. (1993). What is episodic memory? *Current Directions in Psychological Science, 3*, 67–70.

Tulving, E., Kapur, S., Craik, F. I. M., Moscovitch, M., & Houle, S. (1994). Hemispheric encoding/Retrieval asymmetry in episodic memory: Positron emission tomography findings. *Proceeding of the National Academy of Sciences, 91*, 2016–2020.

Tulving, E., & Markowitsch, H. J. (1998). Episodic and declarative memory: Role of the hippocampus. *Hippocampus, 8*, 198–204.

Tulving, E., & Thomson, D. M. (1973). Encoding specificity and retrieval processes in episodic memory. *Psychological Review, 80*, 352–373.

Usher, J., & Neisser, U. (1993). Childhood amnesia and the beginnings of memory for four early life events. *Journal of Experimental Psychology: General, 122*, 155–165.

Utsunomiya, H., Takano, K., Okazaki, M., & Mistudome, A. (1999). Development of the temporal lobe in infants and children: Analysis by MR-based volumetry. *American Journal of Neuroradiology, 20*, 717–723.

Van Abbema, D. L., & Bauer, P. J. (2005). Autobiographical memory in childhood: Development of a personal past. *Memory, 13*, 829–845.

van den Broek, P. W. (1989). Causal reasoning and inference making in judging the importance of story statements. *Child Development, 60*, 286–297.

van den Broek, P. W. (1997). Discovering the cement of the universe: The development of event comprehension from childhood to adulthood. In P. van den Broek, P. J. Bauer, & T. Bourg (Eds.), *Developmental spans in event representation and comprehension: Bridging fictional and actual events* (pp. 321–342). Mahwah, NJ: Lawrence Erlbaum Associates.

van Hof-van Duin, J., Heersema, D. J., Groenendaal, F., Baerts, W., & Fetter, W. P. (1992). Visual field and grating acuity development in low-risk preterm infants during the first 2 1/2 years after term. *Behavioral Brain Research, 49*, 115–122.

Van Petten, C. (2004). Relationship between hippocampal volume and memory ability in healthy individuals across the lifespan: Review and meta-analysis. *Neuropsychologia, 42*, 1394–1413.

Vargha-Khadem, F., Gadian, D. G., Watkins, K. E., Connelly, A., Van Paesschen, W., & Mishkin, M. (1997). Differential effects of early hippocampal pathology on episodic and semantic memory. *Science, 277*, 376–380.

Wachs, T. D., Morrow, J., & Slabach, E. H. (1990). Intra-individual variability in infant visual recognition memory performance: Temperamental and environmental correlates. *Infant Behavior and Development, 13*, 397–403.

Wagenaar, W. A. (1986). My memory: A study of autobiographical memory over six years. *Cognitive Psychology, 18*, 225–252.

Wagenaar, W. A. (1994). Is memory self-serving? In U. Neisser & R. Fivush (Eds.), *The remembering self: Construction and accuracy in the self-narrative* (pp. 191–204). New York: Cambridge University Press.

Wagner, A. D., Schacter, D. L., Rotte, M., Koutstaal, W., Maril, A., Dale, A. M., Rosen, B. R., & Buckner, R. L. (1998). Building memories: Remembering and forgetting of verbal experiences as predicted by brain activity. *Science, 281*, 1188–1191.

Waldfogel, S. (1948). The frequency and affective character of childhood memories. *Psychological Monographs, 62* (Whole No. 291).

Walkenfeld, F. F. (2000). *Reminder and language effects on preschoolers' memory reports: Do words speak louder than actions?* Unpublished doctoral dissertation, City University of New York Graduate Center.

Walker, W. R., Skowronski, J. J., & Thompson, C. P. (2003). Life is pleasant—and memory helps to keep it that way! *Review of General Psychology, 7*, 203–210.

Walker, W. R., Vogl, R. J., & Thompson, C. P. (1997). Autobiographical memory: Unpleasantness fades faster than pleasantness over time. *Applied Cognitive Psychology, 11*, 399–413.

Wang, Q. (2001). Culture effects on adults' earliest childhood recollection and self-description: Implications for the relation between memory and the self. *Journal of Personality and Social Psychology, 81*, 220–233.

Wang, Q. (2003). Infantile amnesia reconsidered: A cross-cultural analysis. *Memory, 11*, 65–80.

Wang, Q., Leichtman, M. D., & Davies, K. I. (2000). Sharing memories and telling stories: American and Chinese mothers and their 3-year-olds. *Memory, 8*, 159–177.

Wang, Q., Leichtman, M. D., & White, S. H. (1998). Childhood memory and self-description in young Chinese adults: The impact of growing up an only child. *Cognition, 69*, 73–103.

Warren, A. R., & Swartwood, J. N. (1992). Developmental issues in flashbulb memory research: Children recall the Challenger event. In E. Winograd & U. Neisser (Eds.), *Affect and accuracy in recall: Studies of "flashbulb" memories* (pp. 95–120). New York: Cambridge University Press.

Warrington, E. K., & Weiskrantz, L. (1974). The effect of prior learning on subsequent retention in amnesic patients. *Neuropsychologia, 12*, 419–428.

Waters, E. (1987). *Attachment behavior Q-set (Version 3.0)* [Computer software]. Stony Brook: State University of New York at Stony Brook, Department of Psychology.

Waters, H. S., Rodriguez, L. M., & Ridgeway, D. (1998). Cognitive underpinnings of narrative attachment assessment. *Journal of Experimental Child Psychology, 71*, 211–234.

Watts, R., Liston, C., Niogi, S., & Uluğ, A. M. (2003). Fiber tracking using magnetic resonance diffusion tensor imaging and its applications to human brain development. *Mental Retardation and Developmental Disabilities, 9*, 168–177.

Webb, S. J., Monk, C. S., & Nelson, C. A. (2001). Mechanisms of postnatal neurobiological development: Implications for human development. *Developmental Neuropsychology, 19*, 147–171.

Webster, M. J., Ungerleider, L. G., & Bachevalier, J. (1991a). Connections of inferior temporal areas TE and TEO with medial temporal-lobe structures in infant and adult monkeys. *Journal of Neuroscience, 11*, 1095–1116.

Webster, M. J., Ungerleider, L. G., & Bachevalier, J. (1991b). Lesions of inferior temporal area TE in infant monkeys alter cortico-amygdalar projections. *NeuroReport, 2*, 769–772.

Weigle, T. W., & Bauer, P. J. (2000). Deaf and hearing adults' recollections of childhood and beyond. *Memory, 8*, 293–309.

Welch-Ross, M. K. (1997). Mother–child participation in conversation about the past: Relationships to preschoolers' theory of mind. *Developmental Psychology, 33*, 618–629.

Welch-Ross, M. K. (2001). Personalizing the temporally extended self: Evaluative self-awareness and the development of autobiographical memory. In C. Moore & K. Lemmon (Eds.), *The self in time: Developmental perspectives* (pp. 97–120). Mahwah, NJ: Lawrence Erlbaum Associates.

Welch-Ross, M. K., Fasig, L. G., & Farrar, M. J. (1999). Predictors of preschoolers' self-knowledge: Reference to emotion and mental states in mother–child conversations about past events. *Cognitive Development, 14*, 401–422.

Wenner, J. A., & Bauer, P. J. (1999). Bringing order to the arbitrary: One- to two-year-olds' recall of event sequences. *Infant Behavior and Development, 22*, 585–590.

West, T. A., & Bauer, P. J. (1999). Assumptions of infantile amnesia: Are there differences between early and later memories? *Memory, 7*, 257–278.

Wetzler, S. E., & Sweeney, J. A. (1986). Childhood amnesia: An empirical demonstration. In D. C. Rubin (Ed.), *Autobiographical memory* (pp. 191–201). New York: Cambridge University Press.

Wheeler, M. A. (2000). Episodic memory and autonoetic awareness. In E. Tulving & F. I. M. Craik (Eds.), *The Oxford handbook of memory* (pp. 597–608). New York: Oxford University Press.

White, R. (1982). Memory for personal events. *Human Learning, 1,* 171–183.

White, R. (1989). Recall of autobiographical events. *Applied Cognitive Psychology, 3,* 127–135.

White, R. (2002). Memory for events after twenty years. *Applied Cognitive Psychology, 16,* 603–612.

White, S. H., & Pillemer, D. B. (1979). Childhood amnesia and the development of a socially accessible memory system. In J. F. Kihlstrom & F. J. Evans (Eds.), *Functional disorders of memory* (pp. 29–73). Hillsdale, NJ: Lawrence Erlbaum Associates.

Wickelgren, W. A. (1974). Single-trace fragility theory of memory dynamics. *Memory & Cognition, 2,* 775–780.

Wickelgren, W. A. (1975). Age and storage dynamics in continuous recognition memory. *Developmental Psychology, 11,* 165–169.

Williams, J. M. G. (1996). Depression and the specificity of autobiographical memory. In D. C. Rubin (Ed.), *Remembering our past: Studies in autobiographical memory* (pp. 244–267). New York: Cambridge University Press.

Winograd, E., & Killinger, W. A. (1983). Relating age at encoding in early childhood to adult recall: Development of flashbulb memories. *Journal of Experimental Psychology: General, 112,* 413–422.

Woodruff-Pak, D. S., Logan, C. G., & Thompson, R. F. (1990). Neurobiological substrates of classical conditioning across the life span. In A. Diamond (Ed.), *Development and neural bases of higher cognitive functions* (pp. 150–178). New York: New York Academy of Sciences Press.

Yasuno, F., Hirata, M., Takimoto, H., Taniguchi, M., Nakagawa, Y., Ikerjiri, Y., Nishikawa, T., Shinozaki, K., Tanabe, H., Sugita, Y., & Takeda, M. (1999). Retrograde temporal order amnesia resulting from damage to the fornix. *Journal of Neurology, Neurosurgery, & Psychiatry, 67,* 102–105.

Zecevic, N. (1998). Synaptogenesis in layer 1 of the human cerebral cortex in the first half of gestation. *Cerebral Cortex, 8,* 245–252.

Zhang, L. X., Xing, G. O., Levine, S., Post, R. M., & Smith, M. A. (1997). Maternal deprivation induces neuronal death. *Society of Neuroscience Abstracts, October: 1113.*

Zola, S. M., & Squire, L. R. (2000). The medial temporal lobe and the hippocampus. In E. Tulving & F. I. M. Craik (Eds.), *The Oxford handbook of memory* (pp. 485–500). New York: Oxford University Press.

Zola, S. M., Squire, L. R., Teng, E., Stefanacci, L., & Clark, R. (2000). Impaired recognition memory in monkeys after damage limited to the hippocampal region. *Journal of Neuroscience, 20,* 451–463.

Zola, S. M., Teng, E., Clark, R. E. et al. (1998). Impaired recognition memory and simple discrimination learning in monkeys following lesions limited to the hippocampal region made by radio frequency, ischemia, or ibotenic acid. *Society for Neuroscience Abstracts, 24,* 17(Abstract).

Zola-Morgan, S., & Squire, L. R. (1990). The primate hippocampal formation: Evidence for a time-limited role in memory storage. *Science, 250,* 288–290.

Zola-Morgan, S., Squire, L. R., & Amaral, D. G. (1986). Human amnesia and the medial temporal region: Enduring memory impairment following a bilateral lesion limited to field CA1 of the hippocampus. *Journal of Neuroscience, 6,* 2950–2967.

Zola-Morgan, S., Squire, L. R., & Ramus, S. J. (1994). Severity of memory impairment in monkeys as a function of locus and extent of damage within the medial temporal lobe memory system. *Hippocampus, 4,* 483–495.

Zola-Morgan, S., Squire, L. R., Rempel, N. L., Clower, R. P., & Amaral, D. G. (1992). Enduring memory impairment in monkeys after ischemic damage to the hippocampus. *Journal of Neuroscience, 9,* 4355–4370.

# Author Index

*Note:* *f* indicates figure, *n* indicates footnote, *t* indicates table.

## A

Abelson, R. P., 229, 244, *409*
Ablin, D. S., 336, 338, 372, *407*
Abson, V., 41, 69, *384*
Ackil, J. K., 38, 369, *384*
Adams, S., 284, 293, 294*t*, 365, *384, 393*
Adlam, A.-L. R., 101, *384*
Aguirre, G. K., 132, *384*
Aicardi, J., 164, 165, 166*t*, 167, 168, 181, 207, 211, *394*
Alexander, G. E., 136, *394*
Alkire, M. T., 171, *389*
Allen, J. G., 291, *384*
Allen, J. J. B., 129*f*, *384*
Alsop, D. C., 132, *384*
Altman, J., 185, 256, *384*
Alvarez, P., 141, 147, 151, 154, *384, 410*
Alvarez-Royo, P., 141, *384*
Amaral, D. G., 6, 8*f*, 123, 126, 127, 139, 145, 146, 148*f*, 162, 167, 209, *390, 399, 411, 414*
Andersen, P., 149, *385*
Angevine, J. B., 183, *385*
Anglin, J., 271, *385*
Arenberg, D., 370, *395*
Arnold, S. E., 184, 186, 256, *385*
Astington, J. W., 270, *405*
Augustine, A., 121, *385*

## B

Babinsky, R., 127, *389*
Bachevalier, J., 99, 182, 186, 189, 191, *385, 413*
Baddeley, A. D., 25, *399*
Baerts, W., 211, 212, *412*
Bahrick, H. P., 10, *385*
Bahrick, L. E., 93, 275, *385, 393*
Baillargeon, R., 89, 226, *394*
Baker-Ward, L., 243, *385*
Bangston, S. K., 104, 106, 112, 113, 197, 198, 199, 327, 357, *387*
Barclay, C. R., 36, *385*
Barkovich, A. J., 180, *385*
Barnat, M. P., 100, *385*
Barnett, M. P., 159, *385*
Barr, R., 102, 192, 193, 248, 357, *385, 386*
Bartsch, K., 366, *386*
Bates, E., 113, 254, *386, 392*
Bates, J. E., 115, 296, *408*
Bauer, P. J., 21, 35, 38, 41, 47, 48, 52*t*, 65, 66, 67, 68, 69, 70, 73, 97, 98, 99, 100, 101, 102, 103, 104, 105, 106, 107*t*, 108, 109*f*, 111, 112, 113, 114, 116, 117, 118, 119, 182, 185, 194, 196, 197, 198, 199*f*, 199, 200*f*, 201, 201*f*, 202, 203, 204, 205, 206*f*, 209, 211, 212, 212*t*, 213n1, 215, 236, 243, 244*f*, 246*f*, 248, 250, 251*f*, 259, 260,

## F

Faassen, A. E., 209, *394*
Fagan, J. F., 93, 104, *392*
Fagen, J. W., 96, *408*
Fajnsztejn-Pollack, G., 370, *392*
Fallon, J., 171, *389*
Fanselow, M. S., 146, 147*f*, 154, 157, *398*
Fantz, R. L., 92, *392*
Farol, P., 256, *387*
Farrant, K., 285, 296, 300, *392*
Farrar, M. J., 231, 251, 266, 362, *392, 413*
Fasig, L. G., 266, 362, *413*
Feirinig, C., 298, *399*
Feldman, J. F., 104, *407*
Fenson, L., 113, *392*
Fernández, G., 150, *392*
Fetter, W. P., 211, 212, *412*
Fielder, A., 212, *394*
Fink, G. R., 155, 171, 172, *392, 406*
Fischer, K. W., 61, *392*
Fitzgerald, J. J., 39, 40, *392*
Fivush, R., 37, 46, 47, 48, 62, 99, 230, 231,
     232, 232*t*, 233, 234, 235*t*, 235, 236,
     237, 238*f*, 238, 239, 240, 241, 243,
     246, 248, 249, 250, 251, 252, 267,
     269, 272, 273, 274*f*, 275, 276, 281,
     282, 284, 285, 286, 287, 289, 292,
     293, 294*t*, 294, 295, 295*f*, 298, 299,
     300, 307, 319, 326, 327, 335, 336*f*,
     337, 338, 339, 339*t*, 340, 341, 342,
     343, 344*f*, 345, 351, 357, 358, 359,
     361, 362, 365, 366, 367, 369, 384,
     386, 388, 392, 393, 395, 397, 399,
     403, 404, 407
Flannagan, D. A., 243, *385*
Flavell, J. H., 225, 270, *393, 405*
Fletcher, C. R., 245, *393*
Fletcher, P. C., 138, 160, 161, 162, *391,
     393, 408*
Foley, M. A., 67, *398*
Fong, S. S., 209, 211, *391*
Foreman, N., 212, *394*
Foster, J. C., 223, *394*
Fox, N., 350, *405*
Frackowiak, R. S. J., 132, 160, 161, 400,
     *408*
Francis, D., 215, *389*
Frank, L. R., 254, *394*
Frank, M., 73, *405*
Freeman, N. H., 290, 291*t*, 366, 367, *399*

Freeman, R. B., 159, *398*
Freud, S., 50, 51, 58, 59, 64, 65, 68, 263,
     315, *394*
Friedman, A., 73, *394*
Friedman, W. J., 269, *394*
Friston, K. J., 155, *388*
Frith, C. D., 132, 138, 155, 156, 160, 161,
     162, 170, *393, 400, 408*
Fromhoff, F. A, 232, 235, 272, 282, 284,
     319, *393*
Fujita, F., 47, *394*
Fuster, J. M., 136, 137, 151, 158, 194, 238,
     *394*

## G

Gabrieli, J. D. E., 150, 174, *388, 394*
Gadian, D. G., 139, 164, 165, 166*t*, 167,
     168, 181, 207, 211, *394, 402, 412*
Gaensbauer, T., 315, 316, *394*
Galkin, T. W., 137, *395*
Gall, F. J., 122, *394*
Galton, F., 24, 25, 223, *394*
Garavan, H., 171, *394*
Gelman, R., 89, 226, *394*
Georgieff, M. K., 209, 211, 212, 212*t*,
     213*n*1, *391, 394*
Gerhardstein, P., 95, 96, *408*
Ghaemi, M., 137, *401*
Giambra, L. M., 370, *395*
Giedd, J. N., 256, *395*
Glover, G. H., 150, *388*
Gluck, M., 174, *394*
Gluck, M. A., 158, 185, *395*
Gochin, P. M., 94, 191, *402*
Goldberg, A., 275, 337, *393*
Goldman, P. S., 137, *395*
Goldman-Rakic, P. S., 186, 189, 190, *388,
     395*
Goldsmith, H. H., 117, *395*
González, R. G., 6, 8*f*, 123, 127, 146, 162,
     *390*
Goodenough, F. L., 223, *395*
Goodman, G. S., 231, 243, 251, 252, 336,
     338, 372, *392, 407, 408*
Goodman, S. H., 293, *393*
Gordon, K., 73, *395*
Gordon, R., 243, *403*
Gore, J. B., 155, *395*
Gottfried, A. W., 93, 195, *408*

# Subject Index

*Note:* *f* indicates figure, *n* indicates footnote, *t* indicates table.

## A

*Activity Level*, 116t, 117–118, 297
Adopted infants, 214–216
Age-related
  changes in autobiographical memory, 18,
    277–278, 314
  changes in preschoolers' recall of specific
    past events, 234–242, 263
  in consolidation, 197, 203, 260
  differences in amount remembered, 110
  differences in encoding, 195, 259–260,
    345, 372
  differential loss of information over time,
    205
  increases in long-term recall, 111, 118,
    196, 203, 205, 216, 259–261, 270
  in memory behavior, 178, 181
  in narrative structure, 308, 342
Alcohol-related clinical syndrome, 30
Amnesia, 20, 49, 94, 101, 127, 154,
    162–163, 174, 179, 207
  anterograde, 17, 139, 143–145, 147, 150,
    380
  childhood, 17–19, 31, 33, 49, 87–88, 179,
    190, 222, 225, 228, 234, 236, 240,
    255, 278, 280, 309, 315, 317, 320,
    330, 335, 338–345, 348–349,
    369–371, 374–375, 378, 380–381

  cognitive development as explanation
    for, 60–62
  different lenses as explanation for,
    59–60, 79–80
  Freud's explanation of, 57–59, 79
  gender differences in, 73–74
  group differences in, 71–72
  Hobbesean theory of, 57, 63, 87
  individual differences in, 72–73
  phenomenon of, 51–56, 313–314,
    332–333
  sociocultural perspective on, 62–63
  theories as to the source of, 56–63,
    78–82
  universalities of, 70–78
  infantile, 17–18, 31, 33, 50–52, 58, 177,
    380–381
  retrograde, 17, 146–147, 156, 159,
    196–197, 260, 383
    temporally graded, 143–144, 383
  temporal lobe, 131, 139–140, 161, 208
Association cortex, 135, 137–138, 149–150,
    152, 156–157, 159, 164, 175, 182,
    186–187, 194, 263, 382–383
Atatürk, Mustafa Kemal, 43–44
*Attachment Behavior Q-set*, 299–300
Augustine, Saint Aurelius, 121, 124
*Autobiographical Interview*, 25
Autobiographical memory, 4, 9, 14, 16–19,
    56, 58, 61–64, 74, 75f, 75, 77–78,
    81–83, 88, 284–290

# W